Deploying and Managing Microsoft.NET Web Farms

Barry Bloom

SAMS

201 West 103rd St., Indianapolis, Indiana, 46290

Deploying and Managing Microsoft.NET Web Farms

International Standard Book Number: 0-672-32057-6

Library of Congress Catalog Card Number: 00-107955

Printed in the United States of America

First Printing: June 2001

04 03 02 01 4 3 2 1

Trademarks

Warning and Disclaimer

Publisher
Don Fowley

Acquisitions Editor
Neil Rowe

Development Editor
Steve Rowe

Managing Editor
Matt Purcell

Project Editor
George E. Nedeff

Copy Editor
Gene Redding

Indexer
Eric Schroeder

Proofreader
Candice Hightower

Technical Editor
Garth Hughes

Team Coordinator
Vicki Harding

Media Developer
Dan Scherf

Interior Designer
Aren Howell

Cover Designer
Anne Jones

Page Layout
Steve Geiselman
Ayanna Lacey
Lizbeth Patterson

Overview

Contents

About the Author

Barry Bloom (MCP) has worked in the Information Technology field for over five years. At the age of 12, he started his first online business, a bulletin board system, which ran on an Atari 800. He is currently employed as Chief Architect of E-business for Richmont Web Services and Mary Kay, a billion dollar company in Dallas, Texas. He leads projects like network and server infrastructure, software architecture and design, and platform interoperability. In the past three years he has helped Richmont Web Services and Mary Kay grow their online business to over 1 billion in total revenue serving over 300,000 individual businesses, and 20 million end consumers. This effort currently ranks fourth in retail sales on the Internet and will likely move into second place by the end of 2001.

Dedication

To my family Sheila, Carl, and Connor, without your support, patience, love, and understanding, I could not have written this book.

Acknowledgments

I would like to start of by thanking my technical editors, Garth Hughes, David Findley, Bart Barber, Morris Koeneke, and Eric Brock. Without their efforts and suggestions, this fine guide to Web farms would be incomplete. These gentlemen are the best in their field and I am honored to have worked with them.

I would also like to thank Bill Brown, Kregg Jodie, and Mary Kay Inc. for affording me the time and support to make this book a reality. I hope that my efforts here pay off in our teams continued success. I would also like to acknowledge Mary Kay Ash. Without her vision to enrich women's lives we would never have had the opportunity to create some of the best sites on the Internet.

This work is a technical memoir of a three-year effort to build the fourth largest retail site on the Internet. There is no way an accomplishment of this magnitude is achievable without an incredible team. While I have led this effort, my co-workers are the real people who deserve the credit. While I can't list them all here, I would like to name a few who have especially contributed to what I have presented here in this book: Robert "Bobo" Tabor, Roy Bomberger, Jason Bentrum, James Whatley, Gary Hartley, Gary Mills, Daryl Myrick, Eric Wiley, Michael Abdelmalek, Lance Wilson, Ed Garcia, Kevin Austin, Joe Campos, Mark Stolle, Venkat Rangaswamy, Mark Wheeler, and all the other great people at Richmont Web Services and Mary Kay.

Tell Us What You Think!

As the reader of this book, *you* are our most important critic and commentator. We value your opinion and want to know what we're doing right, what we could do better, what areas you'd like to see us publish in, and any other words of wisdom you're willing to pass our way.

As Publisher for Sams Publishing, I welcome your comments. You can fax, e-mail, or write me directly to let me know what you did or didn't like about this book—as well as what we can do to make our books stronger.

Please note that I cannot help you with technical problems related to the topic of this book, and that due to the high volume of mail I receive, I might not be able to reply to every message.

When you write, please be sure to include this book's title and author as well as your name and phone or fax number. I will carefully review your comments and share them with the author and editors who worked on the book.

Fax: 317-581-4770

E-mail: `feedback@samspublishing.com`

Mail: Don Fowely
Publisher
Sams Publishing
201 West 103rd Street
Indianapolis, IN 46290 USA

Introduction

In this age of the Internet, people and corporations have, in many ways, just begun to tap into the true "business power" that the Internet provides. At an enterprise level, many businesses are choosing to go online as an option of doing business with customers, suppliers, or both. Often the online presence is used as a time-saving measure, offering ease of purchase for customers and streamlining business processes with business partners.

With this move to business online, IT professionals within these organizations are faced with building, maintaining, upgrading, and administering the hardware and software used for an online business presence. As more customers and business partners use your online presence to conduct business, you, as the IT professional, must ensure both that adequate system resources exist to handle the load and that the Web presence stays available. As these system and performance needs grow, you gradually—or sometimes very quickly—have the makings of a Web farm.

With Web farms, there are certainly many ways to create these entities. Yet, if you are not careful, poor choices in determining your architecture, hardware selection, software creation and deployment, and future needs can quickly generate a site that fails to perform and, thus, fails to provide online business needs to customers. An online business presence that is not prepared to handle a growing number of users or that crashes too regularly can impact your business's profits quite dramatically.

What is the answer? This book intends to show you, the IT professional who might currently be running a "makeshift" online business presence or who has been saddled with creating an online business presence, how to properly plan the architecture of your systems. It gives you an in-depth look at tools and concepts to help you maintain the system infrastructure. You will explore ideas and practices to ensure that your system is scalable and ready to meet the demands of a growing user or customer base, and you'll explore items to help keep your systems running more than 99% of the time, to ensure constant availability to your business's products and services.

Best practices covering issues such as server redundancy, hardware and network load balancing, performance monitoring, and clustering, are demonstrated in this book as well. These practices are included to help you achieve a highly scalable and available online business presence. In addition, this book demonstrates new tools from the Microsoft .NET Enterprise Server family to help you centralize, cluster, and manage your Web farm. You will discover the power of Application Center 2000, IIS, Windows 2000 Clustering and Network Load Balancing, and SQL Server 2000 Clustering. These tools are discussed in depth because they were designed for professionals, like you, who are in charge of a highly visible and important part of business.

Who This Book Is For

To maximize your experience with this book, you, the reader, should be very familiar with networking fundamentals; you might be a developer in charge of making applications destined for the online business presence. As a networking professional, you will cover advanced topics such as clustering, architectural design, and load-balancing techniques system scalability and availability. Developers will gain a strong understanding of the systems and architecture used to deploy and manage the applications that you will be creating. By understanding this infrastructure, you can create applications that will take advantage of the system structure that supports these applications.

Conventions Used

As you read the text, you will encounter several elements used to enhance your learning:

NOTE

One element you will see is the note element, shown here. Notes give you extra information on a topic currently being discussed or point you elsewhere to get extra information related to the current topic.

TIP

Tips are used to point out new or different ways to do a task.

CAUTION

Cautions throw up a "red flag" on a topic being discussed. They point out possible trouble spots or pitfalls that you might encounter as you create your Web farm.

NEW TERM The new term box plucks a term or concept from the text and sheds a little more light on it. The term or concept highlighted could be something that you have never encountered or something that you might have heard but not been formally introduced to.

The sidebar is used to cover a topic in more detail. Case studies or further instruction often are provided with this element.

Microsoft .NET: Today and Tomorrow

CHAPTER

1

IN THIS CHAPTER

In the summer of 2000 in a gathering of media from across the world, Bill Gates announced the new technology direction of Microsoft. In a speech aimed at everyone, Gates delivered his vision of the coming paradigm shift at Microsoft and consequently business on the Internet. Gates made it clear that, as business on the Internet changes, Microsoft is changing. He clarified that Microsoft was not defeated and that there was much life and vision left in Redmond. He likened this new direction to the move from Windows 3.1 to Windows 95: something completely different.

As usual, this new direction has a great name: Microsoft .NET. Pronounced *Microsoft dotnet*, this new marketing architecture has everything to do with the Internet and nothing to do with the .NET domain. .NET is about .COM and business on the Internet, but it's not just another great way to build Web sites; .NET is about a service-based Internet where Web sites are constructed from disparate Web-based services linked together by the .NET platform. .NET is about using Microsoft's .NET enterprise servers to host .NET services and .NET devices to interact with those services.

The goals of this chapter are to help you

- Understand the Microsoft .NET vision. .NET is a completely new direction for Microsoft and affects its entire product line. Understanding this new direction prepares Microsoft's customers for the changes ahead, enabling better planning for a successful migration to the .NET world.
- Understand the .NET platform. Microsoft describes the .NET platform as a collection of .NET devices, .NET framework, and .NET building block services, all built and supported using .NET enterprise servers.
- Understand the overall layout and goals of this book, starting with Web farm fundamentals like application and network architectures and ending with practical application of Microsoft .NET enterprise servers like Application Center 2000.

Understanding the Microsoft .NET Vision

Microsoft .NET is an umbrella term. It already means different things to different people. In classic fashion, Microsoft has crafted an overloaded term that is catchy and confusing. Terms like this are great because they spark discussions and create a buzz. Microsoft has attached the .NET moniker to at least five distinct terms discussed in this chapter: .NET platform, .NET framework, .NET services, .NET devices, and the main topic of this book, .NET enterprise servers. As .NET becomes the focal point of the Microsoft marketing strategy, be prepared for other terms, including Visual Studio.NET, VB.NET, and ASP.NET. The ActiveX marketing campaign in 1996 pales in comparison to what Microsoft plans for .NET.

NOTE

The critical paradigm shift of .NET is that it is a service-oriented Internet operating system that spans multiple traditional platforms.

.NET is about the Internet. The current Internet is a loosely coupled collection of Web sites and services that are difficult to integrate and use as a cohesive unit. For Microsoft, .NET takes the Internet to the next logical step. .NET is about creating tools, servers, and services to make building .NET applications easy. .NET applications span the Internet, and Microsoft's goal is to make building these applications as easy as building traditional Windows programs.

.NET already exists on the Internet in a primitive form. There are numerous .NET-like services for businesses and people to use. Examples include Microsoft Passport, an authentication service that business can use to store and retrieve customer passwords, e-mail addresses, and other such information. Other existing services include discussion forums, e-mail lists, calendar services, credit card authentication services, and so on. The problem with these services is that there is no standard way for them to be consumed, and therefore each integration effort is unique.

How can Microsoft possibly provide a solution for building .NET applications when the Internet is built with all flavors of operating system? The answer lies with standards and the World Wide Web Consortium (W3C). The W3C develops interoperable technologies (specifications, guidelines, software, and tools) to lead the Web to its full potential as a forum for information, commerce, communication, and collective understanding. The W3C owns the deliberation process for all existing standards on the Internet, such as HTML and XML. It conducts hearings and debates about proposed changes and ensures that services on the Internet can interoperate. With .NET, Microsoft has made a commitment to creating new and open standards for all. Microsoft does not own the means by which Web sites interoperate in a .NET world; it is available for anyone to use.

The main standard that drives .NET is Extensible Markup Language (XML). XML is a broadly adopted open standard for universal data exchange. XML has the potential to affect the development of all new software and technologies, especially those that are Internet based. With XML, .NET ensures that its interoperability will be cross platform, unifying the Internet under one data paradigm. XML will change data access as significantly as HTML has changed the user experience.

What About SOAP?

What does SOAP have to do with .NET? SOAP is an acronym for Simple Object Access Protocol and is poised to replace DCOM and CORBA as an Internet-based software communication protocol.

SOAP is an XML standards–based way for two .NET services to interact and exchange information across different platforms. By creating a SOAP service, a .NET application provider can provide services to customers in a way that any platform that understands SOAP can use. A SOAP service sends method invocation data streams that travel over TCP/IP in XML format. In .NET, these services are called Web services because they use port 80, the HTTP port, as their traffic channel.

SOAP is the glue that makes .NET work. SOAP describes the programmatic entry points to a Web site using an XML-based contract language. It has been submitted to the W3C as a standard and is currently under review.

NOTE

The W3C can be found on the Internet at `http://www.w3c.org`.

Because Microsoft cannot own the Internet, how will it compete when the operating system is the Internet? Microsoft's goal is to make the traditional Windows platform the best for delivering services and applications to the Internet through .NET. Microsoft is shifting its focus from making tools and technologies that interoperate on Windows to tools and technologies that do so on the Internet. Microsoft calls these tools, services, server technologies, and devices the *.NET Platform*.

NEW TERM The *.NET Platform* is a collection of Windows tools, services, servers, and devices that is used to build .NET applications.

Understanding the Microsoft .NET Platform

The Microsoft .NET Platform is the strategy the Microsoft will use to compete in the Internet services space that .NET is predicting. By applying its experience with tools, servers, and services, Microsoft will take the development of rich e-business solutions to the next level with the .NET platform.

Within the Microsoft .NET Platform there are four main technology areas that change the way business is conducted on the Internet. First, Microsoft announced the new .NET application framework for building custom solutions on the Windows Platform. Second, to help drive the vision of .NET and prove the value of its tools, Microsoft is deploying .NET building block services both for the general Internet and with MS core products. Third, Microsoft has announced with their core partners initiatives to bring .NET enabled devices to every aspect of Internet life. Finally, Microsoft changed the name of its existing line of server technologies from Windows DNA to Microsoft .NET enterprise servers and promised to incorporate .NET concepts and Internet-enable them. Figure 1.1 shows the four different initiatives of the .NET platform.

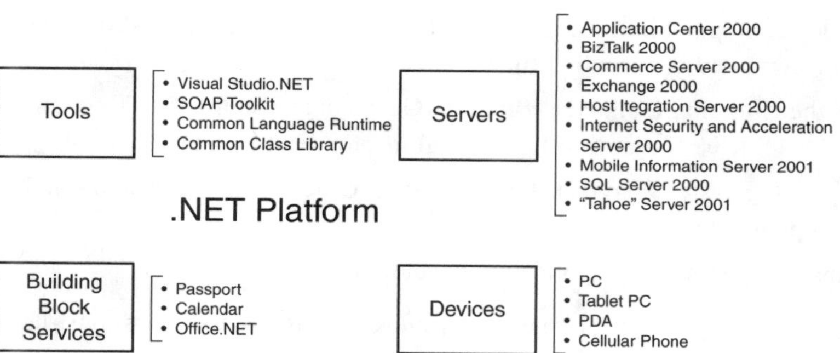

FIGURE 1.1
The four initiatives of the Microsoft .NET Platform.

Understanding the Microsoft .NET Application Framework

The Microsoft .NET application framework is a set of development tools for building .NET applications and services. These tools will be delivered in 2001 as a part of the Visual Studio 7 or Visual Studio.NET package. From these tools, developers will begin creating the next generation of Web-enabled services and applications that will implement the rest of the .NET platform.

The .NET application framework solves some of the most challenging problems of application development for the Windows platform. Most importantly, the .NET framework eliminates traditional Windows programming, which has become fragmented and increasingly difficult. But rather than creating yet another programming style, the .NET framework unifies C-style Windows programming, component-based programming, and Web programming under one common model without forcing programmers to learn new languages. Programmers are able to change from one model to another without learning an entirely new programming style. From a productivity standpoint, this is the most significant change in Windows programming since the introduction of Windows.

It is important for the administrator to be familiar with a number of new concepts introduced by the .NET application framework. Understanding these concepts helps any administrator better plan and support the .NET application framework when it becomes available. The .NET application framework has the following characteristics:

- It is language independent, so existing developers won't have to learn new syntax to use it.
- It provides a common class library that all programming languages use to interact with operating system services.
- It is XML and SOAP based, so network configuration is simple (uses port 80), and data exchange is standards based.
- All code is compiled into the Microsoft Intermediate Language (MSIL). This code is then JIT compiled at execution time.
- It uses the Common Language Runtime (CLR) that executes all JIT-compiled MSIL code. The CLR is similar to a Java virtual machine but language neutral.
- It is operating system and distribution neutral. Other operating systems and platforms could implement a .NET CLR.
- It dramatically simplifies application development.

The Windows .NET application framework provides a unified model for constructing e-business solutions. Creating Web-based services is as easy as traditional Windows programs for any solution provider familiar with the .NET application framework. Understanding the framework services helps him to make deliveries on time, decrease redundant code, and use .NET Internet services across an application. The .NET application framework is poised to become the dominant solution platform of the Internet.

Understanding Microsoft .NET Building Block Services

The .NET building block services are the newest line of software products offered by Microsoft. These products are similar to operating system services but are designed to be Internet based. These services use SOAP and XML to provide an operating system–neutral Internet component architecture.

The example most used by Microsoft is the Passport authentication service. This service provides customer authentication, tracking, and management of Web sites over the Internet. Plus Passport provides a single sign on and password. This is useful because many sites employ custom user tracking. As users interact with more Web sites, the process of joining and authenticating is slightly different for each site, and each site will have its own password. The goal is for existing Web sites to use the Passport system without a complicated integration process. Dragging and dropping a .NET Web service onto an existing Web site is how this is accomplished with Visual Studio.NET, for example.

The long-term strategy for .NET building block services is to move the rest of Microsoft's product line in that direction. There are plans for Office.NET and a Windows.NET server. Information on these services is sketchy, and many of them are in the planning phase. Rest assured that the services provided by these new building blocks will greatly simplify the construction of .NET applications.

Understanding .NET Devices

.NET devices provide the user interface experience of .NET. Going beyond common user interfaces such as HTML and the keyboard, .NET devices will provide a more natural human interaction by using handwriting and voice recognition. With the advent of more and more powerful mobile devices and the move to embedded Windows 2000, the possibility of these ideas becoming reality is on the horizon.

With these human-like user interfaces are numerous hardware devices. These include tablet PCs, cellular phones, desktop PCs, and PDAs. These user interface access points will link the .NET platform to anyone, anywhere. This is significant because the current wireless industry is fragmented. By using XML standards, Microsoft can help bring a common consistent methodology to an industry that sorely needs standardization. Microsoft is joining with major device manufacturers to ensure that the .NET platform concepts and standards are integrated into the next generation of devices.

Understanding Microsoft .NET Enterprise Servers

.NET enterprise servers complete the technological offerings and direction of the .NET platform. .NET enterprise servers host the .NET building block services for Internet-enabled applications. They host the application framework, providing developers a rich server platform for business processes. Finally, they provide connectivity and applications for .NET-enabled devices. Properly configured and deployed, they deliver a highly scalable and easily manageable Web farm. .NET enterprise server technologies are the means by which reliable, scalable business is conducted on the Internet. An application's accessibility, availability, reliability, and scalability are dependent on a properly constructed Web farm using .NET enterprise servers.

At the core of the .NET Enterprise Server suite are the original Windows 2000 Server offerings. Windows 2000 Server, Advanced Server, and DataCenter Server all provide valuable services to the .NET Platform. The core operating system services that contribute to the .NET Platform are Internet Information Services 5.0, COM+, Active Directory, Media Services, Network Load Balancing, and Cluster Service.

Creating a powerful Web farm is possible with these services alone. Internet Information Server is used to serve dynamic or static HTML content, COM+ can host business components that connect to existing backend business systems, and Active Directory has group- and user-management features. Cluster Service and NLB provide scalability and availability for a Web farm.

Along with the core Windows 2000 servers are eight server technologies that are either new or have been renamed. Each of these servers must be deployed onto a core operating system. These technologies solve different problems and, by understanding the purpose and scope of each offering, an administrator can build a world-class Web farm.

Microsoft Application Center 2000

Application Center 2000 is the deployment and management tool for high-availability Web applications built on Windows 2000. Application Center simplifies the management and deployment of simple or complex Web farms. Application Center's primary goal is to make the management of many servers as easy as managing one.

Microsoft BizTalk Server 2000

BizTalk Server 2000 orchestrates business processes and Web services within and between organizations. BizTalk understands many standard EDI documents and can use XML for B2B transactions. BizTalk is integrated with Microsoft Visio to provide a graphic user interface for building business processes.

Microsoft Commerce Server 2000

Commerce Server 2000 is the solution for quickly building an effective online business. Commerce Server provides a set of tools needed to manage, modify, and build a great e-commerce site.

Microsoft Exchange 2000

Exchange 2000 is a reliable, easy-to-manage messaging and collaboration solution for bringing together users and knowledge. With Exchange, an organization can effectively manage all the e-mail both incoming and outgoing that a Web farm generates.

Microsoft Host Integration Server 2000

Host Integration Server 2000 is used to integrate with host systems. Renamed from Microsoft SNA Server, Host Integration Server provides comprehensive managed host access and an application integration platform and is an easy and affordable solution for integrating with legacy systems.

Microsoft Internet Security and Acceleration Server 2000

This is an integrated firewall and Web cache server built to make the Web-enabled enterprise safer, faster, and more manageable. Internet Security and Acceleration Server 2000 provides secure Internet connectivity, fast Web access, and a unified management scheme.

Microsoft Mobile Information 2001 Server

Microsoft Mobile Information 2001 Server is a reliable and scalable platform for wireless solutions that brings mobile users and information together—anytime, anywhere, on any device. Mobile Information 2001 Server provides mobile access for the enterprise, mobile access to Outlook, and custom mobile access solutions.

Microsoft SQL Server 2000

Microsoft SQL Server 2000 is the complete database and analysis solution for delivering scalable Web farms. SQL Server 2000 provides solutions for data warehousing, e-commerce, and other line-of-business applications. SQL Server 2000 has the best management tools and dependability in the industry.

NOTE

The latest information regarding Microsoft .NET is located at `http://www.microsoft.com/net`.

Using This Book

The goal of this book is to teach the reader how to build a successful Web farm capable of hosting both traditional Windows DNA applications and newer .NET applications like Web services. The network, security, deployment, and application architectures of these Web farms are explored using solutions that employ .NET enterprise servers.

This book is intended to be a foundational architecture guide and reference for the .NET Enterprise Server technologies that directly affect Web farms. It is focused on those issues that directly affect the overall robustness of a Web farm. This book will not discuss the complete feature sets of the .NET enterprise servers such as SQL Server 2000 and BizTalk Server 2000. Features that are discussed relate directly to Web farm management and construction.

Understanding Introductory Concepts

Many concepts are introduced throughout this book. The first three chapters introduce concepts of .NET and the motivation for adopting the .NET enterprise servers. Chapter 2, ".NOT: Web Farms the Wrong Way," is a broad overview of a poorly designed Web site using the fictitious .NOT architecture. Chapter 3, "Scalability and Availability of Web Farms," discusses availability and scalability in general terms, because these concepts are used throughout the book.

- Chapter 2 presents common problems faced by Web farms created with the .NOT platform. This discussion is intended to familiarize the reader with the host of problems faced when deploying a Web farm. The suggestions throughout this book address the issues related to .NOT Web farm deployments.
- Chapter 3 discusses how .NET Enterprise and Windows 2000 servers achieve scale by coordinating the efforts of many servers. The concept of availability is introduced and used as a metric for organizations that support Web farms to gauge their ability to keep a site functioning 24 hours a day.

Designing Successful Infrastructures for Web Farms

Chapters 4–10 outline best practices for network, deployment, and application infrastructure designs for Web farms that use .NET Enterprise and Microsoft Window 2000 server technologies. Using these concepts increases the health and growth potential of a Web farm. Chapters 9, "Using Internet Information Services in a Web Farm," and 10, "Using Component Services (COM+) in a Web Farm," describe how IIS and COM+ are best applied in the Web farm environment. Administrators who support Web farms that use these technologies will find these chapters invaluable.

- Chapter 4, "Planning a Web Farm Network," discusses the DMZ-style network architecture and introduces general network problems faced when deploying a Web farm. Best performance, throughput, availability, and manageability are key concepts for this network architecture discussion.
- Chapter 5, "Using Microsoft Network Load Balancing in a Web Farm," discusses Microsoft's Network Load Balancing. Network Load Balancing is a software-based load-balancing technology used by Application Center 2000 to build and manage clusters. This chapter discusses different Network Load Balancing configuration options, how it is deployed, and advanced configuration options.
- Chapter 6, "Using Hardware Load Balancing in a Web Farm," discusses features of hardware load balancing devices. Features covered include load balancing algorithms, connection persistence options, and the effect on network topology. This chapter also provides pros and cons of hardware load balancing devices versus Network Load Balancing.
- Chapter 7, "Dissecting Web Farm Application Architectures," discusses the application architecture of Web farms that use classic Windows 2000 technologies like COM+ and Microsoft .NET technologies. Included is the presentation of a diagramming system to help map application constructs to servers in a Web farm.

- Chapter 8, "Designing Web Farm Application Deployment Environments," introduces the concept of the deployment architecture. Included are different options for handling deployment change control procedures and application deployment processes. One-, two-, three-, and four-tier deployment architectures are compared and contrasted.
- Chapter 9, "Using Internet Information Services in a Web Farm," discusses advanced IIS configuration options related to Web farms. Understanding IIS security, application architecture, and the IIS metabase is key to successful Web farm management. Many examples for manipulating the IIS metabase through scripting are presented.
- Chapter 10, "Using Component Services (COM+) in a Web Farm," discusses COM+ services as they relate to Web farm applications and deployment. COM+ provides administrative control and automated deployment and extends classic COM components. This chapter covers all the features of COM+ and how they affect Web farms.

Solving Web Farm Deployment Problems Using Application Center 2000

Chapters 11–16 discuss using Application Center 2000 to build highly available and scalable Web farms. Key to this concept is the ability to manage a farm of servers like a single server. These chapters provide an experienced administrator insight into Application Center 2000 deployment and implementation issues.

- Chapter 11, "Introducing Application Center 2000," introduces the deployment and management tool of choice for Web farms based on Microsoft DNA and .NET technologies. Installation and a high-level overview of the administrative console are presented.
- Chapter 12, "Deploying Application Center 2000 Web Clusters," outlines a step-by-step process for creating a Web cluster. Web clusters are Application Center groupings of servers that share content and increase the scalability of Web farms. This chapter covers the management of membership, the deployment of applications, and the creation of abstract Application Center 2000 applications in a cluster.
- Chapter 13, "Deploying Application Center 2000 COM+ Clusters," outlines a step-by-step process for creating COM+ clusters. COM+ clusters come in two forms: clusters that use Component Load Balancing—a new technology for achieving scale out for COM+ components—and Network Load Balancing. How to use a COM+ cluster, creating a COM+ routing cluster, and deploying and using COM+ applications are also covered.
- Chapter 14, "Monitoring a Web Farm with Application Center 2000," introduces a monitoring tool that integrates with Application Center 2000. Based on Windows Management Instrumentation (WMI), Health Monitor enables the creation of monitoring scripts and actions that better enable administrators to track and discover problems with Web farms before major outages occur.

- Chapter 15, "Performing Common Health Monitor Tasks," discusses all the tasks that an administrator can perform with Health Monitor 2.1. Creating data collectors for monitoring the event log to COM+ applications is covered, along with creating actions that occur when data collector criteria are met.
- Chapter 16, "Performing Advanced Application Center 2000 Tasks," discusses advanced tasks in Application Center 2000. Using the command-line interface, working with Site Server 3.0 applications, and deploying application security are covered.

Using Windows Cluster Server for High Availability Systems

Chapters 17–22 discuss Windows Cluster Service, which is used to provide high availability for server applications. Cluster Service provides redundancy for file shares, message queues, IIS virtual directories, and COM+ applications. Cluster Service is the only clustering option for SQL Server 2000.

- Chapter 17, "Introducing Windows Server Clusters," introduces Windows Server clusters, the server high-availability solution for Windows Advanced and DataCenter server. Cluster server clusters are shared nothing clusters that require special hardware that is shared between members of the cluster. Topics include a feature overview, installation of cluster service, and limitations of cluster service.
- Chapter 18, "Creating a Windows 2000 Server Cluster," discusses the steps required to create a cluster service cluster. Topics include using the Clustering Wizard, configuring groups, configuring resources, and testing failover scenarios.
- Chapter 19, "Clustering Application Resources," provides step-by-step instructions for adding standard server resources that can be clustered. These resources include file shares, generic Windows applications, generic Windows services, print spoolers, COM+ applications, IIS virtual roots, distributed transaction coordinator, and Microsoft Message Queue Service.
- Chapter 20, "Architecting Databases for Web Farms," discusses highly available database architectures for Web farms using Microsoft Windows Server clusters. Included is a discussion of RAID, SANs, and the growing hardware-based clustering and scalability options for SQL Server 2000.
- Chapter 21, "Clustering SQL Server 2000," provides a step-by-step process for creating a SQL 2000 cluster. Using multiple SQL 2000 instance configurations is covered, along with using the SQL Server Install Wizard to set up SQL on a Windows Server cluster.
- Chapter 22, "Maintaining a Cluster," covers best clustering practices, removing resources from a cluster, upgrading applications and the operating system on a cluster, and migration strategies for applications to and from a Windows Server cluster.

Securing Web Farms

- Chapter 23, "Securing a Web Farm," discusses security problems of Web farms, including best practices for solving security problems, using firewalls, server hardening, security policy, and the concept of defense in depth. A great Web farm without proper security is just a shiny prize for hackers.

Summary

.NET is the future of Microsoft: a broad technology strategy refocusing Microsoft's efforts to integrate businesses on the Internet. With the .NET framework, Microsoft takes advantage of its experience in integration technologies like COM to integrate Internet objects using SOAP. Through the .NET building block services, Microsoft offers distributed Internet software as a service. Using .NET devices, Microsoft will open the door to embedded platforms to access .NET services and applications over the Internet. Finally, the .NET Enterprise Servers provide the platform for delivering any Internet-enabled .NET solution. The only company capable of executing the .NET vision, Microsoft successfully united the desktop and is attempting to conquer the Internet in the same fashion.

.NOT: Web Farms the Wrong Way

CHAPTER

2

IN THIS CHAPTER

A Web farm is a collection of servers dedicated to providing Web-based content for end users. Some servers are dedicated Web servers that provide static HTML content; others are database servers that store and retrieve customer data or provide dynamic content. Web farms are complicated machines that have incredible flexibility in construction and design. This flexibility breeds diversity, which ensures the possibility of constructing a quality Web farm. Diversity in architecture also guarantees Web farms that are destined to fail. Knowing the path to failure is as important as knowing the path to success. Hence, .NOT is born.

.NOT is the opposite of .NET. A .NOT Web farm was built without .NET principles in mind. Many different problems that .NOT Web farms face are presented throughout this chapter. The solutions to .NOT problems come from reading this book. Read this section to better understand the problems of .NOT Web farms.

New Term A *.NOT Web farm* is a Web farm that was designed incorrectly using .NET enterprise servers. .NOT Web farms perform poorly, have many problems, and lack the characteristics of a well-designed Web farm.

Most Web farms contain many Web sites. A Web site is an online application that runs on the servers of a Web farm. As with Web farms, Web sites have incredible flexibility in construction but are susceptible to failure if poorly designed. A .NOT Web site exists on a .NOT Web farm, and each can affect the success of the other. In a sense, their fates are intertwined.

The goals of this chapter are to help you

- Characterize .NOT by identifying problems with application, server, network, and deployment architectures and by providing a list of mistakes made by .NOT business and technology decision makers.
- Identify the downtime problems of .NOT by discussing change-management problems, lack of redundancy, and bad coding practices.
- Identify the capacity, load, and scaling problems of .NOT by discussing reasons for slow performance and suggested ways of addressing it. Limitations to scaling .NOT Web farms are also discussed.
- Analyze .NOT sites that fail and those that succeed to help decision makers determine how to improve their existing Web farms.

A .NOT Site Is Born: Foo.com

Foo Incorporated is a fictitious company that is in the business of supplying foo to the world. Of course, its main competition is from Bar Incorporated, which supplies bar to the world. Foo Inc. is a traditional business and has a corporate headquarters, distribution centers, and regional sales offices. Bar Inc. recently launched a successful Web site to move its business to the Internet. In an effort to catch up, the president of Foo Inc. mandated that Foo.com would launch in record time.

The IT staff at Foo Inc. was ill prepared for such an announcement, but he took the task in stride. He had little time to plan Foo.com, and the budget was limited. A few of the IT staff had minimal experience building Web sites for the company intranet. These poor individuals were assigned the task of transferring this knowledge to the online business. The corporate intranet was a single server using Access and IIS. This server, for all intents and purposes, was never very busy, so a single server looked like all the Foo.com effort would need.

This initial site design was done so fast and the president was so impressed that he decided not to wait any longer. Foo.com was launched, and customers began using it. At first, only a few customers ever used the site at one time, and most had a decent experience. Soon, however, as word spread about the new site, more and more customers started using Foo.com. The site started slowing down, and people began complaining about strange errors that didn't show up when the site was less popular.

The president was concerned, and the IT staff was baffled. How could they solve these problems? What had they done wrong?

Characterizing a .NOT Site

Most .NOT sites have a number of common characteristics. .NOT sites have simple application frameworks that are constructed from basic HTML and the intrinsic ASP objects. They usually exist on a single server and have small operating budgets. .NOT sites typically work well with a few users and fail with large numbers of users. .NOT sites resemble intranet sites and are usually rushed to market.

Application Framework Problems

There is considerable application power in the initial configuration of Windows 2000 Server, which includes Internet Information Services (IIS). The default Web site of IIS is easily modified with a simple HTML editor. A minimal understanding of HTML, a connection to the Internet, and IIS are all that is required to join the Internet community. This power is great for small, simple user communities. However, when larger user communities are expected, an ASP object such as Session can fail outright if it is not used properly. The failure to understand and use this power properly is the reason most .NOT Web sites are unsuccessful.

Another common application framework problem is where to store persistent data. Typically, with .NOT, persistent data is stored in files or file-based databases like Access. These databases fail to scale correctly with larger user communities. Even if SQL Server 2000 is used, this will not ensure success. Most .NOT SQL Server implementations perform poorly because they are missing indices, lack referential integrity, and require normalization.

Finally, .NOT application frameworks suffer because businesses fail to provide the proper time to plan robust application architectures. Even a simple Web site can fail if the application framework is inadequate.

NOTE

Application frameworks and architectures are discussed in Chapter 7, "Dissecting Web Farm Application Architectures."

Server Architecture Problems

Problems with .NOT server architectures include slowdowns under load, intermittent crashes, and server thrashing. Thrashing is caused when individual services on the same machine compete for limited resources like CPU, disk I/O, and memory. Frustrating intermittent bugs and complete site meltdowns are common under single-server configurations. Overestimating the business need of an e-business application is likely if a .NOT site does not stress a single-server configuration.

NEW TERM *Server thrashing* is the process in which the software services in use on a single machine consume all of a server's resources.

How Can You Tell a Server Is Thrashing?

Symptoms of server thrashing are easy to detect. From the perspective of the user, the Web site experience includes many timeouts, intermittent errors, and server not responding errors (such as 404 and 502). Sometimes the problems may come in spurts as the thrashing corrects itself over time, only to start again when the condition that caused the thrashing reoccurs.

Every server has a thrashing point, and a load test is a good way to determine when a server will thrash. When a good load test is not possible, it is best to observe the server during the peak load hours. Peak load hours will vary from site to site, so use Performance Monitor to tell when a site is under heavy use. A good counter used to determine the amount of load a Web server is under is Web Services, Current Connections, Total Connections. This counter will tell you the average number of user connections to a Web site over time. Once peak load times are determined, use Task

Manager to track the memory and CPU utilization of the server. Processes to watch include `inetinfo.exe` (the main IIS process), `sqlservr.exe` (the main SQL Server process), `dllhost.exe` (the COM+ process wrapper), and any other process that takes more than 50% of the CPU on a consistent basis. Determining which processes are using the most server resources leads to what may be wrong.

Other symptoms of thrashing occur because of low memory. In a low memory situation, determined by looking at total memory utilization in Task Manager, a hard drive may have excessive activity. This is called hard-drive thrashing, and it occurs because memory is being swapped to disk constantly. The easiest way to tell if a hard drive is thrashing is to watch the hard drive indicator on the server for constant activity.

Simplicity, cost, and convenience are the main considerations when building .NOT server architectures. The database, Web server, and messaging server reside on a single physical computer. Some businesses want to avoid expensive initial deployments on multiple machines in case the market for its Web site was overestimated. While this is shrewd decision making, no business can succeed without the proper investment.

Network Architecture Problems

Although the network architectures that underlie the .NOT site can vary widely, generally they consist of simply connecting the corporate network to the Internet. While other network architectures can be hidden from the business owner because the site is hosted at an offsite location, the potential benefits of a hosting company's network are often negated by .NOT application design problems.

Choosing to host a site internally presents a number of difficult questions for the network administrator. Most businesses with Internet connectivity restrict Internet activities of employees using proxy servers and firewalls. A .NOT site offers services to customers over the Internet and, when placed on the same network as an employee's computer, poses a network and security risk. Connection sharing by outbound employee activity and inbound site traffic is dangerous because any spike in bandwidth utilization from both directions could affect network performance. Figure 2.1 shows a typical .NOT site configuration.

NOTE

Network architecture for a Web farm is discussed in Chapter 4, "Planning a Web Farm Network."

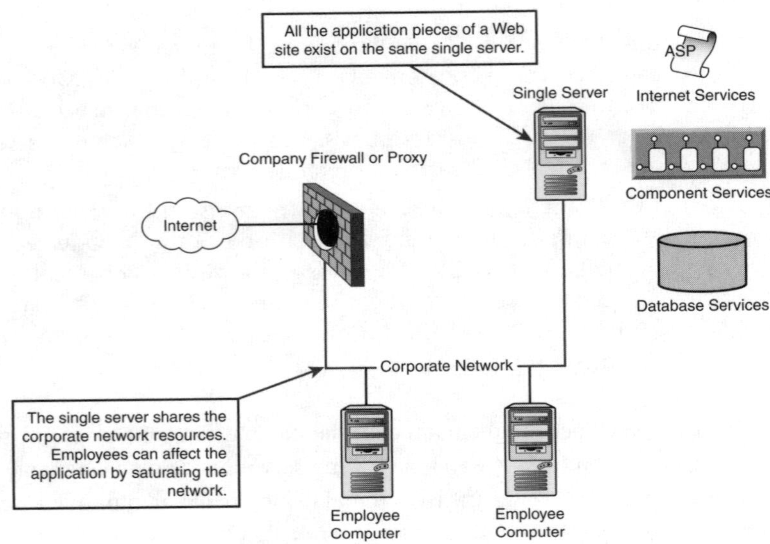

FIGURE 2.1
A typical .NOT site.

Deployment Architecture Problems

Deployment is the process of moving the application components from a development environment to a production environment. With a .NOT site, this is similar to the server architecture; all deployment stages exist on a single server. Most .NOT sites lack a process for approving and testing site changes as new features are released.

Without a deployment plan, changes to a .NOT site happen quickly and dangerously. An errant click, improper configuration, or coding error could affect the health and availability of a site. In worst-case scenarios, rebuilding the entire server is the only alternative; contingency planning at that stage is non-existent.

NOTE

Web farm deployment is discussed in Chapter 8, "Designing Web Farm Application Deployment Environments."

Avoiding .NOT Business Mistakes

While effectively migrating a .NOT site to a Web farm that uses .NET enterprise servers is unlikely, avoiding a few common mistakes in the beginning will allow a business to react better to the growth and lifecycle problems of a burgeoning online presence.

- *Define requirements of a site* cleanly to ensure that the requested functionality is delivered. Piecemeal requirements lead to sloppy code, missed delivery dates, and unhappy customers.
- *Spend money effectively* by understanding both the long-term goals of an e-business initiative and the short-term needs for success. It is much easier to spend twice the amount up front than four times the amount in the end. Building a Web farm is like building a house. It is much easier and cheaper to add a room in the beginning than at the end.
- *Setting proper business goals* is the best way to manage and measure e-business application success. If a goal is to handle all business-to-business transactions of a billion-dollar company in the next two years over the Web, it is unrealistic to expect a two-month solution to meet all business needs. Phased deliverables and realistic milestones are the best ways to manage the change that moving to a .NET Web farm will bring to a business.

Avoiding .NOT Technology Mistakes

All .NOT sites share some common technology design flaws. With a few simple guiding principles being employed from the start, the transition to a .NET Web farm can be much easier. The problem areas include thinking single server, lacking a component-based approach, and using ASP session. The following list highlights these problem areas further:

- *Thinking single server* means a developer includes code in a site that ties the disparate components of a site together in a way that renders them incapable of functioning separately. For example, sloppy ASP code that does not use abstracted data connection techniques, like Data Source Names (DSNs) and Universal Data Links (UDLs), can be written in such a way that it forces the SQL server to be installed locally. The minimal effort required using DSNs and UDLs when connecting to a database far outweighs any misperceived benefit to not using them.
- *Lacking component design* means not taking advantage of the power of component-based applications. With components, sites have improved performance because, unlike ASP, the code in components is compiled. Applications are easier to deploy and segment because business logic is encapsulated inside components. Finally, a component-based approach greatly simples any transition from a .NOT site to a .NET one.

- *The use of ASP session* is the biggest reason sites will not scale. ASP session is a simple way to maintain state across multiple ASP/HTML pages of a site. However, ASP session is tied to a single server. If the number of visitors to a Web site grows beyond the capacity of a single server, use of ASP session can limit the scalability choices of a business. The session object in ASP.NET is designed to handle these scenarios. Many existing sites will have to migrate to take advantage of ASP.NET.

NOTE

For more information on ASP.NET, see Appendix A, "Preparing for ASP.NET."

Foo.com Is Down Again!

Foo.com is having serious problems keeping its site up and running. As complaints come pouring in, the IT staff is desperately trying to fix the problems as they are reported. In doing so they made changes to some of the ASP pages and caused another problem. A cascading effect occurred and the whole site had to be closed because of the volume of customer complaints and errors that appeared in the orders. Their lack of change control and deployment process was causing site downtime.

Outside of the deployment process, users were reporting seeing other customer's orders and a loss of their personal customer data. They were using ASP session to track a user's progress through the site, but because the code was poorly designed, it was almost impossible to track down the bug that produced the reported result. They created a COM component that stored session information in the Access database of the site and put that object in a user's session object. This seemed to fix the problem, but because they stored this object in ASP session, they stared having slowdowns, lockups, and other problems on Foo.com.

Finally, the server that was running Foo.com failed. A hard drive malfunctioned, and the server had to be rebuilt. Without a backup, the site was down for 24 hours as the IT staff worked feverishly to repair the box. The president was furious.

How is Foo.com going to fix its deployment problem? How will they address their bad coding practices? How will they introduce redundancy to their environment?

Reasons for Site Downtime

The challenges of a .NOT site will continue even after deployment and go-live are complete. A single-server Web farm will have problems that cause site failure. Many sites perform well and function perfectly with a few users interacting on the server. Add hundreds of simultaneous users and the application begins to choke on the volume of transactions. Software and hardware under stress are more likely to fail. Over time, administrators make mistakes. A .NOT site at this phase is difficult to manage, maintain, and enlarge. All Web farms have downtime. Web sites in this phase experience unmanaged change, hardware failures, and coding problems.

Change Management Problems

Ineffective change management is the biggest cause of site downtime. In a single-server Web farm, changes to servers and applications occur in the production environment. Unmanaged changes that cause downtime include service packs to the OS, service packs for server applications, configuration changes to server applications, and new application releases. Testing change with the single-server environment is impossible. There is no predicting success or failure. Change happens *ad hoc*, with business managers hoping those involved know the expected outcome. Deployment architectures solve these problems by providing a mechanism for managing change throughout the Web farm lifecycle.

Lack of Redundancy Problems

In the single-server scenario, hardware failure equates to downtime and poor availability. Sites dependent on a single point of failure at the hardware level are guaranteed to fail. Thinking single server is expensive. The only way to address single points of failure in .NOT sites is by purchasing a cold spare server. A *cold spare* is a fully configured, up-to-date server that is used only when there is a hardware failure. Managing and maintaining the cold spare requires the same effort as a multiserver Web farm.

Bad Coding Problems

Coding errors can cause serious downtime issues. Using ASP session state with COM objects, improper use of multithreading, memory leaks in custom code, and over allocation of precious server resources can cause intermittent site failures and server crashes.

Solving Downtime Dilemmas

Every .NOT site has experienced downtime. Some downtime is unavoidable, no matter what preparation and planning a business might make. Other downtime is avoidable and correctable. Changing business processes and adding simple methodologies help prevent downtime. .NOT sites can prevent some downtime by developing a simple release-and-deployment strategy, purchasing a second production server, and addressing improper custom-coding issues. The following expands on these items further:

- *Develop a simple release and deployment strategy* to manage the change-release process. Figure 2.2 shows the addition of a development server. A development server is an exact copy of the production server used by an internal business team for development and testing of new features, service packs, and server configuration changes.

This development server acts as a first defense against downtime from mismanaged releases into production. While this is not the ideal deployment architecture, it is better than a single server. Advanced deployment architectures are discussed in Chapter 8.

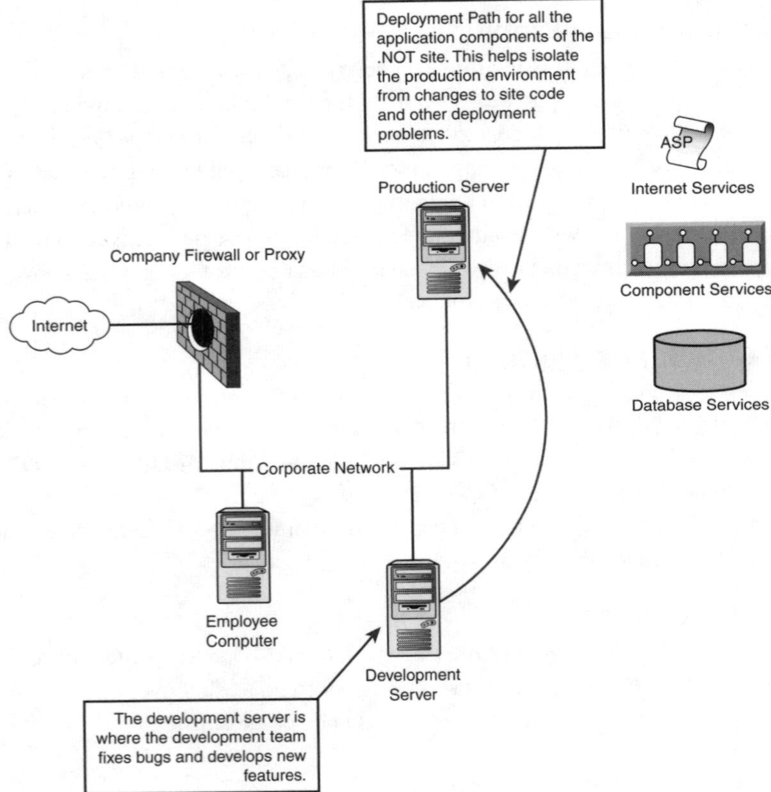

FIGURE 2.2
A .NOT site with a simple deployment path.

- *Purchase a second production server* to provide a cold spare when production hardware fails. While this is not the ideal solution and does not solve any scalability problems, it starts an organization down the right path to building highly available Web farms. With a cold spare, hardware is not fully utilized. Figure 2.3 shows the evolution to multiple production replicas for increased availability. Keeping production servers in sync will become the biggest challenge with this new strategy. For a more in-depth discussion of availability and scalability, see Chapter 3, "Scalability and Availability of Web Farms." For help managing a multiple-server Web farm, see Chapter 11, "Introducing Application Center 2000."

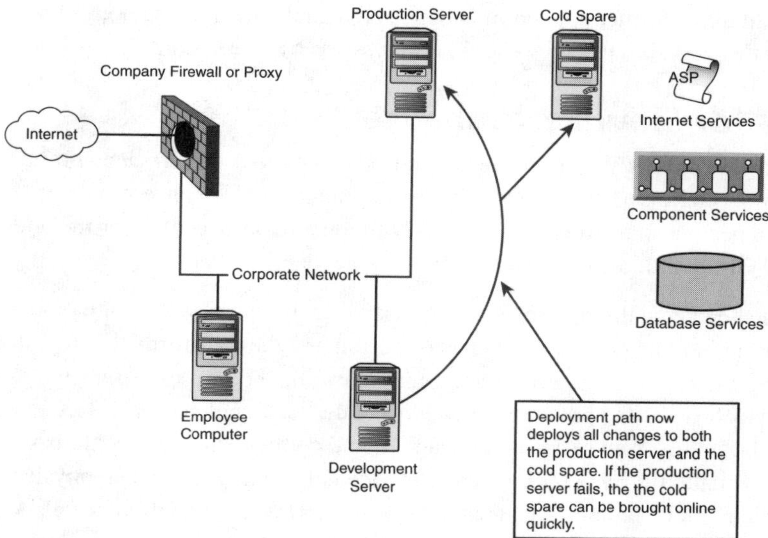

FIGURE 2.3
A .NOT site with a cold spare.

- *Address custom code problems* where possible and eliminate bad coding practices. See Appendix B, "Addressing Custom Code Problems in ASP 3.0," for more information.

Foo.com Cannot Handle the Load

Foo.com is having problems again, and this time the site is very slow. They were able to fix most of the bugs after addressing their deployment problems. They purchased a new primary server and a cold spare for Foo.com. They were smart and took the old server and made it a development server. They added a few components to speed up the slower portions of the site and quit storing them inside ASP session. Things improved for a while, customers quit complaining, and the president was happy again.

Then the user community grew to a point where the server was constantly at 90–100% CPU utilization. They looked at the IIS process, and it was using 90% of the CPU. They couldn't figure out what inside this process was so processor intensive. In development they tried to simulate the load and removed features one by one. Finally they determined that data access was causing most of the CPU utilization. They would have to move to a dedicated SQL Server 2000 implementation and purchase a database server. This would require a complete rewrite of the database code, and the president was not happy.

As they were planning this rewrite, the Foo.com IT staff realized the cold spare was a wasted resource. They wanted to create a site that used all their available resources. They determined that they could make further application changes to enable them to use both servers simultaneously. While this added to their rewrite time, it was the right decision.

Reasons for Slow Performance

Performance problems of Web farms never end. The causes of performance problems change as a site grows. Single-server sites exhibit a few common performance problems. Primarily, single servers become starved for resources. Symptoms of a starved server include high CPU utilization, hard-drive thrashing, and low memory availability.

A successful site eventually outgrows a single-server configuration. When the performance of a single server can no longer meet the needs of customers, the transformation to a distributed Web farm begins. To enhance performance and relieve the bottlenecks of a single server, a tiered or service-oriented approach is best. Physically, each application service exists on a separate server. Database, Web services, messaging, and component services are isolated from one another. This is called *service scaling*; each service is localized to a single physical computer and is a single point of failure. This technique will improve the scalability of a site, but it is only a small step toward true scalability and availability. Figure 2.4 depicts service scaling a Web farm.

NEW TERM *Service scaling* is the isolation of .NET services like IIS, SQL Server, and Exchange onto separate physical servers.

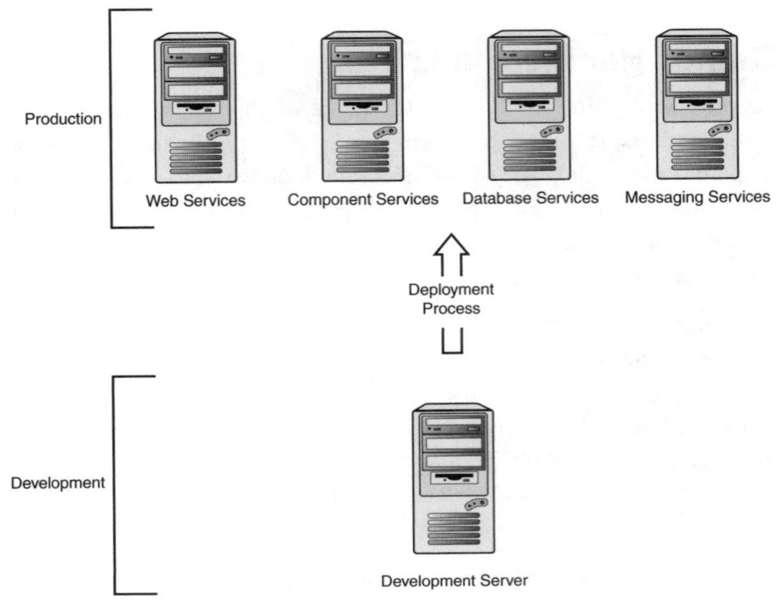

FIGURE 2.4
A .NOT Web farm with simple service scaling.

Poor database design also causes slow performance. As the number of and time to execute queries grow with increased use, overall site response time increases. Finally, excessive ASP scripting keeps IIS busy running business logic and unable to handle HTTP requests.

Scaling Problems with .NOT Sites

Scaling means increasing the capacity of the site to handle more visitors and complex business logic. All scaling is accomplished through distribution of work across multiple servers. Scaling a site is a step toward evolving to a Web farm that uses .NET enterprise servers. This is when difficult choices are made concerning the overall direction of the site. Figure 2.5 shows a fully scaled site.

FIGURE 2.5
A fully scaled site.

Scaling is accomplished in two ways: scaling up or scaling out. Scaling up means increasing the CPU power, memory, network speed, and hard drive quality and capacity of a single server. In the Windows 2000 space, there is an upward limit to scaling up, because 8-, 16-, and 32-way processor servers are available only now. Scaling out is the process of adding servers that have similar responsibilities to a collection or farm. For example, a Web server handles incoming HTTP requests on the TCP/IP port 80. There are tools and technologies that can manipulate the flow of TCP/IP packets targeted at one specific IP address to many IP addresses. In a scaling out scenario, many Web servers handle the requests of a single URL. This is the preferred method for solving performance problems because it also increases the availability of a site.

Solving Performance Issues

Every Web site faces performance problems during its lifecycle. With .NOT sites, it is sometimes possible to correct these situations. In the majority of cases, the performance issue is related to a fundamental problem with the site architecture or code. When these problems are identified, it may be necessary to redesign or recode portions of a site. Adding more hardware can solve performance issues sometimes. In cases of a starved server, excessive ASP scripting, problem databases, or an inability to service scale a site, a careful analysis of site capacity usually provides the best answer. The following will help detail these ideas further.

- *Correcting a starved server situation* is accomplished by increasing server capacity. Moving units of work to a different server increases capacity. Most starved server situations are due to problems that are exacerbated by heavy user load.
- *Databases have many unique challenges* in resolving site performance problems. Sites that rely on SQL Server for important e-business functionality are well on their way to success. If a site relies on a flat-file database or Access, the challenge is much more difficult because these technologies don't have a server component. Queries against these database engines are designed to run locally and share resources with the originating server. They are not distributable. To improve site performance properly, applications that rely on Access or flat files must be migrated to a distributable database engine like SQL Server. Once any necessary migration is complete, distributing the database engine onto a single dedicated server begins the process of creating a .NET Web farm. When using SQL Server or Oracle, this is a relatively simple process because these database engines are designed to exist on dedicated server machines.
- *Beyond the database server configuration choices* are difficulties a custom application has when dealing with the change from a local database engine to remote. If developed application logic relies on close proximity, code changes are necessary. Also, security will likely become a problem as secured authorization to database resources changes in scope with a dedicated database server.
- *Excessive ASP scripting* affects performance of even dedicated Web servers. ASP scripting is an excellent and viable tool for building custom Web applications. However, until the wider adoption of ASP.NET, many existing sites suffer performance problems due to ASP scripting. Solving the scripting problem involves creating compiled components using VB or VC++/ATL that encapsulate the same functionality as the scripting. These components can be created and used from within the same scripting page that executed the original script. This will greatly improve site performance. If an ASP page has more than 10 lines of consecutive scripting logic, it is a good candidate for componentization. In ASP.NET, all code is compiled, which will improve site performance dramatically.

Analyzing the Success of Foo.com

Foo.com is far from an ideal Web farm built with .NET enterprise servers. However, it is a booming, successful site. In its current form it has limited scaling capabilities and many problems with redundancy. With a scalable application tier, Foo.com will be able to add more Web servers to handle increased traffic. The Web tier can grow, but without a good deployment engine like Application Center 2000, administrators will struggle to keep all the servers in sync, increasing downtime. What happens when the database fails? SQL Server 2000 requires cluster server for high availability, and techniques for doing this are discussed in Chapter 21, "Clustering SQL Server 2000." Foo.com does not have the proper network architecture to handle growth, and it is not ready for hackers and security problems. Foo.com is in for a wild ride!

Scrapping a .NOT Site

If a site is in the process of scaling, many changes occur to the server architecture and application. For servers to scale well, the network infrastructure must be ready for additional server resources. For an application to scale well, the application code must be able to handle running on multiple servers simultaneously. If the application or server architecture does not meet these requirements, these sites should be scrapped and rebuilt to scale properly.

Scrapping a site is an individual business decision. However, there are some fundamental issues that help center this discussion on the correct topics.

- *Site functionality is complete* and working correctly. If this is true, then scrapping the site is not a viable option. However, if intermittent problems plague a site, it is likely that the process of enlarging the site to handle the load has rendered much of the code and functionality suspect.
- *Current site code prevents scaling* and significant rework is necessary to allow scaling beyond a single server. Here, the choice has to be made to fix a poorly designed site or redesign a site correctly. Many businesses choose to fix a poorly designed site. This is not the correct decision. For example, if a site relies on the ASP session object, it can scale effectively to multiple Web servers. However, because of the session object, users will be tied to a specific box. If this box were to fail, all session information would be lost. Because it is likely that every page of a site will have some ASP session object code, every page will have to be changed. This equates to a poor man's redesign. Patching a site that won't scale to allow scaling increases the debugging and testing cycle. If significant rework is required, start the site over. Dealing with a few months of scaling and performance problems is worth the effort it will take to build a properly designed scalable site.
- *Faster hardware exists.* If the hardware a site was deployed with is obsolete, then upgrading to the fastest servers could correct some scalability problems. Remember that single server and service scaling don't address any availability issues. Faster and bigger servers will still fail as often as slower ones. Always buy the best hardware, but don't rely on hardware to keep a Web farm available.

Critiquing a Booming Site

A booming site is one that far exceeds the expectations and needs of a business and its customers. Determining such success is dependent on individual metrics that vary from business to business. While all sites are different, most successful ones are built in a similar way. Figure 2.6 shows the ideal architecture of a successful site. Compare this to other site architectures in this chapter. Many of the concepts depicted here are discussed in the first seven chapters of this book.

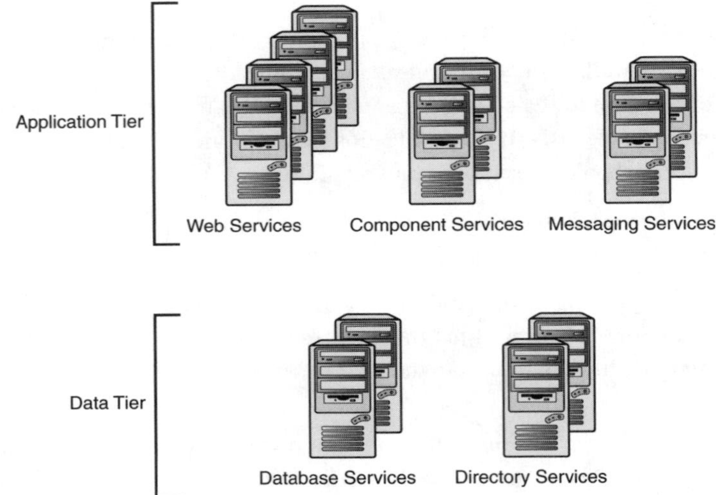

FIGURE 2.6
The ideal architecture of a successful site.

Careful examination of a booming site is useful for information gathering. It is helpful to examine a site with certain criteria in mind so that an informed judgment about what improvements to make can be made. Booming sites have availability concerns, single points of failure, deployment issues, network architecture problems, and security vulnerabilities. Careful site scrutiny leads to development of good, continuous improvement processes. To generate a report card on a booming site, consider the following points.

- *Single points of failure* will cause downtime. A single point of failure is any link in the flow of information from customers to a Web farm that is not redundant. Examples of single points of failure include firewalls, non-clustered databases, DNS servers, and remote COM+ objects. On a server level, a single point of failure includes CPUs, power supplies, network cards, and hard drives. In almost all cases, eliminating a single point of failure is possible, with a trade-off in cost.

- *Deployment issues* will cause downtime. Every Web farm experiences deployment problems. The old adage "if it ain't broke, don't fix it" applies to Web farms. A Web farm is a complicated machine with many moving parts. If one piece fails after a deployment, the entire site may become unavailable. Some deployment steps, like changes to the structure of a database, will require downtime, but a bigger problem is when scheduled changes and fixes cause downtime. Having a well-defined, repeatable deployment process helps eliminate problems that occur when Web farms change.
- *Network utilization and capacity problems* can cause site failure. If network utilization reaches saturation, a Web farm will slow down. Points to consider when critiquing a network include Internet bandwidth use, internal network use, and router/switch capacity problems. Solving network capacity problems is a slow and arduous process. Create a two-year plan to estimate the Web farm's network growth. Without this plan, increased site use could saturate the network.
- *Availability affects the profitability* of a Web farm. Availability is a measure of the site's uptime compared to scheduled and unscheduled maintenance. Improving these areas is an ongoing process for any Web farm. A Web farm's availability should also be a measure of success for the IT team supporting it.
- *Security vulnerabilities* must be dealt with; otherwise a business risks having sensitive information compromised, mistrust from customers, and extended downtime. Having sensitive information such as credit card data compromised would affect sales from online business. If the application and data tiers were damaged, days of uptime could be wasted restoring them. Just as with a physical storefront, a proprietor would never leave the doors unlocked.

Defining the Ideal Site

In an ideal site, application services and server configuration information are organized into tiers. Tiers form a logical organization of the physical and conceptual pieces of a Web farm. The complete picture for any Web farm can be reduced into four distinct tiers.

Application Tier Basics

The application tier is comprised of custom and .NET services. These services define the functional breadth of an application. In cases where the content of a site is simple HTML, the application tier is the HTML content and IIS. A more complex example is an e-commerce site. For e-commerce, the application tier includes custom HTML and ASP, messaging services, Web services, and custom COM+ applications. Figure 2.7 compares a simple and a complex application tier.

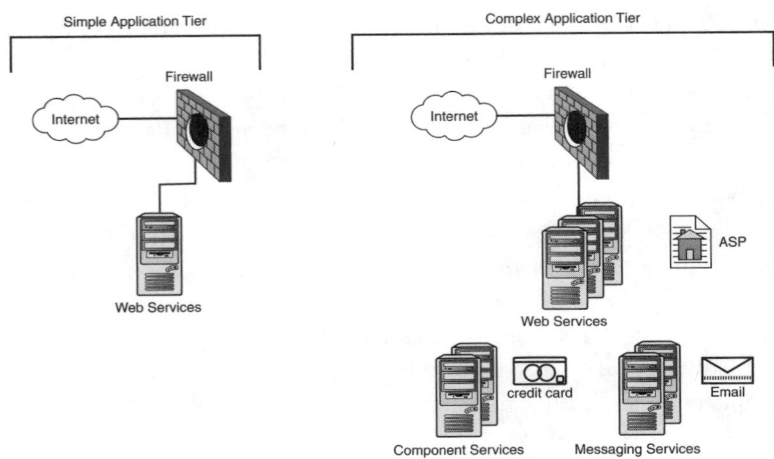

FIGURE 2.7
A comparison of a simple and a complex application tier.

Data Tier Basics

The data tier includes databases, directory services like LDAP and Active Directory, and OLAP providers. Most of the services in this tier are structural or foundational in nature. A database is a special case because some application logic is embedded in schema elements. Stored procedures, views, and tables are custom elements of an application that exist in the data tier. Active Directory is another special case of the data tier. An Active Directory describes networks, businesses, or any hierarchical system. With the .NET platform, Windows 2000 Active Directory provides security services for authenticating users to Web farms. Figure 2.8 shows a simple data tier.

Security Tier Basics

The security tier protects a Web farm from malicious activities and manages defined network access points. Abstractly, the security tier is the traffic cop of a Web farm. Services in the security tier include user authentication, management of IP traffic, and intrusion detection. Among the physical servers in the security tier are domain controllers, proxy servers, and firewalls. See Figure 2.9 for an example of a security tier.

Network Tier Basics

The network tier includes routers, switches, hubs, bridges, and cabling. The network is the nervous system of a Web farm. For example, the network tier enables the application tier to communicate with the data tier. The network tier provides the connectivity required by the Internet.

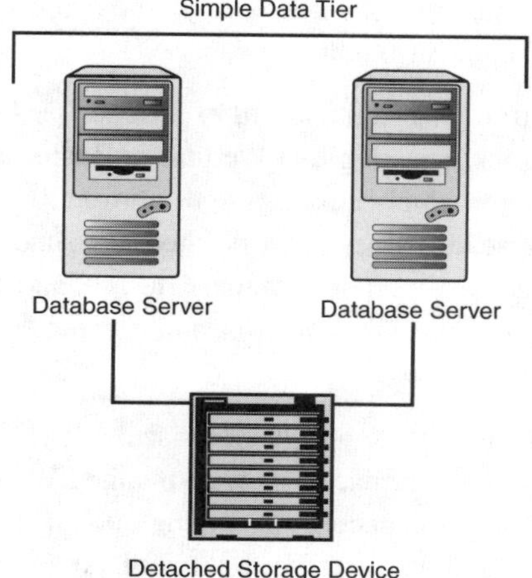

FIGURE 2.8
A simple data tier in the .NET framework.

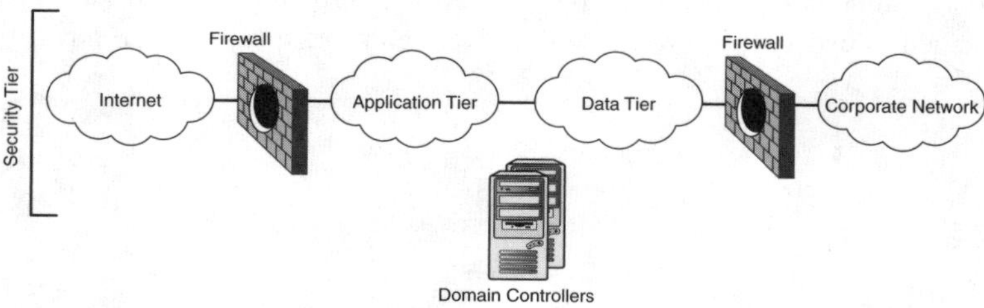

FIGURE 2.9
An ideal security tier.

Summary

When starting a site, the administrator is challenged with delivering a Web site from a business idea. Initial sites are similar to the default configurations of Windows 2000 Server and run on a single server. It is unfortunate that this configuration is not conducive to building a successful Web farm.

Once the site is live on the Internet, the administrator's job becomes keeping the site running. This is a challenging task because problems with hardware and software, the capability to handle the load, and a poor deployment process affect a site's availability. Sites in this phase typically address problems by developing a deployment process, purchasing a second server, and fixing custom code issues. Managing a site becomes a holistic endeavor, as all aspects of the application and infrastructure can cause downtime.

When a site's uptime begins to improve, most will experience performance issues. When this happens, the site begins the transformation to a Web farm. Businesses usually purchase a number of servers and isolate different application services onto individual servers. This is called service scaling. When service scaling doesn't work, there are fundamental reasons for slow performance, including starved servers, poor database design, and excessive ASP scripting. Adding servers, fixing common database problems, and componentizing ASP code can solve these problems.

If performance issues are solvable, a site will begin to scale. It is at this point in the evolution that some sites will be scrapped and replaced by well-planned Web farms using .NET enterprise servers. Businesses will make decisions on scaling up and scaling out and in some cases have to change the entire site architecture to be successful. At some point, faster hardware will not solve all the problems of scaling a site.

A Web farm that uses .NET enterprise servers correctly is a highly scalable, highly available Internet application. Unfortunately, the configuration and construction of this type of Web farm are not trivial. Understanding what a .NOT site is will help an administrator understand the challenges faced in evolving a .NOT site to a .NET enterprise server Web farm.

Scalability and Availability for a Web Farm

CHAPTER

3

IN THIS CHAPTER

Availability and scalability are the two most important concepts to understand when planning a Web farm using .NET enterprise servers. Success of an online business is dependent on a site's capability to meet the needs of a customer when that customer first browses the site. If a customer's initial experience is met with site unavailable messages and slow response times, confidence is decreased, no money exchanges hands, and return visits are unlikely. While not the direct concern of the administrator, any business owner will eventually demand that the site be highly available and perform well. Success in this area requires a thorough understanding of how the .NET platform handles scalability and availability.

The goals of this chapter are to help you

- Understand the concept of availability as it relates to a Web farm. Concepts introduced include the availability rating as it relates to the network, servers, and applications in a Web farm. Using the availability rating as a metric for success in a Web farm is also covered.
- Understand the concept of scalability as it relates to a Web farm. How scaling helps handle increased user load is covered, along with using scale to become a Web farm.
- Understand the techniques used in scaling a Web farm to handle increased user load. Network load balancing, hardware load balancing, component load balancing, and Windows Server clusters are all introduced as means to achieve scalability and availability in a Web farm.

Understanding Availability

When a user browses to a Web site and encounters any error or unexpected message, this results in a perception problem. This is equivalent to a customer walking into a store and finding all the employees in disarray and nothing getting done. Offline businesses have expected hours for business operations. For online businesses, operating hours are 24 hours a day. The expectation is for an online business to accept money whenever a transaction is executed. This capability to accept transactions 24 hours a day is called *availability*.

When a site is unavailable, it is said to have taken an availability "hit." When a site takes an availability hit, it is said to be "down." It is helpful to divide availability hits into two categories: scheduled and unscheduled downtime.

NEW TERM *Unscheduled downtime* is any time that site availability is affected except during scheduled maintenance, upgrades, new software releases, or other planned outages.

The Dot9s Scale

Availability is a ratio of the uptime of a site to unscheduled downtime over a given time period. This is referred to as the "dot9s" scale. A site is given an availability rating such as .9, which is "one nine," or .9999, which is "four nines." A "four nine" site is 99.9999% available. The formula for calculating this ratio is 100 – (Unscheduled Downtime/Period of Time)×100. For example, if a site is down for one hour in a day, the availability of that site in one day is 100 – (1/24)× 100 = 95.83333%. If a site is down one hour in a week, the availability is 100 – (60/10080) × 100 = 99.404%.

Is 100% Availability Realistic?

For a Web farm to obtain 100% availability, it cannot have unscheduled downtime. This should always be the goal of any Web farm, but it is unlikely. From the availability formula, a "four nine" site can have 31.536 seconds of downtime in a year, long enough to replace a network cable! This availability comes at considerable cost in redundant systems, and most businesses accept one or two nines as the goal. Table 3.1 shows some availability measurements.

TABLE 3.1 Availability Measurements

Percent Available	*Downtime Per Year*
90%	36.5 Days
95%	18.25 Days
98%	7.3 Days
99%	3.65 Days
99.9%	8.76 Hours
99.99%	52.56 Minutes
99.999%	315 Seconds
99.9999%	31.5 Seconds

Assessing a Web Farm's Availability

Availability measurements are useful only if an organization uses them properly. A successful strategy for considering availability statistics is to break the measurements into categories. These categories will differ for each Web farm, but basic categories include server availability, application availability, and network availability.

The disjointed nature of these categories means each measurement can be considered separately. This separation provides hard numbers for where money and resources should be spent to improve availability. If network availability is low, it doesn't make sense to invest time and effort in solving application availability problems.

All complex systems fail. Any failure can affect a Web farm's availability rating if the failure has no contingency. Realistic availability goals are achievable through redundancy.

Redundancy is the first line of defense for any site failure. In hardware systems, redundancy comes from complete copies of critical components. For example, a system with a redundant CPU has a spare CPU that is not used unless the primary CPU fails. If this failure occurs, the spare CPU takes over, enabling the system to continue processing without missing an instruction. With software systems like SQL Server 2000, redundancy comes from a cluster of servers, each capable of owning the database of the others. Redundancy eliminates single points of failure in complex systems. Each availability area has different ways to solve this problem.

Monitoring is the final step in assessing the availability of a Web farm. Without monitoring, it is not possible to determine when a component fails. Each area of a Web farm has different methodologies for error reporting.

Understanding Network Availability

The majority of network systems in a Web farm are physical. When building a network for high availability, redundancy must be considered at every level. Every point in the network should have a backup. From the connection, to the Internet, to the routers that move traffic throughout the farm, each level must be considered. Not every system in a Web farm network has to be redundant, however, and a cost-benefit analysis is the best way to determine at which points to build in redundancy.

For example, Foo.com has a front-end router that handles traffic from the Internet. If this router fails, the site is down. However, router failures are rare, and Foo.com decides to take a calculated risk and not have a cold spare sitting unused. A four-hour response time agreement with the router manufacturer is Foo.com's reason why they accept this downtime if it occurs. However, Foo.com decides that having redundant connections to the Internet is important, so they spend the extra money to have two connections to the Internet at all times. Each business will make the same decisions differently.

The most common area of failure in any network system is at the cable level. It is usually cost prohibitive to have redundant network cables between every point in a network. Luckily, it is relatively easy to diagnose and replace a faulty cable in a network.

Vendor-specific tools best handle monitoring the network for failures. There are tools that exist today that take the pulse of the entire network, ensuring that each connection is functioning correctly. When a failure does occur, these tools can alert an administrator to the problem.

NOTE

More information for building Web farm networks is found in Chapter 4, "Planning a Web Farm Network."

Understanding Server Availability

Single points of failure in server hardware include CPUs, hard drives, motherboards, and network cards. Hardware redundancy is purely a cost issue. Available on the market today for a price are servers that have three levels of redundancy for every internal system. Some businesses will invest considerable dollars to achieve complete hardware redundancy.

With .NET enterprise servers it is possible to create redundant configurations without the need for extreme hardware redundancy. The .NET platform eliminates single points of failure by providing simple software solutions so that multiple servers can handle the same task. With .NET, an administrator can designate two or more servers to provide redundancy and increased availability at the server level. This availability creates a natural pathway to scalability for a Web farm.

Monitoring server availability is best accomplished with the server vendor's tools. As part of the decision to standardize on a particular hardware platform, the monitoring software available should be a factor in the decision. These centralized monitoring tools can inform an administrator when any critical component of a server fails, from the CPU to the power supply. Without tools like this, monitoring for hardware failures is a crapshoot. If the drivers for a piece of hardware log errors to the NT event log, then tools like Microsoft Health Monitor can provide an alert. Watching the NT event log with Health Monitor is a way to alert on failures in redundant software systems like Windows Cluster Server and network load balancing.

NOTE

More Information on Health Monitor is available in Chapter 14, " Monitoring a Web Farm with Application Center 2000."

Understanding Application Availability

A more subtle aspect of building highly available systems is application availability. Application availability measures how the functions and features of a specific application perform throughout the Web site lifecycle. By gauging application availability, actual uptime is measurable. If any functional portion of a site, such as credit card authorization, must function to complete a transaction, then that portion's availability affects the overall site availability measurement. Even if the Web site itself is successfully providing content, if a transaction fails at any point, the site is unavailable.

By considering application availability, a new type of thinking emerges for application design. While load-balancing techniques help eliminate single points of failure in physical systems, software single points of failure are a more difficult problem to solve. With the credit card example, the application must be robust enough to continue the transaction either by deferring credit card authorization or switching to a different credit card service. Availability planning for credit card processing must consider redundant connections to a lending institution and load-balanced redundancy for credit card processing servers, and it must also provide service-level redundancy.

Building software systems that have this level of redundancy is a unique challenge. Each application will have different requirements. However, at the fundamental design level there are a few key points to consider when orchestrating an application availability solution.

- *Create software systems with well-defined boundaries.* This means that in the credit card example it should be fairly easy to tell when an application has entered the credit card processing engine. This enables an application to drop in a different system as long as the boundaries into that system look the same.
- *When an application data path leaves the boundaries of a Web farm,* this process is a good candidate for application availability. For instance, if an application makes a WAN connection to an external bank, this connection is by definition not under the control and management of the IT staff that manages the Web farm. In situations like this, alternative mechanisms from the Network layer to the Application layer should be thought through to provide the highest level of redundancy. This may mean purchasing a second WAN connection of a lesser speed and cost and having an agreement for credit card processing with a second bank.
- *For transaction-oriented systems,* build into the architecture a way to move to a batch-oriented processing engine. This means that in the credit-card example the same information would be gathered to process a credit card authorization, it would just not happen in real-time. The functionality of an application would be decreased in batch mode, but at least the transaction could be completed at a later time. It is much better to switch to batch-oriented processing than tell a customer to come back later. Later may never come.

The most complicated monitoring problem is application availability monitoring. Many applications rely on customer input to determine when critical systems fail. Beyond this, most monitoring endeavors for applications are custom built. Critical application components should add time in a delivery schedule to build and implement the appropriate monitoring. In some cases, there are tools that generate replay scripts that can simulate a user on a Web site. These tools can be used to test the functionality of a site and report when errors occur. Even tools like this will likely demand a full-time resource to manage and maintain these scripts for even remotely sophisticated sites.

Understanding Scheduled Downtime

Scheduled downtime should be the only reason a site becomes unavailable. Whenever a site has a scheduled release, hardware upgrade, planned ISP outage, or other required downtime scenario, this is scheduled downtime. Consider these downtimes as a separate measurement from unscheduled downtime. While it is important to improve this availability number, the goal should stay within what is reasonable in today's Web farms. New .NET Enterprise technologies, like Application Center 2000, will help improve the scheduled availability rating. Most of the improvements are to be made by improving the process for releasing new features into the production Web farm.

Measuring Overall Availability

When measuring overall availability, a business should consider total downtime as a separate measurement from total unscheduled downtime. Each area of availability is calculated separately to help direct where efforts to improve availability should be made. Keep a running total of the network, server, application, unscheduled, and scheduled availabilities. Combine the network, server, and application availability to create the unscheduled availability quotient. Combine all the availability ratings to create the overall availability rating. Table 3.2 has the availability ratings and goals for Foo.com, based on a six-month period.

TABLE 3.2 Foo.com's Availability Goals for Six Months

Availability Type	*Availability Goal*	*Downtime*	*Availability Measurement*
Network	99.9	1 hour	99.97%
Server	99.9	5 hours	99.88%
Application	99.9	10 hours	99.77%
Scheduled	99	70 hours	98.39%
Unscheduled	99.9	17 hours	99.61%
Overall	99	87 hours	98%

Foo.com does a good job of preventing unscheduled downtime. It is 0.3% away from its stated unscheduled availability goal. However, this is approximately 12 hours of downtime. In order to achieve this goal, application availability problems need to be addressed. To improve overall availability, Foo.com needs to work on the time it takes to perform scheduled maintenance tasks. Foo.com needs to make up 43 hours to reach its overall availability goal of 99%.

Understanding Scalability

Stress is a universal term that applies to both natural systems and computer systems. When a human feels stress, his coping mechanism differs according to the type of stress. When a Web farm experiences stress, its coping mechanisms differ according to the type of stress, too. A Web farm becomes stressed under many different scenarios. Some of the following items illustrate such stress factors:

- *Application changes and increased complexity* can cause stress as new features and options affect the performance of a Web farm.
- *Increasing the number of servers* can cause stress in other areas of the farm. Adding Web servers increases the connections to a COM+ cluster or SQL Server.
- *Site success can create stress* when a user community grows beyond the planned capacity of a .NET Web farm.
- *Server failures and crashes* can add stress to specific areas of a .NET Web farm, reducing the overall throughput until repairs are completed.

NEW TERM *Scalability* is a measure of a Web farm's capability to handle stress and the effort required to adjust overall site capacity on demand.

Handling Increased User Load

Increased user load occurs when a site gains popularity or during calendar-sensitive times like Christmas or the end of a fiscal quarter. Of course, meeting this demand is paramount because this is the time when a business earns the most money. To handle this stress and scale to meet the demand, most online businesses will have more server hardware than is required for normal business operations. The .NET platform's scaling strength is the capability to add server capacity seamlessly. It is through this "more is better" philosophy that the problem of single-server diminishing returns is eliminated. Where and how to add extra servers to a Web farm and whether an application can use this additional power are the main challenges when scaling to handle user load.

For example, Foo.com has a simple server architecture, shown in Figure 3.1. The Foo.com Web farm has a single Web server and a single database server. Foo.com has cyclic selling patterns, and during the last quarter users experienced delays in adding foo to their shopping baskets. When the administrators of Foo.com were watching the site, they noticed that the Web server CPU use was consistently 95%–100%. They decided that the best thing was to purchase the fastest server available. This is called *scaling up*. Unfortunately, when the end of the next quarter arrived, they noticed the same CPU utilization problem. The number of users had doubled, but the single fastest server available was still not powerful enough to handle the demand.

NEW TERM *Scaling up* is accomplished by increasing the memory, CPU speed, network speed, and hard drive capacity of a single server to address bottlenecks in performance.

When facing a situation where scaling up is no longer an option on a single server, the .NET platform has an alternative: scaling out. Scaling out means creating a pool of servers that performs the same work as a single server. This is where the term "Web farm" originated. A herd of cows is equivalent to a farm of servers. For Foo.com, this means purchasing a second Web server identical to the original server.

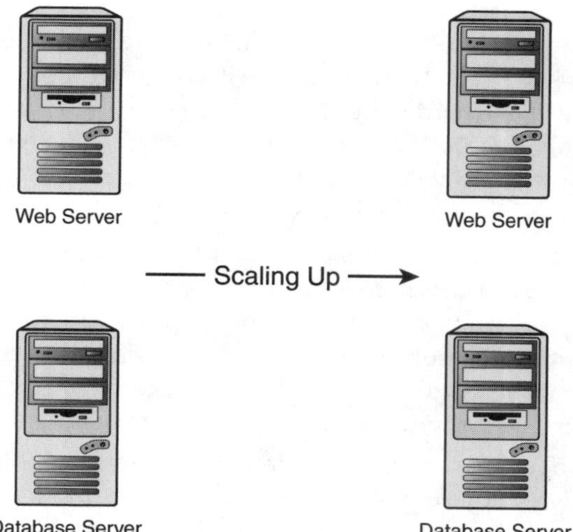

FIGURE 3.1
Scaling up Foo.com's Web Server.

NEW TERM *Scaling out* is accomplished by increasing the number of servers in a layer of a Web farm.

Determining How to Scale Up

When facing a situation where a server is over utilized, there are four different scenarios to consider. Two of the utilization problems come down to a relationship between CPU and memory. In fewer cases, utilization problems can relate to I/O bottlenecks. And even fewer problems relate to network throughput and performance. Knowing a few simple concepts can help an administrator diagnose these problems and make the right choice as to scaling up or scaling out.

In the first scenario, and the most common, the CPU utilization on a box under load with no application problems is stuck at 100%. In this situation, the CPU has too much work to do. There is adequate memory, and thus hard drive usage is not the problem. The only way to address this problem is to buy a bigger CPU or add a second one either to the same server or an additional server. With high CPU utilization situations, there will almost never be problems with memory, network speed, or disk space because the CPU has to wait on these devices and during these wait times cannot perform work. Thus, the CPU would not stay at 100%.

In the second scenario, the server is starved for RAM. In that case, the CPU will not be stuck at 100%, but it is likely the hard drive will be in constant use. This happens because Windows will use hard drive space like memory and swap memory sections in and out of RAM from one CPU request to another. When this happens, the box will perform slowly, but the CPU will not be the cause of the slowdown. The solution is to add more RAM if possible or add more servers.

In the third scenario, usually a problem found on file and print and SQL Servers is using all the I/O of a disk subsystem. The only way to tell this is happening is to monitor disk queue length with Performance Monitor. Disk queuing counters are not turned on by default, so consult the Windows Server help to determine how to do this for a particular server and disk subsystem. The only way to solve this problem is to increase I/O with a better system on a single server or multiple servers.

In the final scenario, usually only with wide area network links, inadequate network bandwidth can slow the performance of a server down considerably. This scenario is really separate from scaling up a server, as it is likely the real problem is with the physical pipe to an external or internal system. The only way to address problems like this is to increase the capacity of the network link.

Becoming a Web Farm

Transitioning from a single server Web site to a Web farm is not an easy task. Applications must be able to distribute functionality across multiple machines and layers. Networks must be able to handle increased traffic and physical connection points. Administrators must learn how to manage multiple servers and the software systems that allow scalability. Businesses must be willing to invest in faster and better hardware. Luckily, the .NET platform provides robust solutions for dealing with the complexity of scaling a Web site.

Scaling is accomplished by increasing the resources in a specific area that is experiencing stress. The majority of scaling technologies rely on creating a layer of abstraction between the source of the stress and the stress point. Usually this layer of abstraction begins in the network layer as these technologies circumvent TCP/IP addressing in one form or another. This type of technology is commonly referred to as “load-balancing.”

Loading balancing works by abstracting the uniqueness of a network address (either a MAC address, an IP address, or a NetBIOS Name) to a software or hardware service. This service answers requests on that network address and then directs the traffic to multiple servers. This “balancing” effectively increases the number of physical machines that answer to a network name. When a collection of servers is balanced, these servers are referred to as a *cluster*. Figure 3.2 shows a Web farm with different types of clusters.

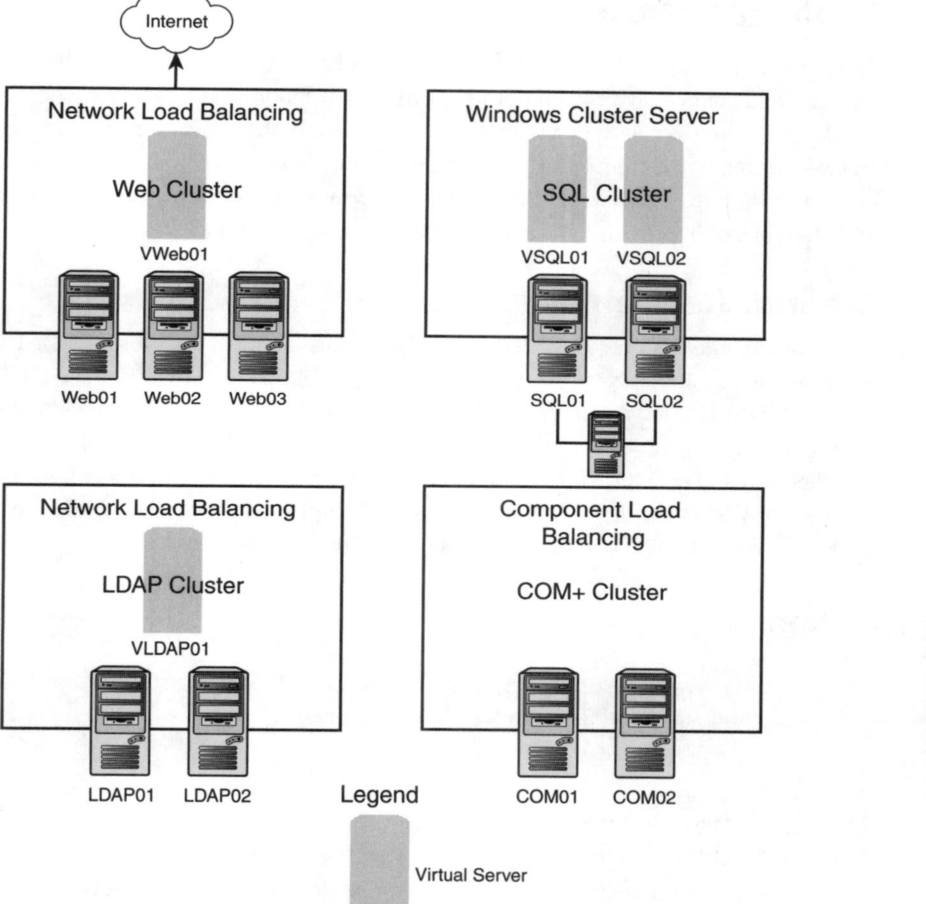

FIGURE 3.2
A simple load-balancing diagram with different clusters.

NEW TERM A *cluster* is a group of servers that act as one entity through software- or hardware-based balancing systems.

The original definition of a Web farm encompassed only the servers that provided HTTP services. The .NET Web farm has evolved into a collection of different cluster types. Just as a real farm has chickens, pigs, horses, and cattle, a .NET Web farm has Web clusters, COM+ clusters, SQL Server clusters, and other clusters.

Scaling a Web Farm

The Application layer of the .NET platform is broken conceptually into Web clusters, COM+ clusters, and data clusters. Each tier uses different technologies to achieve scale. Web clusters are the most familiar, and the technology choices are both hardware and software based. COM+ clusters are available only with Application Center 2000 and finally address the single point of failure that is DCOM. Data clusters vary in size and scope, but the most common, SQL Server 2000, provides ways to scale database servers up and out.

Scaling the Web Tier

Traditionally, the Web tier is scaled out. This tier has the most robust set of load-balancing technologies available. Network Load Balancing (NLB) is the obvious choice. NLB ships as part of Windows 2000 Advanced Server with all the features needed to load balance network traffic on any TCP/IP port. This fits perfectly with HTTP, which by default uses port 80. Another way to scale the Web service tier is with a hardware solution like Cisco's Local Director or CSS, Foundry's ServerIron, and F5's BigIP. These hardware solutions provide the same functionality as NLB, but they work with any operating system.

NOTE

Scaling the Web tier using Application Center 2000 is discussed in Chapter 12, "Deploying Application Center 2000 Web Clusters."

Using Network Load Balancing

Network Load Balancing (NLB) works by creating a virtual network name. This virtual network name is then associated with a fake MAC Address. A MAC address is a network address that uniquely identifies a network interface card on a layer two network. It is a globally unique number that every network interface card has burned into its chips. NLB creates a mangled, fake MAC address that up to 32 machines can listen on for traffic. Then, each machine examines all the packets targeted at the mangled MAC address and a hashing algorithm determines which machine actually handles each packet.

Network Load Balancing has limited options for determining which server will handle an incoming packet. Servers can be designated to handle packets based on percentage of the traffic. There are no options to direct packets based on CPU, memory, or other traditional starved server conditions. NLB lacks the traditional round-robin, weighted algorithm, and response time balancing found on all hardware-based solutions. NLB is not a panacea, but it is a very good solution in most situations.

Figure 3.3 shows an NLB-scaled Web site with three machines listening to the packets directed at Foo.com. To migrate from the original framework in Figure 3.1, the administrators at Foo.com purchased a second Web server and installed Windows 2000 Advanced server with NLB. Then they copied the existing site from the old server onto the Windows 2000 Advanced Server machine. Next they ensured that the site was functioning properly and pointed the Foo.com URL to that new machine. Then they rebuilt the original Foo.com server with Windows 2000 Advanced Server and NLB and joined it to the farm. This created a situation where up to 32 Web servers could handle Foo.com's traffic.

NOTE

Using Network Load Balancing is covered in great depth in Chapter 5, "Using Microsoft Network Load Balancing in a Web Farm."

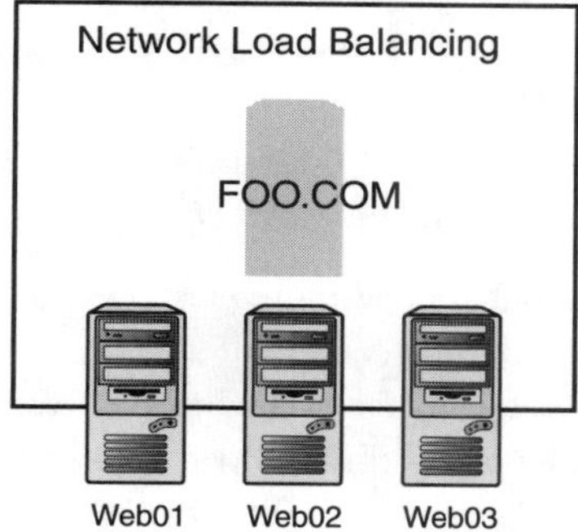

FIGURE 3.3
Foo.com's simple .NET Web farm using Network Load Balancing.

Using Hardware Load Balancing

With hardware load balancing (HLB), the change to a multiserver site happens at the network layer. Commonly referred to as layer 3–7 network switches, hardware load balancing is becoming the norm for successful sites. HLB acts as the traffic cop, handling all the requests for Foo.com and directing them to the servers configured in HLB to handle the traffic. Figure 3.4 shows Foo.com using HLB.

NOTE

Using hardware load balancing is covered in great depth in Chapter 6, "Using Hardware Load Balancing in a Web Farm," and Appendix C, "Hardware Load Balancing Vendors."

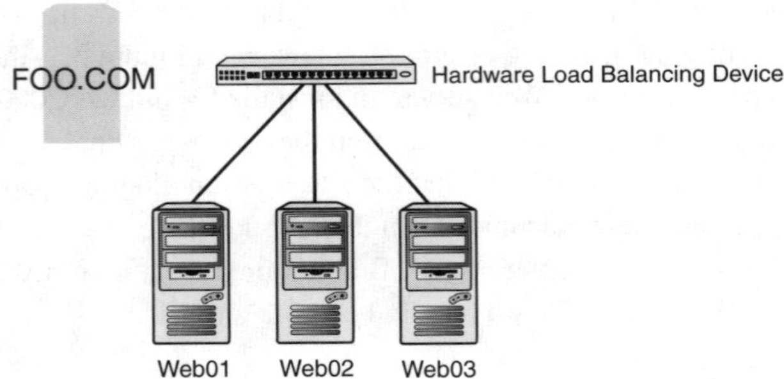

FIGURE 3.4
Foo.com's simple .NET Web farm using HLB.

Scaling COM+ Using Component Load Balancing

COM+ Services via DCOM use RPC, a connected network protocol, for remote COM+ component invocations. This means that once a client and a server have established a connection, they remain connected like FTP. This is the opposite of HTTP, which is a disconnected protocol. A special technology called Component Load Balancing (CLB) was created to provide scalability and availability for COM+ and circumvent the connected nature of DCOM.

CLB works by intercepting component creation requests before they leave the client computer. CLB maintains a list of servers, usually members of a COM+ cluster in an server architecture like that shown in Figure 3.5, to send remote component activations. Through a combination of statistics-gathering using WMI and a round-robin load-balancing algorithm, CLB picks the best server for a component's activation. CLB still uses DCOM, so the client server in Figure 3.5 has a DCOM connection to each member of the COM+ cluster.

NOTE

More information on Component Load Balancing and COM+ clusters can be found in Chapter 13, "Deploying Application Center 2000 COM+ Clusters."

Scaling the Data Tier

Unlike the Web and component tiers, scaling of the data tier is much more complicated. With disparate entities like LDAP directory services and SQL Server 2000, each requires a different mechanism for dealing with scalability problems. Some, like SQL Server, have limited options for scaling out and could force application changes under load. However, careful planning can help prevent situations in which the data tier becomes a bottleneck.

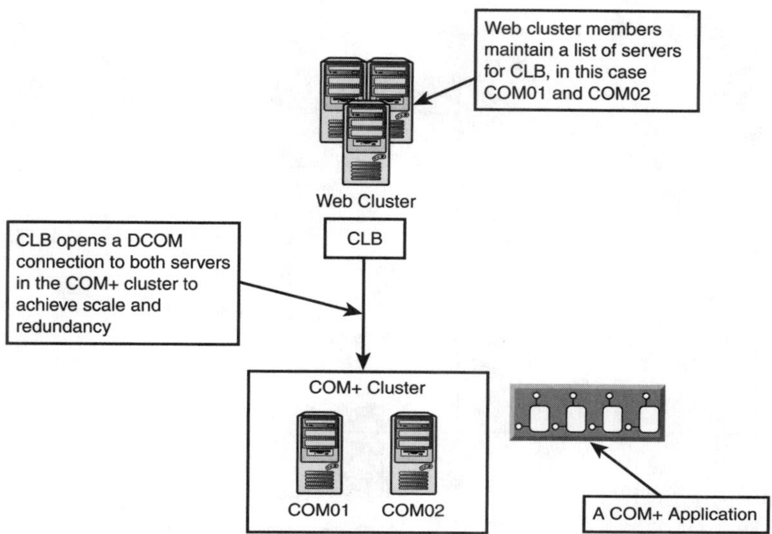

FIGURE 3.5
Component Load Balancing in a Web farm.

Scaling Out Directory Services

LDAP is a TCP/IP–based directory service. Scaling out of directory services like LDAP is accomplished in much the same way as scaling out the Web services tier. Technologies like hardware and software load balancing provide linear scalability for any TCP/IP–based data services system.

Improving Availability Using SQL Server 2000 with a Windows Server Cluster

With SQL Server 2000 and Windows 2000 there are two types of shared-nothing clusters: those that use a disk to maintain cluster state and those that use the network. A shared-nothing cluster that uses a disk to maintain cluster state is called a *Windows Server cluster*. The operating systems of cluster members have access to the same physical data on a shared disk. This systems does not rely on complicated distributed lock management techniques, so even though there is a shared disk, the clusters are considered shared nothing.Windows Server clusters improve the availability of SQL Server by allowing failure of one node of the cluster. Clients make requests of a virtual SQL server through a Windows Server cluster virtual network name. When a SQL server fails, the virtual network name and SQL server are restarted on a different member of the cluster. Availability is greatly improved as new client requests of the virtual name move to the failover cluster member. When the failed node is repaired, the virtual name and SQL server can be moved back to their original cluster member. Figure 3.6 shows a shared-disk SQL Server 2000 cluster and what happens during a fail-over.

NOTE

Chapter 17, "Introducing Windows Server Clusters," discusses clustering Windows 2000 using Windows Server clusters.

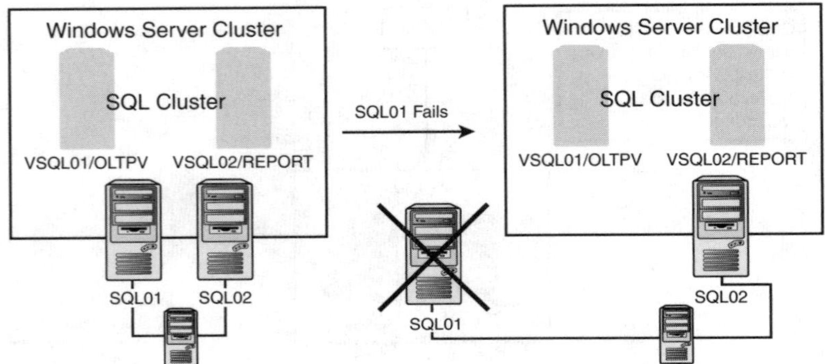

FIGURE 3.6
A Windows Server cluster for SQL Server 2000.

NOTE

More information on SQL Server 2000 distributed partition views and federated database support in SQL 2000 can be found in Appendix D, "Scaling Out SQL Server 2000."

Summary

Scalability and availability go hand in hand in Web farms that use .NET enterprise servers. For availability, the biggest challenge beyond the different technologies is its measurement. If a business can successfully measure and monitor its overall availability, this can be used to measure success and drive Web farm improvement.

Scalability is achieved in the .NET platform by using multiple servers for the same task. This technique provides limitless scale to handle increased user load. Once a Web farm moves to this model for handling growth, there is no upper limit to the number of concurrent users and transactions that it can support and generate.

Network Load Balancing, Hardware Load Balancing, Component Load Balancing, and Windows Cluster Server all provide both availability and scalability. This is an incredible benefit of the .NET platform. By understanding these technologies, an administrator has a roadmap for making the tough scalability and availability choices at each tier.

Planning a Web Farm Network

CHAPTER

4

IN THIS CHAPTER

The network is the nervous system of a Web farm. Every server relies on the network to provide content and services and conduct business. If the network is unavailable, a Web server cannot deliver its content, a database server cannot provide its data, and an application server cannot provide its services. Building a highly reliable and scalable network is required for a Web farm to be a success.

After surveying the hardware options for connectivity and bandwidth, the network administrator has to create the Web farm network. Considerations include how to build a DMZ separate from the corporate network, and connecting the Web farm network to the Internet. Also, the administrator must provide a WAN solution for connecting with external service providers and building a fully redundant network with no single points of failure. Each of these options could require separate hardware and layout planning.

Finally, the network administrator must predict network utilization. This can be the most difficult task because the network is like a road: If it is there, people will use it. With more and more services being provided by e-businesses, the uses for bandwidth continue to increase. What was considered a large amount of bandwidth two years ago is now becoming a bottleneck when trying to implement voice-over-IP solutions and streaming video and audio. Expect the network usage pattern to double every year.

The goals of this chapter are to help you

- Build the right network configuration for a Web farm, including network hardware topology and network security considerations.
- Connect the Web farm network to the Internet, including redundancy options, bandwidth considerations, and quality of service issues.
- Connect the Web farm network to other networks, including the parent corporation and third-party service providers like banks and inventory fulfillment centers.

It is assumed the reader is familiar with basic network hardware such as switches, hubs, and routers. For more information on these technologies, see an appropriate vendor's Web site. Other network terms to be familiar with include packet, protocol, broadcasts, ports, network address, OSI Model, and network topology.

Building a Web Farm Network

Building a Web farm network requires an understanding of a number of different concepts. A Web farm network should have a overriding philosophy that is expressed through best practices. When followed, best practices are reasonable guidelines that produce similar results even if implementation details are dissimilar. When considering the Web farm network be sure to

- *Pick the most appropriate model* for Web farm network topology. Most Web farm network should choose a network DMZ model.
- *Choose familiar network hardware*. Network standards have simplified basic hardware choices; all networks are beginning to share the same characteristics. Traditional network hardware satisfies the requirements for the hardware of a Web farm network.
- *Isolate Web farm network hardware* from the hardware of other networks. Isolation helps ensure high network availability, which is more difficult to achieve in a shared network environment. Isolated networks are inherently more secure because entry and exit points for network traffic are well known.
- *Define secure and well-known entry points* for anonymous and administrative users. Defined access points are critical for any Web farm network in order to monitor network traffic patterns and measure bandwidth utilization successfully.

From these best practices a number of important concepts must be defined. The following sections will address network backbones, DMZ topology, connecting servers to the Web farm network, and dealing with network related issue for IIS. From this, the network administrator can make the right decision concerning hardware and its configuration, software, and network security for a successful Web farm network.

The Web Farm Backbone

Figure 4.1 shows a Web farm backbone. A backbone links one server to the other and connects, through a firewall, router, or other device, to other networks. The backbone is used for intra-server communication and intra-network communications. A backbone is typically a hub, router, or switch. These devices serve as the spinal cord that connects all the servers in a Web farm to each other and the outside world.

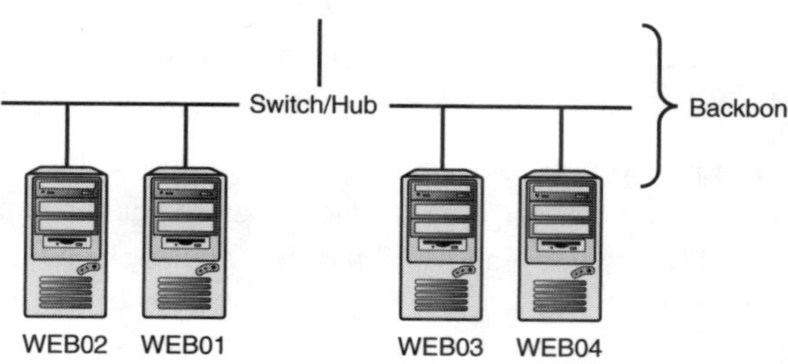

FIGURE 4.1
Web Farm Servers Connected to a Network Backbone.

Beyond choosing and building the backbone of a Web farm network are the complexities of laying out a network DMZ. The network DMZ contains the Web farm backbone and the network topology used for network-to-network communication.

Understanding the Network Topology of a DMZ

In the traditional sense, a demilitarized zone (DMZ) is an area that has restricted use and access requirements. A DMZ is a negotiated location separating two rival factions in wartime. By preventing rival factions from having direct contact with one another, a DMZ helps maintain peace. A DMZ has secure entry and exit points; everyone who enters or leaves a DMZ is verified and recorded.

With networks, a DMZ is an isolated area with well-defined application services. A DMZ controls the types of application services that are presented to the networks external to a DMZ. For the Web farm, most of these services are exposed by standard IP addresses and port designations. For example, all services addressable over the Internet use IP addresses like `208.20.120.29:80`. These services include HTTP, FTP, LDAP, and SQL. Table 4.1 shows some standard services that are available from a DMZ.

TABLE 4.1 Standard DMZ Services

Service	*Port*
HTTP	80
SSL	443
FTP	21
SMTP	25
LDAP	389
POP3	125
DNS	53

NEW TERM A *DMZ, or demilitarized zone,* is an isolated or perimeter network, for Web farm servers, which provides security, reliability, and connectivity to other networks. A DMZ provides a buffer zone for public and private networks to exchange data.

A network DMZ also has controlled access points; not every service in Table 4.1 is exposed from a DMZ. Firewalls, routers, and load balancers can restrict unwanted network traffic from entering a DMZ. A DMZ provides increased physical and application security for a Web farm through physical separation of networks. Simple network devices like hubs and switches should not bridge the gap between the networks a DMZ separates. Construct this bridge by using a higher-level network device, like a firewall, or by creating a topological organization of network hardware connected by Dual-NIC servers. Because of this physical separation, a DMZ is the optimal place to house the servers and applications that comprise the Web farm. Figure 4.2 shows a high-level DMZ topology.

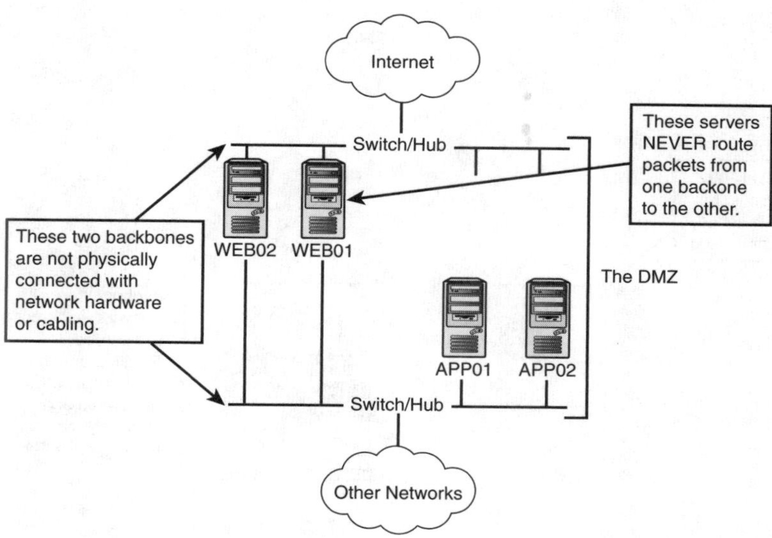

FIGURE 4.2
A high-level DMZ network topology.

To understand the DMZ concept better, it is valuable to consider briefly some alternative and less desirable configurations for a Web farm network. These considerations are viable alternatives to connecting a Web farm to other networks. There are four types of DMZ-like configurations to choose from. Each one has a number of different physical implementations. Each implementation will differ slightly based on the network hardware and security requirements. In some cases, the existing network infrastructure for a corporation and budget will dictate to what level a DMZ is built.

No DMZ

Without a DMZ, the Web farm network is essentially shared with one of the other connecting networks. In most cases this network will be the corporate network that owns the Web farm deployment. Usually these configurations occur only in small businesses where a Web farm is deployed on the same physical network as other corporate resources, like client desktops. Figure 4.3 shows a simple Web farm network without a DMZ.

A No-DMZ Web farm network topology is a high-risk configuration with the following problems:

- *Sharing bandwidth* with corporate resources is problematic. Sharing the bandwidth to the Internet can cause desktop activities to interfere with users accessing the Web farm. Even worse, if the rail depicted in Figure 4.3 is a hub, the bandwidth of the internal network is shared; effectively all traffic is broadcast, and every machine on the network must examine all packets.

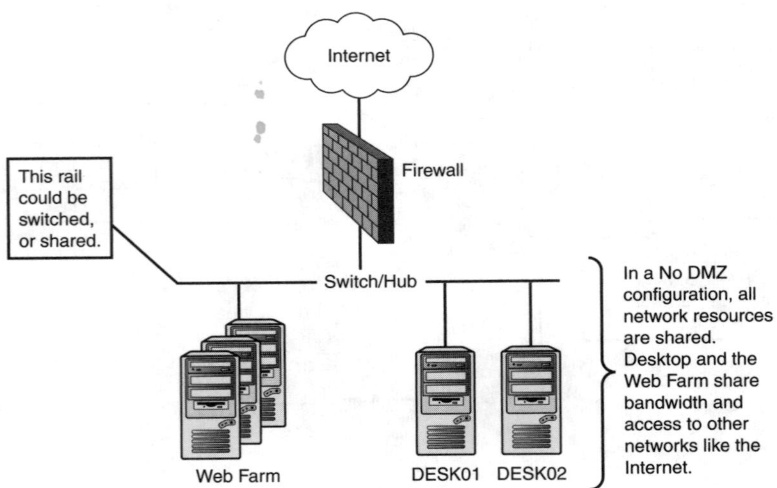

FIGURE 4.3
A No-DMZ Web farm topology.

- *Securing the Web farm servers is difficult* because they share a physical network with desktops and other corporate resources. All the servers in Figure 4.3 can see one another on the network and thus are subject to attack. Because these servers likely share the same network address space, all standard ports, like NetBIOS, are available to all servers on this network.
- *Allowing connection to servers* in the Web farm from the Internet is a risk to the corporate network. If any of the servers in the Web farm are compromised, it puts the other servers in the corporate environment at risk.

Single-Rail DMZ

In a Single-Rail DMZ model, part of a Web farm is isolated from one of the connecting networks through some network construct. In most cases, this is a firewall. A Single-Rail DMZ looks very similar to a Dual-Rail DMZ except much of the resources of the Web farm still exist on some shared network, such as a corporate network. The idea is that servers, which are exposed to uncontrolled networks like the Internet, are isolated from corporate resources like database servers. Figure 4.4 shows a Single-Rail DMZ Web farm network topology. The servers in this model have actual Internet IP addresses as they are on the Internet directly.

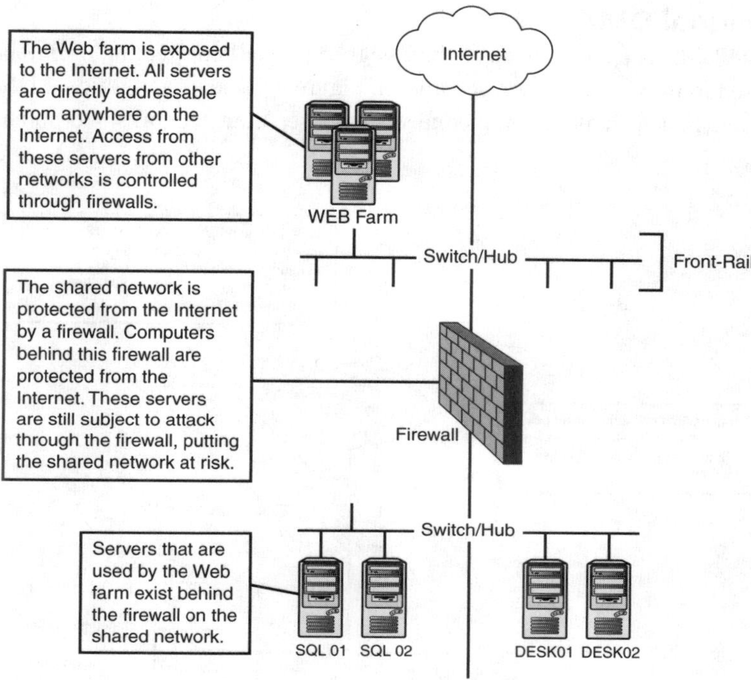
The Web farm is exposed to the Internet. All servers are directly addressable from anywhere on the Internet. Access from these servers from other networks is controlled through firewalls.
Internet
WEB Farm
Switch/Hub
Front-Rail
The shared network is protected from the Internet by a firewall. Computers behind this firewall are protected from the Internet. These servers are still subject to attack through the firewall, putting the shared network at risk.
Firewall
Switch/Hub
Servers that are used by the Web farm exist behind the firewall on the shared network.
SQL 01
SQL 02
DESK01
DESK02

FIGURE 4.4
A Single-Rail DMZ Web farm topology.

A Single-Rail DMZ Web farm network topology is also a high-risk configuration with the following problems:

- *Hacking the servers on the Internet* is easy and a big risk. These servers must be secured or hardened from attacks to prevent them from being hacked. Because administrators use the same network adapters for management traffic as application users, hardening these servers is doubly difficult.
- *Accessing corporate resources* through a firewall is both a potential bottleneck and a single point of failure.
- *Web farm servers in the corporate or shared network* have all the problems of a No-DMZ model: They share bandwidth and are difficult to secure from other servers on the network.
- *Compromised servers exposed to the Internet* put the internal network at risk because traffic for application servers must be allowed to pass through the corporate firewall. These ports are also available for hackers and traffic from a compromised Web server would appear to be coming from a trusted source.

The Traditional DMZ

The traditional DMZ is also known as a three-legged firewall configuration. In this scenario, a Firewall is used to provide the DMZ separation. Figure 4.5 shows a traditional DMZ network topology. Notice how a single firewall connects three separate networks: Corporate, DMZ, and the Internet.

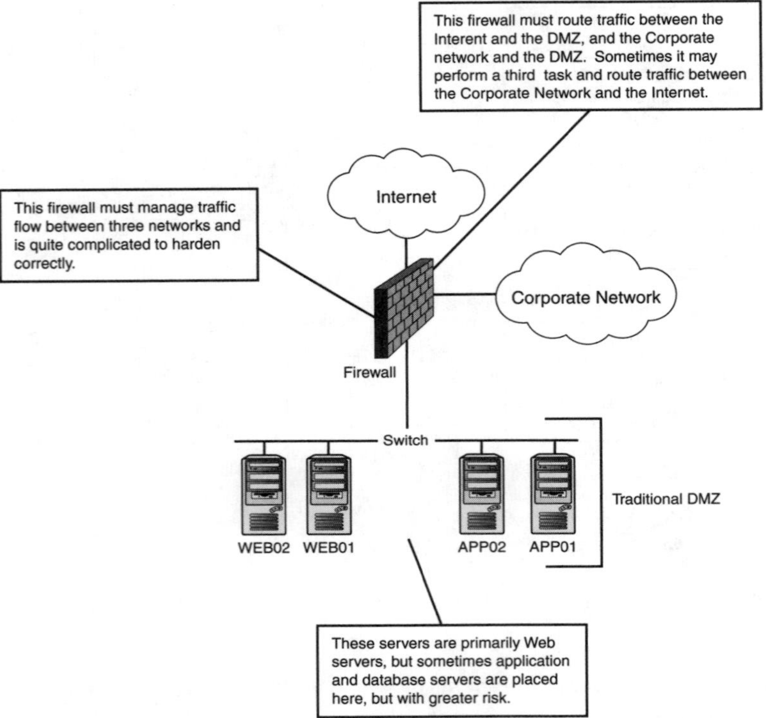

FIGURE 4.5
A Traditional DMZ Web farm topology.

The firewall is the center of this configuration and is quite complicated to configure. The firewall must

- *Route application traffic for specific IP addresses and ports to the DMZ subnet,* defining all the allowed traffic types from the Internet. Administrative traffic must be well defined and not allowed to pass through the connection to the Internet.
- *Route application traffic back to the corporate network* to access servers that are not on the DMZ network. Because the DMZ network is receiving Internet traffic, it is wise to limit the types of servers and data that are stored there.

- *Route administrative traffic from corporate users to the servers in the DMZ* for maintenance tasks. This means that traffic from the corporate network and Internet share the same bandwidth on the single-NIC servers in the DMZ.
- *Protect the corporate network from attacks.* The firewall must not route traffic from the Internet to the corporate network. In the same vein, traffic from the corporate network should not be allowed to travel to the Internet.

There are numerous other disadvantages to the traditional DMZ model including:

- *Adding new servers to the DMZ network means that at least three paths of access to these servers must be secured:* DMZ to Internet, DMZ to Corporate, and Corporate to DMZ. Each path has a different purpose and a different configuration.
- *The types of servers to place on the DMZ network must be carefully considered.* If the firewall that is securing the DMZ is compromised the DMZ servers are now directly accessible.
- *The centralized firewall is a single point of failure* and a potential network bottleneck. Some form of firewall load balancing must be employed, further complicating the configuration.

While correctly configuring the firewalls in a traditional DMZ is not an impossible task, the chance for mistakes and security holes is much greater. The firewall is performing so many roles that any change to the server configuration or requirements means that the whole security model for the DMZ and corporate network could be compromised by one errant entry in the firewall. A traditional DMZ is a complicated yet viable choice for a Web farm network, but the Dual-Rail DMZ is better.

Dual-Rail DMZ

The Dual-Rail DMZ is the ideal network topology for a Web farm. In a Dual-Rail DMZ, all Web farm servers are isolated from other networks by a firewall or router. Figure 4.6 shows a typical Dual-Rail DMZ network topology.

The networks of a DMZ are referred to as the "front rail" and "back rail." A front-rail network is connected to the Internet. Servers on this network are exposed to the Internet but only through a firewall, a router, or a combination of both.

NEW TERM A *front-rail network* is any network segment that is ultimately connected to the Internet.

A *back-rail network* is any network segment that is connected to another secure network. A secure network is considered to be anything but the Internet. "Secure" is used here in the loosest sense, because any network can be insecure. However, for this discussion, it is an important distinction.

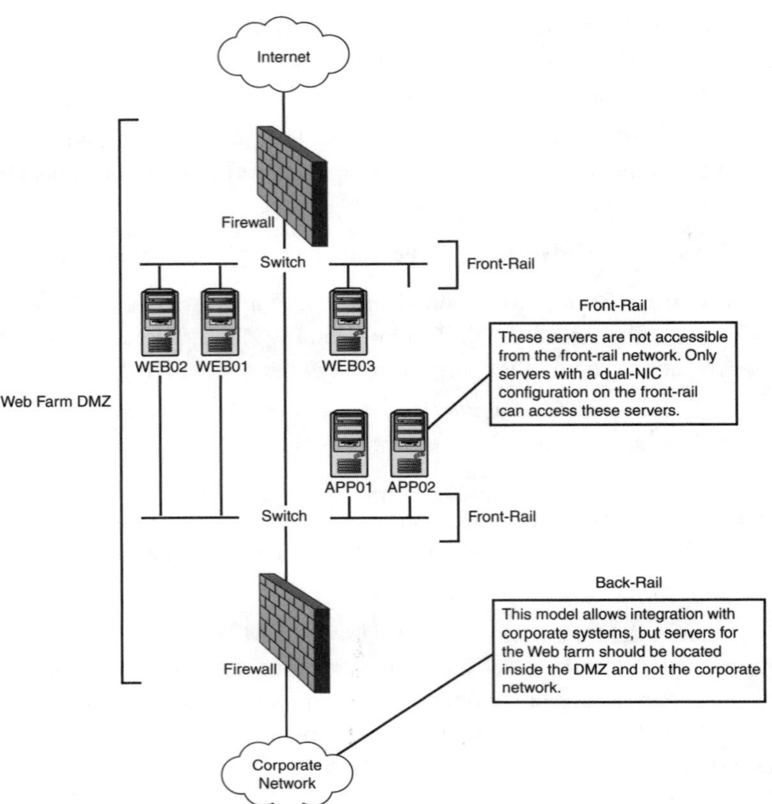

FIGURE 4.6
A Dual-Rail DMZ Web farm topology.

NEW TERM A *back-rail network* is any network segment that is not connected directly to the Internet.

The Dual-Rail DMZ solves all of the problems of No-DMZ and Single-Rail DMZ models:

- *Connecting servers to the Internet* is a low risk because a firewall, a router, or a combination of both manages network access and traffic. Access points to front-rail servers are well defined and thus more difficult to hack.
- *Sharing of bandwidth is eliminated* in a switched environment. Shared environments that use hubs are still subject to bandwidth sharing, but even with hubs, the sharing is isolated to each network segment. Web farm servers on the front rail will not share bandwidth with Web farm servers on the back rail and corporate network.

- *Switching isolates traffic for improved security.* A VLAN can be used to further isolate traffic into separate broadcast domains.
- *Dual-NIC front-rail servers access servers on the back rail without using a firewall.* This eliminates a single point of failure without increasing the security risk because sensitive back-rail servers have no connection to the Internet and are thus not subject to direct attack. Corporate resources are also fully protected because there is no access (in the form of a route) from the Internet to the corporate network.
- *Using corporate resources* does not affect DMZ resources in any way. As long as all Web farm servers exist between the front- and back-rail networks, corporate resources are not involved in Web farm transactions.

From this point forward, the term DMZ will mean the Dual-Rail DMZ model.

The Advantages of Dual-NIC Server Configurations

Dual-NIC servers may seem like an unnecessary configuration hassle considering the already complicated nature of a Web farm network. It is never a good idea to add extra configuration unless the benefits far outweighs the costs. In the case of Dual-NIC servers the benefits clearly make it worth the effort.

A Dual-NIC server enables a Web farm to take advantage of a Dual-Rail DMZ model. This model clearly serves the Web farm best and has numerous advantages over the other DMZ models. This alone is reason enough to introduce Dual-NIC servers to a Web farm network.

Security is greatly enhanced in Dual-NIC configurations because of the physically separate networks with no network layer interconnect between them. Added to this is the additional separation of administrative traffic and application traffic. The front-rail network can be completely secured, denying access to all administrative tool and functions. The only traffic able to travel over this network should be well known like HTTP, FTP, and SMTP. The back-rail network on the other hand is how the applications of the Web farm communicate with database and application services and what administrators use to access the servers for maintenance. By separating these network requirements, securing them becomes a much simpler task and no flexibility is sacrificed as with other DMZ models.

Connecting Servers to the Front Rail

Servers connected to the front rail are usually accessed from the Internet. These servers expose their services through protocols on specific ports like HTTP for Web pages, SMTP and POP3 for mail, FTP for file transfer, LDAP for directory services, and other ports for other Internet-based services. Protocols and services not usually exposed through the front rail include

Terminal Services, SQL Server, COM/DCOM, MSMQ, and other non-standard services and protocols.

There are two types of servers that are connected to the front rail: single-NIC and multi-NIC. A single-NIC server has only one network interface card that connects to the front-rail network. A server like this is completely isolated from the back-rail network and is little or no-risk to other front-rail servers. A multi-NIC server has more than one network interface card, with a least one connecting to the front rail network and others connecting to back-rail networks. Figure 4.7 shows the two types of server configurations that connect to the front rail. Notice that the multi-NIC server connects to the back rail and the front rail network.

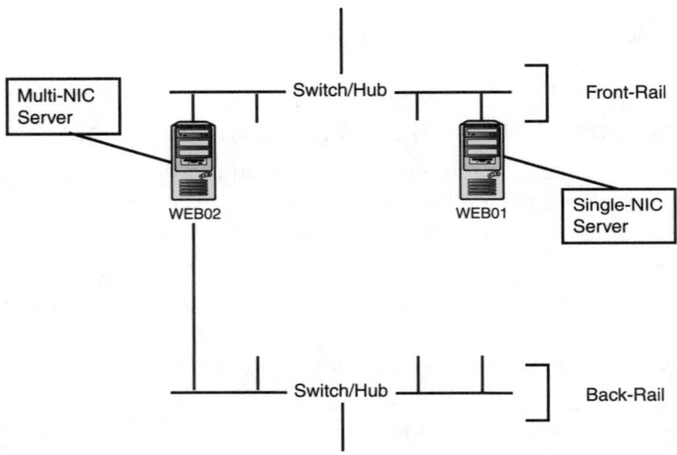

FIGURE 4.7
A Single-NIC and Multi-NIC Server Configuration.

There are special considerations for configuring the network interfaces of multi-NIC servers. Any server connected to a network can have only one default gateway. In a DMZ, the default gateway is used to help direct traffic to networks outside the DMZ. If a server does not know how to communicate with a specific network address, it will forward this request to the default gateway. Most DMZ configurations have the default gateway as the front-rail firewall or router. If these multi-NIC servers need to reach a destination in a network attached to the back rail and the request is forwarded to the default gateway on the front rail, the front rail will not know how to reach the address. To communicate with a network attached to the back rail, each server requires that a persistent route be added to its routing table. This route will point to the firewall or router on the back rail that knows how to communicate with the secure networks attached to it.

The following shows how to add a persistent route from a standard command-line interface.

```
Route -p add 198.168.1.0 255.255.0.0 172.20.1.1
```

In this command, p makes the route persistent, the add command adds the route; 198.168.1.0 is the destination network address, 255.255.0.0 is its subnet mask, and 172.20.1.1 is the gateway. The result is to direct all traffic to the 198.168.1.0 subnet by way of 172.20.1.1, the back-rail firewall.

A multi-NIC server must have a specific binding order for its network adapters. The reason to have a multi-NIC server is so that a mission-critical system such as a database that does not need access to the Internet can be localized closely to servers that do, but without increased security risks. Most multi-NIC servers will need to access these systems as part of the applications they run, so they are members of the back-rail network. In a multi-NIC server there is an order in which network adapters and the attached network are used to resolve network names. This network adapter order is called the *binding order* and can be configured in Network and Dial-Up Connections, found by right-clicking My Network Places on the desktop and selecting Properties. From Network and Dial-Up Connections, select the Advanced menu and then select Advanced Settings from the drop-down menu, as shown in Figure 4.8.

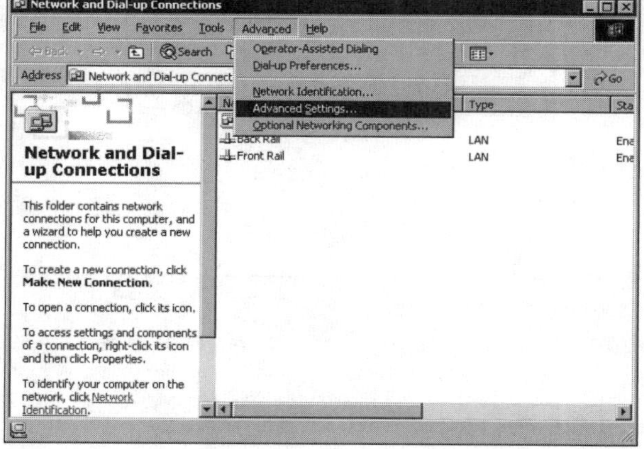

FIGURE 4.8
The location of the binding order configuration in Windows 2000.

If this order has the front rail adapter first, requests to servers on the back rail will travel out the front rail first and eventually timeout. If there is a route for front rail traffic to reach the back rail, then the security of the DMZ network topology is compromised. It is very important that no front-rail routers or firewalls are aware of the back-rail networks.

CAUTION

It is critical to the security of the DMZ model that front-rail routers and firewalls not know how to route requests to back-rail addresses.

Figure 4.9 illustrates an improper binding order for a multi-NIC server that needs access to back-rail servers. Notice that the front rail is first in the list of network adapters.

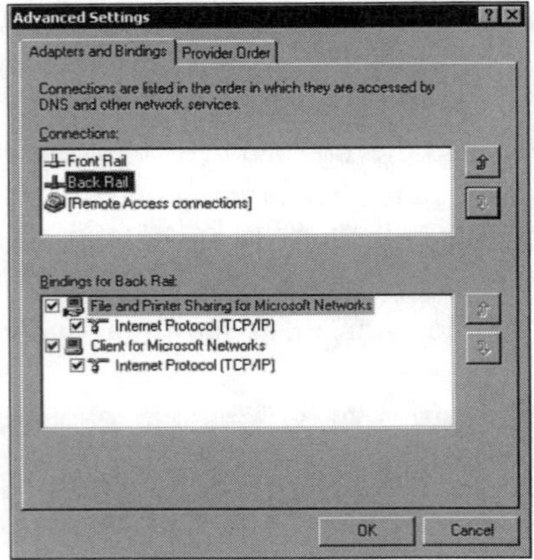

FIGURE 4.9
An incorrect binding order for a multi-NIC server.

TIP

In Windows 2000, the network adapters on a server can be renamed to be more easily identifiable.

A server that has an incorrect binding order will seem sluggish. This is because of the timeout period that must pass before Windows 2000 will try the request on the second network interface. The solution is to bind the back-rail network interface card first; this is shown in Figure 4.10.

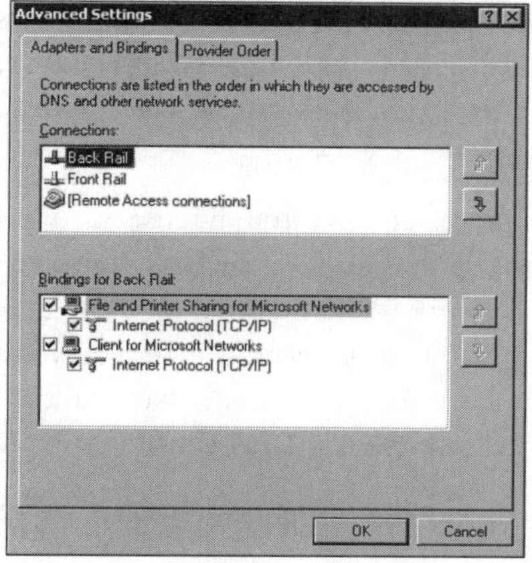

FIGURE 4.10
A correct binding order for a multi-NIC server.

TIP

If a multi-NIC server seems slow or sluggish when accessing resources on the back rail, check the binding order.

Connecting Servers to a Back Rail

Servers connected to the back rail are usually accessed from secure networks or the back-rail NIC of multi-NIC servers on the front rail. They should never be connected directly to the Internet as this violates the security model of the DMZ.

CAUTION

It is critical to the security of the DMZ model that the back rail not be connected directly to the Internet. Back-rail services should only be exposed to front-rail multi-NIC servers and secure networks connected to the back rail.

There are many different types of severs that can be connected to the back rail. Single-NIC servers connected to the back rail could be application servers that have COM/DCOM business objects installed. Microsoft SQL 2000 servers, Exchange Servers, and File servers are other candidates to connect to the back-rail network. It is safe to expose administrative interfaces to the back rail as long as the back-rail network is secure. This means that file and print sharing and Terminal Services can be accessed from the back-rail network. Another useful endeavor is to expose administrative Web sites to the back rail so that administrators can use browsers to administer these servers remotely.

The back-rail firewall protects these servers through its security policies and restrictions. Policies can grant access to application services, such as Terminal Services, only to specific users who exist on the secure network while granting all users access to HTTP and Web services. Because multi-NIC servers are on the back-rail network, it is also possible to grant secure administrative access to these servers from the back rail. It is also possible to expose administrative Web applications from the same IIS configuration that the Web farm applications use.

CAUTION

It is critical to the security of the DMZ to configure the back-rail firewall to only let defined administrative, application, and network specific traffic travel from the secure network into the DMZ.

Summarizing Connectivity Options

Table 4.2 shows an overview of the different server configurations that connect to the back rail only, front rail only, and back-rail/front-rail networks. Each type is presented with reasons for connecting servers and the general types of servers having said configuration.

TABLE 4.2 Server Configurations in the DMZ

Configuration	*Description*	*Server Types*
Front Rail/Back Rail	The Dual-NIC server configuration. Choose this type need access to the Internet and access to back-rail application resources.	Web, FTP, SMTP and other traditional for servers that Internet Application protocols.
Front Rail Only	A single-NIC server configuration used for simple servers that need access only to the Internet. Useful for isolating an application completely.	Web, FTP, SMTP and other traditional Internet application protocols.

TABLE 4.3 Continued

Configuration	*Description*	*Server Types*
Back Rail Only	A single-NIC server configuration used for application services like COM+, database, directory services, and any other application service that is not traditionally to put any exposed to the Internet, or is used only by Web farm Applications.	Application, COM+, File Servers, SQL Servers, .NET Web services, and any other application protocols. It is safe type of server on the Back Rail of a DMZ.

Configuring IIS for the DMZ Network

Internet Information Services (IIS) is Microsoft's general-purpose Internet services server application. IIS is well suited for DMZ networks because it is easy to configure and very flexible. Because the servers on the front rail are usually multi-NIC and primarily serve HTTP requests from clients on the Internet, IIS requires advanced configuration to operate properly. IIS is a very complicated application, and it is assumed that you are familiar with the basics of configuring and using IIS.

NOTE

For more information on IIS in the Web farm, see Chapter 9, "Using Internet Information Services in a Web Farm."

There are some advanced IIS configuration options that are important for a DMZ network. To explore these options, it is important to discuss briefly the different options for organizing Web sites with IIS.

A Brief Overview of IIS Organization

IIS is very flexible in how Web sites can be organized. At the highest level, shown in Figure 4.11, IIS defines a Web site. What makes a Web site unique is that it is bound to an IP address. Virtual directories, files, and folders are part of a Web site and cannot have a different IP from their parent Web sites. Since a Web site is bound to an IP address, it is the only top-level item in IIS that is accessible from the Internet. Clearly files, folders, and virtual directories under a

Web site are accessible from the Internet, but they depend on the top-level Web site to be accessible. These other items have little importance when considering a Web farm network.

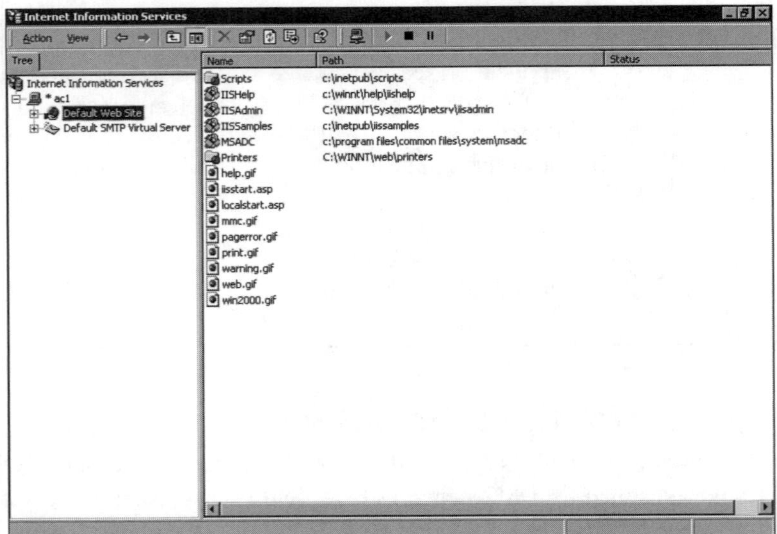

FIGURE 4.11
The top-level organization of IIS.

Using the Default Web Site

The Default Web Site is Microsoft's playground. Everything from the online IIS documentation to famous examples of huge security holes is found on the Default Web Site. The IIS and Site Server 3.0 Web-based administration are located here. Every tool and server product that has Web-based components installs itself to the Default Web Site. It is the wrong place to build the organization of a Web farm site.

Ironically, Microsoft encourages the use of the Default Web Site because of its development tools. Both FrontPage 2000 and Visual InterDev connect with the default Web site and encourage developers to build their applications with this mindset. Not only does this make the transition to a dedicated Web site problematic, it confuses the issues of what a Web site is versus a virtual directory under a Web site. Figure 4.12 compares a Web site and a virtual directory. For a DMZ network, use a Web site for any custom Web farm IIS configuration.

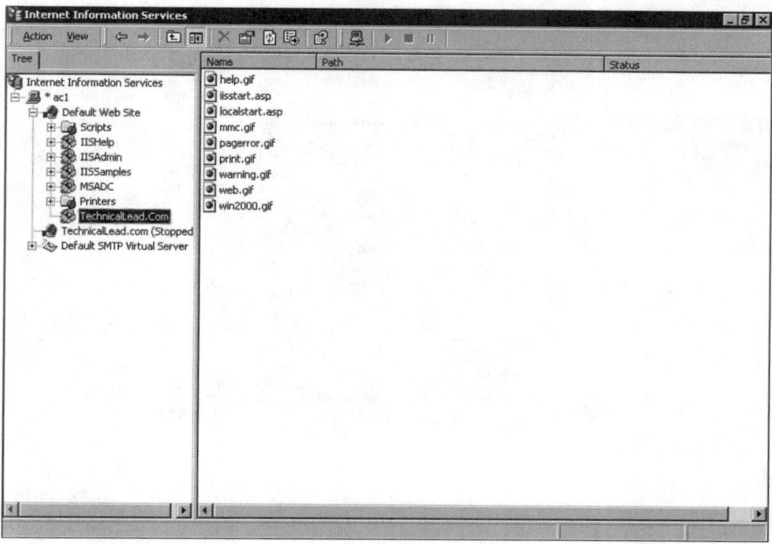

FIGURE 4.12
Comparing a Web site to a virtual directory.

Binding a Web Site to a Specific IP Address

Web sites expose their services to networks that are attached to the DMZ. Some Web sites are exposed to only the front rail, only the back rail, or both. If a Web site needs to expose its services to a back-rail network, it must bind to a back-rail IP address. To expose its services to just the front rail, it must bind only to a front-rail IP. To expose services to both rails, a Web site must bind to a back-rail and a front-rail IP address.

To bind a Web site to a specific IP address, go to the IIS console, right-click a specific Web site, and select Properties. Figure 4.13 shows the properties of a specific Web site. The Web Site tab shown is where to pick a specific IP address to bind to a site. Bind a site to a specific IP address from the Web Site tab by selecting an IP address from the IP address drop-down combo box.

To bind a site to more than one IP address, click the Advanced button next to the drop-down combo box. Advanced Multiple Web Site configuration allows the addition of multiple IP addresses to the same Web site. Add an IP address by clicking the Add button, selecting an IP address, and specifying the appropriate port, usually 80.

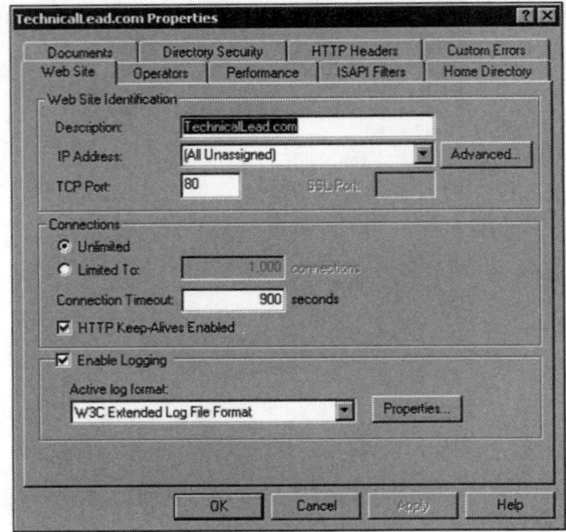

FIGURE 4.13
The Web Site property page of an IIS Web site.

Providing Administrative Web Access to the Back Rail

It is valuable to bind the default Web site and all other administrative Web sites to the back-rail network. This provides a consistent way to access the administrative Web-based tools provided by a number of Microsoft's server tools, including IIS, Site Server 3.0, and Application Center 2000. This also means that these sites are not accessible through the front-rail and not open to attack from the Internet.

Connecting the Web Farm Network to the Internet

The connection to the Internet from the front rail of a DMZ is the most important point of access to an online business. Through this connection, information flows in and out of the Web farm servers to and from the rest of the Internet. This connection is the front door used by customers to obtain access to goods and services that an e-business provides, and customers expect this door to be open, reliable, and secure. Providing a reliable and secure connection requires an understanding of the roles and responsibilities of the network infrastructure for this bridge between the DMZ and the Internet.

Understanding Important Network Concepts

Internetworking bridges between open and closed networks are built from organizations of different network hardware and share common characteristics. In general, a connection between the Internet and the front rail of a DMZ may require at least one of each of the following network concepts: quality of service, packet blocking and filtering, address translation, and load balancing.

Understanding Quality of Service

Quality of service (QoS) is a term used to describe the allocation and management of bandwidth through parameters defined at the application layer of a network by some network device. QoS guarantees that designated network traffic always have fixed amounts of bandwidth available.

NEW TERM *Quality of service* is the management and allocation of bandwidth resources.

For example, a business with 1.45Mbps of bandwidth can guarantee through a QoS device that business-critical traffic such as SSL maintains .45mbps of bandwidth. If the total bandwidth of the pipe is overloaded and the network cannot maintain this rate, bandwidth from less critical activities is transferred to requests for SSL traffic. This ensures that servers that process credit card transactions would always receive their money-generating data. Other uses for QoS include global bandwidth sharing between a corporate network and an e-business DMZ like that shown in Figure 4.14.

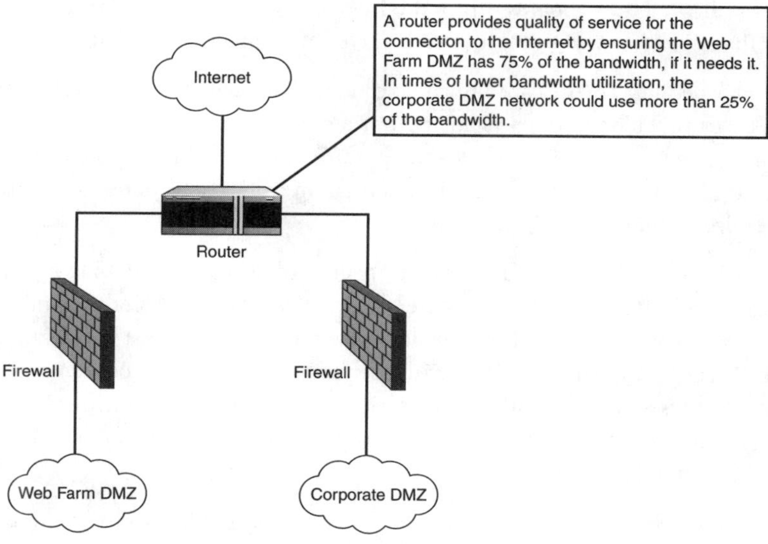

FIGURE 4.14
A quality of service example.

Notice that the hardware used in Figure 4.14 is a router. Most newer routers and load balancers have robust QoS features. It is important to understand QoS requirements up front in order to build the internetworking bridge between the DMZ and the Internet.

Understanding Packet Blocking and Filtering

Every network-connected host transmits and receives data in the form of packets. A packet contains information that describes the packet's source, destination, and data. The overall packet spectrum is limited by the applications that exist on a network. When a network is well understood and secure, the packet spectrum is small and easy to predict and control. When a network is connected to an insecure network like the Internet, the packet spectrum changes considerably and is unpredictable.

Packets are like little commands and requests made from one server to another. For instance, commands in an HTTP request are usually very safe. *Get me this HTML page* is a perfectly valid and acceptable command for one server on the Internet to issue to another. Others, such as NetBIOS commands, are more dangerous and provide information and commands that only trusted servers in a secure network should access.

A server that is connected to the Internet should always have an intermediary filter and block unnecessary packets. If a server is primarily responsible for Web content, why should FTP or Ping packets be allowed to bombard it from the Internet? While it may be safe to let through packets other than HTTP and HTTPS to a Web server, it is unnecessary and should be avoided.

Examples of intermediary devices are firewalls, routers, and switches with VLAN functionality. There are cases in which a router is an appropriate packet management tool. For example, in Figure 4.14, the router filters and blocks all IP traffic intended for the e-business DMZ from the corporate DMZ. This could be accomplished by a firewall, but a router is built to blocking and filtering entire IP ranges at a QoS level.

It is recommended that a firewall be the primary packet-filtering and blocking agent, even in an internetworking topology that contains a router. A firewall makes it easier to administer application protocols across a particular IP range and is better suited for most packet filtering and blocking tasks because of a simpler GUI geared toward application protocol management. But some form of Network device, usually a router, should sit in front of the firewall. This entry routers directly connected to the Internet should be configured securely so they don't become a DoS weak spot or an attack point.

There are numerous advantages to equipping the internetworking layer between a DMZ and the Internet with a packet-filtering and blocking device. In general, packet filtering helps secure a server from unwanted attacks and conserves server resources by preventing inappropriate application requests like Ping or FTP.

NOTE

For more information on packet filtering and blocking, see Chapter 23, "Securing a Web Farm."

Understanding Network Address Translation

Network Address Translation (NAT) is used to solve a number of problems facing the Internet. NAT was originally conceived in RFC1631 to help conserve the limited number of IP addresses available on the Internet. NAT in this form enables one public registered Internet address to handle many private non-registered addresses. It does so by translating the packets from the private network into packets that look like they came from the single public Internet address. For example, corporate client desktops that need access to the Internet can use NAT to make requests from Web servers and other Internet-based applications but do so as if they all came from a single IP address.

For a Web farm, NAT is used to map the public address of a Web site to a private address or addresses. Typically it is used not for IP conservation purposes but for security and network privacy. For example, if the public Internet address for TechnicalLead.com is `208.20.120.29`, anyone can find this IP address and examine the network signature of whatever server answers to requests from this address. If this address was bound to the network card of the server that ran the TechnicalLead.com Web site, then this server is considered to be directly accessible from the Internet. Figure 4.15 shows a server in this configuration.

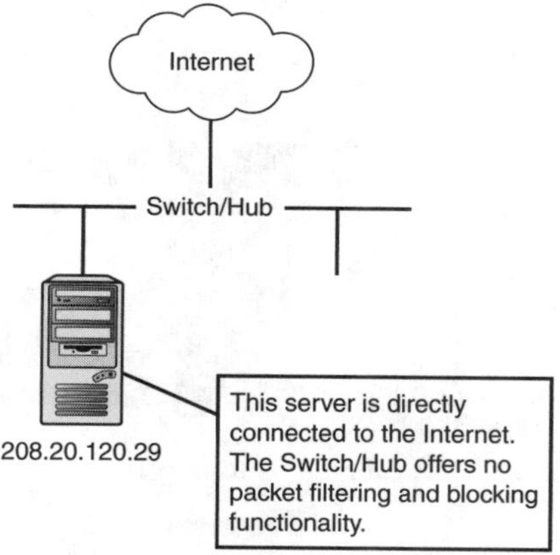

FIGURE 4.15
A server directly connected to the Internet.

If TechnicalLead.com were protected by NAT, then some other intermediary network device would actually bind to the IP address `208.20.120.29` and translate any requests to it to a hidden private address such as `172.20.1.100`. This is called *static NAT*. Static NAT provides additional security, effectively hiding the entire internal network from the rest of the Internet behind one public address. Table 4.2 shows a typical static NAT table.

TABLE 4.3 A Static NAT Table

Unique Internet Address	*Private Address*
208.20.120.29	172.20.1.100
207.46.230.219	172.18.1.200
64.28.67.48	192.168.1.1

There are a number of different devices that can use NAT. Routers, firewalls, and load balancers are all candidates in a Web farm environment. It is even possible and desirable to use multiple levels of NAT. Figure 4.16 shows two levels of address indirection. In this case, the firewall is the Internet server that owns all the public IP addresses. All packets are examined and filtered based on the firewall settings, totally isolating the internal Web farm from the insecure network. A load-balancing device holds all the private addresses that the firewall uses for its NAT. The load balancer then distributes traffic across a second translated list of addresses, requiring two address translations before a packet finally reaches the destination server.

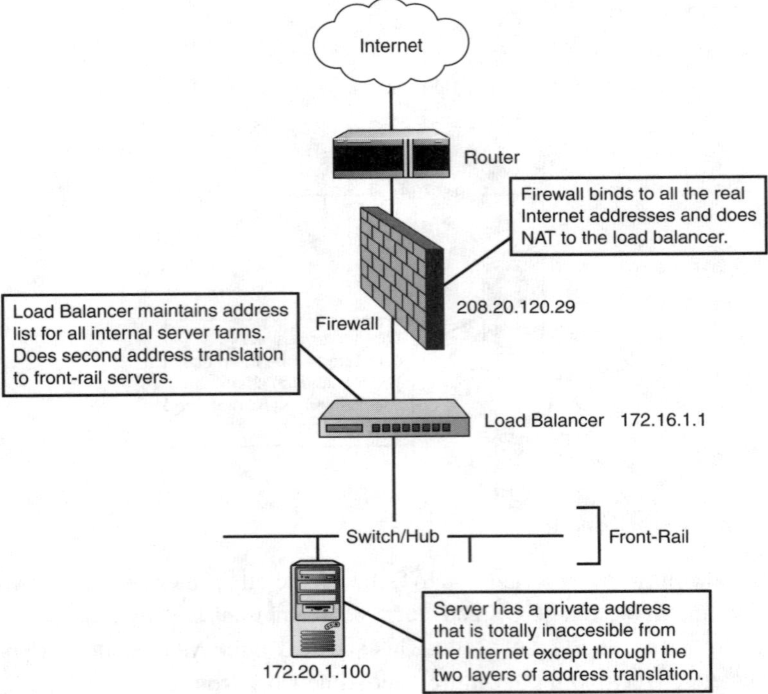

FIGURE 4.16
A front-rail connection to the Internet with multiple address translations.

Load Balancing as Address Translation

Load balancing is another form of address translation. It takes the traffic of a single IP address and distributes it across multiple IP addresses. This enables multiple servers to act as one virtual server, handling the requests of a single IP address. When connecting a DMZ to the Internet, load balancing provides another layer of IP address indirection like that in Figure 4.16.

NOTE

For more information on load balancing and load-balancing technologies, see Chapter 5, "Using Microsoft Network Load Balancing in a Web Farm", and Chapter 6, "Using Hardware Load Balancing in a Web Farm."

Designing the Network Interconnect Between a DMZ and the Internet

The first step in designing Internet-to-DMZ internetworking architectures is to gather requirements from the perspective of quality of service, packet filtering and blocking, network address translation, and load balancing. Once these requirements are understood, begin to think about how network traffic will flow into and out of the Web farm. At what points should packets be filtered? When should a packet be denied access due to bandwidth limitations? When does a packet reach the actual address? Are there multiple levels of NAT? How a packet flows through a network determines which network devices are required. Use Figure 4.17 to help visualize a packet's path from the Internet to the front-rail Web farm servers.

In more complex networks there may be many different points where quality of service, packet filtering and blocking, network address translation, and load balancing occur. For example, some Web farm networks will load balance firewalls for greater redundancy and throughput. Others will have QoS points at the initial connection from the Internet and at a load-balancing device for finer control of bandwidth at a Web site's specific layer. Some will have a single layer of NAT and use Network Load Balancing, a software-based approach that bypasses a second layer of address translation to achieve load balancing. With every network being unique, there are some general guidelines that should be following when designing a DMZ-to-Internet network.

- *Stress redundancy for most* of the physical layer, including a duplicate Internet pipe. This does not mean that every physical device should have a duplicate cold or hot spare ready in case of a failure. As a general rule, the Internet pipe, firewalls, and load-balancing devices should have hot or cold spares on hand. Routers and other switches should have replacement equipment on hand or a service agreement with a response time of four hours or less.

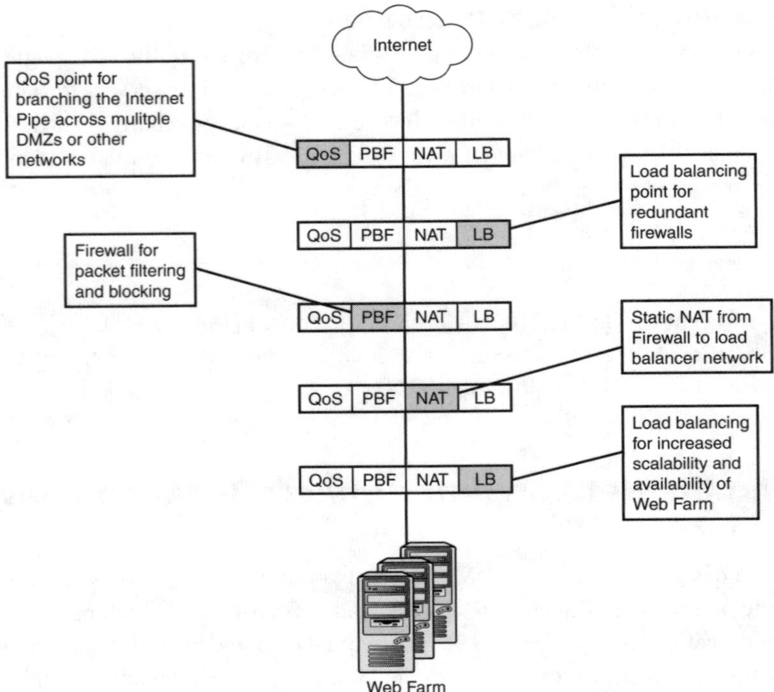

FIGURE 4.17
An example of packet flow for a DMZ-to-Internet network.

- *Plan around the limited bandwidth* of an Internet connection. Almost exclusively, the bandwidth of the closed or DMZ network is much greater than an Internet pipe. Be sure that increasing the bandwidth of an Internet connection is part of any network architecture plan. Especially important is the throughput on any device that funnels traffic, like a firewall or load-balancing device. These should be able to handle the maximum bandwidth of an Internet pipe.
- *Reserve plenty of network addresses* for any NAT and front-rail/back-rail networks. A full class B address such as `172.20.x.x` is appropriate for any medium-size to large Web farm. The task of readdressing all the servers in a DMZ can cause considerable downtime and headache. These internally approved IP addresses are free, and there are plenty available for private networks.

- *Build a DMZ-to-Internet network* so that availability is determined by the uptime of the Internet service provider supplying the connection to the Internet. If the network connecting the DMZ to the Internet is fully fault tolerant, its uptime should be the same as that of the ISP. Consider having a backup ISP for sites that require the highest availability and fault tolerance.
- *Secure the front rail by judiciously* using firewalls and NAT. Don't let unnecessary packets waste server resources and glean information from a network that isn't absolutely necessary. The cost of NAT and a firewall on a network is minimal compared to the increased gain in security. Protecting the DMZ network with a firewall will secure it from unwanted traffic and provide a first layer of defense from network-based attacks and hacks.

Connecting the Web Farm Network to Secure Networks

Connecting the Web farm network to a secure network is much easier than connecting it to the Internet. The same principles and devices used to connect to the Internet are good choices for secure network connections. The back rail is another access path to the same set of servers. It is not unreasonable to create the same internetworking architectures for each connection.

Every connection to a secure network will need an intermediary packet-filtering and blocking device. For general-purpose activities such as administrative access, this device should be a firewall, as shown in Figure 4.18. Without a firewall, the DMZ network is susceptible to the same problems faced by networks directly exposed to the Internet.

There are a number of factors that influence the robustness of a connection to a secure network. Cost is an important consideration, because if a secure network can access the services of a DMZ network from the Internet, it might be a better strategy to keep the connection to the secure network simple. Factors also include the type of access required by users in secure networks. Finally, if you are connecting to another secure network that is not under direct control, that network might have special access requirements.

Connecting to the Web Farm Network from a Corporation

Corporate users have different requirements than customers when connecting to a Web farm network. These requirements depend on the type of users and the task. An administrator might need full privileges and access to all servers in the DMZ. A business analyst or knowledge worker might be restricted to a Web interface that provides the tools needed to complete his tasks. In either case, the user accessing the DMZ is probably well known and can be tracked easier than a user from the Internet.

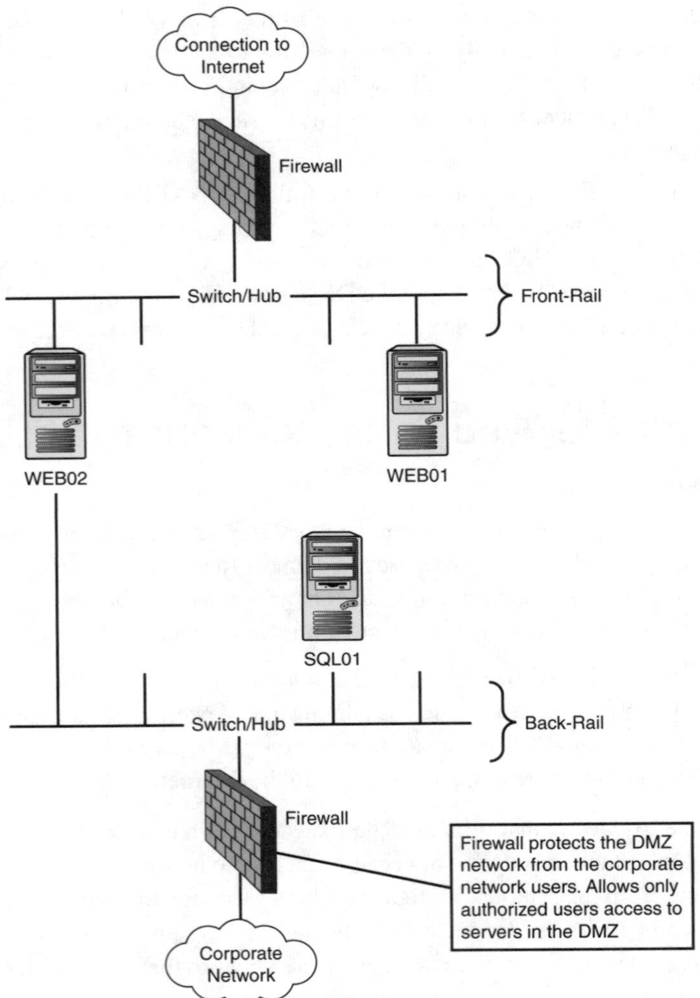

FIGURE 4.18
Using a firewall to filter packets from a secure network.

Connecting to External Service Providers

External service providers are more and more a fact of life for the Web farm. Service providers already exist in a myriad of forms. Banks, fulfillment centers, remote storage providers, user authentication services, and ad management services are only a few of the many available external service providers. As .NET building block services become more widely available,

Microsoft and other companies will begin offering even more services. This means that secure and reliable connections to these services are important.

There are numerous ways to connect to external service providers. These options include

- Connecting across secure networks through a WAN firewall.
- Connecting across the Internet using a secured network protocol like SSL.
- Connecting across a leased line that bypasses a firewall.

The following examples describe two ways Foo.com connected to external service providers.

Connecting to a Bank

Foo.com made the decision that credit card authorization across the Internet was too risky. It chose to connect over a secure, fully owned and operated connection of the bank itself. Figure 4.19 shows how this was accomplished. The bank simply installed a black-box router that connects securely to the bank network. A dedicated network adapter in each credit card server attached to a hub communicates the requests from the Web farm to the bank. In this case, a multi-NIC server on the back rail of a DMZ communicates with two separate secure networks.

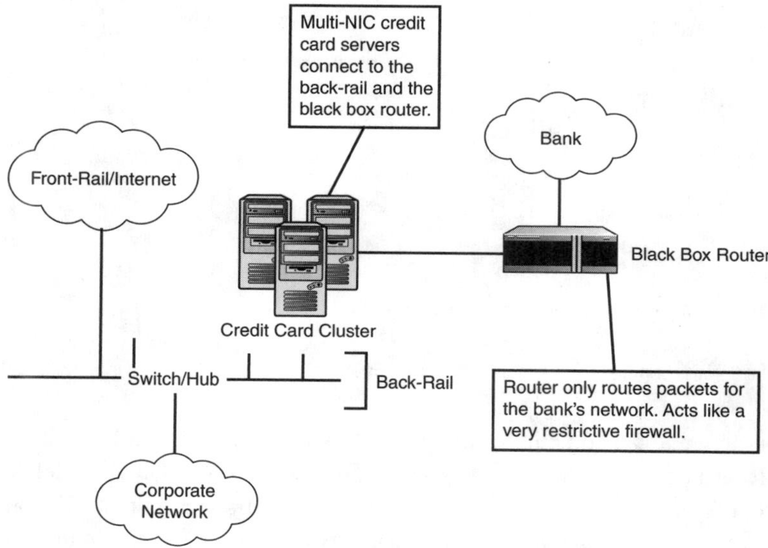

FIGURE 4.19
A configuration for a direct connection to a bank.

Connecting to an Inventory Fulfillment Center

Foo.com connected to an inventory fulfillment center when it outsourced all of its inventory management. Instead of communicating directly to corporate resources to manage inventory, it communicated over the a secure network to a third-party inventory fulfillment center. In this case, as seen in Figure 4.20, the inventory reservation requests traveled from back-rail servers, through the back-rail firewall, and over to another WAN firewall that handles all request to WAN services.

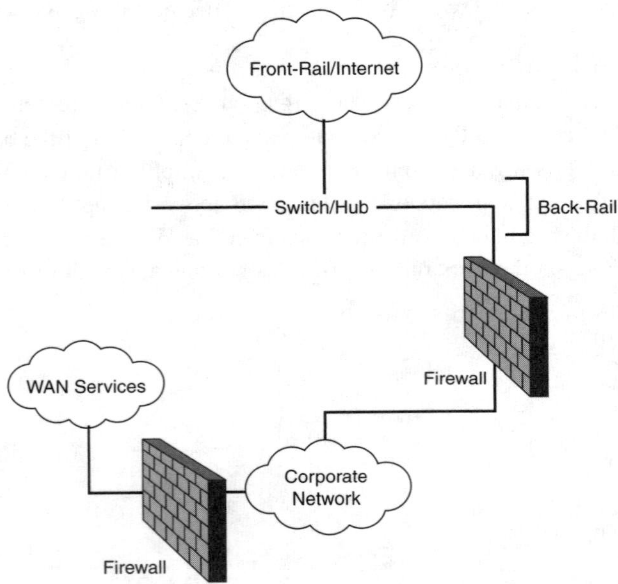

FIGURE 4.20
A WAN firewall used to connect to external service providers.

Summary

The Web farm network can come in a variety of forms. The DMZ model is the best suited from a growth, security, and reliability perspective. In the Dual-Rail DMZ model, servers exist on a front rail, a back rail, or both. Users on the Internet access servers that exist on the front rail. Servers on the front rail and users in a secure network access servers on the back rail.

The front rail connects to the Internet. How this connection is built depends on quality of service, packet filtering and blocking, network address translation, and load balancing requirements. Connections to a secure network are built like connections to the Internet. Sometimes they are simplified due to use requirements and cost. In any case, this connection should be reliable and secure so that the front door of a Web farm is always open.

Using Microsoft Network Load Balancing in a Web Farm

CHAPTER

5

The PC has brought a new age to server-side technologies and applications. Servers originally were large standalone entities, such as mainframes or minicomputers, with built-in redundancy and a high per-unit cost. They were very expensive to replace and upgrade long term. These servers were proprietary and tied a company with a vendor for a considerable period of time.

The software that was built for mainframe servers established a mindset for design that still affects software today. Mainframe software developers assumed a shared memory and disk configuration. These design decisions have affected modern Web farms because many of these mainframe technologies are still in use. These software limitations are the reason so many technologies have been developed to overcome mainframe shortcomings. Network Load Balancing is one technology created to overcome single-server limitations.

The attraction of many small servers running Windows 2000 in a Web farm is clear. Many servers are better than one large server for the following reasons:

- Having many inexpensive servers makes upgrading easy, and replacing failed servers is inexpensive.
- Having many servers provides flexibility as Web farm needs change and grow. Server tasks can be broken up among numerous servers, and the resources used to address different application needs can be scaled independently from one another.
- Initial investment is small. Doubling the power of most Web farms costs as much as the initial server investment. This is small compared to the initial investment in a large single server.
- Many smaller servers take advantage of the current trend toward faster and cheaper hardware, enabling Web farms to decrease physical space requirements while increasing overall Web farm application capacity.

The goals of this chapter are to help you

- Understand Microsoft Network Load Balancing. An overview of special terms, features, and system requirements is provided.
- Configure a Microsoft Network Load Balancing cluster with one or two network adapters using different configuration options.

Understanding Microsoft Network Load Balancing

Microsoft Network Load Balancing (NLB) is a Windows 2000 network service built to scale IP services such as HTTP and FTP. NLB eliminates reliance on single-server configurations for mission-crucial systems, enabling administrators to build highly scalable and available Web farms by combining the power of multiple servers. With NLB, an administrator can combine up to 32 servers to act as one virtual server instance. Web servers, FTP servers, and other network applications that use a TCP/IP-based protocol can use NLB to provide redundancy at the server level and scalability at the application level.

NOTE

Each unique Windows Network Load Balancing cluster can consist of 1 to 32 servers.

Originally known as Windows Load Balancing Services in Windows NT, NLB is now a part of Windows 2000 Advanced Server, Windows 2000 Datacenter Server, and Application Center 2000. Because Application Center 2000 can install onto Windows 2000 Server, it is possible to have NLB balance a Windows 2000 server farm.

TIP

Application Center 2000 provides the Windows 2000 Server product with the Network Load Balancing services so Advanced Server is no longer required.

Concepts of Network Load Balancing

The following sections describe some of the more common concepts of Microsoft Network Load Balancing. Network Load Balancing introduces a number of terms such as cluster IP address, dedicated IP address, and management IP address. Other terms that are important for NLB include convergence, multicast mode, and host priority. A successful installation of NLB requires that the administrator have a firm understanding of the differences in these terms along with other important NLB concepts.

NOTE

Many of these concepts are similar to those discussed in Chapter 17, "Introducing Windows Server Clusters."

Cluster IP Address

Use the cluster IP address to access services that are load balanced across a cluster from a client. This address has the same value across all members of a cluster. In fact, every member of the cluster will bind this address to the network adapter that has the NLB driver installed and active. This driver prevents IP address conflicts from occurring in Windows 2000 with the other members of the cluster.

Another name for this address is a *virtual IP address (VIP)*. When a client makes a request to a VIP under Network Load Balancing, the individual packet travels to every adapter that is bound to the cluster IP address in the cluster. The NLB service ultimately decides which server handles the request based on configuration options.

Network Load Balancing supports multiple-cluster IP addresses per cluster. In this scenario, any IP address that is not the dedicated IP address but is bound to the cluster adapter is addressable as a VIP.

Dedicated IP Address

Use the dedicated IP address to communicate directly to the cluster adapter that is bound to the cluster IP address and has Network Load Balancing enabled. Without this address, a cluster adapter can never be inspected over the network without using the load-balancing algorithms of Network Load Balancing. This address is useful for monitoring the load-balanced services of individual members of the cluster. Also, in some network topologies, it is impossible to measure the availability of the cluster adapter from networks attached to the management adapter. The dedicated IP address would be the only way to ensure that a server is still present and functioning on the network that the load-balanced service is intended to serve.

In all configurations of servers with single or multiple network adapters, the dedicated IP address is always bound to the same adapter as the cluster IP address. This is an important point because the terminology *dedicated* is overloaded and in some help documentation is used interchangeably with the management IP address and adapter. In single-adapter scenarios, the dedicated IP address and the management IP address are the same.

Management IP Address

A management IP address is the real IP address of a server in a cluster. This address is used to communicate directly with the server in question for administrative support, content updates, and any other network operations that would be specific for a cluster member. This is the address that DNS and WINS queries should resolve to.

The management IP address can exist on a single network adapter along with the cluster IP address and in this case is the same as the dedicated IP address. The preferred configuration, and the one that performs best from a network perspective, is to bind the management IP address to a separate network adapter in a multiple adapter server.

Single Network Adapter Servers

A single network adapter or single-NIC server has only one network adapter for handling the load-balanced traffic and traffic directed at individual members of the cluster.

In a single-NIC configuration, the cluster IP address and the management IP address are bound to the same adapter. In this scenario, the dedicated IP address and the management IP address are the same.

NOTE

Microsoft recommends not using a single-NIC server configuration because overall network performance may suffer.

There are advantages to running an NLB cluster with a single adapter machine. It is the default configuration and is easy to set up. However, this configuration is not recommended by Microsoft and not supported in Application Center 2000.

Multiple Network Adapter Servers

A multiple network adapter or multi-NIC server has two or more network adapters. In this configuration, one network adapter is dedicated to the traffic intended to be load balanced and is called the *cluster adapter*. The other network adapter is dedicated to traffic intended for an individual server and is called the *management adapter*. Web farms that use NLB should use a multi-NIC server configuration, especially if using Application Center 2000's managed NLB mode. More information on the cluster and management adapters is found later in this section.

In a multi-NIC configuration, the cluster IP address is bound to the cluster adapter and the management IP address is bound to the management adapter. In some scenarios, a *dedicated IP address* is also bound to the cluster adapter. Don't confuse the dedicated IP address with the management IP address. More information on cluster, dedicated, and management IP addresses is found earlier in this section.

Table 5.1 shows how the cluster, dedicated, and management IP addresses relate to multiple- and single-adapter servers.

TABLE 5.1 Network Load Balancing IP Address Assignments

Server Type	*Cluster IP Address*	*Dedicated IP Address*	*Management IP Address*
Single Adapter Server	Bound to the single adapter and designated as the cluster IP address in Network Load Balancing.	Bound to the single adapter and designated as the dedicated IP address in Network Load Balancing.	The management IP address is the same as the dedicated IP address in a single adapter server.

TABLE 5.1 Continued

Server Type	*Cluster IP Address*	*Dedicated IP Address*	*Management IP Address*
Multiple Adapter Server	Bound to the cluster adapter and designated as the cluster IP address in Network Load Balancing.	Bound to the cluster adapter and designated as the dedicated IP address in Network Load Balancing.	Bound to the management adapter. This IP address is different from the dedicated IP address in Network Load Balancing.

NOTE

Application Center 2000 introduces managed Network Load Balancing mode, which requires multiple adapters. Any installation of Application Center 2000 should plan for a dedicated management IP address and adapter.

The Management Adapter

The management adapter is the network adapter that is used to handle administrative requests to a specific cluster member. This traffic includes any management console traffic such as IIS or Component Services. It also includes terminal server sessions and file share access. Any deployment traffic should travel across this adapter. Separating management traffic and cluster load-balancing traffic prevents overall performance of the cluster from degrading.

The Cluster Adapter

The cluster adapter is the network adapter that is used to handle all requests for services of the cluster. A cluster adapter can be dedicated to the cluster with a management adapter that handles requests directed at the individual servers in the cluster.

In a multi-NIC server, one card is dedicated to application traffic that is being load balanced, such as HTTP traffic. The other cards are dedicated to handling traffic that is not balanced across all members of the cluster. This traffic could include administrative Terminal Service access or remote administrative Network Load Balancing access. In a server with only one network card, this single card performs both roles. Figure 5.1 shows both configurations.

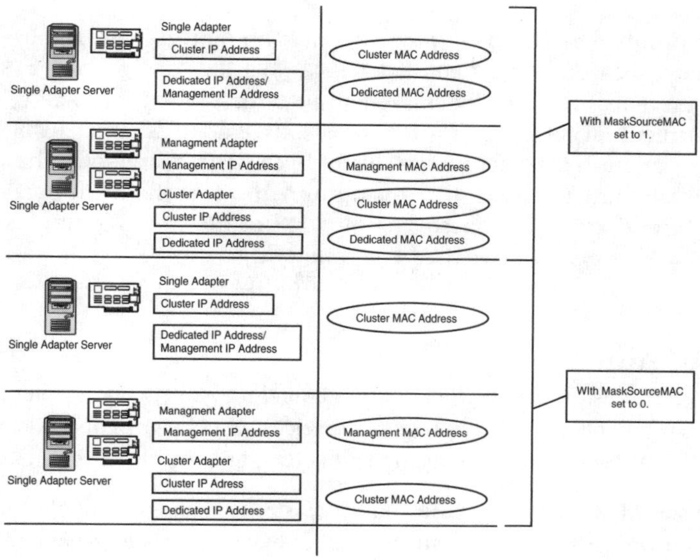

FIGURE 5.1
Single and multi-NIC server configuration for NLB.

In a single network adapter configuration or with a dedicated cluster adapter, the dedicated IP address and the cluster IP address are bound to the same network adapter. Network Load Balancing creates two fake MAC addresses for these two types of IP addresses. One is the cluster MAC address and is used by all cluster members for cluster traffic. The other is a replacement for the MAC address of the network adapter itself and is unique to each host. From the switch port perspective, a single adapter will have two MAC addresses mapped to the same port. This configuration can cause problems with certain switch configurations, so check the vendor specifications before using Network Load Balancing.

Using NLB on Problematic Switches

Certain switches do not support the techniques that NLB uses to distribute traffic to all members of the cluster. This is usually caused by the cluster MAC addresses being advertised on more than one switch port. In other cases, switches do not support multiple MAC addresses resolving to the same port, the technique NLB uses to direct traffic to individual members' cluster adapters.

To solve the problem with more than one MAC address resolving to the same port, use a hub. Connect both cluster adapters to the hub, and connect the hub to the switch. This makes the cluster MAC address resolve to a single port on the switch but introduces a single point of failure.

To solve the problem of a single switch port owning multiple MAC addresses, there is a Registry entry located in `HKEY_LOCAL_MACHINE\SYSTEM\CurrentControlSet\Services\WLBS\Parameters` called `MaskSourceMAC` that, when set to zero, will turn off the MAC address that is created for the dedicated IP address on a cluster adapter. This must be done on each member of the cluster because Registry entry changes are not propagated automatically. With this setting turned off, each switch port will show only one MAC address. Sometimes a combination of these two techniques is the only way to make NLB work in a switched environment.

Cluster MAC Address

The cluster MAC address is the network address bound to the network adapter that processes network packets of clients making requests for services of a cluster. This address is automatically generated by Network Load Balancing and is based on the cluster's primary IP address.

Because the cluster MAC address is based on the cluster IP address, multiple Network Load Balancing clusters on the same subnet are ensured of having uniquely generated cluster MAC addresses. If NLB is running in unicast mode, the cluster MAC address is a standard unicast MAC address beginning with 0x02. If the cluster is running in multicast mode, the cluster MAC is a standard unicast MAC address beginning with 0x03. The remaining digits in the MAC address are determined by the first cluster IP address.

This generation of fake MAC addresses places special requirements on the network adapters used for NLB. If a network adapter does not support dynamically changing its MAC address, it cannot be used in a Network Load Balancing cluster.

NOTE

Network Load Balancing requires that the cluster adapter support dynamically replaceable MAC addresses.

Virtual Network Name

The virtual network name specifies a full Internet name for a Network Load Balancing cluster (for example, `vcluster.foo.com`). Clients use the virtual network name when addressing this cluster at the TCP/IP layer. The virtual network name resolves to the cluster IP address through a DNS server or Hosts file. This name can also be a single NetBIOS name without the fully qualified domain name.

Unicast Mode

Unicast is a network term that describes the sending of packets from one host to one receiver. Unicast mode is the default configuration for NLB, and it defines how intracluster communication works. In unicast mode, cluster members communicate to each other their current status by sending unicast broadcast messages to the fake cluster MAC address once a second. These broadcast messages are of ether type 886f and are 1510-byte packets. Because all hosts in an NLB cluster advertise the same cluster MAC address, they all receive these status messages from one another.

In a switched environment with large broadcast domains (many network ports on the same subnet), unicast broadcast messages can soon become the largest single source of traffic. The nature of broadcast forces each and every server on this subnet to inspect these messages and see if it is a destination. This adds overhead on each server's network adapter and CPU. In a large Web farm with many NLB clusters on the same network, broadcasts can cause problems.

Multicast Mode

Multicast is a network term that describes the sending of packets from one host to many hosts. When NLB runs in multicast mode, the cluster MAC address changes to a multicast MAC. This multicast MAC is still owned by all cluster members, but the way the cluster members communicate becomes much more efficient. Instead of creating a fake dedicated MAC, the real MAC address is used for the dedicated portion of a cluster adapter. These real MAC addresses send status packets to the multicast MAC address instead of using a broadcast message. Only machines that advertise the multicast MAC address receive these status messages, and the load on the network and other servers is considerably reduced or eliminated altogether.

Multicast mode eliminates the broadcast problem of unicast mode. However, multicast mode places special requirements on the network hardware layer. If the clients of the Network Load Balancing cluster travel through a router, it must be able to route packets from a server that has two MAC addresses on a single network adapter. Some routers will not route packets destined for a physical connection with two different MAC address designations (unicast and multicast). If such a router receives an ARP reply that has a multicast MAC address (the fake cluster MAC address) and already has entries for the real MAC address, a unicast MAC address, it will not route the packets to the cluster. In this condition, the cluster MAC address will appear unavailable to the rest of the network. A router must be able to support the resolution of unicast IP addresses to multicast MAC addresses. A router that does not support this configuration may require a static ARP entry to the multicast MAC address for a Network Load Balancing cluster to work.

Cluster Convergence

Cluster convergence is the process of Network Load Balancing hosts periodically exchanging broadcast or multicast messages to monitor the status of the cluster. Whenever a host fails, joins, or leaves the cluster, the servers reestablish cluster membership, status, priority, and other state conditions of a cluster. These messages result in the election of the default host, and each host adjusts the parameters used to determine what traffic it handles. Once convergence is complete and all hosts have reset their operating condition, the cluster will report the convergence in the Windows 2000 event log.

Convergence is a transactional process, so when the status of a cluster changes, the remaining hosts don't adjust their operating parameters until all active members are ready. While convergence is transpiring, hosts remain responsive and healthy under the old balancing configuration. Once all hosts acknowledge the successful adoption of new operating parameters, they all assume their new cluster status and role. Load-balanced traffic is redistributed to achieve the best possible new load balance for specific TCP or UDP port rules.

The convergence process provides the following benefits:

- When a new host is added to the cluster, convergence enables this new host to begin handling traffic seamlessly without disturbing the cluster.
- Hosts can be removed from a cluster in a graceful manner. By gradually changing the priority of a specific host over time, the convergence process will effectively remove connections from the host until it no longer maintains any active ones. This process is called *draining*.
- If a host does not respond to the convergence process for the default five missed message exchange periods, the host is removed from the cluster and its load redistributed to the rest of the cluster.

Host Priority

The host priority is a unique number between 1 and 32 assigned to each member of the cluster. The cluster member with the lowest number handles all the default traffic of a cluster. Default traffic is any traffic that is not governed by port rules. Port rules define how traffic is balanced across members of a cluster. Traffic without a port rule will go only to one member of the cluster, the default host. For more information on port rules, see the "Understanding Port Rules" section later in this chapter.

Default Host

The default host is the server with the highest host priority. This server handles all traffic that is not governed by port rules. There is nothing else special about the default host, and it does not act as a Cluster Controller or master.

Distribution of Network Traffic

NLB uses a fully distributed load-balancing methodology to direct network traffic to each host of a virtual server or cluster. This enables a fully parallel implementation that uses the resources available on each host. Because all hosts are capable of running the balanced service alone or in a cluster, there is no concept of a master or cluster owner that directs the flow of network traffic to each cluster member. Instead, the distributed Network Load Balancing algorithm examines every packet that arrives at a host machine and determines if a particular packet should be handled. If it is not handled, then the packet is discarded; no other communication is sent to other members of the cluster.

For example, Foo.com created a virtual cluster called `VCluster` that is depicted in Figure 5.2. Both members of the cluster always handle traffic that is directed at the `VCluster` network name. The distributed algorithm determines which server should actually process the incoming packet.

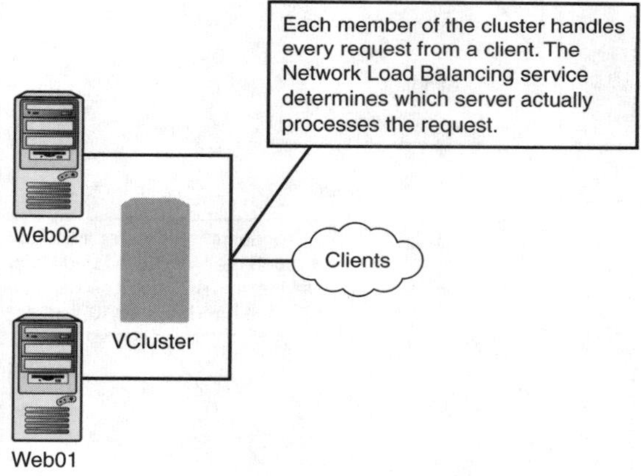
Each member of the cluster handles every request from a client. The Network Load Balancing service determines which server actually processes the request.
Web02
VCluster
Clients
Web01

FIGURE 5.2
Foo.com's `VCluster`.

Because Network Load Balancing is distributed, Microsoft claims that a Network Load Balanced cluster has a higher throughput than centralized hardware solutions and will take full advantage of the bandwidth in a switched environment. Figure 5.3 shows the differences between a hardware-based solution and a fully distributed Network Load Balanced solution. Network Load Balancing is different from a centralized hardware solution because all traffic to a virtual server travels to every server in the farm. It is true in this configuration that there are no inherent network bottlenecks, but this means that the effective bandwidth of a 32-node cluster on a 100Mbps network is 100Mbps. There are no throughput gains from using Network Load Balancing as it is the same as a hardware solution.

NOTE

For more information on hardware load-balancing solutions, see Chapter 6, "Using Hardware Load Balancing in a Web Farm."

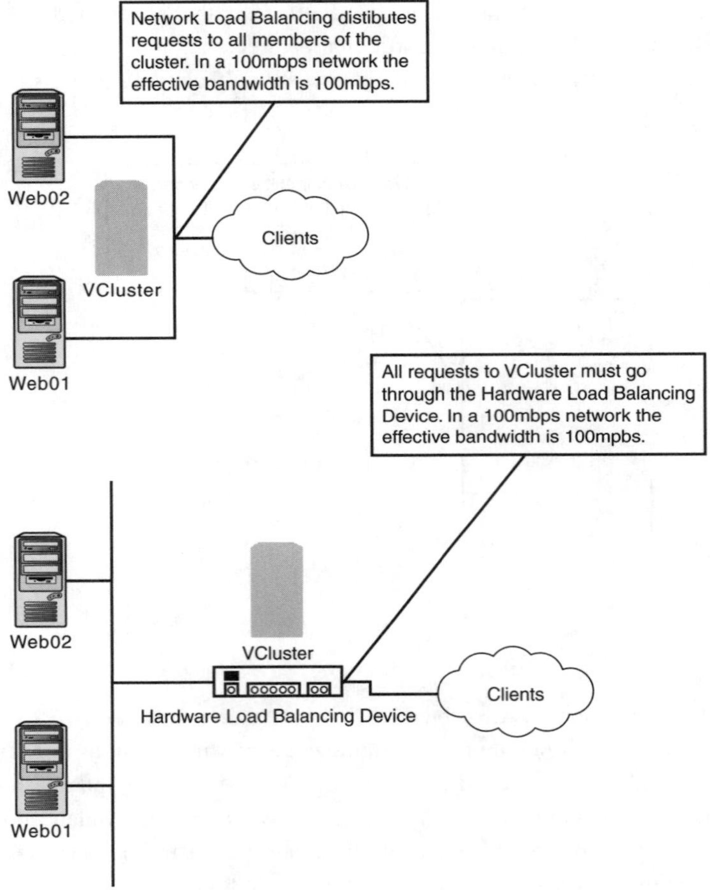
Network Load Balancing distibutes requests to all members of the cluster. In a 100mbps network the effective bandwidth is 100mbps.
Web02
VCluster
Clients
Web01
All requests to VCluster must go through the Hardware Load Balancing Device. In a 100mbps network the effective bandwidth is 100mpbs.
Web02
VCluster
Hardware Load Balancing Device
Clients
Web01

FIGURE 5.3
Network Load Balancing versus hardware load balancing.

Understanding Port Rules

Port rules are the configuration parameters that Network Load Balancing uses to balance a specific port of the cluster IP address. Port rules are made up of seven options. Table 5.2 shows all the port rule parameters and how they affect the load balancing of a Network Load Balancing cluster.

TABLE 5.2 Port Rule Parameters

Port Option	*Possible Values*	*Description*
Start	0–65535	The start port value of a port range for a rule.
End	0–65536	The end port value of a port range for a rule.
Protocol	UDP, TCP, Both	The protocol to balance for this port rule.
Filtering Mode	multiple, single, disabled	Assigns the port rule to multiple hosts or a single host or disables a port, blocking it on all servers in the cluster.
Host Priority	1–32	The priority used when balancing ports that don't have rules defined or when the mode of the rule is set to single. One (1) is the highest priority.
Load Weight	Equal or 1–100	The amount of traffic for a specific host to handle. Equal sets each host to handle the same amount of traffic.
Affinity	None, Single, Class C	The affinity of a connection to a specific member of the cluster. With none, each request is sent to a random server. Single affinity port rules force all request from the same user to the same server. Class C affinity forces all traffic from a Class C address to the same server.

Each of the options changes the behavior of a cluster IP address port.

Start and End Port

The start port and end port are used to define the TCP/UDP port or port range that Network Load Balancing applies a specific rule against. By default, Network Load Balancing has a default rule that covers all the ports on a cluster IP address. To define a rule for a specific port, create a rule that has the start and end port values shown in Figure 5.4.

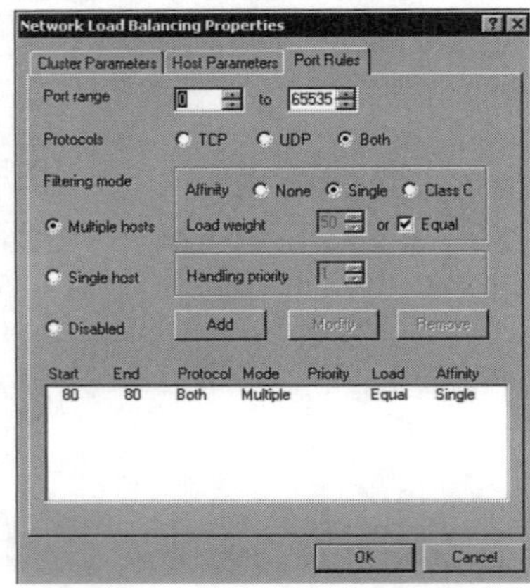

FIGURE 5.4
A port rule for one port.

The start and end port values allowed range from 0 to 65535. A port may only have one rule associated with it, whether it is within a range or for a specific port.

Protocol Choices

The protocol parameter of a port rule determines which TCP/IP protocol—UDP, TCP, or both—a port rule governs. If a rule specifies either UDP or TCP, then the default host handles the other protocol. For example, in a Network Load Balancing cluster of two servers with a port rule on port 80 that is set for TCP-only traffic, a filtering mode of multiple, and the load weight set to equal, TCP traffic will travel equally to both hosts. UDP traffic will travel only to the host with the lowest numerical host priority or the default host. Network Load Balancing allows only one rule per port, so in the just given example, it is impossible to create a second rule on port 80 that is for UDP only.

Filtering Mode

The filtering mode parameter has the most dramatic effect on the behavior of a port rule in a Network Load Balancing cluster. Filter mode can have three values: multiple hosts, single host, and disabled.

When filtering mode is set to multiple hosts, the load-balancing algorithm ensures that network traffic for this port will travel to all the hosts in the cluster. The setting provides redundancy by distributing traffic to all cluster members. It also provides scalability because up to 32 servers can handle traffic for this port rule. When multiple hosts is selected, affinity and load weight determine how the traffic is balanced among multiple servers.

When filtering mode is set to single host, the load-balancing algorithm directs all traffic to the host with the lowest numerical host priority. In this mode, only one server will handle traffic, and the other hosts in the cluster wait in case the default host fails. It is also possible to manipulate the host priority values and change which cluster member is the default host. This mode provides only redundancy and does nothing to help scale a Web farm.

NOTE

Choosing a filtering mode of single host results in a Network Load Balancing cluster in which all traffic is handled by the default host for a particular port rule. Load balancing does not occur.

When filtering mode is set to disabled, the load-balancing algorithm prevents a host from responding to traffic for the port ranges of the rule. This effectively hides this port from other computers in the network and is similar to the behavior of a firewall.

Host Priority

The host priority is a numerical value from 1 to 32. It is used in two specific instances. The host with the highest host priority (the lowest numerical value) will handle all the traffic to a specific port when

- A port does not have a rule associated with it.
- A port rule specifically has been set with the filtering mode of single host.

In either case, the host priority setting is used to determine the order in which servers handle traffic when a failure occurs.

NOTE

Host priority has no effect on rules that specify a filtering mode of multiple hosts.

When the host with the highest host priority fails, a convergence occurs and a new host with the highest host priority becomes the default host. This host will begin to handle traffic for those port rules that meet the criteria specified earlier in this section.

Affinity

Affinity determines how client sessions against a cluster are maintained. A client session is considered to be any request made from the same unique IP address outside the boundaries of a persistent network connection. When a client makes the second and all subsequent requests against a Network Load Balancing cluster, this setting determines whether that client is directed to the same server that handled the first request or to some other server, determined by load weight settings. Affinity applies only to rules that have a filtering mode of multiple hosts. Affinity has three possible settings: none, single, and class C.

When affinity is set to none, Network Load Balancing does not maintain session consistency. Every request is directed to the most appropriate server based on load weight. This means that any session information stored locally on a server will likely be lost when moved to a different server. In the example of a Web site that maintains session state in an old-style ASP session object, an affinity of none will cause the site to appear to behave erratically. When an application session is maintained with client-side cookies or a database, this is the preferred setting.

CAUTION

An affinity of none will cause applications that use ASP sessions to work incorrectly.

If Affinity is set to single, Network Load Balancing maintains session consistency across client requests. Once a server handles a request for a client, the same server will handle all subsequent requests to that client. In other words, the same cluster member handles multiple requests from the same client IP address. In cases of failure, any state that is maintained in the memory of the failed server is lost, and it is likely that the user's current session will be lost. Network Load Balancing will direct the next request after a host failure to the most appropriate host, based on the load weight setting, but it can do nothing to recover application-specific state information from the failed host. This is not a limitation of Network Load Balancing; it is an application design flaw.

When Affinity is set to class C, all requests from the same class C IP address go to the same server. This is used because some Internet service providers use a different proxy server for each client request. This will appear to the Network Load Balancing cluster to be a different client request because each proxy server has a unique IP address. Because it is unlikely the ISP will have a different class B address for each proxy server, class C affinity will handle this problem effectively because all requests from customers of that ISP are directed to the same server. For a large ISP, this could be a problem because of the sheer number of people who would be using the same server. Figure 5.5 illustrates the farm or proxy server problem and how affinity changes the behavior of NLB in these scenarios. Once again, if a Web site is server dependent, it is not a problem with Network Load Balancing; it is a fundamental application design flaw.

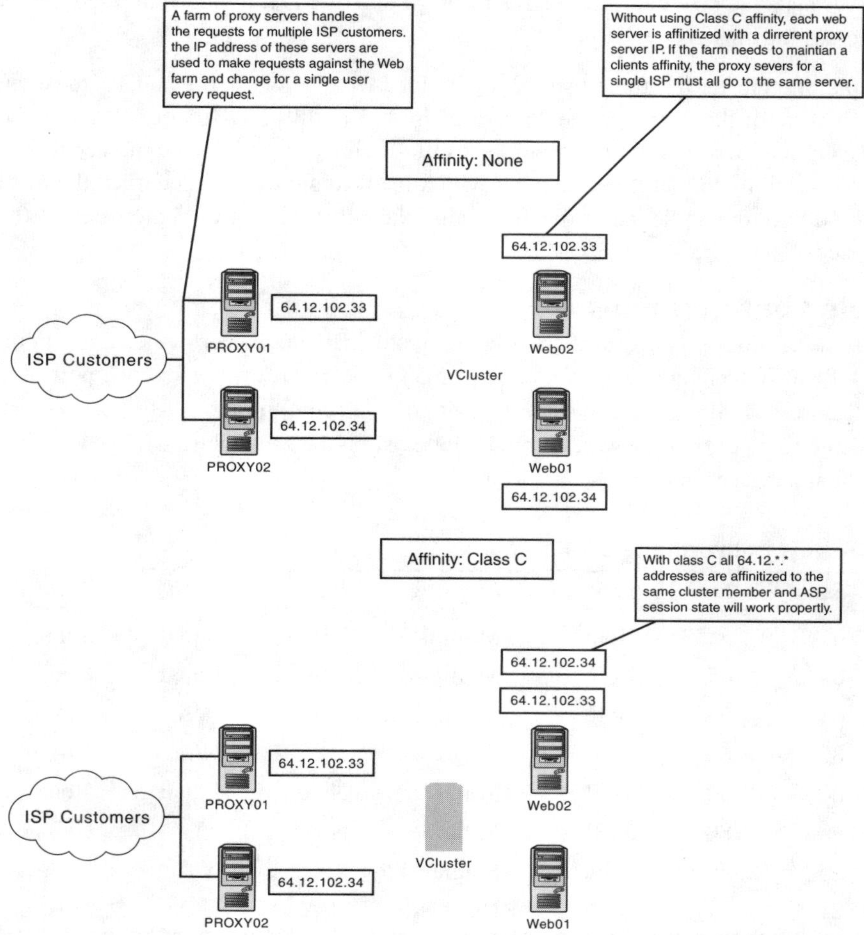

FIGURE 5.5
A farm of proxy servers and the affinity setting.

Load Weight

Load weight is used by Network Load Balancing to determine which host should handle an incoming request. Load weight applies only to rules that use the filter mode multiple hosts.

There are two options for load weight settings. The first is equal, which distributes traffic equally across all servers in the cluster. This is the optimum setting and should be used if all servers in a farm are of like configuration. The second option is a numerical value from 0 to 100. This is not a hard percentage; it is a the local load percentage. To calculate the amount of load a server handles, take the local load percentage and divide it by the sum of all the load weights across the cluster.

For example, if a cluster has three members with load weights of 95, 60, and 40, the actual load percentages for the members are 95 divided by 195 or 48%, 60/195 or 31%, and 40/195 or 21%. Using load weights in this fashion is useful if cluster members are of varying computing power. Bear in mind that if the member with a load weight of 95 failed, then the rest of the cluster would have to handle the traffic, and their load percentages would increase to 60% and 40%, respectively.

Port Rule Configurations

Combinations of different port rules are used to create different clustering behavior. In theory, a Network Load Balancing cluster could have 65,535 port rules, or one for each port of the cluster IP address. Table 5.3 shows some typical port rule configurations. Because a cluster can have only one rule per port, these rules could not exist on the same cluster. They are provided for discussion purposes only.

TABLE 5.3 Typical Port Rule Configurations

Rule	*Start*	*End*	*Protocol*	*Filtering*	*Host*	*Load*	*Affinity*
1	0	65535	Both	Multiple	N/A	Equal	Single
2	0	65535	Both	Multiple	N/A	Equal	None
3	0	65535	Both	Single	1	N/A	N/A
4	80	80	TCP	Single	1	N/A	N/A
5	80	80	TCP	Multiple	N/A	Equal	None
6	80	80	TCP	Multiple	N/A	75	Class C
7	25	25	Both	Single	2	N/A	N/A
8	21	21	Both	Disabled	N/A	N/A	N/A

Rule 1 defines a complete load-balancing cluster. Network traffic directed to all ports of the cluster IP address is balanced, and all TCP/IP protocols are covered. Host priority is unimportant when the filtering mode is multiple. The load is distributed evenly among all members of the cluster. In this rule, once a client makes a connection to a host in the cluster, it will always be directed back to the same host.

Like rule 1, rule 2 defines a complete load-balancing cluster. The only difference is that with an affinity of none, a different cluster member could handle every client request.

Rule 3 defines a complete availability cluster. Network traffic directed to all ports of the cluster IP address is sent to the host with the highest host priority. All TCP/IP protocols are covered. Load and affinity parameters do not apply to rules that use a filtering mode of single.

Rule 4 defines an availability cluster for port 80, the standard port of HTTP. Because this rule uses a filtering mode of single and is balancing only the Transmission Control Protocol, the host with the highest priority will always handle requests. UDP will be handled in the same way, so for rules with filtering mode set to single, the end result is the same as if the protocol was set to both.

Rule 5 defines a load-balancing cluster for port 80. In this case, TCP traffic will be balanced across all members of the cluster, but UDP traffic to port 80 will go to the host with the highest host priority. As with rule 2, subsequent requests from the same client could go to any host in the cluster.

Similar to rule 5, rule 6 defines a load-balancing cluster for port 80 except for special load weight and affinity. With load weight set to 75, the host will likely handle more of the load than others in the cluster, depending on their settings. With class C affinity, all traffic from a class C address will always go to the same host in the cluster.

Rule 7 defines an availability cluster with a host priority of 2. It is likely that this rule would be found on the cold spare in a two-node cluster. Typically, the default host has a host priority of 1. This brings out the important point that the rules on an availability cluster will all be different because the host priority must be different. This is a rule that could be used to provide redundancy for SMTP traffic.

Rule 8 blocks all traffic on port 21 because the filtering mode is disabled. If the port range were 0 to 65535, this cluster would not respond to any network request because all ports would be blocked. This is accomplished by setting the filtering mode to disabled.

Comparing Cluster Types

In Microsoft Windows Server clusters, there are well-defined ways to organize a cluster. Active/Active clusters have both nodes working together, usually doing very different tasks, but during failover a single node can handle the jobs of both nodes. For example, suppose that an Active/Active SQL 2000 cluster running multiple instances has both servers as instance owners. During failover, the failed node's SQL 2000 instances start up on the functioning node. Active/Passive clusters are just an automated way to do a cold spare. One node is in standby mode waiting on the other cluster node to fail.

NOTE

For more information on deploying Microsoft Windows Server clusters, see Chapter 18, "Creating a Windows 2000 Server Cluster."

Network Load Balancing supports configurations that behave like Active/Active and Active/Passive clusters. However, there are some critical differences:

- Membership in a cluster is not restricted to two members (or four with DataCenter Server). Up to 32 servers can exist in a Network Load Balancing cluster.
- Load balancing occurs per port, which means that multiple applications could be balanced across the same cluster in different ways.
- Cluster types are not defined as Active/Active or Active/Passive. There is no obvious way to create these different cluster configurations. It is possible to simulate the two cluster types through port rules.

The cluster types available in Network Load Balancing could be called *load-balancing clusters* and *Availability clusters*.

Load Balancing Cluster

A load-balancing cluster is one in which all members handle cluster traffic at the same time. Every node is active and functioning, similar to an Active/Active Microsoft Server cluster.

Port rules are used to create the load-balancing characteristics for a cluster. Figure 5.6 shows a port rule property page with the default port rule that creates a load-balancing cluster for all the cluster IP address ports. This is the default configuration and the only port rule present from the install of Network Load Balancing. A load-balancing cluster is created using the filtering mode property of a port rule. When filtering mode is set to multiple hosts for a specific port rule, this creates a load-balancing cluster for this port.

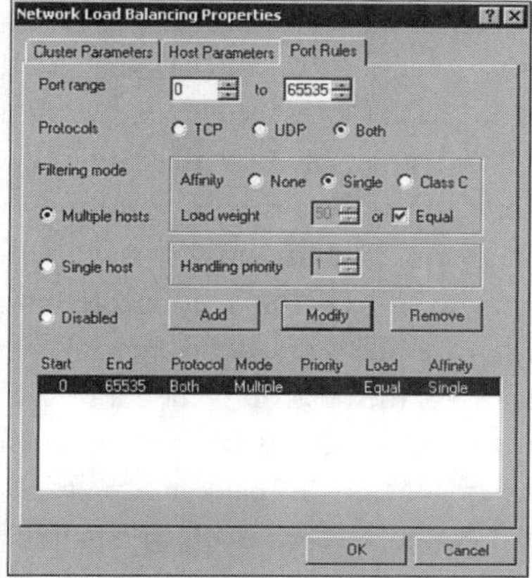

FIGURE 5.6

A port rule used to create a load-balancing cluster.

Availability Cluster

An Availability cluster is one in which only one cluster member at a time handles network traffic. This configuration is very similar to an Active/Passive Microsoft Server cluster. As with a load-balancing cluster, port rules are used to create an Availability cluster configuration. Figure 5.7 shows the port rule for a complete Availability cluster. The host with the highest handling priority handles all traffic directed to the cluster IP address of this cluster.

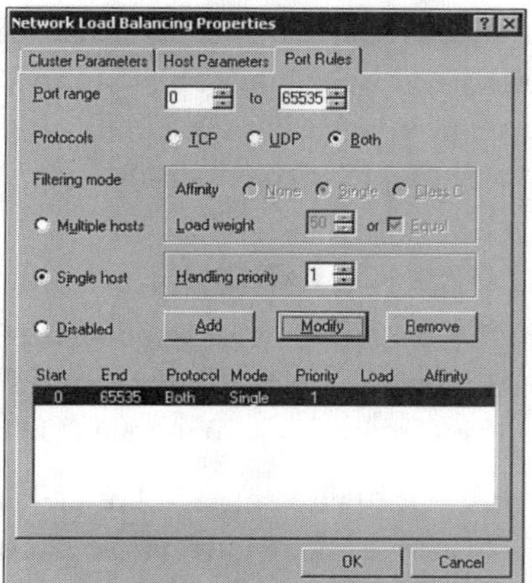

FIGURE 5.7

A port rule used to create an Availability cluster.

For example, Foo.com has two Network Load Balancing clusters in its Web farm. The first cluster is a Lightweight Directory Access Protocol (LDAP) cluster, and the second one is an Exchange 5.5 e-mail cluster. In the LDAP cluster, each server has a copy of the LDAP software, configured exactly alike. This is the same for the e-mail cluster except the server software is Exchange 5.5. LDAP services support running multiple instances against a common data store, so Network Load Balancing is configured to load balance the requests as a load-balancing cluster. In this case, however, LDAP is a connected protocol like FTP, so once a server establishes a session, further requests from this server go to the same member of the cluster until the client or server resets the session. When a member of a two-node LDAP cluster fails, all of the session moves to the other member of the cluster. When the failed member returns to service, the session does not transfer back automatically. Over time, they will balance out, but this is the nature of connected protocols versus disconnected protocols.

Exchange 5.5 does not support simultaneous access from multiple hosts against the e-mail data store. In this configuration, Network Load Balancing is configured as an Availability cluster and only provides redundancy. One host at a time handles mail traffic. However, if the primary host fails or is taken offline, the cold spare or host with the next highest host priority will handle the mail traffic seamlessly.

Configuring Microsoft Network Load Balancing

Configuration of Network Load Balancing can be a confusing and daunting task. It does not have simplified configuration interfaces such as wizards. The interface to configure Network Load Balancing, the three property pages found in the properties section of the Network Load Balancing service, is not easy to use. This section covers installing and locating the Windows 2000 network service for Network Load Balancing. Then it provides a step-by-step explanation of how to configure a two-node single adapter cluster. Finally, it gives a step-by-step explanation of how to configure two-node multiple adapter cluster.

Installing Network Load Balancing

Network Load Balancing is installed by default with Windows 2000 Advanced Server and Windows 2000 Datacenter Server. Network Load Balancing is also available as a part of Application Center 2000 and can be installed onto Windows 2000 Server.

NLB is a Windows 2000 network service that is installed by default on all supported platforms, but it is not enabled by default. This service is located in the Network and Dial-up Connections properties for a network adapter. Figure 5.8 shows the property page of a network adapter with an enabled Network Load Balancing service.

CAUTION

Do not enable network load balancing without configuring it correctly. If it is enabled, it will attempt to function as a `0.0.0.0` IP address with a `02-bf-00-00-00-00` MAC address and will send broadcasts out across the network.

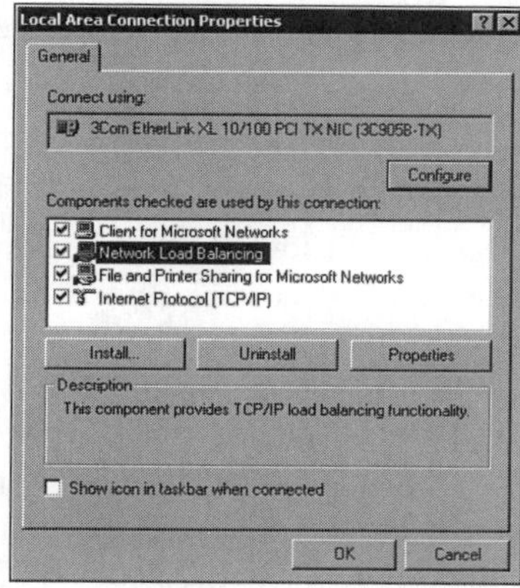

FIGURE 5.8
A network adapter with Network Load Balancing installed.

If the property page of a network adapter does not have the Network Load Balancing service installed, then it will need to be reinstalled from the install CD of the operating system or from the Application Center 2000 CDs. Adding Network Load Balancing is accomplished just like any other Windows 2000 network service or driver.

Creating a Multicast Single Adapter Cluster

This section will describe the process of creating a two-node cluster using Network Load Balancing. In this case, each node of the cluster is equipped with only one network adapter. Three IP addresses are required for this example. One is the cluster IP address used to address the server application being balanced. It will be the same on both servers. The other two are dedicated/management IP addresses that are assigned to each server in the cluster. These IP addresses are used to address the server independently for maintenance and support. Network Load Balancing does not support DHCP addressing for either cluster IP addresses or dedicated IP addresses. Table 5.4 shows the breakdown of IP addresses used in this section.

TABLE 5.4 IP Addresses for the Single Adapter Example

IP Address	*Installed To*	*Purpose*
192.168.1.120	Host 1	Dedicated/management IP address of cluster host 1
192.168.1.121	Host 2	Dedicated/management IP address of cluster host 2
192.168.1.151	Hosts 1 and 2	Cluster IP address or virtual server address

These IP addresses are provided as examples and may vary according to the requirements of different networks. Change them to suit your particular installation.

This example requires at least two servers. They should have similar hardware, but it is not required. It helps when troubleshooting if the network cards are the same. The server application that is the target of the load balancing should be installed and configured on each server. In this example, a Web site will be balanced, so each server should have the same copy of the site installed.

Adding IP Addresses to the TCP/IP Network Driver

The first step in configuring in Network Load Balancing cluster is to register all the IP addresses with the appropriate adapters. Use the TCP/IP network protocol property page to add IP addresses to the network adapter. Selecting Internet Protocol (TCP/IP) from the list box on the network adapter's property page shown in Figure 5.8 and clicking the Properties button shows the initial property page of the TCP/IP network protocol. This page is shown in Figure 5.9.

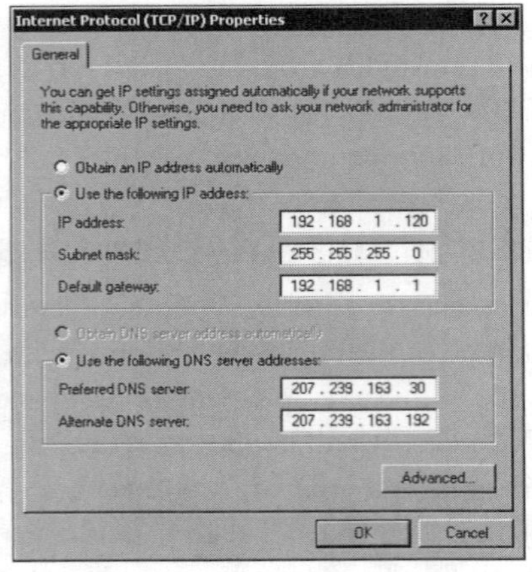

FIGURE 5.9
A network adapter's Internet Protocol (TCP/IP) Properties page.

From the page shown in Figure 5.9, select Use the Following IP Address. On host 1, use the dedicated IP address `192.168.1.120` and for this example a subnet mask of `255.255.255.0`. The network that the cluster is attached to will provide the default gateway, preferred DNS server, and alternate DNS server. Click the Advanced button, which displays the Advanced TCP/IP Settings dialog box, shown in Figure 5.10.

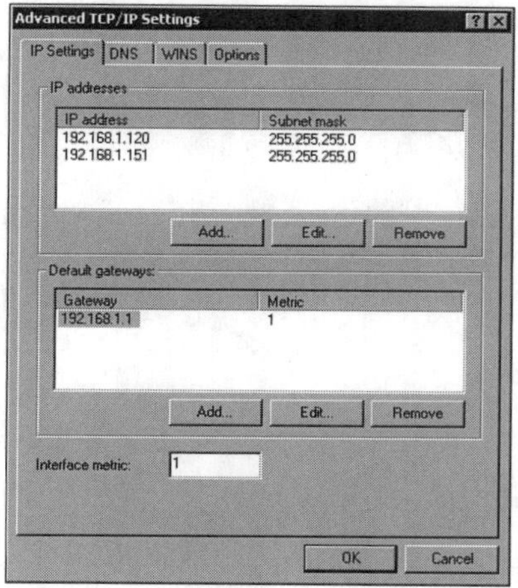

FIGURE 5.10
The Advanced TCP/IP Settings dialog.

Add the cluster IP address to the TCP/IP network protocol from the Advanced TCP/IP Settings dialog. Click the Add button and type in **`192.168.1.151`** for the IP address and **`255.255.255.0`** for the subnet mask. Click OK twice to return to the network adapter property page to configure Network Load Balancing.

On cluster host 2, repeat these steps except use `192.168.1.121` for the dedicated IP address of the machine. Do not forget to add the cluster IP address `192.168.1.151` to host 2. If all network properties dialogs are closed, it is likely an application pop-up will warn of an IP address conflict. Ignore this because Network Load Balancing will eliminate this problem once it is completely configured.

This completes the process of adding the IP addresses needed to configure Network Load Balancing.

Configuring Cluster Parameters

To configure cluster parameters, click on the Network Load Balancing service in the network adapter's property page. The properties of Network Load Balancing page is broken into three tabs. The first tab contains all the information required to configure a host to converge or create a new Network Load Balancing cluster. This is called the Cluster Parameters property tab and is shown in Figure 5.11.

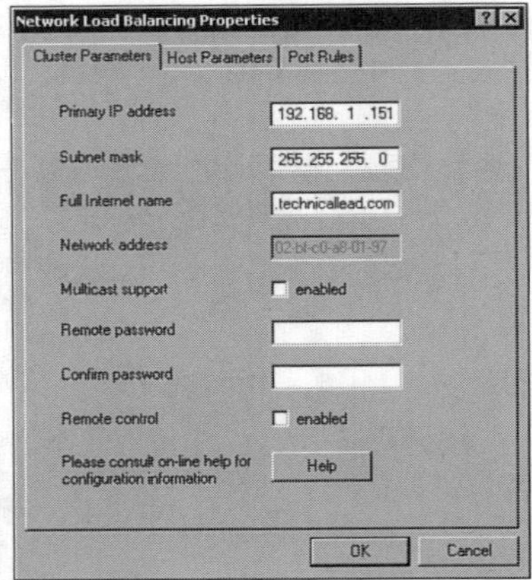

FIGURE 5.11
The Cluster Parameters property tab.

On cluster host 1, in the primary IP address box, type in **`192.168.1.151`**. This is the cluster IP address. The subnet mask for this example is `255.255.255.0`, and the full Internet name is `www.technicallead.com`. Change this Internet name accordingly. It is not necessary for the full Internet name actually to exist in a DNS server at this point. Once the cluster is completely configured, address the cluster by its cluster IP address to prove it is functioning correctly. Finally, enable multicast support by clicking the enabled check box. The Remote Password, Confirm Password, and Remote Control options are covered later in this chapter, so ignore them at this point.

Repeat these steps on cluster host 2. Everything should be exactly the same. Double-check everything; one mistake can cause the cluster to function erratically. This will complete the cluster parameter configuration for both hosts.

CAUTION

Be sure that all IP addresses are correct and that the full Internet name is spelled correctly on all cluster members.

Configuring Host Parameters

To configure host parameters, select the Network Load Balancing property tab labeled Host Parameters. This tab is used to configure properties that are unique to each cluster member. Figure 5.12 shows the Host Parameters property tab.

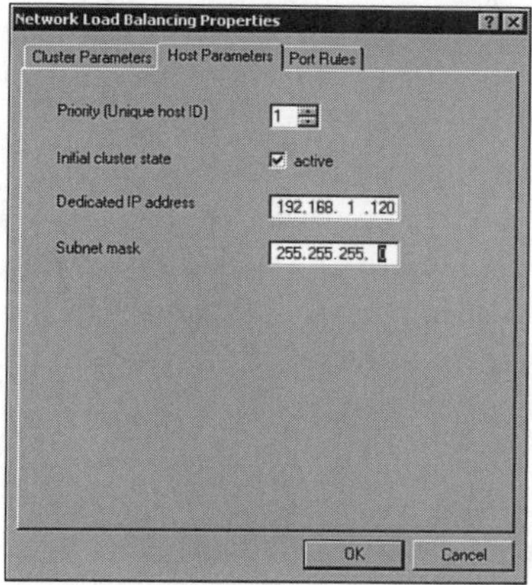

FIGURE 5.12
The Host Parameters property tab.

For the host with IP address `192.168.1.120`, enter **`1`** in the Priority box. This will make this host the default host, and it will handle all traffic that is governed by rules that use a filtering mode of single. In the Initial Cluster State check box, make sure that it is marked Active. In the dedicated IP address box, enter the address **`192.168.1.120`**. Use a subnet mask of `255.255.255.0` for this example.

In the second host, the one with IP address `192.168.1.121`, the Priority box should be set to 2. Any unique number between 2 and 32 is fine, but using 2 is more consistent. Ensure that the Initial Cluster State check box is marked Active. For Dedicated IP Address, use `192.168.1.121`, and set Subnet Mask to `255.255.255.0`. That completes the configuration for the Host Parameters property tab on both hosts.

Changing the Default Rule

At this point, the cluster is completely configured. However, the only port rule is the default one shown previously in Figure 5.12. This default rule uses an affinity of single, which means that once a client IP address has made a request from the cluster, it will always be directed back to the same host. It will appear that no load balancing is occurring unless multiple client machines are used to test the cluster. By default, Network Load Balancing creates a single affinity cluster that will load balance across all members but is difficult to test.

CAUTION

The default rule for Network Load Balancing creates a single affinity load-balancing cluster. Unless many client computers are used to test the cluster, it might seem that all connections are going to one host.

To change this rule and add others, use the Port Rule property page. This page can be confusing, and this task would be better suited to a wizard. Manipulation of the UI on this page has no effect unless the Add or Modify button is pressed. If an existing rule is selected and Remove is pressed, the rule is removed. If an existing rule is selected and the controls such as filtering mode and affinity are changed, pressing Modify will change that rule. To add a new rule, set up all controls with the desired values and click the Add button. Figure 5.13 shows the default changed to have an affinity of none.

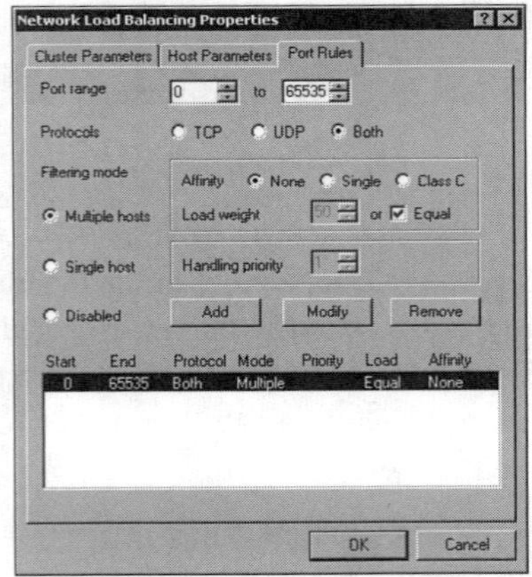

FIGURE 5.13
The Port Rules property tab with a modified default rule.

To modify the existing default rule so that the cluster has an affinity of none, first select the default rule, then select a the None radio button in the Affinity section. Be sure that all the other options are set correctly and press the Modify button. This process must be repeated on all members of the cluster or an error will be reported in the event log, like the one shown in Figure 5.14.

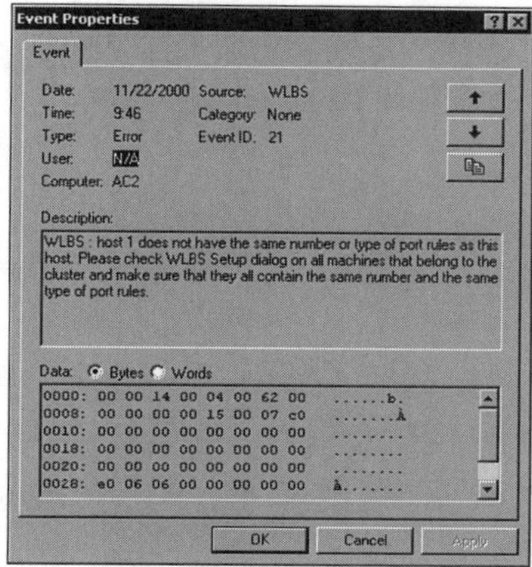

FIGURE 5.14
An error in the event log due to conflicting port rules.

Once the rule has been modified, close all the open dialogs by pressing OK. Be sure to go to the Network and Dial-up Connections page. In Windows 2000, there will likely be a brief delay as the network drivers reload with the new configuration options.

> **TIP**
>
> There is no reason to reboot a server when configuring Network Load Balancing under Windows 2000.

After the network card is back online, the cluster is ready to begin handling traffic as a Load Balancing cluster, with no client affinity. If everything has been entered correctly, there will be a message in the event log similar to that shown in Figure 5.15. This message says that the cluster has converged and the hosts are ready to receive traffic. Any time cluster parameters, host parameters, or port rules are modified, the cluster converges and an entry in the event log signals success or failure.

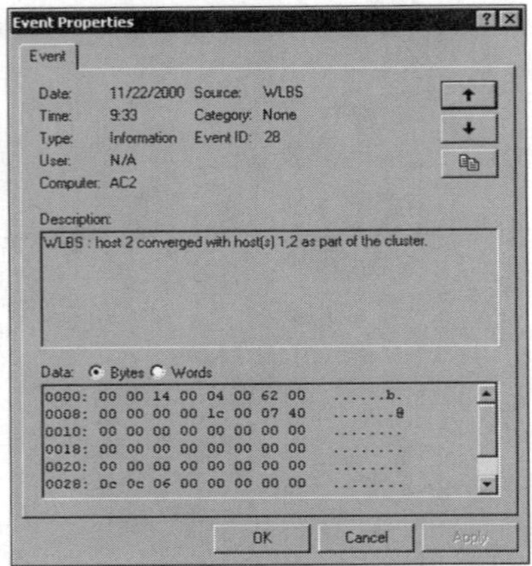

FIGURE 5.15

A message in the event log showing cluster convergence.

Testing the Cluster

Once Network Load Balancing has converged the first time, the cluster is ready to test. It is very easy to misunderstand how a cluster is supposed to act and assume that it is functioning correctly. There are a number of basic tests that will help determine that the cluster is fully operational.

The first test of a Network Load Balancing cluster should prove that both servers are behaving correctly individually. First, each server should be addressable by network name, similar to other servers that are not in a cluster. The simplest way to do this is also the best way to determine if a cluster is load balancing. Use Performance Monitor to watch counters for each server from a third machine outside the cluster. If a cluster is configured correctly, it is possible to watch individual counters for each member of the cluster. This proves that both servers are able to receive network traffic intended for individual members of the cluster. The counters watched are unimportant for this test.

The second test is to try and access services through the cluster IP address. This means that any TCP/IP service should be accessible from the cluster IP address if the default rule is the only rule applied to the cluster. The easiest TCP/IP service to test with is HTTP. The default configuration has the default Web site responding to all unassigned IP addresses. The cluster IP is one of those addresses. Also by default, an "under construction" page is displayed if the default Web site is accessed from outside the cluster. Always test the cluster from a server outside the cluster.

The third test is to watch the connection attempts to each member of the cluster from Performance Monitor. Once again, it is best to do this from a server outside the cluster. The counters to use are part of the Web Service Performance Object, Current Connections Counter, and Total Instance. The Current Connections Counter displays connections to a Web server in real time. Add this counter to a performance graph for both members of a cluster. Then launch at least four copies of Internet Explorer and request the default page of IIS from the virtual IP address. As each browser makes a request, and if the rule has an affinity of none, the requests should be distributed evenly across both nodes of the cluster. It is OK if one node has three connections and the other has only one. Try the test again and it probably will even out over time. If all requests go to one node of the cluster, the rule may not be configured correctly. Check the event log on both members of the cluster for details. Note that the event log still records Network Load Balancing entries as if they are from the WLBS service.

The fourth test is to unplug from the network the member with the highest host priority and try the third test again. All requests should be redirected to the second node. Watch the performance counters to verify this. If for some reason some of the requests return Server Not Found errors, check the event log of the functioning server for any convergence errors.

Creating a Unicast Multiple Adapter Server Cluster

The recommended way to build a Network Load Balancing cluster is with multiple adapters. Microsoft Application Center 2000 can set up clusters with this configuration automatically. This example is similar to the single adapter example except that each host requires two network adapters. Both plug into the same network and can use the same IP addresses as in the single adapter example but must add two more addresses for the dedicated IP address. Table 5.5 shows the IP addresses used for this example.

TABLE 5.5 IP Addresses for the Multiple Adapter Server Example

IP Address	*Installed To*	*Purpose*
192.168.1.120	Host 1 management adapter address of cluster	Management IP host 1
192.168.1.150	Host 1 cluster adapter used	Dedicated IP address to address the cluster adapter directly
192.168.1.121	Host 2 management adapter address of cluster	Management IP host 2
192.168.1.151	Host 2 cluster adapter used	Dedicated IP address to address the cluster adapter directly
192.168.1.200	Host 1 & 2 cluster adapter	Cluster IP address or virtual server address

In a multiple adapter server, Network Load Balancing runs on one adapter, called the cluster adapter. The other adapter is called the management adapter. In this configuration, all administrative access, content updates, intracluster communication, and general network traffic directed at a single cluster member occurs across the management adapter. Binding order and the TCP/IP addresses on each adapter determine which adapter is the cluster adapter and which is the management adapter.

In a multiple-adapter host, each adapter has its own TCP/IP network driver. Figure 5.16 shows a Network and Dial-up Connections screen with two adapters. Notice that these adapters have been renamed Cluster Adapter and Management Adapter. Deciding which adapter is Management and which is Cluster is purely arbitrary for this example. The binding order determines the correct network behavior.

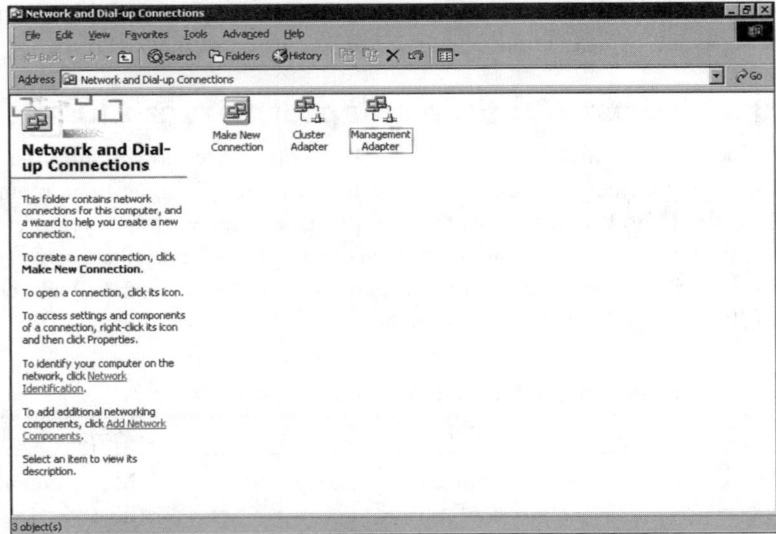

FIGURE 5.16

A multiple-adapter server's Network and Dial-up Connections window.

To set the binding order in a Windows 2000 server, select Advanced, Advanced Settings options in the Network and Dial-up Connections window. Figure 5.17 shows the Adapters and Bindings tab of the Advanced Settings window. Use the up and down arrows to position the management adapter above the cluster adapter.

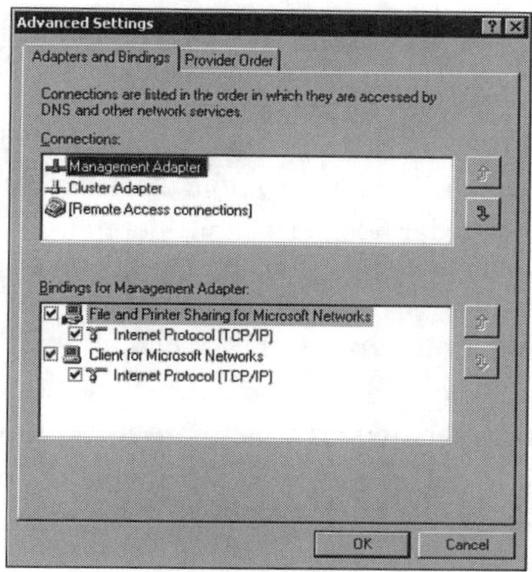

FIGURE 5.17
Configuring the binding order of network adapters in Windows 2000.

On the adapter labeled Cluster Adapter, add the IP address `192.168.1.200`, which is the cluster or virtual IP address of the cluster. Do the same on both hosts. On the adapter labeled Management Adapter, add the IP address `192.168.1.120` to the first host and add the IP address `192.160.1.121` to the Management Adapter of the second host. At this point, configure the Cluster Parameters page exactly like a single adapter server. The Host Parameters page is a bit different. Notice how on a single adapter server the dedicated IP and management IP addresses are the same. In a multiple adapter server, these IP addresses serve different purposes. In effect, the dedicated IP address is used only to address the cluster network adapter directly. This is useful for testing individual members of a cluster or addressing the cluster administratively from a different network segment, as is likely in a two-adapter configuration.

NOTE

At this point, the configuration continues the same as with a single adapter.

NOTE

For more information on using Application Center 2000 with Network Load Balancing, see Chapter 12, "Deploying Application Center 2000 Web Clusters."

Assigning a Multiple Virtual IP Address to a Cluster

Network Load Balancing supports multiple cluster IP addresses per cluster. This enables the administrator to configure multiple Web sites or other applications on the same set of servers. To do this, first specify a dedicated IP address on the cluster adapter. Any other address added to the TCP/IP properties of the cluster adapter is considered by Network Load Balancing to be a cluster IP address. Then bind each Web site to the appropriate cluster IP address.

There are some limitations. Port rules are per cluster and not per IP address. If two or more Web sites are on a cluster, they have to support the same client affinity and filtering mode. Also, the more sites a single adapter supports, the more likely it is that the network adapter could be a bottleneck, because every adapter has to examine all requests for all applications that are balanced across the cluster.

Using Remote Control Features

Remote control features of Network Load Balancing enable the administrator control of individual hosts or the cluster as a whole from remote servers running Windows 2000 Advanced Server, Datacenter Server, or any server with Application Center 2000 installed. With remote control, port rules can be enabled or disabled, hosts can be removed or added, and individual hosts can be started and stopped.

Remote control is disabled by default. Microsoft cautions against using remote control because it can be a serious security breach if a server with remote control is compromised. It is recommended that any cluster with remote control enabled be behind a firewall and that the remote control port 2504 be blocked from receiving UDP packets. Remote control requires a password, and the property page has the standard Confirm Password text box, along with the Password text box. To enable remote control, enter the same password into both boxes on the Cluster Parameters property page of the Network Load Balancing service and check the Remote Control check box.

To address clusters remotely, use the `WLBS.EXE` command-line utility. This utility is covered in depth in Appendix E, "Using the `WLBS.EXE` Command-Line Interface." Listing 5.1 shows a few common `WLBS.EXE` commands that can be executed on any member of a cluster.

LISTING 5.1 Common `WLBS.EXE` Commands

```
WLBS.EXE QUERY myclustername 'queries the status of a cluster
WLBS.EXE STOP myclustername 'stops Network Load Balancing on a cluster
WLBS.EXE START myclustername 'starts Network Load Balancing on a cluster
'stops traffic from getting to port 80 on myclustername
WLBS.EXE DISABLE 80 myclustername
WLBS.EXE HELP 'returns help infomormation
```

Use the /PASSW [password] command-line switch to remote control a cluster from a server outside the cluster. Other than that, the commands are the same as in Listing 5.1.

Summary

Load balancing is a critical component to providing high availability and scalability for Web farms. In the Microsoft world, Network Load Balancing is a key component to this strategy. Network Load Balancing is a software technology that works at the Network layer to make many servers appear as one. Network Load Balancing works on servers with one network adapter or many. Port rules define how a packet is distributed to members of the cluster. Hosts can be removed from or added to the cluster without interrupting service. Network Load Balancing is a flexible, reliable choice as a load-balancing strategy for any Web farm.

Using Hardware Load Balancing in a Web Farm

CHAPTER

6

IN THIS CHAPTER

Hardware load-balancing devices are an alternative to Network Load Balancing. These hardware devices provide all the functionality of Network Load Balancing and more. Over the last two years, the number of new options and features available for these devices has exploded. Administrators must learn to pick the best load-balancing technologies to solve each scaling problem. Hardware load-balancing devices have the most robust configuration options in the load-balancing space and are an important tool for any size Web farm. Learning the types of features available on hardware load-balancing devices is important to help make the choice to use such technology.

The goals of this chapter are to

- *Explore hardware load-balancing devices* and their features. Hardware devices are a key component in any load-balancing strategy.
- *Compare the advantages and disadvantages* of Network load-balancing clusters versus hardware-based clusters.

Exploring Hardware Load-Balancing Features

Hardware load-balancing devices can manage the traffic for any size Web farm. These devices have the most features and capabilities of any network device class introduced over the last two years. Clearly, these devices have defined a new class in the network hardware space: the hardware load balancer.

There are a number of major vendors that offer comparable devices, including Cisco, F5, and Foundry Networks. Fierce competition has helped this market grow, and now most devices have generally the same types of features. Understanding these features is the best way to pick the right vendor for a Web farm.

Load balancers are usually based on switching technology. Many come in PC-sized cases and use Unix kernels that run the load-balancing algorithms. Others are traditional standalone proprietary hardware self-contained units. Because load balancers work at Layers 2–7 of the OSI model, they require considerable processing power to implement some of the more advanced features. Today's balancers do much more than packet redirection and Network Address Translation (NAT); they actually examine protocol layer information such as HTTP headers when making routing decisions.

The feature sets discussed in this section cover the meat of most load-balancing hardware offerings. There are some esoteric features that separate the major vendors, but most features discussed here are available on all devices. The important point is for administrators to understand how valuable these devices have become in creating a successful Web farm network.

Availability and Scalability of Web Farm Servers

Load-balancing devices are prevalent in almost every Web farm implementation because they provide features that greatly improve a Web farm's availability and scalability. These devices distribute traffic across servers in the Web farm, enabling an array of servers to act as one virtual server. Improving availability and scalability is the number one reason all Web farm networks should use a hardware-based load-balancing solution.

Beyond simply creating virtual server arrays, load balancers are beginning to detect server and application failures. From these failures, administrators can have these devices automatically direct traffic to functioning servers and applications or to entirely different server arrays. With the proper configuration, these devices will help make sure a site is always available to customers by verifying that all network components are working properly, based on data gathered from network traffic and server responses.

Load balancers improve scalability by enabling many inexpensive servers to function as a virtual server. Scale-up is no longer the only option for improving the performance of a server in a Web farm. Instead, these devices simplify greatly the task of making many smaller servers work as one large server. They also remove a single point of failure and expense inherent in a single large server.

Load balancers also reduce the availability hit when deploying new applications or additional features to existing ones. They enable the systematic addition of new servers through a centralized management console. Downtime is reduced even during non-peak times because at no point does the Web farm have to become completely unavailable. Even routine maintenance or upgrades of servers can be performed without disrupting service to the end user.

Most load balancers can scale and increase the availability of a large number of application protocols. Table 6.1 lists some of the protocols supported by the major vendors. Because they allow control and management of multiple servers and applications from a central location, all these disparate application protocols are managed in exactly the same way. Some load balancers also allow complete balancing of other network devices, including firewalls, routers, and standard switches.

TABLE 6.1 Application Protocols and Devices Supported by Most Load Balancers

Protocol	*Devices*
HTTP	Firewalls
SSL	Proxy Servers
FTP	Caching Servers
SMTP	Switches
LDAP	Routers

TABLE 6.1 Continued

Protocol	*Devices*
POP3	VPN Servers
FTP	
UDP	
DNS	
Streaming Audio and Video	

Load Balancer Redundancy

All balancers provide some type of built-in redundancy for device failures. Almost all are built with redundant systems, such as power supplies, in an individual unit. Most vendors recommend a pair of units for every installation. Figure 6.1 shows a dual load balancer configuration as a part of the DMZ's connection to the Internet.

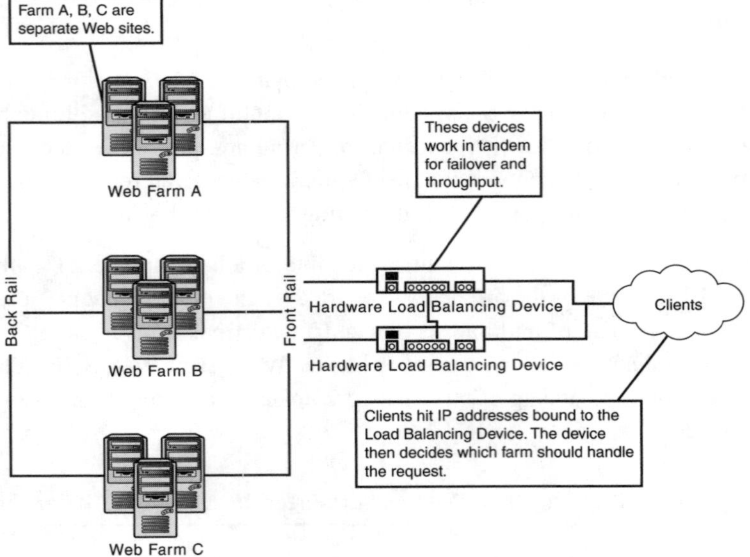

FIGURE 6.1
A pair of load balancers managing the load in a DMZ.

With a pair of load balancers there are a number of redundancy features to consider. Most devices will communicate state across a dedicated serial or ethernet network connection. Many can operate together, doubling the bandwidth and throughput of the device. The following sections cover the redundancy features of hardware load-balancing devices.

Session State Mirroring

Most load balancers provide the capability to failover to a standby controller in the event of device failure. However, if the state of the incoming connections is not maintained during this time, end user service will be interrupted. For most applications, such as streaming media, HTTP, and FTP, this loss of connection will result in an error or unexpected result being displayed to the end user.

To combat this problem, load balancers communicate in real-time through a high-speed direct connection. This connection communicates all current states of the traffic on a Web farm. By doing this, both devices handle each incoming request. When a device failure forces a failover, the connection and data being transferred are maintained and the application is not interrupted. Many devices mirror session state in RAM, so recovery is quick and no end user sessions are lost.

Some load balancers can also maintain state over a network connection. This allows for session state management across physical locations for disaster recovery scenarios. A load balancer with this feature could transfer all the existing connections to another server room over the Internet.

Active/Passive Mode

When a pair of load-balancing controllers is in Active/Passive mode, one of the balancers is idle. If a device supports only Active/Passive configuration, it is not likely to have session state mirroring. Active/Passive is the recommended configuration for most Web farms because it guarantees that a single unit will have all the horsepower needed to handle the traffic of a Web farm. As long as one unit can handle the traffic requirements of a Web farm, an Active/Passive configuration ensures that when failover occurs, the passive node will be able to handle the full traffic of a Web farm.

Active/Active Mode

In Active/Active mode, the load-balancing tandem shares the burden of simultaneously managing traffic for the different virtual servers. This option takes advantage of the throughput of both controllers. When one controller fails, the connections and traffic transfer to the remaining active controller, usually without interruption of service.

NOTE

If traffic utilization on the controller pair goes beyond 50%, a single controller can no longer properly handle the load during a failover.

Organizing the Farm

As discussed previously, load-balancing technologies group servers into farms that handle the same applications. Those farms of servers are addressed from clients by some unique identifier. This unique identifier comes in different forms, depending on the features of the load-balancing device. By presenting an abstraction layer for organizing the farm between the client and the server, a load-balancing device can interject special routing behavior into the flow of network packets. The first step in defining this special routing behavior involves grouping servers into logical application partitions. Hardware load-balancing devices make these farm organization tasks easy to complete.

One IP-to-Many

In most cases, the unique identifier for a farm of servers is an IP address. IP addresses are usually bound to one server and one network adapter. The IP address that uniquely identifies a grouping of servers is bound to the load-balancing device. This IP is like the cluster IP address of Network Load Balancing and is also called a VIP. Requests for services on this IP address are directed to the pool of servers associated with the VIP. Usually each device has a GUI or command-line interface for setting up a VIP and the servers related to it.

HTTP Header Parsing

Another common way to group servers into farms is through HTTP header parsing. The HTTP header contains information about the HTTP version, URL, HTTP cookies header, HTTP uniform resource identifier (URI), client source IP address, and the HTTP method used in the request. All of these values can be examined and a rule applied to determine which farm of servers should handle the request. These features are sometimes referred to as URL parsing, URL switching, or URL hashing. Figure 6.2 shows a Web farm organization that uses HTTP header parsing.

One use of HTTP header parsing is to group content onto dedicated servers. For example, all the images in a farm could be addressed from `www.technicallead.com/images`. In the load-balancing device, any request for images from this URL is directed to a defined group of servers, eliminating the need to distribute the image content to all servers in a farm.

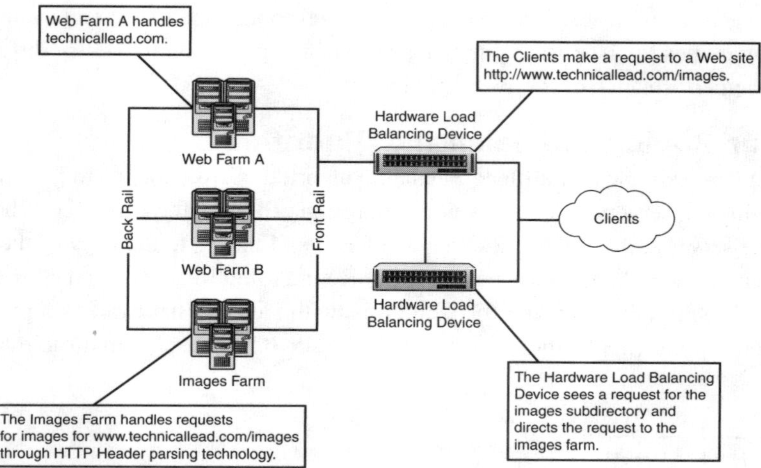

FIGURE 6.2
A Web farm organized with HTTP header parsing.

Rulesets are defined to determine how the structure of the HTTP header is interpreted to find the correct farm of servers. The rules that are applied in HTTP header parsing look at all portions of the URL. Usually devices support regular expression searching of URLs and pattern matching. For example, a rule could look for the word *images* and redirect all requests to a bank of caching servers. This rule could be applied across all farms so that multiple URLs could use the same bank of image servers. The result is a decision by the load-balancing device as to what group of servers should handle the request.

Load-Balancing Algorithms

All load-balancing devices offer a suite of algorithms for distributing load among a group of servers. These algorithms provide a variety of options for how load is distributed. Some are static, meaning they distribute traffic the same way regardless of conditions on the servers in the farm. Others are dynamic—they watch response times and other performance criteria before determining which is the best server to handle the next request.

Determining which algorithm to use for a Web farm is dependent on a number of factors. If all the servers are the same and the application is primarily HTML content, a static algorithm such as round robin is probably best. With servers of differing configuration, a weighted strategy would probably make better use of the resources of a Web farm. For sites with dynamic content and lots of server-side processing, a more dynamic approach might be better. The goal of any load-balancing strategy is to provide scalability by making many servers behave as one.

A secondary goal is to create a user perception that response time is fast and availability is constant. Sometimes the best way to pick a load-balancing algorithm is to try different ones and gauge the performance of the Web application.

The Round Robin Load-Balancing Algorithm

Round robin is the simplest of all load-balancing algorithms. To understand how round robin works, imagine the servers in a farm waiting in a single file line for a request. When a request comes in, the server at the front of the line handles it and moves to the back of the line. The next server in line then handles the next request. Round robin treats all servers as equal. Choose round robin load balancing for Web farms with identical hardware, simple applications, or connection-oriented applications such as FTP. Figure 6.3 shows a round robin load-balanced Web farm.

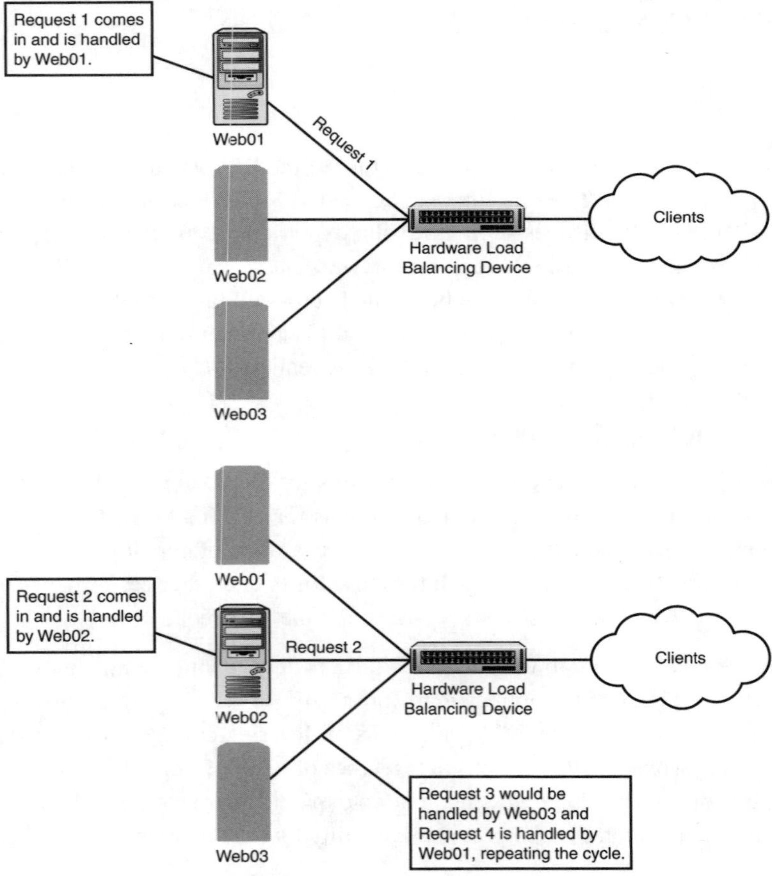

FIGURE 6.3
A round robin load-balanced Web farm.

The Least Connections Load-Balancing Algorithm

Most load-balancing devices track the open connections to each server in a farm. This enables tracking connections as a means of determining utilization of a server. In general, servers with the most open connections are doing more work than other servers. The *least connections algorithm* uses server connection counts to determine which server in a farm should handle the next request. Use least connections with Web sites with dissimilar performance capabilities. Least connection ensures adequate distribution and avoids server overload by sending connections to the server with the smallest number of current connections and potentially the most server resources to handle the job. Figure 6.4 shows a Web farm configured with the least connections algorithm.

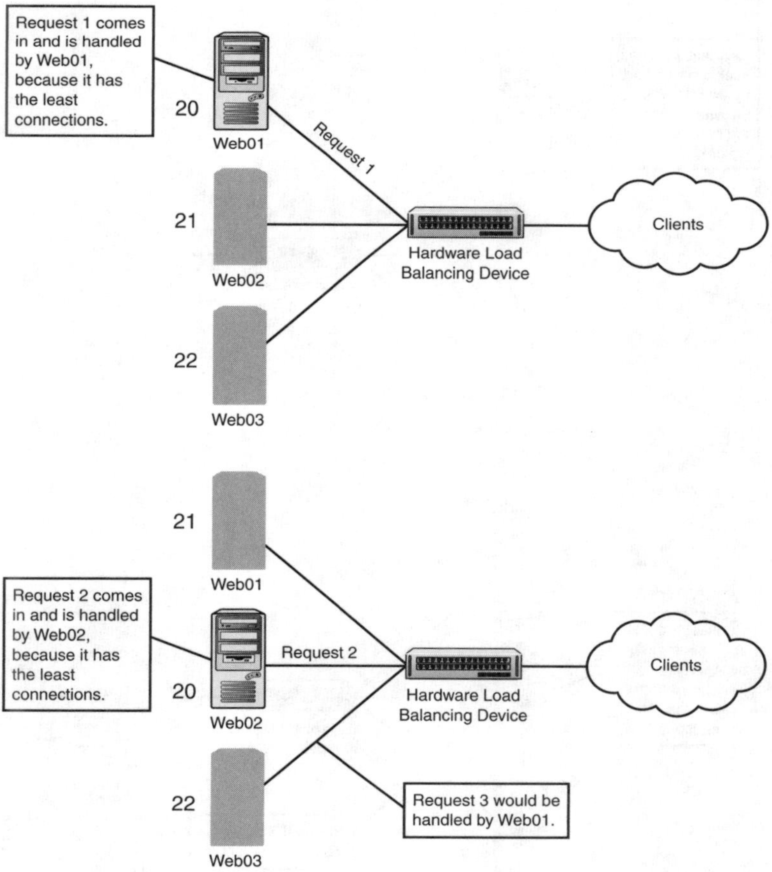

FIGURE 6.4
A least connections load-balanced Web farm.

The Weighted Percentage Load-Balancing Algorithm

When algorithms such as least connections or round robin do not adequately balance a farm, weighted percentage might be a viable choice. Weighted percentage works by assigning weights to each member of a farm and then using the total of all those weights to assign percentages of the load to individual members. For example, if a farm with four servers has each member weighted equally, then each member will handle 25% of the load. If a farm with three servers has one weighted with a value of 2 and the others with a value of 1, then the first server handles 50% of the load and the others 25% each. Use weighted percentages when connections are not a good indicator of server stress and round robin is wasting resources on more powerful servers. Figure 6.5 shows a server farm configured with weighted percentage and the respective load percentage.

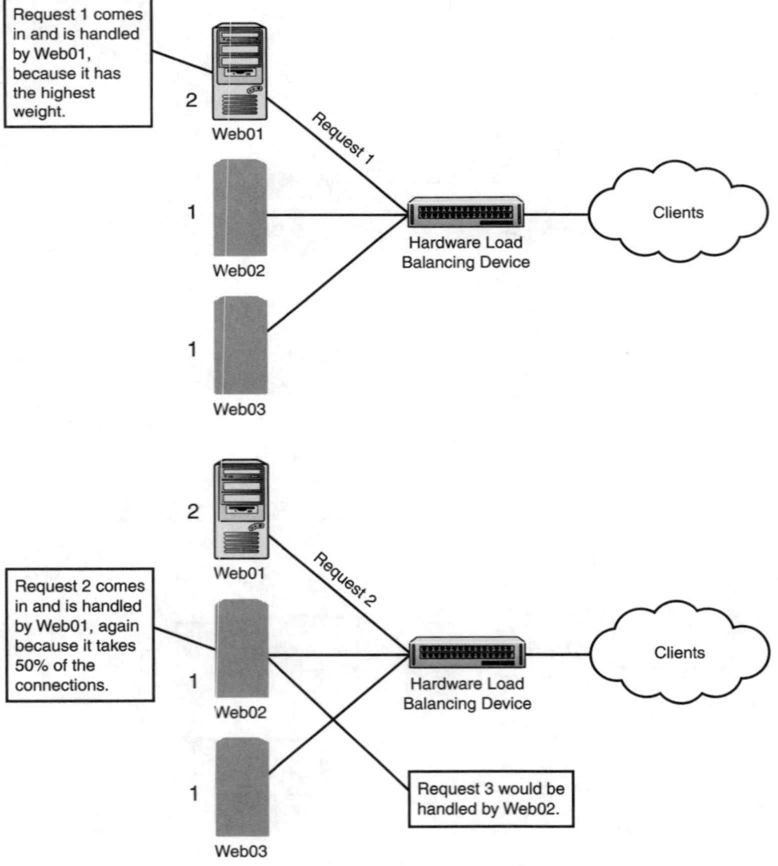

FIGURE 6.5
A weighted percentage load-balanced Web farm.

The Priority Load-Balancing Algorithm

A priority-based algorithm is similar to weighted percentage except it works with groups of servers. Each group is assigned a priority level and a maximum number of connections that the entire group can handle. Connections are distributed in a round robin fashion to all servers in the highest priority group. If all servers in this group are handling more than the predetermined number of connections, the group with the next-highest priority begins handling requests. This provides a mechanism for Web farms organized as shown in Figure 6.6. A pool of servers could be called upon to handle the overflow requests from a dedicated farm in times of heavy load.

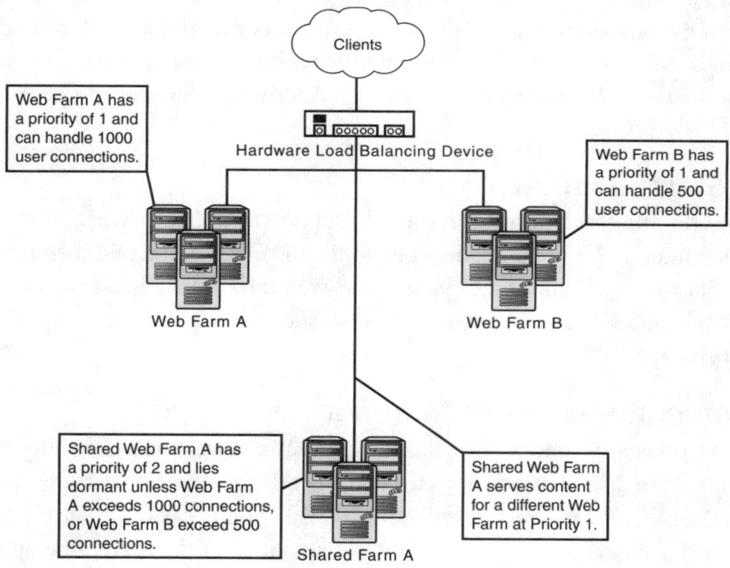
Clients
Web Farm A has a priority of 1 and can handle 1000 user connections.
Hardware Load Balancing Device
Web Farm B has a priority of 1 and can handle 500 user connections.
Web Farm A
Web Farm B
Shared Web Farm A has a priority of 2 and lies dormant unless Web Farm A exceeds 1000 connections, or Web Farm B exceed 500 connections.
Shared Web Farm A serves content for a different Web Farm at Priority 1.
Shared Farm A

FIGURE 6.6
A priority-based load-balanced Web farm.

The Response Time Load-Balancing Algorithm

Response time is a dynamic algorithm supported by most load-balancing devices. Response time is primarily a measure of network latency. The idea is that if a request takes longer to handle on a particular server, it must be busier than other servers in the farm. Load balancers track this response time and make decisions based on it when a new request is directed at the Web farm. Some balancers can look at other server statistics. CPU and memory use can help determine the server with the best response time with more advanced load-balancing devices.

The Combined Response Time and Least Connections Load-Balancing Algorithm

To refine a response time algorithm even further, some load-balancing devices use combinations of algorithms to determine the next server to handle a request. A combination of response time and least connections uses both algorithms to pick the best server in the farm at a given moment in time.

Load-Balancing Modifiers

Load-balancing modifiers are actions that load-balancing devices perform on incoming requests based on extraneous conditions in the farm. These modifiers are used when servers are added or removed from service, when the farm is under considerable load, or to determine which group of servers are responsible for requests based on application layer data. These modifiers occur before a load-balancing algorithm determines the appropriate server to handle a request.

The Slow-Start Modifier

Slow start is used to protect a server returning to service from being overwhelmed. Most slow-start modifiers gradually build up connections to the balanced point, and then the server is balanced using whatever algorithm is assigned to the Web farm. Since most servers cannot handle more than 2,000 new connections per second, slow start helps ensure stability when bringing a server into service.

The Maximum Connections Modifier

The Maximum Connections modifier is used to prevent a server from thrashing because it is overloaded with users. Maximum Connections is the relative number of connections that a server can handle before it becomes overwhelmed. This number is different for each server configuration and is based on varied criteria. Use the power of the server, the applications run on the server, and the response time service level of a Web farm application to determine the Maximum Connections modifier for a load-balancing algorithm.

Connection Persistence

Once a load-balancing algorithm has selected the initial server for a new client request, many load balancers have a number of connection persistence features that help determine how subsequent requests from a client are handled by the farm. Simple HTML or even ASP that does not use the Session object usually does not require connection persistence. When no connection persistence is required, the load-balancing algorithm determines server assignments for every request from a client.

Most Web farms will encounter applications that require some form of connection persistence. These applications challenge the capabilities of load-balancing technologies to provide scalability successfully. Examples of applications that might require connection persistence include the following:

- *Shopping carts* maintained locally on a server for a particular client. Once a client establishes a session to a particular server, all requests must return to the same server so that the shopping cart information is not lost.
- *FTP* is a connection-oriented protocol. Once the client establishes a session, this session must remain on that server until the client disconnects. Passive FTP requires at least two open connections to the same server; load-balancing devices must redirect multiple session requests to the same server.
- *SSL* requires that a client and server perform an encryption handshake to establish the secure data transfer. Once this session is established, load-balancing devices must be intelligent and keep this session alive throughout the client's lifetime.

Connection persistence is the suite of features, present in one form or another on all load-balancing devices, that makes these applications function correctly in a load balanced scenario. The challenge for load-balancing devices is to manage session persistence at the same time as they provide scaling through load balancing.

IP/Port Persistence

An IP address is a unique Internet-based address. Load-balancing devices can recognize individual IP addresses as unique client requests. A port is an application subdivision of an IP address in a TCP/UDP network. All common TCP/UDP applications such as HTTP, FTP, SMTP, and so on are assigned a specific port or a range of ports. Custom applications sometimes place special requirements on the use of IP addresses and ports. Load-balancing devices have many options for handling IP address– and port-based persistence problems.

Source IP

Source IP address persistence is the simplest form of IP/Port persistence and is supported by most load-balancing devices. In source IP persistence, the client IP address is used as the key for determining which real server handles the incoming request. Once an IP address has made a request to a server farm, all subsequent requests use the same real server. Source IP persistence is independent of port. For instance, if a client makes a request for a Web page on port 80 that is handled by server A, a subsequent request from the same client IP address for FTP services on port 21 would also be handled by server A.

One of the challenges of source IP persistence is properly servicing ISPs that use proxy servers to cache or make requests on behalf of users. In this scenario, each user from such an ISP is behind a proxy server and will appear as the same IP address to the load-balancing device.

Source IP persistence can cause these two problems when used in conjunction with proxy server farms:

- Users may move to a different proxy server if they are load balanced like the servers in a Web farm (called a proxy server farm). This can cause the source IP persistence model to fail unless the IP address range can be restricted to include Class C addresses. For example, if two proxy servers are load balanced and have IP addresses such as `172.20.2.2` and `172.20.2.1`, the users of these proxy servers would need to be balanced to the same server in a Web farm. The source IP persistence mechanism must be smart enough to send those requests from both proxy IPs to the same servers.
- Users from a single large ISP may end up on the same server, causing a disproportionate amount of traffic to one server and a degradation of performance for that ISP user community.

To handle this problem, many load-balancing devices have a separate persistence mechanism, which is covered later in this section under "Large ISP IP Source Persistence."

Source IP/Port

In source IP/port persistence, the combination of IP address and port is used to determine which real server handles an incoming request. Most devices that support source IP persistence allow port persistence. This means that the combination of IP address and port is used to determine which real server handles incoming requests. For example, if server A has been assigned port 80 for client IP address `63.68.136.171` and that client makes a request for services on port 21, the load-balancing device could choose to use server B.

Sticky Port Persistence

With sticky port persistence, all subsequent requests for services on ports by a single client are handled by the same real server, based on source IP or session identification features. This persistence mechanism is easily configurable to support only a sequential range of ports. If a client makes a request outside this range of ports, that request could arrive at a different real server. Many load-balancing devices support an arbitrary range or set of ranges for sticky port configurations.

Transactional Port Tracking

Some applications maintain the state of a single transaction across multiple ports. These conjoined ports are sometimes called *lead* and *follower* ports. For example, a browser makes a request on port 80, supplying unsecured data for a Web-based transaction. This particular application stores this information locally on a specific server waiting for the same client to send secured data over port 443, the common SSL port. Port tracking persistence ensures these two client requests are directed to the same server as required by the application. Figure 6.7 shows a typical port tracking application.

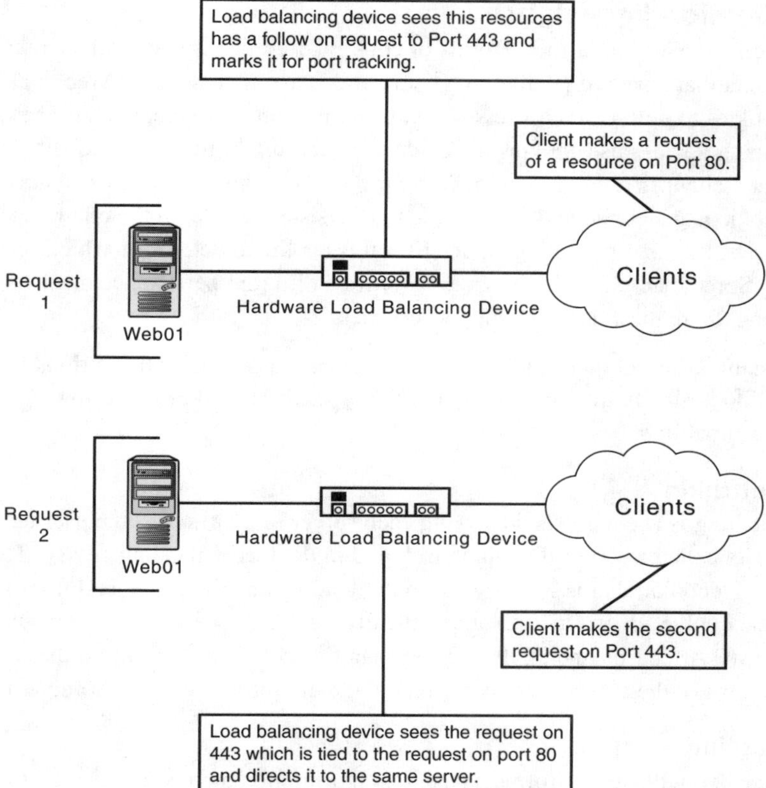

FIGURE 6.7
Port tracking in a Web application.

Large ISP IP Source Persistence

Some large ISPs use proxy servers to provide improvements to speed and limited bandwidth for their Internet connections. With proxy servers, each client request might be assigned a different IP address from a range of IP addresses. To solve this problem, load-balancing devices allow a range of source IP addresses to all go to the same server.

URL Hashing Persistence

Load balancers examine information in an HTTP request and internally map that information to a group of real servers bound to the virtual server. The HTTP request and all future HTTP requests that contain that information are always directed to the same real server.

Cookie Session Persistence

Load-balancing devices have many forms of cookie-based persistence. A *cookie* is a small amount of data that is stored locally on a client and is associated with a Web application. Web sites use cookies to help maintain session state and provide a personalized user experience. Load-balancing devices use cookies to decide to which server to send a request. For example, suppose that a client first connects to a Web farm that is using cookie persistence. A session-oriented cookie is generated and stored in a non-persistent cache on the client machine. On future requests, the load-balancing device uses this cookie to determine which server handles the request. Some load-balancing devices revert to a different persistence mechanism if the client making the request does not support cookies.

There are many different modes of cookie persistence supported by the various load-balancing devices. All do basically the same thing, but the types discussed in the following sections are provided for flexibility.

Cookie Switching

Cookie switching is accomplished by tying each server in a farm to some user-definable configuration data called a server ID, which is stored in the load-balancing device. Then the application creates a cookie that is well known to the load-balancing device and inserts the server ID tag in that cookie. Browsers will automatically send the cookie string with subsequent HTTP requests. A load-balancing device can scan this cookie string to find the well-known cookie and retrieve the server ID to determine the real Web server for that request.

Cookie Hashing

The load-balancing device performs a hashing algorithm on a cookie issued by the Web application to determine what server handles a client's requests. All subsequent HTTP requests with cookies that resolve to the same hash value will be sent to the same real Web server. This enables an application to manage its session persistence by ensuring that given sets of cookies resolve to the same real Web server across client requests.

Cookie Rewrite

Cookie rewrite is similar to cookie switching in that a well-known cookie is used to communicate information from the servers in the farm to the load-balancing device. In this technique, the server inserts a placeholder cookie on the client machine and the load-balancing device replaces it with a cookie that has information the load-balancing device uses to determine to which server it should send that client's requests. This simplifies the configuration process because the Web application and the load balancing have only a common cookie between them and no server-specific information is exchanged.

Cookie Insert

Cookie insert totally disconnects the Web application from any responsibility for handling cookie-based session persistence. Any Web application can use this form of cookie-based persistence because the load-balancing device manages the cookies used to determine to which real server to send client requests.

SSL Session

Load balancers can manage the session requirements of SSL separately from other application traffic. SSL has become such an important part of Web commerce that it is available on most load-balancing devices. SSL works through a client and a server, first exchanging keys for encryption and decryption. Then the Web server assigns an identity to the newly established session called an SSL ID. Load-balancing devices maintain the relationship between SSL IDs and the Web server that established the session in hash tables for quick access. This ensures that all subsequent traffic for that SSL ID is directed to the same Web server.

NAT

Many load-balancing devices support the various forms of Network Address Translation (NAT). NAT is the process of looking up an address in a table and translating it to a different address. Assigning real servers internal non-routable private addresses enhances security and conserves address space in public networks, where banks of IP addresses are costly. Other uses of NAT include port mapping, which maps well-known ports such as 80 and 443 to totally hidden ports, increasing the overall security of the site. Many load-balancing devices now support NAT for generic UDP, TCP, and Windows Media Services.

Security Features

Security features of load-balancing devices provide increased security for Web farms. Load-balancing devices protect a Web farm from common attacks such as TCP SYN, Denial of Service, Ping of Death, Teardrop, Land, and IP spoofing. Load balancers provide limited forms of packet filtering and blocking like a firewall. Some provide features that allow access control list filtering, limiting ranges of IP addresses from certain applications.

Packet Filtering

Many load-balancing devices can act as rudimentary firewalls by filtering packets. This technique limits or denies access from blacklisted sites by monitoring the traffic source, destination, or port from which malicious threats originate. A whole range of IP addresses can be denied access to resources in a Web farm by a load-balancing device. Along the same lines, these devices monitor the frequency of attempts and what ports were hit, acting as a rudimentary intrusion detection system.

Access Control List (ACL) Filtering

An ACL in a load balancer lists the applications (that is, ports) that a specific group has access to. By applying these ACLs, a network administrator can deny or grant access to a specific range of IP addresses. This granularity of control provides the capability to expose different functionalities to different groups without compromising the security of a site.

Manageability

All load-balancing devices provide a variety of improvements to management of a Web farm. Web farm manageability is improved by centralizing common management tasks such as adding and removing servers from service, organizing and defining server groupings for handling application traffic, creating load-balancing rules, assigning persistence options to server groups, and monitoring health and availability of multiple servers from one location.

Load-balancing devices expose these centralized options through many different console types. The network administrator can

- *Use a GUI,* usually written as a standard Windows application. This interface has the richest UI and is usually the simplest to use.
- *Use a Web-based interface* accessible from the device. A Web server, present in most load-balancing devices, serves up this interface without requiring a dedicated server external to the device. Designed to be easy to use, most Web-based interfaces are simple but effective.
- *Use a command-line interface* for high-speed configuration and scripting access. Some command-line interfaces can be scripted with standard scripting languages, and some have proprietary scripting options. Many devices can be configured remotely through the command-line interface—a useful feature for advanced integration with Application Center 2000.

Application availability monitoring is another feature that many load-balancing devices are now offering. These devices watch for common Web site errors such as 404 and 500. With user configurable thresholds, a Web server can be removed from service when it has too many of those errors, and an administrator can be notified. Features like this are invaluable for large farms that load balance each client request dynamically because determining a single server that has errors is difficult when there are many to choose from.

Caching Services

Many load-balancing devices provide caching services for static content in Web farms. Caching static content can free busy servers to perform more useful work than serving up GIFs and JPEGs to users. By organizing a Web farm with an array of caching servers, the administrator can scale this group of servers separately from those doing application processing.

Some load-balancing devices include the capability to designate a bank of servers as a cache either automatically or through some form of HTTP header parsing. For example, a Web farm could organize all its image content into an image directory. Then the administrator would create a rule for all Web sites that use the cache to redirect requests for anything in the image directory to this bank of servers.

Some devices perform this caching automatically by determining what content is highly requested. This provides an automated way for a Web farm to see great benefit if serving up static content is a large part of what the Web farm does.

Comparing Network Load Balancing with Hardware Load Balancing

Network Load Balancing and hardware load balancing perform the same task but accomplish it completely differently. Network Load Balancing is a software-based solution installed on every server; hardware load balancing is centralized into a device.

How They Work

Both load-balancing technologies rely on abstraction to make many servers appear as one. Table 6.2 shows the steps that a packet might take from the client to the target load balanced server.

TABLE 6.2 A High-Level Description of How Load-Balancing Technologies Work

Step	*Hardware Load Balancing*	*Network Load Balancing*
1	Client makes a request of a VIP.	Client makes a request of a VIP.
2	All servers in farm examine the incoming packet using port rules to determine which server handles the request. All others discard the packet.	Device determines which farm of servers handles the request with rulesets for VIP and HTTP header parsing.
3	Client affinity setting determines if subsequent requests return to the same server or are redistributed across the farm.	Device uses load-balancing algorithm to determine which real server handles the request in the selected pool of servers.

TABLE 6.2 Continued

Step	*Hardware Load Balancing*	*Network Load Balancing*
4		Device uses persistence rules to determine how and whether the next request from a client returns to the same server or is redistributed across the farm or to a different farm.

Pros and Cons

All load-balancing technologies have pros and cons. The choice for a Web farm should be made on a case-by-case basis. It is likely that both technologies will end up in service for medium to large Web farms.

TABLE 6.3 Pros and Cons of Network Load Balancing and Hardware Load Balancing

Network Load Balancing		*Hardware Load Balancing*	
Pros	*Cons*	*Pros*	*Cons*
Application Center 2000 requires only two network adapters.	Requires Advanced Server or Application Center 2000, which is very expensive.	Robust features that provide great flexibility.	Two devices required, eliminating a single point of failure.
Simple and effective for different types of load balancing needs.	Very simplistic and limited features compared to hardware devices.	Centralized management for greater control of Web farm topology.	Funnel for network traffic and could be a bottleneck.
Does not force all traffic through a single network pipe.	Confusing to configure without Application Center 2000.	As the farm grows, cost does not increase.	Not integrated with Application Center 2000.
Integrated with Application Center 2000.	Difficult to maintain without Application Center 2000.	Features in devices increase over time as new revisions are made.	

TABLE 6.3 Continued

Network Load Balancing		*Hardware Load Balancing*	
Pros	*Cons*	*Pros*	*Cons*
	Can cause port flooding on some switches and routers.		
	Large farms can get very costly.		

Summary

Hardware load balancing is an alternative to Network Load Balancing. Hardware load balancing works with special network devices that focus on the management and reliability of Web farms. These devices have numerous features that make them much more powerful than Network Load Balancing. A hardware load-balancing device can enhance the availability and scalability of any size Web farm.

Load-balancing technologies are becoming more and more standard in the application provider space. With the cost of servers low and the speed to market fast, Web farm flexibility and robustness is no longer complete without a solid load-balancing strategy. A Web farm without load balancing is becoming a Web farm without the Web.

Dissecting Web Farm Application Architectures

CHAPTER

7

IN THIS CHAPTER

Every .NET application is different. Some applications are database-centric, requiring large and robust database architectures. Others may concentrate the load on the Web servers, meaning the number of Web servers is directly proportional to the performance of the application. Many applications have high network bandwidth requirements, sending large amounts of data to users. Some are more balanced, requiring robust services on all tiers. Because each .NET application is different, the Web farm that is built to meet the needs of each application is different. The challenge for the administrator is to build the right Web farm for the application at hand.

Building application architectures is about understanding what construes an application, where these pieces execute in the environment, and their functional requirements. Most environments support many applications of different forms, each with differing functional and operating requirements. Some applications are transactional, and others have a more batch-oriented nature. With this amount of diversity and complexity, visualization of the environment is critical for management and support.

Visualizing an application layout is vital for planning server architectures. If an application requires large amounts of online storage, then the environment must provide an extensible external storage array. Applications that are computationally expensive might need four- or eight-way CPU configurations. Media-driven applications such as streaming video and audio will require large amounts of bandwidth and a low latency on the network. Each application will have different requirements, but understanding the components of an application is the first step to anticipating compatible server architectures.

Monitoring and alerting requirements are tied to the visualization of an application. Administrators are responsible for the uptime of an application in the production environment. This responsibility translates into building and creating monitoring and alerting processes that inform administrators to potential problems with an application in real-time. Without visualization of the application, administrators are blind to what problems can occur and will not be able to respond properly to application failures. Visualizing an application is a tool administrators use to catalog application components and develop alerting processes for component failures.

The goals of this chapter are to help you

- Visualize an application architecture using a simplified n-tiered model. The presentation, business, and data layers provide a simple but useful model for understanding components in an application.
- Understand more complex application constructs that identify key components in all .NET applications. Foundational and service-level application constructs are presented graphically. These constructs are then mapped onto real-world server architectures, completing the application visualization process.

Simplifying Application Architectures into N-Tiers

The first step to visualizing application architectures is to break the application into conceptual tiers. In any complex discussion about real-life application architectures, it is important to first establish a frame of reference for the discussion. Dividing an application into a tiered model simplifies a complex discussion of application services into manageable parts.

In the discussion of tiered models there are three layers: the presentation layer, the business layer, and the data layer. These tiers can be divided into three distinct types of .NET servers: Web, application, and database. A Web server provides the presentation layer, the business layers are provided by the application servers, and the database layer is handled by the data servers.

The value of this model is to help describe the different high-level actions that servers in an environment might take. It can also be a guide for an initial server architecture design. The requirements of these three tiers for most applications are similar, so a best-guess estimate of hardware requirements can be made once the different application components are assigned to appropriate tiers.

The risk with this model is that it oversimplifies the discussion, as there is considerable overlap throughout the layers when deployed on server hardware. This doesn't mean that—heaven forbid—data access logic is combined with business logic. Instead, it means that the servers that provide these services might be shared between layers. Figure 7.1 shows how multiple tiers can exist on one server or be spread among many servers.

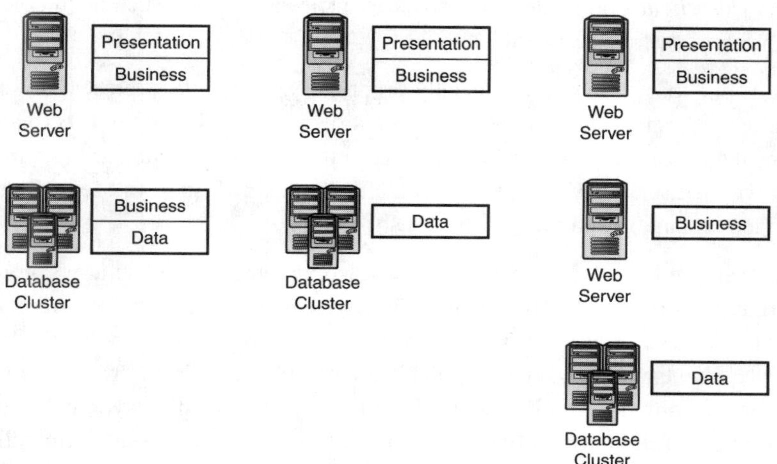

FIGURE 7.1
Different tier organizations.

The Presentation Layer

The presentation layer is where the user interacts with a Web farm. It is composed of user-interface elements of varying complexity and function. The presentation layer also has limited and well-defined techniques for accepting data from users. Lastly, there are a number of different Windows 2000 and .NET enterprise servers that can serve user interface content.

Reach Versus Rich Client

For simple clients, such as HTML-based Web sites, any Web browser can provide the user interface to a Web farm. This is called a "reach" Web site. In other cases, a special user interface is required to gain access to the user interface of a Web farm. These user interfaces can be described as "rich."

NEW TERM A *reach client* caters to the least common denominator of user interface like any browser that supports HTML 3.2. A reach Web site will work with Internet Explorer, Netscape, and Opera.

A reach client must conform to some well-defined standard. Usually, this is an HTML 3.2 specification. This HTML standard provides a limited set of functionality compared to the next-generation HTML 4.0 specification. In most cases, an HTML 3.2 site will have limited capabilities on the client. This means that a reach client will not have user interface functionality like drop-down menus or roll-up text areas. Reach clients also use a server-side component such as IIS to present dynamic content or handle user interface requests such as a form submission.

NEW TERM A *rich client* is any client that requires a special browser such as Internet Explorer 5.5 or a custom client such as Flash.

A rich client is one that has a special, usually proprietary, technique to present a user interface. Internet Explorer is a great example of a rich client because, while it conforms to all HTML specifications better than any other browser, it has a number of non-standard features that greatly improve the user experience. Other rich clients include Windows Media Player for streaming video and audio and Shockwave Flash.

Applications that require a rich user interface are also targeted at specific user communities. In the case of Internet Explorer 5.5, this community consists of all those users who have upgraded to IE 5.5. Most of these users use Windows for their operating system, and since IE is a platform itself, rich clients take advantage of platform-specific features. In the case of streaming media, the user community is composed of those users with a media player and large enough bandwidth to realize fully the benefits of this media form. In either case, the rich client is targeted at specific users and takes advantage of platform-specific functionality.

Servers of the Presentation Layer

There are many examples of servers in the presentation layer. Internet Information Services, Windows Media Services, and Mobile Information 2001 Server all directly interact with users using a client application. To interact with IIS, users use a Web browser application. Users use Windows Media Player to access streaming video and audio content from a server running Windows Media Services. .NET devices communicate with Mobile Information 2001 Server to present data in a structured format for manipulation and display. The following section describes in more detail how each client application might interact with a server in the presentation layer:

- IIS 5.0 is the Web server in Windows 2000. The Web server is the primary server that is used to transmit data back and forth to the client browser in the presentation tier. In the simplest example, a client running Internet Explorer requests the URL `http://www.technicallead.com` and downloads the default file for the `technicallead.com` site. Next, this file loads into the browser and executes whatever client-side script is on the page. Any further requests to `technicallead.com` from this page will send data back to the server for processing or request a different page from the site.
- Windows Media Services is another Windows 2000 server technology. Media Services provides streaming video and audio to clients that understand audio or video compression standards like MPEG-4. Microsoft provides an implementation of this called Microsoft MPEG-4. These files have the extension `.ASF`. Windows Media Player is the client application that understands these `.ASF` files, and it requests these files using a URL similar to an HTML page: `mms://www.example.com/file.asf`. There is no way to send data back to Windows Media Services.
- Mobile Information Server (MIS) 2001 is used to provide user interfaces for .NET devices. Data from this server is transmitted in XML format, and the information is presented on the respective device. For example, a cellular phone maintains a list of contacts over the Internet and stores them on MIS. When a user looks up a contact, the phone makes a request of MIS to get the detail of the contact and download it to the phone's memory for display.

Data Transfer to the Presentation Layer

All data is transferred to and from clients with some Internet-based application protocol, such as HTTP. To get data from a Web server, browsers use a `GET` request for a specific file. To send data to a Web server, a browser uses either a `POST` request, in which data is transferred in a the body of the `POST` request, or a `GET`, in which data is sent with the URL.

For Windows Media Services, data is transferred using the MMS transport protocol. MMS is Microsoft's native audio and video streaming protocol. MMS is a connected protocol that allows Windows Media Player to play video and audio in real-time without download all the media at once. Windows Media Services also supports HTTP streaming, which is similar to MMS but uses port 80 to bypass firewalls.

In some cases, data is sent and consumed in XML format, as with Mobile Information Server 2001. Custom clients such as a cellular phone and a tablet PC can communicate with Mobile Information Server 2001 natively. There are developing standards, such as Xforms and XHTML, that will greatly simplify the transmission of structured data from browsers and will change the way data is transmitted to Web servers. Figure 7.2 shows how data moves in and out of the presentation layer.

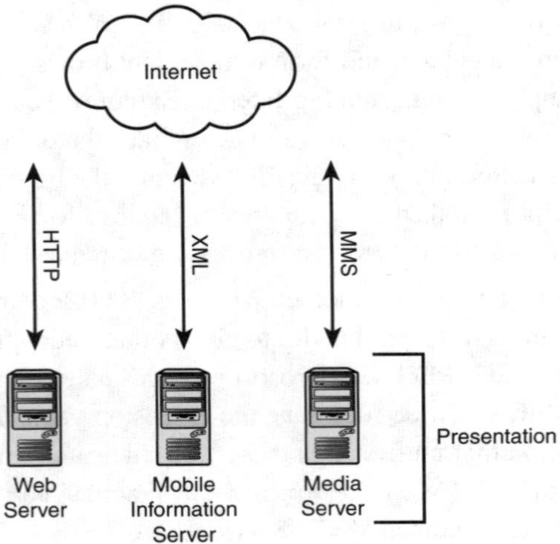

FIGURE 7.2
Data transfer: the presentation layer.

The Business Layer

The business layer is a conceptual subdivision of an application where all business logic resides. Business logic is simply the process by which a specific business accepts and manipulates data from a user or other program with specific rules. For example, a bank applies a $2.00 surcharge for every ATM transaction. This surcharge is a business rule. The business logic for this surcharge is to subtract $2.00 from the ATM user's account and transfer it to the bank's account.

Because all businesses are different, business rules and logic will be different for every application that is hosted in a Web farm. For application architecture, the important concept is that the business logic and rules should be separate from the other layers. This separation comes in many forms, including COM components, ASP.NET/ASP pages, .NET Web services, NT services, and others.

Servers of the Business Layer

The servers of the business layer are similar to the presentation layer. IIS and Mobile Information Server 2001 also host the business layer. This is a great example of servers that have multiple purposes. Just because a server has both presentation layer logic and business logic doesn't mean these layers are combined. The separation occurs at the boundaries of the individual application components or their interface layer. For example, all COM components have a set of well-defined application programming interfaces. Other application components, like ASP pages, use these interfaces to instruct the components to do work by calling methods on the COM component. These methods encapsulate the business logic that the application developer has embedded within the COM component. So even though the COM component might exist on the same IIS server as the ASP page, there is a separation between these two entities because of the COM interface. For .NET Web services, this interface is called SOAP and is based on XML.

Other servers that host business logic include custom COM+ application Servers, BizTalk Server 2000, Commerce Server 2000, and Microsoft SQL Server. Each server has strengths and weaknesses for creating and handling business logic, and every application will find different uses for these server technologies in the business layer. A brief example of these technologies and business logic follows:

- COM+ Application servers host custom COM+ applications that have business logic in the form of COM components. These components are units of code that functionally encapsulate the business rules of a specific portion of a Web site. The bank transaction is the classic example of a custom COM+ application server. In that situation, the COM components handle moving the money in and out of specific accounts, and COM+ ensures that the transaction is completed. Another good example is a suite of components that encapsulates access to a database table, such as customer information.
- BizTalk Server 2000 is a B2B integration technology. In a simple example, BizTalk can be used to define the rules that businesses use to communicate procurement requests to each other. BizTalk Server can link a Web site to an external vendor that handles fulfillment and product warehousing, manage all the requests, and even transfer the funds. BizTalk Server is a tool to build business logic through document exchange; COM+ is a generic business logic broker and runtime for custom business components.
- Commerce Server 2000 provides a set of business components for creating custom e-commerce sites. With Commerce Server 2000, a shopping cart is already built, so sites can use this functionality out of the box. Other features include built-in inventory management, shipping, and profile management.
- Microsoft SQL Server 2000 can encapsulate business logic in stored procedures. Stored procedures are snippets of code that execute on the SQL server to interact with data.

These stored procedures are the classic business interface into a database. Many sites have moved away from embedding business logic in stored procedures and prefer the other business layer server technologies. Poorly written stored procedures and excessive business logic force SQL Server to do more than just manage access to data.

With the advent of .NET, the IT world has encountered a new item called a *Web service*. A Web service is like any other service except its interface is XML/SOAP and can be consumed over the Internet. Common .NET Web services that a Web farm may host include credit card processing, order submission and processing, inventory management, tax calculation, order status information, reporting, custom alerting, and many more. Web services create the programmable Web and enable developers to write code easily to interact with Web sites over the Internet.

NEW TERM A *Web service* is a business layer service that uses a SOAP/XML interface for consumption by Visual Studio .NET and other SOAP-aware applications on the Internet.

Data Transfer to the Business Layer

Data is transferred from clients and other application layers in many different formats and protocols in the business layer. Typically these protocols are XML or COM/DCOM based. Web services for example, use an XML-based contract called SOAP Contract Language. This structured document provides information concerning all the entry points into a Web service. For SQL Server, the client typically does not have direct access. Instead, servers in the presentation layer access the SQL server through stored procedures. BizTalk Server 2000 uses XML to facilitate the exchange of business documents. Other servers such as Commerce Server use COM/DCOM as the interface into their business components. Figure 7.3 shows a typical business layer with different access points and data transfer protocols.

The Data Layer

The data layer is the realm of databases. In this layer, the services focus on providing secure, reliable, and fast access to data. A database is specialized for all-purpose data handling tasks. Databases organize data into tables and views. They provide indexes to speed access and stored procedures to provide a programmatic interface.

Servers in the Data Layer

The main server in the data layer is SQL Server 2000. SQL Server's focus is on the data needs of the rest of the application and how the data should be organized. If a database is transactional, then there will be fewer indexes so that inserts, updates, and deletes are fast. In reporting-type databases, more indexes means faster queries and better response times for queries.

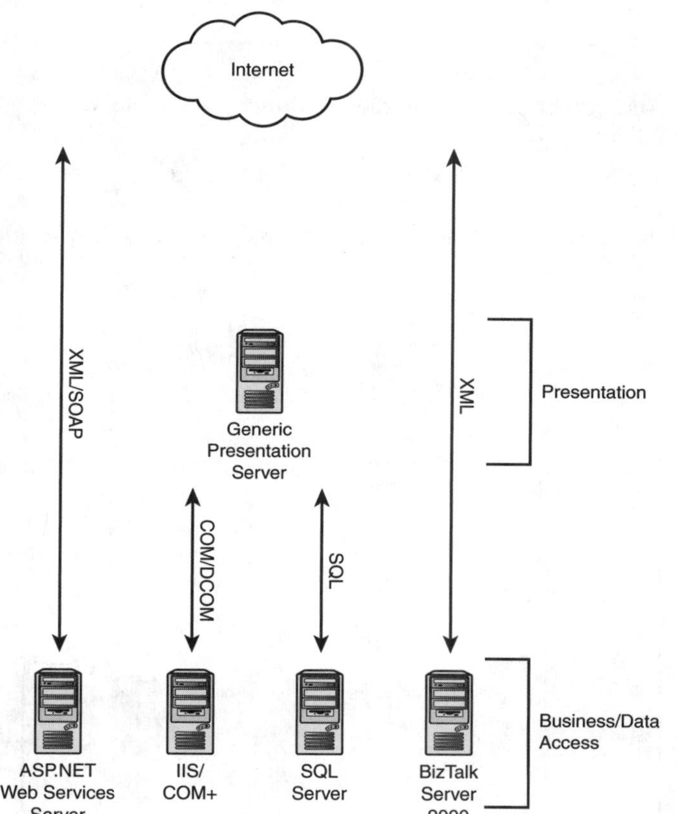

FIGURE 7.3
Data transfer: the business layer.

Data Transfer to the Data Layer

Data is accessed through SQL Server in a number of ways. Structured Query Language (SQL) and XML are two common ways used to manipulate data in SQL Server. Each method has the following characteristics:

- Structured Query Language provides a cross-platform, standards-based language used to access data from SQL Server. SQL can be used to retrieve, update, delete, and insert data. SQL can also help create new tables, indexes, stored procedures, and views.
- XML is natively supported in SQL Server. XML can be generated for any request. An XML document provides a human-readable format in plain text for any SQL query. The data is consumable cross-platform by any service that understands XML. With OpenXML, a feature available only in SQL Server 2000, relational views, XML joins, and updating a database are now possible, all from XML.

NOTE

More information on SQL Server 2000 features is available at `http://www.microsoft.com/sql`.

Figure 7.4 shows the data layer, the different access points, and their relationship to other application tiers and clients.

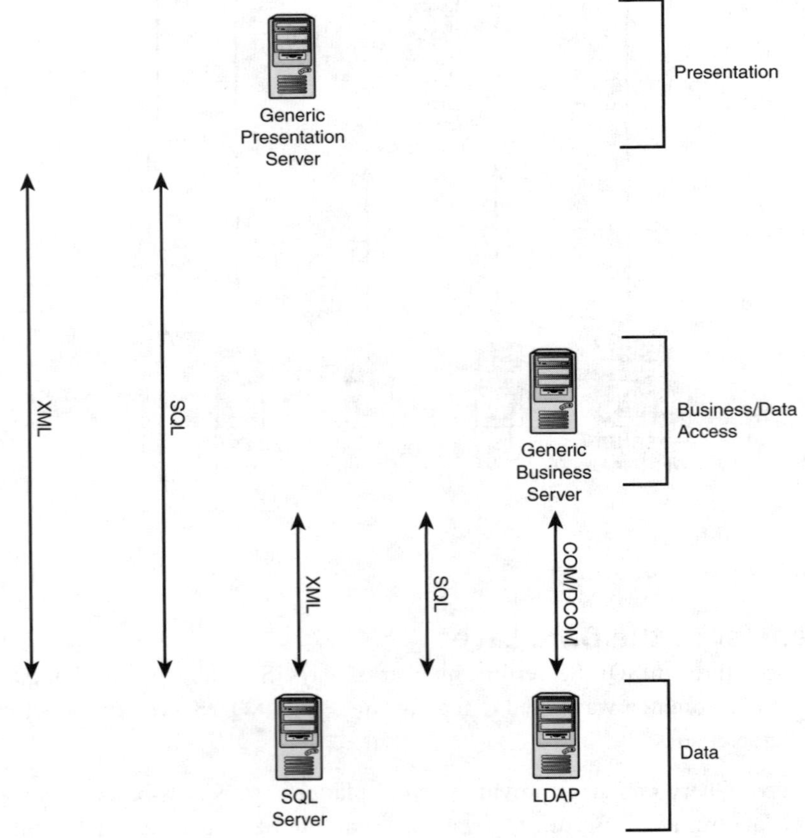

FIGURE 7.4
Data transfer: the data layer.

Together, these three layers provide a good foundation for understanding the organization of.NET applications. The presentation layer provides user interface services, the business layer provides business logic and data access services, and the data layer provides access to databases. This layered approach is great for simple views of an application. A more useful discussion is to break the application into fundamental constructs and examine how constructs are actually deployed onto real-life server architectures.

Defining Application Constructs

Building the right Web farm can come only from understanding common application architectural constructs. Fortunately, .NET application architectures can be reduced to a few general configurations. Each configuration has advantages and disadvantages that pinpoint the architectural constructs that best meet an application's requirements.

All architectural endeavors are similar; each one involves combining discrete building blocks into larger functional constructs. For example, each room in a home is built with different elements for different purposes. In a bathroom there is a toilet, a bathtub, a sink, tile, a mirror, walls, pipes, and a door. As individual elements, these building blocks provide simple services, but combined they provide all the services of a bathroom. Each room of a house will have different constructs, and some constructs exist in all rooms. Each room also provides different services; the kitchen is for preparing meals, the bedroom for sleeping, and the living room for living. As rooms are combined, they form a home, which provides all the services required for people to live.

Applications are very similar to homes in that they provide services for customers. Like the home, each application may contain many "rooms," and these rooms are referred to as services of the application. Each service is composed of foundational constructs.

The Foundational Constructs

All application services are built from the foundational constructs. These foundational constructs are the basic building blocks of Web farm applications. There are many core constructs to choose from, and not all constructs will be found in a .NET application.

The Datum Construct

The datum construct is a singular piece of data used in a .NET application. Datum examples in a .NET application include customer records, product information, pictures, video, documents, XML, and audio. Datum has little use without a user interface construct that understands how the datum should be interpreted.

Depending on the type of datum, a Web farm will have to provide the vehicle to deliver the datum to the user. If the datum is video, Microsoft Media Services and a large pipe to the Internet are required. A simple `.JPG` file is delivered with IIS and viewed with a browser. Each datum will place different requirements on a Web farm; most of those requirements are obvious.

The User Interface Construct

The user interface (UI) construct is a client-side program that understands how to interpret a particular datum. Examples of client-side programs include Windows Internet Explorer for viewing Web pages and Windows Media Player for listening to and watching streaming audio and video. User interface constructs can also be custom programs that must be deployed to user desktops before interfacing with the Web farm.

Usually user interface constructs place no burden on the .NET Web farm. Custom UI constructs could require automated deployment across the Internet, which means more network bandwidth. With .NET Devices, the breadth of user interfaces increases in complexity. Now, tablet PCs and cellular phones will be accessing information in a Web farm. Web farms that use Mobile Information 2001 Server will provide data to these devices in different ways from traditional PC-based devices. This adds complexity to a farm, but it is manageable because of a .NET MIS enterprise server.

The HTML Page Construct

The HTML page construct is one element in the presentation layer of a Web farm application. HTML pages contain images, form fields, script, text, cascading style sheets, and other standard HTML elements. All these combine to provide the interactive experience that is a Web page. HTML pages are static from a Web farm perspective but may contain dynamic elements that execute on the client.

HTML is delivered from a Web server to a Web browser. The only requirement for a Web farm is the network bandwidth and server capacity to deliver the page to the user.

The ASP/ASP.NET Page Construct

The traditional ASP page is a presentation layer construct similar to HTML. ASP is like HTML because a Web server delivers it and it can provide dynamic content. ASP is different from HTML because, while some HTML provides dynamic content that executes on the client desktop, the ASP page provides dynamic content that is generated on the server. An ASP page is dynamically built on the Web server at the time it is requested. ASP pages may interact with components, databases, XML, and other server-side constructs to form the pages sent to clients.

The application requirements for an ASP page will differ according to the breadth of the functionality provided and whether it is a traditional ASP page or an ASP.NET page. With ASP, the pages are built from script elements, and execution is not compiled. Just this fact can place a tremendous burden on the CPU of a Web server. If an ASP page is complicated, it is usually better to use ASP as the glue to connect smaller, foundational constructs together to form larger service constructs. Calculating the impact of these ASP pages, on the Web server's limited processing resources, requires that the construct's impact be considered separately. Once this is complete, the overall impact of the ASP service construct can be estimated.

ASP.NET pages are compiled runtime objects that use the .NET framework to deliver content. This means that running an ASP.NET page is very close to running a standard Windows application in terms of performance and speed. Simple ASP.NET pages will place little burden on the Web server, and CPU utilization should not be a problem. Complicated pages, with lots of business logic, could stress a Web server, but due to the compiled nature of ASP.NET, the effects of most pages will be light, especially when compared to similar pages in traditional ASP 3.0.

The CGI Construct

Common gateway interface (CGI) is another presentation layer construct with the same characteristics of an ASP.NET page. CGI is an executable or DLL that is accessed by client applications over the Web. CGI programs deliver dynamic content, depending on the API or "methods" called on the CGI program by the client. The big difference between CGI and traditional ASP is that CGI is compiled code like ASP.NET, and ASP is script.

The ISAPI Construct

The Internet Server Application Programming Interface (ISAPI) provides a set of interfaces that are used to create extensions and filters for IIS. ASP.NET itself is an example of an ISAPI extension that hosts the .NET runtime. These ISAPI components are installed on an IIS server in the form of a DLL. For example, `asp.dll` is the ISAPI extension for the traditional ASP processing engine. Whenever a request for a file with the ASP extension is made from a browser, IIS turns control over to `asp.dll`. `asp.dll` processes the request and executes the ASP page. Once `asp.dll` is finished processing the page, it returns control to IIS.

An ISAPI filter differs from an extension in that it sits in front of all requests made to IIS. A filter is called an *interceptor* because it looks at and performs some action on every request. Actions could include logging to a file or database, performing a security authentication, or redirecting a user to a different page. An example of an ISAPI filter is the Commerce Server 2000 authentication filter. This filter ties members of a Web site to users in a Windows 2000 domain. It allows the administrator to protect file system content on a Web site with standard Windows 2000 security. Each request that comes in goes through this authentication filter, and the filter checks the security of the files and compares that to the credentials of the requesting user. If they don't match, then the filter denies access to the file and redirects the user to a page for an explanation of the denial.

Depending on its scope and function, an ISAPI application construct can place different levels of load on a Web server. Web farm impact analysis should be done in the same way as for ASP pages, because an ISAPI construct could be as simple as other fundamental constructs or it could be composed of many fundamental constructs.

The Local COM Object Construct

A local COM object is a fundamental construct that is used by ASP, ISAPI, CGI, and any other consumer of COM objects. COM objects are registered on a server, and programs that execute on the server can use whatever features the COM object provides. COM objects that are registered locally, in DLL form, run in the caller's Windows NT process space. For example, `dllhost.exe` is a Windows NT process; when it creates a COM component, the DLL associated with that component is loaded into the memory of that process. A COM object in EXE form runs in its own process. The DLL form of a COM object is the most common.

A COM object typically encapsulates business logic or data access logic. Object consumers use the COM object's well-defined application interfaces to access its functionality. Most COM objects provide some common functionality that is accessed from multiple locations within a larger application. A good example of a COM object is one that retrieves customer data from a database. Most .NET applications will need customer data more than once, and a COM object is best suited for this purpose. A COM object is a great way to build common, reusable libraries of code. For example, `Customer.Data` is the name of a COM object that has methods to retrieve data from a database called `Customer`. On the Web server, there is an administrative tool, in the form of an ASP page, that lists all the customers of a Web site for a particular day. When a customer service representative requests this page from the Web server, the ASP page creates a copy of the `Customer.Data` component and calls the method `RetreiveCustomerRecordsforToday`. This method accesses the data in the `Customer` data and returns a dataset containing all the relevant customer data. Then the Web page parses this data and returns a grid containing the information the customer service representative requested.

COM objects are mostly compiled code, so they execute much faster than script-based programs such as ASP. A COM object can call other COM objects, access databases, create and read local files, manipulate the Registry, and anything else a Windows 2000 program is allowed to do. Everything a COM object uses internally must be considered when attempting to estimate its impact on the Web farm.

The Remote COM Object Construct

The remote COM object construct is exactly like the local COM object except that it does not execute on the server where it is created. This means that when the COM object is registered on a server, the registration information instructs the COM runtime libraries to instantiate any requests on the designated remote machine. This remote location can be a single machine or, with Component Load Balancing, a cluster of machines. A remote COM object runs on another machine whether it is in DLL form or EXE form.

All remote COM objects are instantiated using the Distributed Component Object Model (DCOM). DCOM is a collection of services in Windows 2000 that manages the communication between components and other application constructs across process (EXE) boundaries and machine boundaries (over the network). DCOM provides location transparency for COM objects by hiding the complicated details of opening a connection to a remote machine, creating an object on that machine, and then calling methods on that object. To the application developer, a DCOM object is used no differently than a local COM object. For example, DCOM manages the network plumbing that is required anytime a component creation request is forwarded to a different server.

The .NET Component Construct

The .NET component construct is a class in the .NET framework. A *class* is a set of code or business logic that encapsulates this functionality behind an object-oriented interface. The words "class" and "component" are interchangeable. The .NET framework provides a unified, object-oriented, hierarchical, extensible set of class libraries (APIs) for .NET components to use. A .NET component can create a window for traditional Windows programming or interface with a database for Web-based reporting.

All .NET components in either EXE or DLL form behave similarly to traditional DLLs. These .NET components are not like other DLLs in that the standard Windows Explorer shell cannot load or execute code in them. Instead, loading and execution of .NET components occur in the .NET Common Language Runtime (CLR). The .NET CLR is a service construct discussed later in this chapter.

.NET components can access anything that a COM object can access, including databases, file systems, other Common Language Runtimes through remoting, and COM objects. .NET components have access to TCP/IP and XML libraries for interfacing with network services and SOAP.

The Database Element Construct

A database element construct is a discrete unit of a database. For SQL Server, these main elements include tables, views, indexes, and stored procedures. These elements are used by all parts of a .NET application. An ASP page can interact with a database element as easily as a CGI program or a COM object.

A .NET application uses SQL statements and database elements to interface with a database. .NET applications retrieve, insert, update, and delete data in a database. A transactional application that performs primarily inserts, updates, and deletes requires a database with fast I/O, but less CPU horsepower. The application servers that execute these queries are little more than brokers of the data and spend most of their time waiting on the database. In contrast, a reporting application can place a burden on both the CPU of the SQL Server and the application servers. To return the data in a reporting query, the SQL server must pull data from multiple tables and perform complex relations, costing CPU and disk I/O resources. The application server must format for display the data that is returned from the database, another expensive process.

A Graphical Representation of Foundational Constructs

Figure 7.5 shows icons for all foundational constructs presented in this chapter. These icons are used in other diagrams throughout the chapter to help facilitate an understanding of common application architectures.

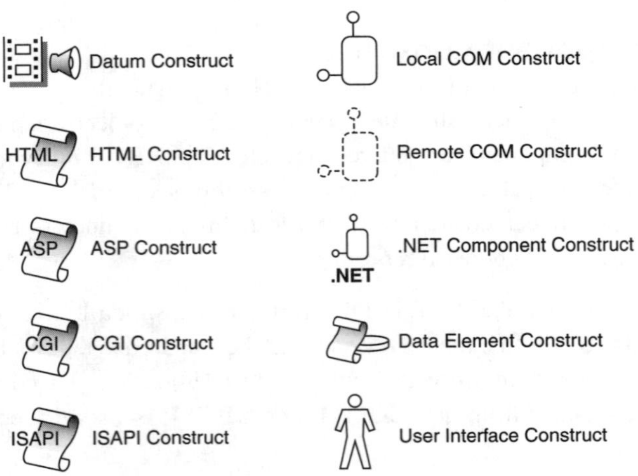

FIGURE 7.5
The fundamental constructs of applications.

The Service Constructs

Service constructs are built from combinations of foundational constructs. A service construct is a functional subset of an application. In this case, the word "service" is an overloaded term that means any functional application piece. For example, a database or traditional NT service can be a service construct in a Web farm. The approach of this section is to describe all the services that a Web farm can provide, for both internal Web farm operations and external overall application functionality.

Key points to consider when thinking about services include

- A service is composed of foundation constructs. Some services are composed of other services and could be referred to as *meta-services.*
- A service is unique, and the Web farm server architecture best suited will be unique for each service.
- A service has an interface. This interface is the means by which a service consumer uses the service functionality. Examples of interfaces are TCP/IP, COM/DCOM, and XML.
- A service has a redundancy methodology. This can be as simple as a cold spare or as complicated as Windows Cluster Service.

Figure 7.6 shows the graphical representations of all the service constructs described in this section.

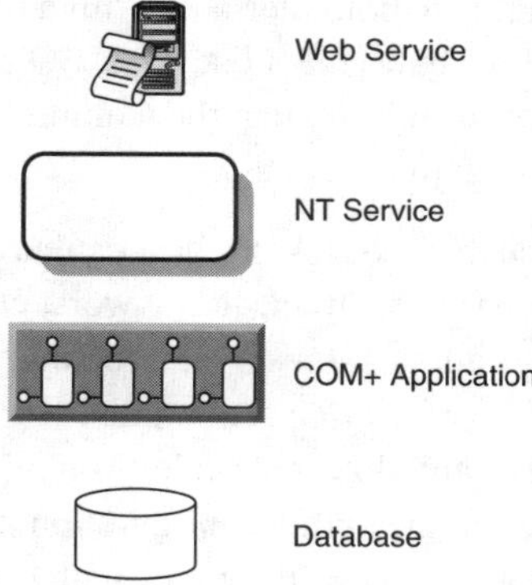

FIGURE 7.6
Symbols for service constructs in this section.

A Database

A database is a collection of database elements and datum organized by a database engine, such as SQL Server 2000. A database may contain many types of datum and data elements. These fundamental constructs describe the form and function of the database. Figure 7.7 shows a simple database built from fundamental data elements and datum.

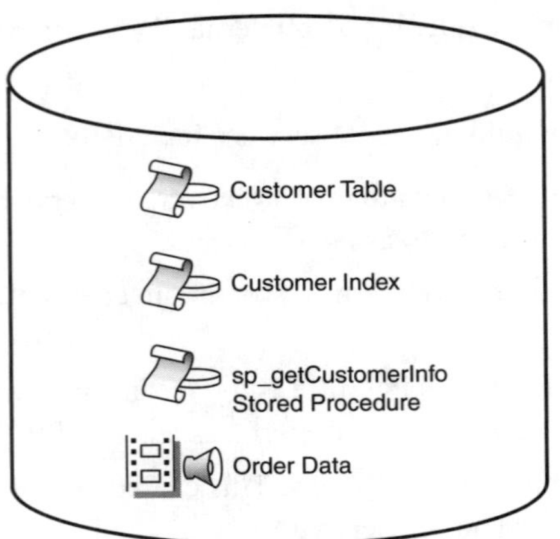

FIGURE 7.7
The simple database built from fundamental constructs.

A consumer of database information interfaces with a database through SQL or TCP/IP. SQL is a well-defined standard for querying a database. SQL Server 2000 also has a native TCP/IP language that some Microsoft objects, like the Commerce Server 2000 Orderform object, use to communicate with the data in a database.

A highly available and scalable .NET Web farm can have a number of different server configurations to support the database construct. In the worst case, the database construct exists and shares resources with other application servers, including a Web server. Of course, this configuration violates the principle of service scaling discussed in Chapter 3, "Scalability and Availability of Web Farms," and does not scale. At a minimum, the database construct should have a dedicated database server. In this configuration, this database server is a single point of failure, but at least it no longer shares resources with other servers. The database construct's resource requirements (CPU, disk I/O, memory) scale separately from other application components. For mission-critical applications and most Web farms in general, SQL Server (or any other database for that matter) should be clustered for high availability. This means that there are two or more servers acting in a failover capacity for a single database construct. When one fails, the other steps in and handles the application request for data. Windows Cluster Service provides this capability for SQL 2000 and is covered in Chapter 21, "Clustering SQL Server." Figure 7.8 shows a database on a single server and one on a cluster: two viable server architectures to support the database construct.

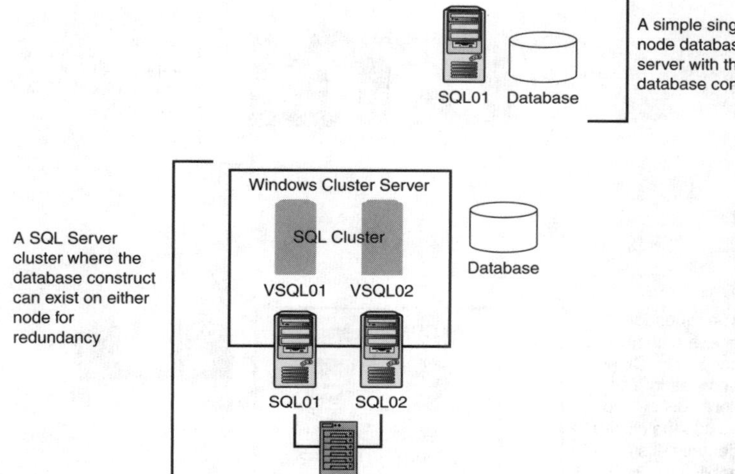

FIGURE 7.8
The server architecture required to support a database construct.

A second form of redundancy available only with SQL Server 2000 is a shared-nothing cluster, or federated database. This type of cluster distributes the load of database queries across multiple independent servers, but it maintains a view to client applications of one single database. This technology is called *distributed partitioned views* and is discussed in Appendix D, "Scaling Out SQL Server 2000."

The COM+ Application Service

In the early days of COM, creating a COM-based application service was an individual endeavor. Each development team would re-create the server part of the application, limiting the amount of time spent working on the functionality the service was supposed to provide. On top of the wasted time, COM services tended to be difficult to write and error prone.

With COM+, Microsoft has created a way for developers to focus on writing the business objects that meet the requirements of the business and not worry about creating a robust service architecture. COM+ provides this service architecture in the form of the COM+ runtime. The COM+ runtime allows developers to create business objects and administratively insert them into user-defined application services, effectively creating a COM+ application service. Chapter 10, "Using Component Services (COM+) in a Web Farm," explores the configuration of COM+ applications in detail. Figure 7.9 is an example of a COM+ application service.

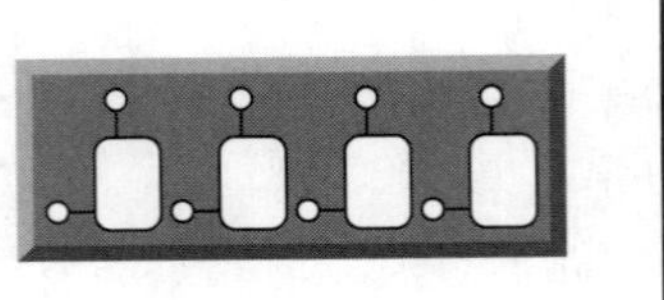

A COM+ application with multiple local COM objects

The redundant server architecture supports a COM+ application. The construct symbol next to the cluster denotes this application is deployed here.

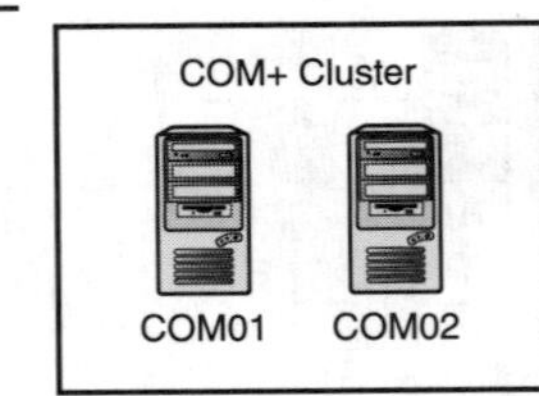

FIGURE 7.9
The COM+ application service.

Almost any local DLL-based COM object construct can be inserted into a COM+ application service. Most COM+ application services access database element constructs from the local COM objects that they are composed of. Some COM+ application services use remote COM object constructs and even other COM+ application services.

COM+ applications expose their services through DCOM when they are configured as server applications either locally or remotely. They use COM for library applications because the components in a library application run in-process to the caller. In a sense, a library application is just like a collection of local COM objects. However, a COM+ library application provides a graphical interface for local COM objects in the COM+ application and a simple deployment process.

NOTE

For more information on COM+ applications, see Chapter 10.

A COM+ application uses Component Load Balancing (CLB), a feature of Application Center 2000, to achieve redundancy, scaling, and fail over. In its native form, DCOM itself is a single point of failure, in which standard load-balancing techniques that address availability do not address scalability. For remote COM+ application services, a cluster of CLB-managed COM+ servers is the only viable option for true availability.

The first example, seen in Figure 7.10, shows a data access service that contains many components. These local COM objects encapsulate database access for reporting, alerting, and customer information. This is a common technique for centralizing the code to access a database and from an application perspective provides an object-oriented–like way of accessing the data in a database. Also in Figure 7.10 is the server architecture required to support a data access service with the constructs associated with each server. All of the remaining examples will show both the service and how they are deployed to sample server architectures.

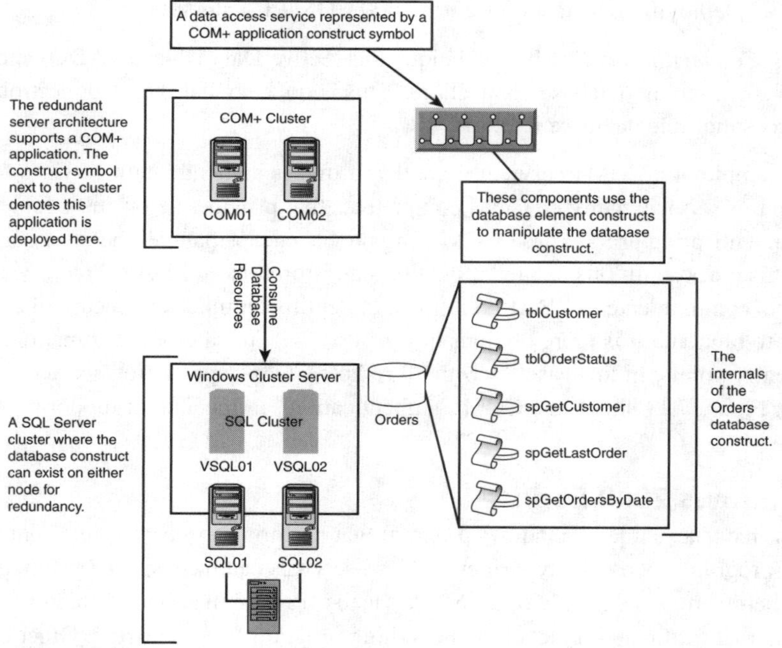

FIGURE 7.10
A COM+ data access service.

It is interesting to note that the data access service could also run remotely on a cluster of COM+ application servers. While this adds a network hop between the frontend servers and the database, increasing the number of network calls, it can help centralize connecting to the database. Connecting to the database is a relatively expensive process compared to issuing queries. That is why much effort has been placed in Microsoft Active Data Objects (ADO) to pool database connections. If a farm has 30 Web servers that create 30 connections each to a SQL Server database, that's 900 connections for SQL Server to maintain. If those same data access COM+ services could be accessed remotely on a cluster of three COM+ application servers, the number of connections could decrease to 90! This tenfold decrease in connections happens because multiple servers make requests for the same remote data component in succession sharing the same database connection. When the components run locally on the Web server, this connection sharing does not happen across server boundaries, and thus each server opens its own set of pooled connections, increasing the load on the SQL server. It is important to understand that this sharing of database connections does not always outweigh the additional network traffic. In fact, a remote component invocation is considerably slower than a local one, due to network latency. For more information on best practices for COM+ clusters, see Chapter 13, "Deploying Application Center 2000 COM+ Clusters."

NEW TERM *Connection Pooling* is a technique that Active Data Objects (ADO) and ODBC use for caching database connections. This is done so that these connections can be reused across multiple database requests.

Another example of a COM+ service is one that provides authentication services for Web site visitors. In this service, there are COM components that provide the business logic for validating and authenticating users. These COM components encapsulate all the necessary business logic for this purpose. In this example, the users are stored in an LDAP directory, so the COM components communicate to LDAP to retrieve the entire datum. The concept of a service is beginning to blur, and it is more obvious how a service is just a group of functionality that has different entry points. In this case, as with all remote COM+ application services, the interface is DCOM. Figure 7.11 shows the COM+ authentication service and its supporting server architecture.

The Windows 2000 Service

An NT service is a standard Windows program that performs specific system functions to support other programs. Most likely written in C++, services can have special privileges and interface with hardware. An example of an NT service is IIS Admin service, which listens for TCP/IP Internet traffic and directs it to a handling program for processing. Other examples include Indexing Service, File Replication Service, and Print Spooling Service. Some services host specialized COM objects or provide interfaces to legacy systems.

An NT service can be composed of local COM objects, remote COM objects, database elements, COM+ application services, and datum. Figure 7.12 shows a sample NT service that provides a TCP/IP interface for a mainframe to access functionality in a local COM+ application service.

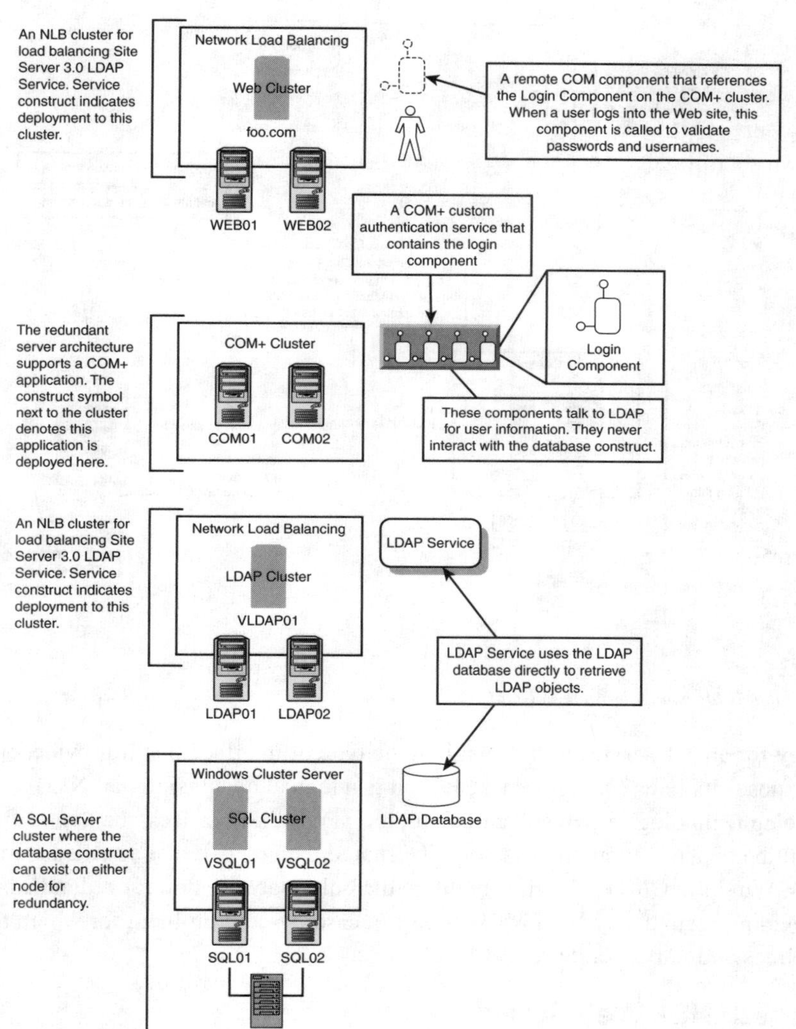

FIGURE 7.11
A COM+ authentication service.

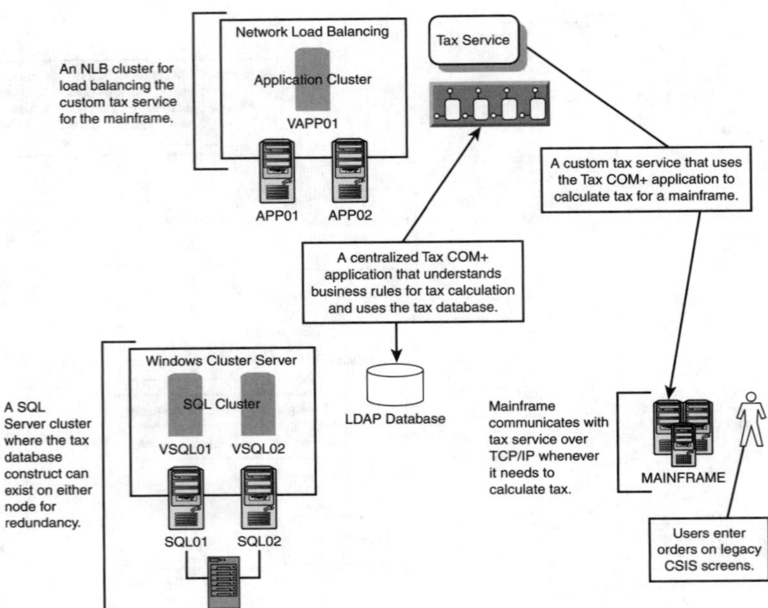

FIGURE 7.12
An NT service that bridges a mainframe to COM.

Redundancy for an NT service will depend on the type of interface that it provides. For a service that exposes its interface through TCP/IP, it is a logical conclusion that NLB or other load-balancing technologies will solve this problem. For other services, the application redundancy might be dependant on other factors like shared data on external attached storage. In these cases, Windows Cluster Service might be the only viable option for redundancy. In other words, providing redundancy for a NT service is a case-by-case problem for which there are only guidelines and not concrete rules for solutions.

A Managed .NET Web Service

A managed .NET Web service provides runtime services for native .NET components and exposes them using SOAP and HTTP. The Web service executes inside the Common Language Runtime (CLR). The runtime is responsible for managing memory allocation, creating and destroying threads and processes, enforcing security policy, and interoperating with COM components or other non-managed operating system services. The CLR also provides a unified environment across multiple programming languages.

A managed Web service is composed exclusively of .NET components, database elements, and datum. The components are either custom built or from the .NET common class library. This means that a managed Web service is very stable because the .NET runtime handles all memory access and allocation, reducing the possibility of memory leaks and access violations in developer code. In unmanaged code (traditional COM+ components, ASP pages, and so forth), the onus is on the developer to access and free memory. Managed Web service stability comes from the elimination of malicious or poorly written code that can corrupt a Windows 2000 process. With managed-code implementations, all external constructs are forbidden because they could introduce such code and crash the CLR.

Other services and constructs can interface to the Web service through SOAP. SOAP stands for Simple Object Access Protocol and is an XML-based language for executing code in a Web service. Web services use the SOAP specification to expose an interface in XML format. Using HTTP as a transport protocol, a client of a Web service can discover all access points by simply downloading the SOAP contract document and consuming it. Visual Studio .NET will do this natively.

NOTE

For more information on SOAP and Web services, please see `http://www.soapwebservices.com`.

Because managed Web services use SOAP and HTTP for an interface, standard load-balancing technologies like NLB and other hardware solutions are sufficient. Figure 7.13 shows a managed Web service using NLB to provide redundancy.

.NET components are powerful enough to create any application. In Figure 7.14, a Web service implements an inventory reservation and management system that communicates with a legacy mainframe through TCP/IP to reserve inventory. Notice that all the constructs are managed code, so this Web service is very stable.

A Non-Managed .NET Web Service

A non-managed .NET Web service is exactly like a managed one except that it can be composed of any foundation construct, including local COM objects, remote COM objects, database elements, ASP, ISAPI, CGI, COM+ application services, and datum. Therefore, non-managed implementations are less stable because a foundational construct can access the operating system outside of the .NET CLR.

Interfacing and redundancy of non-managed .NET Web services are handled in the same way as managed .NET Web services described previously.

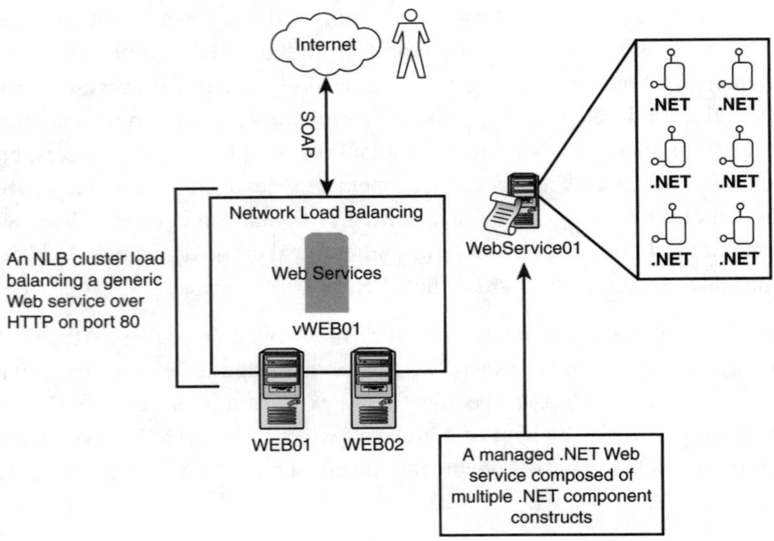

FIGURE 7.13

A Web service using NLB for redundancy.

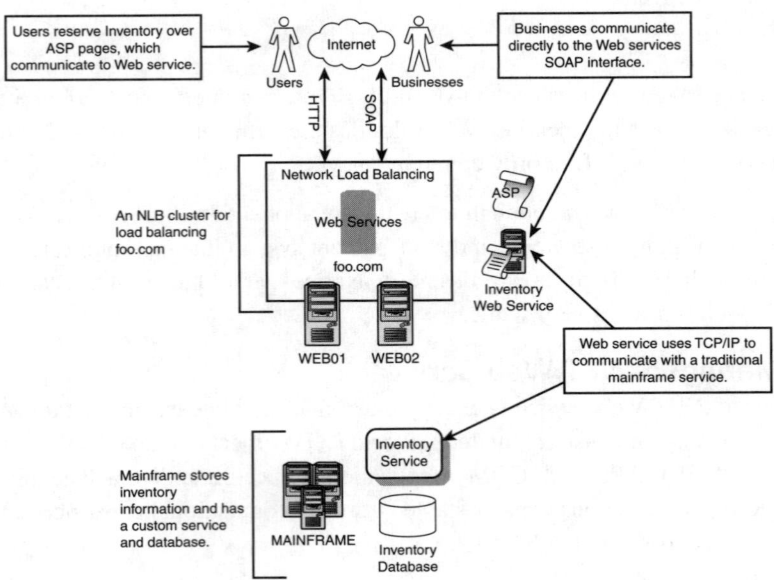

FIGURE 7.14

A managed Web service for inventory reservation.

During the migration to managed .NET Web services, there will be a significant number of non-managed Web services that integrate with legacy systems. A .NET Web service can be just another way that an application exposes its services. A legacy credit card system composed of a COM+ application could create a .NET Web service that wraps the COM+ application but doesn't re-implement the core functionality. That is left up to the COM+ objects. Figure 7.15 shows a credit card Web service that wraps legacy components.

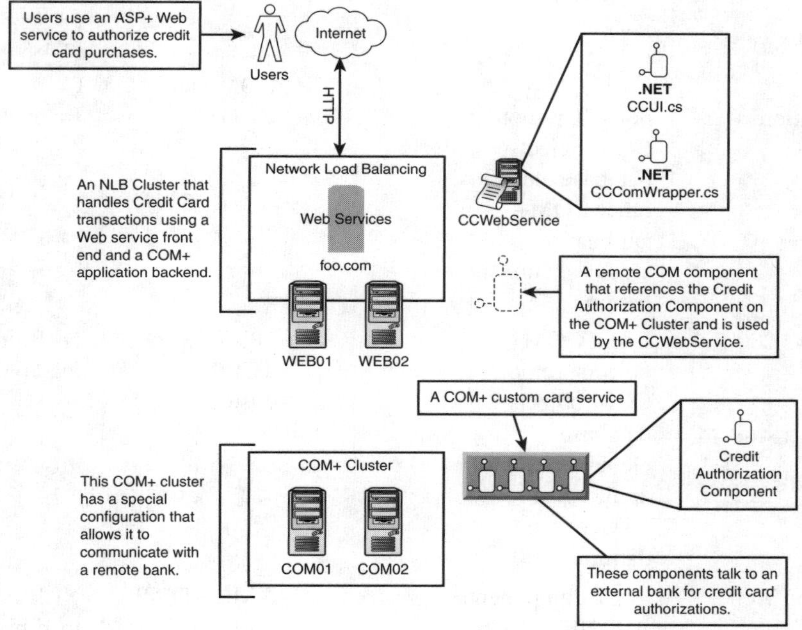

FIGURE 7.15
A non-managed Web service for credit card authorization.

Summary of Service Constructs

Table 7.1 gives a summary of all the service constructs discussed in this chapter. This table is invaluable to help determine an initial analysis of an application's architecture requirements. Use this table to determine potential service interfaces how to plan for redundancy.

TABLE 7.1 Service Constructs Summary

Service Type	*Foundational Constructs*	*Interface*	*Redundancy*
Database	Database elements and datum	SQL, XML, native	Cluster Service, NLB with distributed partitioned views
COM+ Application	Local COM objects, remote COM objects, database elements, other COM+ application services, and datum	COM and DCOM	Component Load Balancing
Windows 2000 Service	Local COM objects, remote COM objects, database elements, COM+ application services, and datum	DCOM, TCP/IP, custom	NLB or hardware load balancing
Managed Web Service	.NET components, ASP.NET, database elements, and datum	XML, HTTP, .NET remoting	NLB or hardware load balancing
Non-managed Web Service	Local COM.NET components, objects, remote ASP.NET COM objects, database elements, COM+ application services, and datum	XML, HTTP, .NET remoting	NLB or hardware load balancing

Understanding common application architectures can lead to better understanding server architecture requirements. This understanding can lead to better performance, simplification of troubleshooting, higher availability, and increased scalability.

Summary

Every .NET application is different. An administrator's challenge is to construct server architectures, troubleshoot, and monitor every application supported. The first step is to understand the various roles of conceptual application layers. The presentation layer is for interfaces either for users or businesses. The business and data access layers are about business logic and services that are COM/DCOM based or SOAP based. The data layer is databases and data. Servers here provide fast access, reliable service, and scalable architectures.

Where the layered architecture fails is when describing real application architectures. Visualization of applications using fundamental constructs is the best way to communicate design and function. Functional constructs range from datum to .NET components. While more simplistic than other designs, application visualization provides key insight into server architecture requirements and key areas to consider when planning monitoring initiatives. Visualization is the bridge between developers and administrators.

Designing Web Farm Application Deployment Environments

CHAPTER

8

IN THIS CHAPTER

> If we slide into one of those rare moments of military honesty, we realize that the technical demands of modern warfare are so complex a considerable percentage of our material is bound to malfunction even before it is deployed against a foe. We no longer waste manpower by carrying the flag into battle. Instead we need battalions of electronic engineers to keep the terrible machinery grinding.
>
> Ernest K. Gann, *The Black Watch*

In the winter of 1990, the United States military began the most massive troop deployment effort of all time with Operation Desert Shield. In less than three months, 400,000+ troops and their gear were moved from the United States to the desert of Saudi Arabia. The logistical problems faced and overcome paved a great foundation for the most effective and bloodless war of all time.

Any logistics operation of the complexity and magnitude of Desert Shield requires in-depth planning and flawless execution. The procurement of goods required a thorough step-by-step repeatable process. It was necessary to track the ebb and flow of goods as they moved from phase to phase in the deployment process. Even with great systems and planning, this mighty deployment process was a hulking bureaucratic beast that only through sheer will and determination—because lives were at stake—enabled success. This is the nature of logistics and deployment.

Webster's defines *deploy* as

1. To position (troops) in readiness for combat, as along a front or line.
2. To bring (forces or material) into action.
3. To base (a weapons system) in the field.
4. To distribute (persons or forces) systematically or strategically.

v. intr.

To be or become deployed.

In a Web farm, deployment is defined as the process of moving application code, data, and configuration information from one server to another. It can be a complicated process, as the logistical challenge of managing the release process is directly proportional to Web farm complexity. The administrator has to bring site changes into action quickly and effectively. Deployment is like renewing the site, as unique problems confront each version. Just like a military operation, a deployment team must act quickly, follow a step-by-step repeatable process, and execute the changes with perfection. It is this logistical challenge that requires every successful Web farm to build deployment architectures to facilitate change.

The goals of this chapter are to help you

- Justify the deployment environment by outlining how it helps an organization successfully maintain a Web farm.
- Define the typical deployment stages of development, testing, staging, and production. The scope and purpose of each environment are discussed in detail.
- Consider different deployment architectures, including one-, two-, three-, and four-stage configurations. Choosing the right architecture for a Web farm, fitting in performance testing, and dealing with deployment adversity are also covered.

Setting the Stage for Deployment

Critical to the success of a deployment is the concept of stages. A *stage* is a step in the process of propagating site change. These steps facilitate the following deployment actions:

- Ensuring that new features and functionality work as coded.
- Practicing change-control procedures.
- Ensuring that overall site functionality works as described.
- Managing the logistics of the release process without affecting the site availability.

Developers begin the release process by coding new site features and functionality. Usually, this development occurs on a single developer workstation. In any reasonably complicated Web farm, a single-machine site configuration is unlikely. A developer needs an environment, similar to the live one, in which he can deploy initial site changes. Once the developers and business people have agreed upon the features of a release, they compile a *change control document* for the rest of the deployment team. This document describes in detail the step-by-step deployment process. Without a staged deployment effort, the development staff makes changes to the live environment. Because developers work with site code, this can cause serious outages, and the site will eventually take an availability hit.

In the early days of Foo.com, before they used a staged deployment process, developers made changes to the live production environment. In one particular release, a change prevented orders from successfully completing on the back-end order processing systems. This problem was not discovered for many days, and manually adjusting over 1000 orders caused Foo.com to experience a logistical nightmare. Developers should make changes to a dedicated development environment because they can dramatically affect a site like no other team involved in the deployment process.

NEW TERM A *change control document* is the list of new features and functions in a particular Web site version. It also describes the step-by-step process for deploying those changes.

Practicing change control procedures is the only way to determine the cause-and-effect relationship in multiple configuration or site changes. A stage gives the administrator the flexibility to try a change and spend the appropriate time understanding its affect. If the change control documentation is incomplete, practicing in a staged environment will flush out the inconsistencies. Without a stage, the changes happen on the live environment and eventually cause an availability hit. No matter how experienced and seasoned an administrator, at some point an unexpected result of changes will disable a site. Even for sites already using tools like Application Center 2000 to manage deployments, a stage to practice change control in is necessary to prevent downtime.

NOTE

For more information on Application Center 2000, see Chapter 11, "Introducing Application Center 2000."

Before Foo.com practiced change control procedures, it experienced serious availability hits due to administrator mistakes. These poor administrators who were with Foo.com initially were to blame for many problems that a staged deployment effort prevents. In one instance, a single misstep in an IIS configuration change caused four hours of downtime. It wasn't that the change was difficult or time consuming to perform; it was determining through troubleshooting what went wrong. Troubleshooting change control procedures should happen in a deployment stage and not production.

Once the changes for a particular release have been made to a stage, some form of quality assurance should determine the success of the deployment effort. This quality assurance team, composed of dedicated testers who understand technology and business needs, is a key component of the deployment staff. They understand at a business level how a site should behave, but they have enough technical savvy to communicate problems to developers. This group has a list of business requirements, which is part of the change control document that it uses in testing the site. If any of these business requirements are not met in a particular stage, the development and administrative teams must determine at what point the deployment effort failed. Some business changes are complicated to test, and it could take hours to verify that the functionality is correct. Without a staged deployment, this testing occurs in the live environment, and when a new site version fails a test, redeploying the fix will cause an availability hit.

When Foo.com developers were the primary testers of new site versions, many times problems went unreported. When managers and business people tested the site, it was challenging for them to demonstrate repeatable problems. In one instance, a manager found a problem and sent the development staff off to fix it. After three hours of effort, the developer finally realized that the manager's testing was flawed, and a problem existed on his machine, but not the site. Once Foo.com established a true quality assurance team, it still had problems because it lacked staged deployment. In one particular instance, a complicated inventory problem was missed because it took placing an order, inserting it into a back-end system, and analyzing the resulting inventory record to determine if reservation occurred correctly. By the time the problem was found in the live environment, 50 orders had items that were no longer available. Testing site functionality should happen in a deployment stage and not production.

Deploying a new version of a Web site is clearly a logistical challenge. Development, administrator, business, and quality assurance teams all have to work together for a successful release. Figure 8.1 brings the deployment business process together, showing the flow of a change control document throughout the deployment cycle.

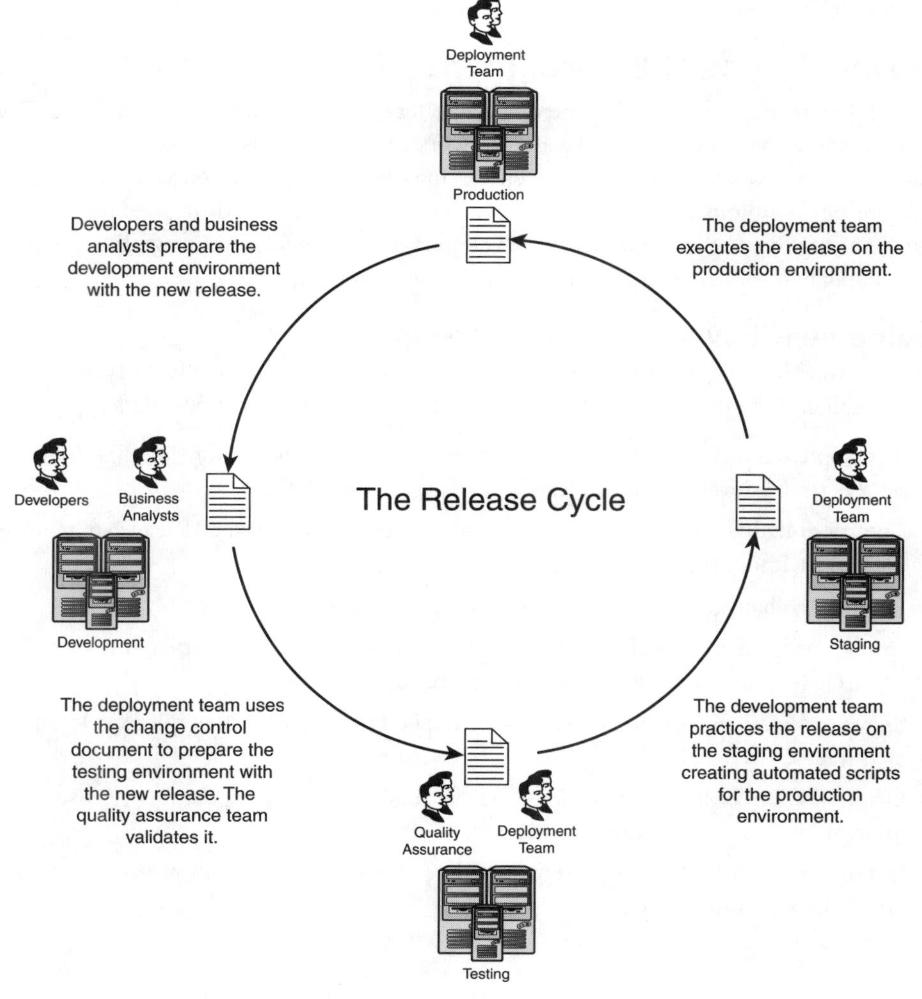

FIGURE 8.1
The deployment process change control cycle.

Defining Typical Deployment Stages

A number of different stages can be derived from the deployment process change control cycle. It is important to think of these stages conceptually. Don't assume that a conceptual stage translates into a physical stage of dedicated server resources. As the roles and responsibilities of each stage are defined, permutations into physical configurations will become clear. In the ideal case, each stage has the luxury of a complete copy of the live environment. However, if a live Web site has a Web cluster, a COM+ cluster, and a SQL cluster, duplicating these clusters throughout every stage requires significant server resources and is expensive. It is possible to combine and simplify the architecture of each stage to save money. This will be explored where appropriate.

The Development Environment

The development stage is typically where new site features and functionality originate. The development environment is where developers work on a daily basis. Developers and business analysts determine what improvements each version of a Web site will provide for the business. From this requirement gathering, a change control document is developed and used to propagate change to downstream stages. Development also provides an integration point for the application and developers that is similar to a live environment.

Development Environment Ownership

A developer has free reign in the development environment. He is typically an administrator in this environment. The developer is the master of this domain and must be able to

- Add application constructs like files and components to his machine and the shared servers of the development staff.
- Control domain and server security so that new configurations and ideas can be tested with and without security implications.
- Iterate site changes at will to deliver new features and functionality.
- Apply service packs and hot fixes if doing so eliminates bugs in server software like IIS and COM+ and is required for the coming release.
- Leave applications in a broken state for extended periods of time while developing the next release.
- Install new server technologies to help meet requirements for upcoming releases or to improve the overall capability of the site.
- Install developer tools to server equipment to troubleshoot difficult problems and diagnose poor performance areas.

New technologies, release requirements, and ideas have to be examined somewhere, and the development environment is the perfect place.

Determining Requirements and Coding Practices

In order to begin a deployment, business analysts and developers determine the requirements for a new Web site version. Requirements come from many different sources, including customer requests, business requests, site improvements, and new technologies. These requirements translate into units of time for development, testing, and deployment. The challenge is in determining the timeframe for completing proposed changes and allowing time for these changes to be tested and deployed. This challenge will be unique for each team and deployment, but thorough testing can take as long or longer than a development effort. Be sure to provide adequate testing time to a quality assurance team. Practicing a deployment should also be given adequate time so that mistakes can be made in the staged environments and not in production. If all these processes are rolled up into the development environment, increase any estimates accordingly.

When the developer begins delivering the code for the new requirements, development usually occurs on an isolated development machine. This developer server may or may not share database and component resources with shared development resources. Most importantly, a developer has to be able to make changes and experiment at will, without affecting other developers or the environment as a whole. Figure 8.2 shows a typical development environment.

Development Integration Points

Integration between developers and site changes is required any time a development environment supports more than one developer or more than one effort. In general, any development environment must overcome the following logistical challenges:

- Interaction on shared development equipment can cause integration problems. However, if developers use their local machines for the majority of development and use the shared server as a deployment point, this becomes less important.
- Management of source code should use a central repository such as Source Safe. These systems allow multiple developers to work freely on the same site without accidentally deleting or modifying other developer changes.
- Upgrading server software might require interaction between development teams if teams share the development servers. In many cases, this is desired because keeping sites on the same version of server software simplifies troubleshooting later.

Once the code is considered complete, it is deployed manually to the shared development environment. This environment should mirror the live environment as much as possible. In the development environment, developers have full administrative privileges to all machines. They must be free to make changes and experiment, making sure to document any configuration changes required to deploy the new release.

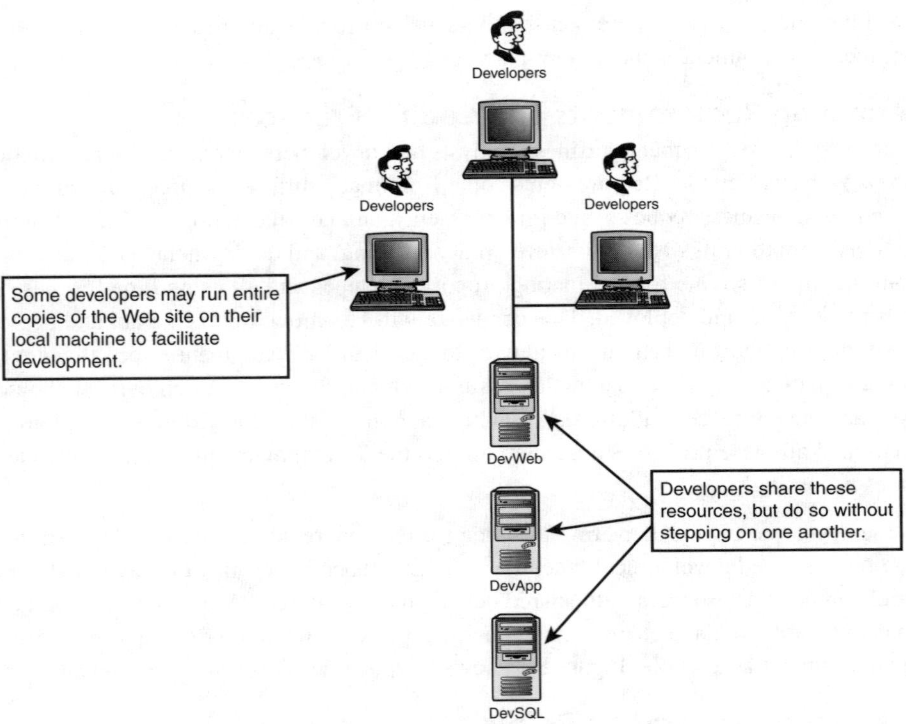

FIGURE 8.2
A developer's machine in the development environment.

Creating the Change Control Document

From the deployment into the development environment, the developer and business analyst build the change control document. This includes all the required changes and a list of new features in the release. The deployment and testing team uses this document to perform the release into the next stage. An example change control document is available for download on this book's Web site (`www.technicallead.com\webfarms`).

The Testing Environment

The testing environment is used to test a site independently of developers and the free-form nature of the development environment. Testing is when the deployment team takes the first practice run at implementing the change control documentation. The quality assurance team also uses the testing environment to validate features of a new release. Using this environment correctly greatly improves the speed to market and deployment downtime of any new release.

Testing Environment Ownership

Testing is different from development in that multiple groups that comprise the deployment team own it. The deployment team uses the testing environment to practice the changes in the change control document. This process is similar to what happens in the development environment. Much of what the deployment team does is experiment with the changes, making sure they understand the change's scope. In testing, they begin to consider building scripts to automate the deployment process as much as possible into the live environment.

Unlike with the development environment, developers should not have administrative access to the testing environment. The deployment team should manage this environment. It is important to separate the duties here because, if the deployment team cannot own the change control, the development staff will end up owning any problems in the production environment. This will slow down the cycle of new features and releases if developers spend time troubleshooting release problems.

For example, when Foo.com created its first testing environment to help improve the deployment process and improve its availability rating, it gave both developers and administrators full administrative access. This seemed like a good idea because sometimes change control documents were incomplete and when the quality assurance team went to test and found problems, they could use either the developers or deployment staff to troubleshoot the problem. However, more than once the development staff would fix a problem directly in testing and not inform the deployment team. When the release was moved to the next stage, many of these original problems happened again. Once the developers and the testers had to involve the deployment team in managing changes, these problems ceased.

Testing from the Quality Assurance Team

The quality assurance team has different ways to test a release. Functionality testing assures that each feature works as described. Regression testing scrutinizes a complete software system, ensuring that new features haven't broken old ones. System testing determines the effects of new third-party technologies, service packs, and hot fixes. Finally, load testing ensures that the new release performs as well as the previous one under heavy load conditions.

The Staging Environment

A staging environment is the original second stage in most deployment methodologies. It is this stage that protects the production site from outages by isolating the change control. Simply put, the staging environment is used to practice the deployment. To practice the deployment, administrators develop and test automation scripts, maintain and build application replication projects, and configure application security.

Staging Environment Ownership

The deployment team has complete administrative control of the staging environment at the exclusion of other groups. This ownership forces the deployment team to configure and manage all releases fully. The deployment team should resolve any problems that are encountered deploying to this stage. If any change requires development intervention, then the change control should be modified and redeployed into testing. Ownership here is key to ensure the deployment team can support the production environment.

Scripting Changes to Staging

Microsoft has made Windows 2000 the most scriptable operating system of all time. There is almost no change that can't be scripted. Scripting is the only way to guarantee that a change was made correctly. Typical scripting tasks include IIS metabase configuration, application account creation and management, application component installation, and Registry and INI file manipulation.

In our first example, a simple command file is used to enter Registry entries, change file attributes, and move configuration files. The following command line is used to execute a command or batch file.

```
C:\scripts\mybatchfile.cmd argument1 argument2
```

All of these tasks are easily completed manually without creating a batch file. This batch file ensures that a series of simple changes will be applied correctly. Notice our example in Listing 8.1.

LISTING 8.1 A Simple Command Script Example

```
REM *** %1 = Server's Environment

REM *** Insert Entries in registry with regsrv32
regsrv32 /s c:\scripts\configfiles\%1\regentries.reg

REM *** Copy the general diagnostic files into Inetpub
xcopy c:\scripts\webfiles\servertest.asp D:\inetpub\anthemroot /i /y

REM *** update the browsecap.ini file
xcopy c:\scripts\webfiles\browscap.ini c:\winnt\system32\inetsrv\ /i /y

REM *** update site UDL Files
xcopy c:\scripts\udls \%1\*.udl c:\config\udl\ /i /y

REM *** Attrib all the inetpub file from read-only to full access
attrib -r d:\inetpub\*.* /s
```

LISTING 8.1 Continued

```
REM *** remove extra DBMSSOCN.DLL for Site Server 3.0
ren c:\winnt\system32\inetsrv\DBMSSOCN.DLL DBMSSOCN.dll.newer

REM *** remove the old mfc.dll and replace it with the new one
attrib -r c:\winnt\system32\mfc42.dll
ren c:\winnt\system32\mfc42.dll mfc42.dll.older
xcopy c:\ISTWebs\configfiles\mfc42.dll c:\winnt\system32\ /i /y

REM *** Configure custom isapi filter
regsrv32 /s c:\scripts\webfiles\%1\Filter.reg

REM *** Set Passwords
call c:\scripts\webfiles\setpasswords.cmd
```

In our second example, a Visual Basic script is used to modify the COM+ catalog. A Visual Basic script (VBS) file is executed from the command line using either `cscript.exe` or `wscript.exe`. To launch a script and have any output directed to a console window, use `cscript.exe` as in the following:

```
cscript.exe c:\scripts\ConfigIIS.vbs
```

Use `cscript.exe` to run scripts in the background from deployment tools like Application Center 2000. When running scripts like this, it is invaluable to log the output to a local file to examine later. Use the following to log output from a VBS:

```
cscript.exe c:\scripts\ConfigIIS.vbs >c:\scripts\logs\configIIS.log
```

To launch a script and have any output directed to a Windows message box, use `wscript.exe` as in the following:

```
wscript.exe c:\scripts\ConfigIIS.vbs
```

The main disadvantage to using `wscript.exe` is when running scripts in the background. If any errors or messages boxes are generated from a script running under `wscript.exe`, they will never finish because in the background there is not a user present to click the OK button. Even if an administrator is logged in interactively, the message boxes are not displayed if the script is launched from a service or system process.

Visual Basic scripting is available with all versions of Windows 2000. VBS allows the creation of external COM objects, interfacing with Active Directory objects, modification of the Registry programmatically, and modification of IIS metabase information. Listing 8.2 provides an example VBS script.

LISTING 8.2 A Simple VBS Example: `ConfigIIS.vbs`

```
'use CScript from the command line so echos won't pop-up message boxes
Dim oIIS

WScript.Echo "Start: ConfigIIS.vbs"

WScript.Echo "Getting the IIS Administration Object"
Set oIIS = GetObject("IIS://LocalHost/W3SVC")

WScript.Echo "Turning Buffering Off GLOBALLY so client will see pages as
➥they are generated"
oIIS.AspBufferingOn = FALSE

WScript.Echo "Setting Default Docs Globally"
oIIS.EnableDefaultDoc = TRUE

WScript.Echo "Setup the list of default documents for this server"
oIIS.DefaultDoc = "default.asp,default.htm,index.htm"

WScript.Echo "Commit Changes to IIS"
oIIS.SetInfo

WScript.Echo "Done: ConfigIIS.vbs"
```

NOTE

For more information on Windows scripting options, see `http://msdn.microsoft.com/scripting`.

Automated Deployment Options

Most deployment teams use a content replication tool to manage the moving of application components from one stage to another. Tools range from simple file copy utilities that can sync two directories to Application Center 2000. Any tool requires some degree of configuration to initiate the deployment. With each release, the deployment team creates whatever new replication configuration items are required. Once again, the keys to success with content replication are automation and repeatability.

NOTE

For more information on replication options with Application Center 2000, see Chapter 12, "Deploying Application Center 2000 Web Clusters."

Handling Password Problems

A staging environment may exist in a separate security domain in order to stage and test security changes. With tiered security architectures, it becomes easier to manage changing passwords used by application accounts. There is nothing more difficult than understanding all the points in an application where changing an application account password causes functionality to fail. Being able to test these changes is very important for both application availability and security of the DMZ.

For example, Foo.com recently added a security boundary between staging and production by creating a separate NT domain. It added new domain controllers and joined all the staging servers into this new domain. It can now change passwords for application accounts in staging without affecting the passwords in development or production. This allows administrators to change passwords in staging and understand the impact on Foo.com. They discovered application areas in which password information was being stored. It took them an entire day to analyze and troubleshoot the password change problems, thus preventing a costly outage in the live environment.

If a separate security boundary in staging is not an option, then the deployment teams will need to maintain a checklist of application passwords. These checklists should have information on what each application account does and where to change the password information. For instance, IIS maintains an NT account to grant access to Web pages that exist within a Web. When the password is changed using the Windows 2000 User Manager, it must also be changed inside IIS. In scenarios like this, changing passwords will be successful only with complete application architecture documentation.

The Production Environment

The production environment is where customers and businesses interact. It is secured and owned by the deployment team; access to other teams is restricted, except for emergencies. This level of separation is necessary if the deployment team is held accountable for the availability of the production site. If other groups can freely interact with the production environment, they are bound to introduce changes that could affect overall site availability.

No changes happen directly to this environment except during scheduled releases or emergency situations. With a proper staging area, the deployment team can create a checklist of scripts and tasks to be completed with each release. As long as these steps were practiced and repeated in the staging environment, the deployment to the production environment will be smooth.

Considering Different Deployment Architectures

There are four conceptual deployment stages, which do not necessarily translate to four physical stages. Development, testing, staging, and production can be combined, depending on the complexity of an application and the amount of resources allocated to deployment. Each Web farm will use a different strategy for successful deployment. However, it is useful to consider the differences in deployment architectures with one, two, three, and four stages. Usually, cost will be the most influential factor in making the deployment architecture decision.

Using a One-Stage Deployment Architecture

A one-stage deployment environment consists of only production. It is never recommended and no Web farm should choose to use one-stage deployment architectures. The one stage serves for development, testing, staging, and production. It is likely that as new features are delivered to this stage, users will experience problems. With no way to test and stage changes, the site will experience considerable downtime.

Using Two-Stage Deployment

A two-stage deployment environment has combined development, testing, and staging environments and an isolated production environment to protect it from release changes. By using the first stage to develop new code, test site changes, and practice deployment, the move to production is likely to have problems. This is because with so many people having access to a single environment, it becomes difficult to track changes, and it is likely that some important changes will be missed. When this happens, the deployment will fail, and the site will become unavailable until the problem is resolved. Two-stage deployment is usually effective only with simple Web farms composed of static HTML or very small applications. Figure 8.3 shows a two-stage deployment architecture.

With two-stage deployment, it is possible to manage the process. With solid change control and a locked-down first stage, tracking release changes is possible. Considerable effort is spent managing the time that different groups have access to this environment. Testing cannot occur at the same time developers are releasing new code. The deployment team can't practice the release during testing. Most deployment teams won't have the diligence to manage the first stage to this extent. This necessary control can also stifle development, because developers must be careful what changes they make and thoroughly document everything.

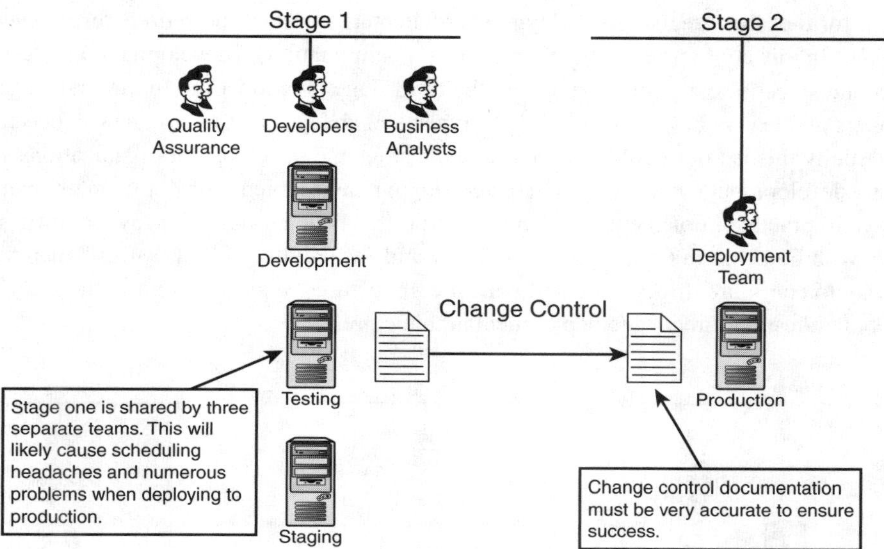

FIGURE 8.3
A two-stage deployment architecture.

Foo.com's initial deployment architecture was in two stages. When it was time for a new release, the developers and business analysts would plan the new features and set a timetable for moving the new site to production. When the developers began work on this new release, the changes to the development environment made it functionally different from production. Unfortunately, it was discovered that a serious bug in production required immediate attention. With the development environment unavailable, the developers were unable to test any fix with absolute certainty except for in production. In this case, it took two or three times to get the fix in because other factors were missed. This is in large part true because the development environment was not like the production one. During this time, the application availability of Foo.com took a major hit.

Using Three-Stage Deployment

There are two distinct forms of three-stage deployment architectures. With three stages, only two stages have to be combined. Production should never be combined with another stage, so the choice is between combining development and testing or testing and staging. Three-stage deployment may be the most cost effective deployment architecture for medium-size Web farms.

The first form of the three-stage deployment architecture is called the *shared development/testing model*. In this configuration, the first stage is a combination of development and testing. The second stage is solely for staging, and the third stage is production. In the first stage, developers and testers have to work closely to test site changes and release new code successfully. Usually this is not a problem, because the testing and development organizations share the same development cycle. With an isolated staging environment, the deployment team has a full stage to practice implementing change control. If scheduled downtime availability is a concern, as with Foo.com in Chapter 3, "Scalability and Availability of Web Farms," then this is a great way to configure three-stage deployment architectures. Figure 8.4 shows the shared development/testing three-stage deployment architecture.

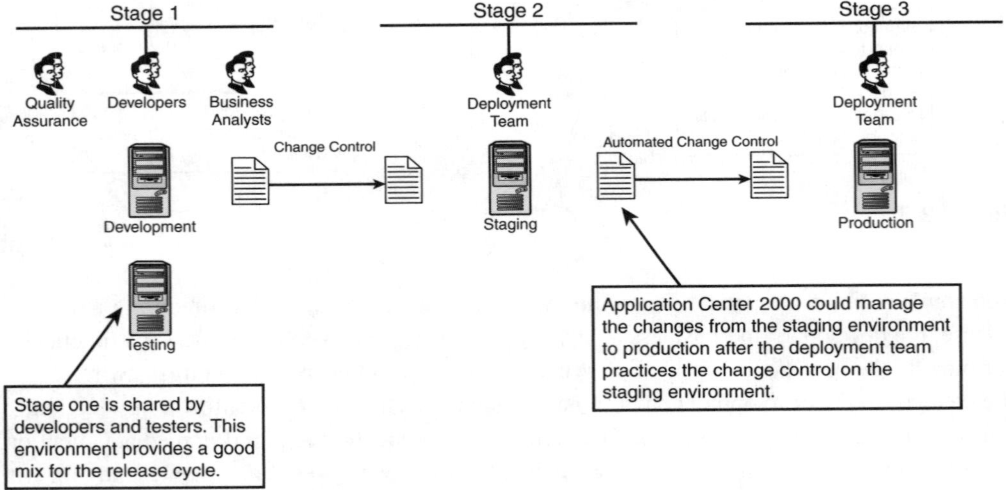

FIGURE 8.4
The shared development/testing three-stage deployment architecture.

The second form of three-stage deployment architecture is called the *shared testing/staging deployment model*. In this configuration, the first stage is dedicated solely to development. The second stage is a combination of testing and staging, and the third stage is production. In the first stage, developers have complete control and can move and work very quickly on new site changes. This is great for large Web farms with many different applications and development cycles. In the second stage, testers have to schedule time to test the site, usually after the deployment team has implemented the initial testing change control. The most difficult challenge in this configuration is practicing the deployment. Many times, the release change control will be repeated in the shared testing environment to test the automated scripts that were created after the initial deployment. Figure 8.5 shows the shared testing/staging three-stage deployment architecture.

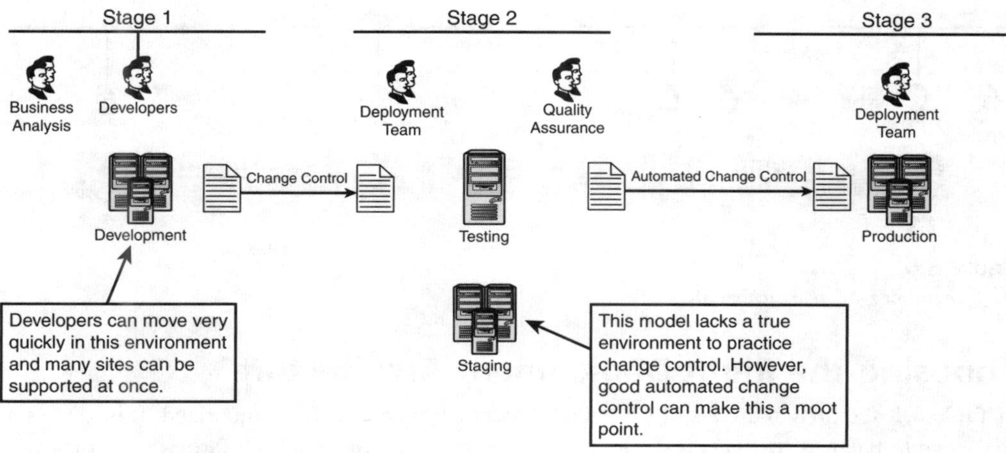

FIGURE 8.5

The shared testing/staging three-stage deployment architecture.

Using Four-Stage Deployment

In four-stage deployment, a physical stage represents each conceptual stage. This provides the greatest separation and the most flexibility in the release process. For very complex applications and ASP type data centers, this is the only way to deploy successfully.

Four-stage deployment allows each functional team an environment in which to perform its job. Developers are completely isolated in the development environment and can make changes and use new technology at will. In testing, the deployment team only has to move the changes into this environment for the quality assurance team. At this point, the quality assurance team can test the release without worrying that the deployment team is making changes and practicing the deployment. In the staging environment, the deployment team can build automated scripts and practice the deployment at will. Figure 8.6 shows the typical four-stage deployment architecture.

One of the drawbacks of the four-stage deployment architecture is increased server cost, because any new deployment requires a total of at least three extra servers, not counting production. More servers mean more administrators to manage server configuration. More servers also mean more deployment and time spent making sure the releases are consistent across all the stages.

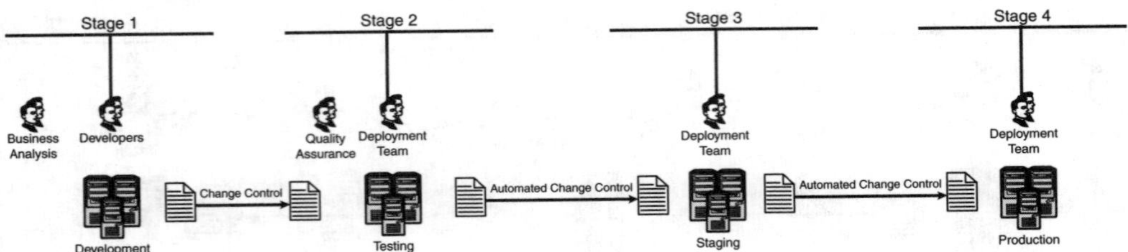

FIGURE 8.6
The four-stage deployment architecture.

Choosing the Right Deployment Architecture

In Table 8.1, the pros and cons of each deployment architecture are summarized. It is always a challenge to balance cost versus deployment effectiveness. For each Web farm, this choice will be different.

TABLE 8.1 A Simple Deployment Architecture Decision Matrix

Architecture	*Cost*	*Effectiveness*	*Other*
One-Stage	Low	Very Low	Terrible choice, not suitable for any Web farm.
Two-Stage	Low	Low	Can work for sites that are only HTML, no ASP or components.
Three-Stage Dev/Test	Med	Med	Require coordination between developers and testers. Good for single-site Web farms.
Three-Stage Test/ Staging	Med	High	Requires coordination between testers and deployment team. Allows for deployment of many sites concurrently.
Four-Stage	High	High	Requires considerable resources to manage all the stages. Great flexibility.

Fitting In Performance Testing

One of the most challenging tasks in the deployment process is load testing. Load testing is the process of simulating a large number of users and evaluating the effects of site stress. For complicated applications, a separate load testing stage is critical.

It is important to load test because, with distributed systems, the behavior of a feature with one user can be completely different with multiple users. Many organizations find that each major application revision must go through a rigorous load test evaluation.

To perform a proper load test requires an environment capable of handling the desired number of users and generating it. Also required is the tool to generate the load. There are many options for load testing tools, and each tool has different features and benefits. Figure 8.7 shows a typical load test environment.

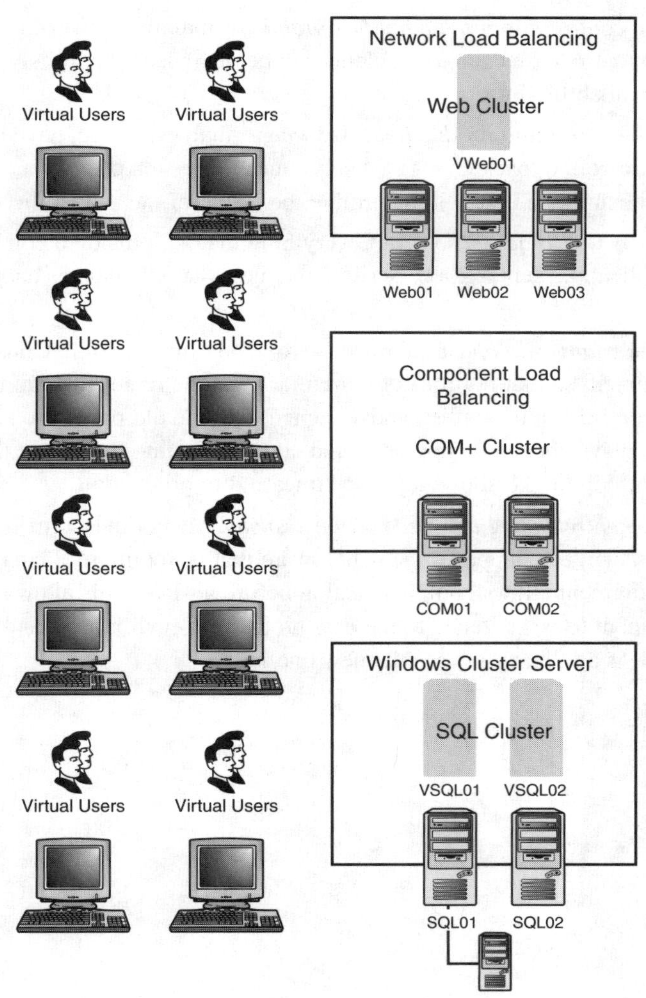

FIGURE 8.7

The typical load testing environment.

Dealing with Deployment Problems

Good deployment architectures allow for problems during the release process. Every release will have some problems, so expect them. They might include incomplete documentation of change control procedures, underestimation of time constraints, and human error.

- *When change control into production has problems*, maintain a list of responsible parties to contact so that release change problems can be diagnosed in a timely fashion, limiting application availability hits.
- *When change control into production takes longer* than estimated, have contingency plans ready for rolling back changes. Many times a decision of whether to roll back changes or finish the release will determine the extent of the availability hit.
- *Human error is unavoidable*, so script everything that isn't handled completely by a GUI tool like Application Center 2000. Scripting assures that all changes happen to every server.
- *Releasing site changes in phases* allows a zero downtime situation. Construct a deployment environment so that portions of a Web farm can be removed from production and the change control can be applied and switched with the old production system. Then the old production system can be upgraded and added back into the mix at the deployment team's leisure. Figure 8.8 shows a phased release into production.
- *Be creative when releasing new production systems*. Many times a major release of a new production system can happen on new hardware that is not in use. Planning a release with new equipment allows complete testing before go-live. This allows the old production environment to be switched to the new production environment and keeps the old one available as a fallback in case the new one fails.

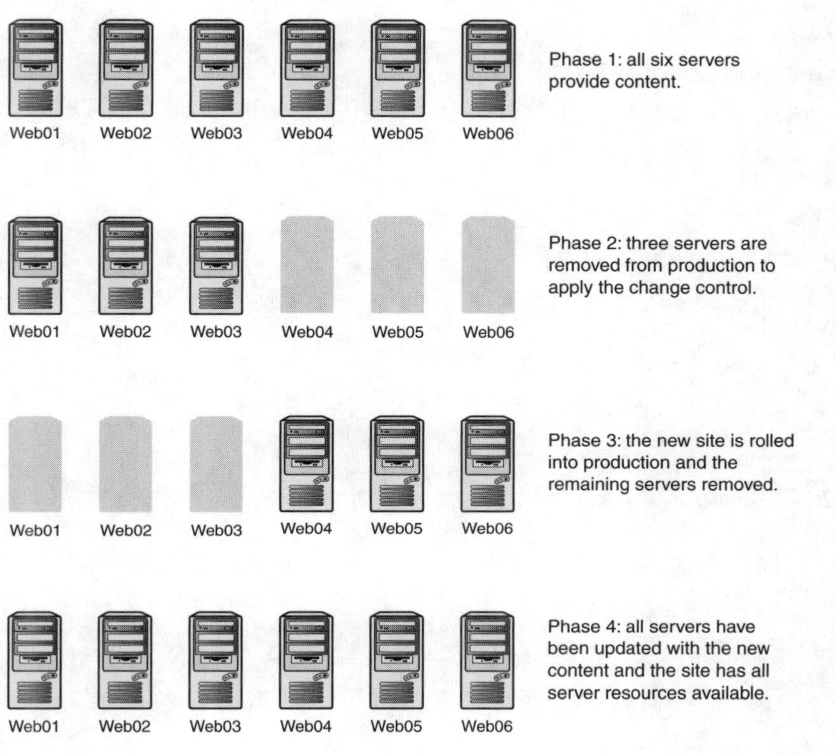
Phase 1: all six servers provide content.
Web01 Web02 Web03 Web04 Web05 Web06
Phase 2: three servers are removed from production to apply the change control.
Web01 Web02 Web03 Web04 Web05 Web06
Phase 3: the new site is rolled into production and the remaining servers removed.
Web01 Web02 Web03 Web04 Web05 Web06
Phase 4: all servers have been updated with the new content and the site has all server resources available.
Web01 Web02 Web03 Web04 Web05 Web06

FIGURE 8.8
The phased release into production.

Summary

Good deployment architectures are critical for the success of a Web farm. Understanding the four conceptual stages for successful deployment is the first step in choosing a deployment architecture. Development, testing, staging, and production all serve unique roles in the deployment process. An organization should invest in building a three- or four-stage deployment architecture as described in this chapter. These architectures provide the highest level of flexibility, availability, and manageability for any Web farm deployment effort.

Using Internet Information Services in a Web Farm

CHAPTER

9

IN THIS CHAPTER

Internet Information Services (IIS) is a key component in a Web farm. IIS provides the base services Windows needs to serve content to Internet users. Without IIS, a Web farm cannot communicate with users over any of the standard Internet protocols supported by IIS. It includes built-in support for the HTTP, FTP, SMTP, and NNTP Internet protocols. It is flexible enough to listen for network traffic on any port and hand off the request to the appropriate processing engine, depending on the protocol of the incoming network request. IIS has an advanced administrative console that provides complete control over all its features.

IIS is the platform of choice for custom Internet applications. It uses Active Server Pages (ASP), the most popular programming paradigm for applications on the Internet. Combined with high availability and ease of use, custom ASP applications run some of the largest Web sites in the world. IIS provides quick development time for simple applications and is still robust enough for more complicated endeavors. IIS handles serving static HTML pages as well as it does custom applications. With the coming .NET platform, IIS plays a key role here as well. IIS is the preferred application platform for ASP.NET, the next generation of ASP built on the .NET framework. To learn more about the role IIS plays in Web farms, let's explore the goals for this chapter.

The goals of this chapter are to

- Cover advanced topics relating to IIS, including the metabase, security, ISAPI extensibility architecture, custom applications, and monitoring IIS.
- Establish best practices for using IIS in a Web farm. Topics include creating multiple sites, using application protection, using default documents, and setting custom error pages.
- Script changes to the IIS metabase using the programmatic interfaces of IIS. This includes learning how to create a Web site, change properties of virtual directories, and modify global parameters of IIS.

Advanced IIS Concepts

IIS is a very robust and complicated server technology. There are many books written completely on administering IIS. Many of these books cover some of the topics covered in this section. This section summarizes some of the more challenging tasks and explains the inner workings of IIS. A basic understanding of IIS administrative concepts is assumed.

NOTE

For more information on administering IIS, check out *IIS 5.0 Administration* (ISBN: 0-672-31964-0)

This section covers the most important concepts for administering IIS in a Web farm environment. Topics include analyzing the structure of the metabase from the Local Machine object to the folder and file objects in a Web site. IIS security is reviewed in depth, with a focus on techniques that apply to Web farms, such as anonymous authentication and SSL. IIS's robust application architecture used for custom applications is diagrammed with an emphasis on understanding how the architecture evolved and how it provides high availability for Web sites. The Internet Server Application Programming Interface (ISAPI) is covered. ISAPI filters and extensions are explained from the administrator's perspective. Finally, monitoring IIS is considered with an in-depth analysis of all the Performance Monitor counters that provide information for the performance and availability of IIS itself.

Analyzing the Structure of the Metabase

The *metabase* is a local repository of configuration settings for various Microsoft Server technologies. The goal of this section is to become familiar with how the information contained within the metabase is organized and to understand the important information it contains.

The metabase is similar to the Windows Registry in that data is stored in a hierarchical manner with nodes containing subnodes. Each node in the metabase is called a *key*. Each key is a specific type, such as `IIsComputer` or `IIsWebFile`. Each key type has a corresponding defined set of properties called *metabase properties*. Metabase information is stored in a local file called `METABASE.BIN` by default.

IIS uses the hierarchical structure of the metabase mostly by mirroring it to the structure of a Web site. Each folder or file in the layout of a site can have a corresponding key in the metabase. This provides a mechanism for uniquely identifying configuration information for any object in a Web site. Figure 9.1 shows the metabase hierarchy for IIS, mapped to the administrative console. Most of the mappings are one to one, but a Web site and the Web service actually map to multiple keys. The Web site in the administrative console maps to three IIS objects: the `IIsWebServer`, `IIsWebVirtualDir`, and potentially the `IIsCertMapper` keys. The Web service maps to three objects: the `IIsWebService`, `IIsWebInfo`, and `IIsFilters` keys.

Configuring metabase properties at a particular key, such as an `IIsWebDirectory` key, affects how this directory and all its children behave. Changes to the parent are propagated to the children because the metabase uses property inheritance. For example, the top-level metabase key for the entire Web server is called the `IIsWebService` key and is represented by the computer node in the ISS administrative console. This key contains information about the security authentication schemes configured for the entire Web server. By default, Windows Integrated Authentication is checked, which means that all the `IIsWebServer` keys under the `IIsWebService` key also use Windows Integrated Authentication. To override this setting for the entire server, uncheck Windows Integrated Authentication at the `IIsWebService` level. To override this setting for say, the Default Web site a single `IIsWebServer` instance, uncheck it at the Default Web site level in the IIS administrative console.

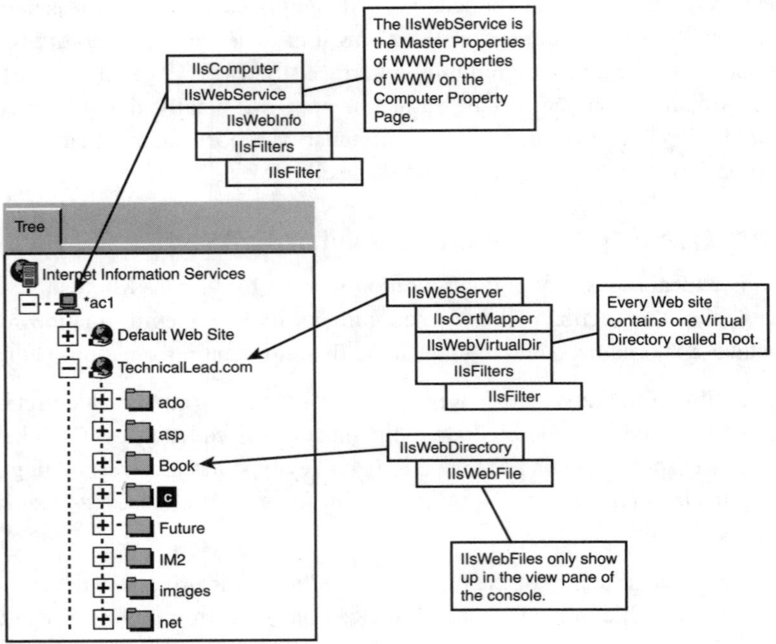

FIGURE 9.1
The hierarchical keys of the metabase.

Objects in the metabase are addressable through a path, similar to a file system path. This path is called an `ADsPath` because the administrative interfaces that enable programmatic manipulation of metabase configuration are based on the Active Directory COM interface specification. Active Directory is more than just a tool to manage users and computers on a network; it is a specification for creating a generic object model to represent hierarchical systems. All references to object paths in the metabase begin with `IIS:`. To address the `IIsWebService` by `ADsPath`, use `IIS://LM/W3SVC`. To address the first `IIsWebServer` by `ADsPath` inside the `IIsWebServices` key, the path is `IIS://LM/W3SVC/1`.

Using MetaEdit 2.1

MetaEdit 2.1 is a metabase configuration tool available as a free download from Microsoft. This tool enables editing of the metabase directly and is similar to the Windows Registry tool `REGEDIT.EXE`.

> **NOTE**
>
> To download MetaEdit 2.1, visit `http://download.microsoft.com`. Microsoft has further information regarding using MetaEdit 2.1 at `http://support.microsoft.com/support/kb/articles/Q232/0/68.ASP`.

Be sure to backup the metabase of IIS before making any changes using MetaEdit 2.1. To backup the metabase, right click on the computer node in the IIS console and select Backup/Restore Configuration from the menu. This launches the Configuration Backup/Restore dialog shown in Figure 9.2. Click the Create Backup button and fill in an descriptive name to create a backup. For example, in Figure 9.2, the Clean Install backup was created before making any changes to the metabase. Selecting this entry and clicking restore returns the metabase to the state it was right after installing IIS.

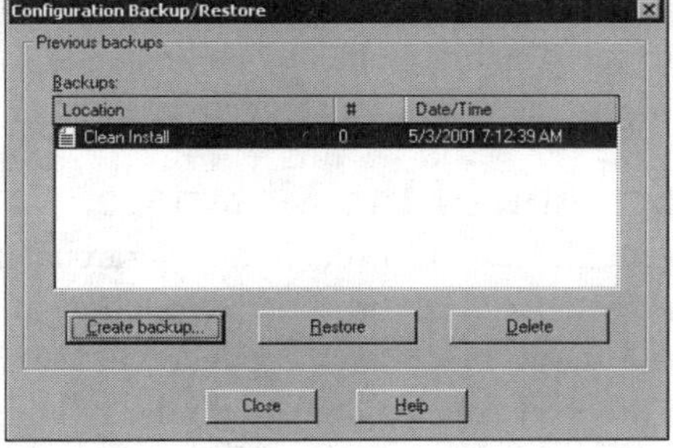

FIGURE 9.2
The Configuration Backup/Restore dialog.

> **CAUTION**
>
> Incorrectly configuring the IIS metabase using MetaEdit 2.1 can cause catastrophic failures and render IIS unable to start. Be sure to back up the metabase before making any changes.

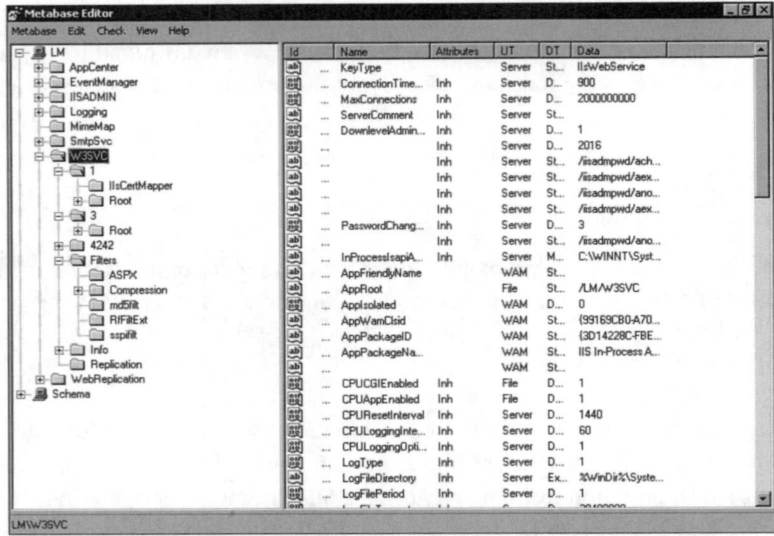

FIGURE 9.3

The main screen of MetaEdit 2.1.

Figure 9.3 shows the Metabase Editor with the top-level key, `LM`, expanded. LM corresponds to the `IIsComputer` key. The rest of the keys are for different applications, including Application Center 2000, IIS, and Site Server. The hierarchical view in MetaEdit corresponds to the `AdsPath` for an individual object.

Understanding the Schema of the Metabase

There are a number of different classes of objects in the hierarchical organization of the metabase. The schema of the metabase is defined on a branch located at the root level of the metabase hierarchy. Figure 9.4 shows this branch expanded in MetaEdit 2.1. This schema is a simple collection of Active Directory schema objects similar to what is found in the Active Directory for Windows 2000. Notice that `IIsComputer` is selected. In the property pane, two properties define the properties possible for an `IIsComputer` object and the other objects that can be contained within an `IIsComputer` object.

An *Active Directory Schema* is a collection of objects that describes the properties, methods, and hierarchical relationship among objects in an Active Directory implementation.

Important Objects of the Metabase

The metabase for IIS 5.0 contains at least 50 distinct classes of objects. Many of the objects relate to other services such as FTP, NNTP, and SMTP. The IIS 5.0 documentation contains a complete list of metabase objects, their properties, methods, and hierarchical organization. The goal of this section is to point out a few important objects that relate to the functioning of IIS in a Web farm. This is by no means intended to replace the complete reference. To find this complete object reference, use the IIS help that is installed at the default Web site located locally on a server that has IIS installed at `http://localhost/iishelp/iis/misc/default.asp`. From there, select the Index tab and type **`IIS Admin Objects`**; then select the Reference topic.

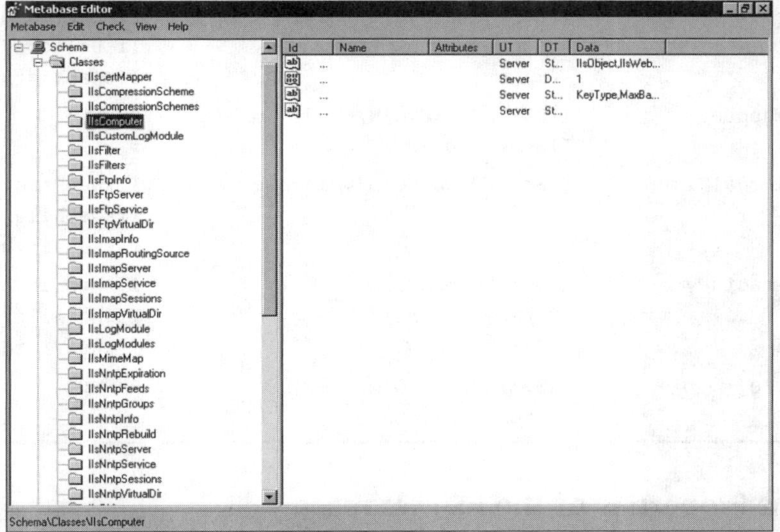

FIGURE 9.4

An `IIsComputer` object with its schema definition.

Table 9.1 lists the metabase objects of importance for configuring IIS. Included are the generic `ADsPath` and hierarchical organization information for `IIsComputer`, `IIsWebService`, `IIsFilters`, `IIsFilter`, `IIsWebInfo`, `IIsWebServer`, `IIsCertMapper`, `IIsWebVirtualDir`, `IIsWebDir`, `IIsWebFile`. In the `ADsPath` column of Table 9.1, substitute `LM` with `localhost` or a remote machine name.

TABLE 9.1 General Information for Metabase Objects of IIS

Name	ADsPath	*Can Contain*
IIsComputer	IIS://LM	IIsWebService
IIsWebService	IIS://LM/W3SVC	IIsFilters, IIsWebServer, IIsWebInfo
IIsFilters	IIS://LM/W3SVC/Filters	IIsFilter
IIsFilter	IIS://LM/W3SVC/Filters/FilterName	None
IIsWebInfo	IIS://LM/W3SVC/INFO	None
IIsWebServer	IIS://LM/W3SVC/N (where N is a number for each Web site)	IIsCertMapper, IIsFilters, IIsWebVirtualDir
IIsCertMapper	IIS://LM/W3SVC/N/IIsCertMapper	None
IIsWebVirtualDir	IIS://LM/W3SVC/N/vDirName	IIsWebDirectory, IIsWebFile, IIsWebVirtualDir
IIsWebDirectory	IIS://LM/W3SVC/N/vDirName/DirName	IIsWebDirectory, IIsWebFile, IIsWebVirtualDir
IIsWebFile	IIS://LM/W3SVC/N/vDirName/FileName	None

Important Properties of the IIS Metabase

All the metabase objects contain standard ADSI methods and properties when accessed through script. Because metabase properties are inheritable and can be found on multiple object types, the next section covers important properties in the IIS Web server portion of the metabase. Configuring the metabase programmatically is covered later in this chapter.

AspAllowSessionState

The AspAllowSessionState property enables session state persistence for the ASP application as a Boolean value. By default, session state is enabled, and each new connection results in a new session object. This enables access to the session object and causes Session_OnStart and Session_OnEnd to fire from the Global.asa. Finally, a session-oriented ASPSessionID cookie (it expires when the browser is closed) is sent to the client. If the value is FALSE, session state is disabled. This property is can be set on the IIsWebService, IIsWebServer, IIsWebVirtualDir, and IIsWebDir objects and is inheritable. To disable session state for the entire server, edit the master properties of the WWW service and select the Home Directory tab. From this tab, click the Configuration button and select the App Options tab. From this tab, uncheck the Enable Session State check box. Figure 9.5 shows the Master WWW Properties App Options tab from the IIS console.

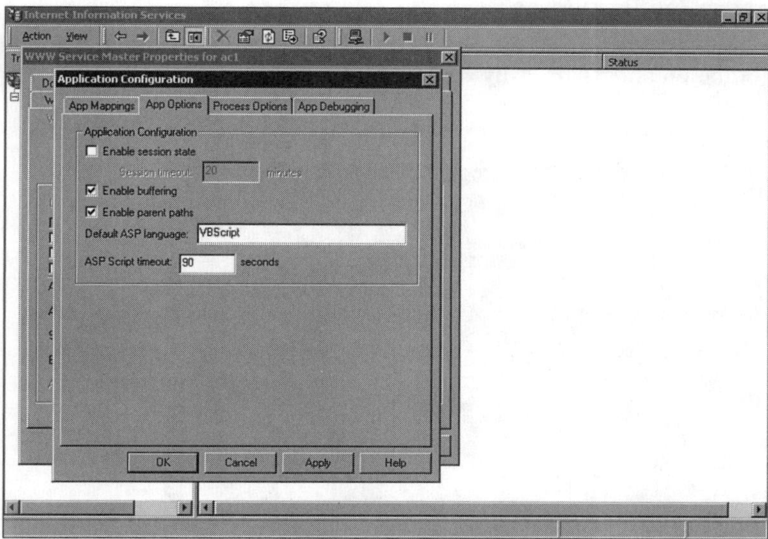

FIGURE 9.5
Disabling session state from the console.

`AspProcessorThreadMax`

IIS uses the `AspProcessorThreadMax` property as the maximum number of worker threads per processor to create. `AspProcessorThreadMax` cannot be set from the IIS console. It is a long number that by default is set to `25`. This property is available on `IIsWebService`, `IIsWebServer`, `IIsWebVirtualDir`, and `IIsWebDirectory`.

The true nature of this property is a topic of much debate. According to the IIS help, this property actually controls the number of ASP requests that can execute simultaneously. Meaning that regardless of processor utilization, if more than 25 ASP pages are being processed, some form of context switching (a thread can switch from processing one ASP page to another) must occur for all the requests to finish. It cautions that changing this value is unnecessary in most circumstances unless the ASP pages make out-of-process calls to external processes locally or otherwise that lock threads waiting for results. In contrast, according to the IIS 5.0 Resource Kit, `AspProcessorThreadMax` is tied to the new thread-gating features of IIS and is adjusted automatically based on load.

NEW TERM *ASP thread gating* is the process by which IIS automatically increases and decreases the number of threads handling ASP requests based on CPU utilization, never exceeding the `AspProcessorThreadMax` setting.

IIS Performance Tab Properties

IIS supports a number of performance options for Web sites of differing configurations and sizes. Some of these options are easily configurable from the Performance tab shown in Figure 9.6.

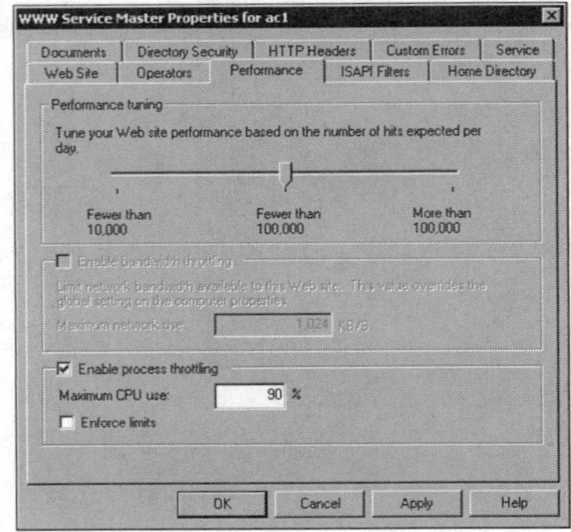

FIGURE 9.6

The Performance Tab of the `IIsWebService` *object.*

The first portion of this dialog affects the number of outstanding sockets that can be queued. The Performance Tuning slider corresponds to the `ServerSize metabase` property. This property can have three values, 0, 1, and 2. These values correspond to the expected number of hits per day that can have the values fewer than 10,000 hits, fewer than 100,000 hits, and more than 100,000 hits respectively. These values are used to determine the `ServerListenBacklog` property, which determines the number of outstanding sockets that can be queued. These properties can be set on the `IIsWebService`, and `IIsWebServer` objects.

TIP

To get an estimate for the number of hits for a Web site, look at a single day's log in the c:\winnt\system32\inetsvr\logs directory and count the number of lines in the log file which corresponds to the number of hits.

The second portion of this dialog enables bandwidth throttling. The goal of bandwidth throttling is to limit the amount of network traffic from a Web site or Web server. The end result is the site still serves content from all users, but at a maximum rate governed by the metabase property `MaxBandwidth` that can be set on the `IIsWebService` and `IIsWebServer` objects.

This property does not behave as prescribed. Instead of slowing down the transfer of requests, any requests that exceed the bandwidth limit imposed by this property are dropped. These drops show up as failed requests, like missing images, stylesheets, or other GET requests on a HTML page. Simply enabling bandwidth throttling on the top-level IIS object and setting the value to 1KBps, and then doing the same for the target Web site, can demonstrate this behavior. Once these settings are configured and IIS is restarted, browse to a page that is heavy in images and content and refresh the page repeatedly. Eventually some of the images will fail to display due to exceeding the bandwidth limit.

There is a property mentioned in the IIS help called `MaxBandWidthBlocked` that appears to prevent the dropping of requests and sets the length of the request queue. According to the IIS help, the default behavior of this property is to queue all pending requests until bandwidth is available, but instead it appears that the default value is zero, which means to drop all requests. Even after using MetaEdit and adding this property to the top-level `IIsComputer` node and setting it explicitly to -1 (the default value to queue all requests), the dropped requests continued to occur. The conclusion is that this feature does not work as described and while it will limit bandwidth, there is no way to queue pending requests. The dropping of request renders this feature useless for any real Web farm.

The final portion of the Performance tab is used to limit CPU utilization for a particular `IIsWebService` or `IISWebServer` object. There are numerous properties that affect the way CPU limits work, but the user-interface only allows the configuration of `CPULimitsEnabled`, `CPULimitLogEvent`, `CPULimitPriority` and `CPULimitProcStop`. If the Enable process throttling checkbox is checked the `CPULimitsEnabled` property is set to 1. The Maximum CPU use corresponds to the `CPULimitLogEvent` which in the metabase is stored as $1/1000^{th}$ of the actual percentage (100% corresponds to 100,000). This property is used to determine when to mark the event log that a CPU limit was exceeded. The enforce limits check box sets the `CPULimitPriority` and `CPULimitProcStop` to values that correspond to the `CPULimitLogEvent` value. The `CPULimitPriority` is used by IIS to determine if a CPU limit was exceeded, and, if so, sets the offending process to Idle Class priority, which means it will sleep till the next processing account reset as specified by the metabase property `CPUResetInterval`. The `CPULimitProcStop` metabase property corresponds to the amount of CPU percent (in $1/1000^{th}$ again) a process must exceed before IIS halts the process until the next `CPUResetInterval` has passed.

ASP Thread-Gating Properties

The ASP thread gate is a new feature of IIS 5.0. IIS uses thread gating to tune the performance of IIS based on CPU use trends. A thread gate is IIS deciding from a maximum thread threshold compared to a lower and upper bound CPU utilization how many threads will effectively handle the current volume of requests. For example, an IIS server is currently under light load, with a CPU utilization of 25%. During this condition, IIS will create as many worker threads (per processor) as it can with an upper limit specified by `AspThreadProcessorMax`. In the case of a dual processor server, IIS creates 50 threads to handle incoming requests. As CPU utilization grows to 85%, the number of requests far exceeds the number of threads, and context switching becomes a major factor that can negatively affect performance. To eliminate this problem, IIS scales back the number of threads available to handle requests, effectively freeing the CPU from handling expensive thread context switching.

Six properties control how IIS handles thread gating outside of `AspThreadProcessorMax`. These properties are available on `IIsWebService`, `IIsWebServer`, `IIsWebVirtualDir`, and `IIsWebDirectory`. Table 9.2 summaries these properties and explains how they affect ASP thread gating.

TABLE 9.2 Summary of ASP Thread Gating Metabase Properties

Name	*Data Type*	*Default Value*	*Notes*
`AspThreadGateEnabled`	Boolean	`False`	The IIS help says this is enabled by default, but it is not correct.
`AspThreadGateLoadLow`	Long	`50%`	Lower end of CPU utilization range in which to keep the server. IIS increases thread count to reach this level if possible.
`AspThreadGateLoadHigh`	Long	`80%`	Higher end of CPU utilization range in which to keep the server. IIS decreases thread count as CPU utilization approaches or exceeds this level.

TABLE 9.2 Continued

Name	*Data Type*	*Default Value*	*Notes*
`AspThreadGateSleepDelay`	Long	`100msec`	When thread gating is in effect, this property specifies how long to defer thread requests, in milliseconds.
`AspThreadGateSleepMax`	Long	`50` times	This property controls the number of times a thread can be deferred.
`AspThreadGateTimeSlice`	Long	`1000msec`	This property specifies the interval during which IIS checks the current CPU utilization for thread-gating statistics.

IIS does not provide an interface for configuring these properties so they must be configured through script. Enable these features cautiously because they can dramatically affect the performance of a site under load. In some cases, these settings could negatively impact the performance of a site even though the server would function normally under the load that caused thread gating to fire.

CAUTION

Be sure to performance test any use of ASP thread gating. In some instances, enabling this feature might be detrimintal to a Web site.

ASP Queuing Properties

As requests for ASP pages are made of an IIS server, they are stored in a queue. This is called the *ASP request queue*. Under normal load conditions there should be little or no activity in this queue because there are ample CPU and threads to handle all requests. During heavy load, there are three main properties that IIS uses to determine how to treat requests in the queue.

These properties are available on `IIsWebService`, `IIsWebServer`, `IIsWebVirtualDir`, and `IIsWebDirectory`. Table 9.3 summaries these properties and explains how they affect the ASP request queue.

TABLE 9.3 Summary of ASP Request Queuing Metabase Properties

Name	*Data Type*	*Default Value*	*Notes*
`AspRequestQueueMax`	Long	`3000`	The IIS help is incorrect and says `500`. If there are more than 3000 items in the queue, then clients receive the `Server Too Busy` error.
`AspQueueConnectionTestTime`	Long	`3` seconds	If a request has been in the queue longer than this value, IIS will test the connection to make sure the client is still waiting for the response.
`AspQueueTimeout`	Long	`-1` (none)	The time in milliseconds before a request will be flushed from the queue. By default, requests are never flushed from the queue.

ASP Script Engine Properties

The metabase provides control of how ASP caches script engines, how it caches ASP files, and how long a script runs before it times out. For example, when an ASP page request comes in, ASP creates a scripting engine to process the request. It then stores this scripting engine in the scripting engine cache for reuse by other requests. The ASP page that is requested is compiled and stored in the ASP script file cache.

These properties are available on `IIsWebService`, `IIsWebServer`, `IIsWebVirtualDir`, and `IIsWebDirectory`. Table 9.4 summarizes these properties and explains how they affect ASP script engine properties.

TABLE 9.4 Summary of ASP script engine metabase properties

Name	*Data Type*	*Default Value*	*Notes*
`AspScriptEngineCacheMax`	Long	`125` engines	The maximum number of script engines to cache.
`AspScriptFileCacheSize`	Long	`250` files	The number of precompiled scripts to cache. A value of `-1` means to cache all ASP files.
`AspScriptTimeout`	Long	`90` seconds	The maximum time before the ASP engine terminates a script and writes an event to the event log.

`MaxBandwidth`

The `MaxBandwidth` property is used to set the maximum amount of network bandwidth available for applications under IIS. This property is available at the `IIsComputer` level and when set controls the entire bandwidth available for all Web sites on the server. Figure 9.7 shows the default property page of the `IIsComputer` object on a server. This property page is accessible by right-clicking the computer name and selecting Properties in the IIS console. `MaxBandwidth` is also a property of `IIsWebServer` (a Web site in the console) and when set at the Web site level overrides the settings at the global level. The default value of this property is `-1`, which means Enable Bandwidth Throttling is unchecked. A positive value checks that box and sets the value in bytes. For example, a setting of `1024` puts a 1 in the Maximum Network Use text box. Stop and restart IIS for a changed `MaxBandwidth` value to take effect.

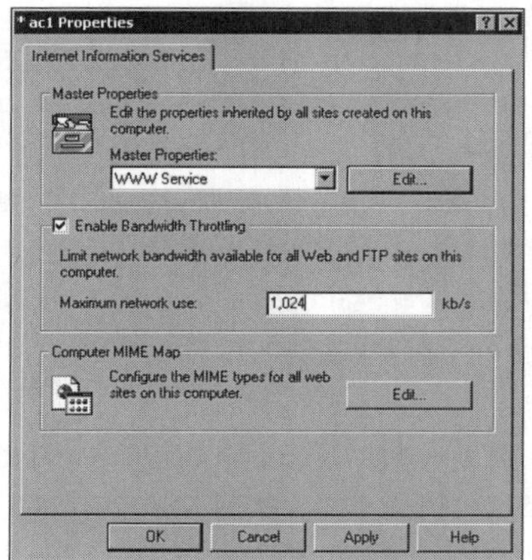

FIGURE 9.7

The `MaxBandwidth` property setting at the server level.

`ServerComment`

The `ServerComment` property is the friendly name of a Web site (`IIsWebServer` object) in string form. This property is set from the console properties of a Web site in the Web Site tab, Web Site Identification section, and Description text box. The `ServerComment` property is used in the console as the top-level name of a Web site. This property is available at the `IIsWebService` level but has no affect on the console. Surprisingly, this property is inheritable.

`AppFriendlyName`

The `AppFriendlyName` property is the friendly name of a Web application in string form. This property is set from the console properties of a Web application in the Home Directory tab, Application Settings section, and Application Name text box. This property is available at the `IIsWebService`, `IIsWebServer`, `IIsWebVirtualDir`, and `IIsWebDirectory`. It is not inheritable.

Understanding IIS Security

IIS Security has three components: Anonymous Access and Authentication Control, IP and Domain Name Restrictions, and Secure Communications Using SSL. Anonymous Access and Authentication Control handles the methods for authenticating users to the resources in a Web farm. IP and Domain Name Restrictions allows administrators to restrict access by IP address or top-level domain name to resources in a Web farm. Finally, Securing Communications provides an easy and standards-based mechanism for encrypting communications between clients and the Web server for commerce and other personally sensitive transactions.

IIS has a rich set of security options available at every level in a Web site. With public Internet sites, security settings are normally maintained at the root level. These settings cascade to all virtual directories, directories, and files under the root site. Changing the security at any level means that certain folders or even single files of a site could use completely different access mechanisms. This is a viable option for creating an administrative Web site that has special access requirements but is located under the same domain as the public site. For example, `www.technicallead.com`, an anonymous access site, could have administrative pages for submitting articles located at `www.technicallead.com/admin` that require Client Certificates to gain access. This example also applies to domain and IP address restrictions and securing sites with SSL.

IIS 5.0 supports four basic strategies for authenticating users to Web content and applications. They are called Anonymous, Basic Authentication, Digest Authentication, and Windows Integrated Authentication.

IIS 5.0 supports denying access to everything but a list of specific IP addresses, groups of IP addresses, and domain names (requires a reverse DNS lookup, an expensive process). By default, all IP addresses and domain names are allowed access.

IIS 5.0 supports secure communications using SSL and provides a fifth way to authenticate users using Client Certificates. It provides a simple way to import a security key from one of the many registered Certificate Authorities (CA) on the Internet.

Locating Security Options in the IIS Console

Security options are configured from the properties of any object in the IIS namespace, including the Web server, Web site, virtual directory, folder, and file level. For example, right-click on the default Web site and select Properties. Then select the Directory Security tab, shown in Figure 9.8. The Directory Security tab controls anonymous access and authentication control, IP address and domain name restrictions, and secure communications using SSL.

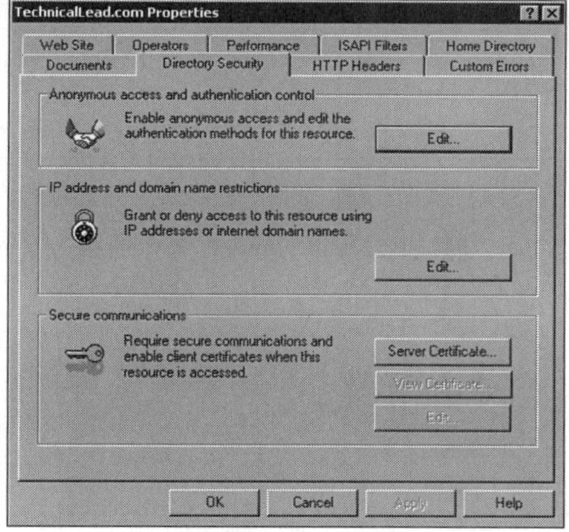

FIGURE 9.8
The Directory Security tab of a Web site.

Configuring Authentication Methods

Authentication methods are means by which IIS establishes an identity to users of resources from the Web. These methods are configured from the Authentication Methods dialog shown in Figure 9.9. To access this dialog, click the Edit button in the Anonymous Access and Authentication Control section of the Directory Security tab.

IIS supports multiple levels of security per resource. By default a new Web site is configured to use anonymous access and Integrated Windows Authentication. IIS follows a set of rules to determine which form of authentication to use when anonymous access is used along with other authentication methods. These rules are shown in Table 9.5. Anonymous access takes priority over all the other forms of access, so uncheck Anonymous Access to use any other form.

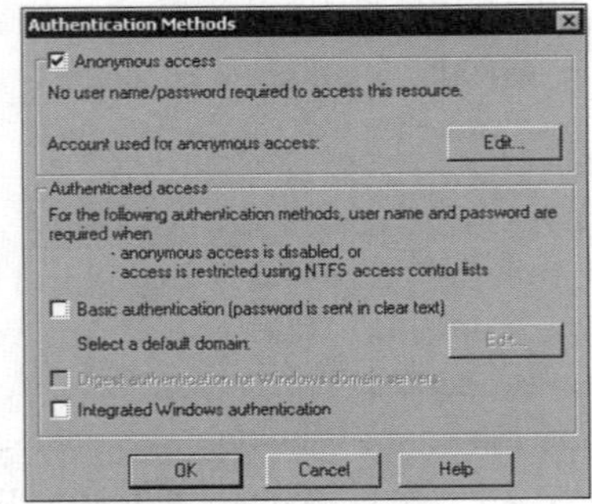

FIGURE 9.9
The Authentication Methods dialog.

TABLE 9.5 Using Anonymous Access with Other Authentication Methods

Security Mechanism	*Rule*
Client Certificates	If Require Client Certificates or Allow Client Certificates is enabled, this security mechanism overrides anonymous access.
Windows Integrated Authentication	Used only if Anonymous Access fails.
Digest Authentication	Used only if Anonymous Access fails.
Basic Authentication	Used only if Anonymous Access fails. If Windows Integrated Authentication is used in conjunction, that too must fail before Basic is used.

Using Anonymous Authentication

Anonymous access is the access mechanism used with most public Internet sites. Any user from the Internet can gain access to Web site content. IIS creates a proxy account when IIS is first installed on a server. The account is named `IUSR_<servername>` and is a member of the Guests group. Whenever a Web with anonymous access receives a request from a user on the Internet, IIS will access the resource using this account. Use NTFS file system security to restrict access to resources by explicitly removing the Everyone special user designation and granting access only to specific users and groups. This effectively prevents Guest group members from accessing a particular file or folder in a Web farm.

The details of anonymous access are handled from the Anonymous User Account dialog. This dialog is located under any Web site or virtual directory's Directory Security tab as shown in Figure 9.6 earlier in the chapter. From this tab select the Edit button in the Anonymous Access and Authentication control. This launches the Authentication Methods dialog shown in Figure 9.7 earlier in the chapter. From this dialog, click the Edit button in the Anonymous Access section, which launches the Anonymous User Account dialog shown in Figure 9.10.

FIGURE 9.10
The Anonymous User Account dialog.

There are actually two forms of anonymous access, depending on whether IIS controls the password. The Allow IIS to Control Password check box actually does much more than just control the password. IIS uses a special security authentication DLL to simulate the access to local and remote resources when this box is checked. Even if the IUSR_<servername> account is disabled, resources previously enabled for anonymous users are still available. When this check box is not used and the administrator controls the password, all standard security rules and behavior apply. Verify the difference by creating a local account and changing it to be the anonymous access user and enter the password. When this account is disabled, the files on the local machine for the Web site will no longer be accessible by anonymous users.

Having IIS control the password also changes the behavior of the Web site when accessing remote COM+ applications. If IIS is not controlling the password, then the account that runs as the Web site must be present on the remote machine to gain access. This is not true if IIS controls the password. In effect, all COM+ applications are available to users from this site if the remote machines have the proper DCOM ports exposed in both directions. This is an obvious security risk but, because DCOM is not considered a viable Internet protocol and because it simplifies security for public sites that use Anonymous Access, it is recommended to allow IIS to control the password. See Chapter 10, "Using Component Services (COM+) in a Web Farm," for more information on COM+.

CAUTION

Be sure that any Web server exposed to the Internet limits access only to ports that need to be exposed such as 80 and 443. RPC, and hence COM+ use any port above 1024 by default and port should be blocked from users on the Internet.

Using Basic/Clear Text Authentication

If a Web site allows Basic Authentication and a user requests resources with ACLs that don't match the IUSR anonymous account, the browser displays a user authentication dialog. This dialog is a standard user challenge dialog and expects a username and password that is sent to the server in clear text. The server then attempts to impersonate the user with those credentials and gain access to the resource. If a file has ACL restricting access to only a specific group or user, then the username and password sent to the server must match with a valid member of the group or user in question. If this user has rights to the resource, then IIS will process the request. If not, the user is either challenged again or eventually receives an HTTP 401.3—Access Denied by ACL on Resource message. With Basic Authentication, the username is sent in clear text unless the request is issued to a page that requires SSL. In that case the whole conversation is encrypted.

Using Digest Authentication

Digest Authentication is a more advanced form of Basic Authentication that uses a hashing algorithm to transmit an encrypted password to the Web server. This hashing process mangles the user password in such a way that determining the original value cannot be deciphered from the hash. This is called a *one-way hash.*

Digest Authentication works because the client and server communicate well-known information that is used in the hashing process. A requirement of Digest Authentication is that the domain controller of the server know the user password in clear text. When a client connects to the server, the server sends the client information that is used to compute the hash along with the user name, password, domain, time stamp, and other information. This hashed value and the information used by the client to create the hash are passed to the server in clear text. The server then adds the client information to a plain text copy it has of the client's password and hashes all of the information. If the password is correct, this should produce an exact copy of the hash performed on the client.

The advantage of Digest Authentication is that the password is not sent to the server in clear text, so it can't be intercepted and used. Firewalls, proxy servers, and WebDAV all support Digest Authentication because its nature doesn't require any special configurations. Support is primarily dependent on the browser used to access the resources. Digest Authentication is an HTTP 1.1 feature, and many browsers do not have support for this security mechanism. Users of non-compliant browsers receive an error from the server when accessing resources secured in this manner.

For a Web farm, Digest Authentication could be used to lock down administrative areas of a Web site. But because this mechanism requires a Windows 2000 domain controller to store the passwords in clear text and a user account in Active Directory, this mechanism would likely be too expensive to support a members-only area of a Web site. If cost is not an issue, then create a Windows 2000 domain account for each member to use Digest Authentication from a public Web site.

Using Windows Integrated Authentication

Windows Integrated Authentication uses standard Windows NT accounts and requires that the client browser establish an NTLM authentication with the server. This method works only for intranets and will not work across firewalls or proxy servers. Use Windows Integrated Authentication to use existing user accounts in a Windows 2000 domain for intranets.

Configuring IP Address and Domain Name Restrictions

Blocking access to Internet resources such as a Web server, Web site, virtual directory, folder, or file for a specific IP address is a powerful feature of IIS. It is used to grant or deny access to Web sites from an IP Address layer. It can either deny access to IIS resources from IP addresses that have attacked the Web server in the past or grant access only to specific IP addresses, such as a group of administrators. For example, `www.TechnicalLead.com` has an administrative portion of the site that allows the publishing of articles by contributors over the Internet. This administrative site is simply a subdirectory under the main site. It has special domain and IP address restrictions that deny access to all IP addresses accept those of contributing authors.

From the Directory Security tab, click Edit in the IP Address and Domain Name Restrictions section to launch the IP Address and Domain Name Restrictions dialog, shown in Figure 9.11.

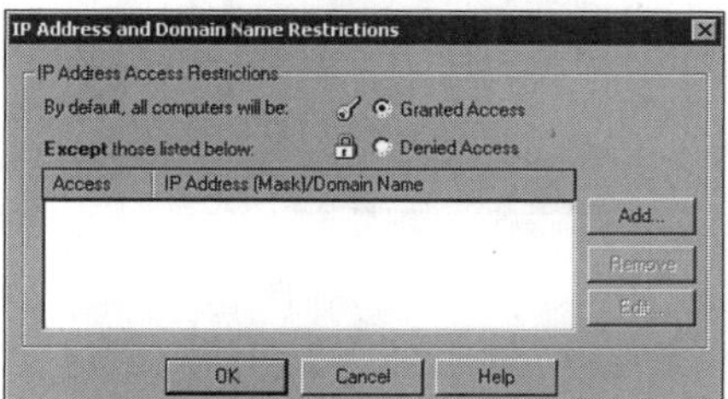

FIGURE 9.11
The IP Address and Domain Name Restrictions dialog.

By default, all computers will be granted access except those that are listed in the exception box. This means that any IP address, group of computers, or domain name added to this list receives an HTTP 403.6—Forbidden: IP Address Rejected error when it attempts to access the IIS resource. Select the Denied Access radio button to restrict access to everyone except those listed in the exception box.

Add IP Addresses, groups of computers, and domain names by clicking the Add button on the IP Address and Domain Name Restrictions dialog previously shown in Figure 9.11. Figure 9.12 shows the Deny Access On dialog where single computers, groups, and domains are restricted. For a single IP address, type it in the IP Address box.

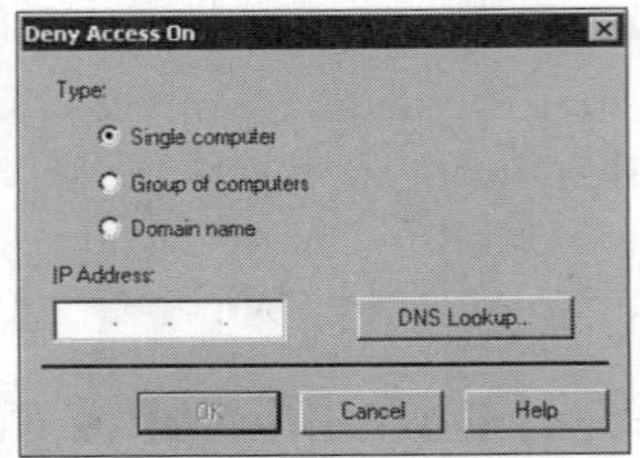

FIGURE 9.12
The Deny Access On dialog for a single IP address.

Select the Group of Computers radio button and the dialog changes to the one seen in Figure 9.13. Type the appropriate network address and subnet mask to restrict an entire range of IP addresses. For example, to restrict an entire class C address type **`172.20.1.1`** in the Network ID box and use the subnet mask of `255.255.0.0`. All computers from the `172.20` subnet will be restricted from accessing this resource.

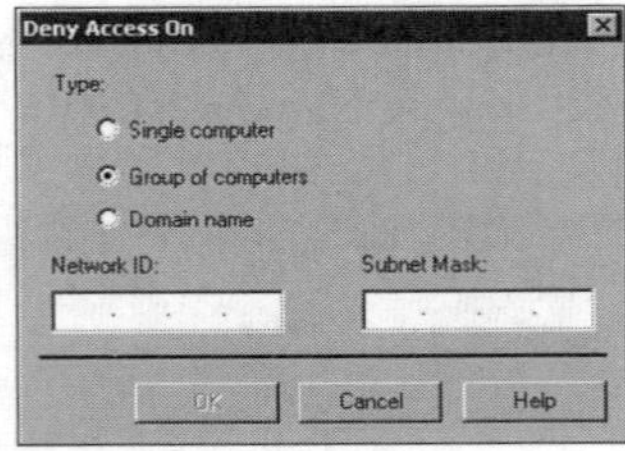

FIGURE 9.13
The Deny Access on dialog for a group of computers.

To restrict access for an entire domain, such as `www.technicalLead.com`, requires a reverse DNS lookup. Use this feature conservatively because every access attempt to the server costs considerable resources to perform this reverse DNS lookup in the process of handling a request.

Configuring Secure Communications Using SSL

Secure Sockets Layer (SSL) is a transport protocol developed by Netscape Corporation that has been adopted by the Web community for all secure transactions. SSL is intended to provide privacy and reliability between two communicating applications (such as a browser and a Web server) in a secure manner. SSL is not an approved RFC, but a derivative work called Transport Layer Security that was developed and is available for review at `ftp://ftp.isi.edu/in-notes/rfc2246.txt`. Netscape also has information on SSL at `www.netscape.com`.

SSL is used to secure transactions between clients of a Web farm. Any communication that involves private confidential user information is a candidate for SSL encryption. Examples today include registration information, e-mail, and credit card information.

SSL uses a server-side root certificate to establish creditability and authenticity of the secure transaction. This certificate is generated and guaranteed by a third party called a Certificate Authority (CA). When a client establishes a secure connection to a resource that uses SSL, typically by using the HTTPS URL designation, this certificate is compared with a list of known CAs installed on most browsers. Figure 9.16 shows an Internet Explorer Certificates dialog with a list of root certificates that are installed by default with Internet Explorer 5.5. To find this dialog, select Tools, Internet Options from the menu, pick the Content tab, click the Certificates button, and select the Trusted Root Certificate Authorities tab. This means that a Web farm that purchases a certificate from one of these well-known CAs will be recognized and authenticated without any intervention from a user's perspective.

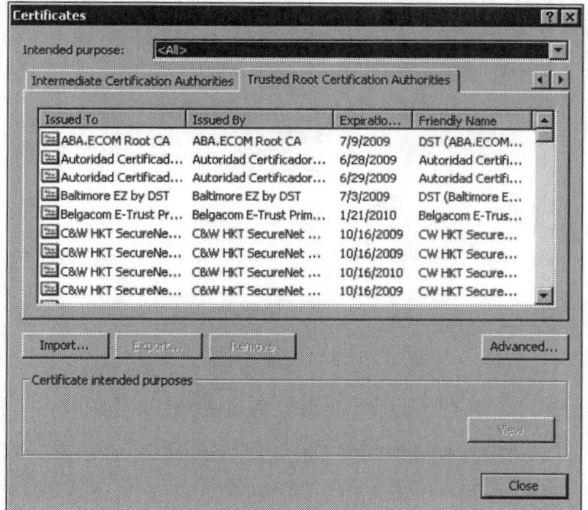

FIGURE 9.14
The Certificates dialog on Internet Explorer 5.5.

> **NOTE**
>
> For a list of Certificate Authorities, see Appendix F, "Well Known Certificate Authorities."

Installing a New Server Certificate

Installing a new server certificate to a Web site is a complicated process. To begin the process for a brand new certificate request, select the target Web site from the console and bring up the Directory Security tab from its properties. From the Secure Communications section, select the Server Certificate button. This launches the Web Server Certificate Wizard, shown in Figure 9.15. Unlike other welcome screens, this one actually changes according to the status of a pending certificate request, so read it carefully.

FIGURE 9.15
The welcome screen of Web Server Certificate Wizard.

The second page of this wizard shows the three options for installing a server certificate. The first option is for creating a new certificate. Certificate creation is a three-step process. The first step is creating the certificate request for a CA using the wizard. The second step is sending the certificate request to the CA, usually by a secure online sign-up process. The final step involves taking the response file from the CA, which is the actual server certificate, and installing it to the target Web site.

To complete the certificate request, select the first option from the Server Certificate page. On the Name and Security Settings page, fill in a name for the certificate and its security bit length. On the Organizational Information page, fill in the organization (a company) and organizational unit (a department) for the certificate. From the Site's Common Name page, file in either the Internet name (such as `www.technicallead.com`) or its NetBIOS name (such as `TLINTERNAL`). On the Geographical Information page, fill in Country/Region, State/Province, and City/Locality. Once all these pages are filled out, fill in Certificate Request File Name. This file contains the cryptographic information that a Certificate Authority needs to fill a certificate request. Submit this file to a well-known Certificate Authority; it will send a response file with the server certificate. Figure 9.16 shows the actual data for a Generate Certificate

Request from the Web Server Certificate Wizard and the response file data from the Certificate Authority. Be sure not to change the content of the certificate requesting even avoiding extra carriage returns and line feeds in these files because this will affect the success of the sign-up process.


```
-----BEGIN NEW CERTIFICATE REQUEST-----
MIICjDCCAjYCAQAwfDEXMBUGA1UEAxMObXlzaXRlLmZvby5jb20xFjAUBgNVBAsT
DVRlY2huaWNhbExlYWQxHjAcBgNVBAoTFVJpY2htb250IFdlYiBTZXJ2aWNlczEP
MA0GA1UEBxMGZGFsbGFzMQswCQYDVQQIEwJ0eDELMAkGA1UEBhMCVVMwXDANBgkq
hkiG9w0BAQEFAANLADBIAkEA1pQOiwSWtM5Gq7gJhz8jChoDCm/G5oCaddT/8YjD
c3kIS2rk7PfRmiLZDnirkuXobE0okzISXLthiiFdRFxdzQIDAQABoIIBUzAaBgor
BgEEAYI3DQIDMQwWCjUuMC4yMTk1LjIwNQYKKwYBBAGCNwIBDjEnMCUwDgYDVR0P
AQH/BAQDAgTwMBMGA1UdJQQMMAoGCCsGAQUFBwMBMIH9BgorBgEEAYI3DQICMYHu
MIHrAgEBHloATQBpAGMAcgBvAHMAbwBmAHQAIABSAFMAQQAgAFMAQwBoAGEAbgBu
AGUAbAAgAEMAcgB5AHAAdABvAGcAcgBhAHAAaABpAGMAIABQAHIAbwB2AGkAZABl
AHIDgYkA0jwwllPCwtmzxrLJ/2/rpGCvHrqzYzASmxr2ltdVP4OJogQKKcWQz5vk
wdEPmEY23Ivam+3jSC5oZ6+I54thine5YzNLyHZ5lZK11nalKu/dN6hbwBhBemxU
oi4NpIFfdw6MIxm1bmlcLFxaI4jtJ7UDIg+pMMiMraSAo4zAaBMAAAAAAAAAADAN
BgkqhkiG9w0BAQUFAANBAFLKpH/YaO2eLJF47bugNm7ZQLtGNwPLck1eO2SK37pc
KdWjElTCesQjGUjX+u4MJ4Ifmwk/OyeMP3iUwaqckXI=
-----END NEW CERTIFICATE REQUEST-----
-----BEGIN CERTIFICATE-----
MIICXTCCAcagAwIBAgIDfeQrMA0GCSqGSIb3DQEBBAUAMIGHMQswCQYDVQQGEwJa
QTEiMCAGA1UECBMZRk9SIFRFU1RJTkcgUFVSUE9TRVMgT05MWTEdMBsGA1UEChMU
VGhhd3RlIENlcnRpZmljYXRpb24xFzAVBgNVBAsTDlRFU1QgVEVTVCBURVNUMRww
GgYDVQQDExNUaGF3dGUgVGVzdCBDQSBSb290MB4XDTAxMDIxMDAzMDcyNVoXDTAy
MDIxMDAzMDcyNVowfDEXMBUGA1UEAxMObXlzaXRlLmZvby5jb20xFjAUBgNVBAsT
DVRlY2huaWNhbExlYWQxHjAcBgNVBAoTFVJpY2htb250IFdlYiBTZXJ2aWNlczEP
MA0GA1UEBxMGZGFsbGFzMQswCQYDVQQIEwJ0eDELMAkGA1UEBhMCVVMwXDANBgkq
hkiG9w0BAQEFAANLADBIAkEA1pQOiwSWtM5Gq7gJhz8jChoDCm/G5oCaddT/8YjD
c3kIS2rk7PfRmiLZDnirkuXobE0okzISXLthiiFdRFxdzQIDAQABoyUwIzATBgNV
HSUEDDAKBggrBgEFBQcDATAMBgNVHRMBAf8EAjAAMA0GCSqGSIb3DQEBBAUAA4GB
AFvT+v8IAWlQMfswmzxAx0FWLAcMA8ZIdP4E7je0zo/Xv0xmUweGIErV7XhGzSA2
4bZU13Ltbs7yrb2U4lZaJFXDQky+ila7eVhu0OwhRJhFG/Lm6CzFvPmh7MPQhdNR
98gulvV2VngxbJtr0Qao6Hqxle5kkMcG+FaheBI2EbPU
-----END CERTIFICATE-----
```


FIGURE 9.16

A Certificate Request file and Response file.

NOTE

Server Certificates cost money. Many Certificate Authorities provide free test certificates. Go to `https://www.thawte.com/cgi/server/test.exe` and follow the online process to get a test certificate from Thawte.

Once the CA supplies a response file, click the Server Certificate button again. Now the wizard presents a Pending Certificate Response page like that shown in Figure 9.17. Select Process the Pending Request and Install the Certificate and click next. Then enter the path to the file that contains the certificate response file. Complete the wizard, and now the Edit and View Certificate buttons are no longer grayed out.

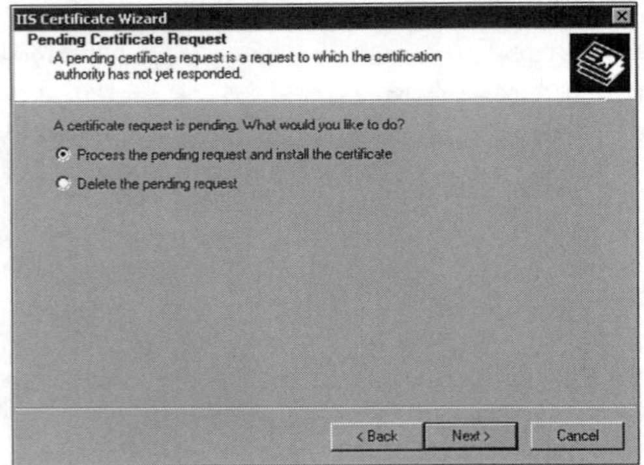

FIGURE 9.17
A Pending Certificate Response page from the Web Server Certificate Wizard.

Use the Assign an Existing Certificate option of the Web Server Certificate Wizard to associate a Web site with a certificate that has already been installed to a server. Use the Import a Certificate from a Key Manager Backup File option to import old keys generated under IIS 4.0.

Forcing a Resource to Require SSL for Access

Once a server certificate is installed on a Web site, it is easy to configure a resource to require the use of SSL for access. Click the Edit button in Secure Communications section of the Directory Security tab to launch the Secure Communications dialog, shown in Figure 9.18.

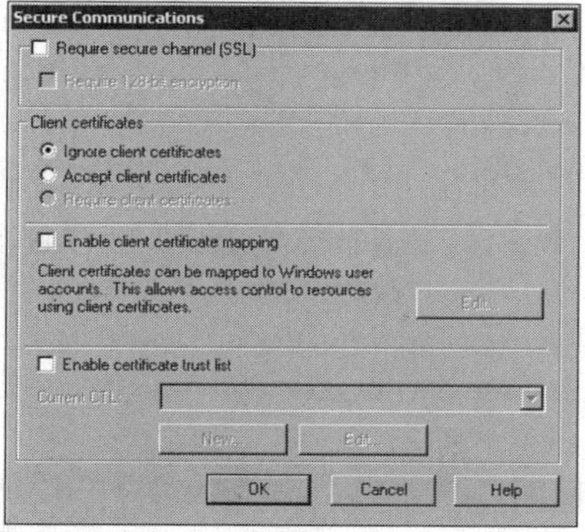

FIGURE 9.18
The Secure Communications dialog.

Click the Require Secure Channel (SSL) check box to force the use of HTTPS on a particular resource. This can be configured at the Web site, virtual directory, folder, and file levels. For 128-bit encryption, select the Use 128-bit Encryption check box.

Using Client Certificate Authentication

The final authentication mechanism supported by IIS is Client Certificate Authentication. A client certificate is a well-known token that corresponds to a key installed on a server and mapped to resources such as files and folders. Client certificates uniquely identify a user, and IIS provides a mechanism for mapping these certificates to Windows accounts for access to secured resources.

Client Certificate Authentication is configured separately from other authentication methods by pressing the Edit button in the Secure Communications section of the Directory Security tab. From the Client Certificates section of the Secure Communications dialog, there are three options: Ignore, Accept, or Require Client Certificates. Each affects the access to the resource in a different way.

- Select *Ignore Client Certificates* and any client certificate sent by the browser is discarded and the normal settings, such as anonymous access for example, in the Authentication Methods dialog takes precedence.
- Select *Accept Client Certificates* and any client that sends certificates will be authenticated using Client Certificate Authentication. If no client certificate is sent, then once again, the Authentication Methods dialog takes precedence.
- Select *Require Client Certificates* and authentication to this resource is denied if the client does not have an appropriate certificate or it is not mapped to an appropriate Windows NT account.

To accept or require client certificates, each client browser must have a copy of the client certificate and its private key. The server will require a server certificate and any number of client certificates, depending on the mapping scheme. The root certificate of the CA issuing client certificates being used must be installed to the server using the Web Server Certificate Wizard.

IIS 5.0 supports two mapping schemes that are important for Web farms: *basic* and *advanced.* Basic is simply a one-to-one mapping of certificate to Windows NT account. Figure 9.19 shows the 1-to-1 tab on the Account Mappings dialog. Basic mapping is absolutely secure because each client requires a unique certificate.

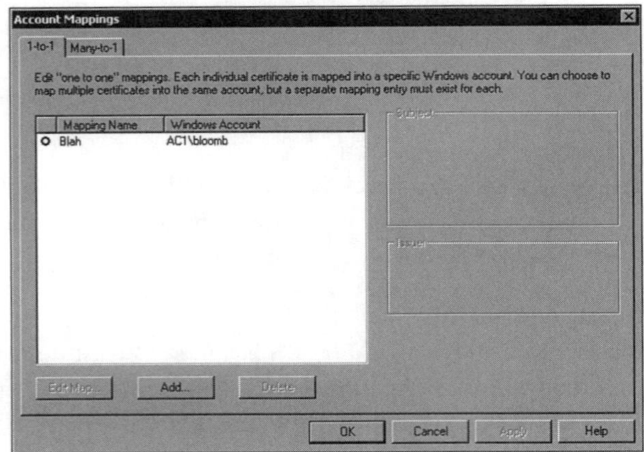

FIGURE 9.19
The 1-to-1 tab of the Account Mappings dialog.

To create a 1-to-1 mapping, click the Add button on the 1-to-1 tab. This launches a standard file browse dialog to browse to the certificate file. Selecting a valid certificate file displays the Map to Account dialog, shown in Figure 9.20. Enter a mapping name, account name, and password to complete the mapping.

Advanced Mapping, or Many to-1 mapping, creates a rule based on a characteristic of the server certificate, such as the organizational unit, and maps all certificates that meet the rule criteria to a specific Windows NT account. This means that any client certificate that comes from the appropriate organizational unit, as specified in the server certificate creation process, is authenticated to the resource using the mapped account. Figure 9.21 shows the Many-to-1 tab of the Account Mappings dialog. This method is reasonably secure because an unauthorized user would have to obtain a valid certificate that matched the rule(s) for the advanced mappings.

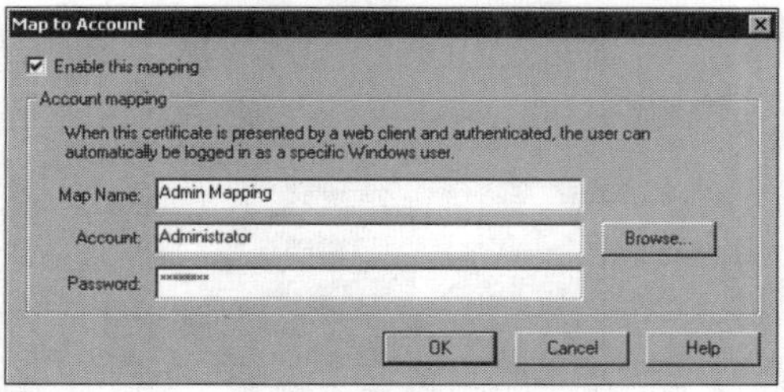

FIGURE 9.20
The Map to Account dialog.

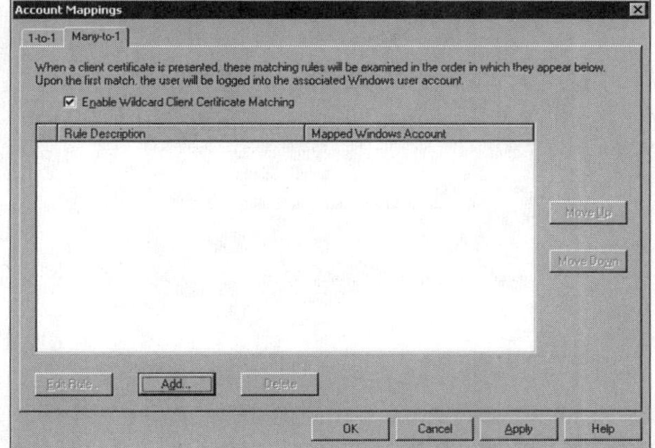

FIGURE 9.21
The Many-to-1 tab of the Account Mappings dialog.

To create an advanced certificate mapping, select the Many-to-1 tab and click the Add button. This launches an unnamed wizard that helps in the creation of rules for advanced mappings. On the first page, enter a description for the rule, such as "Map to Organizational Unit," and click Next. Then rules are created with the Edit Rule Element dialog by clicking the New button shown in Figure 9.22.

From the Edit Rule Element dialog, select either Issuer or Subject. Then select a subfield from the Sub Field combo box. Choices include O, OU, CN, C, S, and L for Organization, Organizational Unit, Common Name, Country/Region, State/Province, and Locality, respectively. Then a string is specified in the criteria that matches the subfield being mapped to. After the rule criteria is complete, a Mapping dialog allows a Windows NT account to be mapped to this rule or for all client certificates that match this rule to be denied access to the resource. Figure 9.23 shows the Mapping dialog.

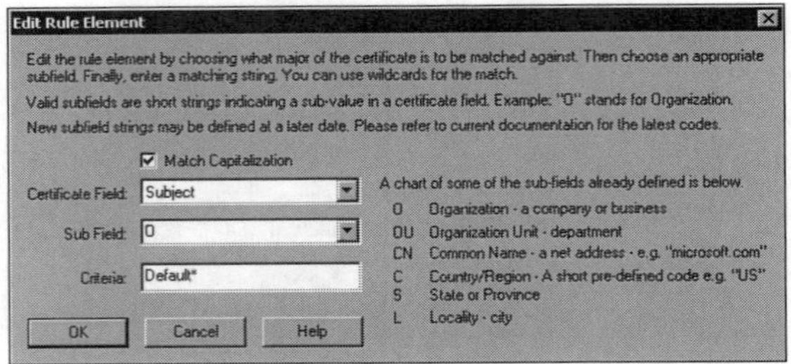

FIGURE 9.22

The Edit Rule Element dialog.

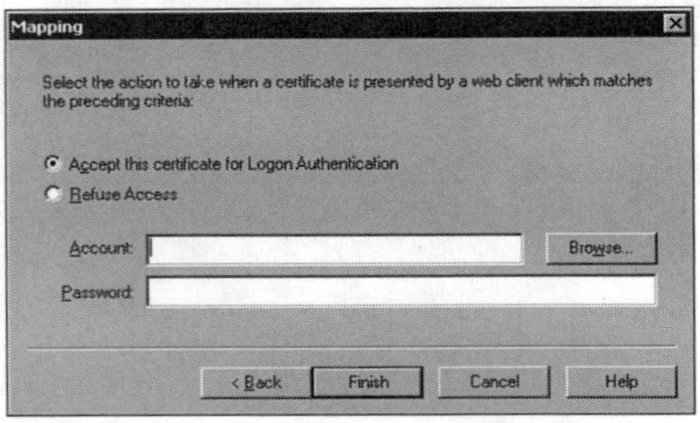

FIGURE 9.23

The Mapping dialog.

For example, TechnicalLead.com wants to grant access to a particular directory to all the client certificates from the Richmont Web Services organization. They selected Subject for Certificate Field, O for Sub Field, and set Criteria to Richmont*. Once Criteria is set, the Mapping dialog allows the Web server to accept the certificate for logon using a specified Windows NT account that had access to the directory. This effectively maps all client certificates from the Richmont Web Services organization to the NT account specified in this mapping.

Understanding IIS Applications Architecture

One of the strengths of IIS 5.0 is the ease of developing custom applications. Custom applications written in ASP (and now ASP.NET) are simple to create and deploy. The problem has always been that, once custom applications are introduced to a Web environment (even to Web servers outside of the Microsoft world), they tend to cause unexpected failures and lower the availability of the Web server itself.

Understanding how IIS handles custom applications and Web server availability requires a review of the concept of a *Windows NT process*. A process is a self-contained application that has fault protection and its own memory space separated from other processes. Windows protects individual processes from access by other applications on the same machine. In NT, it is impossible to accidentally address or erase memory of another process's code and data. An NT process is anything in the Task Manager list, `EXPLORER.EXE` for example. In the IIS 5.0 world there are two process names that are important: `INETINFO.EXE` and `DLLHOST.EXE`.

Knowing the history of IIS helps reveal the motivations behind the architecture of IIS 5.0. The goal from the beginning has been twofold: easy application development and high availability of Internet services. IIS 2,3, and 4 all had serious problems with application protection and high availability. Easy application development has existed from the start, which was part of the problem.

In IIS 2.0 and 3.0, all custom application code ran in the process `INETINFO.EXE`. Even today, `INETINFO.EXE` is the main engine in IIS that listens for requests for HTTP, FTP, and other Internet-based services on specific ports and IP addresses. When a request for an ASP page is made of a particular Web site, `INETINFO.EXE` sees this request and hands it to the appropriate engine for processing. For static content, `INETINFO.EXE` processes all requests. For ASP it is a DLL named `ASP.DLL` that does the work of dynamically generating ASP page content. Figure 9.24 shows a simplistic view of how IIS handles requests.

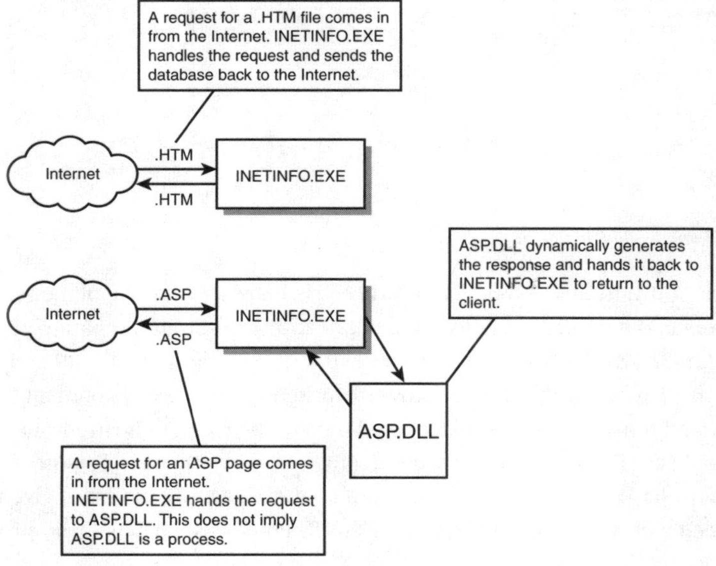

FIGURE 9.24
`INETINFO.EXE` *handling requests from the Internet.*

When an ASP page generates a runtime error or some other exception that causes a protection fault to occur, the Web server fails. This failure is tied to the `INETINFO.EXE` process space causing the portion of IIS that listens for requests to crash. Of course, this made IIS look bad because it was hard to determine if the crash was caused by sloppy IIS code or sloppy custom code. Figure 9.25 illustrates a custom application running the same process as IIS.

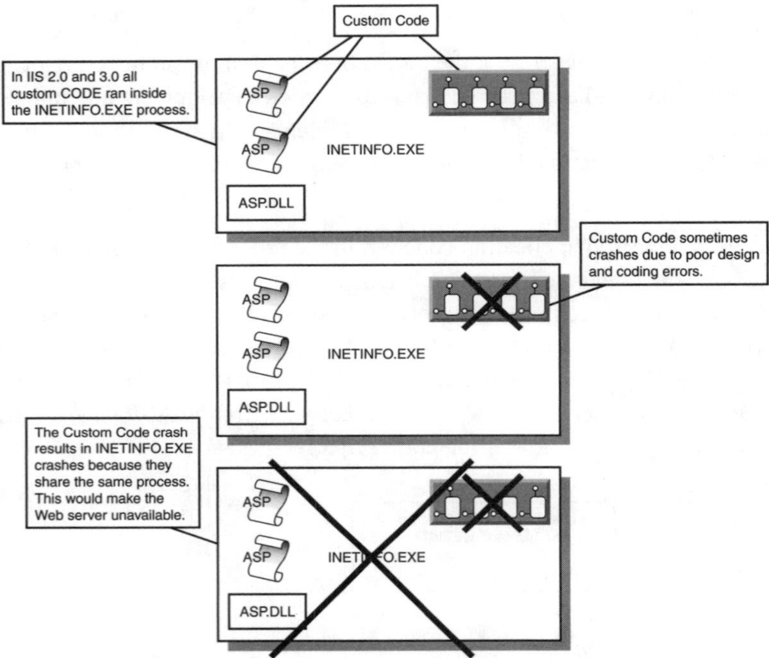

FIGURE 9.25
The IIS 2.0 and 3.0 application architecture.

In IIS 4.0, Microsoft introduced the idea of process isolation. Process isolation enabled application developers and administrators to force applications to run in a separate process space outside of `INETINFO.EXE`. In IIS 4.0, this process is `MTX.EXE`. In fact, IIS 4.0 and MTS 2.0 were joined at the hip because MTS was now the primary hosting environment for custom applications. An administrator could make any Web site or Web application run out of process from the primary `INETINFO.EXE` process by a simple property change. This greatly enhanced the availability of the Web server and the custom applications that ran on it. Even better was the fact that when a custom application did crash, IIS could just spawn a new process to handle the next request.

There were drawbacks to isolation. Not everything was totally isolated, so some custom applications could still crash IIS. Furthermore, out of process applications were slower than in process ones because of the cross-process communication required between `INETINFO.EXE` and `MTX.EXE`. Figure 9.26 shows an IIS 4.0 custom application isolated from `INETINFO.EXE`.

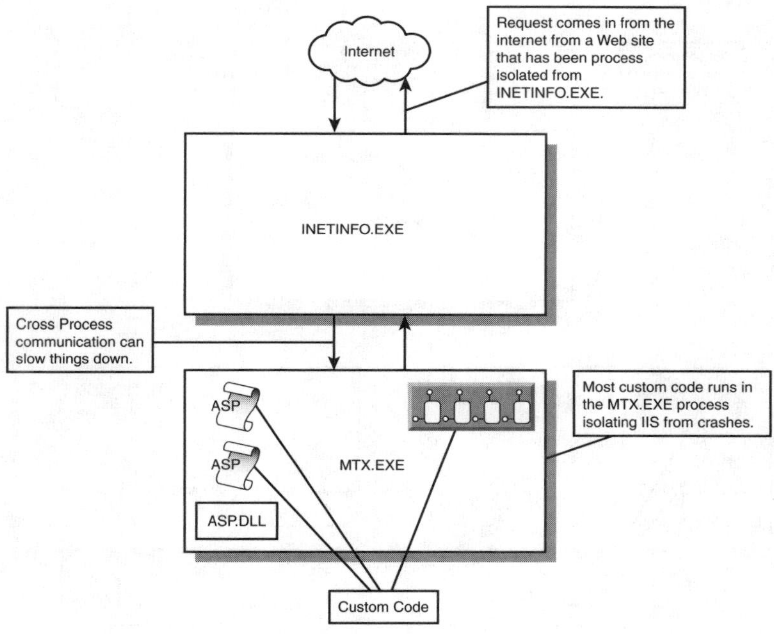

FIGURE 9.26
The IIS 4.0 application architecture.

IIS 5.0 further improved application protection and performance by creating three levels of process isolation. It is still possible to run custom applications in the `INETINFO.EXE` process space by setting the application protection low. The default setting is now medium pooled, which means all applications run out of process to `INETINFO.EXE` by default but multiple applications share a pooled process. This process is called `DLLHOST.EXE`.

`DLLHOST.EXE` is the replacement for `MTX.EXE` because IIS and COM+ are still tightly integrated. The third form of application protection is called *High Isolated*. In this form, a dedicated `DLLHOST.EXE` process is created for each application marked as High. This provides the greatest level of availability for the applications on a Web server. IIS 5.0 also solves most of the performance issues with out of process applications because of the reduction in the number of cross-process calls. Even today, the best-performing applications are those that run in process to `INETINFO.EXE`, but just due to the well-documented improvements in threading in Windows 2000 and architecture changes to IIS itself, out of process applications in IIS 5.0 run at the same speed as in process applications in IIS 4. Figure 9.27 shows the IIS 5.0 application protection features in a process diagram.

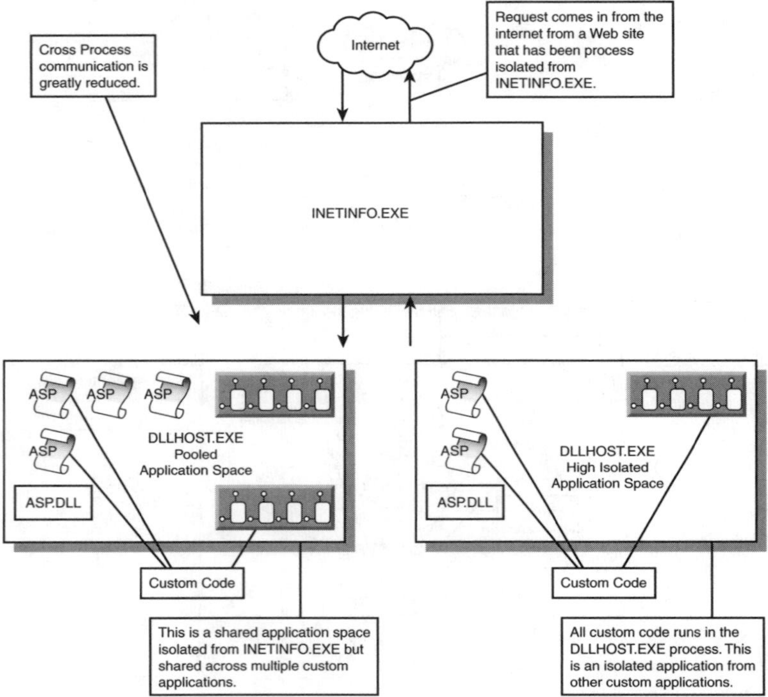

FIGURE 9.27
The IIS 5.0 application architecture.

Understanding the ISAPI Extensibility Architecture

As explained earlier, ISAPI stands for Internet Server Application Programming Interface. ISAPI is used to extend the functionality of IIS through custom DLL programs. ISAPI enables developers to hook in to key areas of the request-processing pipeline IIS uses to handle requests for HTTP traffic. IIS supports two types of ISAPI programs: extensions and filters.

Extensions

An ISAPI extension is a DLL program that is mapped to a particular file extension such as ASP. When a request is received by IIS for a file type that is mapped to an ISAPI extension, IIS passes the request to the ISAPI extension for processing.

Extensions are called applications in the IIS console and are configured from the Home Directory tab of a Web site or Web application. Click the Configuration button to launch the Application Configuration dialog, shown in Figure 9.28. The active tab is App Mappings, which contains all the current ISAPI extensions installed on this IIS object.

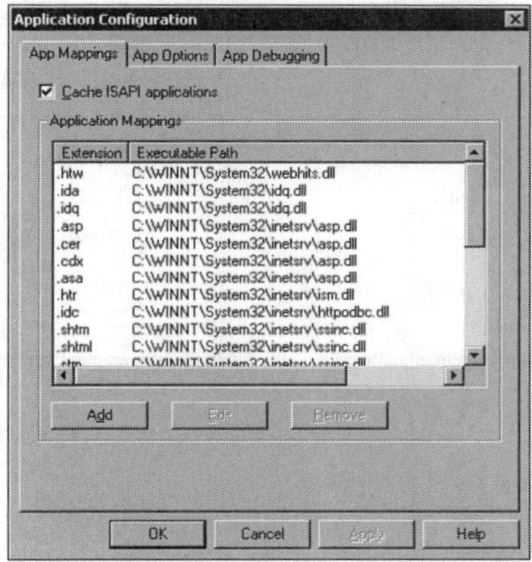

FIGURE 9.28
The App Mappings tab of the Application Configuration dialog.

Because ISAPI extensions are associated at application protection boundaries, they will run inside `INETINFO.EXE` if, for example, the ASP page requested is inside a Web site configured for low application protection. If the page requested is inside a Web application set for medium application protection, the extension loads into `DLLHOST.EXE` and is outside the `INETINFO.EXE` process. ISAPI extensions load into whatever process is handling the file being requested. Figure 9.29 shows how a request is handled by IIS and then passed to an ISAPI extension.

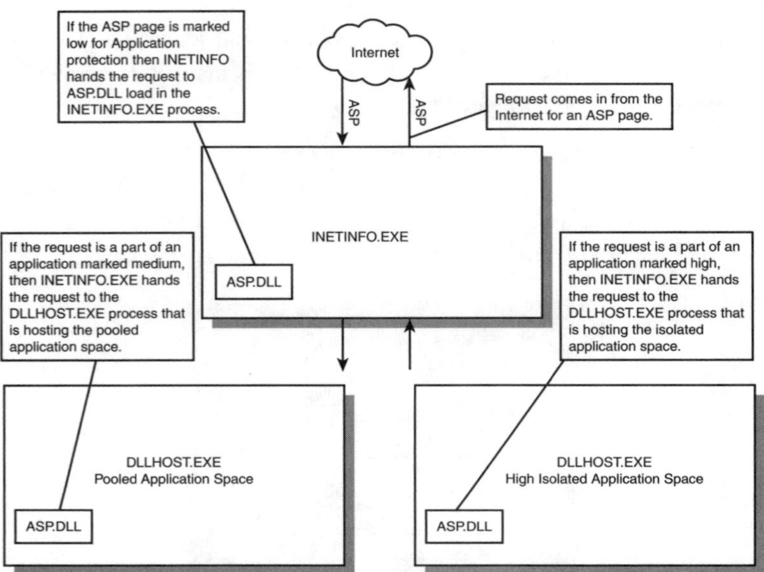

FIGURE 9.29
The flow of a request to an ISAPI extension.

For example, `ASP.DLL` is the ISAPI extension that IIS passes requests for files with an ASP, CDR, CDX, or ASA extension. When a request comes in for an ASP file, IIS uses the settings seen in Figure 9.30 to determine what actions to take before passing the request to `ASP.DLL`.

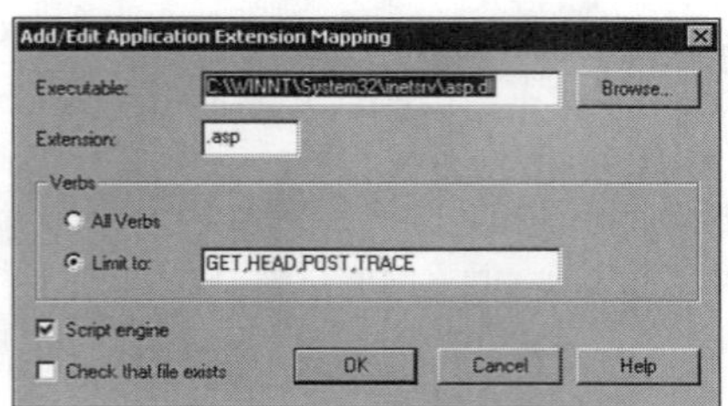

FIGURE 9.30
An application extensions' mapping settings.

Access this dialog by selecting the ASP mapping and clicking the Edit button. IIS first checks whether the request is using one of the HTTP verbs assigned to the extension, such as `GET`, `HEAD`, `POST`, or `TRACE`. Then, it checks the permissions on the folder, looking for execute or script access checks. If the Script Engine check box is not checked, the directory must have execute permission assigned explicitly for the request to be processed. Since ASP is script based, with this checked, ASP programs can be executed in directories without execute permissions for a higher level of security. Finally, if the Check That File Exists check box is selected, the Web server attempts to access the `PATH_INFO` portion (the full file path as known by the client) of the URL. If the file can't be opened due to security or does not exist, an error is returned to the client. Once all the verification procedures are completed, IIS calls an entry point function in `ASP.DLL` and hands the request over for processing. ASP then parses the file, compiles the script code, and executes the page, returning the results to the user.

Add and remove extensions with the Add and Remove buttons on the App Mappings tab. To add a new extension, specify the path to the DLL, the appropriate HTTP verbs, whether it is a script engine or not, and if it should attempt to verify the file exists. To remove an extension, select the extension and click the Remove button.

Filters

ISAPI filters differ from ISAPI extensions in that they are used during the process of handling a request for a page on a Web site. They are not associated with a particular file extension but with events that occur during the processing pipeline before and after a file is processed by IIS (in case of static files) or an extension as with ASP files.

An ISAPI filter registers programmatically to listen for events from IIS during the processing of a request. These events include the reading of raw data, preprocessing of HTTP headers, notification of anytime a server is converting a URL to a real file path (a URL map), notification of authentication, and completion of authentication. These event notifications occur in any order, depending on the condition at the time of the event, and are managed by the internals of the ISAPI filter. These events occur before and after IIS passes the request to the appropriate processing engine.

ISAPI filters have a priority that is used by IIS when many filters have registered for the same events. IIS notifies filters that request high priority first, medium priority second, and low priority last. For situations in which many ISAPI filters have the same requested priority level, IIS uses the `FilterLoadOrder` property in the metabase to resolve any ties. Filters are configured per Web server and Web site at the IIS level. Filters at the Web server level are called *global* and are used in the processing of all requests to a Web server. Filters at the Web server level have a higher overall priority than those at the Web site level. Figure 9.31 shows the processing pipeline with many ISAPI filters.

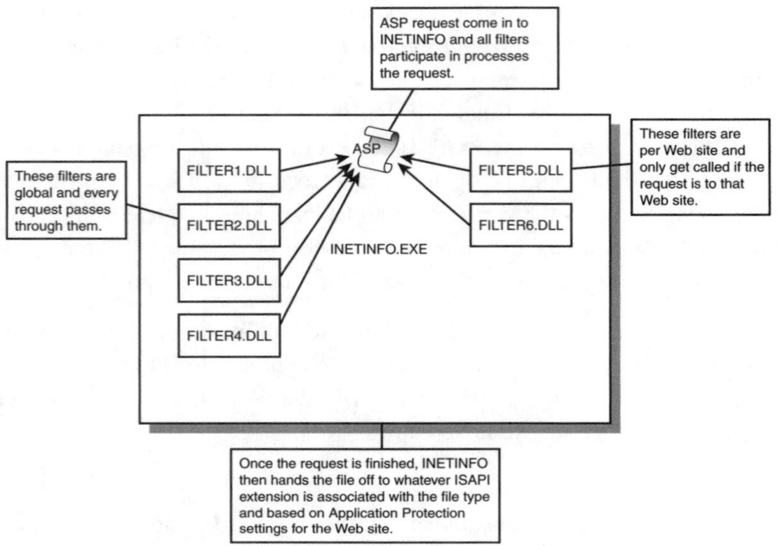

FIGURE 9.31

The processing pipeline for many ISAPI filters.

For example, at the end of the processing request after all the events in the pipeline have fired, IIS logs the request to the IIS log according to the settings for logging. Many third-party vendors have created specialized logging ISAPI filters that log statistical information to a custom repository outside the IIS logs. Site Server 3.0 has an ISAPI filter that ties authentication of users to members in an external database using cookies and caching. This filter allows the restricting of access to groups in LDAP that have corresponding NT groups to file resources. Filters are very flexible and provide the low-level hook in IIS needed to change its behavior dramatically.

Add a filter to IIS through the ISAPI Filters tab found on the Web server for global filters and the Web site for normal filters. Figure 9.32 shows the global ISAPI Filter tab for a Web server. Click the Add button, give the filter a name, enter the fully qualified path for the filter, and click OK. To remove a filter, select the filter and click Remove.

All filters load into the `INETINFO.EXE` process space even if they are associated with a Web site that uses medium or high application protection. Reset IIS when changing ISAPI filter configurations.

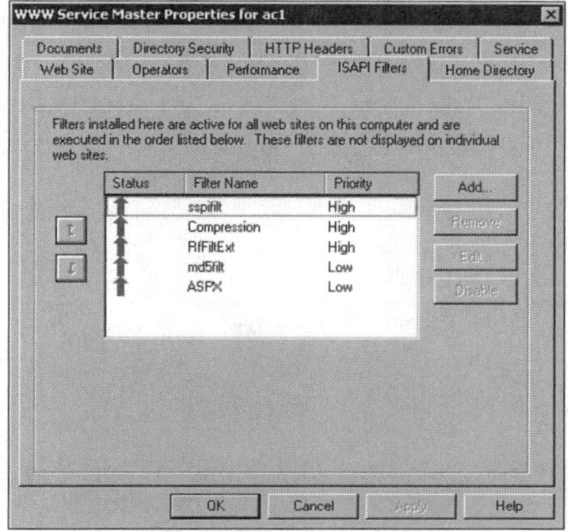

FIGURE 9.32
The global ISAPI Filters tab.

Understanding How to Monitor IIS

Monitoring IIS is a complicated process. A quick look at Performance Monitor shows that there is a plethora of counters. Determining the important counters is an almost impossible task. The first step is to create functional counter groups and then pick important counters that fit these groups.

Placing counters into five groups reduces the number required for successful monitoring of IIS. These groups are as follows:

- *Processor counters* report information about the CPU and how it is being used.
- *Memory counters* report information on memory utilization both from an efficiency and amount-available perspective.
- *Web service counters* relate specifically to the activity of the Web service such as number of connections and `GET` requests.
- *ASP counters* report statistics on how well the `ASP.DLL` ISAPI extension is handling the generation of dynamic ASP pages.
- *Miscellaneous counters* cover other areas such as network use and disk performance.

Processor Counters

The processor is the heart of IIS. IIS uses the processor for requests and to do the work of ISAPI filters and extensions. In general, a Web server with high processor utilization is desirable because the processor is not waiting on network and memory access. When CPU utilization is low but the overall response time is high, this suggests that IIS is waiting on the network, disk, or memory, in that order. Table 9.6 shows the important counters for monitoring IIS with regard to the processor(s). The Performance Monitor description is taken directly from Performance Monitor. (more) indicates that there is more information in the Performance Monitor description. To see this text, select the performance object and counter and click the Explain button.

TABLE 9.6 Useful Processor Counters

Performance Object—Instance	*Counter*	*Performance Monitor Description*	*Thresholds*
Processor	% Processor Time	The percentage of time that the processor is executing a non-idle thread. (more)	Should be less than 90%.
Processor	% Privileged Time	The percentage of non-idle processor time spent in privileged mode. (Privileged mode is a processing mode designed for operating system components and hardware-manipulating drivers.) (more)	High numbers could indicate a failing device due to excessive interrupts.
Processor	% User Time	The percentage of non-idleprocessor time spent in user mode. (User mode is a restricted processing mode designed for applications, environment subsystems, and integral subsystems.) (more)	This should be as close to % Processor Time as possible.

TABLE 9.6 Continued

Performance Object—Instance	*Counter*	*Performance Monitor Description*	*Thresholds*
System	Processor Queue Length	Processor Queue Length is the number of threads in the processor queue. (more)	More than two for a sustained period suggests processor congestion.

Memory Counters

Memory is where all the work of manipulating data for Web applications should occur. Memory utilization should be high on most Web servers but not over the available physical memory. Hard page faults where memory is swapped to disk should be avoided at all costs. Table 9.7 shows some useful memory counters that help monitor the memory performance and utilization of IIS.

TABLE 9.7 Useful Memory Counters

Performance Object—Instance	*Counter*	*Performance Monitor Description*	*Thresholds*
Process—`INETINFO`	Private Bytes	Private Bytes is the current number of bytes this process has allocated that cannot be shared with other processes.	Must be compared against baseline value.
Process—`DLLHOST`	Private Bytes	Same as above.	Same as above. There could be multiple `DLLHOST` processes for a single instance of IIS.

TABLE 9.7 Continued

Performance Object—Instance	*Counter*	*Performance Monitor Description*	*Thresholds*
Memory	Available Bytes	Available Bytes is the amount of physical memory available to processes running on the computer, in bytes. (more)	Optimal value is 10% of the total memory available.
Memory	Page Faults/sec	The overall rate at which the processor handles faulted pages. A page fault occurs when a process requires code or data that is not in its working set (its space in physical memory). (more)	Must be compared against baseline value.

Web Service Counters

Web service counters have information about the performance of the Web service itself. Table 9.8 shows some useful Web service counters. These counters provide an overall indicator of the use and activity of a Web site from the HTTP perspective.

TABLE 9.8 Useful Web Service Counters

Performance Object—Instance	*Counter*	*Performance Monitor Description*	*Thresholds*
Web Service —_Total	Bytes Total/sec	The sum of Bytes Sent/sec and Bytes Received/sec. This is thetotal rate of	Depends on network and baseline. Could be indicator of

TABLE 9.8 Continued

Performance Object—Instance	*Counter*	*Performance Monitor Description*	*Thresholds*
		bytes transferred by the Web service.	need for caching servers.
Web Service —_Total	Current Connections	Current Connections is the current number of connections established with the Web service.	Requires baseline and is application dependent.
Web Service	Get requests/sec	The rate at which HTTP requests using the `GET` method are made. Get requests are generally used for basic file retrievals or image maps, though they can be used with forms.	Requires baseline and is application dependent.
Web Service	ISAPI Extension Requests/sec	The rate at which ISAPI extension requests are simultaneously being processed by the Web service.	Requires baseline and is application dependent.

ASP Counters

ASP Counters indicate the performance and activity of custom applications written is ASP that run on a Web server. These counters are a great way to tell when the Application layer in a site is taxing the server. Table 9.9 shows useful ASP counters.

TABLE 9.9 Useful ASP Counters

Performance Object—Instance	*Counter*	*Performance Monitor Description*	*Thresholds*
Active Server Pages	Errors/sec	The number of errors per second.	Requires a baseline as some errors always occur. Can be an indicator of application problems.
Active Server Pages	Request Execution Time	The number of milliseconds that it took to execute the most recent request.	Can show expensive individual ASPs. More than 10,000 msec is bad.
Active Server Pages	Request Wait Time	The number of milliseconds the most recent request was waiting in the queue.	Long wait times in the queue can indicate an overtaxed server. If CPU is low and wait times are high, increase the thread count for IIS.
Active Server Pages	Requests/sec	The number of requests executed per second.	Requires baseline.
Active Server Pages	Requests Queued	The number of requests waiting for service from the queue.	More than 2 or 3 could indicate a problem.

Miscellaneous Counters

Table 9.10 shows some miscellaneous counters that are important when monitoring IIS. Be sure to check using the DISKPERF command-line utility that disk performance counters are enabled. Type **`DISKPERF`** at a command line; it reports the status of these counters. Use `DISKPERF /?` to enable or disable disk performance counters on a system. Windows 2000 enables disk performance counters by default.

TABLE 9.10 Important Miscellaneous Counters

Performance Object—Instance	*Counter*	*Performance Monitor Description*	*Thresholds*
TCP	Connections Established	The number of TCP connections for which the current state is either `ESTABLISHED` or `CLOSE-WAIT`.	Requires baseline.
Physical Disk	Current Disk Queue Length	The number of requests outstanding on the disk at the time the performance data is collected. (more)	This value should average less than 2.
Network Interface	Bytes Total/ Sec	The rate at which bytes are sent and received on the interface, including framing characters.	For 100Mb networks this number should remain under 4,000,000 bytes for optimal performance.
Network Interface	Output Queue Length	Output Queue Length is the length of the output packet queue (in packets). (more)	Shouldn't be larger than 2 unless this value is invalid. Consult network adapter manufacturer for details.

IIS Best Practices for a Web Farm

Using best practices, learned from hands-on experience and appropriate knowledge enables administrators to:

- Establish consistency and stability for any server technology, including IIS.
- Enhance the reliability of the process for handling application change and of the application itself.
- Enhance the experience of the customer by providing consistency across the Web farm.

Best practices exist for a reason, so don't ignore them for no reason. For example, storing files somewhere other than `c:\inetpub\wwwroot` enhances the security of a site because that directory is well known.

Lay Out the File Structure for a Web Site

The file structure of a site is actually much more important than the flexibility of IIS would indicate. Using IIS, it is possible to store files anywhere and create a virtualized view of the files that corresponds to the Web site structure. However, it is easy to maintain, enhances security, simpler to move, and easy to troubleshoot if the files of a Web site are grouped together in one place.

> **TIP**
>
> Store Web site files in one central location because it simplifies management and enhances security.

Microsoft stores most of the files that are part of the default Web site in the `inetpub/wwwroot` directory. Don't store custom applications in this directory because it is a security risk and it keeps them out of the way of Microsoft stuff in the default Web site location.

Keep the file location consistent throughout the deployment process. For example, don't store files on the E drive on one layer and then on D on the other.

Use Metabase Property Inheritance

Most properties of objects in the IIS hierarchy are inherited from a parent object. A new Web site object inherits the properties from the Web server object. Changes to any property override the parent's setting.

TIP

Set properties that apply across IIS metabase objects to the top-most parent item.

Set the properties on the parents, not on all the objects. If a property applies to every Web site, set that property on the Web server level. If a property applies to all the files in a Web site, set that property at the Web site level. Set properties sparingly and only when necessary.

When changing a property of a parent item, use the Inheritance Overrides dialog seen in Figure 9.33 to override the new setting in any child item that has different settings. This dialog appears whenever a parent property override affects the value of previously configured child items.

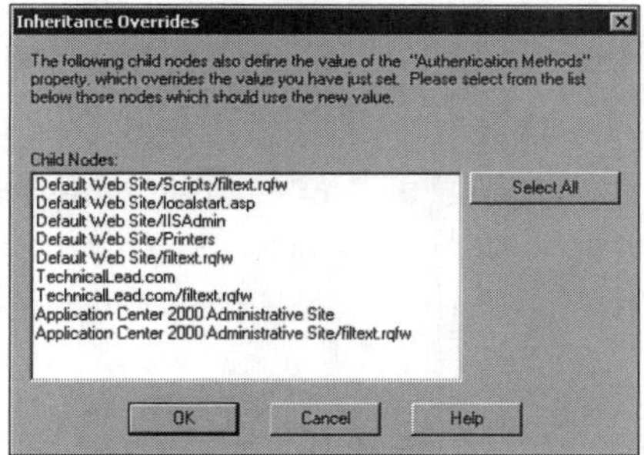

FIGURE 9.33
A property override dialog.

Create Multiple Web Sites

All IIS configurations come with a default Web site. The default Web site is the playground for every Microsoft product that needs Web capability. Microsoft uses the default Web site for many things, so don't use it for production Web sites at all.

TIP

Create a dedicated Web for each Web site in a Web farm.

There are many different ways to structure a virtualized Web site in IIS. The Web site object can bind to a specific IP address and is the only object with that capability. Create a Web site object for each IP address exposed on the Internet. For example, the top-level domain name `www.technicallead.com` has its own Web site. If a Web server handles more than one top-level domain name, then there should be a one-to-one ratio between domain names and Web sites.

Because IIS is flexible, multiple Web sites can coexist in the same IIS configuration and on the same physical server. Whether to run multiple sites on the same server is a matter of opinion and choice for a business. In some cases, this is an efficient use of resources and appropriate for many small sites. In others where complex custom applications can sometimes interfere with one another, Web site isolation per server is the best choice.

To create a Web site, run the Web Site Creation Wizard. Use this wizard to enter a Web site description, IP address and port settings, Web site home directory, and Web site access permissions.

Increase Availability of Web Applications Using Application Protection

Application protection is the IIS term for the configuration setting relating to the application architecture a Web site or Web application runs under. Application protection applies to Web sites and Web applications. Figure 9.34 shows the application configuration option on the Home Directory tab.

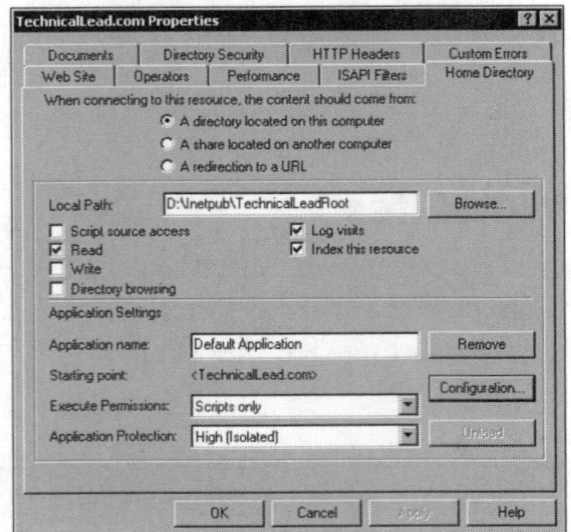

FIGURE 9.34

The Home Directory tab in a Web site or application.

There are three settings for application protection, low (IIS process), medium (pooled), and high (isolated). When an application is run low, it runs in the INETINFO.EXE process. For medium (pooled) applications, they all share the same DLLHOST.EXE process. High (isolated) applications have a dedicated process. By default all applications on a Web server run at medium. This protects the INETINFO.EXE process from poorly written custom code. In some cases, two medium pooled applications could cause each other to fail. In those cases, run both applications as high. The flexibility to give each Web application its own process space greatly enhances the availability of the Web server. INETINFO.EXE should only listen for incoming requests and hand those requests to medium and high applications.

TIP

Run new applications high for the greatest application availability. Once an application is stable, change it to medium pooled to improve performance.

Any subdirectory or virtual directory of a Web site can be turned into a Web application. Be warned that this creates a new application instance and can break an existing application. Consult the support developer of the custom application to find out if it supports this level of application isolation. Click the Create button on the Home Directory tab to turn a directory into a Web application.

Use Default Documents

Default documents are used to ease navigation through a site. When a user requests a URL such as http://www.technicallead.com, he is not specifying a particular document. When IIS sees a URL like that, it uses the settings shown in the Documents tab in Figure 9.35 to determine what document to return or whether to generate a 404 error.

If Enable Default Document is unchecked, then the request will fail and generate a 404 error. If not, then IIS goes down the list looking for each file and returns the first one it finds. Documents can be configured at the Web server, Web site, Web application, virtual directory, and folder level.

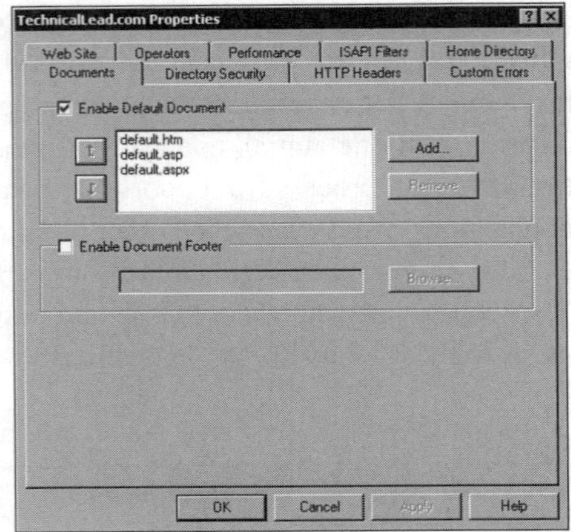

FIGURE 9.35
The Documents tab.

TIP

Always specify a default document because it reduces the number of errors generate by IIS, improving the perceived availability of a Web site.

To add a new default document, click Add and specify the document name. Use the arrow keys to move around the search order of the documents. Select a document and click Remove to remove a document.

Use Custom Errors

Every request to a Web server from a browser involves a request and a response. A request comes in the form of a `GET`, `POST`, and so on, in which the browser is asking the server for a specific file-based resource on the server. The Web server has a set of standard number-based responses it can give to any request. For example, if a browser requests the existing page `/default.htm` and the requesting browser has properly authenticated for access, the server returns a 200 response along with the content of the page. If `/default.htm` does not exist, then the server returns a 404 error response, along with a message explaining the reason for the error. If the requesting page does exist but the browser credentials don't match the ACL on the page, the server returns a 401;3 error along with a message explaining the reason for the error.

NOTE

Appendix G, "Supported IIS 5.0 HTTP Error Responses," lists the class of standard error messages that IIS supports.

IIS 5.0 supplies a set of standard error messages installed by default to `C:\WINNT\Help\iisHelp\common`. These messages look like the 404 error shown in Figure 9.36.

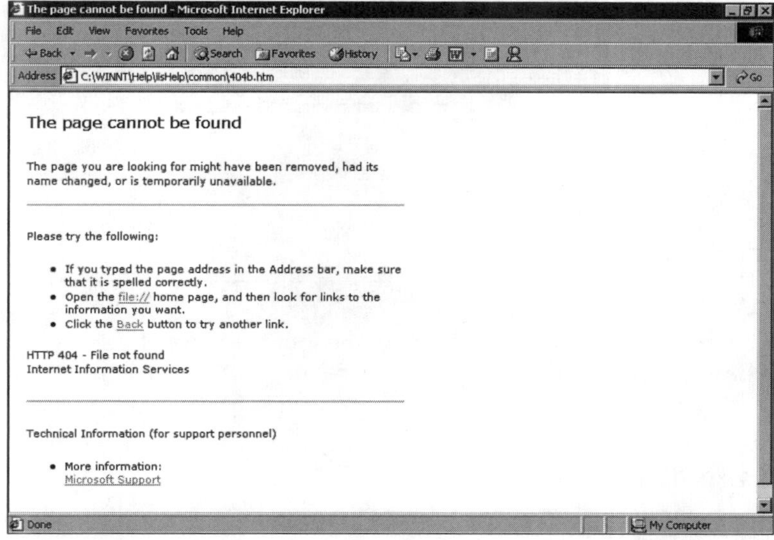

FIGURE 9.36
The default 404 error from IIS 5.0.

Most sites will want to customize these error messages to make them look like the site the error came from. This is done through the Custom Errors tab, shown in Figure 9.37. To substitute a default error for a custom one, select the error and click the Edit Properties button. From this dialog, choose either File or URL to associate the error with a custom message. Choose Default to return the setting to its default state. Custom error messages can be set at all container levels, including virtual directories and directories.

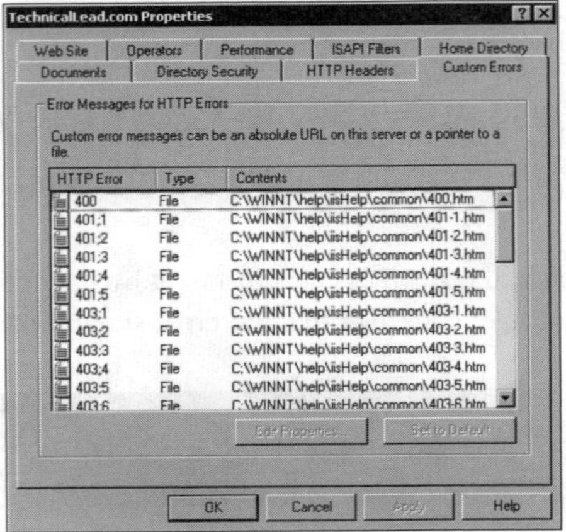

FIGURE 9.37
The Custom Errors tab.

> **TIP**
>
> Use Custom Errors to maintain consistency in the look and feel of a site even when errors and unexpected requests occur.

Eliminate the 404

It is possible to eliminate 404 errors by replacing the error message for 404 with a custom error page. This custom error page could direct the user to submit an error report or provide a link back to the home page of the site. The 404 custom error page can also be used to provide a site with "fake" URLs. The custom ASP page assigned to handling 404 examines the URL, checks it in a database or local XML file, and redirects the user accordingly, using a 302 Redirect response.

Help the Debugging Process

A custom error message can also help the debugging of complex problems in large Web farms. If one single server is having trouble severing pages, it can be a tedious process to find the affected server. A simple ASP script using the Window Scripting Host components can retrieve the server name from an ASP page. Listing 9.1 shows two methods for retrieving a server's name.

LISTING 9.1 Programmatically Retrieving the Server Name

```
dim shell, serverName

serverName = ""
On Error Resume Next
set shell = CreateObject("Wscript.Shell")
serverName = shell.RegRead("HKLM\SYSTEM\CurrentControlSet_
\Control\ComputerName\ActiveComputerName\ComputerName")
Set shell = Nothing
On Error Goto 0
'OR
set shell = CreateObject("WScript.Network")
serverName = shell.ComputerName
```

Once an ASP page has the server name, it can write it out to the page as an HTML comment as in the following code line. Make sure to obfuscate the name because it will be sent to Web browser and viewable in clear text from the source of the page. For example, if the name of a server is `W2WEB01`, it would be as valuable to return only `WEB01`, hiding the true name of the server but identifying it enough for troubleshooting purposes.

```
serverName =  "<!-- Server name: " & serverName & " -->" & vbCrLf
```

TIP

Write out an obfuscated server name to all ASP pages to help troubleshoot large Web farms.

Remove the Default Web Site from the Internet

The default Web site is the playground of Microsoft. Many of the samples that come with IIS are the subject of well-known exploits for IIS. Never install them to a production server and never point the rest of the default Web site to the Internet. In a single NIC server, disable the default Web site or move it to a different port that is not accessible from the Internet. On a Dual NIC server, bind the default Web site to a back-rail IP address. It is not wise to remove the default Web site entirely, because many administrative tools use it and so does IIS for help.

Remove Unneeded ISAPI Extensions

By default IIS installs a number of ISAPI extensions. Many of these extensions, such as `.ASP`, are used on most every IIS site. Others, such as `.HTR` and `.IDC`, are less frequently used. Many of these less frequently used extensions are the subject of well-known exploits and should be removed from the Application Configuration tab, shown previously in Figure 9.28. This tab is available at the global level and at any Web application.

To remove unneeded extensions for the entire server, select the IIS computer name in the console and edit the Master Properties of IIS. Select the Home Directory tab and click the Configuration button. Select the unneeded extensions and click Remove. When prompted, select all Web sites and apply the changes to them as well. Most sites should remove everything but those bound to `ASP.DLL`. Sites that use Application Center 2000 will have a binding to `RfFiltExt.dll` that should remain intact if they use the request forwarder. To use the .NET framework, anything bound to `aspnet_isapi.dll` should also remain.

TIP

Remove unneeded ISAPI extensions to eliminate unnecessary security risks and unused configurations.

Configuring the Metabase Programmatically

Configuring the IIS metabase programmatically is an advanced administrator task. It requires an understanding of creating scripts and basic programming tasks. Programmatic metabase administration

- *Is the best way to apply* complex piecemeal changes when a targeted metabase replication tool such as Application Center 2000 is unavailable and `IISSYNC.EXE` is too generic or fails under complex conditions.
- *Removes human error* from the deployment process, especially when complex changes are applied to multiple sites.
- *Creates a repeatable process* and is self documenting.
- *Promotes a deeper understanding* of IIS, how it works, and how it is configured, which helps the troubleshooting process.

Why Not Just `IISSYNC.EXE`?

`IISSYNC.EXE` is a great tool for replicating simple IIS configurations across multiple servers. `IISSYNC.EXE` is installed by default to `c:\winnt\system23\inetsrv`. `IISSYNC.EXE` is a command-line tool that copies the IIS specific contents of the metabase from one server to another. It is easy to use; just type **`IISSYNC.EXE <COMPUTERNAME>, <COMPUTERNAME>`** to target one or many destination servers.

However, `IISSYNC.EXE` is not a viable solution for all Web sites. It works great with simple configuration but is error prone when dealing with complex sites. During failures it can leave the target metabase corrupt, requiring at worst a reinstallation of

IIS. Make sure to back up the metabase on the target servers before using IISSYNC.EXE. IISSYNC.EXE is great for initial deployments and brand new servers, but for ongoing site operations, using a tool such as Application Center 2000 or administering the metabase programmatically is a better method to introduce change to a production metabase.

There are many different tasks that are appropriate for programmatic administration of the metabase. For example, creating a Web site without using the New Web Site Wizard is a great way to understand what steps are required and how IIS is organized. Disabling session state for a Web server is a simple script to create and provides an easy way to demonstrate applying changes at the root level and propagating those changes using property inheritance. Setting global logging parameters is also useful to script because it creates a document that defines what properties to expect in the IIS log.

There are two ways to configure the metabase programmatically. The first is the more difficult and involves creating scripts that use native ADSI methods and properties to configure changes. The second uses a VBS script called ADSUTIL.VBS.

Using ADSI to Configure the Metabase

Active Directory Services Interfaces (ADSI) is a standard set of COM interfaces that are accessible from script. ADSI uses the GetObject command to retrieve the ADSI COM object associated with a path such as IIS://LOCALHOST/W3SVC. From that point, the standard IADs and IADsContainer methods are used to interact with the object returned. Listing 9.2 shows how to retrieve the IIsComputer object from the metabase, display the MaxBandwidth property setting, and change it.

LISTING 9.2 Using ADSI to Set the EnableDefaultDoc Property

```
dim oWebService

set oWebService = GetObject("IIS://LOCALHOST/W3SVC")
MsgBox "Enable Default Document is set to: " & oWebService.EnableDefaultDoc
OWebService.EnableDefaultDoc = False 'a Boolean property
OWebServcie.SetInfo
```

Notice that the oWebService object has the property EnableDefaultDoc; this is how any property is addressed for all objects in the metabase. The SetInfo command commits the changes to the object; without it, the EnableDefaultDoc is never actually changed. While it is easy to change property values with native ADSI, it is much more difficult to create new objects such as an IIsWebServer. ADSUTIL.VBS is much better suited for that task.

Using ADSUTIL.VBS to Configure the Metabase

ADSUTIL.VBS is an administrative script that encapsulates the calls to ADSI with a large number of command-line parameters. ADSUTIL.VBS is installed to the c:\inetpub\adminscripts directory by default. Perform the following command to retrieve a list of commands supported by ADSUTIL.VBS.

```
CSCRIPT.EXE c:\inetpub\adminscripts\adsutil.vbs HELP
```

It is best always to address the ADSUTIL by full path so the script will work on any server with IIS installed regardless of path. ADSUTIL.VBS does not work with WSCRIPT, the command-line scripting engine associated by default to VBS files. Changing the association of VBS files to CSCRIPT.EXE might cause scripts launched from Explorer not to function correctly. It is best to leave the associations at defaults and always address a command-line VBS script with the CSCRIPT.EXE designation.

Listing 9.3 shows how to retrieve the EnableDefaultDoc property and set it. Notice how few lines of script this actually takes compared to Listing 9.2.

LISTING 9.3 Using ADSUTIL.VBS to Set the EnableDefaultDoc Property

```
CSCRIPT.EXE c:\inetpub\adminscripts\adsutil.vbs GET W3SVC/EnableDefaultDoc
CSCRIPT.EXE c:\inetpub\adminscripts\adsutil.vbs SET W3SVC/EnableDefaultDoc
➥FALSE
```

Some Examples of IIS Programmatic Administration

Clearly, ADSUTIL simplifies the creation of scripts and programmatic administration of IIS overall. The following examples will use ADSUTIL primarily because it creates much shorter scripts and is easy to understand. Where appropriate or valuable, examples written in native ADSI are presented.

Creating a Web Site

Listing 9.4 shows the steps required to re-create a Web site like the New Web Site Wizard. This is useful for farms that have to support many different sites and sometimes need to move them from server to server quickly. Notice how the Web site number is specified as 3. Use a unique number for each site supported. The full path to ADSUTIL.VBS is c:\inetpub\adminscripts\adsutil.vbs so modify this listing accordingly.

LISTING 9.4 Creating a Virtual Server or Web Site

```
cscript.exe adsutil.vbs CREATE_VSERV w3svc/3
cscript.exe adsutil.vbs SET w3svc/3/ServerComment "Technicallead.com"
cscript.exe adsutil.vbs SET w3svc/3/AccessScript "TRUE"
```

LISTING 9.4 Continued

```
cscript.exe adsutil.vbs SET w3svc/3/ServerBindings ":80:"
cscript.exe adsutil.vbs SET w3svc/3/SecureBindings ":443:"
cscript.exe adsutil.vbs CREATE_VDIR w3svc/3/Root
cscript.exe adsutil.vbs SET w3svc/3/Root/Path "D:\Inetpub\TLRoot"
cscript.exe adsutil.vbs SET w3svc/3/Root/AuthAnonymous "TRUE"
cscript.exe adsutil.vbs APPCREATEPOOLPROC w3svc/3/Root
cscript.exe adsutil.vbs SET w3svc/3/Root/AppFriendlyName "Technicallead.com"
```

Listing 9.4 shows that a Web site is a collection of three objects in IIS: a virtual server, a virtual directory, and a Web application. The `CREATE_VSERV` command is used to create the virtual server. The `CREATE_VDIR` command is used to create the virtual directory, which must be called `Root`. The `APPCREATEPOOLPROC` command is used to create the Web application and associate the site with the IIS pooled out-of-proc COM+ application.

Setting Global Logging Parameters

Listing 9.5 shows the modification of global logging parameters. It is a good idea to modify the default parameters because many of the useful columns are turned off by default. This script moves the log file directory to the D drive to prevent logging of data from consuming all the space on the operating system drive. This helps prevent the logs from crashing the system due to lack of disk space. Notice that this script changes logging parameters of the Web service; as long as no Web sites override the global parameters, this will apply to the entire Web server. This is a good example of properly using property inheritance. The full path to `ADSUTIL.VBS` is `c:\inetpub\adminscripts\adsutil.vbs` so modify this listing accordingly.

LISTING 9.5 Modifying the Global Logging Parameters

```
cscript.exe adsutil.vbs SET w3svc/LogFileDirectory "d:\logfiles"
cscript.exe adsutil.vbs SET w3svc/LogExtFileServerIP "TRUE"
cscript.exe adsutil.vbs SET w3svc/LogExtFileServerPort "TRUE"
cscript.exe adsutil.vbs SET w3svc/LogExtFileBytesRecv "TRUE"
cscript.exe adsutil.vbs SET w3svc/LogExtFileTimeTaken "TRUE"
cscript.exe adsutil.vbs SET w3svc/LogExtFileWin32Status "TRUE"
cscript.exe adsutil.vbs SET w3svc/LogExtFileDate "TRUE"
cscript.exe adsutil.vbs SET w3svc/LogFilePeriod "1"
```


Setting Default Documents

Some sites have special default document needs, including custom names and extensions. Listing 9.6 shows how to set a default document at the Web service level and for a specific Web site. Because IIS specifically sets the default documents of the default Web site to include `iisstart.asp`, changing the default document of the Web service level has no effect on the settings in the default Web. The order of documents in the `DefaultDoc SET` command determines the order that IIS serves the pages from a directory. The full path to `ADSUTIL.VBS` is `c:\inetpub\adminscripts\adsutil.vbs` so modify this listing accordingly.

LISTING 9.6 Setting Default Documents Programmatically

```
REM ** THIS SETS THE GLOBAL DEFAULT DOCUMENT TO INDEX.HTM AND DEFAULT.ASP
cscript.exe adsutil.vbs SET w3svc/DefaultDoc "index.htm,default.asp"
cscript.exe adsutil.vbs SET w3svc/EnableDefaultDoc "TRUE"

REM ** THIS SETS THE NUMBER 3 WEB SITE'S DEFAULT DOCUMENT TO DEFAULT.ASP ONLY
cscript.exe adsutil.vbs SET w3svc/3/DefaultDoc "default.asp"
cscript.exe adsutil.vbs SET w3svc/3/EnableDefaultDoc "TRUE"
```

Disabling Session State and Enabling ASP Buffering

A common task for administrators is to disable ASP session state and turn on ASP buffering. Listing 9.7 shows how to do this at the Web service level. The full path to `ADSUTIL.VBS` is `c:\inetpub\adminscripts\adsutil.vbs` so modify this listing accordingly.

LISTING 9.7 Disabling Session State and Enabling ASP buffering

```
cscript.exe adsutil.vbs SET w3svc/AspAllowSessionState "FALSE"
cscript.exe adsutil.vbs SET w3svc/AspBufferingOn "TRUE"
```

Changing Security Settings

Most Web sites have a few isolated files that require special security settings. For example, a page that users post credit card information to usually requires SSL. Another site might have a special directory that has write permissions for uploads. Listing 9.8 shows how to set a specific file to require SSL and grant a specific directory write permissions. Notice that setting specific properties on a file that has never been modified with the console requires the creation of all the objects in the hierarchy, including the directory and the file itself. The full path to `ADSUTIL.VBS` is `c:\inetpub\adminscripts\adsutil.vbs` so modify this listing accordingly.

LISTING 9.8 Setting SSL and `AccessWrite` Permissions

```
REM** MUST CREATE THE OBJECTS IN THE HIERARCHY
cscript.exe adsutil.vbs CREATE w3svc/3/Root/Home "IIsWebDirectory"
cscript.exe adsutil.vbs CREATE w3svc/3/Root/Home/purchase.asp "IIsWebFile"
cscript.exe adsutil.vbs SET w3svc/3/Root/Home/purchase.asp/AccessSSL "True"
REM** HERE WE CREATE ANOTHER IISWEBDIRECTORY OBJECT FOR THE UPLOADS DIRECTORY
cscript.exe adsutil.vbs CREATE w3svc/3/Root/Home/Uploads "IIsWebDirectory"
cscript.exe adsutil.vbs SET w3svc/4/Root/Home/Uploads/AccessWrite "True"
```

Changing the Anonymous Account and Password

Some sites change the Anonymous account and password. Listing 9.9 shows how to do this at the Web server level. The full path to `ADSUTIL.VBS` is `c:\inetpub\adminscripts\adsutil.vbs` so modify this listing accordingly.

LISTING 9.9 Setting SSL and `AccessWrite` Permissions

```
REM** MUST CREATE THE OBJECTS IN THE HIERARCHY
cscript.exe adsutil.vbs SET w3svc/AnonymousUserName "TLUser"
cscript.exe adsutil.vbs SET w3svc/AnonymousUserPass "tlrocks"
cscript.exe adsutil.vbs SET w3svc/AnonymousPasswordSync "FALSE"
```

Enabling ASP Thread Gating

ASP thread gating must be enabled through the command line. See section "ASP Thread-Gating Properties," earlier in this chapter for a review of how thread gating works. Listing 9.10 shows how to enable ASP thread gating and set the upper and lower bounds for the CPU to 45 and 95 respectively. The full path to `ADSUTIL.VBS` is `c:\inetpub\adminscripts\adsutil.vbs` so modify this listing accordingly.

LISTING 9.10 Setting SSL and `AccessWrite` Permissions

```
REM** MUST USE SCRIPT TO DO THIS. USE CAUTION
cscript.exe adsutil.vbs SET w3svc/ASPThreadGateEnabled "True"
cscript.exe adsutil.vbs SET w3svc/ASPThreadGateLoadLow "45"
cscript.exe adsutil.vbs SET w3svc/ASPThreadGateLoadHigh "95"
```

Summary

IIS is an integral part of any Web farm. Successful Web farm management requires a deeper understanding of IIS than just what is gleaned from the management console. At the top of the list is the structure of the IIS metabase. The metabase is the center of all configurations for IIS, and administrators who use and understand its structure are among the best.

Understanding advanced concepts helps administrators to use IIS fully. The administrator must understand IIS security concepts, including the five authentication methods and configuring IIS for SSL. Administrators must also understand the application architecture of IIS to provide high availability and scalability. ISAPI filters and extensions provide a way to extend the functionality of IIS; understanding how they work helps the administrator troubleshoot problems with these low-level applications. Finally, administrators must monitor the performance of IIS to provide better feedback to application developers to improve their applications.

Once administrators understand the metabase, advanced IIS concepts, and how to configure the metabase programmatically, IIS best practices become second nature. A best practice from the outside can seem like overkill or a waste of time, but during a crisis a best practice can save the day. IIS is the center of any successful Web farm, and proper care and configuring will lead to success.

Using Component Services (COM+) in a Web Farm

CHAPTER

10

IN THIS CHAPTER

The Component Object Model (COM) is a standards-based specification for defining and building business components. COM has grown from a specification for communication between Windows applications (OLE) into COM+. COM+ has become an application platform to host business objects with the COM+ runtime.

NEW TERM A *runtime* is a place where code can execute within a defined set of operating parameters. The COM+ runtime is an environment for COM objects; the VB runtime is for Visual Basic components.

The COM+ runtime allows a business component to be configured at runtime with transaction support, concurrency support, just-in-time activation, component- and application-level security, and other configurable attributes. Transaction support provides components the capability to ensure that any business process will execute to completion or not execute at all. Concurrency support prevents multiple client requests from interfering with existing client requests. Just-in-time activation allows caching of frequently used components. COM+ security provides an administrative way to control access to an application or an individual component. All of these features give the administrator considerable options when configuring components that exist in the business or presentation layer.

These COM+ runtime features can be added to COM components through the Component Services console. Once a component is added to the Component Services console, it gains attributes from the COM+ runtime. Attributes are the configuration options of a COM+ application or the components. Components that have COM+ attributes are called *configured components*.

COM+ applications are collections of components organized through the Component Services console with application requirements in mind. The administrator chooses options based on application requirements and can take ownership of tasks that are traditionally developer specific. This empowerment also increases the responsibility of the administrator to better understand the parts of a COM+ application.

For example, Foo.com creates a custom COM object that handles login requests to its B2B Web site. The initial COM+ application is created in the testing environment. The Foo.com administrators configure component-activation parameters to increase performance. They configure the security context the component is created with for the testing environment. Then, because transaction support is being developed for a future version of the component, they disable transactions to increase performance. There are no code changes required to configure these options. The developer is completely unaware of these changes and thus is free to focus on solving the problem of authenticating users to the Web site. When it is time to deploy to production, the administrator creates a copy of the COM+ application in the production environment and reconfigures the options required by the application, duplicating the testing environment except for the security context. The security context is of a different user in the production environment than in testing. Before jumping any further, let's take a look at what you will be experiencing throughout this chapter.

The goals of this chapter are to help you

- Build a COM+ application using the COM Application Install Wizard in the Component Services console. Installing a prebuilt application and creating an empty application are covered.
- Configure a COM+ application after it has been installed. Topics include understanding activation, security, identity, and advanced options of a COM+ application.
- Install COM components into a COM+ application shell so that they become configured components. Installing classic COM components and COM+ components is covered.
- Understand all the attributes of configured components once they are installed into a COM+ application. Transaction, security, activation, and concurrency attributes are covered.
- Deploy a COM+ application to another server using the export command. Exporting server, library, and proxy applications is covered, with an example of using the `MSIEXEC.EXE` tool and the `COMREPL` tool.

Building a COM+ Application

COM+ applications are built with the Component Services console. The Component Services console is standard on a Windows 2000 server. It is located in the Start menu under Programs, Administrative Tools, Component Services.

In standard Windows 2000, the Component Services console has three default nodes. Under the Component Services node is the Computers node. At this node, all the servers in a farm can be configured and managed from one central console. Under the Computers node are the individual servers that have been added to this Component Services console. By default, the only computer configured is the local machine, called My Computer. Expanding the My Computer node reveals two more nodes, one called COM+ Applications and the other Distributed Transaction Coordinator. Expanding the COM+ Applications node reveals the main tree view for building a COM+ application. By default, the fully expanding COM+ Application node looks like Figure 10.1. Depending on the Windows 2000 options installed, different COM+ applications are installed on individual systems.

NOTE

The Component Services console cannot administer Microsoft Transaction Server, the precursor to Component Services and COM+, on Windows NT 4.0.

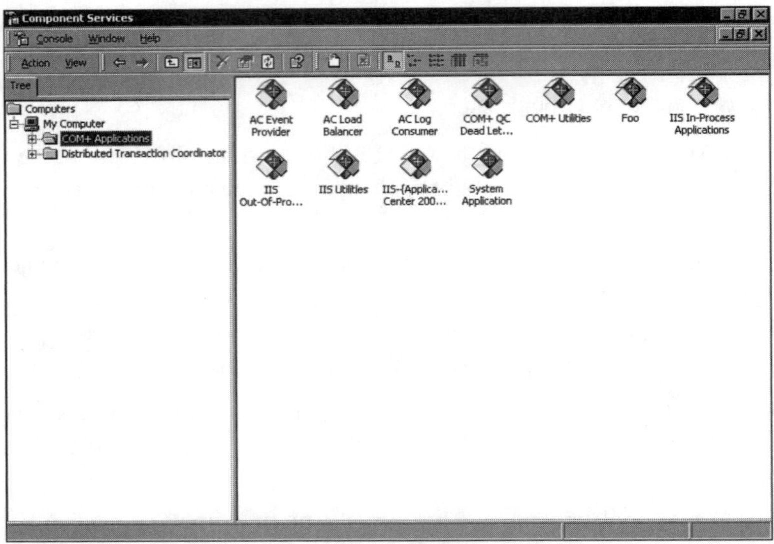

FIGURE 10.1
The COM+ Application node of the Component Services snap-in.

There are two methods for creating a framework for a COM+ application. The first method is to build a new application using the COM+ New Application Wizard and create an empty application. The second method is to install prebuilt application(s) using the New Application Wizard. To start the wizard, right-click on the COM+ Application node in the Component Services console under the desired computer node. Select New, Application, acknowledge the welcome screen, and click Next. The options on the second screen of the wizard are where the two paths in the wizard diverge. Figure 10.2 shows this pane in the wizard.

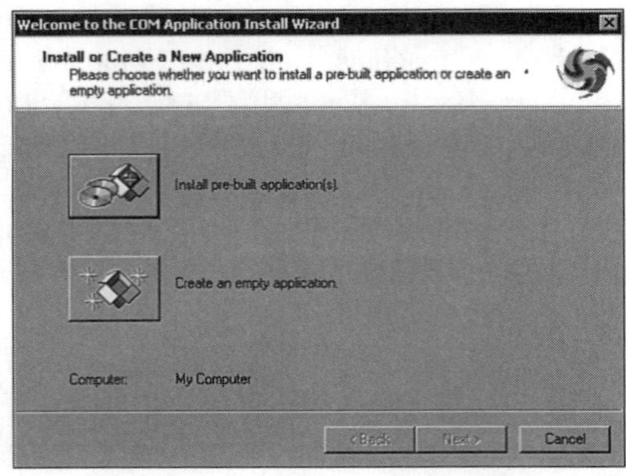

FIGURE 10.2
The COM+ Application Wizard's Install or Create Application pane.

Building a New Application

From the COM+ Application Wizard's Install or Create New Application pane, click the button labeled Create an Empty Application. Select Build a New One, which automatically shows the third page of the wizard. Select a name for the new application and the activation type. Figure 10.3 shows the third page of the wizard. Notice the description for Server Application and Library Application. In the default, a server application, the components added to this COM+ application will be activated inside a dedicated COM+ process space. In a COM+ library, application components are activated within the client application process that created the component.

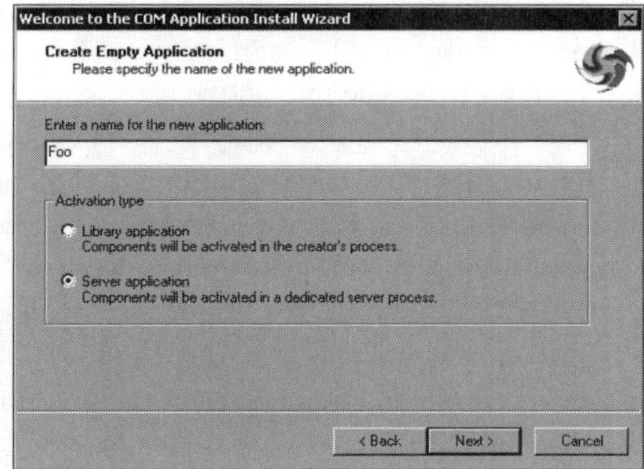

FIGURE 10.3
Important configuration choices for a COM+ application.

> **NOTE**
>
> A *dedicated COM+ process space* is a Windows 2000 executable named `dllhost.exe` that hosts the components separate from client applications. Each application configuration receives a different instance of `dllhost.exe`.

For example, if Internet Information Server activates a component in a library application, then that component is loaded into the IIS process. With COM+ server applications, the dedicated process provides process isolation, protecting the calling process from component crashes at the cost of speed due to out-of-process calls. If IIS activates a component in a server application and it has a critical failure, IIS will not be affected. This choice is clearly a tradeoff of performance versus stability.

TIP

Start a new COM+ application as a server application to isolate it from potentially crashing the client application. When fully confident of stability, switch the COM+ application to a library application for better performance.

After you choose a name and activation type for a new COM+ application, step four of the COM+ Application Wizard presents configuration options for the security context. A security context provides the authentication credentials for components in a COM+ application. These credentials are used to gain access to protected resources like the file system and other COM+ applications either locally or on other servers. The administrator has two security context choices: interactive user or a specific user. The interactive user security context will change depending on who is logged into the server interactively. If there is not an interactive user, and thus no one is logged in locally, then the COM+ application will not have a security context and be refused access to protected resources. Use the interactive user account option in the development environment to simplify the initial debugging process. In the rest of the deployment environment, it is a bad idea to create a COM+ application with the interactive user security context. These servers typically have no interactive user so the COM+ application won't work properly. Instead, pick an appropriate domain or local account that the objects run under.

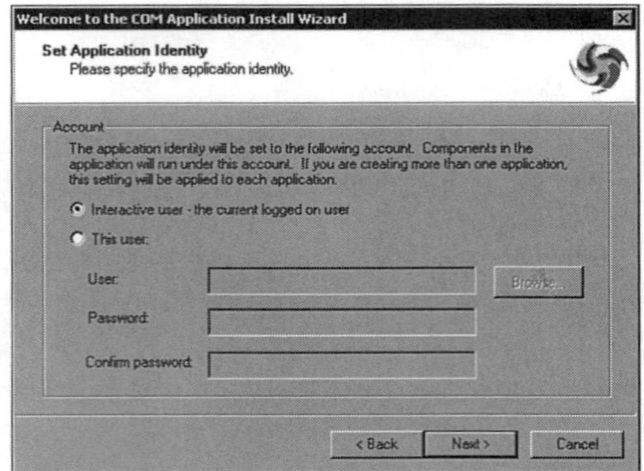

FIGURE 10.4
The Security Context dialog of the COM+ Application Wizard.

Picking an appropriate account in a Web farm for a COM+ application security context requires a good understanding of how IIS manages anonymous access in IIS 5.0. If the COM+ application is part of the Web Services tier and runs locally but out of process, on the same box as IIS, create a local account for the security context. If the COM+ application is distributed from the Web Services tier, create a local account on the remote server without any group membership and run the application under that security context.

As long as IIS controls the password and COM+ security is not being used (the only appropriate way for anonymous sites), the Web server should be able to access these components without additional configuration. If the IIS anonymous account has been changed and IIS no longer controls the password, then the local account that IIS runs as and the local account on the remote server for the COM+ application must have the same username and password for the Web server to create the components. If access to the components in the application seems restricted or the component seems to function incorrectly, it is likely a security problem due to changing the anonymous user account and not letting IIS control the password. It is not recommended to change the anonymous account as this complicates the configuration and does nothing to increase security.

CAUTION

The default configuration of IIS and COM+ is most suited for anonymous Web sites. Leave the anonymous settings in IIS at default to ensure success when accessing remote COM+ applications from the Web tier.

When troubleshooting security problems with COM+ applications, understand what steps are taken to reset the environment to ensure a reliable test. Excessive rebooting of servers is not required to verify security configurations changes under Windows 2000. Shutting down the COM+ application and restarting the IIS services (if IIS is involved) ensures a valid test. To shut down a COM+ application, right-click on the COM+ application name and choose Shut Down. The next attempt to access any components in this application will cause a new `dllhost.exe` process to be created, restarting the application.

After picking the security context, the COM+ application framework and the new COM+ Application Wizard are complete. An entry using the name of the new COM+ application appears in the COM+ Applications node of the Component Services console. From this point, components can be added, configuration options changed, and the application shut down or removed from the server.

Installing a Prebuilt Application

From the COM+ Application Wizard's Install or Create New Application pane, click the button labeled Install Prebuilt Application(s). This button launches a standard Windows file browser dialog. From this dialog an administrator can pick any number of MSI and PAK files. An MSI file is used by Microsoft Installer to re-create a COM+ application that was exported from another server. Exporting a COM+ application is explained later in this chapter. A PAK file is a legacy installation package that was created by exporting a package from Microsoft Transaction Server. Both of these files are similar and contain all the necessary information to re-create an application and configure it as it was when it was exported. These files are like scripts that are executed by the COM+ wizard, and an MSI file contains all component DLLs needed for the application to function. This dialog allows the administrator to add and remove as many of these files as needed to configure more than one application at a time.

After picking all the installation files, the next page in the wizard is the standard COM+ dialog for picking the security context that an application runs under. Security contexts are described in the section "Building a New Application," earlier in this chapter.

After you pick the security context, the next dialog enables the administrator to pick the installation directory for all the files associated with the installation scripts. Files in MSI packages are installed by default to `C:\Program Files\ComPlus Applications\{GUID}`. `{GUID}` is a globally unique identifier that has the form `{21D61CE6-A517-11D1-9D8B-0020781039AF}`.

NEW TERM A *GUID* (pronounced G-U-I-D, gwi-d, or goo-id) is a globally unique identifier. COM uses GUIDs for names of COM+ applications, classes, interfaces, and type libraries, among others things.

The administrator can also change the default destination directory like any standard installation program. Figure 10.5 shows the Application Installation Options dialog of the COM+ Application Wizard. If an MSI file contains roles, then the check box labeled Add Windows Users Saved in the Application File will be available to turn on or off. Roles are discussed later in this chapter.

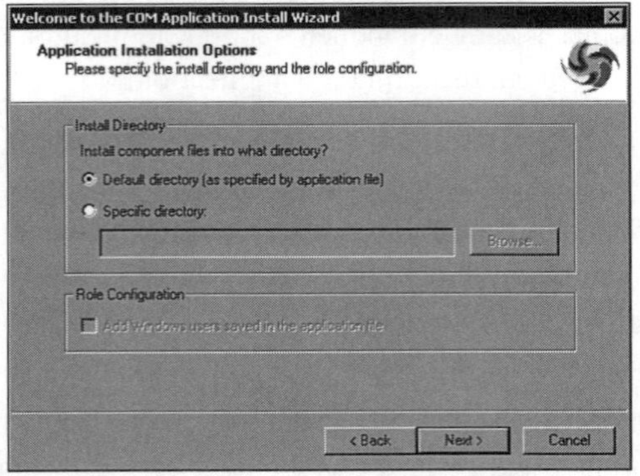

FIGURE 10.5
Application installation options of the COM+ Application Wizard.

Configuring a COM+ Application

A thorough understanding of the configuration options for a COM+ application is necessary to build robust applications. Right-click on a COM+ application's name and select Properties to see all the configuration options. From the initial tab, the administrator can change the name of the COM+ application, add a description, and view the GUID of the COM+ application.

TIP

It is possible to highlight the GUID of a COM+ application and copy it to the Clipboard. This is useful for searching the Registry for entries relating to this application when troubleshooting.

Understanding Activation Options

The Activation tab is used to define how a COM+ application will start up when first called. It also determines the options that are available for the application and components. The settings in this tab determine how the COM+ runtime wraps activation calls from client applications. Figure 10.6 shows the Activation tab. There are two main options for local activation: Server Application and Library Application. The Remote Server Name text box is used by COM+ proxy applications.

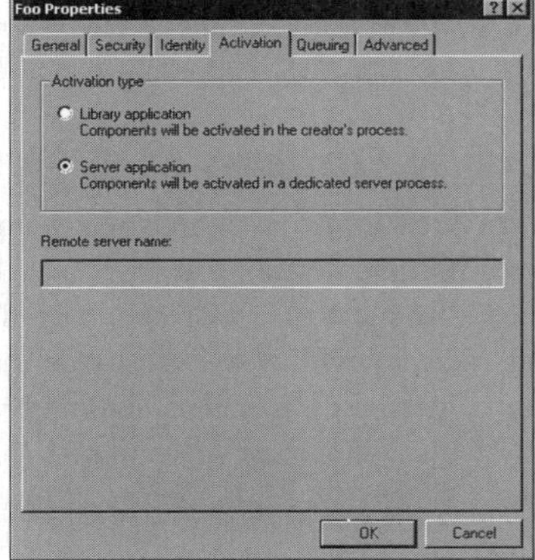

FIGURE 10.6
The Activation tab of a COM+ application.

Activating Server Applications

Classic COM components are typically in dynamic link libraries (DLLs) and are loaded into the process space of the client application upon creation. When a client activates a server application, the COM+ runtime creates a separate operating system process. This and all further requests for application components are instantiated inside this process, even from different clients. This process appears in Task Manager as `dllhost.exe`. There could be many `dllhost.exe` processes, one for each configured COM+ application that has been activated. By isolating components inside a dedicated process, COM+ provides a high degree of fault tolerance from any application errors. If any catastrophic error occurs that forces the shutdown of the `dllhost.exe` process, another one will be created by the COM+ runtime on the next activation. In contrast, termination of the client process happens if a catastrophic error occurs without server applications. The downside to server applications is out-of-process calls. Because the server application has a dedicated process, all component calls must cross process boundaries. Crossing server process boundaries is called *marshaling*.

Activating Library Applications

Library applications activate inside the caller's process, similar to classic COM. However, unlike classic COM, library applications benefit from some of the features of the COM+ runtime. Configuration options for library applications are much more limited. The identity and some security settings are inherited from the client process.

The biggest advantage to a library application is the speed improvement from activating the application in the client process. Disadvantages are that any problems with the application could cause the client to fail. Also, most of the advanced features of COM+ are not available to library applications.

Understanding Security Options

From the original DCOM, security configuration options were configured at two levels: machine-wide and for individual COM applications. It was through a utility called `DCOMCNFG.EXE` that these settings were managed. Unfortunately, this utility was very confusing and led seasoned administrators on many wild goose chases. At the very first sign of trouble, administrators changed security options without understanding the effect. Even with the original DCOM, the default machine-wide settings are appropriate for 95% of all COM systems. Figure 10.7 shows the `DCOMCNFG.EXE` DCOM configuration utility.

With COM+ applications, security options are configured through the Component Services console. By right-clicking a computer name in the console tree and selecting Properties, the administrator can examine and modify machine-wide COM+ security settings in the Default Security tab, shown in Figure 10.8. Therefore, the original DCOM model of two-level security configuration exists in COM+.

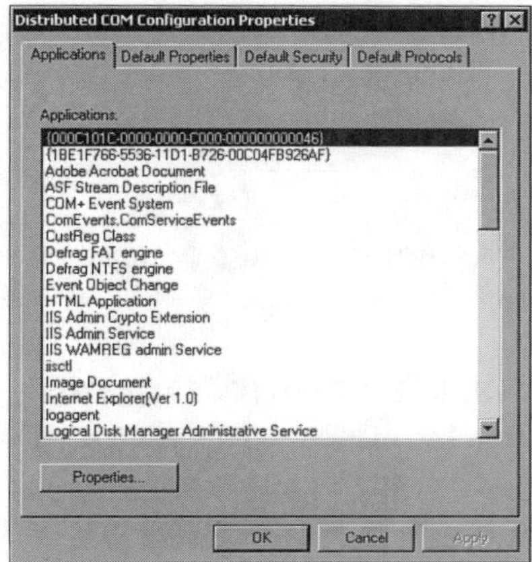

FIGURE 10.7
The DCOMCNFG.EXE *configuration application for DCOM.*

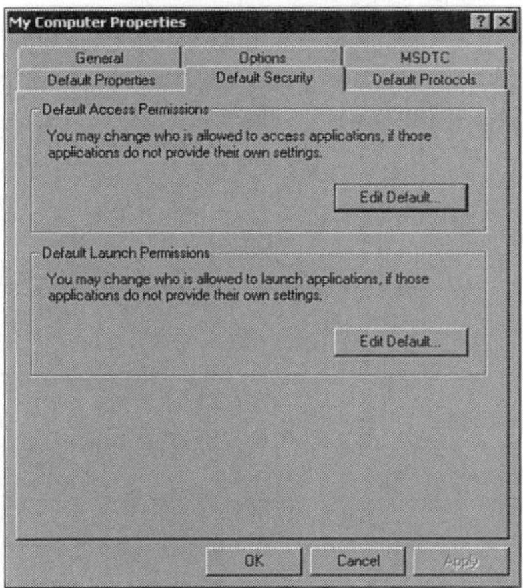

FIGURE 10.8
The Security tab of a computer in the Component Services console.

By default, COM+ application security is configured optimally for a Web farm and uses some of the default machine-wide settings. By eliminating security consideration in the default configuration, it is easier to use COM+. In most instances, it is prudent to avoid additional security when the components of a COM+ application do not require it. Administrators have a tendency when troubleshooting to assume something with security is configured incorrectly and change settings on the tab shown in Figure 10.8. Do not do this; careful examination reveals that, unless an application has special security options defined by developers, the effect of the options on this tab should not affect the functioning of a COM+ application.

CAUTION

Avoid modification of COM+ security settings in most instances.

Choosing the Default COM+ Security Options

The default security configuration for a COM+ application is suitable except in the most esoteric instance. To better understand the default configuration for COM+ security, there are four concepts to consider: authentication level, impersonation level, access permission, and launch permission.

Understanding COM+ Authentication

When a user supplies credentials to log on to a Windows 2000 server, an authentication process verifies identity and resource access rights. In COM+, authentication is the process by which a client and COM+ server application agree on resource access rights. In a library application, the authentication scheme is inherited from the client because those components in the library application are created inside the client process space. Thus, the security context configuration option is unavailable in a library application. COM+ authentication also establishes the encryption level used in communication between the client and COM+ application resources.

COM+ has six distinct levels of authentication, with increasing security and encryption requirements. Table 10.1 shows these levels.

TABLE 10.1 COM+ Authentication Levels

Level	*Description*	*Additional Info*
None	No authentication	Default machine-wide setting.
Connect	Authentication required on initial connection	Similar to an interactive logon. Authentication remains while the client is connected.
Call	Authentication required at each method call into a COM+ application	Slight performance hit; may be worth it in some instances.
Packet	Same as Call, plus verifies all data is received	Default value for COM+ applications.

TABLE 10.1 Continued

Level	*Description*	*Additional Info*
Packet Integrity	Same as Packet, plus verifies data has not changed	Value is questionable. If protection is an issue, use Packet Privacy.
Packet Privacy	Packet Integrity, plus all data is encrypted	Should be reserved for highly sensitive data.

From Table 10.1 we see that the default setting for machine-wide COM settings is None, and for COM+ server applications it is Packet. When a client and a server initially connect, negotiation of authentication occurs by selecting the highest level between the two. For example, if an IIS server is using None and the COM+ server application is using Call, the negotiated authentication level will be Call. The defaults are sufficient for most applications. In all instances, as the amount of encryption increases, performance decreases.

CAUTION

Avoid unnecessary encryption during authentication because it greatly decreases performance.

Understanding Impersonation Level

Impersonation is the process in which the server assumes the identity of the client. A client must explicitly grant the server this right through the Impersonation Level setting. A server needs to do this when it is appropriate to use the client credentials when accessing secured resources. Table 10.2 discusses the different impersonation levels.

TABLE 10.2 COM+ Impersonation Levels

Level	*Description*	*Additional Info*
Anonymous	Any impersonation is anonymous; no client information is used.	Default machine-wide setting.
Identify	The client identity can be used to do ACL checks.	Restricted to resources on server machine only.

TABLE 10.2 Continued

Level	*Description*	*Additional Info*
Impersonate	The server can access resources on the client machine, impersonating the client fully.	Default machine-wide and COM+ application setting. This setting does not allow the server to impersonate the client fully over the network.
Delegate	The server can impersonate the client fully over the network.	This is the feature that caused Microsoft to modify the Kerberos implementation in Windows 2000.

In Windows 2000, for Delegate-level impersonation to work, the server must be marked as Trusted for Delegation in Active Directory, and the client credentials must not be marked as Account Is Sensitive and Cannot Be Delegated. It is highly unlikely that a Web farm application would need any impersonation features at all.

Understanding Access Permission

Access permissions grant the right to access a COM+ application. Access permission is defined by a list of users and groups that are granted access to a COM+ application. As with all COM+ security settings, there are machine-wide settings that apply to any COM+ application that does not specify access permissions.

To configure machine-wide access permissions, bring up the properties of the computer from the Component Services console and select the Default Security tab. Select the Access Permission button. The resulting dialog allows the addition and removal of user accounts and groups in the standard Windows 2000 configuration.

Understanding Launch Permission

Launch permission is the right to start or launch a COM+ application. Launch permission is defined by a list of users and groups that are granted launching privileges to a COM+ application. By default, all user accounts on a local server have the right to launch programs. As with all COM+ security settings, there are machine-wide settings that apply to any COM+ application that does not specify Launch permission.

To configure machine-wide Launch permission, bring up the properties of the computer from the Component Servers administrative tool and select the Default Security tab. Select the Launch Permission button. The resulting dialog enables the addition and removal of user accounts and groups using the standard Windows 2000 procedures. Changing this configuration is necessary only when using COM+ applications outside a Web farm.

Overriding Machine-Wide COM+ Security Options

The Security tab of the COM+ application Properties panel is used for configuring application-specific security settings. Changing settings in the tab overrides the default machine-wide security settings. Figure 10.9 shows the Security tab of a COM+ server and library application.

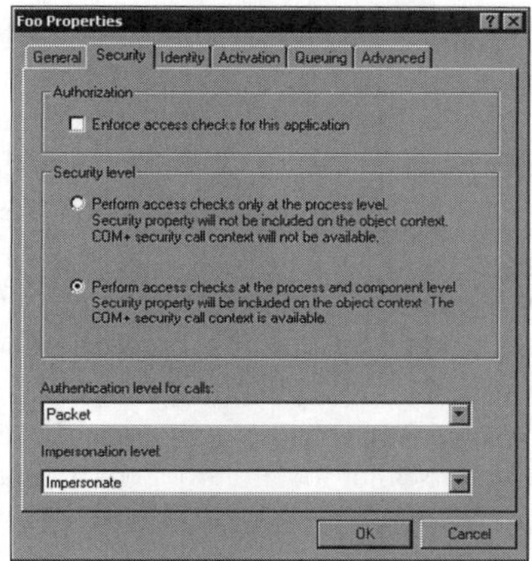

FIGURE 10.9

Security options for a COM+ server and library application.

For server applications, in the Authorization section of the Security tab, the Enforce Access Checks for This Application check box is unchecked by default. If this option is unchecked, then the security level settings on this page have no effect. In fact, if accessing this COM+ objects from a Web server where IIS is controlling the password for the anonymous account, there is no security required at all. When IIS controls the password, the authorization request comes in as the Local System Authority, which by default can launch COM+ application and create objects. The authentication and impersonation combo boxes still override the machine-wide COM settings. In a library application, these combo boxes are not present and instead are replaced by an Enable Authentication check box. This check box tells COM+ by default to allow the authentication settings of the client process to control how authentication of the COM+ application happens. This setting is unnecessary if the application is not using role-based security.

Understanding Identity Options

The Identity tab is used to configure the security credentials for a COM+ application. These security credentials are used to gain access to any resources that can be protected by an access control list. The default setting for this tab is Interactive User. If this property changed in the original configuration of the COM+ application, then those changes should be reflected here. When deploying a COM+ application, make sure that some account other than the interactive user is specified. Failure to specify an account here will require an active logon session on every server that will run the COM+ application.

For example, a COM+ application requires access to a series of network share points. In succession, the application attempts to find a configuration file located in these share points. If it is unable to locate the file in point A, either because it is not present or the application does not have the appropriate security credentials, it moves on to share point B. This process repeats until all share points have been examined. During initial testing, the COM+ application ran in the interactive user security context. Because an administrator was logged into the server to perform maintenance, access to these share points was granted. However, during a different test, when the administrator had logged off, there was no interactive user security context, and access to these share points was denied. Diagnosing a problem like this is frustrating, due to people logging on and off a server, a normally innocuous activity. Another artifact of the application identity is that, by clever management of access control lists to these share points, an administrator could change the share point location of a configuration file. While this example is purely hypothetical, it serves to explain the importance of a COM+ application identity.

Understanding Advanced Options

Figure 10.10 shows the Advanced tab. From this tab, the administrator can configure how a COM+ server application manages its lifetime. The Permission section controls modification of a deployed library or server application. Developers use the debugging session to help troubleshoot COM+ server applications. The Enable Compensating Resource Managers check box allows a COM+ application to use special resource managers. The Enable 3GB Support check box allows a COM+ application to take advantage of the three gigabytes of memory available in a Windows 2000 Advanced Server.

The Server Process Shutdown section applies only to server applications. Administrators use this setting to control when the `dllhost.exe` process self-terminates. If the Leave Running While Idle setting is selected, the `dllhost.exe` process for a COM+ server application will never self-terminate. If Minutes Until Idle Shutdown is selected, the text box next to this option determines how many minutes until the `dllhost.exe` process self-terminates.

TIP

Always specify the minutes until idle shutdown on all COM+ applications. This helps recover expensive server resources when they are not in constant use.

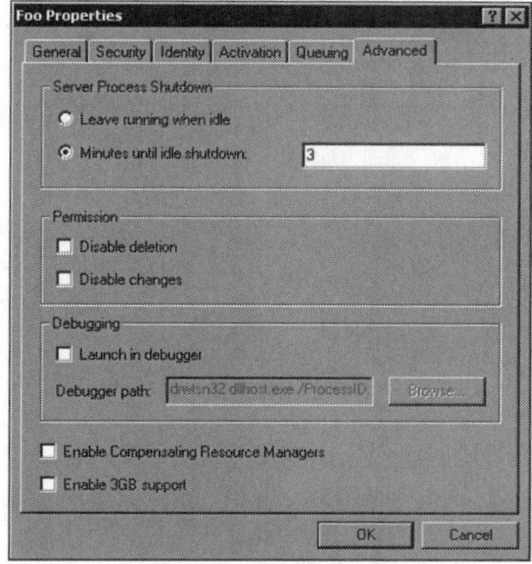

FIGURE 10.10
Advanced configuration options of COM+ applications.

Installing Configured Components

A COM+ application is not complete without classic COM components. Every COM+ application must have one or more components that it manages. Think of the COM+ application as an operating system for COM components. By creating a layer of abstraction, Microsoft has provided a way to extend the functionality of COM components without needing to recompile the code.

Interception is the concept of taking key classic COM APIs and hooking them into COM+. With interception, a component can gain features administratively rather than programmatically. Classic COM components that have attributes granted from the COM+ runtime are called *configured components*. Creating configured components is as simple as running a wizard from the Component Services administrative tool.

NEW TERM A *configured component* is any component that has been installed into a COM+ application. Configured components gain features from the COM+ runtime administratively.

Installing Classic COM Components

Before delving into the installation of COM+ components, it is important to understand how classic COM components are installed onto a server. One of the great features of COM components is that they are self-installing, or in COM terms, *self-registering*. Registering a classic COM component is done using a utility called `regsrv32.exe`, which is installed by default with Windows 2000. `Regsrv32.exe` understands how to look at a COM DLL and extract the appropriate Registry entries required for the component to function. Because COM components use the Registry to hold configuration information, the process of installing COM components to a server is called *registering a COM component*. The following example shows the command line for registering `foocomponents.dll`, which contains COM components.

```
Regsvr32.exe c:\components\foocomponents.dll
```

`Regsrv32.exe` is also used to unregister, or remove, entries that a COM component added to the register when it was registered. The following example shows the command line for unregistering `foocomponents.dll`.

```
Regsvr32.exe /u c:\components\foocomponents.dll
```

COM+ extends the classic COM registration capabilities through the Component Services console. This console simplifies and automates the registration process for COM components and in most cases eliminates the need to use `regsvr32.exe` to register COM components in COM+.

Installing COM+ Configured Components

Making a COM component a configured component is as easy as running the COM Component Install Wizard. Expand any COM+ Application node; inside is a folder called `Components`. Right-click the `Components` folder and select New, Component to launch the wizard.

From the welcome screen, click Next and the Import or Install a Component pane becomes visible, as seen in Figure 10.11. From this pane the administrator has three choices: Install New Component(s), Import Component(s) That Are Already Registered, and Install New Event Class(es). Here COM+ makes an important distinction for deployment between COM components that have already been registered on a server and those that have not. In most instances it is better to let the COM Component Install Wizard register and install new objects, but some poorly designed components don't function properly with the COM+ tools and must be registered manually before they are installed into the COM+ runtime.

TIP

Do not register components with `regsrv32.exe` if they are a part of a COM+ application. COM+ handles all registration tasks.

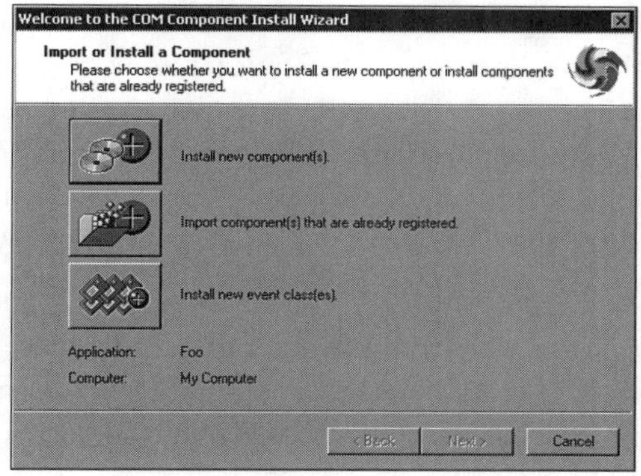

FIGURE 10.11
The Import or Install a Component pane of the COM Component Wizard.

To let COM+ install a new component, it is necessary only to point it to the COM component DLL file, which a developer or third party should supply. Do not register this file with `regsrv32.exe` unless directed to. Registering a COM DLL manually could make the deployment process fail and affect the application's capability to function. Instead, from the wizard, select the Install New Component button. This button launches a standard file-browsing dialog. Browse to the location of the DLL file and select it by clicking Open. Multiple files are added in this way because COM+ allows the conglomeration of COM components from disparate DLL files to appear as one COM+ application. Figure 10.12 shows the Install New Components pane of the wizard with multiple COM components from the same DLL file.

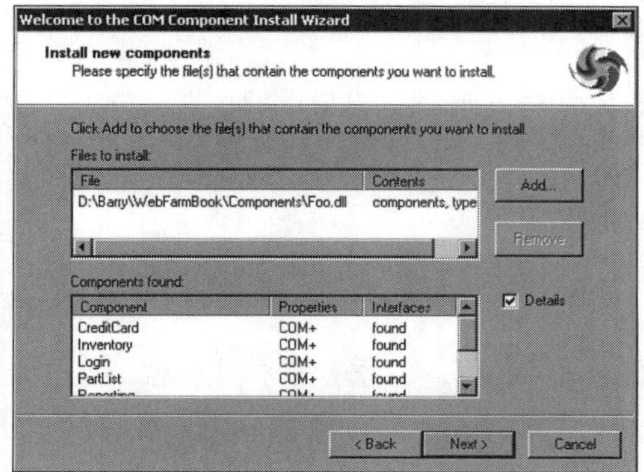

FIGURE 10.12
The Install New Components pane of the COM Component Wizard.

To import a component that is already registered, select Import Components That Are Already Registered from the initial pane. From here, a component browser shows all the in-process COM components that have already been installed on this server in the classic COM fashion. To add a component to a COM+ application, simply find the component desired, select it and any others required, and click Next. The Details check box shows the file path to the DLL file for each COM component and the CLSID. The CLSID is a GUID the COM uses to name a specific component.

One of the disadvantages of importing components is that method and interface information is unavailable when deploying. In some situations, this could render the application unusable. Re-creating this application on every machine would be the only deployment option.

After components have been installed into a COM+ application, it is possible to add others. Each DLL can have any number of COM components that it holds. It is also possible to mix and match installing new components and importing existing ones. However, it is not possible to have the same component in more than one COM+ application. Figure 10.13 shows a COM+ application that has multiple components installed. Note that this is the Property view.

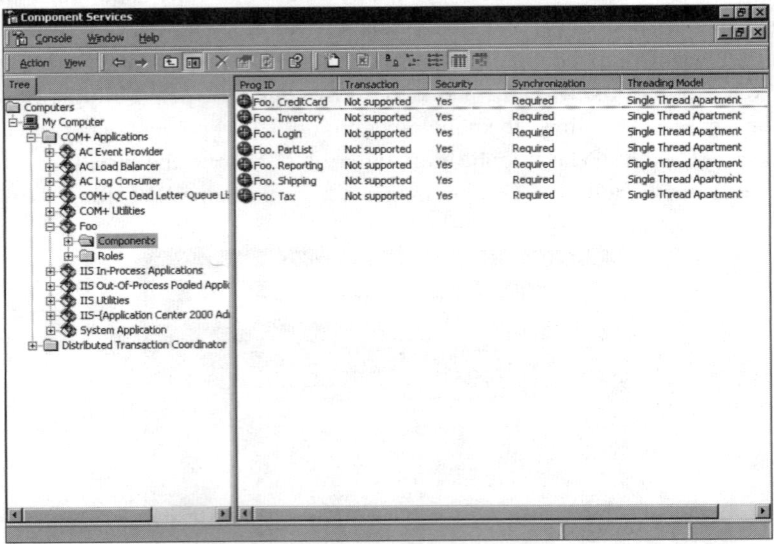

FIGURE 10.13

The Property view of a COM+ application with many components.

Understanding Configured Components

Configured components gain attributes from the COM+ runtime. Attributes for configured components include transaction support, role-based security, object pooling, just-in-time activation, and advanced concurrency support. All of the attributes are configured from the properties of an individual component. To access a component's properties, right-click it in the View pane of the Component Services administrative tool and select Properties.

Understanding Transaction Attributes

Transaction support is one of the main features of the COM+ runtime granted to configured components. When multiple components participate actively in a transaction, they all have a vote in whether the transaction commits or aborts. Each component that participates in a transaction must declare success for the transaction to commit. For example, suppose that a transaction is composed of two components, one that writes to a database and another that writes to a file. If the database portion failed, then that component would vote that the transaction should abort. Even if the component that wrote to the file system voted to commit the transaction, the whole transaction fails and is said to *roll back*. Figure 10.14 shows the Property pane for transactions of a configured component. It is through this pane that the types of transaction support a component uses are declared.

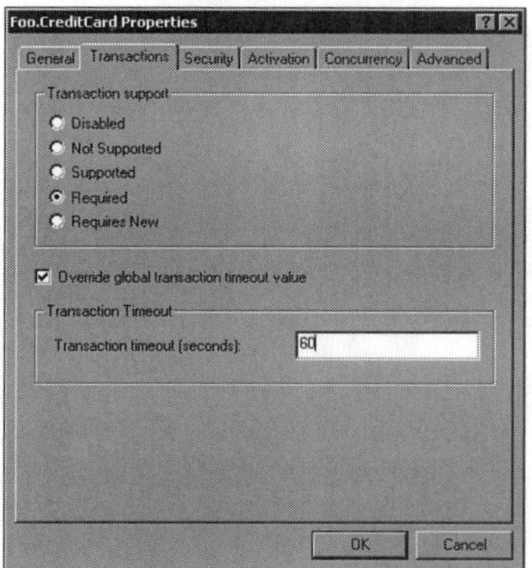

FIGURE 10.14
The Transactions Property view of a COM+ component.

Transaction support is broken into five types, which are listed in Table 10.3.

TABLE 10.3 COM+ Transaction Attributes

Value	*Description*	*Additional Info*
Disabled	Transactions are disabled for this component.	Most effective setting for traditional COM components in COM+ that don't use transactions.
Not Supported	Transactions are not supported, but the component will not affect the outcome of a transaction if activated within the context of one.	Default value.
Supported	Component can participate in an existing transaction but never creates one.	Most flexible; requires that a component be aware of this setting.
Required	Component must be activated within a COM+ transaction. If one exists, it will use it.	
Requires New	Component must be activated within a new transaction. It cannot use any existing transaction context.	Usually reserved for components that begin transactions.

Understanding Security Attributes

COM+ allows security settings to be configured on applications and individual components. Figure 10.15 shows the Security tab for a configured component. This tab will show roles that are configured to have access to this component if using role-based security.

In this tab, the Enforce Component Level Access Checks check box is one step in enabling role-based security at the component level. In order to fully enable role-based security in COM+, the Enforce Access Checks for This Application check box and the Perform Access Checks at the Process and Component Level radio button must be selected in the application's Properties Security tab. Application properties are accessible by right-clicking an application in the Component Services console and selecting Properties from the menu. Table 10.4 summarizes the main security configuration options in COM+.

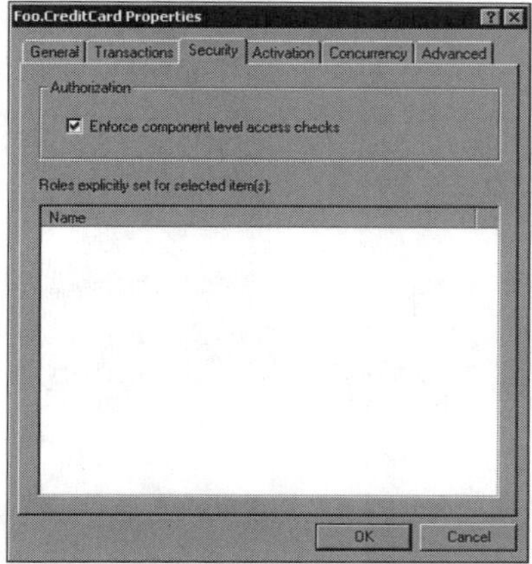

FIGURE 10.15
The Security tab of a COM+ component.

TABLE 10.4 COM+ Security Configuration Summary

Setting	*Area*	*Summary*
Enforce Access Checks for This Application	Application Security tab	Disabled by default. Must be enabled for role-based security.
Perform Access Checks Only at the Process Level	Application Security tab	Role-based security is disabled. COM+ security context is disabled.
Perform Access Check at the Component and Process Level	Application Security tab	Required for role-based security. Enabled by default.
Enforce Component Level Access Checks	Component Security tab	Required for role-based security. Enabled by default.

Role-based security is an advanced feature of COM+. An administrator creates roles that represent the different users of a COM+ component. In a company, roles could be manager, administrator, and employee. If an application uses roles, then roles control access to component interfaces, component methods, and the component.

For example, Foo.com has a credit card component called `Foo.CreditCard`. `Foo.CreditCard` has two methods: `GetAuthorization` and `SettleTransactions`. A method is a programmatic interface that a component uses to expose its functionality to other application areas. Figure 10.16 shows the two methods of `Foo.CreditCard` in the Component Services console and also shows that two roles have been defined: Manager and Web Site.

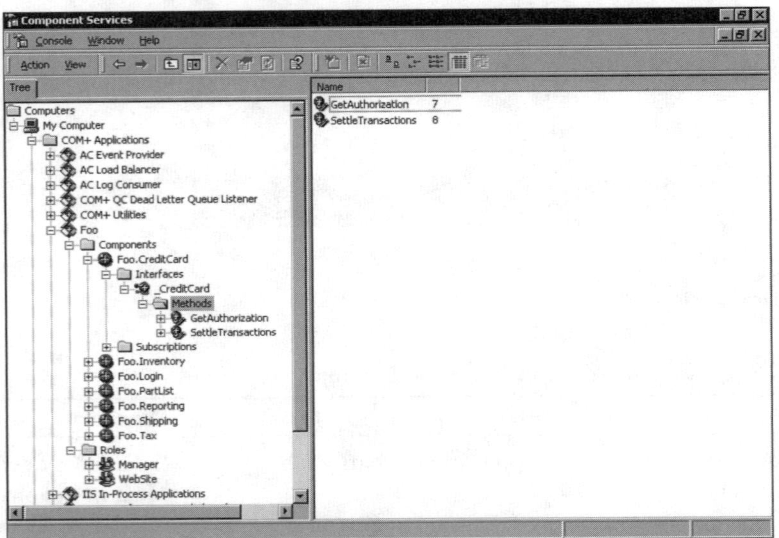

FIGURE 10.16

The methods and roles of the `Foo.CreditCard` *component.*

Foo.com policy allows the Web Site role to get authorization on a credit card number, but only the Manager role has the authority to settle transactions. The administrator of Foo.com can assign these roles to individual methods of the `Foo.CreditCard` component. Figure 10.17 shows the `Foo.CreditCard SettleTransactions` property page with the Manager role assigned. Only one role in role-based security can be assigned to anonymous access Web site users because all anonymous users access resources as the same account. To use role-based security with anonymous sites, change the anonymous account username and password to match the user in the role that is for the Web site. Role-based security is not that useful in an anonymous access Web site and should be used only if absolutely necessary.

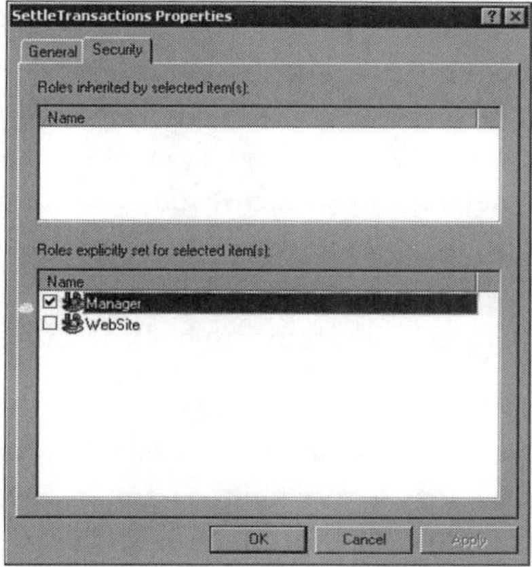

FIGURE 10.17
The `SettleTransactions` *method's Security tab.*

Understanding Activation Attributes

When a COM+ component is created, activation attributes determine which features the COM+ runtime adds to the component. Activation features include object pooling, object construction, just-in-time activation, and support for dynamic load balancing. Figure 10.18 shows the Activation tab of a configured component.

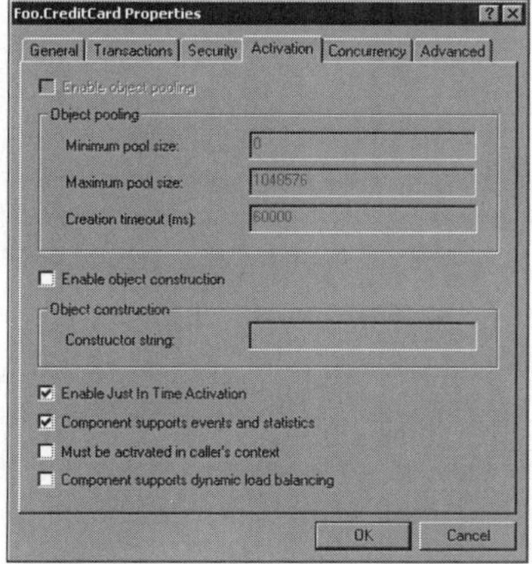

FIGURE 10.18
The `Foo.CreditCard` *component's Activation tab.*

The first section of the Activation property page enables object pooling. A component must be built specifically to support object pooling, and the one in this example does not. If a component supported object pooling, then that object would be recycled and reused instead of destroyed after each object request. Object pooling is great for components that have expensive activations such as making connections to slow distributed systems on startup. It is also possible to set a maximum number of objects that a pool can support and an initial pool count so that at startup objects can be ready for use. The Creation Timeout value is used when the maximum pool size is reached. This timeout must expire before the client will get a Component Unavailable response.

COM+ uses object construction to pass parameterized startup values to configured components. This is useful in deployment situations across multiple environments. The simplest example of a constructor string is an ODBC DSN. A component must be written to use a constructor string so setting this value has no effect unless directed by the developer of the component.

The Enable Just In Time Activation check box is used to specify that an object may be repeatedly deactivated and reactivated just-in-time (JIT) to handle calls from a client. This JIT activation is completely hidden from the client and uses server resources more efficiently. JIT activation can decrease the component activation time.

If an object uses Component Load Balancing, it must enable the component to support dynamic load balancing. At this point, the component will no longer be activated on the local machine, but instead will use the CLB routing list to create the component on a remote COM+ cluster. This is different from creating an application proxy. Component Load Balancing is available with Application Center 2000.

NOTE

For more information on Component Load Balancing, see Chapter 13, "Deploying Application Center 2000 COM+ Clusters."

Understanding Concurrency Attributes

In multithread environments such as IIS, classic COM components had to worry about re-entrancy. Re-entrancy happens when more than one thread executes the same code within a component at the same time. Developers spend considerable effort ensuring that a component can handle these re-entrant conditions. With COM+ concurrency, the runtime provides this functionality through a configurable attribute. Figure 10.19 shows the Concurrency tab for a COM+ component.

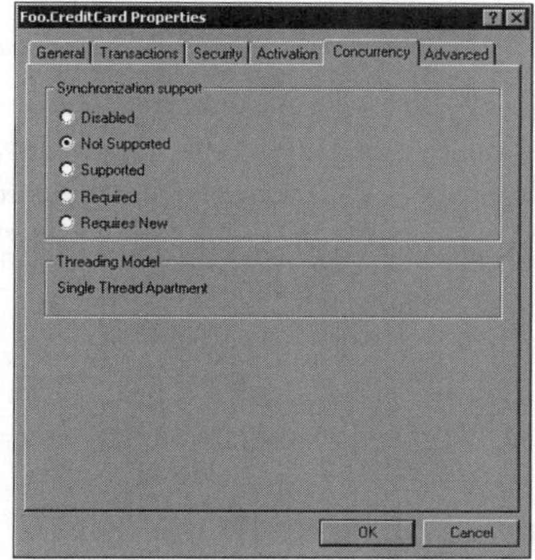

FIGURE 10.19
The Concurrency tab of a COM+ component.

Synchronization support is used to define what level of re-entrant protection a component requires. Which attributes are available is contingent on other attributes of the COM+ runtime. For instance, if transactions are supported or required for a component, then the only synchronization attribute available is Required. Table 10.5 shows the dependency between COM+ attributes.

TABLE 10.5 COM+ Attribute Dependency for Concurrency

Setting	*Synchronization Options Available*	*Notes*
Transaction Required or Supported	Required	Also requires just-in-time activation.
Transaction Requires New	Required or Requires New	Also requires just-in-time activation.
Just In Time Activation Enabled	Required or Requires New	Transaction support level is not important.
Transactions Disabled or Not Supported and Just In Time Activation Disabled	All synchronization options available	Must have transaction support disabled or not supported.

Deploying COM+ Applications

Deploying a COM+ application is easier than building one. The best deployment practice is to build the COM+ application manually in a testing or development stage and then use the COM+ deployment tools to re-create the application in the staging and production environments.

The primary task of deploying a COM+ application is that of exporting. *Exporting* is taking an individual COM+ application and running the COM+ Application Export Wizard. The exporting process creates a Microsoft Standard Installer (MSI) file. This file contains all the relevant component files and the INF files needed to install the application on another server. Running this MSI file will re-create the COM+ application on the target server.

Exporting a Server Application

To export a server application, launch the Export Wizard and bypass the welcome screen. On the second pane, type the path to where the COM+ application configuration information should be exported or browse to a local or network file point. This is the file path to where the MSI is created. Be sure to select Server Application and click Next. The wizard will tell you when it is finished.

Testing the export is as simple as deleting the application and running the MSI file. To delete a COM+ application, right-click on the application name and select Delete. To re-create or install the COM+ application on another server, use Explorer to browse to where the application was originally exported and double-click the MSI file. When the MSI is finished, right-click on the COM+ `Applications` folder and select Refresh. The application should reappear in the console tree.

There is one caveat to exporting and re-creating a COM+ application: For security reasons, the identity information of the COM+ application is reset to the interactive user. The administrator can either change the user information manually at install time or create a script to set the password programmatically using the COM+ catalog objects.

Exporting an Application Proxy

Exporting an application proxy is the same as exporting a server application. The only difference is selecting the Application Proxy radio button. Conceptually, application proxies are completely different from server applications. A proxy application, when installed on another server, creates a COM+ application that is configured to forward component requests to a remote server. By default, this remote server is the same as the server where the application was exported. This is a problem in a multistage deployment environment.

NEW TERM A *proxy application* is a COM+ application that is configured locally on a server to execute on a remote machine.

Luckily, the MSI files can accept command-line parameters using the `MSIEXEC.EXE` utility. One of these parameters, `REMOTESERVERNAME`, enables the administrator to configure what server the application proxy should forward requests to.

TIP

Always refresh Component Services after making configuration changes.

A COM+ Application Deployment Example

Foo.com has a COM+ application called CreditCard that runs on a farm of application servers. These application servers perform credit card authorizations for customers on the Foo.com Web site. They have special configurations for connecting directly to a bank to get authorizations in real-time. Foo.com wants to access these servers remotely from all of the Web servers. Figure 10.20 shows Foo.com's deployment architecture.

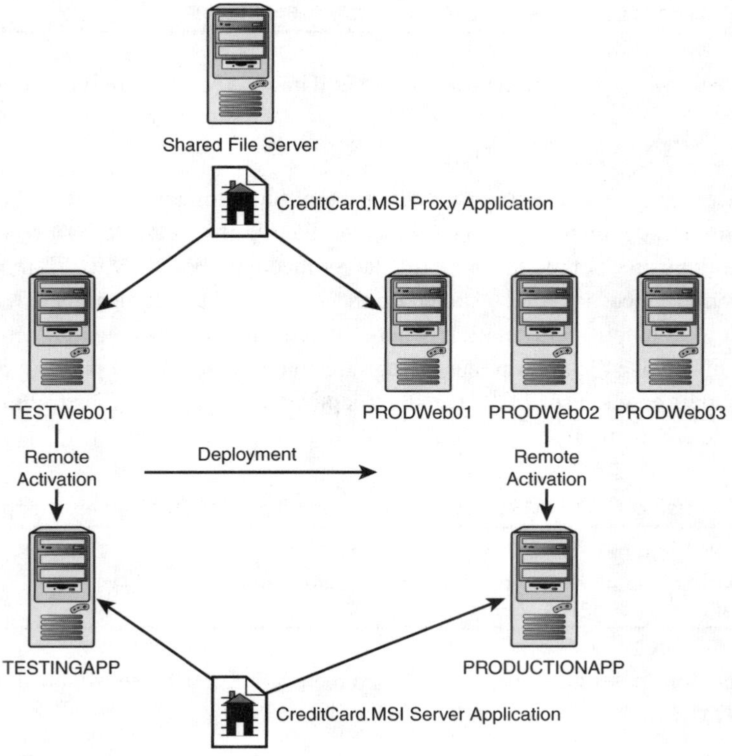

FIGURE 10.20
Foo.com builds a COM+ application deployment architecture.

In the testing environment, the administrator creates the initial credit card authorization application manually, using the COM+ Application Wizard and the COM Component Install Wizard. Then he exports an application proxy to a network share that is available to all the servers in the farm. On the testing Web server, he runs the MSI file, creating the application proxy on the Web server. On the Activation tab, the remote server is `TESTAPP`. He tests the application and prepares to deploy to production application servers and Web servers. For the production application servers, he needs to re-create the actual server application, so he exports the application server MSI file for this purpose. In production, the MSI file for the application servers is used to re-create the server application. He must remember to reset the identity to the appropriate credentials for the production environment. The Web servers use the application proxy MSI and must specify the command-line parameter `REMOTESERVERNAME` to change the configuration information stored in the MSI file. Listing 10.1 shows how he used the Microsoft Installer to install the credit card application.

LISTING 10.1 Using `MSIEXEC.EXE` to Install the Foo.com Credit Card Application

```
Using MSIEXEC command line parameters
MSIEXEC.EXE -I creditcard.msi REMOTESERVERNAME=PRODAPP
```

The code in Listing 10.1 will set the remote server name in the Activation tab to `PRODAPP`.

Using the COMREPL Tool

Component Services provides a very rudimentary tool for automating the replication of COM+ applications through deployment environments and Web farms. `COMREPL.EXE` copies all the COM+ applications on a source machine to a target machine. For COMREPL to work properly, Component Services must be installed on the source and target machines. As with other COM+ services, all identity information is not replicated and reset to the interactive user. The administrator must have the appropriate permissions on all machines to perform replication. Listing 10.2 shows how to use `COMREPL.EXE` to deploy COM+ applications from one server to another with the command line.

LISTING 10.2 Using the COMREPL Command-Line Tool for Deployment: `deploycom.cmd`

```
REM*** COMREPL general command line format
REM*** COMREPL <SourceComputer> <TargetComputerList> [/n [/v]]
COMREPL STGAPP01 PRODAPP01 /n /v
```

COMREPL has four possible command-line parameters. Table 10.6 shows the command-line options for COMREPL.

TABLE 10.6 COMREPL Command-Line Parameters

Parameter	*Description*
`SourceComputer`	The computer that servers as the source of the COM+ applications. For deploying to production, this could be a staging server.
`TargetComputerList`	A list of target computers to which the COM+ applications are to be replicated. For deploying to production, this could be the entire farm.
`/v`	Echo output to console.
`/n`	No prompting.

Application Center 2000 includes all the functionality of COMREPL and more. If Application Center 2000 is used, COMREPL is unnecessary.

Summary

COM+ is a powerful runtime for business components. COM+ adds attributes to traditional COM components just by installing them inside a COM+ application. These attributes enable features such as transaction support, advanced security, and concurrency. These features are traditionally difficult to implement, but COM+ simplifies and generalizes these problems by providing them to any component. In the COM+ runtime, these components are called configured components.

COM+ also simplifies deployment problems. Exporting a server application and installing it on a new server is as easy as running a wizard. The wizard creates a Microsoft Standard Installer file that re-creates and installs the COM+ application and all its components. Installing remote components is made just as easy by creating an application proxy MSI file. The Microsoft Installer uses this file to install the necessary Registry entries and COM+ application configuration on the target machine for remote component activation.

Any administrator will benefit from understanding the different features of COM+. By empowering administrators to control the powerful COM+ configuration options, COM+ has raised attribute-based programming to a whole new level.

NOTE

For more information on COM and COM+, see `http://www.microsoft.com/com`.

Introducing Application Center 2000

CHAPTER

11

IN THIS CHAPTER

Application Center 2000 is a fundamental part of the Microsoft .NET Enterprise Server Architecture. It is a unique offering in the industry that combines a number of disjointed management tools into a centralized, easy-to-use administrative console. What was accomplished with custom scripts, the Site Server 3.0 content replication system, and hard work is now brought together under the umbrella of Application Center 2000.

In this chapter, Application Center 2000 is introduced with a brief overview of the breadth of its features. Web clusters, COM+ clusters, and health monitoring are discussed from a high level. Installation options and server requirements for installing Application Center are covered. A basic Web cluster is created to establish how easy it is to use Application Center 2000. Finally, a tour of the administrative console explores the Application Center 2000 features.

Chapter 12, "Deploying Application Center 2000 Web Clusters," covers Web clusters in great detail, including an exploration of all property pages and wizards. The concept of the application as it relates to Application Center 2000 is explored. Replication and synchronization options are considered, including publishing from one cluster to another. Application Center's integration with Network Load Balancing is covered from hardware requirements to initial setup requirements for adding a new cluster member on-the-fly.

Chapter 13, "Deploying Application Center 2000 COM+ Clusters," examines COM+ clusters and COM+ routing clusters. Details include how Component Load Balancing (CLB) works, COM+ routing clusters, and COM+ client and server options. The fate of COM+ application proxies is revealed.

Chapter 14, "Monitoring a Web Farm with Application Center 2000," covers Health Monitor and Application Center's consolidated monitoring features. Custom and standard alerts are explored, including a complete overview of the Health Monitor console and the centralized logging and event viewing of the Application Center 2000 console. The chapter includes an overview of WMI and how Application Center 2000 uses WMI providers for alerting and custom scripting.

Chapter 15, "Performing Common Health Monitor Tasks," covers managing computers to monitor, configuring custom actions, data groups, and data collectors, and managing alerts. Specific examples are used to illustrate all the different built-in monitors, including a COM+ application monitor, HTTP monitor, and a simple ping monitor.

Chapter 16, "Performing Advanced Application Center 2000 Tasks," discusses creating custom event filtering, defining file and folder exclusions, migrating existing sites to Application Center 2000, using the AC command-line tool, and other advanced topics. Included in that discussion is transferring Site Server CRS projects to Application Center applications.

The goals of this chapter are to help you

- Explore the reasons that Application Center 2000 is the right choice for an administrator who must manage Web farms. Application Center 2000 makes managing a Web farm as easy as managing a single server.
- Install Application Center 2000 on to a server. This section covers the requirements and steps for installing Application Center 2000 onto the servers in a farm.
- Follow an example of creating a cluster controller, one of the most important tasks performed when using Application Center 2000.
- Explore the administrative console in a brief overview of all the features of Application Center 2000.

Choosing Application Center to Manage a Web Farm

Many of the actions and tasks in this book have sorely needed a tool like Application Center 2000. First and foremost, Application Center 2000 solves the application replication problem. Application Center simplifies the process of scaling so that a Web farm can handle its load easily. Application Center centralizes management and monitoring of multiple servers. Finally, Application Center 2000 provides an easy way to stage and deploy new releases.

Replicating Applications with Application Center 2000

Application replication is a serious problem for medium- to large-scale Web farms. When a Web cluster has more than a few members, the process of application replication must be scripted and automated. If it is not, then the process of manually updating a Web site with a new release could take a very long time. Until Application Center 2000, Content Replication System (CRS, also known as Site Server Publishing) was the only tool available from Microsoft that could be used for application replication. However, CRS only replicates the contents of directories and the supporting directory structure. Figure 11.1 is an example of the clunky CRS interface. Eight different tabs with archaic and hard-to-use features make CRS difficult to configure. Just managing file exclude and include paths for directory replication is error prone and poorly designed. CRS cannot replicate other typical application components automatically. Replicating Registry entries, IIS metabase information, Data Source Names for ODBC, and COM+ applications is accomplished by custom scripts. These scripts run before or after a replication job. Clearly, CRS is not good enough to manage a complicated .NET Web farm.

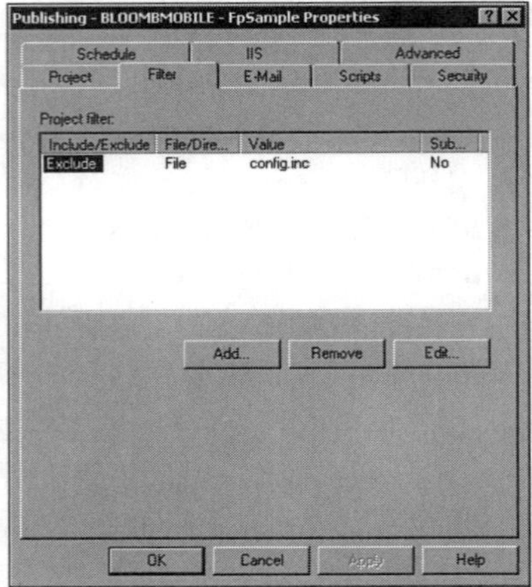

FIGURE 11.1
The CRS user interface, a nightmare.

With Application Center 2000, application replication for Web farms is solved. The clunky interface of CRS has been abandoned for a flashy new explorer interface. COM+ applications, IIS metabase settings, ODBC connection strings, Registry entries, and file system paths are all part of an Application Center application object. This application object is easily configured from one management console, and no custom scripts are required. When deploying, all the pieces of the application object sync with the configuration of the cluster controller. Once an application object is defined, it becomes a conceptual script that Application Center executes on each of the cluster members. Figure 11.2 shows the flow of an application object through an Application Center 2000 cluster.

The application object is easily modified to include new objects. For example, a change control requires a new COM+ application. In the past, the deployment team would likely manually install the exported COM+ application on each machine in the cluster. A manual process is likely to fail at some point. With Application Center 2000, the deployment team manually configures the new COM+ application exactly as needed on the one cluster controller. They add the COM+ application to the application object, telling Application Center 2000 to synchronize the cluster. Within a matter of minutes, the new COM+ application is available on the other cluster members, configured exactly like the cluster controller.

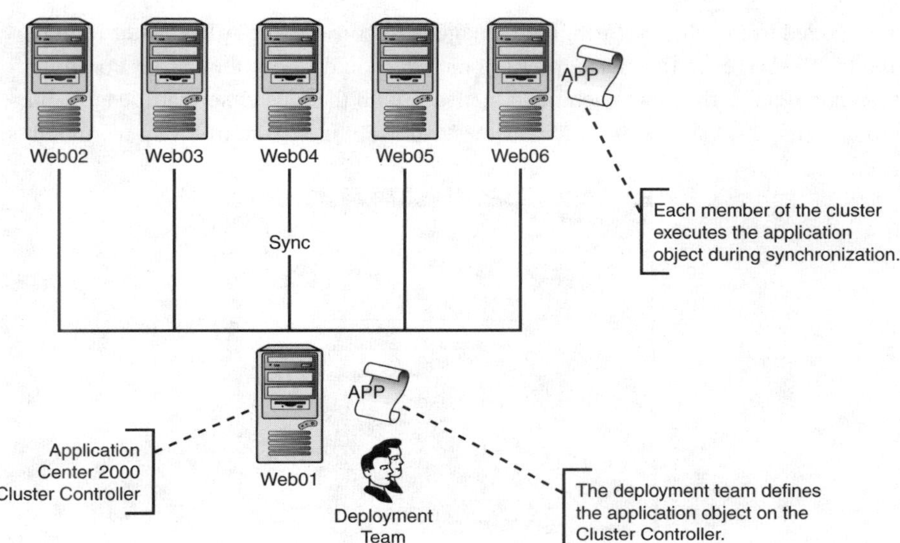

FIGURE 11.2
An application object in Application Center 2000.

NEW TERM A *cluster controller* is an Application Center 2000 server that has the master copy of the application. All deployments and cluster synchronizations originate from this server.

If an application has pieces that don't fit within the scope of the Application Center 2000 object, it is possible to write custom scripts that will be executed from deployment events on each cluster member. Replication of any application configuration is possible with Application Center 2000 custom scripting. More information on custom scripting can be found in Chapter 15.

Scaling with Application Center 2000

Scaling to handle load is a critical success factor for any .NET Web farm. Once an application is able to run across multiple servers, the process of scaling a site is simply adding server capacity to the stressed portion of a site. The challenge then is to replicate the application parts to the new server and add it to the cluster.

Application Center 2000 simplifies adding and removing cluster members for scaling. After installing Application Center 2000 on each new cluster member, a simple two-step process can bring a new server online. In its default configuration, Application Center 2000 uses Network Load Balancing (NLB) as its scaling solution. NLB configuration (see Chapter 5, "Using Microsoft Network Load Balancing in a Web Farm") is done automatically to each server when it is added to the cluster. From the management console, the Add Cluster Member Wizard adds the server to the cluster. During the addition process, the cluster controller configures NLB and readies the new machine to coalesce with the cluster so that it can begin receiving traffic. Figure 11.3 shows the Add Cluster Member Wizard, the first step to smooth scaling.

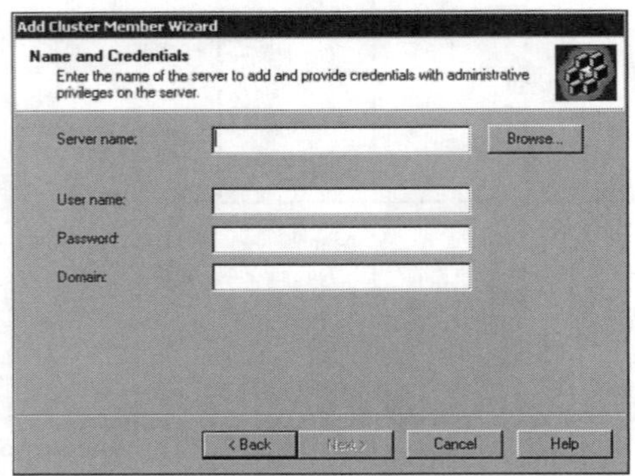

FIGURE 11.3
The Add Cluster Member Wizard.

At this point, if the cluster controller is set up with the default configuration options, the applications on the cluster controller will automatically synchronize to the new member. Once this synchronization is complete, the new cluster member is ready to be brought online through the management console. Since Application Center 2000 is highly integrated with Network Load Balancing, the server can begin handling Web requests immediately. A two-step process scales any Web farm.

This flexibility in scaling allows for some creative management of resources. In a large Web farm, there could be any number of under-utilized servers at one time. With the dynamic cluster member management and automated synchronization processes, those servers could stop serving the under-utilized content and begin serving the stressed content in a matter of minutes. Scenarios like those in Figure 11.4 show creative ways to maximize return on hardware investments.

Using Application Center 2000 for COM+ Load Balancing

COM+ is a great way to create component-based services. COM+ also greatly simplifies the process of deploying and accessing COM+ application services locally and remotely. Application Center adds to this architecture by allowing COM+ applications to replicate with a Web application. For example, if a Web site uses a COM+ application to handle login or credit card authorization, Application Center can be configured to group these objects with the Web pages and replicate them as one unit. Application Center also introduces the concept of COM+ routing clusters and COM+ application clusters to provide fail-over and redundancy.

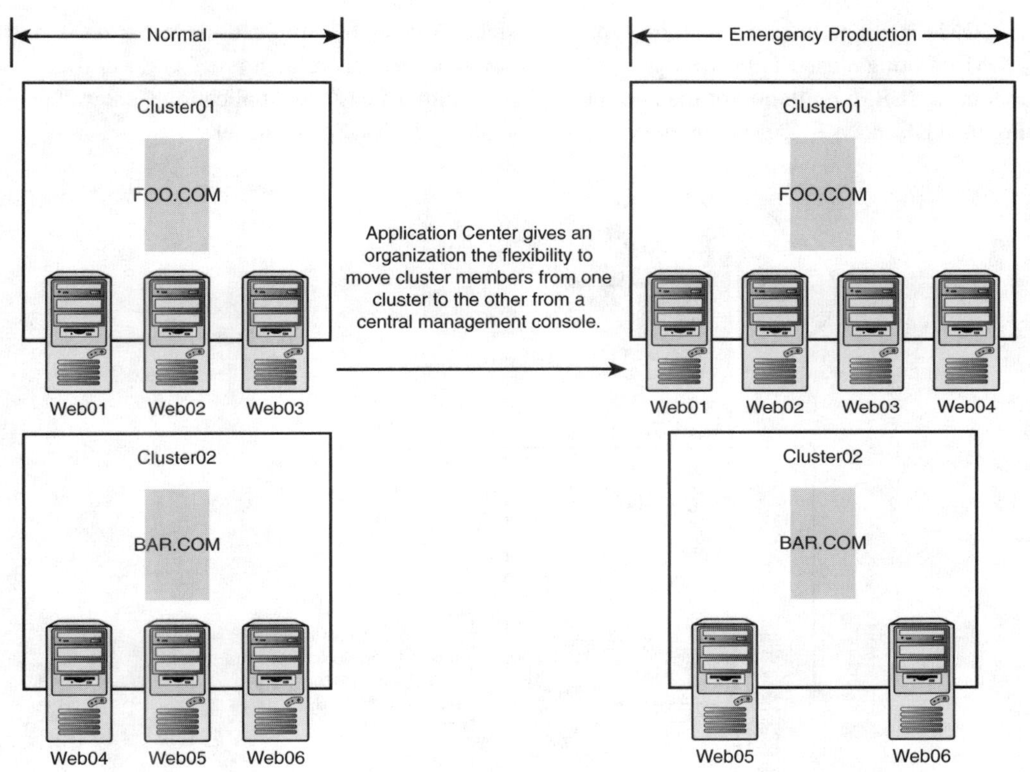

FIGURE 11.4
Using Application Center 2000 to maximize hardware utilization.

Without Application Center, a COM+ application proxy installed on a Web server pointing to a COM+ application server is a single point of failure. If that COM+ application server fails, there is no built-in mechanism for COM+ to begin making remote component requests to a backup machine automatically. While it is possible to use standard load balancing technology like Network Load Balancing to achieve COM+ application server scaling, in reality this only provides high availability. In any case, Application Center solves these problems with COM+ application and routing clusters.

A COM+ application cluster is a group of servers configured with the same COM+ applications. With Application Center 2000, these members are managed and synchronized in the same way as a Web cluster. Once again, a deployment team has only to configure a new COM+ application on the cluster controller. Then, with the same synchronization technology as a Web cluster, Application Center deploys the COM+ application to all members of the cluster. COM+ clusters can use Component Load Balancing or Network Load Balancing to achieve scalability and availability of COM+ clusters.

A COM+ routing cluster is the third type of cluster supported by Application Center 2000. A COM+ routing cluster allows a single client server to address more than one COM+ cluster that uses CLB, a limitation of the current implementation of CLB in Application Center 2000. Figure 11.5 shows a COM+ routing cluster associated with a COM+ cluster.

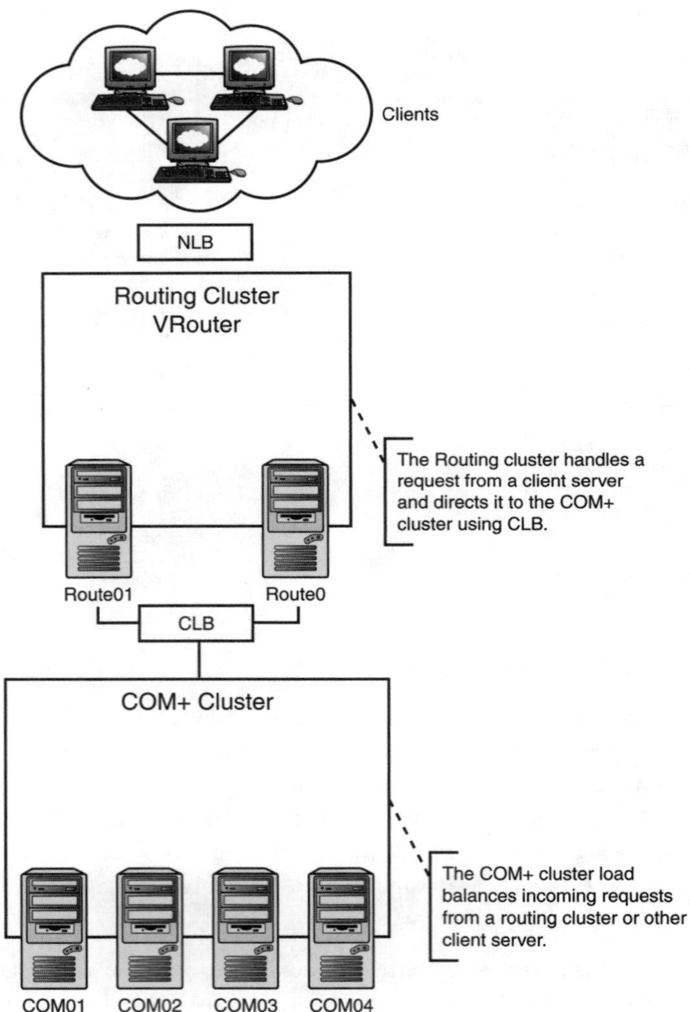

FIGURE 11.5
A COM+ routing and application cluster.

NOTE

For more information on COM+ clusters and Application Center 2000, see Chapter 13.

Another important aspect of the COM+ Application Center enhancements is the addition of a WMI provider (see the following section for more on WMI) for COM+. With this, it is possible to monitor the health of COM+ applications using Application Center 2000. The provider is also used by Application Center 2000 Component Load Balancing to decide which member of a COM+ application cluster activates a component for any request.

By providing scalable COM+ solutions, Application Center eliminates the single point of failure when accessing a COM+ object remotely. When a COM+ application cluster member fails and is taken offline, requests are not sent to the ailing member until the problem is resolved. Application Center 2000 finally delivers a highly available, highly scalable COM+ solution for the enterprise.

Monitoring a Web Farm Is Centralized

Like application replication, monitoring a Web farm is a complex problem. With large application clusters, the administration of monitoring tasks can become time consuming and error prone. Worse than that, monitoring a Web farm for a specific problem is sometimes the only way to tell if an application is failing. Sometimes a problem has no solution, and alerting an administrator who can address the problem manually is the only way to restore functionality. With no simple way to deploy monitoring configurations, the deployment team will bog down in the day-to-day operations and monitoring tasks of a Web farm.

Currently there are a number of different monitoring tools from Microsoft but nothing centralized and useful. For instance, Performance Monitor can alert at different thresholds in a real-time log. This is useful, but hardly an enterprise solution. There are third-party tools that provide an all-in-one solution, but they are proprietary.

With Windows 2000, Microsoft introduced Windows Management Instrumentation (WMI). WMI is Microsoft's unified monitoring API. WMI is a collection of COM interfaces that provide programmatic monitoring information in real-time. Similar to SNMP, WMI provides makers of server technologies, device drivers, and other system-level devices a way to expose monitoring information to a common, scriptable API. All .NET enterprise servers come with some level of WMI support.

With Application Center 2000, Microsoft delivers its unified application health-monitoring console, aptly named Health Monitor. Health Monitor provides a way to examine the state of a

Web farm centrally in real-time. Health Monitor examines each member of a cluster and can report back information to a single management console. This console creates a Web farm command station where deployment status, application health, and availability are measured. Figure 11.6 shows the Health Monitor console.

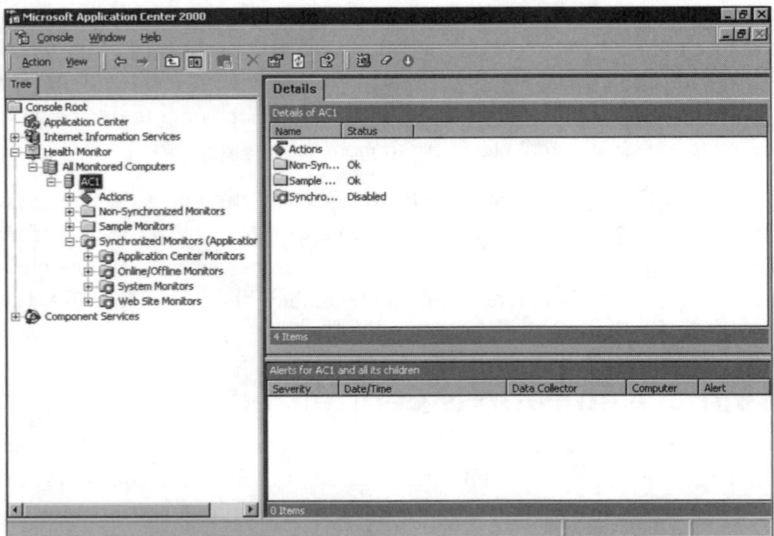

FIGURE 11.6
The Health Monitor console.

Health Monitor can alert on the entire standard performance counter list. Administrators can create alerts for low disk space conditions and on high CPU utilization conditions. Health Monitor reacts to user-definable alerts and responds with user-definable actions. Any WMI provider can be used to generate alerts. Actions include sending e-mail, launching scripts, running batch jobs, writing events to a file, and adding entries in the event log.

Managing the Staging of Releases with Application Center 2000

Application Center 2000 makes multiple stage deployment of Web applications easy. Without Application Center 2000, deployment from testing to staging and staging to production is at best a conglomeration of actions such as copying directories, running scripts, and other manual tasks. The staging of releases is as simple as scheduling a task. Application Center can replicate applications across clusters by using the same technology for deploying applications between members of the same cluster.

Installing Application Center 2000

Application Center itself is simple to deploy. Every server that is a member of a cluster must have Application Center installed. It can be installed onto servers in an existing Web farm for a rolling upgrade or onto new servers for a phased-in rollout. Figure 11.7 shows the Microsoft Application Center 2000 Setup dialog.

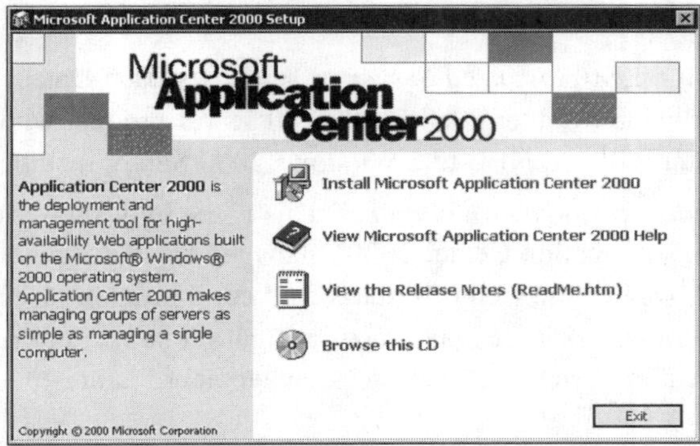

FIGURE 11.7
The Microsoft Application Center 2000 Setup dialog.

The install of Application Center proceeds as any other Microsoft product. There is nothing special or different about installing Application Center. Most deployments will choose a standard installation because the options for a custom install are limited.

Understanding Server Requirements for Application Center 2000

Installation of Application Center 2000 on a server has the following requirements, which are based on the assumption that Network Load Balancing (NLB) is not the load balancing solution for the Web farm:

- *Microsoft Windows 2000 Server is required* for Application Center 2000 for the full server product. The administrative client can be installed on any Windows 2000 offering, including Microsoft Windows 2000 Professional.
- *Internet Information Services (IIS) is required* for the Management Tools and the Application Center 2000 Administrative Web site. This is true even if the Web farm is not using IIS to serve content.
- *Creating Application Center clusters* on domain controllers or Windows cluster servers is not supported. The administrative client can be installed onto Windows cluster servers.

- *Each server requires 256MB of RAM*. For Windows 2000 Server, the maximum supported is 4GB of RAM.
- *Each server requires a minimum 130MB* of free hard drive space for Application Center 2000 operation.

The following additional requirements must be met when using NLB with Application Center 2000. Because Application Center 2000 automates the configuration of NLB, it is recommended that these requirements be met.

- *Microsoft Windows 2000 Advanced Server* or Windows 2000 Datacenter Server are not required for Application Center 2000 for the full server product when using NLB. Application Center will add NLB to a Windows 2000 Server installation.
- *Each server requires two network adapters*. This is the only supported configuration of managed NLB in Application Center 2000. Managed NLB is the name Microsoft uses when describing Application Center's automated configuration of NLB. It is possible to use other configurations of NLB, but these configurations will not be able to take advantage of all Application Center 2000 cluster-management features.

Understanding Install Options

For custom installation, the options for Application Center are limited. It is important to realize that each deployment on a cluster should be identical, so when choosing custom options, ensure that each member has the same installed features. Figure 11.8 shows the Application Center 2000 Setup dialog.

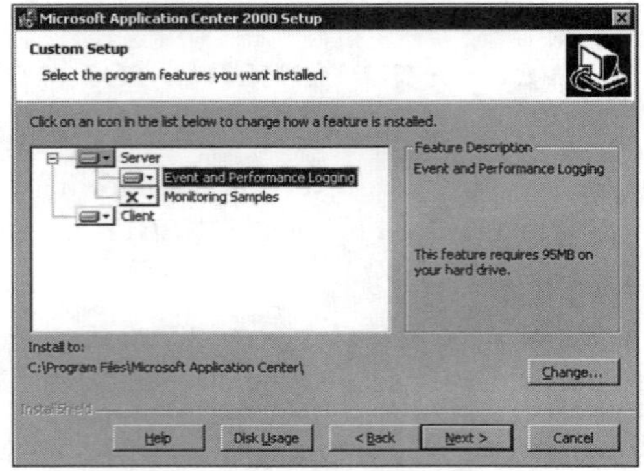

FIGURE 11.8
The Microsoft Application Center 2000 Setup dialog.

Installing the Administrative Client

In network operations centers, it is sometimes useful to install the administrative utilities only to a monitoring server. To install the administrative client, deselect the server node seen in Figure 11.8 and complete the setup process. It is important to note that to install the server component at a later date, the client tools must be completely uninstalled.

Choosing Not to Install Performance and Event Logging

Performance and event logging is the feature of the console that centralizes event and performance data. This makes it easy for administrators to check the pulse of a large number of servers from one place. The Microsoft Desktop Engine (MSDE) is required for the advanced logging features of Application Center 2000. Application Center will function perfectly if the event and performance logging option is removed, but a number of very useful features are lost in the process.

What Is MSDE?

MSDE stands for Microsoft Desktop Engine. MSDE is the SQL Server 2000 runtime environment packaged for deployment to the desktop. With MSDE installed on a server, it is used locally just like a SQL server. A MSDE database is exactly like a Microsoft SQL server. Tables, stored procedures, queries, and other data access methods work with MSDE databases.

How is MSDE different from Access? MSDE is a true client/server database solution packaged on the desktop, and Access is a file server database engine. MSDE is available on all Microsoft operating system platforms from Windows 95 on.

MSDE is limited in that it supports only 2GB databases and lacks support for symmetrical multiprocessing. MSDE supports replication as a replication subscriber but can't publish a replication.

MSDE is designed for use in small workgroup environments as a replacement for the Access data engine. It can be used for mobile users who need replicated data from a master SQL server. It is also becoming the data engine of choice for .NET enterprise servers when local data access improves performance for storing monitoring and application configuration data.

The drawbacks to MSDE are that it can require 20MB+ of RAM on a server. With servers having gigabytes of memory, this is less of a concern, but in older machines with 128MB to 256MB, this can be a drain. Also, the thought of SQL Server on every Web server is troubling for some. Expect MSDE to ship with the next version of Windows.

The disadvantage to removing MSDE is that most of the consolidated monitoring views are not available. For instance, the performance view, which shows the performance of all members of a cluster, is not available. Similarly, a consolidated NT event log view is absent. Included in this list of missing features are the consolidated Health Monitor view and the custom event and performance counter view. These features are clearly valuable; the decision not to install MSDE should be made only when absolutely necessary. The advantages to not installing MSDE are less CPU and memory utilization on the server and a smaller footprint on the local hard drive. Application Center 2000 does not require a DBA to manage the installed databases.

Installing Application Center 2000 Using the Command Line

Microsoft Application Center 2000 supports unattended installation using the Microsoft Installer (MSI). The main MSI file is at the root of the Application Center CD and is called `Microsoft Application Center 2000.msi`. Use this file with `MSIEXEC.EXE`, the Windows Installer program that understands the installation instructions inside the MSI file. All the following examples assume the CD is in the E: drive.

> **NOTE**
>
> For more information on using command-line options with MSIEXEC, see Appendix E, "Using the `WLBS.EXE` Command-Line Interface."

Performing a Default Install

By default, Application Center 2000 installs the server, client, and performance and event logging (MSDE) options. The code line below shows the command line for a default install. Specifying `/q` suppresses the setup user interface.

```
MSIEXEC /I "e:\Microsoft Application Center 2000.msi" /q /lv* c:\apc.log
```

Performing an Administrative Client Install

To install only the client piece, use the following command line. Notice the use of the `ADDLOCAL` switch. The install looks for this switch for a list of options to install. If it is not specified, the default settings (`Client`, `Server`, `ACLogging`) are used. Capitalization is important for the `ADDLOCAL` switch.

```
MSIEXEC /I "e:\Microsoft Application Center 2000.msi" /q /lv* c:\apc.log
➥ADDLOCAL=Client
```

A client-only install requires the logging features. Specifying `ACLogging` is not required.

Performing a No Performance and Event Logging Install

If the centralized performance and event logging features are not important for a particular cluster, or the thought of SQL 2000 on every server is troubling, Application Center supports installation without these options. Use the `ADDLOCAL` switch to specify combinations of `Server`, `Client`, and `ACLogging`. The following code snippet has the command line for specifying no logging options for a server-only install.

```
MSIEXEC /I "e:\Microsoft Application Center 2000.msi" /q /lv* c:\apc.log
➥ ADDLOCAL=Server
```

The next example shows a server and client install without Application Center 2000 logging features.

```
MSIEXEC /I "e:\Microsoft Application Center 2000.msi" /q /lv* c:\apc.log
➥ ADDLOCAL=Server,Client
```

The following line shows a `Server`, `Client`, and `ACLogging` option, which is equivalent to the default with no `ADDLOCAL` switch.

```
MSIEXEC /I "e:\Microsoft Application Center 2000.msi" /q /lv* c:\apc.log
➥ADDLOCAL=Server,Client,ACLogging
```

Performing an Uninstall

To uninstall Application Center 2000, use the command-line switch `/x`. The following line shows how to uninstall Application Center 2000 from the command line.

```
MSIEXEC /X "e:\Microsoft Application Center 2000.msi" /q /lv* c:\apc.log
```

This removes only the Application Center 2000 components. It does not remove the Health Monitor components. The only way to remove the Health Monitor components is through Add/Remove Programs in the Control Panel.

An Example: Creating a New Cluster Controller

The first step to creating a new cluster controller is finding the Application Center 2000 administrative console. Unlike other products, there is no hierarchy of installed programs to choose from in an Application Center Start menu group. The administrative console can be found by navigating the Start menu through Programs to Administrative Tools. Under Administrative Tools is the Application Center management console application. Following the theme of centralized management, all configurations initiate from this tool. Figure 11.9 shows the base Application Center 2000 administrative console, which is perfect for a Webmaster with IIS, Application Center 2000, Component Services, and Health Monitor together in one place.

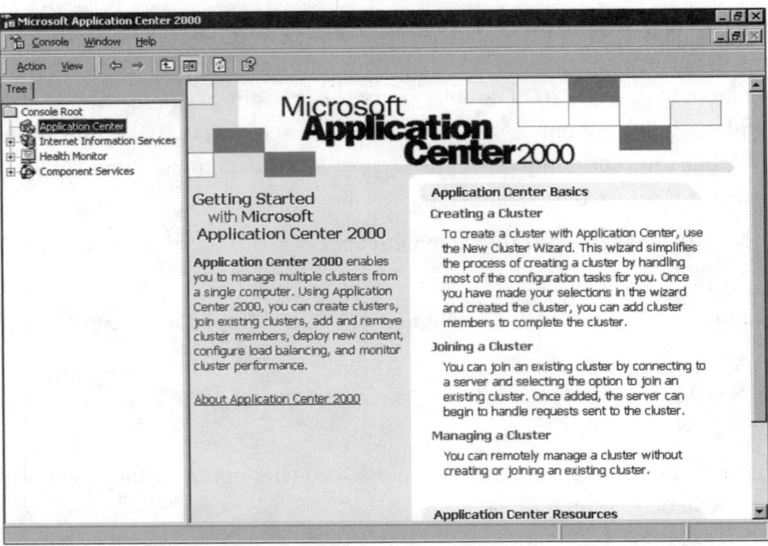

FIGURE 11.9

The Microsoft Application Center 2000 administrative console.

Initially, the Application Center node in the console is empty, and the only action available from the right-click menu is Connect. Connect is used to either connect to existing clusters or create new ones. The initial connection screen is shown in Figure 11.10.

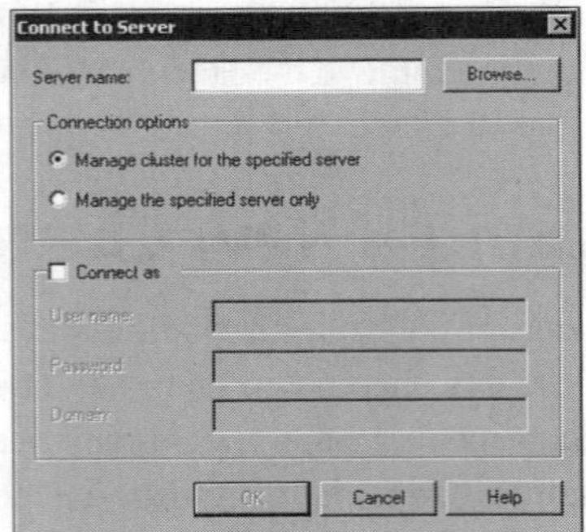

FIGURE 11.10

Connecting to an Application Center cluster.

This connection dialog is poorly named. It not only connects to an existing cluster, it is also the only way to create a new cluster. For purposes of this discussion, select the Connect menu item, fill out the Server Name text box with the name of a server that has a clean install of Application Center 2000, and press OK. The rest of the options on this dialog are fine at their default settings. At the next prompt, select Create a New Cluster and press OK to launch the New Cluster Wizard.

The New Cluster Wizard is a step-by-step process for creating a new cluster. To create the cluster for this example, complete the following steps:

1. Let the the wizard complete an analysis of the target server to understand its network adapter configuration for automated NLB deployment.
2. Choose a cluster name and description to help identify the cluster in the Web farm uniquely.
3. Decide which type of cluster to create. For this example, pick Web cluster.
4. Choose the type of load balancing for the cluster. In this example, make sure to pick None.
5. Fill in the e-mail address and address of the person who will manage and maintain this new cluster.

After completing these steps, the New Cluster Wizard creates the cluster configuration on the target server and adds a cluster node to the administrative console. A more in-depth description of the New Cluster Wizard is in Chapter 12.

Figure 11.11 shows the Application Center 2000 console with the newly added cluster, named `TechnicalLead`. It has been expanded to show the basic sub nodes for any Web cluster. All the management of a Web farm begins from this single node.

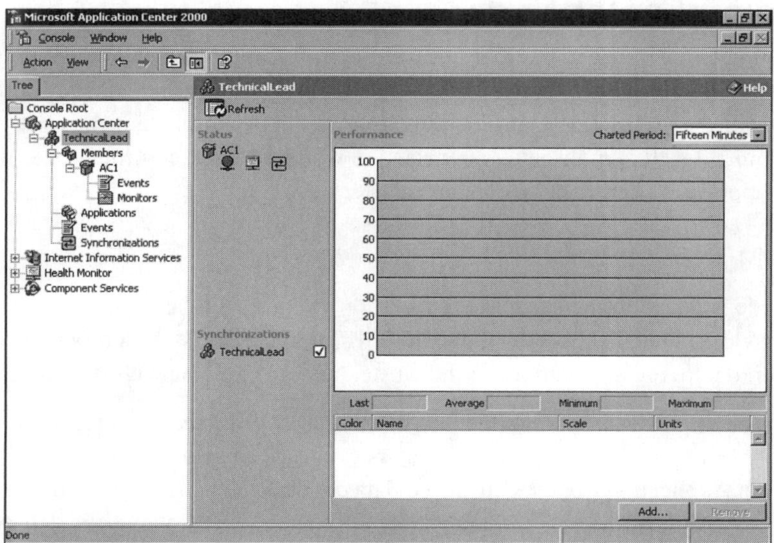

FIGURE 11.11
An expanded cluster node in Application Center 2000.

The Application Center 2000 Management Console

The Application Center 2000 console is the centralized management tool for a Web farm. Creating a cluster, joining a cluster, and managing a cluster are the main tasks performed from the console. The console provides a complete Web farm state overview. Administrators can drill down to a single server to examine performance counters or examine the recent synchronizations for the cluster.

Creating and joining a cluster are done through the New Cluster Wizard. This wizard guides the administrator through all the steps for cluster membership. It simplifies the process of creating and joining clusters by doing a considerable amount of the configuration. All aspects of cluster membership can be done locally or remotely.

It is a difficult task to determine the site-level health of medium to large Web farms. With the health and monitoring features of Application Center 2000, the console has a complete picture of the Web farm. It can remove servers from production so that they no longer accept connections and add them back to receive connections. The vernacular for this process is "in and out of the mix."

NEW TERM *In and out of the mix* means taking a server out of production so that it no longer receives connections and then, after some maintenance task, putting it back into production.

Application Center Node

The Application Center node is the root node of the Application Center management console. The only task available on this node is the `connect` command. Use the `connect` command to add multiple clusters to a single console. The New Cluster Wizard is launched with the `connect` command if the server being connected to is not a cluster controller or a member of a cluster. The application center node contains cluster nodes.

Cluster Node

A Cluster node is added to the console for every cluster in a Web farm. Tasks executed from the Cluster node include disconnecting the cluster from the console, synchronizing all content on the cluster, deploying applications to the cluster, and adding a new cluster member.

In the View pane of a Cluster node is the first consolidated performance chart. This chart can show a history of important performance counters over different time periods. These charts are generated from Application Center's advanced data collection features. Performance data is actually logged to a database on each member of the cluster and then consolidated in this View pane. Some of the more important counters it tracks are ASP request wait time and requests queued. This information is invaluable when looking for performance problems and bottlenecks.

To the left of this chart is a set of graphic status indicators for all members of the cluster. It is possible to tell in a single glance all active cluster members and whether they are accepting new content and logging data. Figure 11.12 shows a console at Cluster node.

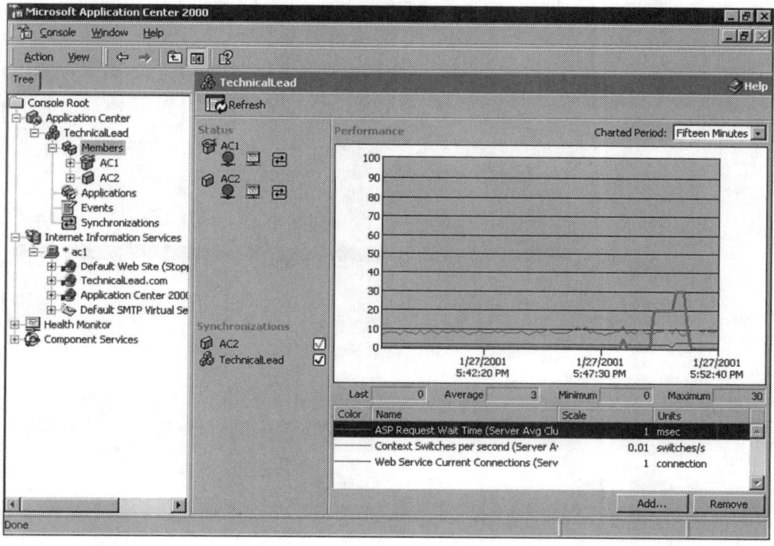

FIGURE 11.12
A Cluster node in the Application Center 2000 console.

The Cluster node contains a cluster Members node, an Applications node, an Events node, and a Synchronizations node.

Members Node

The Members node contains all the cluster members of the active cluster, including the cluster controller. The only action available on the Members node is to add a new member to the cluster. The View pane is the same as the cluster node and shows performance statistics for the entire cluster. Settings transfer from the cluster node to the Members node and vice versa.

Applications Node

The Applications node has a list of application objects defined for this cluster. From the Applications node in the console tree, the only option available is to deploy applications. A deployment can be created using the New Deployment Wizard from the Deploy Applications option. Deployments are used to replicate applications that contain COM+ applications or global ISAPI filters. Deployments are also used for moving content from one cluster to another.

The Applications node View pane is where the cluster manager defines the application deployment objects. New applications are added and existing ones are modified from this pane. Figure 11.13 shows the Applications node with its corresponding View pane. Notice that the TechnicalLead.com application has two parts: the TechnicalLead.com Web site and the TechnicalLead.com COM+ application.

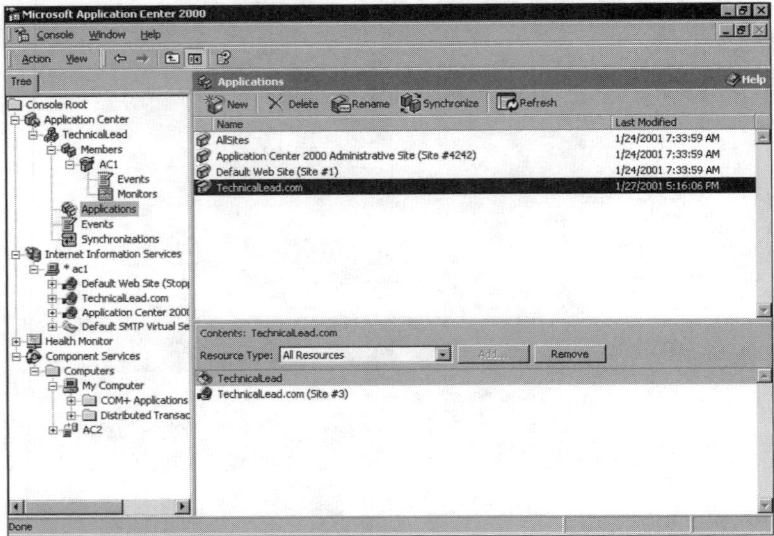

FIGURE 11.13
An Applications node in the Application Center 2000 console.

Events Node

The Events node is a master event viewer from all servers in a cluster. Configuring properties on the Events node lets an administrator set event filters, disable performance logging, and set the number of days to log events. From the Events View pane, the administrator can filter for specific events dynamically across all cluster members. Figure 11.14 shows the Events node of the console.

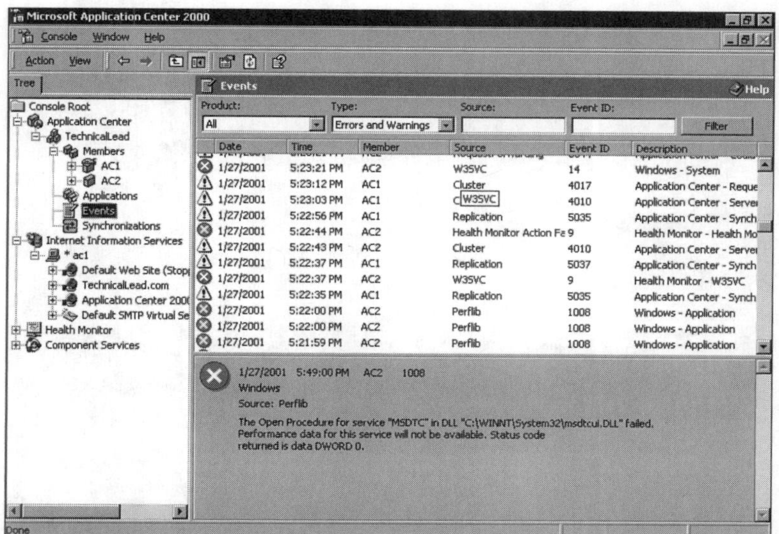

FIGURE 11.14
An Events node in the Application Center 2000 console.

Synchronizations Node

The Synchronizations node is a list of recent cluster synchronizations. Configuring properties for synchronizations lets an administrator set exclusions for files, folders, and file types. Figure 11.15 shows the Synchronizations node of the console. Notice that the AC2 synchronization only partially succeeded. The event pane at the bottom of the screen shows an error that suggests the security identity of the TechnicalLead.com application was not valid on the target machine. This means the target machine needs a local account for the COM+ application or the password is invalid.

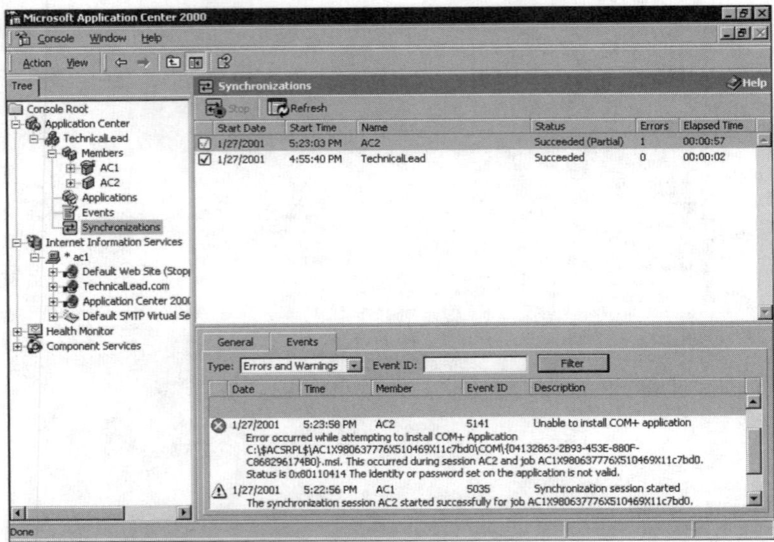

FIGURE 11.15

A Synchronizations node in the Application Center 2000 console.

Summary

Application Center 2000 addresses a number of difficult issues for deployment teams with groundbreaking new technologies. With a myriad of disjointed administrative tools packaged in a simple, centralized console, the management of a Web farm has never been easier. Application replication, COM+ clustering, health and application monitoring, and managed staged deployment are all addressed with Application Center 2000.

Creating and using Application Center is as simple as running the New Cluster Wizard. From the New Cluster Wizard, administrators create and manage the server membership of Web, COM+ application, and routing clusters. With the easy-to-use management console of Application Center 2000, an organization can create a Web farm command center. This command center provides a centralized deployment, management, monitoring, and configuration point for an entire Web farm.

Deploying Application Center 2000 Web Clusters

CHAPTER

12

IN THIS CHAPTER

Deployment teams that manage multiple-server Web farms spend considerable time and effort maintaining the servers and applications. Configuring IIS, keeping application files synchronized, configuring data sources, editing the Registry, and managing COM+ applications are tedious tasks that grow exponentially with the number of servers in a Web farm. There is a strong desire to guarantee that every server is identical. When a problem occurs because of synchronization differences between servers, keeping the servers synchronized becomes the all-encompassing task.

The job of synchronizing severs was never easy with the tools that existed before Application Center Server 2000. Deployments were always error prone, and success depended on the diligence of the people involved. With businesses operating on Internet time, successful Web sites cannot slow down progress for server maintenance. The creation of new Web site features, and thus more deployments, adds value to the customer's experience and keeps the application fresh and profitable. Without time to perfect the replication process, the individual servers begin to show minor differences in behavior and configuration. Server configurations become more and more distinctive, individualizing each server with age. Handling content replication in such a manner, servers soon start to have problems, and eventually they must be rebuilt.

NEW TERM A *Web cluster* is a group of servers whose primary task is to serve Web content such as HTML, ASP, and ASP.NET. Web clusters can be synchronized using Application Center 2000.

Microsoft Application Center Server 2000's Web-clustering capabilities help solve the synchronization and maintenance problem often found in Web farms. Within a Web cluster, content and configuration are replicated to member servers on demand. No longer is the administrator responsible for ensuring that the content and configuration are correct on every server in the farm. Application Center 2000 guarantees that when a cluster is synchronized, all the servers in the cluster are identical. If a server fails to synchronize correctly, Application Center 2000 alerts the administrators, and the servers are removed from service. Application Center 2000 eliminates the individualizing of servers so common with manual deployment.

This chapter is divided into sections describing a step-by-step process for creating an Application Center 2000 Web cluster.

The goals for this chapter are to help the administrator

- Choose a load balancing technology for a cluster. With Application Center 2000, the choices are either Network Load Balancing or a third-party load balancing solution. It is important to make this decision up front to purchase the right hardware for the cluster.
- Build and configure the servers in the Application Center 2000 Web cluster using a repeatable process and making sure to meet the specific operating system requirements for Application Center 2000 clusters.

- Designate a single server as the Cluster Controller. This server is the master of the cluster. Applications installed on this server are synchronized to other cluster members. In every other way, the Cluster Controller is identical to other members.
- Manually deploy the Web applications to a Cluster Controller in the deployment environment. This single step will prepare the Cluster Controller for distributing the application to the other members automatically.
- Identify and create applications in the application list of a cluster, using the Application view of the Application Center 2000 console. An application is a collection of resources such as COM+ applications, data sources, file system paths, Registry keys, Web sites, and virtual directories.
- Add all members to the cluster using the Add Cluster Member Wizard. Once this process is completed for each member of the cluster, an administrator can deploy and synchronize applications to the cluster.
- Deploy applications to the cluster using the New Deployment Wizard. Deployments are very flexible vehicles for synchronizing applications across multiple machines. Deployments are the release mechanism for new application features and updates.

Choosing a Load Balancing Technology

Application Center 2000 uses load-balancing technologies such as those discussed in Chapter 5, "Using Microsoft Network Load Balancing in a Web Farm," and Chapter 6, "Using Hardware Load Balancing in a Web Farm." Application Center 2000 is highly integrated with Windows 2000's Network Load Balancing capabilities, but it also works well with other hardware and software-based third-party load balancing technologies. By determining which load balancing technology to use first, this will help decide what hardware to purchase for an Application Center 2000 Web cluster. Different load balancing technologies may require different hardware.

If a Web cluster is using Network Load Balancing, each server must have at least two network adapters. One adapter is used for management traffic, including synchronizations, deployments, and administrative access. The other is used for application traffic. Even if a Web farm uses a third-party load balancing solution, most DMZ network topologies require two network adapters. Be sure to thoroughly research all hardware requirements a third-party solution may need so no surprises occur while clustering and building a Web farm.

Building the Servers for a Web Cluster

When a Web farm has many servers, it is important to build these servers using a repeatable process to ensure that each server is built with the same items. In simple environments, this process could be a step-by-step build document that provides answers to installation questions for an administrator at each point in the setup. For instance, a simple build document could describe steps to take when installing Windows 2000, any relevant service packs, .NET Enterprise servers, and other third-party system components that are used by multiple services and applications on a server. Having a system like that in place will ensure that all the servers being created will be identical in build.

NEW TERM The *server build* is a repeatable process for creating servers for a Web farm. The server build includes the operating system (OS), service packs, .NET Enterprise servers such as Application Center 2000, and other third-party components.

Unfortunately, using a document checklist is a very tedious and error-prone process for building servers. One of the primary goals of Application Center 2000 is easing management of deployment and maintenance of multiple servers. However, Application Center 2000 does not address any of the issues relating to the server build. Application Center 2000 assumes other technologies have already addressed this need. This chapter explores some of these technologies and how they are used to help create consistency in server builds.

Choosing Technologies to Simplify OS Deployment

Numerous technologies have evolved over the years to simplify management of desktop operating system deployment in corporations. The installation and use of these tools is beyond the scope of this book, but when a simple build document becomes unmanageable, Web farm server builds are greatly simplified by using Windows 2000 unattended installation scripts.

NOTE

To learn more about Windows 2000 deployments, be sure to check out *Windows 2000 Server Unleashed* by Sams Publishing (ISBN: 0-672-31739-7).

Requirements for Adding Application Center 2000 to the Build

The server build prerequisites for Application Center 2000 are Windows 2000 Server, Advanced Server, or Datacenter Server. Application Center also requires Service Pack 1 for Windows 2000 Server/Advanced Server with a variety of pre-sp2 hotfixes. Application Center will also work with Service Pack 2 of Windows 2000. Application Center 2000 must be installed on every member of a cluster.

Requirements for Using Network Load Balancing

Using Network Load Balancing adds a few additional steps to the Web cluster server build. These steps allow Application Center 2000 to configure Network Load Balancing in managed mode. Perform these steps manually on each new server:

- Rename each network adapter located in the properties of My Network Connections. There should be a management adapter for administrative traffic and a cluster adapter for Web cluster application traffic.
- Bind the IP address that maps to a specific cluster adapter, or the dedicated IP address, to the cluster adapter.
- Bind the IP address that maps to the server name, or the management IP address, to the management adapter.

Application Center will manage all the configuration of the cluster IP addresses on the cluster adapter, configure the Network Load Balancing service, and bind the cluster address to Web sites in IIS.

Requirements for Using Hardware Load Balancing

Using hardware load balancing adds a few additional steps to the Web cluster server build. These steps will need to be performed manually on each server:

- Rename each network adapter located in the properties of My Network Connections. In a DMZ network topology as described in Chapter 4, "Planning a Web Farm Network," there should be a back-rail adapter for management traffic and a front-rail adapter for Web application traffic.
- For each Web site active on a server, designate a pool of IP addresses that the hardware load balancer uses to direct traffic to each server in the farm.
- Bind a Web site pool IP address to the front-rail network adapter.
- Bind the IP address that maps to the server name, or the management IP address, to the back-rail network adapter.

For example, a site with 10 Web servers needs 20 unique IP addresses. Ten of these addresses are members of the Web site pool for the hardware load balancer and are bound to the front-rail adapter. The other ten addresses are management IP addresses that should map to the server name in a Windows network. This means that in Dual NIC servers all the front-rail and back-rail IP addresses should be added during the server build.

NOTE

If a Web farm server must support more than one Web site, create additional Web site pools and add these extra IP addresses to the front-rail adapter.

IP addresses from the hardware load balancing pool need to be bound to each server's IIS Web site instance once they have joined the Application Center 2000 Web cluster. When using Network Load Balancing, Application Center 2000 manages the Web site bindings by replicating the Cluster Controller's bindings to all members. This works because all members of the clusters share the virtual IP. With other load balancing support, each member has a unique IP address that is pulled from a pool of IP addresses maintained on the load-balancing device. To remain consistent with the model of managing the farm from one server, bind all the IP addresses for a Web site to that Web site on the Cluster Controller. These IP addresses should not be bound to the network adapter on the Cluster Controller. When the other members of the cluster are added, the Web sites will have all the bindings, too. Only Web site bindings that match network adapter bindings are used by IIS and the rest are ignored. This simplifies the management and configuration of Web site bindings when using other load balancing. This feature eliminates the need to visit each server's IIS configuration after it is added to the cluster.

TIP

Bind all IP addresses for a Web site to the Cluster Controller. Application Center 2000 manages the binding of Web sites to IP addresses in this configuration.

Creating the Web Cluster Controller

The Cluster Controller is a single server in a Web cluster that acts as the "content master" for the cluster. By acting as a "content master," it assumes the responsibility of updating and synchronizing other member servers as new content, and updates are sent to the cluster controller. It is exactly like other members of the cluster in the sense that it can accept connections, be removed from production, and fail. If the Cluster Controller does fail, it is a simple process to designate a different member server as controller. During this failure and change over, cluster synchronizations are unavailable, but the cluster as a whole can still serve existing Web content to customers, and individual member server can receive content through cross-cluster deployments. Designating a new Cluster Controller after failure is described later in this chapter.

The New Cluster Wizard is used to create a Web cluster. This wizard is launched from the Application Center 2000 console. The first step to running this wizard is connecting to the server that will become the Cluster Controller for a new Web cluster. Figure 12.1 shows the right-click menu of the Application Center node of the management console. It is from this point that the New Cluster Controller Wizard is launched. Note that there is not an obvious task called Create New Cluster in the shortcut menu. The connect option is used to connect to or create a new cluster.

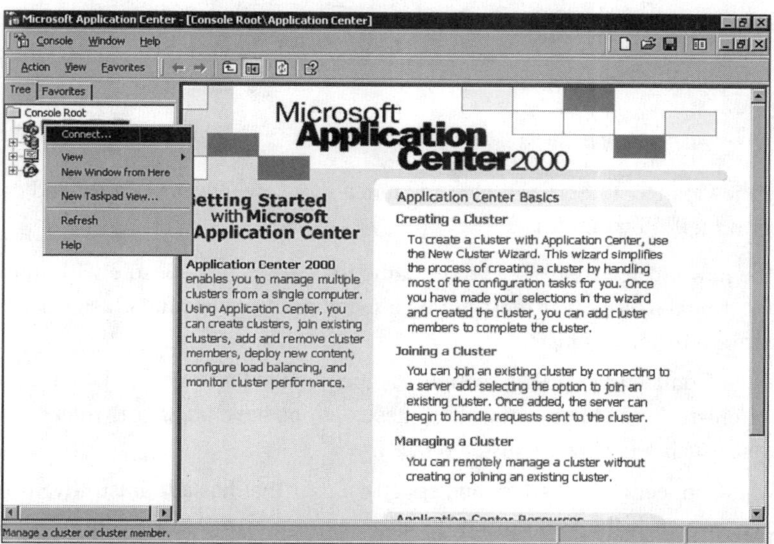

FIGURE 12.1
The launching point for the New Cluster Wizard.

Launching the New Cluster Wizard

Once the Connect option has been selected from Figure 12.1, the Connect to Server dialog box, shown in Figure 12.2, appears. Application Center uses the information specified in this dialog, and the Application Center state on the target server to create a new cluster, join and server to an existing cluster, add to this console an existing cluster, or add to this console a single cluster member.

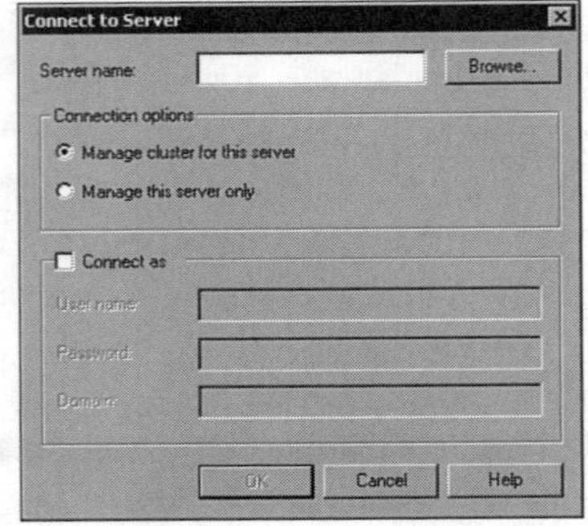

FIGURE 12.2
The Connect to Server dialog of Application Center 2000.

To configure the Connect to Server dialog to launch the New Cluster Wizard and create a new cluster, perform the following tasks:

1. Type the new cluster controller server name to connect this console with in the Server Name text box. This server must not be a member of an existing cluster or a cluster member of a different cluster.
2. Ignore the Connection options section. As long as the target server is not a part of an existing cluster or a cluster controller, these options have no effect when configuring a new cluster using the New Cluster Wizard.
3. Click the Connect as check box and specify a user that has administrative privileges on the target server. If the user currently accessing the console is an administrator on the target server, Application Center 2000 uses these credentials by default so this section can be left blank.
4. Click OK and the console will query the target server and display a dialog that prompts to Start a new cluster on the target server or Join it to an existing cluster. If this dialog does not appear, then either the target server does not have Application Center 2000 installed, it is already configured as a Cluster Controller, or it is a cluster member of an existing cluster.
5. Select the Start a new cluster option and click OK. This launches the New Cluster Wizard.

The Confusing Connect to Server Dialog

The Connect to Server dialog in Figure 12.2 is one of the more confusing UIs that Microsoft has built. Rather than supply simple right-click menu options on the Application Center 2000 top-level console node, Microsoft chose to hide important tasks inside the Connect to Server dialog. This dialog should just be a step in three different wizards. Currently, the connect to server dialog is used to perform these tasks:

- Create a new cluster controller.
- Join a server to an existing cluster.
- Add a cluster controller to the console.
- Add a cluster member to the console.

Quite possibly, a better choice for the top-level node right-click menu would have been to have each of these as a choice rather than a single Connect menu selection.

Accomplishing each of these tasks depends upon how the Connect to Server dialog is configured, and the state of the target server specified in the server name text box. The Connection Options section applies only when adding nodes of existing clusters to the console. If the Manage Cluster for this server radio button is selected, then Application Center determines if this computer is a Cluster Controller and if not finds its Cluster Controller and adds this node in the console window. If the Manage the server only radio button is selected, then the node that is added to the console is only a single member of a cluster. These tasks do not change the state of any cluster member or controller as they are only added to the console, which, of course, can be done on any computer with the administrative tools installed.

To create new a cluster with the New Cluster Wizard or join servers to existing clusters with the Add Cluster Member Wizard, the target server must not be a member of any Application Center 2000 cluster. Choosing which wizard happens after pressing OK on the Connect to Dialog. The Application Center console then displays a simple dialog with Join an existing cluster or Create a new cluster options. Choose Create a new cluster option to launch the New Cluster wizard and choose Join an existing cluster to launch the Add Cluster Member wizard.

Using the New Cluster Wizard

After supplying the necessary information in the Connect to Server dialog box, begin creating the new cluster. This section describes in detail the New Cluster Wizard. To help understand the various steps involved in creation of a Web cluster, Figure 12.3 illustrates the various paths through the wizard. This wizard is very straightforward and easy to use, as the only real decision point involves load balancing options.

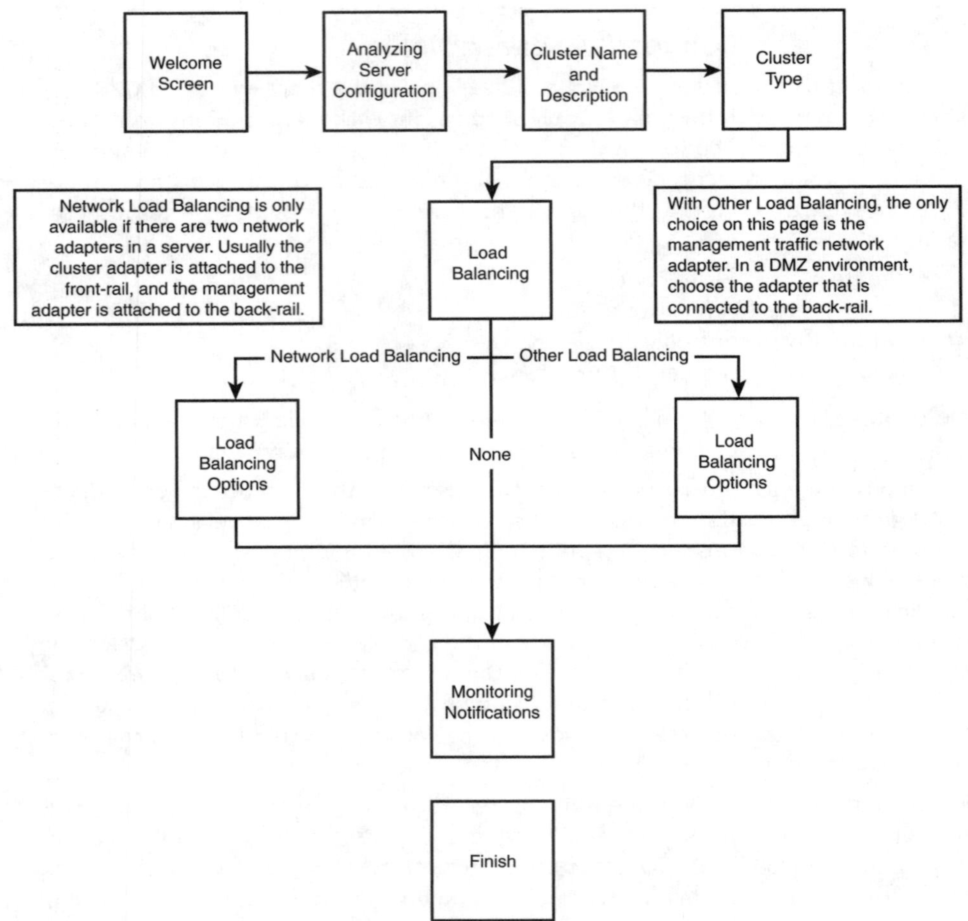

FIGURE 12.3
The paths through the New Cluster Wizard.

Analyzing the Server Configuration

The second pane of the New Cluster Wizard automatically scans the target server, either locally or remotely, for network adapter configuration. It gathers information about installed network devices, drivers, and services. Application Center performs this scan to decide what options are available later in the New Cluster Wizard. If the Network Load Balancing service is found and the network adapters are configured as specified in the earlier section, "Requirements for Using Network Load Balancing," Application Center can manage the Network Load Balancing configuration. Figure 12.4 shows the Analyzing Server Configuration pane of the New Cluster Wizard.

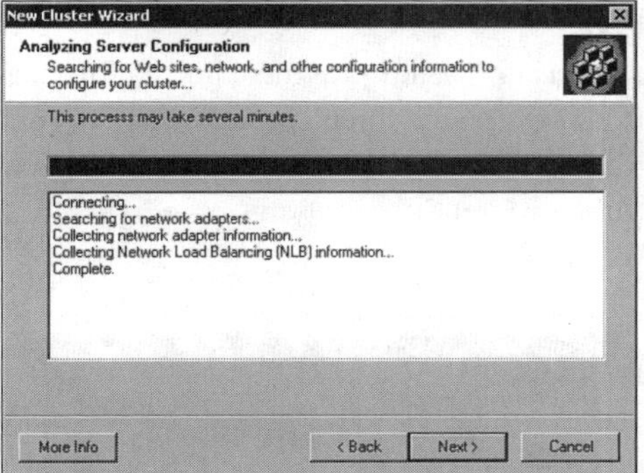

FIGURE 12.4
The Analyzing Server Configuration pane.

Naming a Cluster

The third pane of the New Cluster Wizard provides options for naming and describing the cluster. The Application Center console uses this information for display and informational purposes. Network Load Balancing uses the name as the NetBIOS name of the cluster. The name must be fewer than 15 characters in length and composed of letters and numbers. Names such as `WEB Cluster 1` are invalid because a network name cannot have spaces. If a DNS suffix is specific in the TCP/IP properties of the cluster adapter, this name is concatenated with this value to create the full cluster name. For example, a DNS suffix of `foo.com` with a name of `vcluster` equates to `vcluster.foo.com`. Use an appropriate description, because it is likely most Web farms will have many different types of Application Center 2000 clusters. Figure 12.5 shows the Cluster Name and Description pane with appropriate descriptions for a Web cluster.

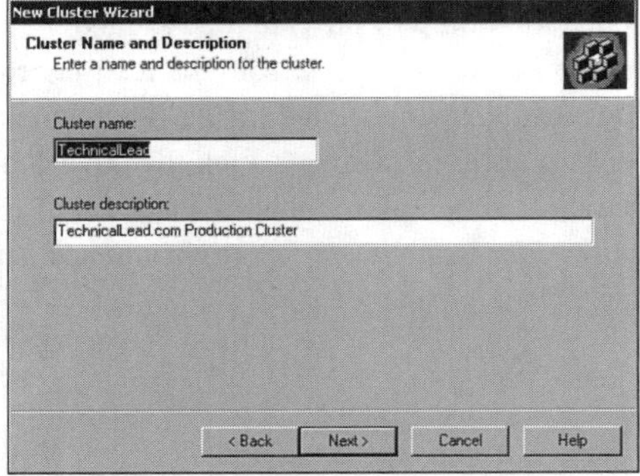

FIGURE 12.5
The Cluster Name and Description pane.

Choosing Cluster Type

In the fourth pane, the New Cluster Wizard presents choices for what cluster type to make this cluster. Application Center 2000 supports three types of clusters: Web, COM+ application, and COM+ routing. The Web Cluster radio button is used to specify creating a Web cluster. The other radio buttons specify the different types of clusters. Figure 12.6 shows the Cluster Type pane of the New Cluster Wizard.

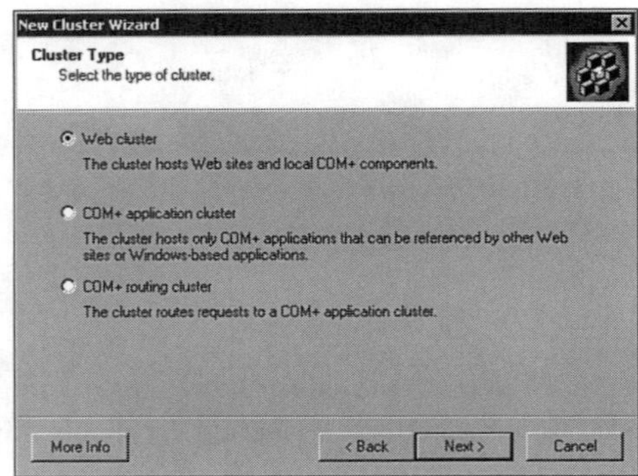

FIGURE 12.6
The Cluster Type pane.

Choosing Load Balancing

Next, select load balancing options for the cluster in the fifth pane of the New Cluster Wizard. These options are shown in Figure 12.7. If a cluster member does not meet Application Center's requirements to integrate with Network Load Balancing, that option is grayed out and cannot be selected. The other load balancing radio button is used to specify that some external, non-integrated, load-balancing solution will provide load-balancing capabilities to this cluster. This option also enables an administrator to pick from the next pane, which network adapter in a Dual NIC server is used for management-related traffic. The None option skips the next pane and assumes that the cluster in question is a stager. Pick the other load balancing or Network Load Balancing options when a staging environment is made up of multiple hosts that are load balanced. Use the None option only in single-server environments, such as development or a simple staging environment.

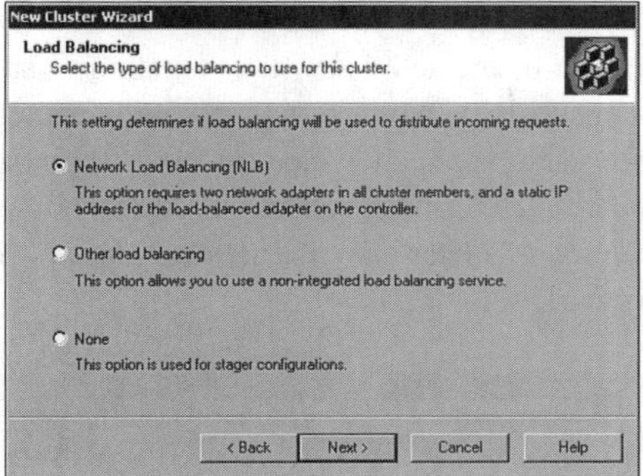

FIGURE 12.7
The Load Balancing pane.

Choosing Load Balancing Options

The sixth pane of the New Cluster Wizard appears only if the Network Load Balancing or Other Load Balancing option is picked in the previous pane. The only option available in the pane is shown in Figure 12.8. Here the drop-down combo box displays all the network adapters on a host. In Dual NIC, DMZ environments, the management traffic network adapter should be the adapter that is connected to the back rail as specified in Chapter 4. In a single network adapter server, this option is grayed out.

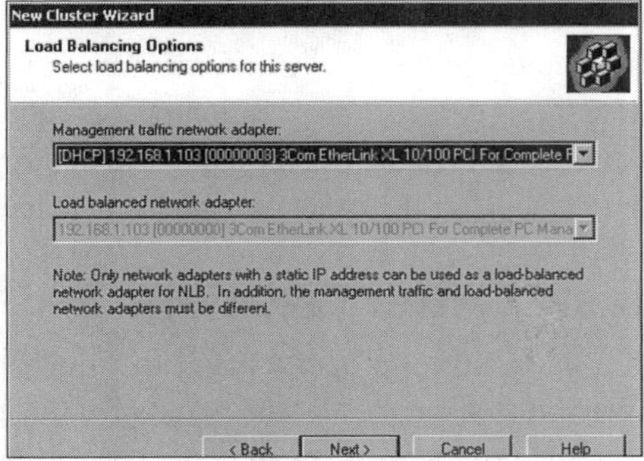

FIGURE 12.8
The Load Balancing Options pane.

Setting Monitoring Notification Information

The Monitoring Notifications pane is the sixth or seventh pane (depending on load balancing choices) in the New Cluster Wizard. Here the E-mail Address text box is used to specify the e-mail address used to send any critical information about the status and health of a cluster.

The E-mail Server Name is used to specify which SMTP server will transmit the message. With Health Monitor, alerts can be created that will use this information. If these fields are left blank, then the Email Administrator default action is not automatically configured. See Chapter 14, "Monitoring a Web Farm with Application Center 2000," for more information on creating custom actions and using alerting. This page can be left blank and the default Email Administrator action configured at a later date. Figure 12.9 shows the Monitoring Notifications pane of the New Cluster Wizard.

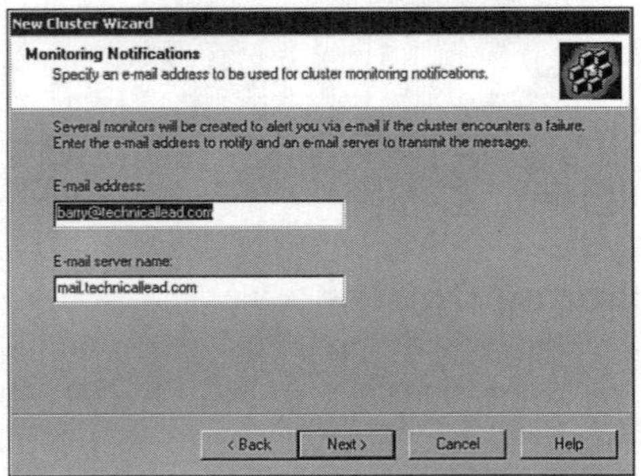

FIGURE 12.9
The Monitoring Notifications pane.

Finishing the New Cluster Wizard

Once all the information is entered and the New Cluster Wizard is finished, Application Center creates the new cluster on the target server. This creation process adds data that uniquely identifies this server as the cluster master. A new cluster node is added to the administrative console once the configuration is complete. It is now possible to manage the new Web cluster.

Configuring a Cluster After Creation

Once the cluster is created, use the cluster property pages to modify a cluster after creation. To access the properties of a Web cluster, right-click the name of a cluster and select Properties. The sections below explore some properties that can be set for configuration purposes.

Using the General Tab

Figure 12.10 is the General Property tab of the cluster. The administrator configures the general properties of a cluster here. In the Cluster Name text box, type the name that this cluster will be referred to in the management console. In the Cluster Description text box, type the brief description of this cluster. Use this to help differentiate this cluster from other clusters.

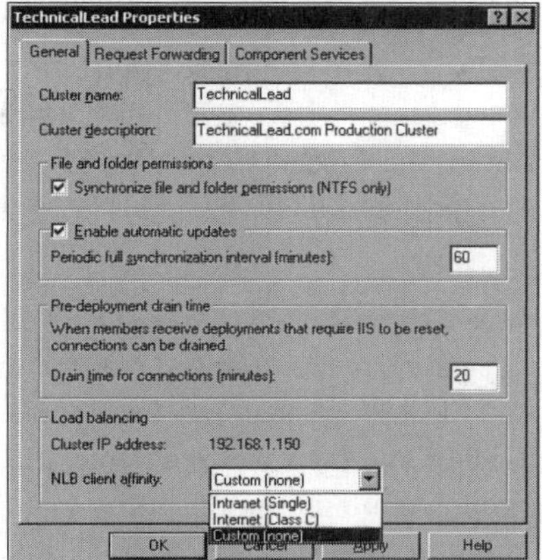

FIGURE 12.10
A cluster's general properties tab.

The File and Folder Permissions Synchronize File and Folder Permissions (NTFS Only) check box is used to propagate file access control lists from the Cluster Controller to the rest of the cluster. This feature greatly simplifies deployments that rely on NTFS permissions to manage access to content. The administrator has to configure the permissions on only one system, and the others will be maintained with Application Center 2000. If this option is not specified when replicating Web content the security access permissions of the files change to that of System authority and the local administrator group. Files that are accessed anonymously from the Web they will no longer be available to the anonymous IIS account. This information will replicate correctly across domains as long as the appropriate trusts are in place between the two deployment domains.

CAUTION

Turning off replication of NTFS file and folder permissions changes the permissions of the replicated files such that anonymous users no longer have access.

The Enable Automatic Updates check box is checked by default for all new clusters. This is a global setting that the Cluster Controller uses to initiate synchronizations of all applications on a cluster automatically. It is recommended to uncheck this setting and manually synchronize any cluster that has complicated deployments. If a site is mostly HTML and ASP content, this setting makes sense because deployments across stages will be simple, and replicating these deployments is simple. In more complicated applications, such as those that contain COM+

applications or ISAPI components, a manual deployment is required because Application Center 2000 does not automatically synchronize these application components. The Periodic Full Synchronization Interval is used to specify the minutes between synchronizations. The default is 60 minutes, so every hour, the Cluster Controller will check for updated content and synchronize the rest of the cluster. Synchronization can also happen automatically when a member is added to a cluster.

The Drain Time for Connections text box is used to disconnect client sessions gracefully during content deployments and when servers are removed from production. This is especially useful when deploying COM+ and ISAPI applications that require IIS to be reset. This provides a much cleaner user experience and increases the perception of a stable and coherent Web farm. The default drain time is 20 minutes, ample time to allow users to move to different servers. The maximum drain period is 1440 minutes. A drain time of 0 (zero) will cause client connections to be terminated instantly, resulting in errors being displayed in users' browsers. Drain time is set and maintained per cluster. When deploying across clusters, Application Center 2000 uses the target cluster's drain time.

NEW TERM *Drain time* is the number of minutes that will pass to allow active connections to disconnect gracefully before taking a server offline.

The Load Balancing section changes according to the load balancing type of a cluster. Clusters that use Network Load Balancing (NLB) show the main cluster IP address and has a combo box where the cluster affinity is specified. Choose the cluster affinity setting based on the description provided in Chapter 5. Clusters that use other load balancing or none will have only a descriptive message in this section.

Using the Request Forwarding Tab

The Request Forwarding tab is used to forward Web requests to specific members of a cluster, depending on application requirements. For instance, an application that uses an ASP 3.0 session state could use the request forwarder to ensure that a user's request is always forwarded to the same server. This is similar to client affinity in Network Load Balancing except that the request forwarder places a cookie on the client. When the client makes a subsequent request to cluster, the server handling the request checks that cookie, and if it was not issued from that server, the request is forwarded back to the original server.

Understanding Session Coherency

Session coherency is the concept of maintaining session state of users across multiple requests to a Web farm. Application Center 2000 calls this concept *Web request forwarding*. As a user browses through a site, each page request can be a completely disconnected network request from the others. Because of this disconnected nature of the HTTP protocol, there are many tricks used to maintain session coherency for users. Some sites will use persistent cookies to hold user information and site-related information. Each page that is requested from a Web farm that uses persistent cookies will also request this persistent cookie to initialize the page with the proper customized content. Other sites use a database and a session-oriented cookie to tie a request back to the session information maintained in a centralized database server. These non-persistent cookies are transmitted with every request, so no additional network traffic is generated with non-persistent cookies. Some sites will maintain session in the URL. This is accomplished by passing from page to page all the session information in the query string for the request.

With IIS and ASP, there is an intrinsic session object that is used to maintain user session information across multiple page requests. IIS will create a non-persistent session-oriented cookie the first time a user requests a page from a site that uses ASP session. This cookie is then automatically sent with every request from that user. From the application, the session object is used to store personalized information so that custom content can be generated. In a simple single-server scenario such as an intranet, the ASP 3.0 session object is very useful. In a multiple-server environment, ASP 3.0 session is less useful unless session coherency is maintained at the server level. This means that all requests for a user must be directed to the same physical server. This also means that if that server fails, the session information is lost forever.

Application Center 2000 provides an ISAPI filter and extension called the *Web request forwarder* to help maintain session coherency on a Web farm that uses ASP 3.0 session state. When the Application Center Web request forwarder is turned on, the Web request forwarder on each member looks for a specific non-persistent cookie generated by Application Center when a user first requested a page, much like the ASP 3.0 session object. If this cookie is associated with the initial member that received the request, it is handled locally. If the cookie is for a different member of the cluster, then the Web request forwarder will send this incoming request to the proper server that has the local session state using standard host header technology.

Using the request forwarder could add considerable overhead on medium-to-large Web farms. Enabling the Application Center Web request forwarder should be done only if eliminating the use of ASP 3.0 session state is not an option at the Application layer.

The request forwarder is a global ISAPI filter installed to the WWW service of Internet Information Services. Every request to the Web server goes through the request forwarder filter. Turn this off if it is not going to be used by a Web farm by unchecking the Enable Web request forwarded check box. Figure 12.11 shows the WWW Service Master Properties ISAPI Filter tab with the highlighted request forwarder.

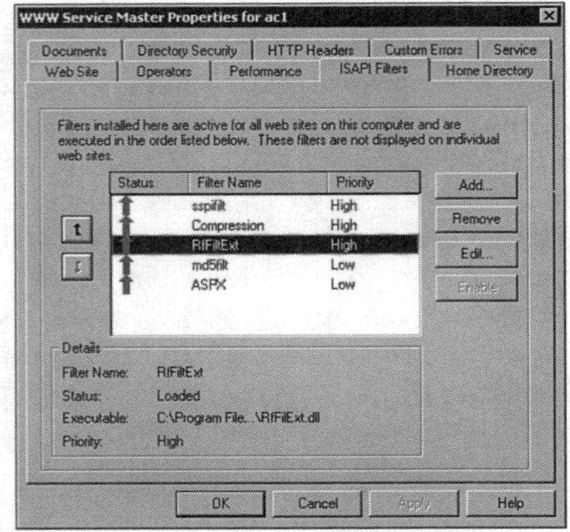

FIGURE 12.11

The request forwarding filter installed in IIS.

It is interesting to note that this request uses host headers to redirect the request to other members of the farm. In heavy traffic farms, forwarding requests could consume considerable bandwidth. It is also likely that some network configurations will not allow the request forwarder to function correctly. In a dual-rail DMZ environment, traffic between the servers on the front-rail could be disallowed for security reasons and would cause the Request Forwarder to fail.

On the surface, request forwarding looks to be a fancy client affinity that is already supplied in Network Load Balancing. This is not the case, as some ISPs use proxy Web caching that spans class C addresses. This means that requests coming in from the same user could look to be from a completely different class C address, and a client affinity of None or Intranet would fail to send this client back to the appropriate server. The request forwarder actually behaves similar to Class C affinity in Network Load Balancing but enables two layers of affinity when used with Network Load Balancing. If the affinity is set to None, considerable forwarding occurs because each incoming request, regardless of the source could be directed to a completely different server. Setting affinity to Intranet should prevent much forwarding from occurring because client requests go to the same server accept for the case where the same users has a different Class C address as when a farm of proxy servers is used. Setting affinity to Class C accomplishes very little when used with the request forwarder accept to tie all requests from a class C address to a single server. Using Class C affinity with the forwarder is a poor configuration choice. Since the Request Forwarder does not tie requests from a class C address to a single server it handles the farm of proxy servers much better than Network Load Balancing for a load distribution perspective.

Request forwarding is turned off by default. Figure 12.12 shows the default state of the Request Forwarding tab. This setting is suitable only for Web farms that have applications that require it. It should be left off for any application that doesn't require session coherency at the server level. Any site that relies on a back-end database, client cookies, or the URL string to maintain session state should not use the request forwarder. For sites that do require session coherency on the server level, there are two options. Enable for Web Sites Using ASP 3.0 Session State Only means that the request forwarder will not function if ASP session state has been turned off in IIS for that particular Web site or virtual directory. Enable for All Web Sites means that the request forwarder forwards requests regardless of the session setting in IIS.

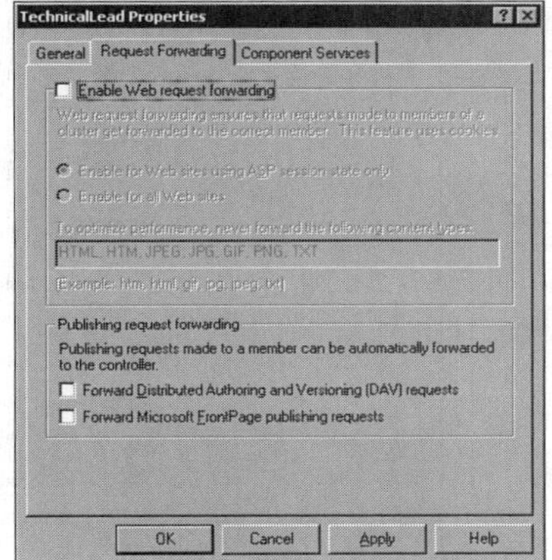

FIGURE 12.12
The Request Forwarding tab.

In order to further optimize performance of the request forwarded, the administrator can specify a list of file types that do not require forwarding. This list includes HTML, HTM, JPEG, JPG, GIF, PNG, and TXT. Any other static content is a good candidate to not be forwarded by the request forwarder.

A second aspect of the request forwarding features of Application Center 2000 has to do with distributed authoring and versioning (DAV) and Microsoft FrontPage server extensions. DAV and Microsoft FrontPage server extensions are two common publishing methodologies for Web sites. What the forwarder does with these requests, when enabled, is forward them to the Cluster Controller. Then the Cluster Controller can synchronize the changes based on cluster settings.

By default the Request Forwarding tab has Forward Distributed Authoring and Versioning (DAV) Requests and Forward Microsoft FrontPage Publishing Requests turned off. These settings do use the request forwarding ISAPI filter and can be controlled independently from the Enable Web Request Forwarding check box. Enable these settings if somewhere in the deployment architecture a Web cluster must accept updates from either of these publishing technologies.

Component Services Tab

The Component Services tab is used to configure routing information for components that use Component Load Balancing. Figure 12.13 shows the Component Services tab. Use the Add and Remove buttons to add or remove COM+ cluster member server names. These names are used to direct remote requests of objects marked for use in Component Load Balancing.

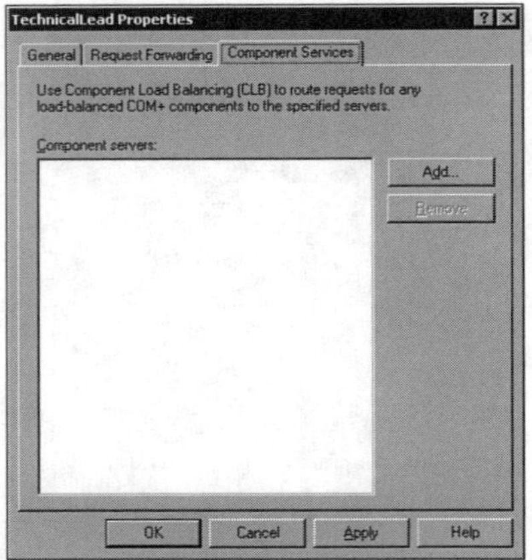

FIGURE 12.13
The Component Services tab.

Performing Cluster Tasks

Once a cluster is established, there are four main tasks that an administrator can perform against a cluster. Right-clicking on the cluster name in the Application Center 2000 console accesses the menu shown in Figure 12.14.

Disconnecting the Cluster from the Management Console

Selecting Disconnect from the menu will remove this cluster from the current Application Center 2000 console. This is only used to remove the ability to administer a cluster from a particular console. Since a single cluster can be configured from multiple consoles, this setting does not affect how the Web cluster functions.

Synchronizing a Cluster

Selecting Synchronize Cluster from the menu will perform a complete synchronization of all applications defined in this cluster. It will not deploy COM+ applications or global ISAPI filters that require IIS to restart. That can only be done with a specific deployment.

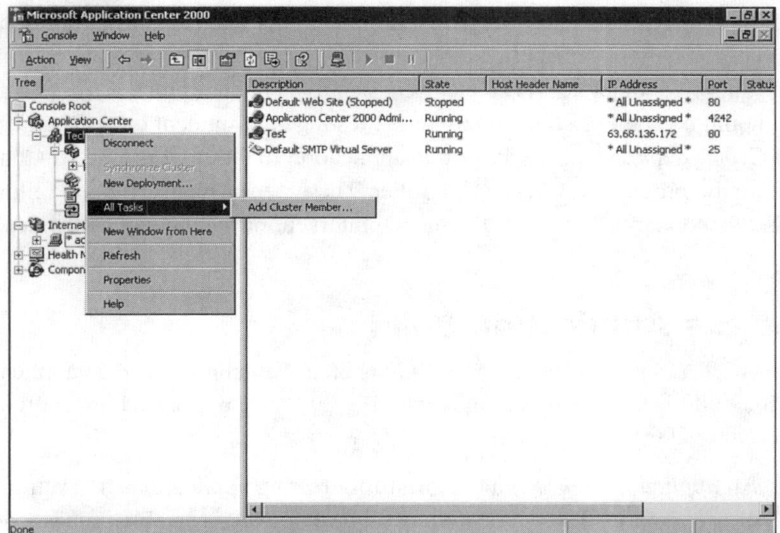

FIGURE 12.14
The right-click menu of an Application Center 2000 Web cluster.

Creating New Deployments

Selecting New Deployment from the menu launches the New Deployment Wizard. Use the New Deployment Wizard to create and schedule deployments of applications within a cluster. The New Deployment Wizard is the only way to synchronize COM+ applications and global ISAPI components. The New Deployment Wizard is covered in the section "Deploying Applications to the Cluster," later in this chapter.

Adding a Member to the Cluster

Selecting the All Tasks menu exposes the Add New Cluster menu. From this menu, administrators can add members to the cluster by using the Add Cluster Member Wizard. The Add Cluster Member Wizard is covered in great detail in the section "Adding Members to the Cluster," later in this chapter.

Deploying Applications on the Cluster Controller

The Cluster Controller is the application distribution point for a stage, like development, staging, and production, in a deployment environment. The applications on this server will be duplicated to other members of the cluster during deployments and synchronizations. Install all application components manually to a Cluster Controller by performing application tasks such as creating Web sites and virtual directories, configuring IIS security, creating Registry settings, copying files, and so on until the application is installed and functioning correctly.

When deploying applications into a staged environment, the manual configuration of an application should occur only once. Application Center 2000 can deploy applications from one Cluster Controller to another across all stages in deployment environment. For example, an application should be configured manually in the testing environment once. Then use Application Center deployments to move this application to the staging Cluster Controller and eventually onto the production Cluster Controller. These deployments, if done following the guidelines in this book, will require little manual intervention on the part of the deployment team.

Creating the Application Build

Just as a server has a server build, the applications on a Web cluster have an application build. An application build is a series of deployment tasks that were performed manually before Application Center 2000

NEW TERM An *application build* is a blueprint for creating applications that run on the servers of a Web farm. The application build describes a repeatable process for creating resources such as file system paths, Registry entries, IIS configuration information, COM+ applications, and many other custom application configuration tasks.

For example, Foo.com's Web site's application build might consist of the following steps:

1. Move and re-create the file structure from development server A located at `d:\inetpub\fooroot`.
2. Create an IIS Web site and set the root directory of the Web site to `d:\inetpub\fooroot`.
3. Bind the Web site to the cluster IP address of the Network Load Balancing cluster that supports Foo.com.
4. Create a virtual directory called `products` under the root of Foo.com on the remote files store `VFileServer01` using the username `SimpleWebAdmin` and the password `123swa890`.
5. Install the SSL key for Foo.com.
6. Mark the directory `c:\inetpub\fooroot\creditcard` as requiring SSL.
7. Start the Foo.com Web site.

This composition of steps culminates in a simple blueprint for creating the Foo.com application on a single server. When these steps must be performed on 10 or 15 servers, the job becomes much more difficult. Not only must each step be repeated on all members, there are numerous opportunities to configure something incorrectly. If any of these steps changes, the application build must be updated. Most application builds contain hundreds of steps if the application does anything other than serve up HTML content.

Application Center 2000 combines the configuration of an application with the application build. The steps needed to configure an application are repeated automatically across all members of a cluster just by defining what resources make up an application. If changes are made to IIS configuration settings, such as passwords, they are automatically replicated during synchronization to all members of the cluster. Application Center 2000 uses the existing configuration of a working application to create a self-documenting application build.

Deploying Special Application Components to All Cluster Members

Application Center 2000 considers applications to be collections of Web sites, virtual directories, Registry settings, data sources, file system paths, and COM+ applications. If a particular Web cluster requires other components such as a mapped drive, classic COM objects, or local account to name a few, Application Center will not automatically replicate these items across the cluster. Application Center can launch custom scripts at deployment or synchronization time as long as an application resource is creatable through script; then each box will not require manual configuration. Custom scripting is covered in Chapter 16, "Performing Advanced Application Center 2000 Tasks." If an application configuration task is not scriptable, then an administrator will need to perform the task manually on each server.

Creating Application Center 2000 Applications

Because applications in the .NET world are composed of many different resources, Application Center 2000 enables administrators to group these resources into a logical application unit. These logical application units are created using the Applications view that appears by clicking on the Applications node of a cluster. Figure 12.15 shows this pane and the Applications node.

The Applications pane contains numerous default applications: AllSites, Application Center 2000 Administrative Site, and every Web site installed to a cluster when it was first created. These applications are created by default for every cluster. The only resources in these applications are Web sites and virtual directories. For simple clusters that consist only of static content, these applications are sufficient. For instance, if the content in a specific site is a part of the default Web site, then by synchronizing the Default Web Site application, this content is replicated to all members of the cluster.

Creating a New Application

Most applications will require a custom Application Center 2000 application object. You can begin this creation of a new application object by selecting the New button on the Applications pane. Enter the name of the application into the resulting dialog. This is the name that will show up in the applications pane's list view for applications.

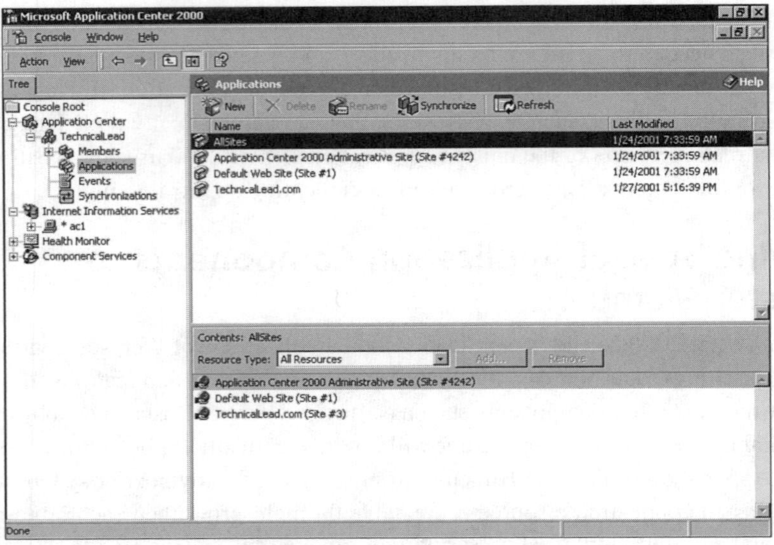

FIGURE 12.15

The Applications view of a cluster.

A new application has no resources assigned to it. To assign resources to it, select the appropriate application and then use the Resource combo box shown in Figure 12.16. Every application can have multiple resources of the same type. To add resources to an application, select the application from the application list and then pick a resource from the drop-down combo box. After selecting the resource type, click the Add button. Depending on the resource type, a Selection dialog is displayed. These dialogs are self-explanatory and easy to use. There is no limit to the number of resources in an application.

Defining Application Resources

Recall that in Application Center 2000 an application has five types of application resources. These resources can include COM+ applications, data sources, file system paths, Registry keys, and Web sites and virtual directories. Table 12.1 summarizes the default application resources.

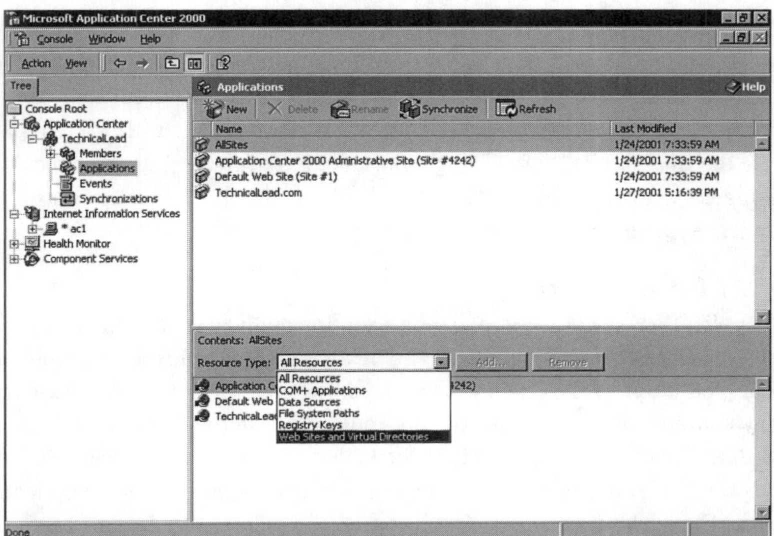

FIGURE 12.16
The Resource drop-down combo box in the Application pane.

TABLE 12.1 Application Resources

Resource	*Description*
COM+ Application	A collection of COM objects organized and managed with Component Services. Discussed in chapter 10, "Using Component Services (COM+) in a Web Farm."
Data Sources	A data source is a preset connection to information, used to connect to ODBC and OLEDB data providers. Data sources provide a layer of abstraction for an application, so this information is not hard-coded within the application.
File System Paths	This resource will point to a directory in the file system of the Cluster Controller. This does not work with mapped drives. This will propagate NTFS permissions unless explicitly prevented.
Registry Keys	A Registry key from the Registry of the Cluster Controller. Does propagate Registry ACLs and will do some account translations.
Web Sites and Virtual Directories	Any Web site or virtual directory defined in Internet Information Services. All metabase information is replicated, including security information.

Removing Resources from an Application

To remove a resource from an application, select the application from the application list, pick a resource in the resource list, and click the Remove button. Removing resources from an application does not delete the real resource. For example, deleting a file system path does not actually delete the files; it just removes the representation of those files from the Application Center 2000 logical application unit. These files will remain on the cluster controller, but no longer be replicated when the application is deployed.

Deleting an Application

To delete an application, select the application from the application list and click the Delete button. All the resources associated with an application are deleted from the Application Center 2000 repository, but none of the resources are actually deleted from the Cluster Controller. Subsequent synchronizations and deployments could result in the deletion of some resources associated with a deleted application only if the Cluster Controller designation changes. Even with a Cluster Controller designation change, deletion occurs only if some application resource overwrites an old application resource. For instance, if a deleted application contained a file system path that is in a new application and the contents of the file system path have changed, when that new application is synchronized, the contents of the file system path are deleted and replaced.

Renaming an Application

To rename an application, select the application from the application list and click the Rename button. Type the new name of the application in the resulting dialog and click OK. A renamed application cannot have the same name as another application already in the view pane.

Synchronizing an Application

To synchronize an application, select it from the application list and click the Synchronize button. Synchronization of an application replicates only data sources, file system paths, Registry keys, and Web sites and virtual directories. COM+ application and global ISAPI filters must be replicated by specifying so in the New Deployment Wizard, described later in this chapter.

Adding Members to the Cluster

Once the applications of a cluster are defined on the Cluster Controller, the next step is to add the rest of the cluster members into the cluster. This is done with the Add Cluster Member Wizard.

Using the Add Cluster Member Wizard

The Add Cluster Member Wizard is launched from the right-click menu of the cluster node and the Members node. Use this wizard to add a new member server to an existing cluster. There is one path through the Add Cluster Member Wizard, shown in Figure 12.17.

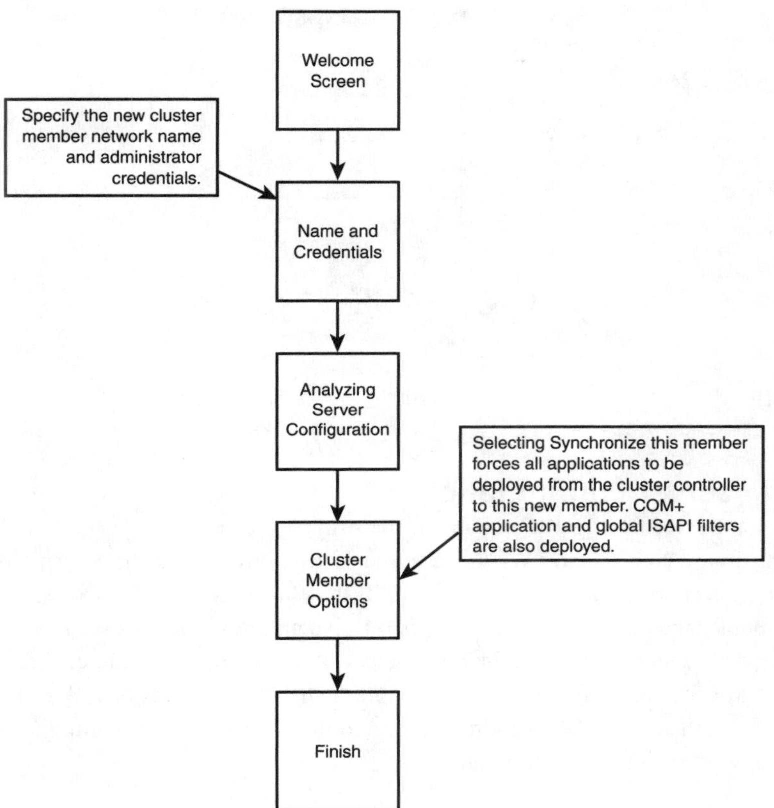

FIGURE 12.17
The paths through the Add Cluster Member Wizard.

Name and Credentials

The first pane of the Add Cluster Member Wizard is used to specify the server name to the new cluster. Figure 12.18 shows the Name and Credentials pane. Type the name of the new member server in the Server Name text box, or use the Browse button to pick from the network the server to add to the Web cluster.

The second portion of this pane is used to specify security credentials that have Administrator privileges on the new member server. These credentials are used to access the new member server remotely so that Application Center 2000 can configure this server as a new member of the cluster.

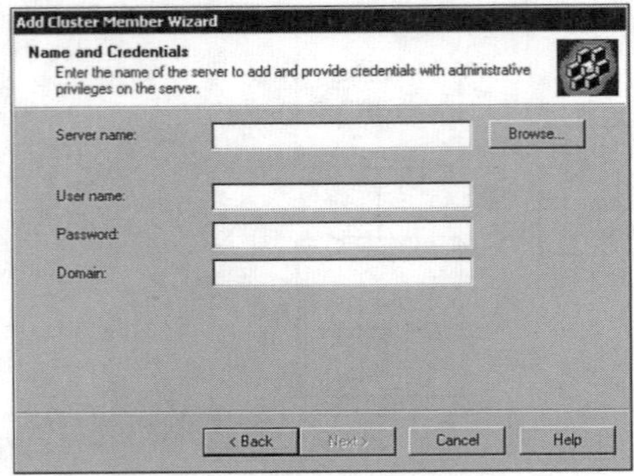

FIGURE 12.18
The Name and Credentials pane.

Analyzing Server Configuration

This Analyzing Server Configuration pane of the Add Cluster Member Wizard performs the same tasks as in the New Cluster Wizard. See the section "Analyzing the Server Configuration" previously in this chapter for more information. If the cluster is using Network Load Balancing the target member must meet the Network Load Balancing requirements for Application Center 2000 managed mode and must have identical network configuration as the cluster controller. The only differences between the members should be the IP addresses bound to the management adapter and the dedicated IP address bound to the cluster adapter. Failure to meet these requirements will cause the wizard to abort.

Cluster Member Options

The Cluster Member Options pane of the Add Cluster Member Wizard has the configuration options shown in Figure 12.19. The Synchronization option section enables an administrator to specify whether a cluster member is automatically synchronized when it is added and when synchronizations are issued from the Application Center 2000 console. The Load Balancing Options section is used to specify which network adapter handles the management traffic generated by Application Center and other administrative tasks. This option is grayed out when a server has only one network adapter.

Choosing not to synchronize the new cluster member means two things:

- After the member is added to the cluster, the normal complete synchronization, including COM+ applications and global ISAPI filters, does not occur.
- The member is not synchronized automatically during cluster synchronization events or when an application is synchronized from the Applications view.

It might be useful to disable this feature if some of the applications in a cluster need not be deployed to every member. This enables the administrator a much finer control over which applications are deployed to a member server. Unless cluster synchronization is left active, the application list is just a collection of logical resource groupings and not necessarily something to be deployed during cluster synchronization.

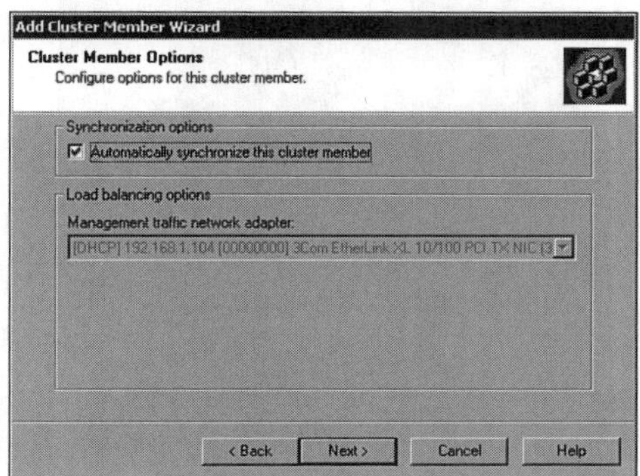

FIGURE 12.19
The Cluster Member Options pane.

Completing the Add Cluster Member Wizard

Once all the information is entered and the Add Cluster Member Wizard is finished, Application Center adds the new member to the target cluster. This process adds data that uniquely identifies this server as a cluster member. A new server node is added to the member node in the console once the configuration is complete. It is now possible to configure, synchronize, and deploy applications to this member.

Configuring Properties of a Cluster Member

Figure 12.20 shows the property page of a cluster member. The only configurable option is whether the member should be a part of synchronizations. If this box is checked, then any synchronization issued from the console happens on this cluster member. If this box is unchecked, then only deployments specifically targeting this cluster member will replicate applications to this member. This panel also shows which network adapter is used by the cluster member for management traffic.

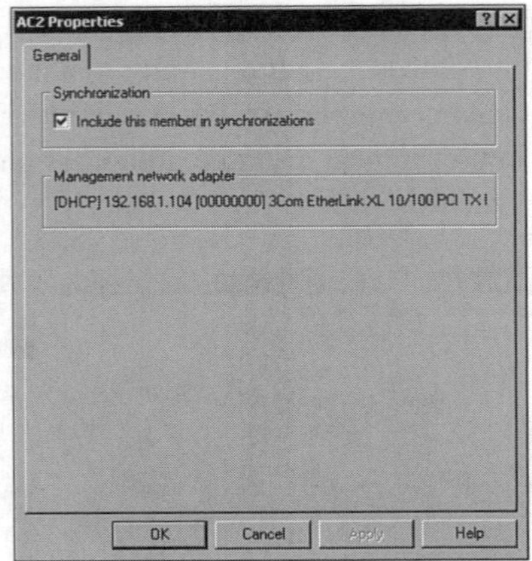

FIGURE 12.20

The property page of a cluster member.

Performing Cluster Member Tasks

Once a member has been added to a cluster, there are eight tasks that an administrator can perform against a member. Right-clicking on the cluster name in the Application Center 2000 console accesses the menu shown in Figure 12.21. Some options are disabled, depending on the type of cluster. If the cluster does not support Network Load Balancing, then the Set Online and Set Offline menu options are grayed out. If the member is not the Cluster Controller, then the Designate As Controller option is available. If there is more than one member server, then the Disband Cluster option is grayed out on the Cluster Controller All Tasks menu.

Set Online

Set Online is used to place servers into online mode from offline mode. A server that is in online mode handles connections to the Cluster IP address. Currently, Set Online is available only in Web clusters that use Network Load Balancing. Set Online modifies Network Load Balancing configuration information on the target member, forcing the cluster to coalesce so the member can begin handling connections again.

To bring a server online, right-click the server name in the Application Center 2000 console and select Set Online. If this command is grayed out, then the Web cluster is not using Network Load Balancing.

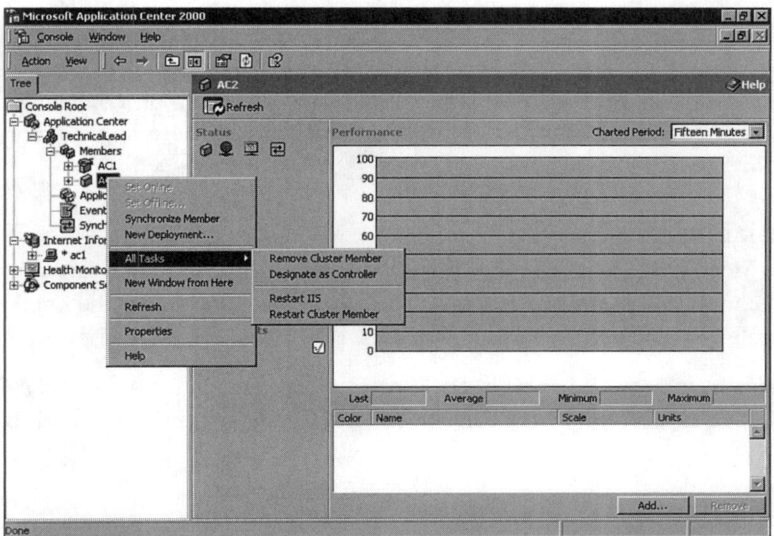

FIGURE 12.21
The right-click menu of a cluster member.

Set Offline

Set Offline is used to place a server into offline mode from online mode. A server in offline mode is not handling connections for the cluster IP address. Currently Set Offline is available only to Web clusters that use Network Load Balancing. Set Offline modifies Network Load Balancing configuration information on the target member, forcing the cluster to coalesce so the member can stop handling connections.

To take a server offline, right-click the server name in the Application Center 2000 console and select Set Offline. If this command is grayed out, then the Web cluster is not using Network Load Balancing.

Synchronize Cluster

Synchronize Cluster launches a replication job that executes all the configured applications in a cluster. Synchronization only copies Registry keys, file system paths, data sources, and Web sites and virtual directories. COM+ applications and global ISAPI filters are not copied because this can require IIS to be stopped and restarted.

To synchronize a cluster, right-click the Cluster Controller server name or the cluster node in the Application Center 2000 console and select Synchronize Cluster.

CAUTION

To deploy COM+ applications and global ISAPI filters, create a deployment using the New Deployment Wizard. Synchronizations do *not* deploy these application resources.

Synchronize Member

Synchronize Member launches a replication job that executes all the configured applications present on a cluster to one specific member. This synchronization copies the same application resources as cluster synchronization.

To synchronize a cluster member, right-click the member name in the Application Center 2000 console and select Synchronize Member. The Cluster Controller cannot be synchronized with itself.

New Deployment

The New Deployment menu item launches the New Deployment Wizard. This wizard is used to create deployments to individual members or other clusters. See the section "Deploying Applications to the Cluster," later in this chapter.

Remove Cluster Member

The next four menu items can be found under the All Tasks submenu, seen in Figure 12.21, starting with Remove Cluster Member. Remove Cluster Member removes a member from the cluster. This process will only mark it as not a member of the cluster; it does not remove applications that have been deployed to the cluster member during its membership period.

To remove a cluster member from a cluster, right-click the target member in the Application Center 2000 console, select All Tasks, and select Remove Cluster Member. The Cluster Controller cannot be removed from a cluster. To remove a Cluster Controller from a cluster, first designate a different member as the Cluster Controller and then remove the old Cluster Controller, which will be a normal member after designation is complete.

Designate as Controller

Designate as Controller transfers the Cluster Controller configuration from one member to another. Use Designate as Controller if the Cluster Controller fails or requires maintenance.

To designate a controller, right-click the target member in the Application Center 2000 console, select All Tasks, and select Designate as Controller. This option is grayed out on the current Cluster Controller.

Restart IIS

Restart IIS recycles the IIS services on the target member. This is useful if issues arise during deployments that cause unexpected failures. Restart IIS is also useful if a Web site is experiencing technical difficulties from bugs or other unexpected failure conditions.

To restart IIS, right-click the target member, select Tasks, and select Restart IIS.

Restart Cluster Member

Restart Cluster Member forces the target cluster member to reboot. To restart a cluster member, right-click the target member in the Application Center 2000 console, select All Tasks, and select Restart Member.

Disband Cluster

Disband cluster removes Application Center 2000 configuration information from a cluster that has only one member. Disbanding a cluster does not destroy any data or applications on the cluster.

To disband a cluster, first remove all the cluster members from a cluster using Remove Cluster Member. Then right-click the Cluster Controller in the Application Center 2000 console, select All Tasks, and select Disband Cluster. The configuration for the cluster is not removed from the Cluster Controller, so re-creating the cluster restores the entire Application Center 2000 application configuration previously created.

Deploying Applications to the Cluster

Once all members of the cluster have been added, it is time to deploy applications. In Application Center 2000, there are two distinct methods for replicating content from the Cluster Controller to other members of the cluster.

The first method is synchronization. Synchronizing a cluster is used to replicate content from the Cluster Controller to all members of the cluster at the moment the synchronization is requested. Because synchronization is an on-demand process, not all application resources are replicated. During day-to-day operation of the cluster, synchronizations are useful for small application updates such as single page changes, simple Registry updates, or changes to file system paths or data sources. Synchronizations do not replicate COM+ applications or global ISAPI filters because these replications might require Application Center 2000 to stop and restart IIS, disrupting service to the Web cluster. Applications that don't contain these resources could use synchronizations to distribute new versions of sites.

The second method of replicating content to members of a cluster is deployments. Deployments are similar to synchronizations except that they are created using the New Deployment

Wizard. The New Deployment Wizard helps the administrator build a deployment. An example of a simple deployment is the standard synchronization. A more complicated deployment includes COM+ applications and global ISAPI filters. All deployments run right after completion of the New Deployment Wizard. The only way to replicate content outside the current cluster is with a separate deployment action.

Using the New Deployment Wizard

To launch the New Deployment Wizard, right-click the cluster node or any member node in the Application Center 2000 console and select New Deployment. If a deployment is started from a specific member of a cluster, that member is the source of the deployment and not the Cluster Controller. To ensure that the Cluster Controller is the source for a deployment, launch the deployment from the cluster node or the application node of a cluster.

The New Deployment Wizard has two paths, as shown in Figure 12.22. Take the first path to deploy content inside the current cluster. Take the second path to deploy content outside the current cluster.

Deploying Content Inside the Current Cluster

The first task to understand in the New Deployment Wizard is the process of deploying content inside the cluster. This is similar to the synchronization process discussed previously. The main difference is that the administrator can choose target members of the deployment and specify to deploy COM+ application and global ISAPI filters.

Deployment Target Options

The Deployment Target Options pane in the New Deployment Wizard is shown in Figure 12.23. The first information supplied in this pane is the source server for this deployment. Make sure that this is the correct server with the latest content because any changes are propagated from this source server to all target members. The deployment name is the name that can be used to refer to this deployment in the Synchronizations View pane in the Application Center 2000 console. Use this name to help reference the deployment later if problems arise or for historical tracking of deployments and releases. When Deploy Content Inside the Current Cluster is selected, the next pane of the wizard will be the Deploy Targets Within a Cluster pane. This also means that content will be replicated only to members of one cluster.

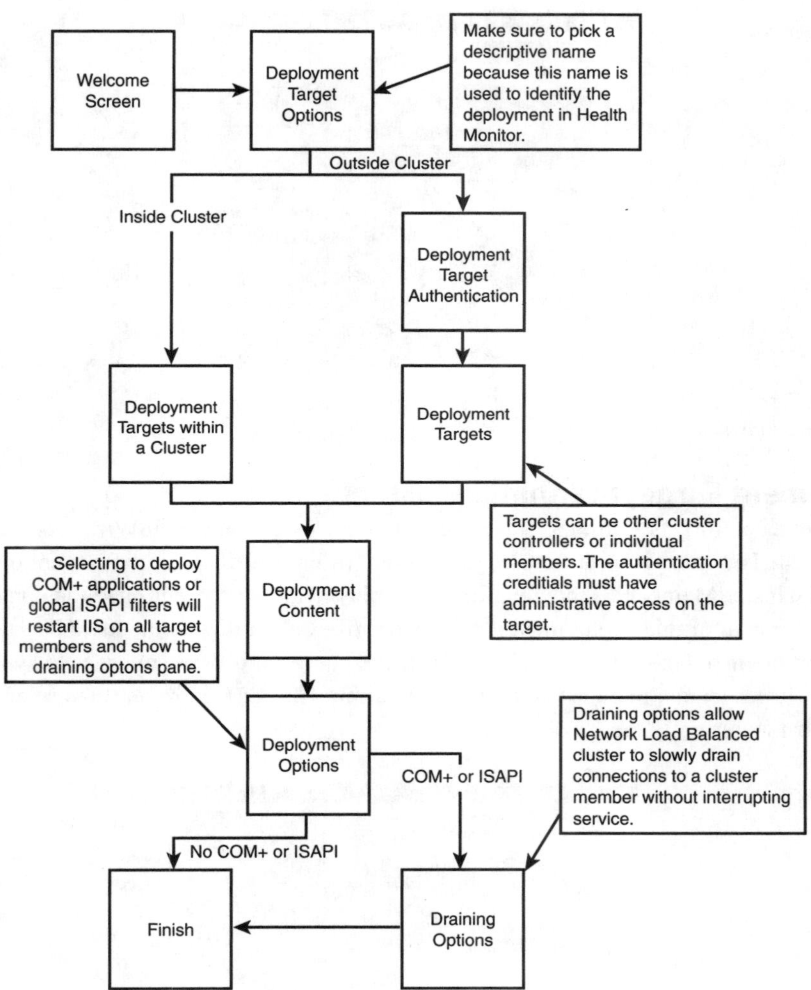

FIGURE 12.22
The paths through the New Deployment Wizard.

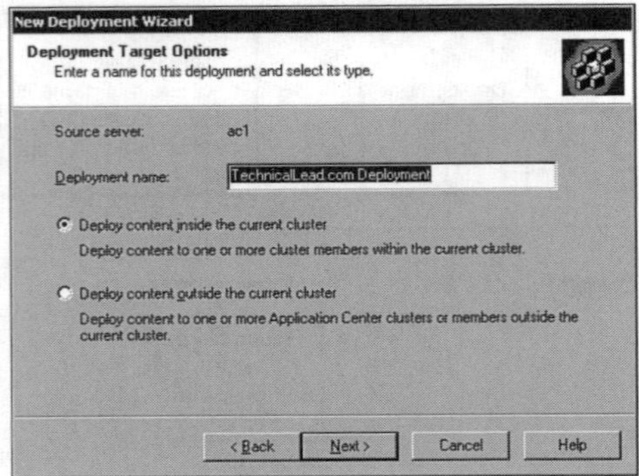

FIGURE 12.23
The Deployment Target Options pane.

Deployment Targets Within a Cluster

The Deployment Targets Within a Cluster pane in the New Deployment Wizard is shown in Figure 12.24. This pane is used to select the targets within a cluster for the current deployment. Select All Cluster Members if the goal for this deployment is to synchronize the content on a cluster. If the goal of this deployment is to synchronize only a few members, then select only the appropriate members for this deployment. If the goal of this deployment is to synchronize the entire cluster from a member other than the current Cluster Controller, then select only the member that is currently the Cluster Controller.

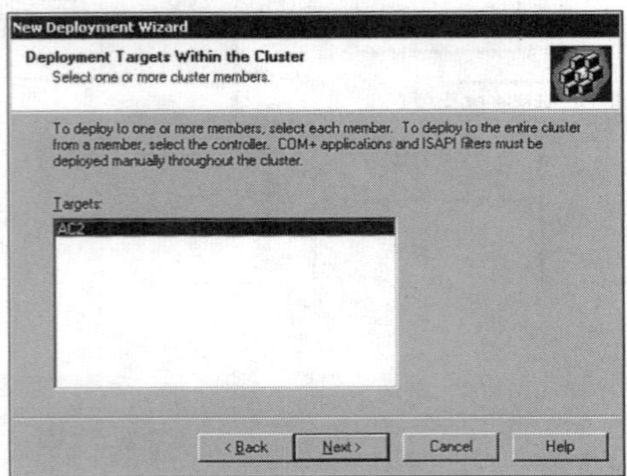

FIGURE 12.24
The Deployment Target Within a Cluster pane.

Deployment Content

After selecting the target members, the Deployment Content pane enables the administrator to select the applications to deploy. Select Deploy All Applications and Related Cluster Configuration to deploy all the configured applications in the cluster. When this option is selected, some deployment options in the next pane are selected with no option of turning them off. Select Deploy One or More Applications to pick which applications are deployed. Figure 12.25 shows the Deployment Content pane.

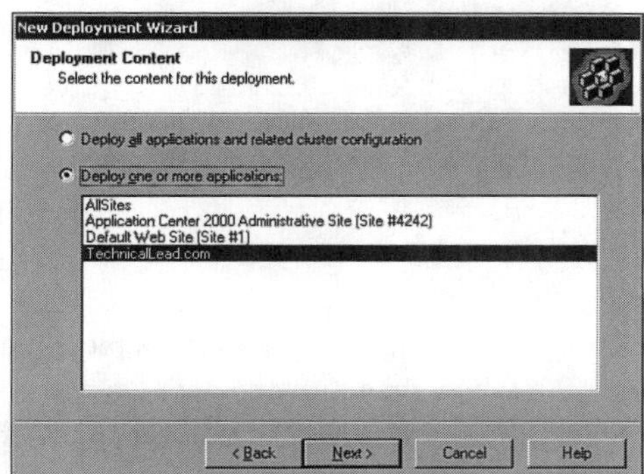

FIGURE 12.25
The Deployment Content pane.

Deployment Options

The next step in the New Deployment Wizard is the Deployment Options pane, as seen in Figure 12.26. This is where administrators determine what types of content are replicated in a deployment. By default the Deploy Folder and File Permissions option is selected. This means that if NTFS security has been configured on specific file system objects that are a part of either file system path or Web site and virtual directories application resources, they will transfer to target members of the deployment. Just like all other deployments, they will override the existing security configuration of any file system object. If this option is unchecked, files and folders will replicate without the configured permissions and change as described in "Using the General Tab," previously in this chapter.

Select Deploy COM+ Applications and Deploy Global ISAPI Filters to force the deployment of these application resources to all target members. If either of these options is selected, then the next pane in the New Deployment Wizard is the Draining Options pane.

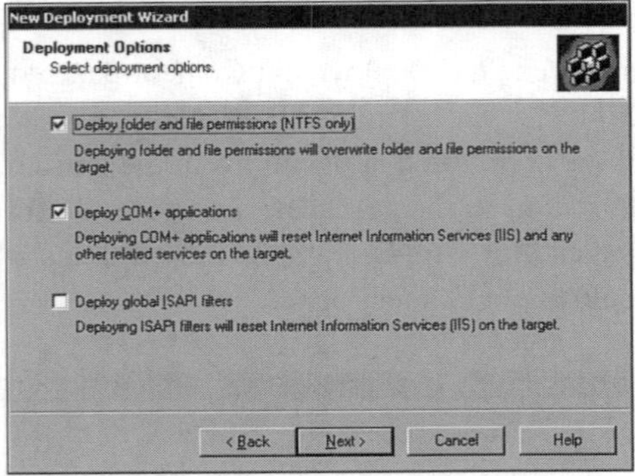

FIGURE 12.26
The Deployment Options pane.

Draining Options

Figure 12.27 shows the Draining Options pane of the New Deployment Wizard. This pane is used to tell Application Center 2000 how gracefully content changes that require IIS to be reset occur. Select Drain Connections Before Resetting IIS to prevent IIS from abruptly terminating user connections. Anytime this occurs, the perception from the user is that the Web site experienced an availability hit. By draining connections from one member to another, the user does not notice any service interruptions. Select Reset the Connections Immediately if the target members or cluster is not in service at the time of the deployment or the changes need to be propagated instantly for some application reason. For instance, if a COM+ application object has a bug that is causing hundreds of orders to have problems requiring attention from customer service personnel, it is probably wiser to force the changes to occur quickly—eliminating the generation of problem orders.

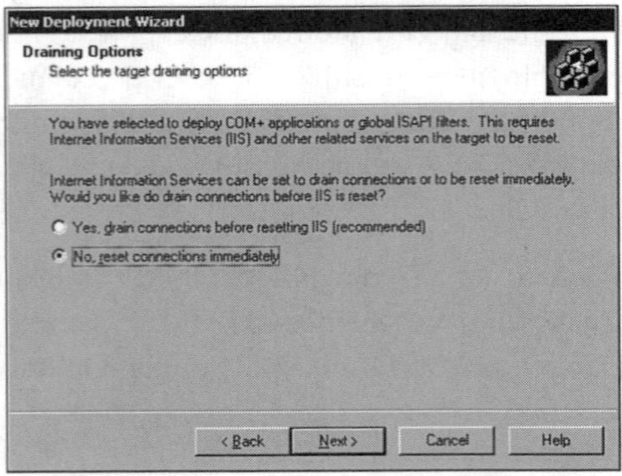

FIGURE 12.27
The Draining Options pane.

Remember that the Draining Options pane is present on the wizard only if the deployment includes COM+ application or global ISAPI filters. Other application resources are deployable without interruption to service.

Deploying Content Outside the Current Cluster

Deploying content outside the current cluster is useful for many scenarios. If the deployment environment is multistage, such as those discussed in Chapter 8, "Designing Web Farm Application Deployment Environments," a cross-cluster deployment saves time and effort for the deployment team. When using Component Load Balancing, the COM+ applications that exist on the COM+ cluster can be deployed to the Web cluster automatically. Cross-cluster deployment eliminates the need to deploy any applications manually to downstream environments such as staging or production, especially in three- and four-stage configurations.

Deployment Target Options

If Deploy Content Outside the Current Cluster is selected, then the next pane is the Deployment Targets Authentication pane. This also means that content could be deployed to a separate cluster. This option is used to replicate content in a multistage deployment environment. For example, this option could be used to move content from the development environment cluster(s) to the staging environment cluster(s). All of the other options in this pane are the same as when deploying content within the current cluster.

Deployment Target Authentication

Use the Deployment Target Authentication pane to supply logon credentials to Cluster Controllers or members in different clusters. Figure 12.28 shows this pane. Supply user name, password, and domain information for an Administrator account on the target server or cluster.

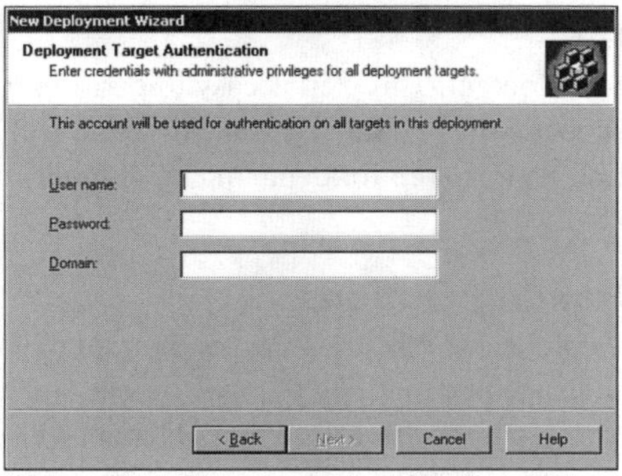

FIGURE 12.28
The Deployment Target Authentication pane.

Deployment Targets

The Deployment Targets pane is similar to Deployment Targets Within a Cluster pane shown in Figure 12.24. The difference on the Deployment Targets pane is target servers are entered by either typing their names manually or by selecting them from a server Browse dialog. To add a deployment target server, the credentials supplied in the Deployment Target Authentication pane must have Administrator privileges on that server. Type the target server name and select Add to add a server to the deployment list. At this time, Application Center will try to log on to this server and verify the security settings you provided. Also, remember that Application Center 2000 must be present on target servers. To remove servers from the Deployment Targets list, simply select the target server and click the Remove button. Figure 12.29 shows the Deployment Targets pane.

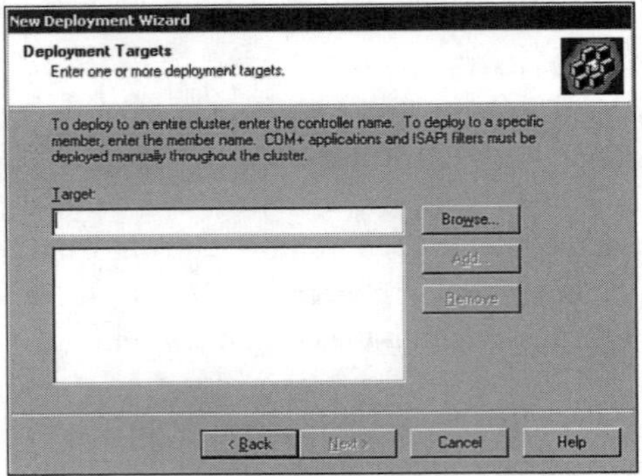

FIGURE 12.29
The Deployment Targets pane.

Deployment Content

The next pane is Deployment Content. This step is easy to perform because all of the options in this pane function the same as when deploying content within a cluster. If this is still unclear, reread the discussion on this item for deployment within a cluster in the previous section.

Deployment and Draining Options

The next step in the New Deployment Wizard is the configuration of deployment options as it was when deploying to cluster members. If deploying from one stage to another crosses security domains, it may be necessary to uncheck Deploy Folder and File Permissions because NTFS permission information may not translate correctly across domain boundaries unless there is a two-way trust between both domains. The same is true for COM+ applications. If the security credentials for a COM+ application are tied to a domain, then the COM+ applications will fail to deploy. Use a local account for security configurations as suggested in Chapter 10. All of the other options in this pane are the same as when deploying content within the current cluster as shown in Figure 12.26.

Monitoring Deployments

In the Application Center 2000 console, every cluster has a synchronizations node. The synchronizations node is where an administrator can check on the status of recent deployments and synchronizations. After the New Deployment Wizard is run, the Synchronization pane will update to show this new deployment. Application Center then analyzes the applications that are part of the deployment and determines which content is new or different from the target members. Figure 12.30 shows the Synchronizations pane in the console.

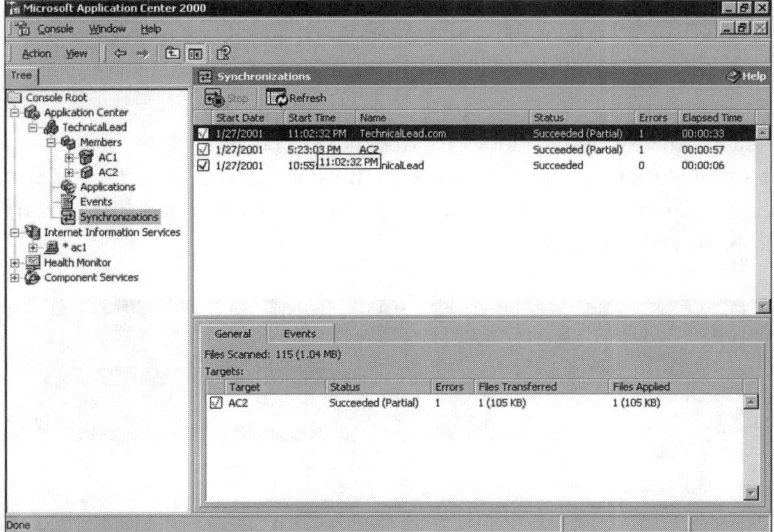

FIGURE 12.30
The Synchronizations pane in the Application Center 2000 console.

As the deployment progresses, it will go through a number of different stages. Table 12.2 summarizes the stages of a deployment.

TABLE 12.2 Stages of a Deployment

Stage	*Notes*
Failed	Occurs only when the connection or credentials don't allow the initialization to occur.
Initializing	Here Application Center 2000 determines what applications components need to be replicated. It will not replicate unneeded files and COM+ applications if they are identical.
Transferring	This stage appears during long deployment with a large number of files or COM+ applications.
Applying	This means that all the content and application components have been transferred to the remote machines and are being applied.
Succeeded	The deployment and all application resources have been installed successfully on the target servers.
Succeed (Partial)	Some of the deployment failed. The errors show up in the Events portion of the Synchronization pane.

Figure 12.31 shows the Synchronizations pane in the process of applying a deployment job to three members of a cluster. Notice in the lower-right pane that the second machine `W2STGLOAD05` is in the process of applying the changes while the others have finished. This is a sign that there might be a problem with this server.

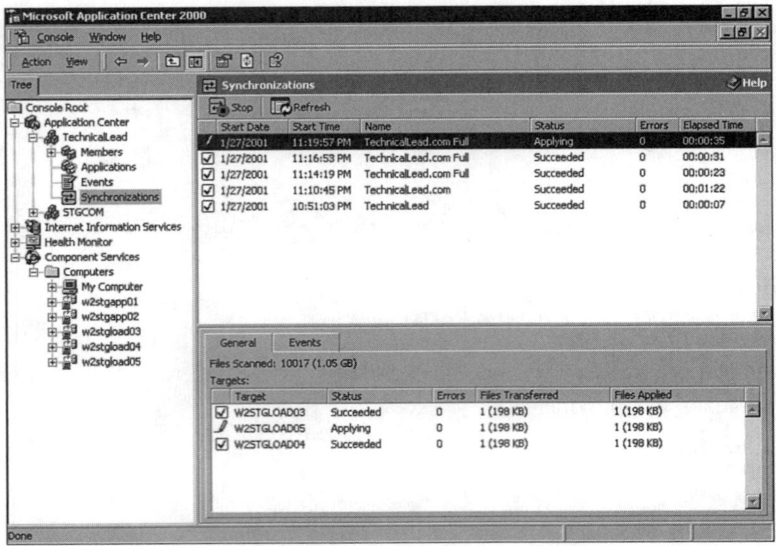

FIGURE 12.31

The Synchronizations pane of a multiple-host deployment.

When a deployment does fail, the General tab in the Synchronization pane shows the individual status for each member of a cluster. Figure 12.32 shows only this portion, with two members deploying successfully and one failing.

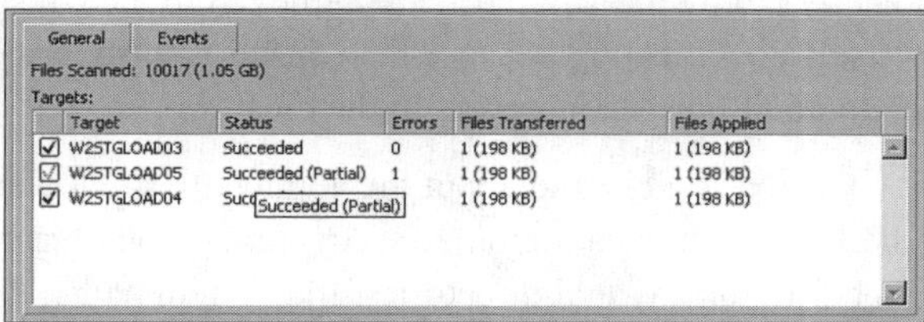

FIGURE 12.32
The General tab in the Synchronization pane.

Look at the Events tab in the Synchronizations pane for details about the errors that caused the deployment to fail for a specific member. The Events pane contains all the events for every node. Figure 12.33 shows the Events tab with the error that caused the deployment to fail to the second member of the cluster. Even though the deployment failed to this member, it is not automatically removed from the production mix. This is accomplished with a custom Health Monitor script, discussed in Chapter 15, "Performing Common Health Monitor Tasks."

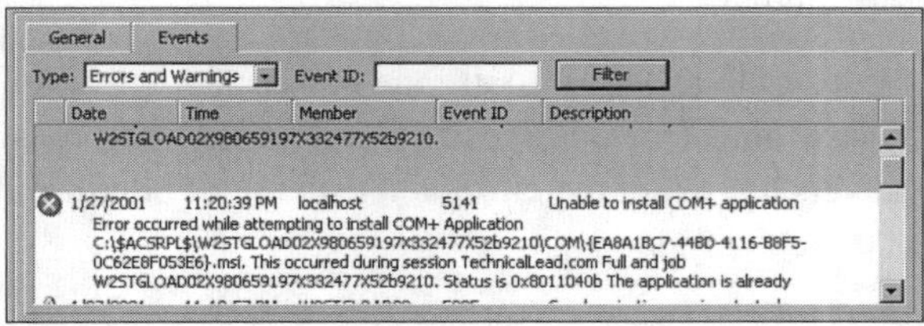

FIGURE 12.33
The Events tab in the Synchronization pane.

Summary

There are seven discrete steps to building a Web cluster. In step one, a determination is made of what load balancing strategy the cluster will use. This helps determine hardware requirements for servers in the cluster.

In step two, a server build process is created, and the operating system, .NET enterprise servers, and other system services are deployed to all members of the cluster. Windows 2000 features like unattended install can help speed this process and prevent errors.

In step three, a single server in the cluster is designated the Cluster Controller, and the New Cluster Wizard is run with the controller as its target. This establishes the key component and central application deployment point for an Application Center 2000 Web cluster.

In step four, applications served by the Web farm are deployed to the Cluster Controller. This one-time deployment is self-documenting because the Cluster Controller becomes the blueprint for creating the application build on other servers in the cluster.

In step five, Application Center 2000 is told about the applications that were deployed onto the Cluster Controller in the form of application objects. An application object is a collection of COM+ components, Web Sites and virtual directories, file system paths, Registry entries, and data sources. Any combinations of these objects can make up an Application Center 2000 application.

In step six, the other members of the cluster are joined with the Cluster Controller, using the Add Cluster Member Wizard. The Add Cluster Member Wizard configures a server as a member of a cluster and prepares it for service.

In step seven, the applications defined on a cluster are deployed to all members of the cluster using the New Deployment Wizard. This wizard creates an Application Center 2000 deployment that replicates applications and ensures that all members are synchronized correctly. In multistage deployment environments, the New Deployment Wizard is used to move applications from one cluster to another.

Follow the outline provided in this chapter to use the power of Application Center 2000 to manage a Web farm. Ease of management, speed of deployment, and consistency of applications across multiple servers are worth the effort and expense of building and deploying an Application Center 2000 Web cluster.

Deploying Application Center 2000 COM+ Clusters

CHAPTER

13

Many organizations have committed considerable time and effort to developing COM+ applications. For years, Microsoft has evangelized the COM+ architecture and component development in general. The mantra was "build middle tier business components using COM and COM+ technologies and scalability is just around the corner." However, the reality is that a COM+ application service did not scale easily until Application Center 2000.

Application Center 2000 is the first technology from Microsoft to address scalability of remote COM+ applications through COM+ clustering and Component Load Balancing. Component Load Balancing solves legacy DCOM issues that prevent remote component invocations from scaling through traditional load-balancing technologies.

The goals of this chapter are to help you

- Understand the motivations behind creating Application Center 2000 COM+ clusters to solve the legacy DCOM scaling problem.
- Create COM+ clusters for server applications and client applications. Learn how server application clusters use Component Load Balancing and provide the ultimate in scalability for COM+ applications. Learn how client application clusters leverage Network Load Balancing to provide high availability for COM+ applications.
- Add COM+ routing clusters to use multiple COM+ clusters for server applications in a Web farm. By default, each Web cluster can reference only one COM+ server application cluster. COM+ routing clusters enable a single Web cluster to use multiple COM+ server application clusters.

Solving the Legacy DCOM Scaling Problem

Before Application Center 2000, remote COM+ applications were mired in DCOM scaling problems. By default, DCOM uses connection-oriented RPC over TCP/IP, a connected protocol, which severely restricts the scalability of load-balancing clusters. Because DCOM holds the connection to a remote server after the first component invocation, further invocations use that same connection, bypassing load-balancing technologies. Currently, all available protocol options for DCOM are connected; thus, DCOM is similar to FTP in that it is session based. It differs from FTP in that this session is established by the COM infrastructure in Windows itself and is shared by all applications on a single server. Once a DCOM connection to a remote server is established, terminating that link requires a failure of the network or servers involved or expiration of the underlying protocol's connection timeout.

Each protocol that DCOM uses has different criteria for reasonable timeout periods and different factors that determine when a connection has timed out. For UDP, if the network or server is not responding to requests, the timeout value is 32 seconds. Server or network failure during a method invocation can extend the timeout period to 96 seconds. Timeouts when using RPC over TCP/IP are in the realm of three to five minutes, depending on the network adapter and other hidden mysteries of the TCP/IP protocol.

Imagine a perfectly viable situation in which Network Load Balancing is balancing requests to a remote COM+ application. The intention of this cluster is to increase performance and scale out the services provided by the COM+ application. If a server fails in this cluster, DCOM calls from the clients attached to the failed member will time out. These clients will reissue requests against the cluster IP address, and the component invocation will happen on a different member of the cluster. Application availability is unaffected, and half the load-balancing promise is fulfilled. This is very similar to what happens when clusters that balance HTTP traffic have member failures.

When the server returns to service, the HTTP and DCOM scenarios sharply diverge. HTTP is disconnected, and each request is independent from the others, so the returning server immediately begins handling requests. DCOM is connected, and there is nothing to signal the return of the failed member to the connected clients. The connections that originally existed on the failed member remain on other cluster members. The returned member accepts requests only from new clients or those that reset their connections through failure or timeout. Figure 13.1 shows the traditional DCOM scaling problem. While DCOM can be highly available, it does not scale.

A seemingly simple solution to the DCOM scaling problem would be disconnected protocol implementation. Probably because of the complexity of managing connections as in the HTML world, Microsoft has not provided this implementation to date. Instead, Microsoft decided to achieve scale with COM+ applications through a different route, separate from load balancing and the network layer. Introduced with Application Center 2000, Component Load Balancing solves the DCOM scaling problem.

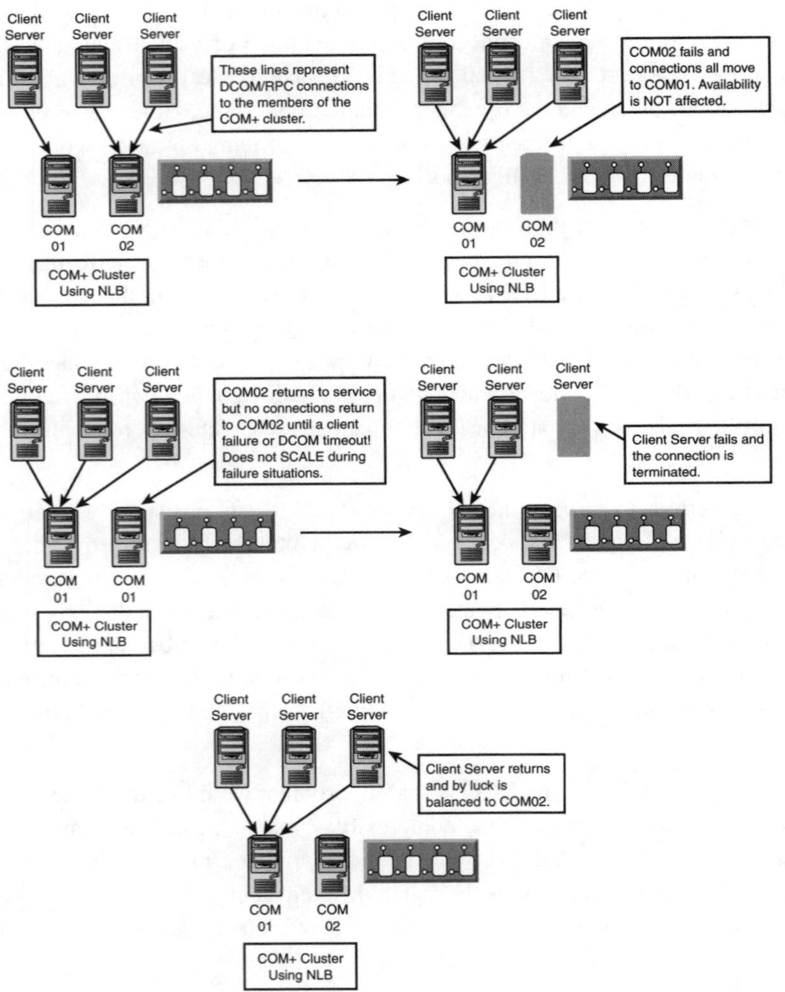

FIGURE 13.1
The traditional DCOM scaling problem.

Understanding Component Load Balancing

Component Load Balancing does not change the fundamental connected nature of DCOM across all protocols. It does change the way clients create components remotely. Traditional DCOM uses the Registry or the COM+ catalog to store the network name or IP address of the server for remote instantiations of DCOM components. Figure 13.2 shows a DCOM component creation call.

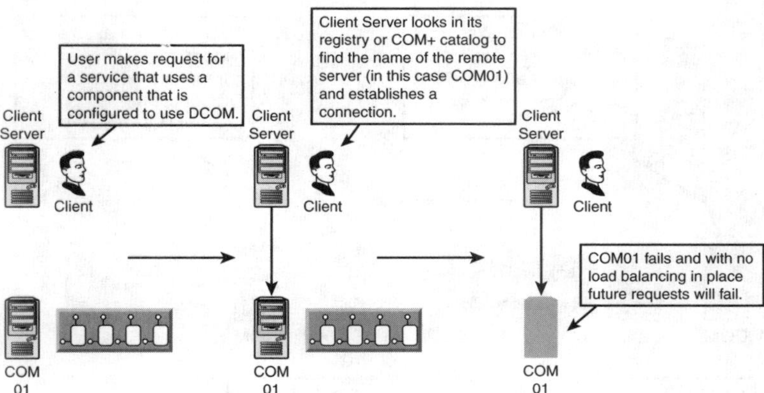

FIGURE 13.2
A DCOM remote component invocation.

Component Load Balancing solves the DCOM scaling problem by intercepting component-creation requests before they leave the client and distributing these requests across the servers in a COM+ cluster. These COM+ cluster server names are stored locally on each client in the COM+ catalog. This list is called a *routing list* because Component Load Balancing routes requests to each member of this list.

Any client that uses Component Load Balancing maintains this internal routing list for a COM+ server cluster. Component Load Balancing communicates through the AC Load Balancer COM+ application every 800 milliseconds to gauge the response time of each member of the COM+ cluster. Servers with the fastest response time move to the top of the list. When a component-creation request comes in, Component Load Balancing uses a fastest response time/round-robin balancing algorithm to assign the creation request to a particular server. If the COM+ server is unavailable, it will move those creation requests to other COM+ servers on the routing list.

Component Load Balancing works because it intercepts component-creation requests. For components configured to use Component Load Balancing, the client machine uses the CLB activator, COM+ load-balancing service, and the routing list to determine the proper COM+ server cluster member to request the component activation on. On the COM+ server side, the AC Load Balancer COM+ application reports availability and performance statistics to each client server. Once a component is created on a remote machine, Component Load Balancing is no longer a part of the picture. The client server can hold this component indefinitely, and all method invocations always occur on the original COM+ server. Figure 13.3 shows how Component Load Balancing handles component-creation requests.

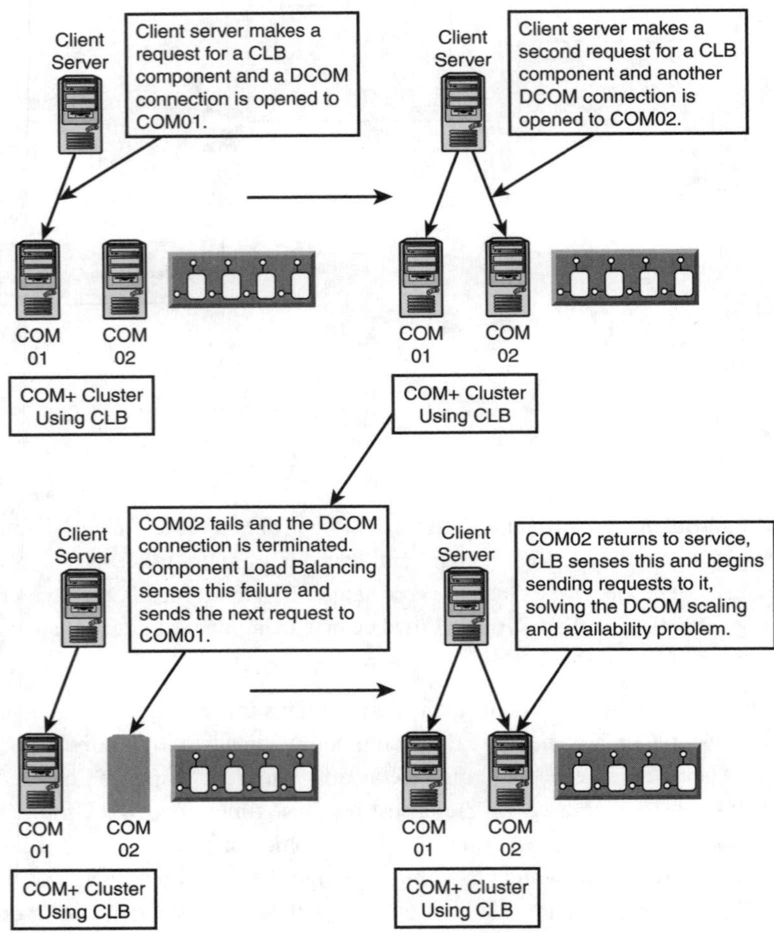

FIGURE 13.3
A Component Load Balancing remote component invocation.

The routing table is maintained on each client machine that uses Component Load Balancing. There is a single list shared by all COM+ applications. For the client server to load balance requests, all servers in a cluster running a COM+ application have to be entered in this routing list. In other words, the client server controls the load balancing, not the COM+ server.

Configuring Component Load Balancing

Clients who use Component Load Balancing require Application Center 2000. Assuming that clients are members of a Web cluster simplifies configuration of Component Load Balancing.

All the steps involved are synchronized by Application Center across a Web cluster environment.

There are three steps to configuring Component Load Balancing. These steps are discussed in the following sections.

Installing the COM+ Application

Installing the COM+ application onto the Web cluster is easy. There are three ways to do so:

- Create the application manually. If the application is simple, creating the application manually on the cluster controller is a viable option. To simplify deployments later, create a new Application Center 2000 application to deploy it throughout the cluster. If the application is installed manually, the cluster controller will be different from the other members of the cluster because a manually created COM application does not have the component DLL files stored in the `c:\Program Files\ComPlus Applications\{Unique GUID}` directory (where `{Unique GUID}` is a special GUID created by the install of the COM+ application export MSI file). To correct this problem, export the manually created application using the COM+ Export Application Wizard discussed in Chapter 10, "Using Component Services (COM+) in a Web Farm." Then remove and delete the existing COM+ application and all its components from the cluster controller. Install the exported application back onto the cluster controller. This installs the application components to the `c:\Program Files\ComPlus Applications\{Unique GUID}` directory on the cluster controller. Now when a COM+ application is deployed using Application Center 2000, the application components are in the same place across the cluster. These steps are not required; they just keep the cluster controller configured in exactly the same way as the rest of the cluster members.
- Export the application from the COM+ server and run the MSI file on the cluster controller. Exporting COM+ applications and installing them on other servers are explained in detail in Chapter 10. Use an Application Center 2000 application to simplify deployment to all the Web cluster members as you would do when creating the application manually.
- Deploy the COM+ application from another Application Center 2000 cluster to the cluster controller. This is the preferred method to install Component Load Balancing COM+ applications to Web clusters. The main advantage is that propagating changes in these COM+ applications to client servers is easy if the remote target is a Web cluster using Application Center 2000. Use a cross cluster deployment to move the COM+ application from the COM+ cluster to the Web cluster.

It is important to understand that installing the application on the Web cluster does not mean that the components in that application are ever instantiated. Component Load Balancing requires this step so that the component can be marked to support dynamic load balancing.

Marking Components to Support Dynamic Load Balancing

Traditional DCOM applications required only that a reference to the remote component be installed on the local machine. This meant that the physical DLL file did not have to be installed locally to the client. In most cases, this was not the practice, so in COM+ Microsoft introduced the *proxy application*. The proxy application looks just like the server application installed on the COM+ server, except the application is set to run on a different server as in DCOM. With Component Load Balancing, Application Center 2000 introduces a third way to configure a component to run remotely.

When you install Application Center 2000 on a server, all COM+ components gain a new check box for enabling dynamic load-balancing support. Enabling this check box for a particular component sends all creation requests to the servers in the routing list.

Adding Servers to the Routing Table

The final step to configure a server to use Component Load Balancing against a COM+ cluster is to add the servers to the routing table for the Web cluster. The routing table is maintained at the cluster node level in Application Center 2000. Access the Component Services tab by right-clicking any cluster node in the console and selecting Properties. Figure 13.4 shows this tab.

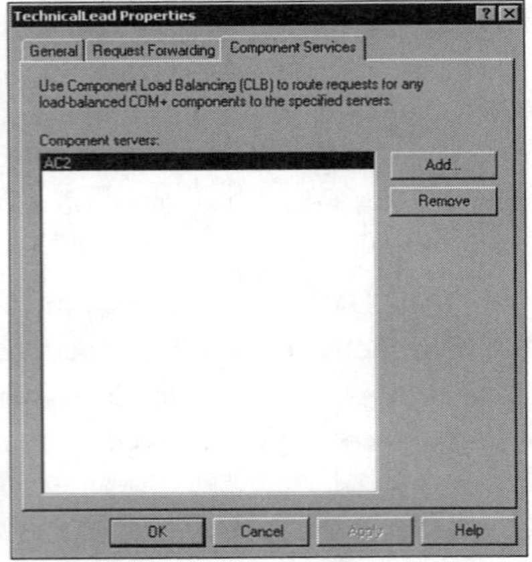

FIGURE 13.4

The Component Services routing table for a cluster.

All components that are configured to support dynamic load balancing use the single routing table that is maintained per cluster.

Limitations of Component Load Balancing

Having a global list of servers per client places a few limitations on Component Load Balancing clusters. There can be only one Component Load Balancing cluster associated with any client server. In environments where COM+ applications reside on servers without special hardware configurations, this provides for real scalability.

However, in environments with different hardware requirements and many different types of remote COM+ applications, such as a credit card authorization application that requires a special connection to a bank or a remote tax application that uses third-party software, Component Load Balancing may not address all needs. To help address this problem, Application Center 2000 provides a third clustering option called a COM+ routing cluster.

Using a COM+ Routing Cluster

A COM+ routing cluster routes COM+ object activations from a client to a COM+ cluster. This cluster is load balanced using Network Load Balancing or any other suitable load-balancing technology. The only requirement is that client components be members of a COM+ proxy application that points to the virtual name of the COM+ routing cluster. By default, Application Center 2000 creates the COM+ routing cluster using Network Load Balancing. Figure 13.5 shows a typical environment configured to use a COM+ routing cluster. Notice that the client application has an independent routing list for the dedicated COM+ cluster, and those components are created using Component Load Balancing. The components on the COM+ routing cluster are created through a proxy application. Using a COM+ routing cluster creates a network hop in the component-creation process by forwarding all these requests to the routing server. This adds a level of indirection between the Web cluster servers and the COM+ cluster.

Client object consumers of components on COM+ routing clusters are unaware of the real location of the COM+ objects until after they are created. The COM+ routing cluster maintains a list of COM+ application servers, usually in a COM+ cluster of their own, that component-creations target. In effect, the COM+ routing cluster forwards creation requests from the client to the server acting as a routing object broker. Once the routing cluster has brokered the creation of a component, method invocations on this component do not use the COM+ routing cluster. All component activations continue to use the COM+ routing cluster as long as the proxy application is marked to do so on the client servers.

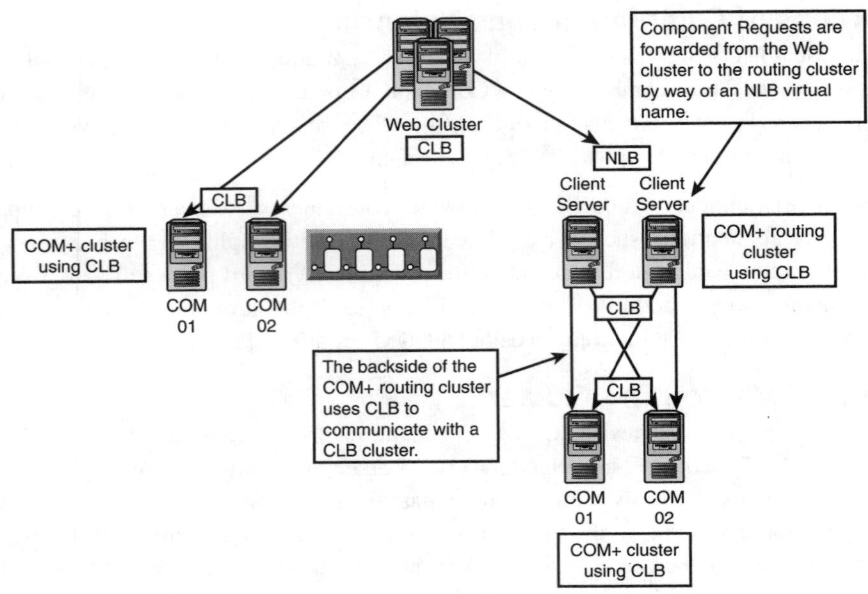

FIGURE 13.5
A Web farm with a COM+ routing cluster.

Creating COM+ Clusters

With Application Center 2000, it is easy to create a COM+ cluster for load-balancing COM+ applications. Like other clusters in Application Center, COM+ clusters are created using the New Cluster Wizard. Many of the New Cluster Wizard pages for a COM+ cluster are identical to those seen when creating a Web cluster.

> **NOTE**
>
> Review Chapter 12, "Deploying Application Center 2000 Web Clusters," for a detailed discussion of using the New Cluster Wizard.

Application Center introduces two types of COM+ application clusters:

- *A server application cluster* uses Component Load Balancing and is a true load-balancing cluster. Each member of the cluster, as long as it is in service, handles the creation, use, and lifetime of COM+ components. COM+ applications can scale to any number of servers for greater throughput and have unprecedented availability.
- *A client application cluster* uses Network Load Balancing and provides load balancing but without circumventing the DCOM scaling problem. All cluster members handle component-creation requests, but on active clients with many DCOM calls, an individual client is tied to a single cluster member, unlike a server application cluster.

Using the New Cluster Wizard for COM+ Application Clusters

New COM+ clusters are built using the New Cluster Wizard on a server that is not a member of a cluster. A COM+ application cluster is a grouping of servers dedicated to particular COM+ applications. Clients of a COM+ cluster could be Web clusters, other COM+ clusters, or routing clusters. Any server with Application Center 2000 can use a COM+ cluster for load-balancing component-creation requests.

Launch the New Cluster Wizard by connecting to a server where Application Center 2000 is installed and following the steps described in Chapter 12. Using the New Cluster Wizard for a COM+ cluster is almost identical to a Web cluster. To create a COM+ cluster complete the following steps:

1. Let Application Center query the target server network configuration on the Analyzing the Server Configuration pane so it can gather information about the network adapters of the target server.
2. Fill in the new COM+ cluster name and description on the Name and Description pane of the wizard.
3. Set the cluster type to COM+ application on the Cluster Type pane of the wizard. Selecting a different cluster type is the first divergence from the Web cluster creation process. Figure 13.6 shows the Cluster Type page of the New Cluster Wizard with a COM+ application cluster selected.

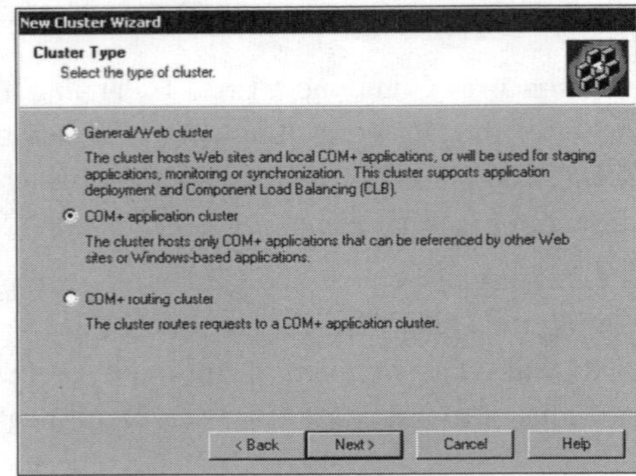

FIGURE 13.6

The Cluster Type page with a COM+ application cluster selected.

4. Choose the type of COM+ application clusters on the COM+ Application Clients pane. This pane is shown in Figure 13.7. From here, the two types of COM+ clusters are created.

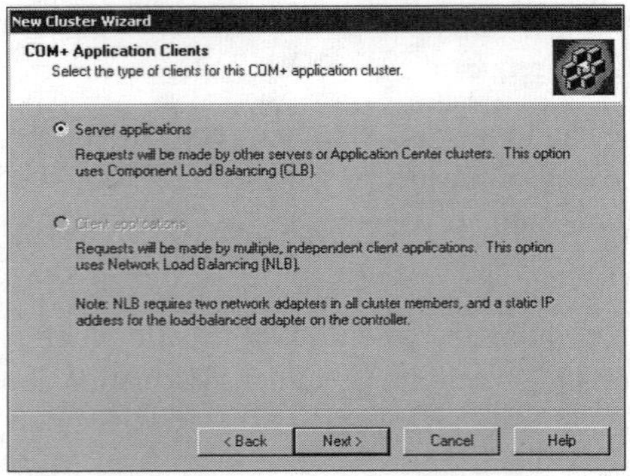

FIGURE 13.7

The COM+ Application Clients page.

Here the wizard diverges depending on the type of COM+ cluster created. The process of choosing a server or client application COM+ cluster is described in the following two sections.

Choosing to Create a Server Application Cluster

Choose Server Applications to create a COM+ cluster that uses Component Load Balancing. A client server can reference only one server application COM+ cluster because of the limitation of Component Load Balancing. This is the preferred type of COM+ cluster, but only one is usable per Web cluster.

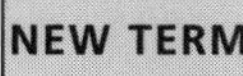
A *COM+ server application cluster* is an Application Center 2000 cluster that uses Component Load Balancing in conjunction with its clients.

Choosing to Create a Client Application Cluster

Choose Client Applications to create a COM+ cluster that uses Network Load Balancing. Figure 13.7 shows the Client Applications choice grayed out. A client application cluster requires that its members have two network adapters so that Application Center 2000 can use Network Load Balancing in managed mode. These clusters provide high availability but suffer from the scaling issues of DCOM, especially during failures. During normal conditions, a cluster like this can have very good balancing success. Make sure that a client application cluster can continue to handle the load of its components during failures. For client application clusters, complete the Load Balancing page as you would for a Web cluster that uses Network Load Balancing.

A *COM+ client application cluster* is an Application Center 2000 cluster that uses Network Load Balancing for high availability of COM+ applications and limited scalability.

Because of the differing COM+ application clusters, the following sections review all wizard choices and finish the cluster creation process for each COM+ cluster type.

Creating a COM+ Cluster for Server Applications

The path through the New Cluster Wizard for creating a COM+ cluster for server applications is shown in Figure 13.8.

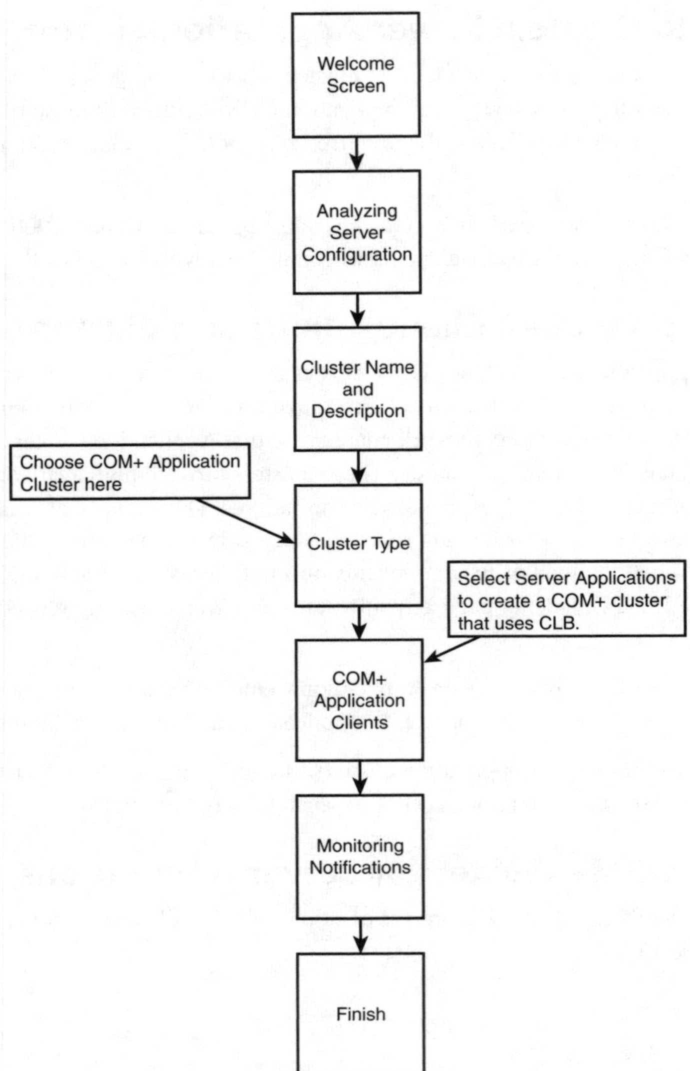

FIGURE 13.8
The path through the New Cluster Wizard for a COM+ cluster for server applications.

Table 13.1 reviews all the steps for creating a COM+ application cluster for server applications.

TABLE 13.1 New Cluster Wizard Steps for a COM+ Application Cluster for Server Applications

Page	*Required Information*	*Notes*
Start	None	Same for all cluster types.
Analyzing Server Configuration	None	Same for all cluster types.
Cluster Name and Description	Name	Must be a valid NetBIOS name composed of letters and numbers with no spaces and fewer than 15 characters.
Cluster Type	COM+ applications cluster	Choose COM+ Application Cluster to create a COM+ cluster.
COM+ Application Clients	Server Applications	Choose Server Applications to create a Component Load Balancing COM+ cluster.
Monitoring Notifications	None	Same for all cluster types.

Installing the COM+ Applications to the Cluster Controller

Component Load Balancing provides scalability only for COM+ server applications; library applications are not supported. The initial installation of applications can be accomplished by installing the components manually, by installing a COM+ application's exported MSI file, or by deploying from another cluster as describe previously in the section "Installing the COM+ Application."

Adding Members to the COM+ Cluster

Use the Add New Member Wizard to add members to the COM+ cluster. The steps are the same for all cluster types; refer to Chapter 12 for more information on adding members to a cluster.

Deploying Applications to the COM+ Cluster

Create Application Center 2000 applications that represent the grouping of COM+ applications on a cluster. For instance, if a cluster has five COM+ applications for one Web cluster and four for another, create two separate applications to manage deployment of these application groups. In some cases, it might be desirable to have an Application Center application for each COM+ application. Use this scenario if the COM+ applications change frequently and to have finer-grain control of the deployment process. This separation also helps troubleshooting of failed deployments. Figure 13.9 shows a failed deployment due to a problem with the COM+ application having unsupported components.

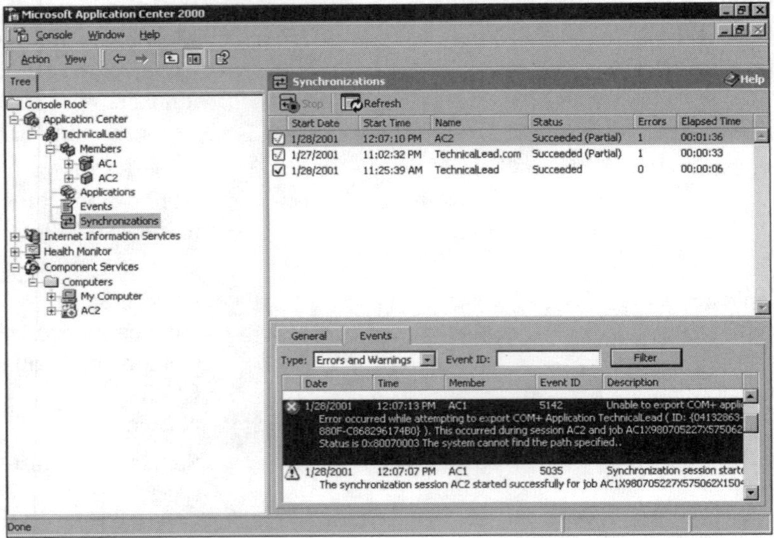

FIGURE 13.9

A failed synchronization event for a COM+ application.

Notice the GUID in the error message. This GUID is the COM+ application GUID that failed to deploy. Match this GUID to the GUID for a COM+ application. It is located in the Component Services snap-in as shown in Figure 13.10.

Even in COM+ application clusters, synchronizations will not deploy COM+ applications automatically. Use the New Deployment Wizard to create a deployment that deploys COM+ applications as in Chapter 12. Make sure to check Deploy COM+ Applications on the Deployment Options pane in the wizard.

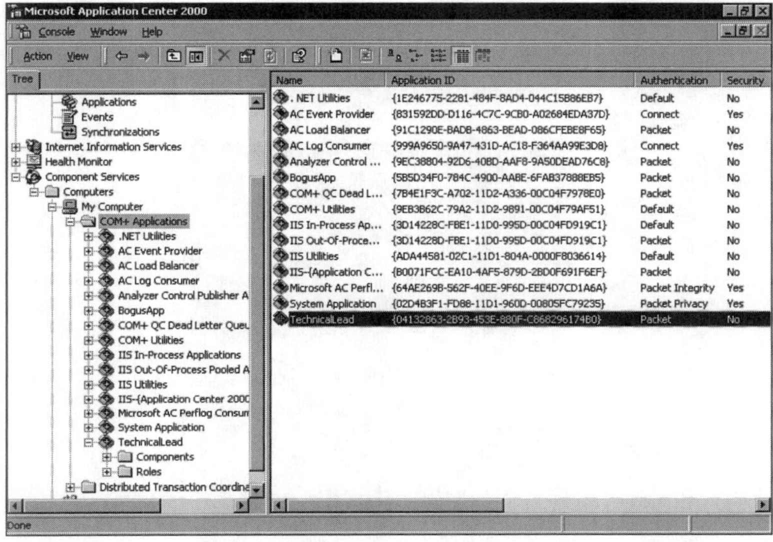

FIGURE 13.10
The GUID list for the COM+ applications on a server.

Using a COM+ Cluster for Server Applications

There are two steps to using components in a COM+ cluster for server applications on a client cluster such as a Web cluster. First, deploy the COM+ applications to the target client cluster. This initial installation of applications can be accomplished by installing the components manually, by installing a COM+ application's exported MSI file, or by deploying from another cluster as described previously in the section "Installing the COM+ Application." Unlike in other DCOM scenarios, use the New Deployment Wizard to move all the COM+ applications to the target cluster controller quickly. Then from the cluster controller, launch another deployment to propagate the change across the cluster. When deploying across clusters, Application Center copies the Application Center 2000 application information and creates the new applications in the Applications View of the target cluster to simplify this process.

> **NOTE**
>
> When deploying COM+ applications from cluster to cluster, a second deployment is required from the target cluster controller to the remaining cluster members.

Second, mark all components to support dynamic load balancing. When you install Application Center 2000 on a server, COM+ server applications gain a new check box, shown in Figure 13.11. This check box can be found on the Activation tab for each component.

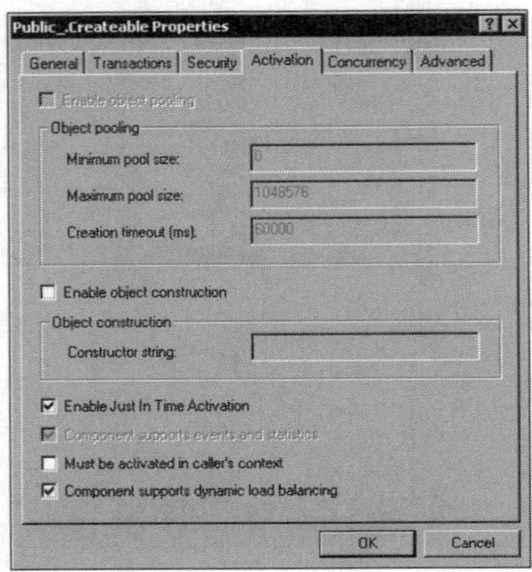

FIGURE 13.11
The Component Supports Dynamic Load Balancing check box.

> **TIP**
>
> Select multiple components in a COM+ application to mark them all at once to support dynamic load balancing.

Table 13.2 shows the steps to take on a client server to use a COM+ cluster for server applications.

TABLE 13.2 Steps for Using a COM+ Cluster for Server Applications

Step	*Description*	*Notes*
Deploy COM+ applications to other client cluster	Chapter 12	To save time, use a cross-cluster deployment to install the COM+ applications onto the Web cluster or other COM+ cluster using the New Deployment Wizard.
Mark applications support dynamic load balancing	Chapter 13	This must be done or the component to creations happen locally.

Creating a COM+ Cluster for Client Applications

A COM+ cluster for client applications uses Network Load Balancing. In this clustering scenario, the COM+ application component-creation requests are balanced by the Network layer at the COM+ servers instead of the COM component-creation layer on the client servers. Once a client connects to a remote server, a cached connection is held open until a timeout expires due to lack of network activity. If continuous component-creation requests occur in time frames under the timeout period, the same COM+ application server handles all requests for a given client.

Like a COM+ cluster for server applications, a cluster for client applications is created using the New Cluster Wizard. There are two main differences to be aware of for client application COM+ clusters.

- First, select Client Applications from the COM+ Applications Client page to create a COM+ cluster for client applications. Because these clusters use Network Load Balancing, all members must have two network adapters. If the Client Application option is grayed out, then it is likely the network adapter configuration for this server does not meet the requirements of Network Load Balancing.
- Second, after choosing client applications and clicking Next, configure the Load Balancing Options page as you would when creating a Web cluster. Figure 13.12 shows the Load Balancing Options pane of the New Cluster Wizard. Select the appropriate management and load-balancing adapters to complete this page. Setting up and configuring these adapters with IP addresses and other network settings is covered in Chapter 12.

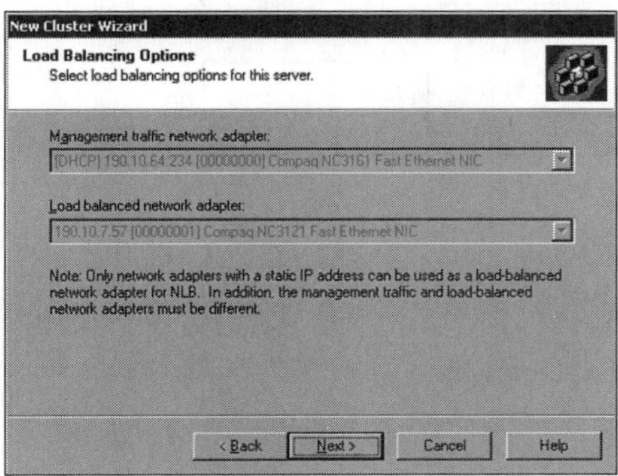

FIGURE 13.12
The Load Balancing Options page.

Figure 13.13 shows the steps through the New Cluster Wizard.

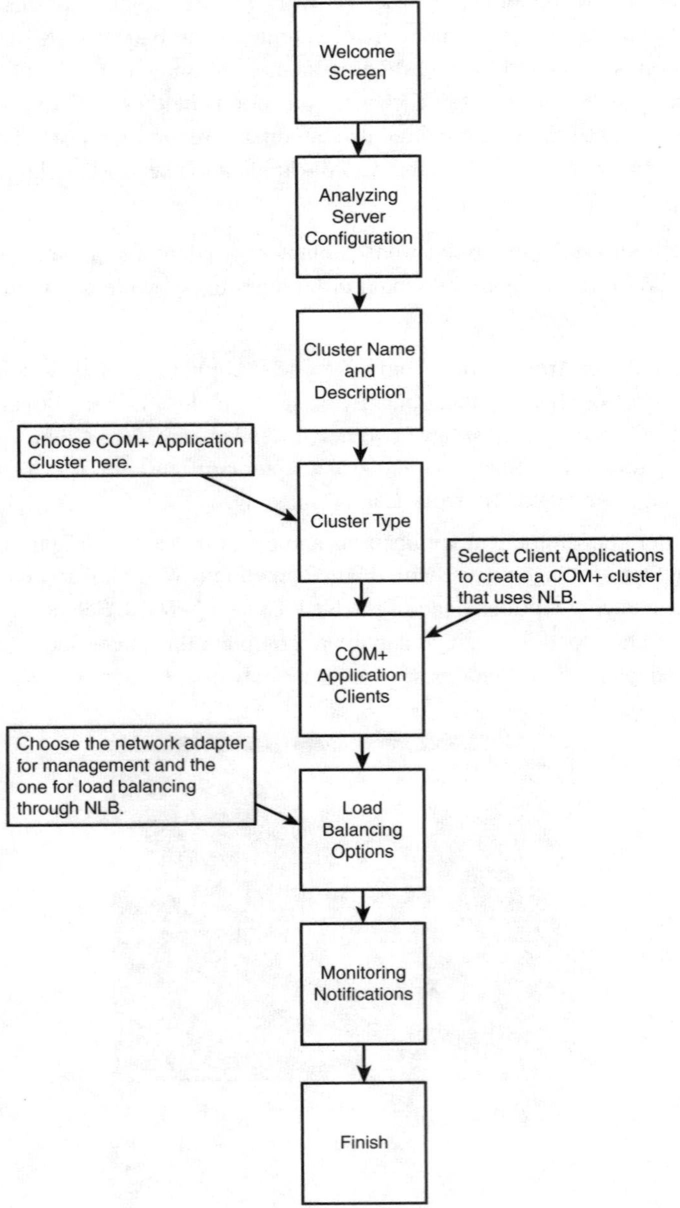

FIGURE 13.13
The path through the New Cluster Wizard for a COM+ cluster for client applications.

Table 13.3 reviews all the steps for creating a COM+ application cluster for client applications.

TABLE 13.3 Steps Through the New Cluster Wizard for a COM+ Application Cluster for Client Applications

Page	*Required Information*	*Notes*
Start	None	Same for all cluster types.
Analyzing Server Configuration	None	Same for all cluster types.
Cluster Name and Description	Name	Must be a valid NetBIOS name composed of letters and numbers with no spaces and fewer than 15 characters.
Cluster Type	COM+ applications cluster	Choose COM+ Application Cluster to create a COM+ cluster.
COM+ Application Clients	Client applications	Choose Client Applications to create a Network Load Balancing COM+ cluster. This option is grayed out if the cluster controller does not have the appropriate network adapters.
Load Balancing Options	Management adapter and cluster adapter	Just like a Web cluster that uses Network Load Balancing.
Monitoring Notifications	None	Same for all cluster types.

Finish installing custom applications to the COM+ cluster controller, adding members to the cluster, and deploying applications to the COM+ cluster, using the same procedures as with a COM+ cluster for server applications.

Using a COM+ Cluster for Client Applications

Using a COM+ cluster for client applications is more involved and requires one step on the cluster and four steps on the client. Unlike a server application COM+ cluster, there is no routing table, and the COM+ application does not need to be installed locally except in its COM+ proxy application form.

Export a proxy application using the Component Services console as described in Chapter 10. Because a COM+ cluster for client application uses Network Load Balancing, the real name that clients use is created from the virtual name of the cluster. For example, if the cluster is called `VCOMCLUSTER`, client applications should reference the objects using the `VCOMCLUSTER` name. It is possible through the properties of the computer object in Component Services to change the default application proxy remote server name for all exports from a particular server in the COM+ cluster. Figure 13.14 shows this property page from the Component Services console. All exports from this cluster are installed with the correct virtual name of the cluster by changing this after COM+ cluster creation. This eliminates a time-consuming step in the deployment process for using a COM+ cluster for client applications.

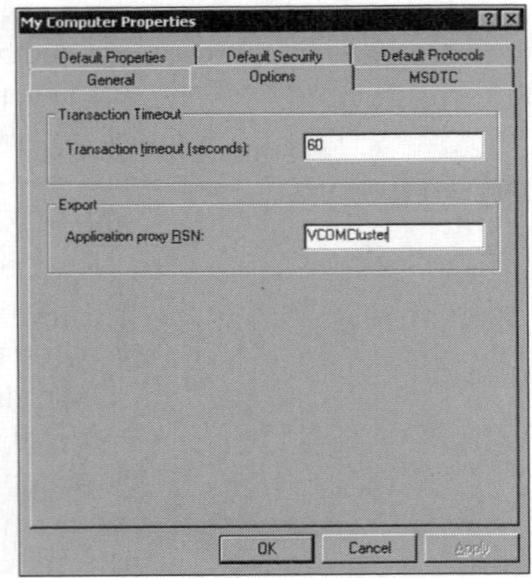

FIGURE 13.14
My Computer Properties Options tab from Component Services.

After exporting the application, install the MSI file onto each member of the cluster by double-clicking it from the member console. Application Center 2000 does not support the deployment of COM+ proxy applications through the New Deployment Wizard. These MSI files have to be deployed manually to all members of the client cluster. An administrator-level account is required to install COM+ proxy applications to Windows 2000 servers, and this account must be logged in locally or through Terminal Services.

TIP

Be sure to change the Application Proxy RSN before exporting the COM+ application to avoid changing this on each cluster member after installing the proxy application.

If the exported application references the machine name of the cluster member it was exported from, the application needs to be changed to use the virtual server name created by Network Load Balancing. Right-click the application in Component Services and select Properties. Choose the Activation tab and change the remote server name to the virtual server name. Figure 13.15 shows the Activation tab with a remote server name of `VCOMCluster`.

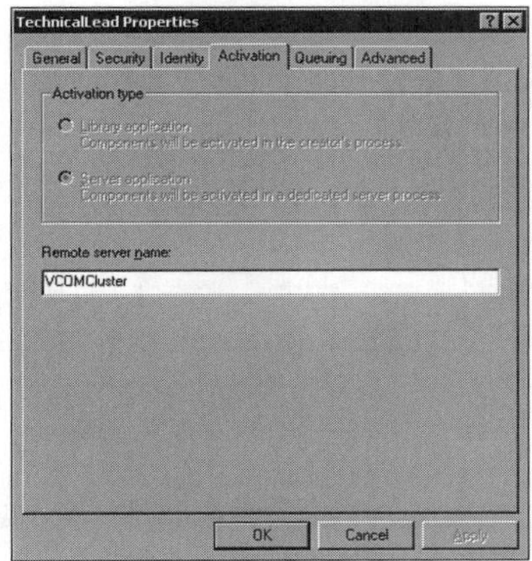

FIGURE 13.15
The Activation property page from a COM+ Application.

Table 13.4 shows the steps to take on a client server so it can use a COM+ cluster for client applications.

TABLE 13.4 Steps Involved in Using a COM+ Cluster for Client Applications

Step	*Description*	*Notes*
Export a COM+ proxy application from the COM+ routing cluster controller.	Chapter 10	Change the remote server name in the Options page of the My Computer node in the Component Services console.
Install the COM+ application proxy to all the Web or COM+ cluster members.	Chapter 10	Run the MSI file locally or through Terminal Services as an administrator.

Creating a COM+ Routing Cluster

The COM+ routing cluster is the third cluster type in the New Cluster Wizard. A routing cluster uses any form of load balancing, including Network Load Balancing. Since a routing cluster is used to route component-creation requests for Web clusters or COM+ clusters that use more than one COM+ server application cluster, the load balancing can be done from the network layer.

The routing cluster is created using the New Cluster Wizard. The path through the wizard is shown in Figure 13.16. The pages in this path are identical to those used to create a Web cluster.

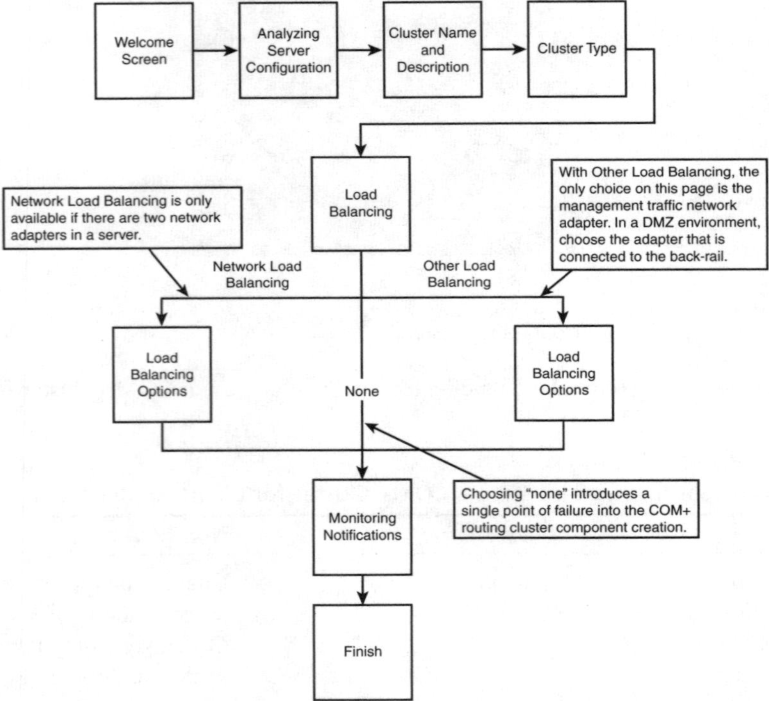

FIGURE 13.16

The path through the New Cluster Wizard for a COM+ routing cluster.

Table 13.5 reviews all the steps for creating a COM+ routing cluster.

TABLE 13.5 Steps Through the New Cluster Wizard for a COM+ Routing Cluster

Page	*Required Information*	*Notes*
Start	None	Same for all cluster types.
Analyzing Server Configuration	None	Same for all cluster types.
Cluster Name and Description	Name	Must be a valid NetBIOS name composed of letters and numbers with spaces and fewer than 15 characters.
Cluster Type	COM+ routing cluster	
Load Balancing	Load balancing technology	To use Network Load Balancing, the cluster members must meet all the requirements for Application Center 2000 to run in managed Network Load Balancing mode.
Load Balancing Options	Management adapter and/or cluster adapter	Just like a Web cluster that uses Network Load Balancing. If Other Load Balancing is selected, only the management adapter needs to be specified.
Monitoring Notifications	None	Same for all cluster types.

A COM+ routing cluster is associated with one COM+ cluster. Install COM+ applications to the cluster controller as if the routing cluster were a Web cluster. Use a deployment from the target COM+ cluster to install the applications locally. Then mark all the components to support Component Load Balancing. Add the servers in the target COM+ cluster to the routing table of the COM+ routing cluster. From there, component creation is handled from the routing cluster just like a Web cluster or other client that uses Component Load Balancing.

To use a routing cluster from a client server or cluster, install the proxy application from the COM+ cluster. Do not install a proxy application from the routing cluster unless the components are first *unmarked* to support dynamic load balancing. If a proxy application is installed with the components marked to support dynamic load balancing, the creation request will fail on the client server.

CAUTION

Do not install proxy applications exported from COM+ applications that support dynamic load balancing. Component creation requests will fail to be routed correctly.

Change the remote server name on the client proxy application to the virtual network name of the routing cluster. Table 13.6 shows the steps to use a COM+ routing cluster from a client server or cluster.

TABLE 13.6 Steps for Creating and Using a COM+ Routing Cluster

Step	*Description*	*Notes*
Create the COM+ routing cluster controller.	Chapter 12	The same wizard steps as a Web cluster.
Deploy COM+ applications from the COM+ cluster to the COM+ routing cluster.	Chapter 12	To save time, use a cross-cluster deployment to install the COM+ applications onto the routing cluster using the New Deployment Wizard.
Mark applications to support dynamic load balancing.	Chapter 13	
Export a COM+ proxy application from the COM+ cluster controller, not the routing cluster.	Chapter 10	Change the My Computer Options page Remote Server Name to the virtual server name of the COM+ routing cluster.
Install the COM+ application proxy to all members of the Web or COM+ cluster.	Chapter 10	Run the MSI file locally or through Terminal Services as an administrator.

Summary

COM+ applications have struggled with scaling problems because at the core all remote component invocations use DCOM. Because DCOM uses connected protocols, traditional load-balancing technologies do not provide the best possible scaling for COM+ applications. To address this need, Microsoft created Component Load Balancing, a client-side technology for intercepting creation requests and selecting a target COM+ application server from a list of available servers called the routing table.

Along with Component Load Balancing, Application Center 2000 makes it easy to create COM+ clusters for client applications that use Network Load Balancing. While Network Load Balancing does not truly balance each request from a single client server, it does provide a good solution for availability needs of COM+ applications.

Finally, COM+ routing clusters provide the ultimate in COM+ cluster flexibility by enabling multiple COM+ server clusters with different application types to be used from the same client cluster. Once you have a good understanding of the COM+ features in Application Center 2000, no Web farm needs to have single points of failure due to DCOM scaling problems. COM+ clustering provides all the options to achieve great availability and scalability for Web farm COM+ applications.

Monitoring a Web Farm with Application Center 2000

CHAPTER

14

IN THIS CHAPTER

Application Center 2000 provides comprehensive tools for performance monitoring, consolidated event log reporting, and programmatic alerting for a Web farm. From the details pane of a cluster or member, it delivers consolidated performance tracking of important counters. From the details pane of the Events node, a consolidated event log reports for all members of a cluster important events from the Windows NT event log. From the details pane of the Monitors node for every member, Health Monitor alerts keep administrators informed of the status of IIS, COM+, and all the .NET enterprise servers. These features are all integrated from the easy-to-use centralized Application Center 2000 console.

Microsoft Health Monitor, shipped as an integrated part of Application Center 2000, provides a centralized alerting tool for custom monitoring scripts and events. It is the first product from Microsoft to address monitoring of a Web farm for the purpose of alerting administrators when errors occur. Before Microsoft Health Monitor, Performance Monitor (Perfmon) was the only general tool that administrators could use to remain informed of the state of the Web farm. Perfmon had limited alerting and custom script creation features. Usually, third-party products, such as NetIQ, were brought in to address a console-oriented, point-and-click style custom monitoring implementation.

Health Monitor 2.1 addresses the needs of Web farm monitoring by providing a customizable, console-oriented programmable alerting and monitoring tool and an agent to gather this information for reporting and alerting. Windows Management Instrumentation (WMI), an implementation of the Web-based Enterprise Management initiative, delivers a robust and extensible monitoring framework. With WMI scripting, administrators can create custom alerts based on COM and VB script. These alerts, coupled with custom actions such as sending e-mail and writing to event logs, complete the monitoring picture. With Application Center 2000's centralized event consolidation and performance data reporting, the monitoring performance and alerting picture for Web farms is complete.

The goals of the chapter are to help you

- Use the details panes of the Events, Cluster, and Monitors nodes in the Application Center 2000 console for the cluster and individual members to monitor cluster-wide and single member events, performance counters, and alerts, respectively. Also covered are any property pages that relate to these detail panes.
- Review the Health Monitor console, including an overview of features in the tree view and list view panes. Different node types are covered, including the Computer, Actions, Data Collector, and Group Collector nodes.
- Understand Windows Management Instrumentation, including its relationship to the Web Based Enterprise Management initiative, its overall monitoring strategy, Application Center 2000 WMI providers, available WMI consumers and agents, script syntax, and coding examples.

Using Application Center 2000 Details Panes for Monitoring Tasks

From the Application Center 2000 console, administrators perform three main monitoring tasks: event log inspection, performance counter reporting, and alert monitoring. These tasks are all performed from the details panes of the various nodes from the Application Center 2000 tree view.

Using the Events Node Details Pane

The Events node comes in two forms in the Application Center 2000 console: a consolidated view across all members of the cluster and the events from a single member. The consolidated Events node is a subnode of the main Cluster node. Expand the Cluster node and click on the Events node to examine the details pane for events. Figure 14.1 shows the cluster Events node details pane. Notice that there are events from multiple cluster members.

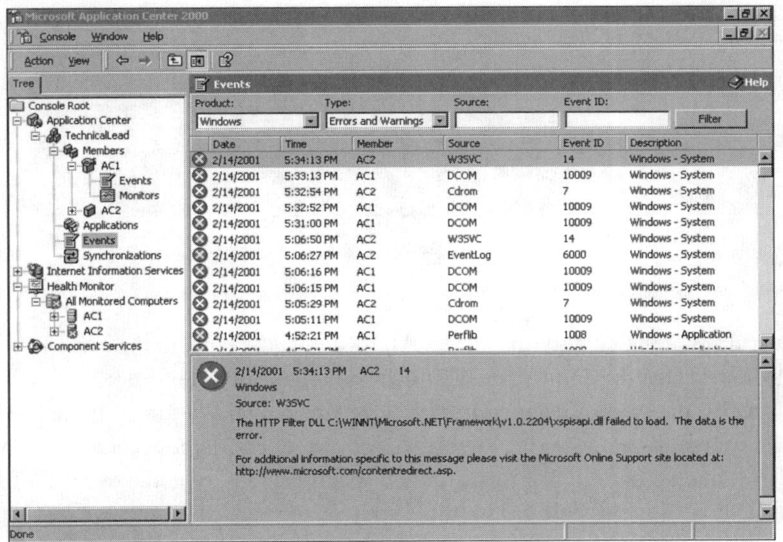

FIGURE 14.1
The Events node details pane of a cluster.

This same view is available on each member of a cluster. Expand the Members node and then the target cluster member's node. Click the Events node under a cluster member to examine a single member's recent events from the NT event log.

Dynamically Filtering an Events Node Details Pane

All events details panes support dynamic filtering (the ability to filter the types of events shown). Dynamic filtering alters only the data shown in the view and not the data stored in the Application Center event log repository. At the top of the detail pane shown in Figure 14.2, there are four criteria that determine the data shown in the view.

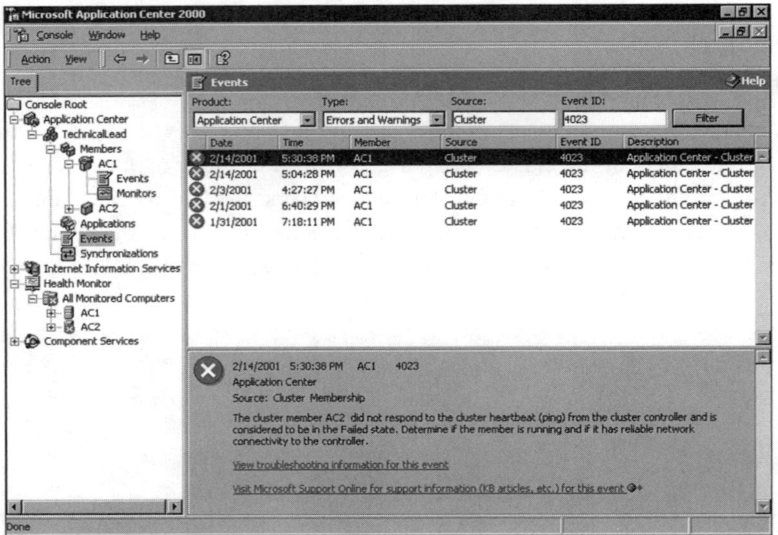

FIGURE 14.2
The Events node details pane with a filter applied.

In the Product drop-down combo box, select All to show all events in the cluster. Select Application Center, Health Monitor, or Windows to narrow the filter criteria at the product level. Then specify the type of event: All, Errors, or Errors and Warnings. In the Source text box, enter the source to see only specific events for a source. Sources include W3SVC, Cluster, Perflib, DCOM, and so on. Finally, to see only a specific event, type the event ID for that event in the Event ID box. It is possible for multiple sources to share the same event ID, so for accurate filters specify as much detail for the criteria as possible. Once the criteria for the filter are specified, press Enter or click the Filter button.

Applying filters has some limitations. There is no way to create reusable filtering criteria and apply them at a later date. Once a filter criterion is applied and another one is entered, the first one is lost until reapplied. Application Center 2000 will remember the last filter criterion specified for an Events node, even for each member of a cluster.

Setting Cluster-Wide Event Logging Criteria

As explained in Chapter 11, "Introducing Application Center 2000," the logging and performance monitoring features of Application Center 2000 use MSDE as the data repository. This means that all cluster members maintain their own copies of all the performance and event data and the console consolidates the data in a true shared-nothing cluster model. In light of this, there are a number of properties that are configurable at the cluster level to help manage the volume of data and the time period it is kept on hand before purging. From the Events node of a cluster, right-click and select Properties to show the dialog in Figure 14.3.

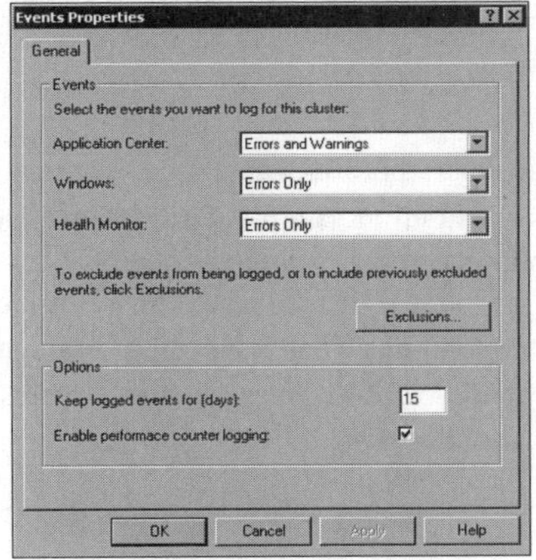

FIGURE 14.3
The cluster-level Events Properties dialog.

From this dialog, configure the cluster-wide settings for logging. This affects only what data makes it into the data repository and not what data is actually logged to the NT event log. In the Events section, global filters are applied to major areas of event reporting. By default, the event data repository stores Application Center warnings and errors, Windows errors, and Health Monitor errors. To change these settings, select the appropriate drop-down and select from the following options: All, Errors and Warnings, Errors Only, and None. Any changes made do not reflect on the existing data in the repository or the details pane. These changes affect only the data that is stored in the repository from the time of the most recent configuration.

In some cases, applications can flood the event log with useless information and render the events logs useless. Other times errors are reported that either have no reasonable resolution or are completely false. To exclude certain events from being logged to the event repository, click the Exclusions button. Figure 14.4 shows the Event Exclusions dialog.

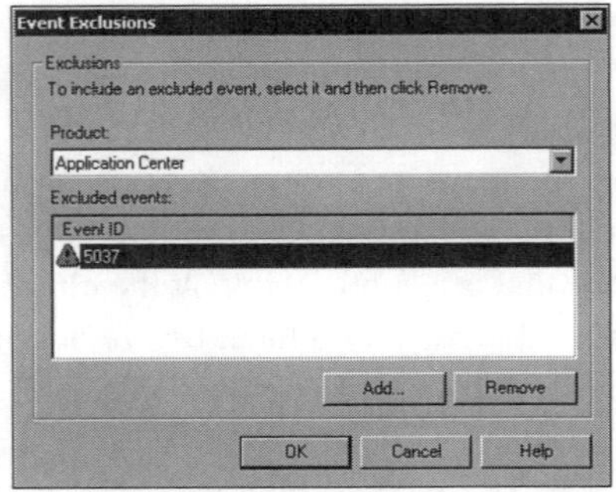

FIGURE 14.4
The Event Exclusions dialog.

To add an exclusion, select the desired product category (Application Center, Windows, or Health Monitor) and click the Add button. A simple dialog prompts you to specify an event severity (Information, Warning, or Error), a source (if the product category is Windows for all others, it is grayed out), and the event ID. Once an exclusion is entered, the changes affect only what will be logged in the future and not what is currently in the details pane. Figure 14.5 shows the Add Event Exclusion dialog. To remove an event exclusion, select the desired category, select the event ID, and click Remove.

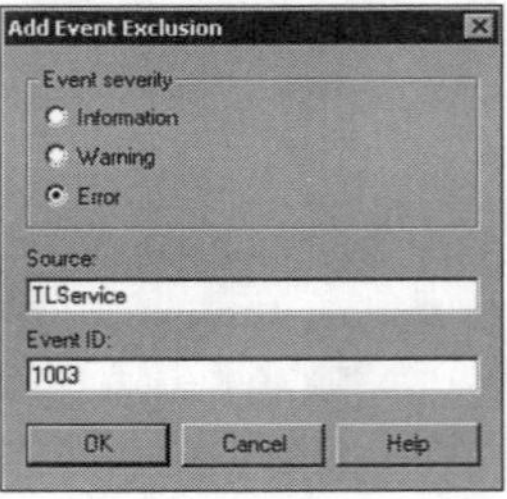

FIGURE 14.5
The Add Event Exclusion dialog.

In the Options section of the Events Properties dialog, seen in Figure 14.3, use the text box to specify the number of days to store event logging information in the repository. The default setting for storing logged events is 15 days. The maximum number allowed is 3650—10 years! To store only the last hour of event log data, set this value to zero. This setting does not affect how long performance counter data is stored or whether it is logged. To disable performance monitoring logging, uncheck the Enable Performance Counter Logging check box in the same dialog.

Using the Cluster and Member Nodes Details Pane

The Cluster and Member nodes details pane shows recent performance data and status information regarding the overall cluster and individual members. To access this pane, click the Cluster node, which has the name TechnicalLead in this case, or click the Members node, or click a particular member server node under the members container. Click a cluster name to show the details pane shown in Figure 14.6. A single-member server shows only the details for one member of a cluster. There are three sections to this pane: overall cluster and member status icons, recent synchronizations status and progress, and a performance graph area.

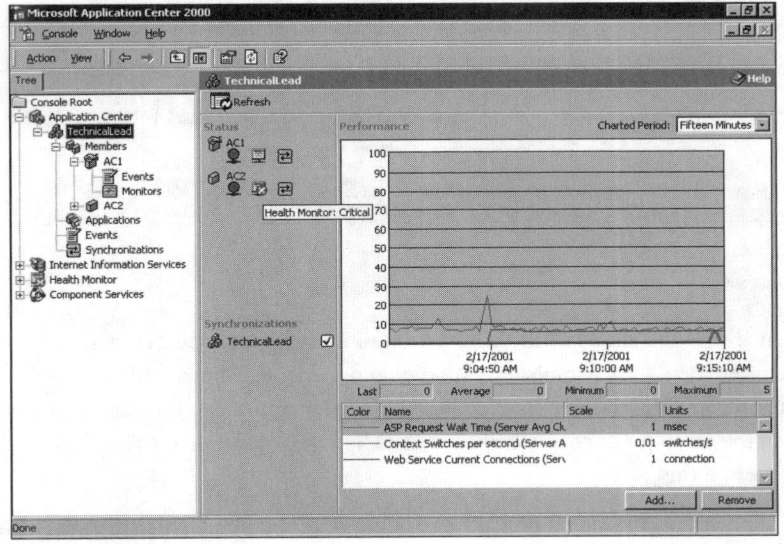

FIGURE 14.6
The Cluster node details pane.

The data in the pane is generated from the ASP pages of the Application Center 2000 administrative site and the local data repositories maintained in MSDE data stores on every member of a cluster. Because of this, the data in the pane is quasi–real-time. To get the latest data, click the Refresh button in the upper-left corner of the details pane.

Understanding Cluster and Member Status

Figure 14.7 shows the cluster and member status area. In this area, a lot of information about members is available. Use this area to keep track of important status information, including connection, load balancing, Health Monitor, and synchronization state. There are four types of status and any number of icons depicting the state of each status type.

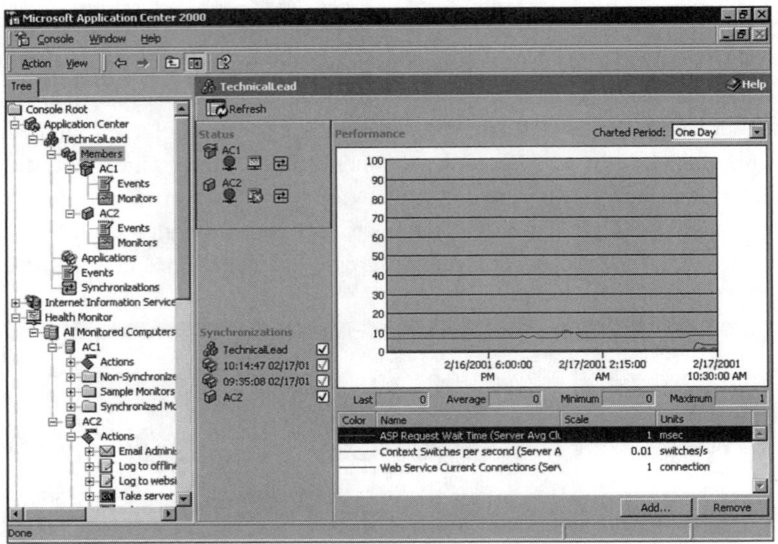

FIGURE 14.7

The cluster status area.

The first icon shows the status of the connection to a particular member. This status has three states: Controller Available, Member Available, and Member Unavailable. If the Cluster Controller is unavailable, the details pane for the cluster returns a 404 Page Not Displayed error because the administrative Web site on the Cluster Controller for Application Center 2000 is used to generate this pane.

The second icon shows the status of load balancing on a member. This status has four states: Online, Offline, Not Installed, and Unknown. The not installed state occurs on cluster members that use third-party load balancing or in stager configurations. Online and offline correspond to the status of the cluster member in either Network Load Balancing or Component Load Balancing. In clusters that use those load balancing types, this icon reflects the offline or online status that is controlled from the right-click menu of a particular member. The unknown status occurs when a member is rebooted or cannot be reached from the Cluster Controller.

The third icon shows the status of Health Monitor alerts on a member. This status has four states: Okay, Warning, Critical, and Unknown. This status corresponds to the overall status of a machine from a Health Monitor perspective. This means that if any warnings or errors are currently unresolved, that state will show here. To change this icon, resolve all alerts from Health Monitor.

The fourth icon shows the current configuration status which determines how a member handles synchronization requests. This status has three states: Enabled, Manual, and In Progress. If a synchronization is in progress, the In Progress icon is displayed. If a particular member was excluded from automatic synchronizations either when it was added to the cluster or from the properties dialog of a cluster member, the Manual icon is displayed. The default state is Enabled.

Figure 14.8 shows all the states of each status type.

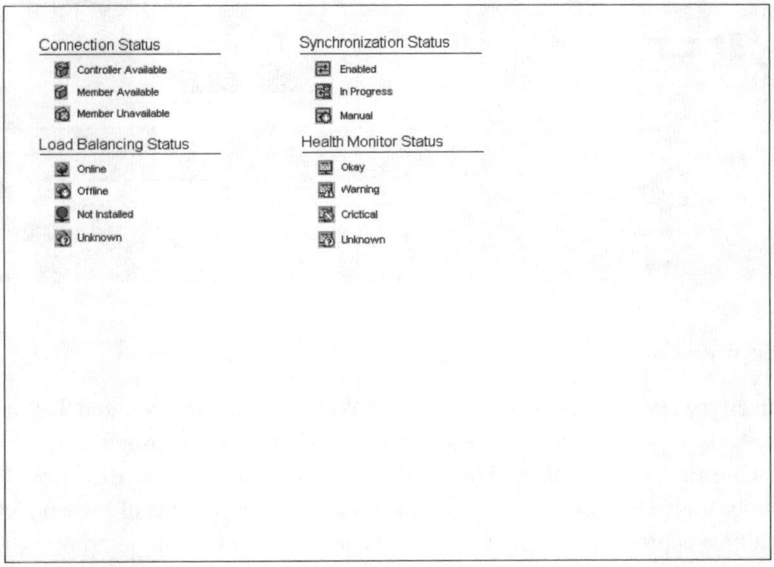

Connection Status
Controller Available
Member Available
Member Unavailable

Load Balancing Status
Online
Offline
Not Installed
Unknown

Synchronization Status
Enabled
In Progress
Manual

Health Monitor Status
Okay
Warning
Crictical
Unknown

FIGURE 14.8
Icons for cluster and member status.

Understanding Synchronization Status

The synchronization status area shows the results of recent synchronizations and deployments. Figure 14.9 shows the synchronization status area of the Cluster and Member nodes details pane. The synchronization status area has two sets of icons that represent the type of synchronization and the status of the synchronizations.

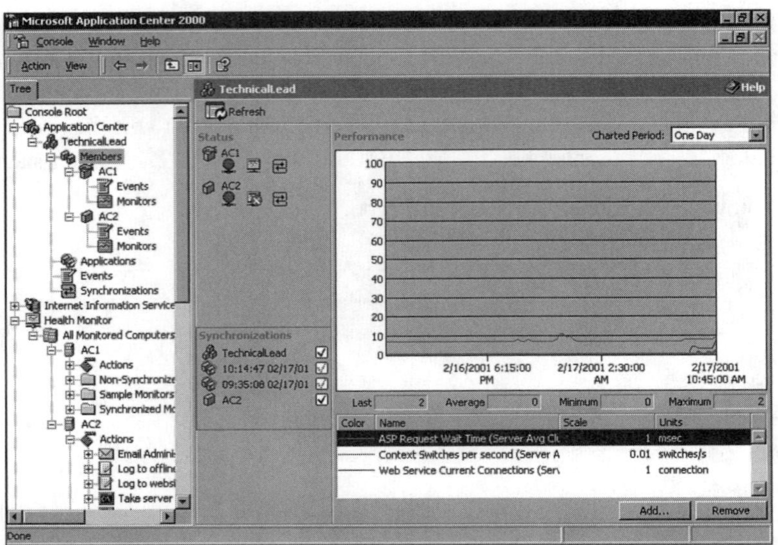

FIGURE 14.9

The synchronization status area.

There are three types of synchronizations: Cluster Wide, Single Member, and Targeted Deployment. A cluster-wide synchronization represents a synchronization that occurs when the Synchronize Cluster option is selected from the right-click menu of the Cluster or Cluster Controller node. It also represents synchronizations that occur periodically when a cluster is set to automatically synchronize content either at cluster creation or from the properties dialog of a Cluster node. A single-member synchronization represents a synchronization that occurs when the Synchronize Member option is selected from the right-click menu of a cluster member or when a new member is added to a cluster. The Targeted Deployment icon represents all deployments generated from the New Deployment Wizard, including cross-cluster deployments.

There are seven states for a synchronization: Succeeded, Partially Succeeded, Failed, Initializing, Scanning, Transferring, and Applying. The first three states represent the status of a completed synchronization. If a synchronization fails, check the reason from the Synchronization node's details pane as described in Chapter 12, "Deploying Application Center 2000 Web Clusters." Initializing, scanning, and transferring all occur during the process of a synchronization. Initializing happens right when a synchronization starts. Application Center 2000 uses this phase to check overall cluster status and determine current member status. When a synchronization is scanning, Application Center is checking for differences between the Cluster Controller and cluster member and building a list of items that need to be transferred to each member. The transferring state signifies that Application Center 2000 is actively copying files to cluster members. The applying state signifies that Application Center is applying the changes to cluster members, usually around COM+ application deployments.

Figure 14.10 shows the icons for the types of synchronizations and the synchronization statuses.

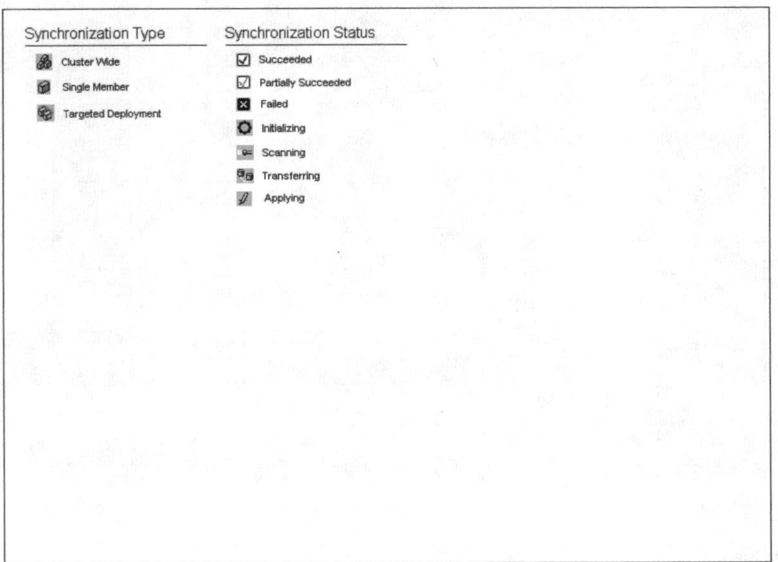

FIGURE 14.10
Icons for the Synchronizations area.

Using the Performance Graph

From this area administrators can track the most important performance counters in quasi–real-time. The performance graph uses the data repository like the events details pane to gather requested counters for a cluster. It does not hook up to the performance counters of the ASP engine in real-time over the network; instead, each member gathers performance data and stores it in the local repository. When the Cluster Controller displays performance data for the cluster, it requests data from each member of the cluster to construct this area of the details pane.

From the time that Application Center 2000 is installed to a member, it automatically tracks this key performance data. At any time, an administrator can examine historical trending data like CPU utilization for individual members or averaged for the entire cluster. This data is very useful for simple trending and capacity planning for members of the cluster.

To view performance data for a cluster, click the Cluster node or the Members node in the administrative console. Figure 14.11 shows the performance graph area of the Cluster and Members node detail pane.

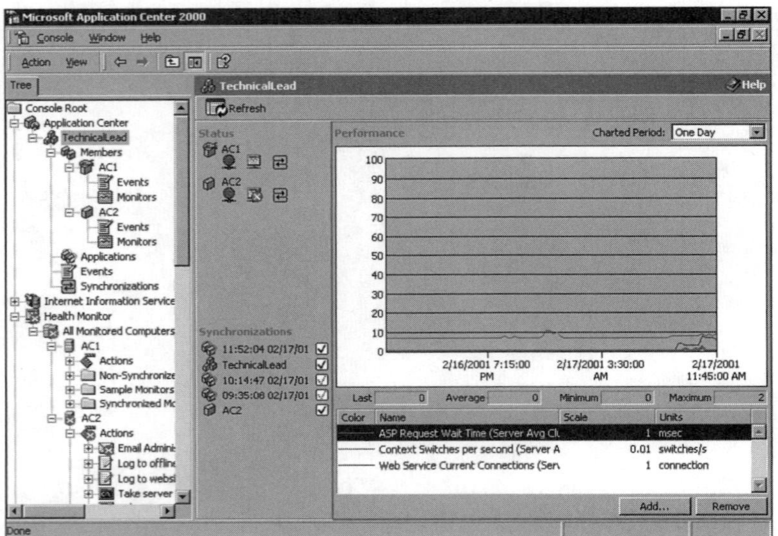

FIGURE 14.11

The performance graph area.

To change the charted period, select the charted period drop-down combo box from the upper-right corner of the performance graph area and choose from the following options: Fifteen Minutes, Two Hours, One Day, One Week, and Three Months.

To change the counters monitored, click the Add button and select a counter from the list of available counters. To remove a counter, select the appropriate counter from the Monitored Counters list and click the Remove button. Application Center does not allow any counter to be tracked. To change this list of counters, see Chapter 16, "Performing Advanced Application Center 2000 Tasks."

Using the Monitors Details Pane

Microsoft Health Monitor 2.1 enables administrators to create a list of monitors that alert when their status changes. To view these monitors, select the particular member node from the Members container, expand it, and click the Monitors node. Figure 14.12 shows the Monitors details pane for a single cluster member. There is no Monitors details pane for the entire cluster.

There are two areas in the details pane: the list of monitors for a particular node and their thresholds. A threshold is a Boolean condition that is used to determine when a monitor status should change, triggering an alert. Monitors cannot be added, removed, or configured from this pane. To configure the monitors for a particular member, see Chapter 15, "Performing Common Health Monitor Tasks."

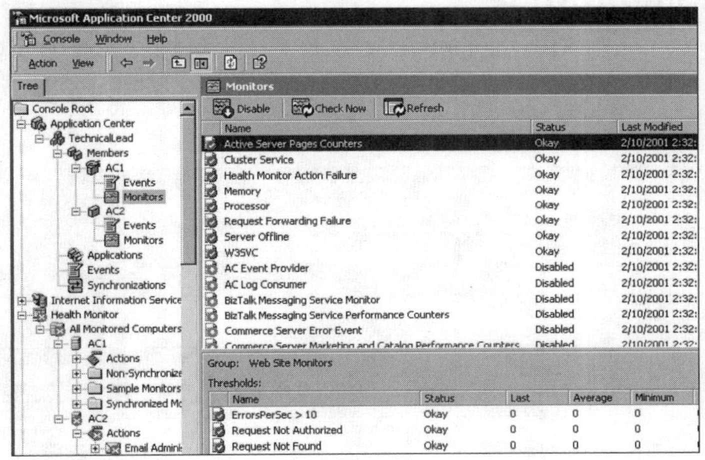

FIGURE 14.12
The Monitors details pane for a cluster member.

From the Monitors details pane, administrators can disable an existing monitor by selecting the target monitor and clicking the Disable button. To check a monitor's status immediately, click the Check Now button. To refresh the list of monitors for a particular member, click the Refresh button.

Health Monitor Console Overview

The Health Monitor console is a subnode of the Application Center 2000 console. The console is broken into two main areas: the tree view and the details pane. The tree view enables navigation across multiple cluster members and through a hierarchy of actions, data groups, and data collectors. The details pane has detailed information about all the nodes in the tree view and enables the configuration of thresholds for data collectors; it also summarizes alerts for child nodes.

NOTE

To perform common tasks using Health Monitor, see Chapter 15.

Health Monitor Node

The Health Monitor node is the top-level node of the Health Monitor console. To show an overall status of all the computers registered with this Health Monitor console, click the Health Monitor node as shown in Figure 14.13.

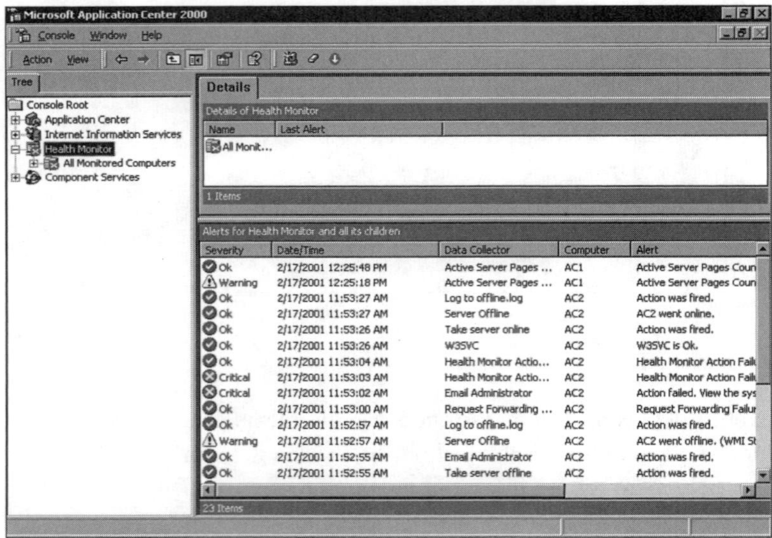

FIGURE 14.13
The Health Monitor node.

In the details pane of the Health Monitor node, the Details tab shows that the Health Monitor node has one child item: All Monitored Computers. Also in the details pane is the alert list for all computers in this console. The Health Monitor node provides a convenient view into all the alerts for a particular set of computers and the status of all recent alerts.

All Monitored Computers Node

By default the Health Monitor console tree view includes an All Monitored Computers node. This node is used to control which servers are configured from this console. A computer does not have to exist in the console for the Health Monitor agent to run. Computers in this console just report alerts to the console and are configured from the console. Figure 14.14 shows the All Monitored Computers node.

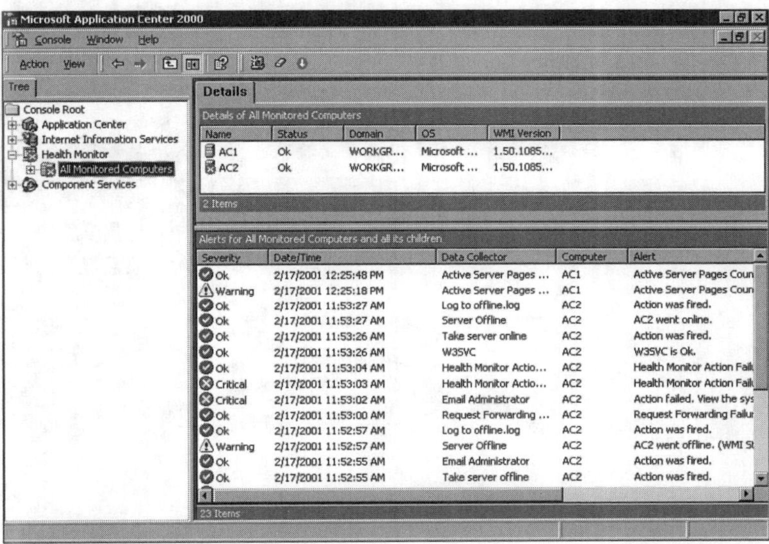

FIGURE 14.14
The All Monitored Computers node.

Notice that this node's Details tab contains all the computers registered in this console. This does not correspond to the members of the Application Center 2000 clusters managed by this console. Each member must be added to control all members of a cluster from the same console.

Computer Node

The Computer node represents an individual computer that this console is managing. Figure 14.15 shows a Computer node with its corresponding details pane.

A Computer node contains the Actions node for a computer and all the Data Group nodes configured. The Details tab shows the status of these nodes and the Alerts list shows all the alerts for a particular node.

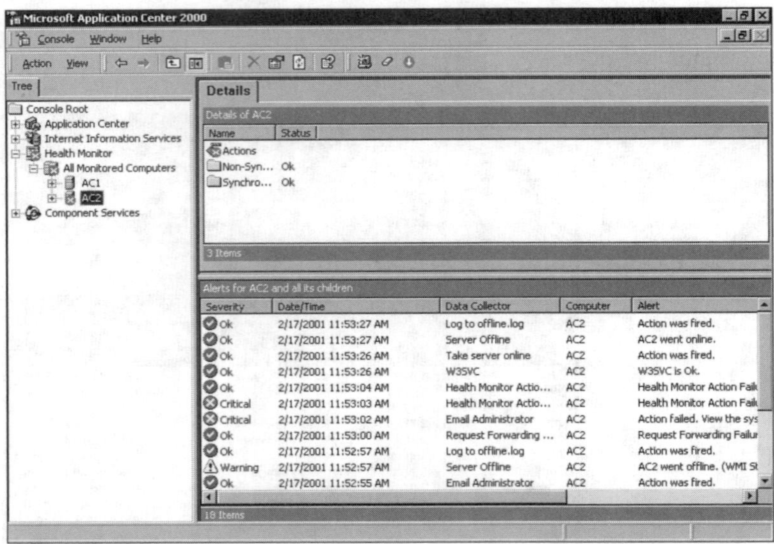

FIGURE 14.15
The Computer node.

Actions Node

The Actions node contains all the defined actions for a particular computer. From this node, administrators create actions that fire in response to alerts that have been triggered because thresholds have been met. Figure 14.16 shows the Actions node expanded to show all the actions defined.

The Actions node supports five types of actions. A command-line action launches a batch file or any other program that runs from the command line such as the Application Center 2000 AC command-line tool discussed in Chapter 15. An e-mail action sends an e-mail to a list of e-mail addresses. A text log action logs a user-definable message to any text file. A Windows event log action logs a user-definable message to the NT event log. A script action runs any Visual Basic Script (VBS) or JavaScript (JS) file.

From the details pane of the Actions node, the Details tab shows the status of all actions. Use this tab to determine whether actions are executing correctly. The actions list shows the most recent actions that have fired and whether they were successful or not.

Email Administrator Action Node

The Action node is a leaf node and contains no child nodes. Figure 14.17 shows the default Email Administrator Action node and its detail pane.

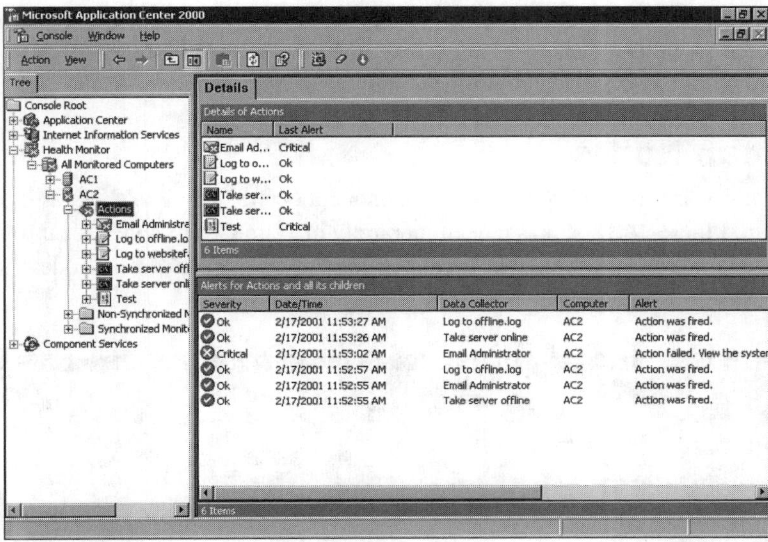

FIGURE 14.16
The Actions node.

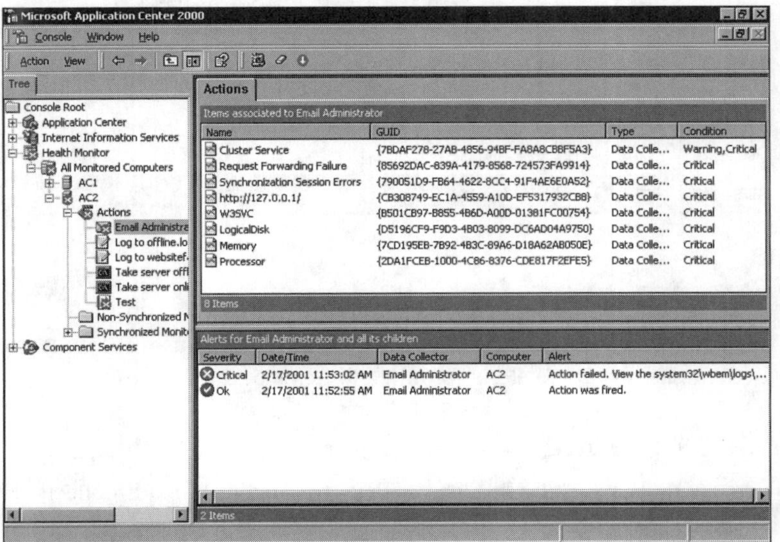

FIGURE 14.17
The Email Administrator Action node.

From the Action node details pane Actions tab, all the data collectors that use this action are summarized across all data groups for this computer. The Alerts list shows all the recent thresholds that have caused this action to fire and the success or failure of the action.

Data Group Nodes

Data Group nodes are simply used to organize data collectors. Think of them as directories in the file system. Figure 14.18 shows a deep hierarchy of Data Group nodes for the TechnicalLead.com Web site. Data Group nodes contain other Data Group nodes and Data Collector nodes.

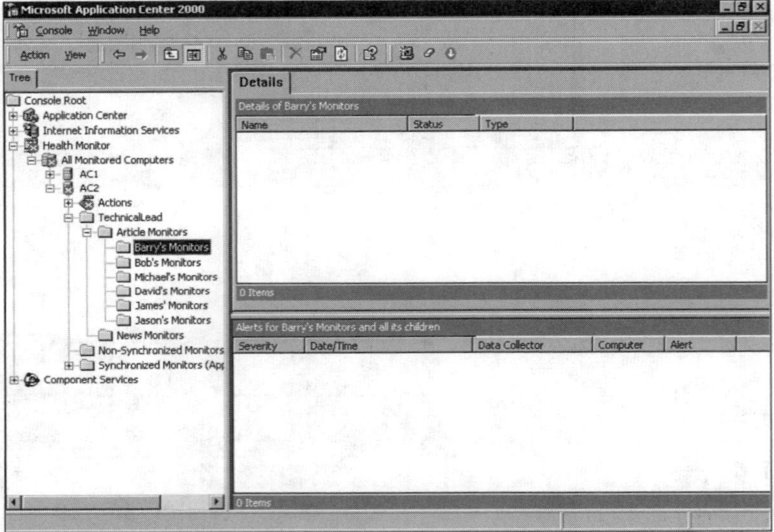

FIGURE 14.18
The Data Group node.

The details pane contains a Details tab that shows all the child items for a specific data group. The Alerts list summarizes all the alerts for all child items of the data group.

Data Collector Nodes

A Data Collector node is a specific instance of data that Health Monitor collects. From a Data Collector, thresholds are defined that trigger actions based on some programmatic condition such as a Boolean expression or string comparison. Data Collectors are the meat of Health Monitor. Figure 14.19 shows a Data Collector node.

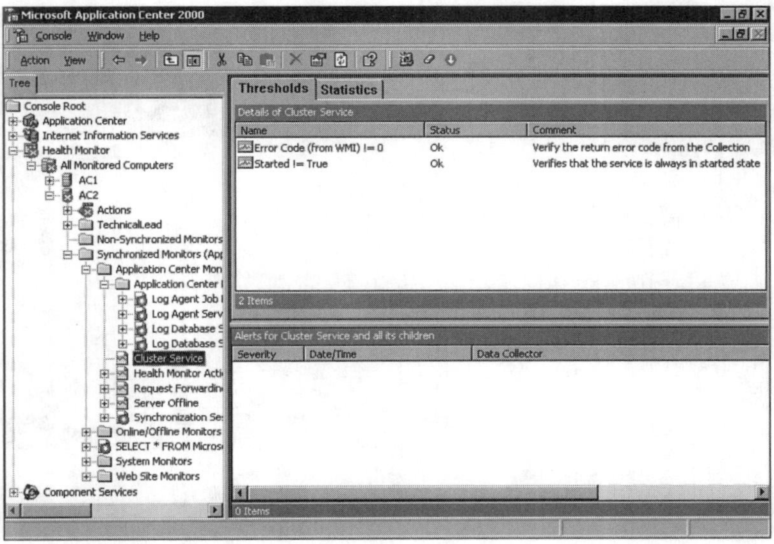

FIGURE 14.19
The Data Collector node.

The Data Collector node details pane contains three separate areas. The Thresholds tab contains all the thresholds created for a specific Data Collector. When a threshold is breached, for instance when a specific condition such as a service is not started or a Health Monitor action fails to fire, actions are fired in response. A Data Collector can have any number of thresholds. The Alerts list shows all the recent thresholds that have been met and the result of the condition.

The Data Collector details pane also contains a Statistics tab, shown in Figure 14.20. This tab shows statistics that are gathered over the lifetime of a Data Collector. Each Data Collector is associated with a specific WMI event, and each WMI event contains a list of properties that can be used to create thresholds.

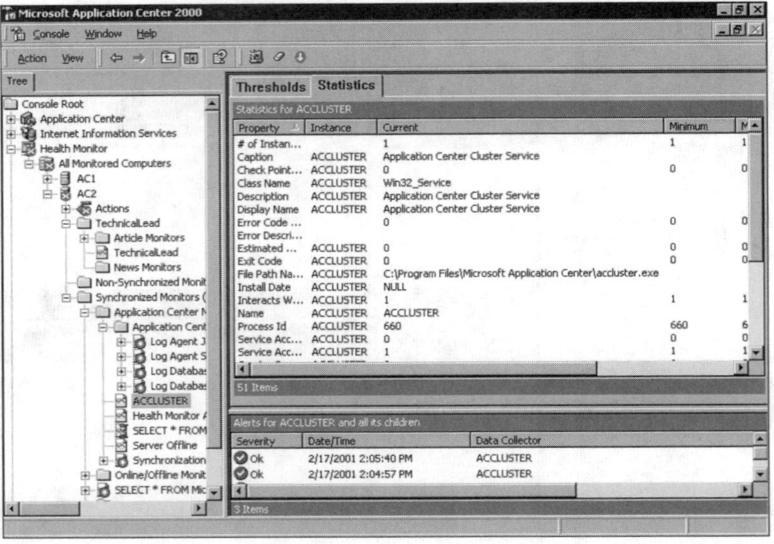

FIGURE 14.20
The Statistics tab.

Understanding Windows Management Instrumentation

Windows Management Instrumentation (WMI) is Microsoft's implementation of the Web Based Enterprise Management (WBEM) initiative. The WBEM initiative is a proposed set of standards for managing the systems on a network. WBEM does not replace existing UIs for managing systems, network management protocols such as Simple Network Management Protocol, or any other component of an existing system. WBEM has little to do with the Web or browsers; it is an enterprise management initiative.

The goal of WBEM is to create a system of standards for retrieving schema information about managed objects and managed object data in an enterprise network from a centralized repository. Clients and management tools exchange data with the repository in a standards-based way, and access to this repository is managed such that, with proper authorization, data can be analyzed and manipulated anywhere.

From the high-level goals of WBEM, the Common Information Model (CIM) was created. The CIM describes a common management standard that unifies disparate system management tools under one CIM specification. The CIM specification is composed of the following parts:

- *A modeling language* for describing the objects in an enterprise network in human-readable form.
- *A naming convention* that standardizes the names of objects in the schema.
- *A mapping methodology* to collect and transport data from standard CIM providers and other non-compliant management tools.
- *A schema* called the CIM schema that defines an object-oriented hierarchy of classes that organizes information about enterprise networks.

NEW TERM The *Common Information Model (CIM)* specification describes the blueprint for creating a WBEM-compliant management system.

Since WMI is Microsoft's implementation of WBEM, it complies with the standards outlined in the WBEM initiative by providing the following:

- *A unified set of COM interfaces* that defines a consistent methodology for accessing managed object data in the CIM across the enterprise through scripting languages like VB Script.
- *Built-in integration with tools* like Health Monitor 2.1 and a well-defined methodology for extending the CIM object hierarchy through WMI providers.
- *Robust event management and a rich query language* so that tools can recognize and listen for changes in object data that signify important conditions like system failure and stress.

Components of WMI

The WMI architecture is composed of the following components:

- *A CIM object manager* to implement the CIM requirements of WBEM.
- *WMI providers* that interface between the CIM object manager and the managed objects of the CIM repository such as hardware devices and operating system components.
- *A WMI security model* that uses Windows 2000 security to control access to managed objects.
- *Event handling* so that management tools can respond to events and errors from managed objects.
- *A WMI query language* for a standards-based human-readable language to access the data exposed through WMI providers in the CIM repository.
- *A Windows scripting host* for creating simple scripts to interact with the CIM object manager.

WMI Providers

WMI providers are COM DLLs that provide the gateway between the CIM object manager and the managed objects they support. Windows 2000 provides a set of core providers that interface with the event log, the registry, and Active Directory, to name a few. Any third party can create a provider, and many have. Application Center 2000 provides COM+, HTTP, and the Port Connect provider.

Standard Windows 2000 Providers

Table 14.1 lists the standard Windows 2000 providers. Through WMI events, these provide reading, writing, and monitoring of all the core Windows 2000 management and system objects.

TABLE 14.1 Standard Windows 2000 Providers

Provider	*Description*
Win32	Manages information for the operating system, file system, computer system, and security information.
WDM (Windows Driver Model)	Provides access to low-level device data for input, storage, network, and communication devices.
Event Log	Provides access to the Windows NT event log. Allows NT events to be read as they occur and responds to these with WMI events.
Registry	Provides access to the Windows Registry for monitoring changes in specific keys with WMI events. Can be used to create, modify, and delete Registry keys.
Performance Counter	Provides a WMI interface to all counters that are exposed through Performance Monitor. WMI Events can respond to thresholds such as CPU and memory.
Active Directory	Provides access to data in the Active Directory. Can create WMI events to watch for changes in the object of the Active Directory such as new users and groups.
Windows Installer	Provides complete control of the Windows Installer and an interface to enumerate all the software installed through `MSIEXEC.EXE` (the Windows installer).
SNMP	Enables access to all SNMP MIBs for reading and writing. SNMP traps can be mapped to WMI events.
View	Can be used to aggregate two or more existing CIM objects into a single new View object.

Application Center 2000 WMI Providers

Table 14.2 lists the Application Center 2000 providers. These providers extend the core Windows 2000 providers and provide a WMI interface into the managed objects of the Web farm, such as COM+ applications and IIS.

TABLE 14.2 Standard Application Center 2000 Providers

Provider	*Description*
COM+	Provides access to COM+ application statistics and WMI events for failure conditions.
HTTP	Provides access to HTTP requests and responses and then sends this information to Health Monitor.
Port	Enables connecting directly to a port (such as 80) and returning the results of the request.

Querying Providers with WMI Query Language

The following section has a few examples that show how to use the WMI Query Language (WQL). A full reference of WQL is found in the WMISDK available at `www.microsoft.com`. These examples are meant to illustrate the wide range of data exposed through WMI.

Requesting a URL with the HTTP Provider

The HTTP provider is a WMI instance provider. This means that there is no data stored in the CIM object repository across provider activations. When an instance of this provider is created, it must be created using the `SWBEMService` object `GET` method. Once it is created, it will make the request specified from the `URL` parameter and return the results of the HTTP request. Listing 14.1 shows how to use the HTTP provider from script.

LISTING 14.1 Using the HTTP Provider

```
Dim objHM, objHTTPProvider
Set objHM = GetObject("winmgmts:root/cimv2/MicrosoftHealthMonitor")

set objHTTPProvider= objHM.Get_
("HTTPProvider.URL=""www.technicallead.com"",ResponseLength=128000")
msgbox Len(objHTTPProvider.TextResponse)
msgbox objHTTPProvider.TextResponse
```

This script first gets the `SWBEMService` object with the `GetObject` command. This object contains all the classes that have been added by Health Monitor to the CIM. Then, using the

SWBEMService object's GET command, the WMI HTTPProvider issues an HTTP GET request for the URL www.technicallead.com and sets the ResponseLength input parameter to 128000. Then, two message boxes display the length of the response and the actual HTML returned with the TextResponse property.

Displaying Current CPU Utilization

Microsoft Health Monitor provides a Performance Monitor namespace for retrieving any performance counter. Similar to the standard Windows 2000 Performance Monitor provider, the Health Monitor provider is a simpler instance provider. Listing 14.2 shows retrieving the "_Total" and "0" CPU instances from the Processor class.

LISTING 14.2 Using the Health Monitor Performance Monitor Provider

```
Dim objHM, objCPU
Set objHM = GetObject("winmgmts:root/cimv2/MicrosoftHealthMonitor/PerfMon")

set objCPU= objHM.Get("Processor.Name=""0""")
msgBox objCPU.PercentProcessorTime
set objCPU= objHM.Get("Processor.Name=""_Total""")
msgBox objCPU.PercentProcessorTime
```

This script gets the Perfmon object from the CIM object repository. Then, using the SWBEMService object, it retrieves the first processor named 0 and displays the PercentProcessorTime parameter. Then the script retrieves the _Total instance, which would include all processors in a multiple processor box. Notice that the instance name corresponds to the instances shown from Performance Monitor in Figure 14.21. Use this technique to retrieve any Performance Monitor counter and instance name.

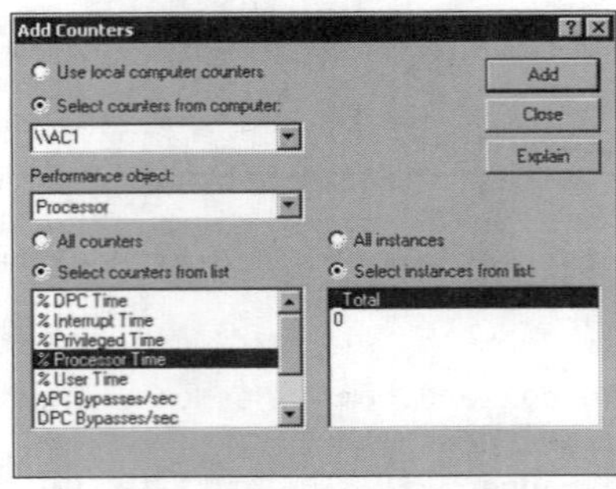

FIGURE 14.21

Performance Monitor showing CPU instances.

Summary

Application Center 2000 provides a great set of tools for monitoring a Web farm. The consolidated NT event and performance reports provide single server–like ease and efficiency for administrators for a cluster of servers. These reports help determine when errors occur across multiple machines and how a Web farm behaves from a performance counter perspective over time. Both of these tasks in the past required considerable effort and time.

Health Monitor 2.1 provides a management tool for Windows Management Instrumentation of not only core Windows 2000 managed objects, but also important objects for Web farms such as HTTP and COM+. The Health Monitor console provides a graphical tool for monitoring and alerting across all the members of a Web farm.

Finally, WMI completes the monitoring picture by providing an implementation of WBEM. With WMI, administrators have complete access to all performance, system, and other important data in Windows 2000. With simple scripts, administrators can retrieve data and respond accordingly. WMI is the core technology upon which Health Monitor 2.1, and Application Center's management features are built.

Performing Common Health Monitor Tasks

CHAPTER

15

IN THIS CHAPTER

It is important to understand the tasks that administrators perform to monitor a Web farm. Using Health Monitor 2.1, administrators perform a variety of tasks such as creating alerts, custom actions, and thresholds. These actions result in a collection of WMI-based mini-programs that monitor the Web farm's status and respond appropriately to failures. It is learning how to perform these tasks, in a step-by-step manner, that is the focus of this chapter. Here are some specific goals to accomplish while learning and performing these health monitoring tasks. The goals of this chapter are to help you

- Manage the servers to monitor in the Health Monitor 2.1 console. Learn how to add, remove, and modify the properties of these servers in regard to Health Monitor.
- Create data groups to organize and manage Data Collectors. Learn how to add, remove, associate actions, and perform other tasks related to data groups.
- Create Data Collectors to monitor and alert when events occur that affect the functionality of a Web farm. Learn how to perform common Data Collector tasks and how to create the 11 different types of Data Collectors.
- Create actions to respond to errors from Data Collectors. Learn how to add, remove, and create the five supported action types. Learn how to associate an action with other Health Monitor nodes.

Managing Computers to Monitor

The Microsoft Health Monitor console can manage any number of servers in a Web farm. For the Health Monitor console to connect to a target server, the Health Monitor Agent must be installed. To install the Health Monitor Agent, install the full version of Application Center 2000 to the target server. This enables the target server to be centrally managed by the Health Monitor console.

After meeting the Health Monitor requirements, servers in a particular instance of the Health Monitor console are managed from the All Monitored Computers node. This node contains a list of all the servers that have been added to a particular console. These servers are Health Monitor computer nodes. Add and remove servers from the All Monitored Computers node.

Adding a Computer

To add a server to the Health Monitor console, perform the following tasks:

1. Right-click the All Monitored Computers node as shown in Figure 15.1.
2. Select Connect to Another Computer to launch the standard New Computer dialog.
3. Select or enter the target server from the New Computer dialog. For multiple computers, use semicolons to separate entries.
4. Click OK.

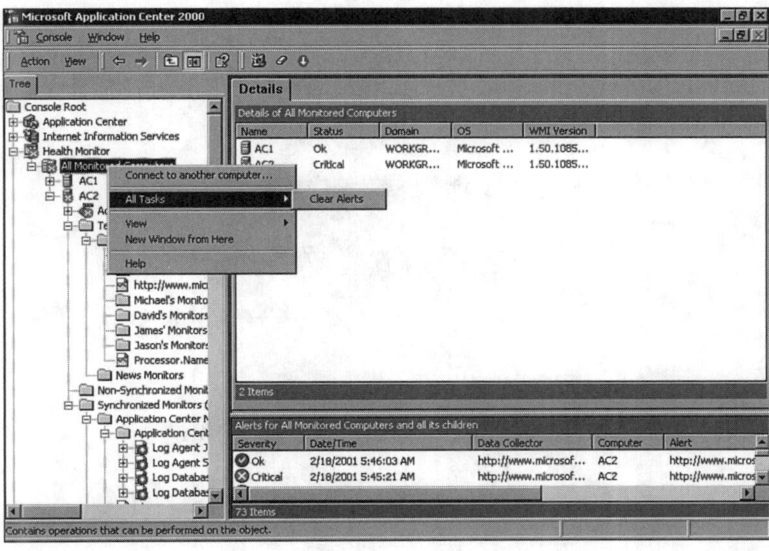

FIGURE 15.1
Tasks for the All Monitored Computers node.

Once a server has been added, a new Health Monitor computer node is created and added to the `All Monitored Computers` folder. This process can fail if target computers don't have the Health Monitor Agent installed or the administrator performing the addition does not have the appropriate security credentials on the Health Monitor WMI provider. This provider is located in the CIM repository at the path `CIMV2/MicrosoftHealthMonitor`. Modify the ACLs on this provider from the WMI Control console. This console is located at `c:\winnt\system32\wmimgmt.msc` by default.

To configure WMI security access permissions for the Microsoft Health Monitor provider, perform the following tasks:

1. Launch the WMI Control console from `c:\winnt\system32\wmimgmt.msc`.
2. Right-click the WMI Control node (the only node in the console) and select Connect to the Target Computer from the WMI Control node right-click menu and select the target computer. This action requires administrative access on the target computer.
3. Once the console is connected to the remote computer, right-click the WMI Control node and select Properties.
4. From the Properties dialog, select the Security tab.
5. From the Security tab shown in Figure 15.2, expand the ROOT node, followed by the CIMV2 node and select the MicrosoftHealthMonitor node.

6. Click the Security tab and add the appropriate domain or local groups to the list of accounts granted access. For Health Monitor to function correctly, assign new users or groups the following permissions: Remote Enable, Execute Methods, and Partial Write. All other permissions are optional.

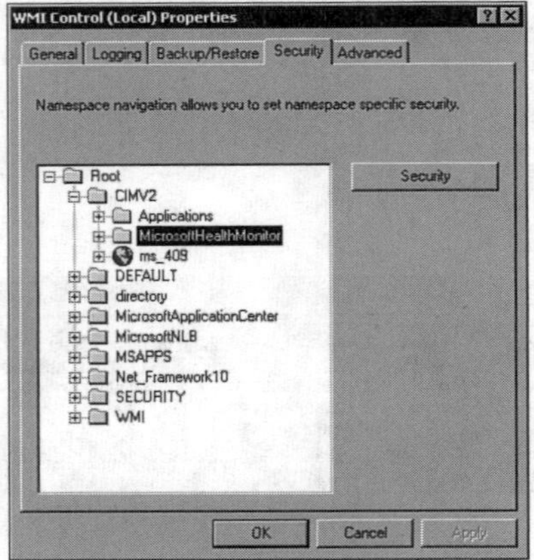

FIGURE 15.2
WMI Control Properties Security tab.

Removing a Computer

To remove a computer from the Health Monitor console, perform the following tasks:

1. Right-click the target computer from the All Monitored Computers node. Figure 15.3 shows the tasks available for a Health Monitor computer node.
2. Select All Tasks from the right-click menu.
3. Select Disconnect Computer.

Clearing Alerts for All Monitored Computers

To clear alerts for All Monitored Computers, perform the following tasks:

1. Right-click the All Monitored Computers node.
2. Select All Tasks from the right-click menu.
3. Select Clear Alerts.

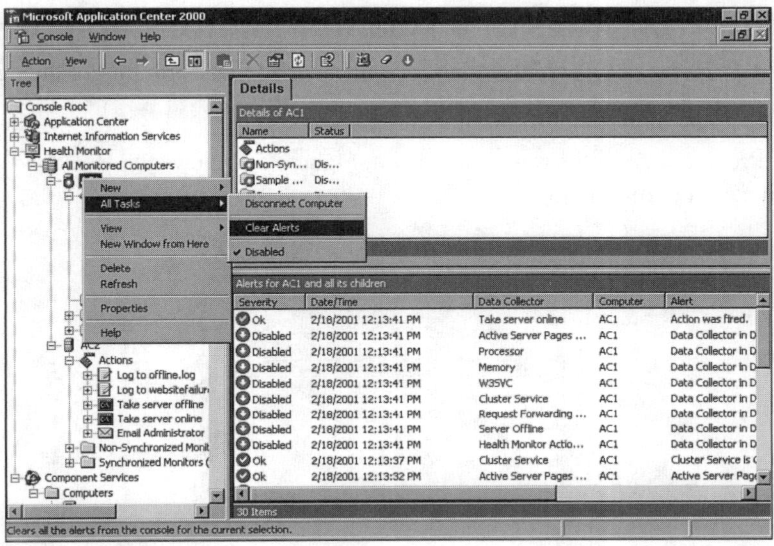

FIGURE 15.3

Tasks for a Health Monitor computer node.

If this fails to clear alerts, then there are likely failures that were immediately tripped again, restoring the console to failed state. A failed state is signified by a red X over the All Monitored Computers node. From the details pane or the tree view, any Health Monitor computer with a red X is considered to be in an alerted or failed state. Follow the red X down the Health Monitor hierarchy from the tree view to find the source of the alert.

Disabling a Health Monitor Computer Node from Reporting Errors

To disable a Health Monitor Computer node from reporting errors, perform the following tasks:

1. Right-click the target Health Monitor computer node.
2. Select All Tasks from the right-click menu.
3. Select Disabled; if already checked, then it is already disabled. To enable this computer, select Disabled again to uncheck the Disabled option.

A Disabled node in Health Monitor is signified by a down arrow next to the node icon that is disabled. Once any node is disabled, it no longer generates alerts or displays a failed red X status.

Modifying Properties of a Health Monitor Computer Node

To modify the properties of a Health Monitor computer node, perform the following tasks:

1. Right-click the target Health Monitor computer node.
2. Select Properties from the right-click menu. Figure 15.4 shows the Health Monitor computer node properties dialog.

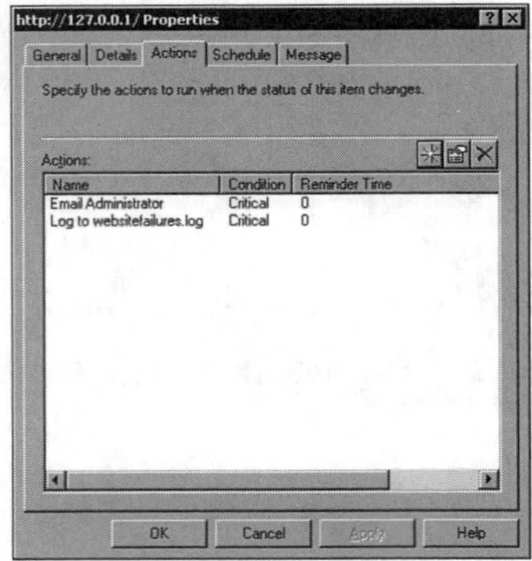

FIGURE 15.4
The Actions Property tab of the Health Monitor computer node.

In Figure 15.4, the Actions tab shows that when the status of this computer changes, the Email Administrator action fires. Creating, managing, and setting actions on Computer, Data Group, and Data Collector nodes in Health Monitor are discussed in the "Configuring Actions" section later in this chapter. The General tab (not shown) provides information about the target server and contains no configuration options.

Configuring Data Groups

Data groups in Health Monitor are simply organization units for managing Data Collectors; the main alerting and reporting mechanism in Health Monitor. Data groups are like file folders because they can contain Data Collectors (the files) and other data groups (the folders). The Health Monitor computer node is the top-level node that can create data groups. Figure 15.5 shows the standard data groups that come with Application Center 2000.

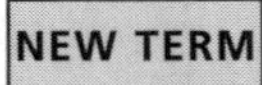

A Health Monitor *data group* is an organization object for grouping Data Collectors into manageable units.

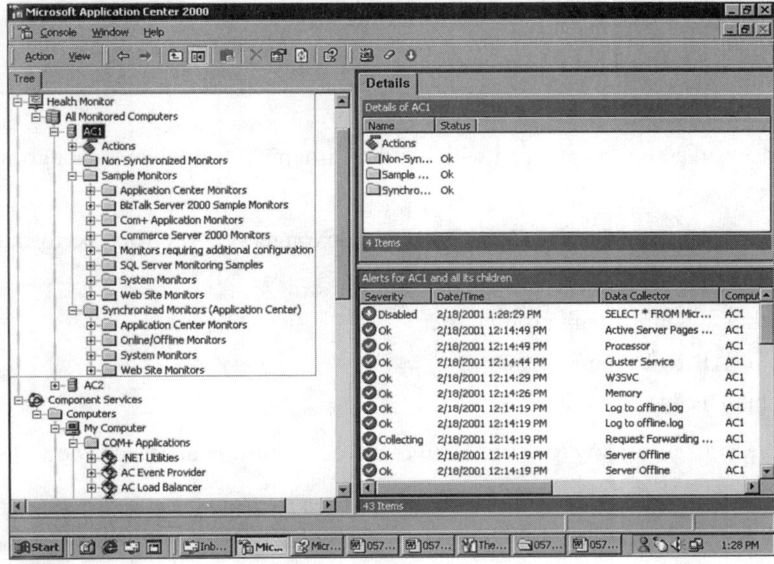

FIGURE 15.5

The data groups shipped with Application Center 2000.

Notice that the `Sample Monitors` folder contains a list of monitors for many of the .NET enterprise servers. Some of the Data Collectors in these samples will not work unless the associated .NET enterprise server is installed. However, these samples are very useful examples for the types of collectors most Web farms need to create.

Adding a Data Group Folder

To add a data group folder to a Health Monitor computer node or another Data Group node, perform the following tasks:

1. Right-click the target parent node for the new data group.
2. Select the New menu item.
3. From the New menu, select Data Group. This launches the Data Group property page.
4. From the General tab, type the name of the data group.
5. Click OK.

Performing Other Data Group Tasks

An administrator can perform all the standard tasks on data groups, including delete, disable, clear alerts, rename, cut/copy/paste, and associate actions with a status change of a Data Collector within a data group.

To delete a data group folder, perform the following tasks:

1. Right-click the target data group folder.
2. Select the Delete menu item.

All child nodes and actions associated with the data group are lost when a data group folder is deleted.

To disable a data group so that the Data Collectors no longer report errors, perform the following tasks:

1. Right-click the target data group folder.
2. Select the All Tasks menu item.
3. Select the Disable menu item.

To clear all alerts from a data group so that it removes all current alerts, perform the following tasks:

1. Right-click the target data group folder.
2. Select the All Tasks menu item.
3. Select the Clear Alerts menu item.

To cut/copy/paste a data group, perform the following tasks:

1. Right-click the target data group folder.
2. Select the Cut, Copy, or Paste menu item.

To change the name of a data group, perform the following tasks:

1. Right-click the target data group folder.
2. Select the Rename menu item.
3. Type in the new name and press Enter.

Select the Properties menu item from the right-click menu of a data group. This property page has a General tab and an Actions tab, similar to a Health Monitor computer node. From the General tab, the name of the data group can be changed. From the Actions tab, an action can be associated with a data group status change. Creating, managing, and setting actions on Computer, Data Group, and Data Collector nodes in Health Monitor are discussed in the "Configuring Actions" section, later in this chapter.

Configuring Data Collectors

A Data Collector is a WMI data abstraction for managing objects of a Web farm. Data Collectors collect and act upon the data supplied by WMI objects based on configuration information supplied in Health Monitor. These Data Collectors provide all the tools necessary to monitor the disparate systems in a Web farm.

NEW TERM A Health Monitor *Data Collector* is an abstract representation of a managed Web farm object. Data Collectors are composed of WMI data, programmatic thresholds, and actions (both custom and default) that provide monitoring and alerting for managed objects in a Web farm.

Data Collectors also define thresholds around the data they collect to provide a means to differentiate the status of a managed Web farm object. These thresholds are little bits of programmatic evaluation that run periodically to test the condition of the managed object. Each Data Collector can have any number of thresholds specified. These thresholds look at the wide range of WMI data provided by managed objects. If any of these thresholds change their status (say from OK to Critical), then the Data Collector's status changes, a message is logged to the Health Monitor console, and any custom actions associated with the Data Collector fire.

There are eight Data Collectors that target specific managed objects in a Web farm. These collectors include a Performance Monitor, a Service Monitor, a Process Monitor, a Windows Event Log Monitor, a COM+ Application Monitor, a HTTP Monitor, a TCP/IP Monitor, and a Ping Monitor. They are called monitors because they monitor the type of managed object in their name, for example, a Process Monitor gather data from a Windows NT process. There are three generic Data Collectors for other managed objects not covered by the specific collector types. They include a WMI Instance Collector, a WMI Event Query Collector, and a WMI Query Collector.

Understanding Common Data Collector Tasks

There are a number of common Data Collector tasks that are similar to tasks performed on other node types. These common actions include adding, deleting, disabling, clearing alerts, cut/copy/paste, and configuring properties.

Each Data Collector type shares these common tasks. Data Collector types are differentiated by a single details property page. The following section covers the tasks associated with all Data Collector types, followed up by a detailed description of each Data Collector type and an example.

Adding a new Data Collector

Data Collectors can be added only to data groups. To add a new Data Collector of any type, perform the following tasks:

1. Right-click the target data group.
2. Select the New menu item.

3. Select the Data Collectors menu item.
4. Select the target Data Collector type.
5. Configure the General, Details, Actions, Schedule, and Message tabs as described in the following sections.
6. Click OK.

Configuring the General Tab

The General tab of a Data Collector is similar to other general tabs in Health Monitor. The only configuration available on this tab is the administrative name of the Data Collector. Application Center does an excellent job of generating a name that makes sense for each of the collector types. For example, a service collector gets the name of the service as its generated name, and an event log collector generates the name from the configuration of the Details tab.

Figure 15.6 shows the general tab of a service collector. Notice that the name of the collector is W3SVC. This is the service name for the World Wide Web Publishing service the main component of IIS for serving Web pages. Use the description field to tell other administrators the job of each collector.

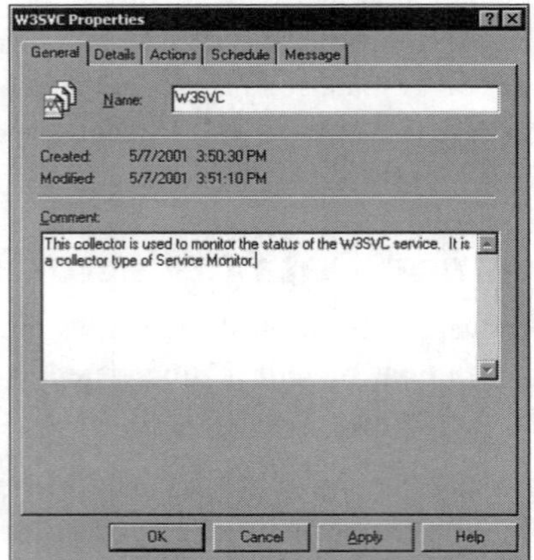

FIGURE 15.6
The General Tab of a Service Monitor.

Configuring the Actions Tab

The Actions tab for a Data Collector is exactly like the Actions tab for a data group. Configuring this tab is described in the "Configuring Actions" section earlier in this chapter.

Configuring the Schedule Tab

Figure 15.7 shows a new Data Collector's Schedule tab. From this tab, schedule the time during which this Data Collector gathers data and alerts when thresholds are met. If a Data Collector threshold has a status change outside the Data Collector's time to run, the Data Collector's status will not change. Figure 15.7 shows a new Data Collector's Schedule tab that will run Saturday and Sunday all day long.

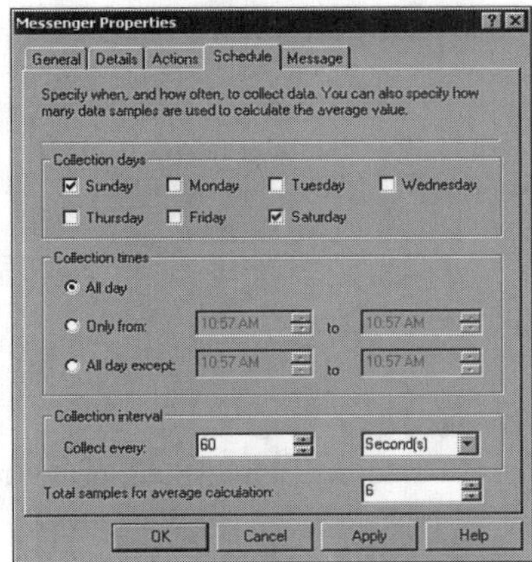

FIGURE 15.7
A scheduled Data Collector.

Specify from the Schedule tab in Figure 15.6 the collection interval for the Data Collector. The collection interval is the time period that Health Monitor waits to recheck the thresholds of a Data Collector. The time period can be seconds, minutes, or hours with the default setting being 60 seconds. For Data Collectors that rely on average values, use the Total Samples for Average Calculation text box to enter a number to use to calculate the average value. This average value is used for thresholds that change status based on an average.

Configuring the Message Tab

Use the Message tab seen in Figure 15.8 to specify a message to send to the Health Monitor console when the status of a threshold changes. When a Data Collector status changes to Warning or Critical, the message in the first text box is sent to the console. This message can be customized by the > button with WMI data from the Data Collector type. Each Data Collector type has different insertion strings that can be displayed here. Specify in the second text box the message to display when the status of the Data Collector returns to OK.

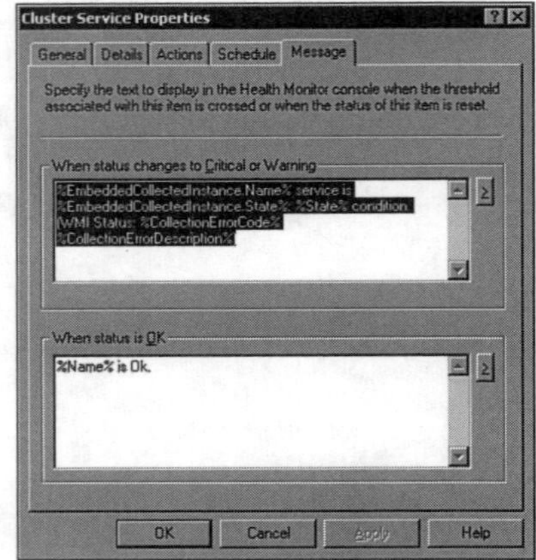

FIGURE 15.8
The Message tab of a Data Collector.

Creating a Custom Threshold

All Data Collectors have thresholds. To create a threshold, perform the following tasks:

1. Right-click the target Data Collector.
2. Select the New menu item.
3. Select the Threshold menu item.
4. Configure the Threshold Properties dialog.

Figure 15.9 shows the Threshold Properties dialog. Set up the criteria for a threshold by selecting conditions and criteria for an alert. To better understand how to configure thresholds, see the examples in the section relating to specific Data Collector types.

Performing Other Common Data Collector Tasks

To delete a Data Collector, perform the following tasks:

1. Right-click the target Data Collector.
2. Select the Delete menu item.

Deleting a Data Collector removes it from the console and deletes all associated thresholds.

To disable a Data Collector so that it does not collect data or evaluate thresholds for status changes, perform the following tasks:

1. Right-click the target Data Collector.
2. Select the All Tasks menu item.
3. Select the Disable menu item.

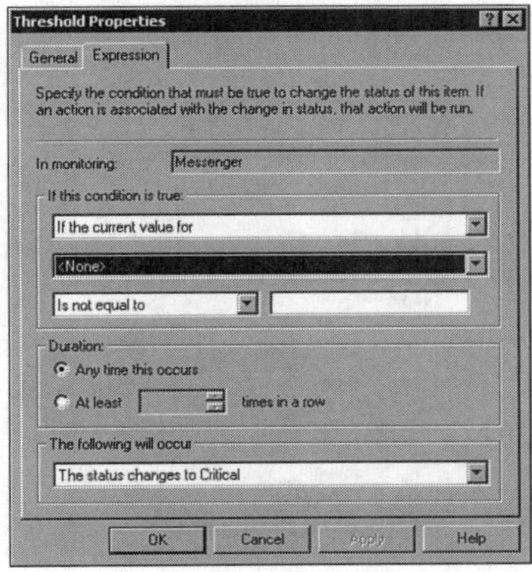

FIGURE 15.9
A threshold's Properties dialog.

The Alerts list in the details pane for a Data Collector shows all the recently triggered alerts that are associated with the thresholds of a Data Collector. To clear these alerts, perform the following tasks:

1. Right-click the target Data Collector.
2. Select the All Tasks menu item.
3. Select the Clear Alerts menu item.

To cut/copy/paste a Data Collector, perform the following tasks:

1. Right-click the target Data Collector.
2. Select the Cut, Copy, or Paste menu item.

To change the name of a Data Collector, perform the following tasks:

1. Right-click the target Data Collector.
2. Select the Rename menu item.
3. Type in the new name and press Enter.

Defining a Performance Collector

Use a performance collector object to monitor all Windows Performance Monitor counters. From this object, create alerts for high CPU utilization, high Web server connection counts, low memory conditions, and any other data provided through Perfmon. Figure 15.10 shows the details page of the Performance Collector object.

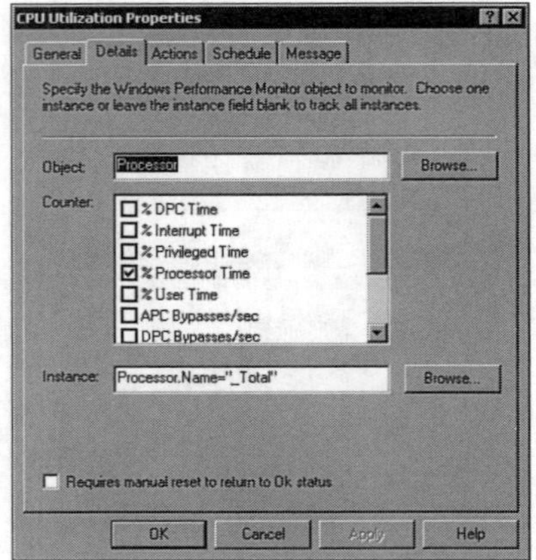

FIGURE 15.10
The Details tab of a Performance Collector.

To create a Performance Collector that monitors for excessive CPU utilization, perform the following tasks:

1. Right-click the target data group.
2. Select the New menu item.
3. Select the Data Collector menu item.
4. Select the Performance Monitor menu item.
5. On the Details tab, select the Processor object by using the Browse button next to the object.
6. From the Counter Selection box, select % Processor Time.
7. Use the Browse button next to the instance box to select the Total instance.
8. Leave Requires Manual Reset to Return Status to OK unchecked.
9. On the General tab, name the collector CPU Utilization.
10. On the Schedule tab, define the time this collector is active. In this case, leave the times for collecting at default and change the collection interval to 30 seconds.
11. On the Actions tab, associate the default Email Administrator action with the collector.
12. On the Message tab, change the Critical and Warning message to say CPU is over 80% for 3 minutes.
13. Change the OK message to say "CPU has returned to normal."
14. Click OK to create the collector.

Now data is being actively collected for this Performance Counter. An average count is being established every three minutes. However, no threshold is in place to monitor the change and set the status of the collector to Critical to fire the alert. To create the threshold that checks for 80% CPU over three minutes, perform the following tasks:

1. Right-click the CPU Utilization collector created in the previous example.
2. Select the New menu item.
3. Select the Threshold menu item.
4. From the Expression page of the Threshold Properties panel in the If This Condition Is True section, change the selection in the first combo box from If the Current Value For to If the Average Value For.
5. In the second combo box, change the selection from None to % Processor Time [Real Number].
6. In the third combo box, change the selection from Is Equal To to Is Greater Than and enter the number 80 in the text box next to this combo box.
7. In the Duration section, select the At Least radio button and enter 6 in the Selection box. The time should show 3 minutes, as in Figure 15.11.
8. Leave the combo box in the section The Following Will Occur set to The Status Changes to Critical.
9. Click OK.

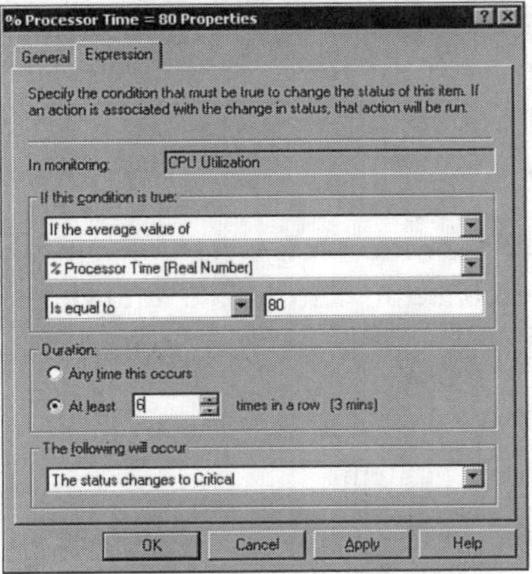

FIGURE 15.11

The settings for monitoring a CPU threshold.

There should be a second threshold in the threshold pane that says `% Processor Time = 80`. If the CPU utilization averages over 80 for three minutes, the status of the collector will change to Critical, the Collector Critical message will be sent to the console, and the Email Administrator action will be fired. If the condition corrects itself, the status will change back to OK automatically.

Defining a Service Collector

Use a service collector to monitor the status and availability of a Window NT service. Service collectors can monitor what state the service is in, whether it's started, and other service-related functionality. Figure 15.12 shows the Details tab of a service collector.

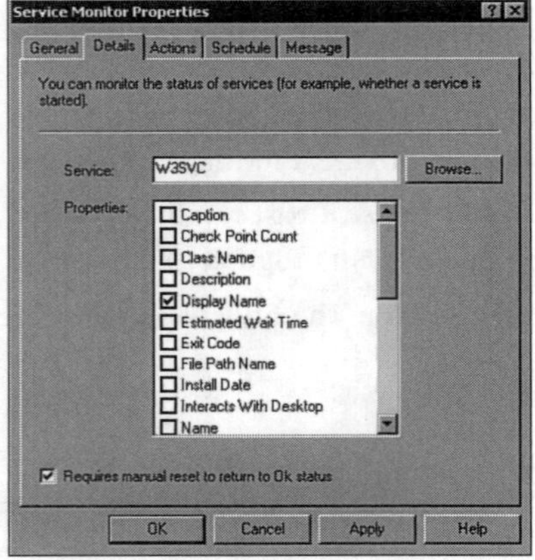

FIGURE 15.12
The Details tab of a service collector.

In the following example, a service collector is created that monitors the started property of the W3SVC service. To create this collector, perform the following tasks:

1. Right-click the target data group.
2. Select the New menu item.
3. Select the Data Collector menu item.
4. Select the Service Monitor menu item.
5. On the Details tab, click the Browse button next to the Service text box and select the W3SVC service.
6. In the Properties selection box, leave the default choices.
7. Check the Requires Manual Reset to Return to OK Status check box.

8. On the Actions tab, associate the default E-mail Administrator action with the collector.
9. Leave the General, Schedule, and Message tabs with the defaults.
10. Click OK to create the collector.

The service's state is now being monitored because a service monitor has a default threshold, shown configured in Figure 15.13, that changes the status of the collector to Critical when the service is not running.

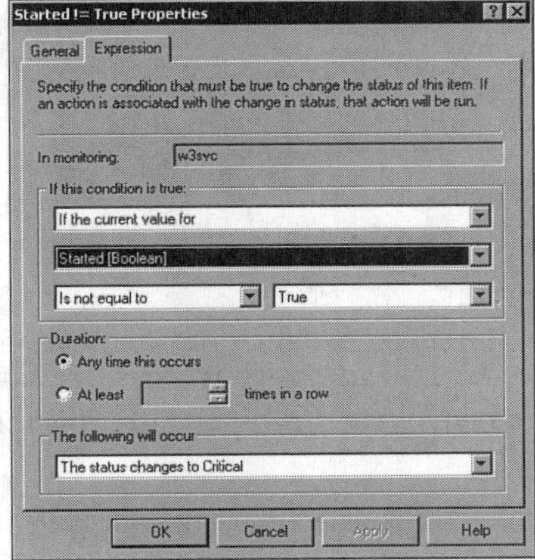

FIGURE 15.13
A default threshold for a service collector.

Defining a Process Collector

Use a process collector to monitor the status of any Windows NT process. A process collector isn't much different from a service collector, and a process collector can be used to monitor a service. The main difference is the list of properties available. For example, a process doesn't have a Started property. Figure 15.14 shows the Details tab of a process collector.

To create a process collector that looks for an excessive number of threads created (a condition that can occur during a deadlock situation) perform the following steps:

1. Right-click the target data group.
2. Select the New menu item.
3. Select the Data Collector menu item.
4. Select the Process Monitor menu item.

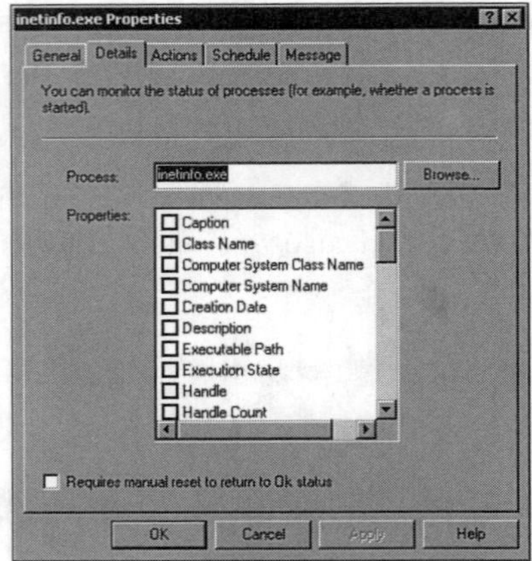

FIGURE 15.14

The Details tab of a process collector.

5. On the Details tab, Select the `inetinfo.exe` process by using the Browse button. IIS must be installed on the target server and running for this service to show up in the Browse dialog.
6. From the Properties selection box, select the Thread Count property.
7. Leave Requires Manual Reset to Return Status to OK unchecked.
8. Leave the General, Schedule, and Message tabs with the defaults. The default name for this collector should be the name of the process.
9. On the Schedule tab, define the time this collector is active. In this case, leave the times for collecting at default and change the collection interval to 30 seconds.
10. On the Actions tab, associate the default Email Administrator action with the collector.
11. On the Message tab, change the Critical and Warning message to say "IIS has created over 80 threads."
12. Change the OK message to say "Thread count returned to normal."
13. Click OK to create the collector.

To create a threshold to monitor for high thread count, perform the following tasks:

1. Right-click the collector with the URL of the Web site being monitored that was created in the previous example.
2. Select the New menu item.
3. Select the Threshold menu item.

4. From the Expression page of the Threshold Properties panel in the If This Condition Is True section, leave the selection at the default If the Current Value For setting.
5. In the second combo box, change the selection from None to Thread Count [Integer].
6. In the third combo box, change the selection from Is Not Equal To to Is Greater Than and enter the number 80 in the text box next to this combo box.
7. In the Duration section, leave the defaults.
8. Leave the combo box in the section The Following Will Occur set to The Status Changes to Critical.
9. Click OK to create the threshold.

Figure 15.15 shows the configuration of the threshold for monitoring a thread count above 80. In some cases, 80 might not be high enough to truly detect a deadlock situation. Adjust this value if when this alert occurs the Web server in question is still responding to requests. Most times when the Web server is deadlocked, no Web pages are returned from the HTTP requests.

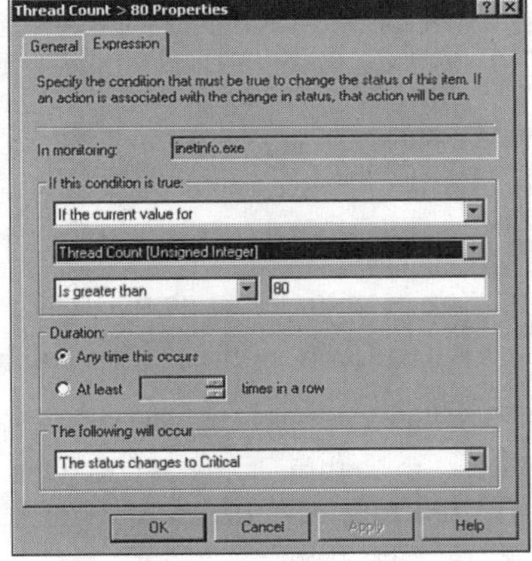

FIGURE 15.15
A threshold monitoring the thread count of a process.

Defining a Windows Event Log Collector

Use a Windows event log collector to monitor the event log of a server. The flexibility of the event log collector enables the creation of monitors that check for specific entries occurring in the log, all of one type of error, or even all errors. It can monitor the security, application, or system logs. As with all other Data Collectors, configure the Details tab with information regarding the particular type of event log monitoring required. Figure 15.16 shows the Details tab of a Windows event log collector.

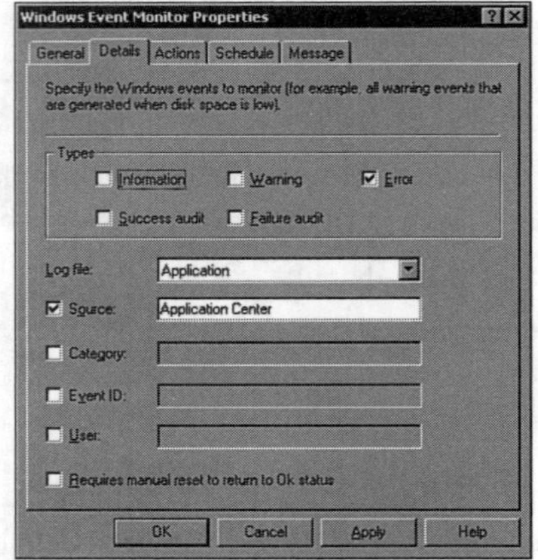

FIGURE 15.16

The Details tab of a Windows event log collector.

To create a Windows event log collector that watches for all errors from Application Center, perform the following tasks:

1. Right-click the target data group.
2. Select the New menu item.
3. Select the Data Collector menu item.
4. Select the Windows Event Log Monitor menu item.
5. On the Details tab, select Application from the log file combo box.
6. Check the Source check box and type **`Application Center`**.
8. Check Requires Manual Reset to Return Status to OK. This enables the status in Health Monitor to stay critical. For this type of collector, the status will change on the next data collection because it does not track event log history.
9. On the Actions tab, associate the default Email Administrator action with the collector.
10. Leave the General, Schedule, and Message tabs with the defaults. The default name for this collector should be Application Center Errors in Application Log.
11. Click OK to create the collector.

Any time an error is reported from Application Center while this collector is active, the administrator will receive an e-mail. There are two ways to further filter this collector. One way is to configure a specific category and event ID for this collector. Then create a collector for each event to be monitored. The default thresholds will catch that event, change the status to Critical, and force the action to fire. The other way to watch for specific events is to create a threshold for each event and remove the default thresholds. To create a event specific threshold, perform the following steps:

1. From the Thresholds View pane, right-click the two default thresholds and select Delete. Now we can configure specific event log thresholds.
2. Right-click the Application Center Errors in Application Log collector created in the previous example.
3. Select the New menu item.
4. Select the Threshold menu item.
5. From the Expression page of the Threshold Properties panel in the If This Condition Is True section, leave the selection in the first combo box at If the Current Value For.
6. In the second combo box, change the selection from None to Event Code [Unsigned Integer].
7. In the third combo box, change the selection from Is Not Equal To to Is Equal To and enter the number 8015 in the text box next to this combo box. Error 8015 is an Application Center error that occurs when the Cluster Controller can't reach a member for logging information.
8. In the Duration section, leave the defaults.
9. Leave the combo box in the section The Following Will Occur set to The Status Changes to Critical.
10. Click OK.

Figure 15.17 shows the threshold created to watch for a specific error. To test this threshold, disable the network adapter on a cluster member. At the next collection point (every 60 seconds by default), the threshold will change the status of the collector to Critical and fire the Email Administrator action. To monitor for more Application Center errors, create additional thresholds in the same manner but change the specified event code.

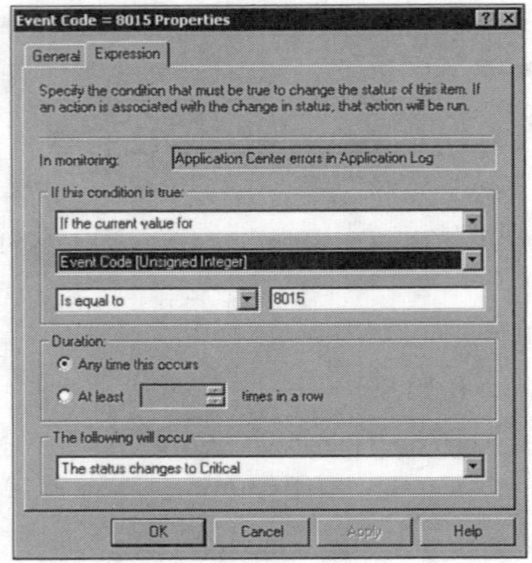

FIGURE 15.17
The threshold for monitoring for an error in the event log.

Defining a COM+ Application Collector

Use a COM+ application collector to monitor the health and status of COM+ applications. The COM+ application collector can gather data relating to aborted transactions, shutdowns due to failures, handle count, object creations per second, object activations per second, and other process-level data, similarly to what is available on the process collector. COM+ application collectors are associated with a single COM+ application. Figure 15.18 shows the Details tab of a COM+ collector.

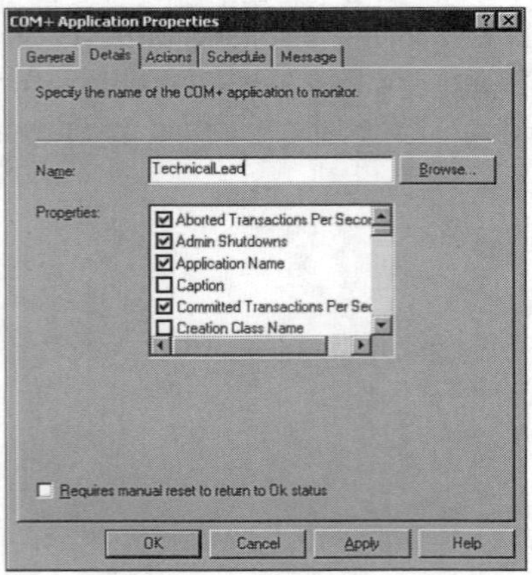

FIGURE 15.18
The Details tab of a COM+ collector.

To create a COM+ collector that changes status when it has too many object activations per second, perform the following tasks:

1. Right-click the target data group.
2. Select the New menu item.
3. Select the Data Collector menu item.
4. Select the COM+ Application Monitor menu item.
5. On the Details tab, click the Browse button next to the Name text box to browse for a specific COM+ application.
6. Leave the selection in the Properties selection box set to the defaults because the Failure Shutdown property is collected by default.
7. On the Actions tab, associate the default Email Administrator action with the collector.
8. Leave the General, Schedule, and Message tabs with the defaults. The default name for this collector should be the name of the COM+ application.
9. Click OK to create the collector.

By default every COM+ collector creates three thresholds: one for aborted transactions, one for WMI errors, and one for failure shutdowns. To create a threshold to monitor the number of object activations per second, perform the following tasks:

1. Right-click the collector with the name of the COM+ application being monitored, which was created in the previous example.
2. Select the New menu item.
3. Select the Threshold menu item.
4. From the Expression page of the Threshold Properties panel in the If This Condition Is True section, change the selection to If the Average Value Of.
5. In the second combo box, change the selection from None to Object Activations Per Second [Real Number].
6. In the third combo box, change the selection from Is Not Equal To to Is Equal To and enter the number 10 in the text box next to this combo box.
7. In the Duration section leave the defaults.
8. Leave the combo box in the section The Following Will Occur set to The Status Changes to Critical.
9. Click OK to create the threshold.

This threshold will fire if the average number of object activations for the COM+ application over a 60-second period is more than 10. This could be used to alert on very high usage and near failure conditions. Figure 15.19 shows the object activations threshold configuration.

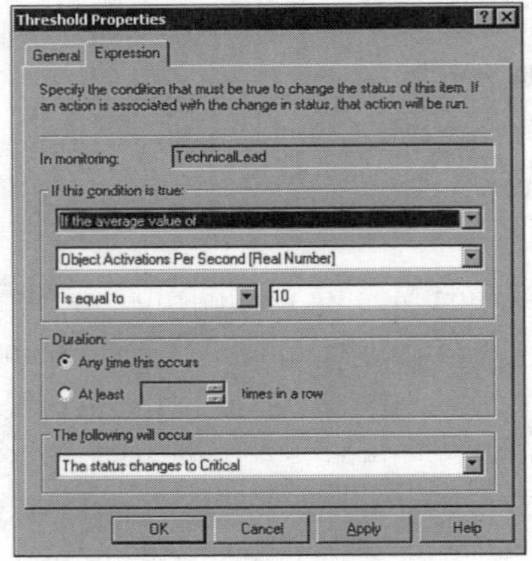

FIGURE 15.19
The threshold monitoring for high object activations per second.

Defining an HTTP Monitor Collector

Use an HTTP monitor to check the availability and functioning of specific pages on a Web site. For example, an HTTP monitor can request a page that returns status information about the applications its supports. Thresholds can look for specific strings in the returned text stream or slow response times and status change information to alert administrators of application failures.

HTTP monitors are special Data Collectors because they don't have a set of WMI properties associated with them that are available outside of a specific request. For example, an HTTP monitor makes requests for a default page of a Web site. No data can be retrieved relating to this until the request for the default page has returned from the Web server. Data is input to the HTTP monitor collector to specify the type of query to perform against the target Web server. When the query is complete, other properties such as raw headers, text response, and response time are filled in with values that resulted from the HTTP monitor collector query.

Figure 15.20 shows the Details tab of an HTTP monitor collector.

To create a HTTP monitor collector that looks for an error code in the returned HTTP data, perform the following tasks:

1. Right-click the target data group.
2. Select the New menu item.
3. Select the Data Collector menu item.
4. Select the HTTP Monitor menu item.

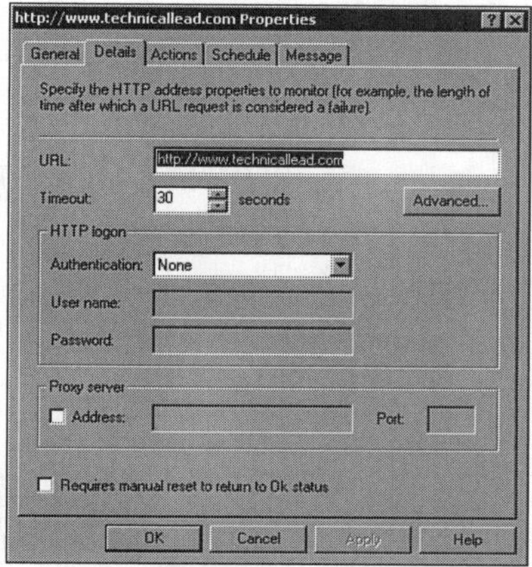

FIGURE 15.20
The Details tab of an HTTP monitor collector.

5. On the Details tab, fill in the full URL to the target Web site to monitor. In this case, use `http://www.technicallead.com`.
6. Leave the rest of the page at the defaults unless a proxy server is required to make a connection to the Internet. In that case, click the Address check box and fill in the address and port of the proxy server.
7. On the Actions tab, associate the default Email Administrator action with the collector.
8. Leave the General, Schedule, and Message tabs with the defaults. The default name for this collector is whatever URL is specified.
9. Click OK to create the collector.

By default, HTTP monitor collectors have three thresholds: One checks for WMI errors, one checks for a Web server response time greater than 30, and the final one checks that the HTTP status code from the Web server is greater than 400. To create a threshold that looks for errors in the response text, perform the following tasks:

1. Right-click the collector with the URL of the Web site being monitored that was created in the previous example.
2. Select the New menu item.
3. Select the Threshold menu item.
4. From the Expression page of the Threshold properties panel in the If This Condition Is True section leave the selection at the default If the Current Value For.
5. In the second combo box, change the selection from None to Text Response [String].

6. In the third combo box, change the selection from Is Not Equal To to Contains the String and enter the word `error` in the text box next to this combo box.
7. In the Duration section, leave the defaults.
8. Leave the combo box in the section titled The Following Will Occur set to The Status Changes to Critical.
9. Click OK to create the threshold.

This threshold changes the status of the HTTP Monitor Collector when the string "error" occurs in the response text. Figure 15.21 shows the configuration for this threshold.

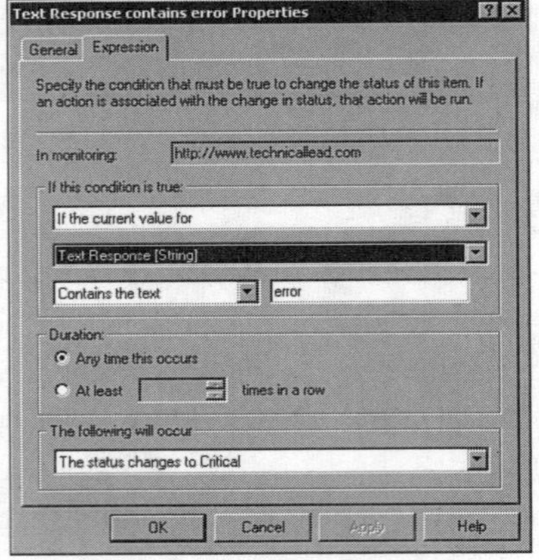

FIGURE 15.21
A threshold to check for the word error in an HTTP response.

Defining a TCP/IP Monitor

Use a TCP/IP Data Collector to monitor any valid TCP/IP port on a network. This collector can ensure that a service is responding at the network level to requests from the outside. Examples of service types to monitor include FTP, SMTP, POP3, IMAP, HTTP, HTTPS, and so on. Figure 15.22 shows the Details tab of a TCP/IP monitor.

To create a TCP/IP monitor that checks the status of port 80 on a target server, perform the following tasks:

1. Right-click the target data group.
2. Select the New menu item.
3. Select the Data Collector menu item.
4. Select the TCP/IP Monitor menu item.

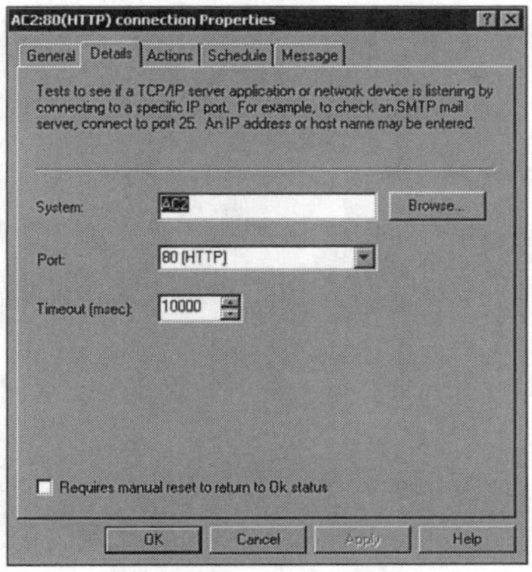

FIGURE 15.22
The Details tab of a TCP/IP monitor.

5. On the Details tab, fill in the machine name or an IP address for the target server. Use the Browse button to display a list of servers to pick from inside Network Neighborhood.
6. Change the Port combo box to 80(HTTP).
7. Leave the Timeout set to the default.
8. On the Actions tab, associate the default Email Administrator action with the collector.
9. Leave the General, Schedule, and Message tabs with the defaults. The default name for this collector type is `MachineName:Port value`.
10. Click OK to create the collector.

By default, TCP/IP monitor collectors have three thresholds: One checks for WMI errors, one checks for response time greater than 15000ms, and the final one checks that the TCP/IP error does not equal zero. These thresholds cover all the necessary conditions to monitor the availability of any port on a target server.

Defining a Ping Monitor

Use a ping monitor to ensure that a server is alive and responding to ping requests. Ping is a simple way to tell that the server's network presence is available, but it does not tell anything about specific ports or network applications. Use the TCP/IP and HTTP collectors for more details of specific network services. Figure 15.23 shows the Details tab of a Ping Monitor.

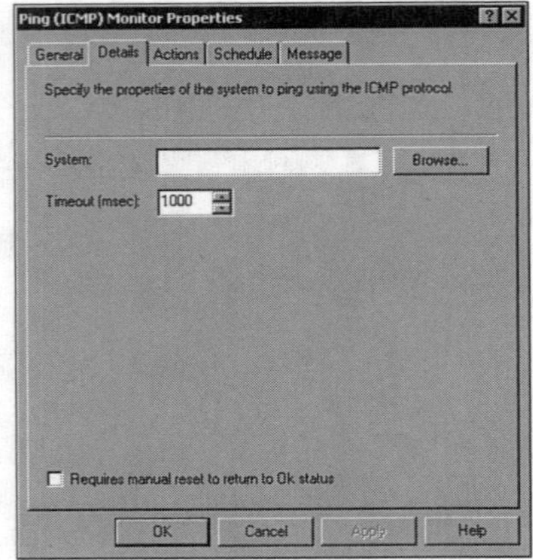

FIGURE 15.23
The Details tab of a Ping Monitor.

To create a Ping Monitor that pings a server, perform the following tasks:

1. Right-click the target data group.
2. Select the New menu item.
3. Select the Data Collector menu item.
4. Select the Ping Monitor menu item.
5. On the Details tab, fill in the machine name or IP address for the target server. Use the Browse button to display a list of servers to pick from inside Network Neighborhood.
6. Leave Timeout set to the default.
7. On the Actions tab, associate the default Email Administrator action with the collector.
8. Leave the General, Schedule, and Message tabs with the defaults. The default name for this collector type is `Ping machine name`.
9. Click OK to create the collector.

By default, a Ping Monitor creates four thresholds to check the status of the ping request. These thresholds check the status of WMI for errors, change status if the ping fails, change status if the ping fails once, and change status if the ping fails twice. These threshold are more than sufficient for any ping monitoring of a server.

Defining a WMI Instance

Use a WMI Instance Data Collector for monitoring a specific WMI instance. A specific WMI instance is similar to an instance in Perfmon. For example, the class that represents logical disk properties, `WIN32_LogicalDisk`, has as many instances as there are logical disks. Use an instance of `WIN32_LogicalDisk` to monitor free disk space or other disk drive properties. As with other Data Collectors, the WMI Instance Data Collectors have a special Details tab that is used to specify the WMI namespace, class, instance, and properties to collect. Figure 15.24 shows the Details tab of a WMI instance.

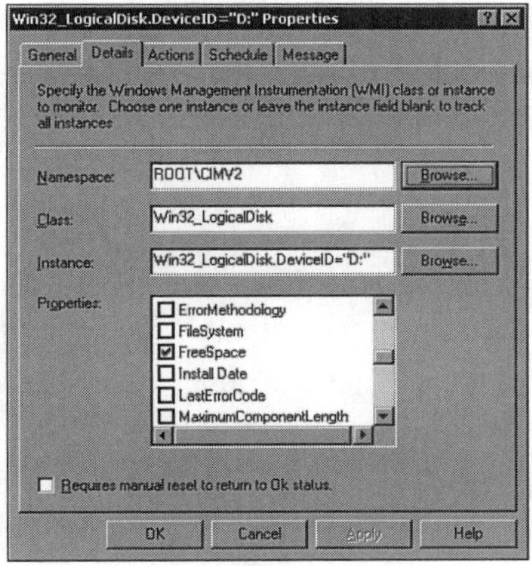

FIGURE 15.24
The Details tab of a WMI instance.

To create a WMI Instance Data Collector that monitors free disk space, perform the following steps:

1. Right-click the target data group.
2. Select the New menu item.
3. Select the Data Collector menu item.
4. Select the Ping Monitor menu item.
5. On the Details tab, fill in the WMI class object. In this case, click the Browse button next to the class text box and pick `Win32_LogicalDisk` as the class name.
6. Use the Browse button next to the Instance text box and select the first hard drive instance on the target server. In this example, `Win32_LogicalDisk.DeviceID="D:"` is selected for drive D:.
7. In the Properties select box, choose FreeSpace as an additional property to collect for this WMI instance.
8. On the Actions tab, associate the default Email Administrator action with the collector.

9. Leave the General, Schedule, and Message tabs with the defaults. The default name for this collector type is `Win32_LogicalDisk.DeviceID="D:"`, which is the WMI instance name.
10. Click OK to create the collector.

At this point only one threshold is created, the on named Default error code from WMI does not equal zero. This only happens when the Data Collector fails completely. To monitor the free space on a particular disk, perform the following tasks:

1. Right-click the collector with the name of the WMI instance being monitored, which was created in the previous example.
2. Select the New menu item.
3. Select the Threshold menu item.
4. From the Expression page of the Threshold Properties panel in the If This Condition Is True section, leave the selection at the default If the Current Value For.
5. In the second combo box, change the selection from None to FreeSpace [Unsigned Integer].
6. In the third combo box, change the selection from Is Not Equal To to Is Less Than and enter the number `50000` in the text box next to this combo box. This corresponds to 50,000 bytes left.
7. In the Duration section leave the defaults.
8. Leave the combo box in the section The Following Will Occur set to The Status Changes to Critical.
9. Click OK to create the threshold shown in Figure 15.25.

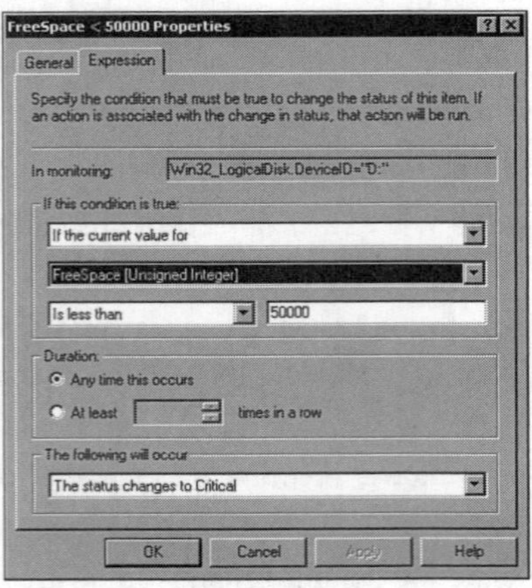

FIGURE 15.25
A threshold for monitoring low disk space conditions.

Now, any time this specific instance of the `Win32_LogicalDisk` class has less than 50,000 bytes of disk space free, the threshold will change the status of the collector to critical and e-mail an administrator. In this case, a custom action that deletes temporary files and log files might be an appropriate response to avoid an administrator intervening on every occasion.

Defining a WMI Event Query

Use WMI event query to respond to WMI classes that support event notifications. A WMI event query establishes a connection between the provider and Health Monitor that says "Let me know when something occurs," instead of polling the WMI class as with a WMI Instance Data Collector. Examples of WMI event queries are CPU utilization, monitoring changes in the event log, and disk space changes.

Figure 15.26 shows the Details tab of the WMI Event Query Collector. From this tab, specify which WMI event class to hook the Health Monitor console with and the type of query to run.

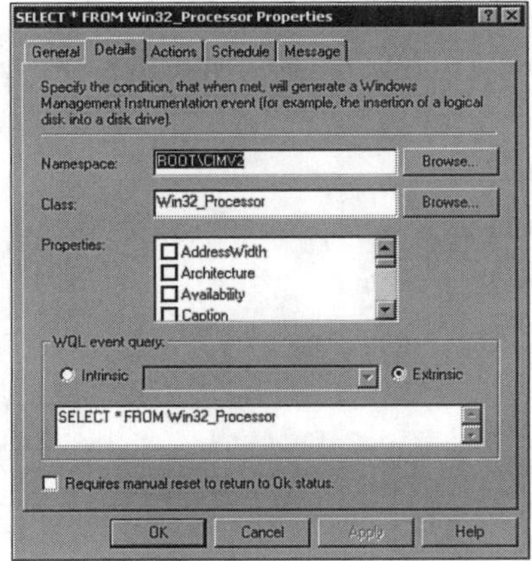

FIGURE 15.26
The Details tab of a WMI event query.

Defining a WMI Query

A WMI query is similar to a WMI event query in that it uses WQL (Windows Query Language) for returning data. It is different in that it works with collections of data instead of events fired from WMI providers. WMI queries are used to monitor a collection of data such as all the space available on every hard disk or the CPU utilization of every processor. Figure 15.27 shows the Details tab for a data query.

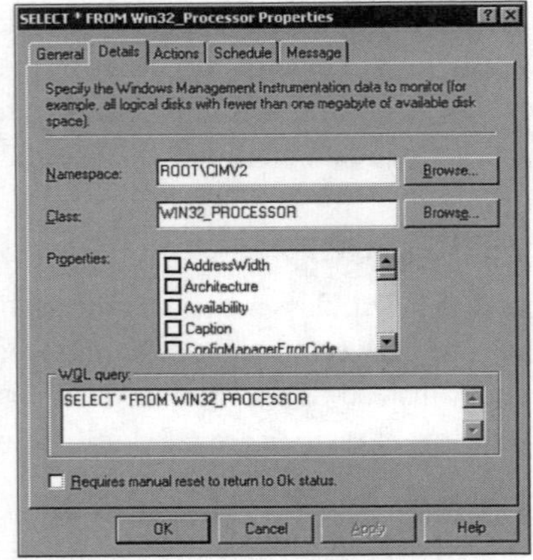

FIGURE 15.27
The Details tab of a WMI query.

To create a data query that monitors for high CPU utilization on all CPUs, perform the following tasks:

1. Right-click the target data group.
2. Select the New menu item.
3. Select the Data Collector menu item.
4. Select the WMI Event Query menu item.
5. On the Details tab, fill in the WMI class object. In this case, click the Browse button next to the Class text box and pick `Win32_Processor` as the class name.
6. In the Properties select box, choose `LoadPercentage` as an additional property to collect for this WMI data query.
7. On the Actions tab, associate the default Email Administrator action with the collector.
8. Leave the General, Schedule, and Message tabs with the defaults. The default name for this collector type is the WQL query, which in this case is `SELECT * FROM Win32_Processor`. This means to return all the data relating to all the processors on the target machine.
9. Click OK to create the collector.

The default threshold for a WMI data query checks only for the status of the Data Collector itself and does nothing to monitor CPU utilization. To create a threshold that monitors CPU utilization on all processors, perform the following tasks:

1. Right-click the collector with WQL query from the data query that was created in the previous example.
2. Select the New menu item.
3. Select the Threshold menu item.
4. From the Expression page of the Threshold Properties panel in the If This Condition Is True section, change the selection from If the Current Value For to If the Average Value Of.
5. In the second combo box, change the selection from None to LoadPercentage[Unsigned Integer].
6. In the third combo box, change the selection from Is Not Equal To to Is Greater Than and enter the number 95 in the text box next to this combo box. This corresponds to 95% processor utilization.
7. In the Duration section, select the At Least radio button and change the value to 5. This means the CPU will average over 95% for 5 minutes before triggering.
8. Leave the combo box in the section The Following Will Occur set to The Status Changes to Critical.
9. Click OK to create the threshold shown in Figure 15.28.

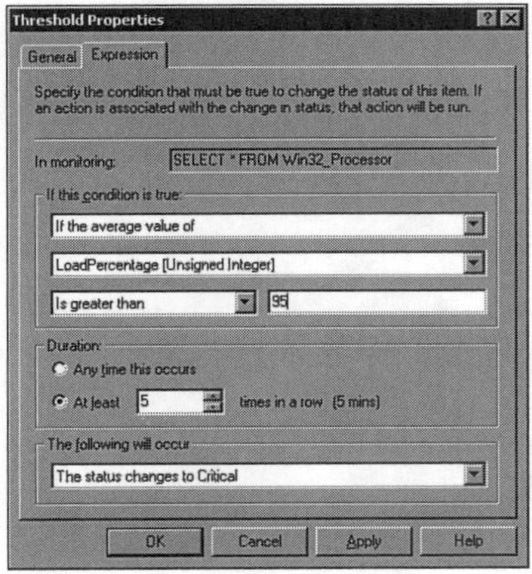

FIGURE 15.28

A threshold monitoring the load percentage of all processors in a system.

Configuring Actions

Actions are Health Monitor responses to status changes from Data Collectors that cross user-defined threshold boundaries. An action can send an e-mail message, create an NT event log entry, create a log entry in a text file, execute a shell script from a command line, or launch a Windows Scripting Host (WSH) script such as a VBS or JS file. For example, these actions are the responses to alerts such as if CPU utilization is over 90% for 5 minutes or an Application Center 2000 deployment task failed.

NEW TERM A Health Monitor *action* is a programmatic response to a Data Collector status change. Actions enable administrators to have programmatic responses such as e-mails, logging, and custom scripting to known error conditions.

Understanding Common Action Tasks

There are a number of common action tasks that are similar to tasks performed on other node types. These common actions include adding, deleting, disabling, clearing alerts, cut/copy/paste, and configuring properties.

Each action type shares these common tasks. Actions type are differentiated by a single Details property page. The following section covers the tasks associated with all action types, followed by a detailed description of each action type.

Adding an Action

To add a new action, perform the following steps:

1. Right-click the Actions node.
2. Click the New menu item and select the type of action. Figure 15.29 shows the Action right-click menu.
3. Fill out the Details tab for each action type as described in each Action type's section below.
4. Name the action from the General tab.
5. Schedule the action's availability window.
6. Click OK.

Configuring the Schedule Tab

Figure 15.30 shows a new action's Schedule tab. From this tab, schedule the time during which this action can run. If an action is associated with a Data Collector that has a status change outside the action's time to run, the action will not fire. Figure 15.30 shows a new e-mail action that will run only Monday through Friday 8:00 a.m. to 5:00 p.m.

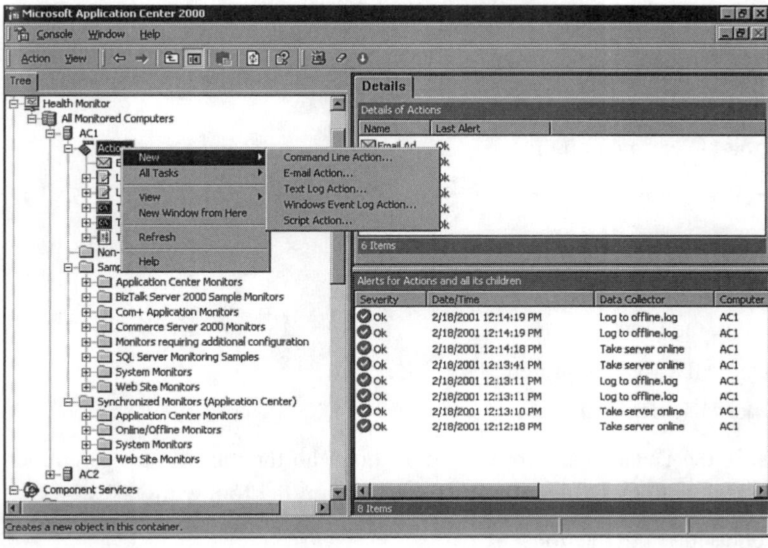

FIGURE 15.29

The Actions node right-click menu.

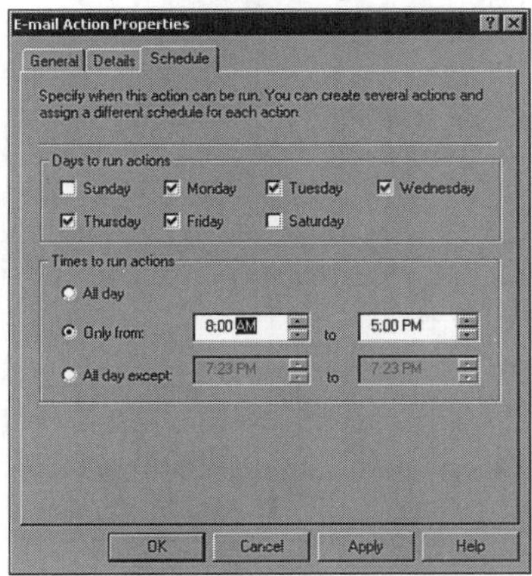

FIGURE 15.30

A scheduled e-mail action.

Performing Other Common Action Tasks

To delete an action, perform the following tasks:

1. Right-click the target action.
2. Select the Delete menu item.

Deleting an action removes it from all the Data Collectors that fire it.

To disable an action so that it does not run when a Data Collector's status changes, perform the following tasks:

1. Right-click the target action.
2. Select the All Tasks menu item.
3. Select the Disable menu item.

The alerts list in the Details pane for an action shows all the recently triggered alerts that are associated with an action. To clear those alerts, perform the following tasks:

1. Right-click the target action.
2. Select the All Tasks menu item.
3. Select the Clear Alerts menu item.

To cut/copy/paste an action, perform the following tasks:

1. Right-click the target Action.
2. Select Cut, Copy, or Paste menu item.

To change the name of an action perform the following tasks:

1. Right-click the target action.
2. Select the Rename menu item.
3. Type in the new name and press Enter.

The Actions tab of the Details pane contains a list of all Data Collectors associated with an action. Use this list to track all these alerts and their current status during failures.

Defining a Command-Line Action

Figure 15.31 shows the Details tab of the default Take Server Offline command-line action. From this tab specify the filename of the program or batch file to run for this action. In this case the filename is `AC.EXE`. No working directory is specified. Specify a working directory if the action needs to run from a particular directory. This action specifies a command-line parameter that tells the `AC.EXE` program to take the server offline.

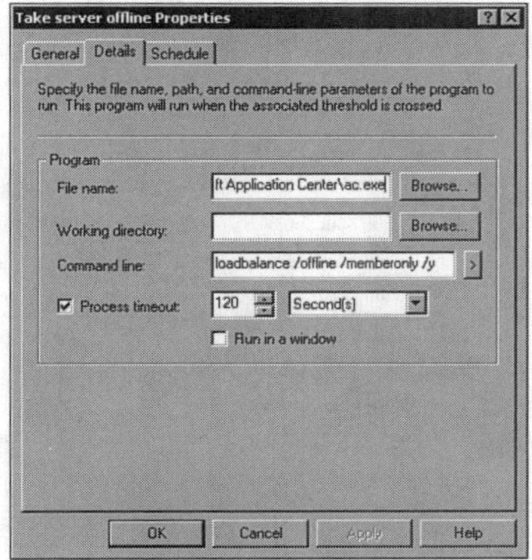

FIGURE 15.31
The Details Tab of a Command-line Action.

If a command-line action can fail, use the Process Timeout check box to tell Health Monitor how long to wait before terminating the action. If one does fail, an error is reported back to the action item in the `Actions` folder. An action that fails shows a red X as part of its icon until the error is resolved or cleared manually.

Defining an E-Mail Action

Figure 15.32 shows the Details tab of the default Email Administrator action. From this tab, specify the parameters required to send an e-mail. In the SMTP Server text box, enter the server name or IP address of a valid SMTP server. Use the From text box to send the e-mail with a particular name or identifier. Use the To text box, CC, and BCC buttons to specify e-mail recipients for the TO, CC, and BCC lists, respectively.

The Subject and Message fields can contain special insertion string codes enclosed in percent signs (%). These codes come from the properties of the WMI event that is associated with an e-mail action. Click the > button for a list of properties that can be embedded in the subject or message body.

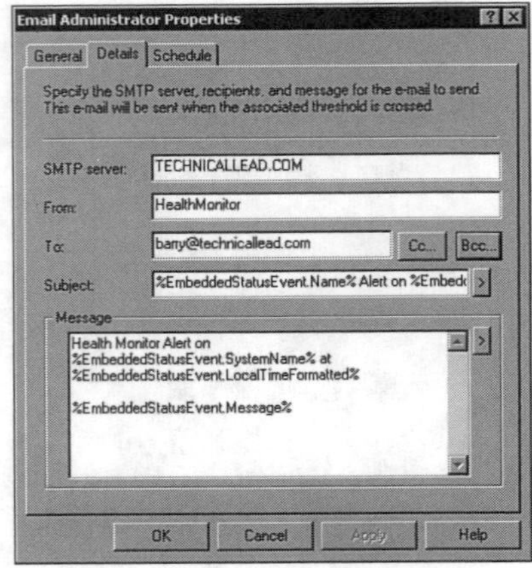

FIGURE 15.32
The Details tab of an e-mail action.

Defining a Windows Event Log Action

Figure 15.33 shows the Details tab of a new Windows event log action. Use the Event Type combo box to specify the type of event: error, warning, or information. In the Message text box, specify the message that is entered into the event log. Use the > button to insert insertion strings to customize the output.

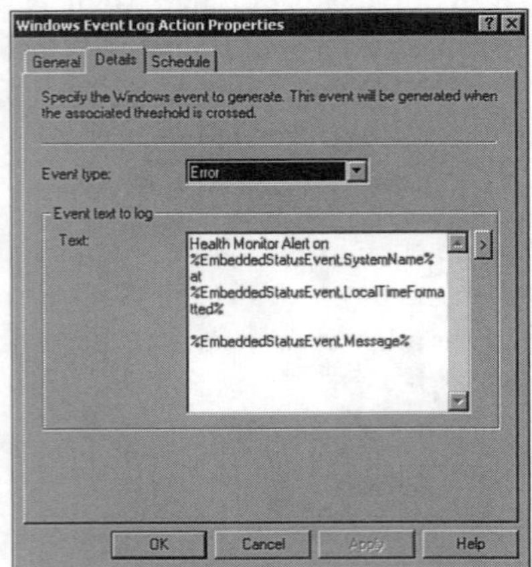

FIGURE 15.33
The Details tab of a Windows event log action.

The default message makes an entry in the log with the format shown in Listing 15.1. This example is an alert that is watching the status of the Messenger service, which was recently stopped or failed.

LISTING 15.1 Default Message Format for a Windows Event Log Action

```
2/21/2001    11:41:11 AM    AC1      2

Windows
Source:  HealthMonitor


Health Monitor Alert on AC1 at 2/21/2001 11:41:11 AM

Messenger service is Stopped: Critical condition.
(WMI Status: 0 )
```

Defining a Text Log Action

A text log action is similar to an event log action except the error message is entered at the end of a specified file. From this Details tab, configure the name of the file in the File Name text box. Use the Browse button to find an already created log file. If a filename is specified that does not exist, Health Monitor will create it. Specify the size in either bytes, kilobytes, or megabytes. When a file fills up, it is renamed with an extension of `.001`, `.002`, and so on, and new one with the active name is created. Logging goes on uninterrupted in the model but will eventually cause the drive to run out of disk space. Figure 15.34 shows the Details tab of a text log action.

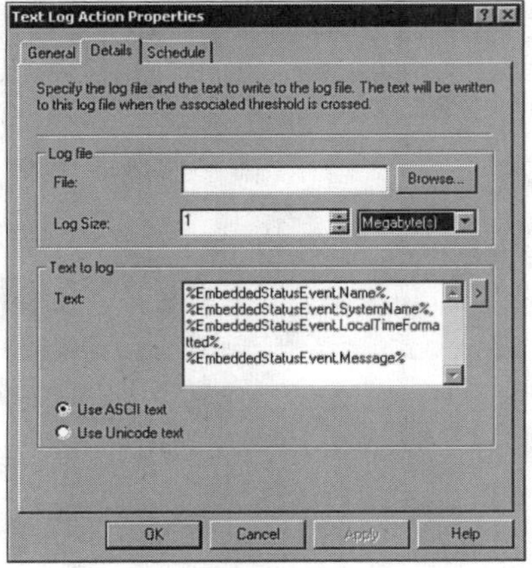

FIGURE 15.34
The Details tab of a text log action.

In the Text to Log text area, insert the message body to log into the file for each event. Use the > button to place embedded insertion strings into the body of the message. By default, a message logged to a text log has this format:

```
%EmbeddedStatusEvent.Name%, %EmbeddedStatusEvent.SystemName%,
➥%EmbeddedStatusEvent.LocalTimeFormatted%, %EmbeddedStatusEvent.Message%
```

And looks like this:

```
Messenger Alert, AC1, 2/21/2001 11:52:16 AM, Messenger service is Stopped:
➥Critical condition. (WMI Status: 0 )
```

A log to text file action also supports using Unicode or ASCII format for the message for internationalized log files.

Defining a Script Action

A script action is the most flexible action type available in Health Monitor. Any custom VBS or JScript file can be executed in response to an alert or status change. Figure 15.35 shows the Details tab of a script action. Specify the type of script in the Script Type combo box. Specify the full path to the script in the Path text box or by using the Browse button. Specify the Process Timeout to set a time frame for Health Monitor to wait for the script to finish before terminating the action.

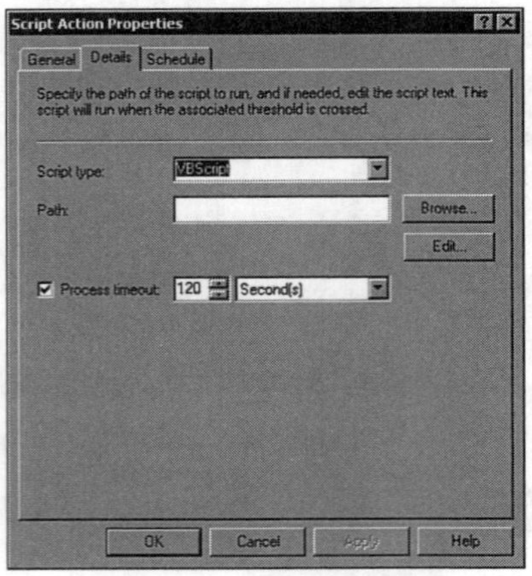

FIGURE 15.35
The Details tab of a script action.

Associating Actions with Computer, Data Group, and Data Collector Nodes

To associate a Health Monitor action to a computer, data group, or Data Collector status change, perform the following actions:

1. Right-click the target data group folder.
2. Select the Properties menu item.
3. Select the Actions tab from the Property dialog.
4. Click the New Action button and configure the Execute Action Properties dialog shown in Figure 15.36.

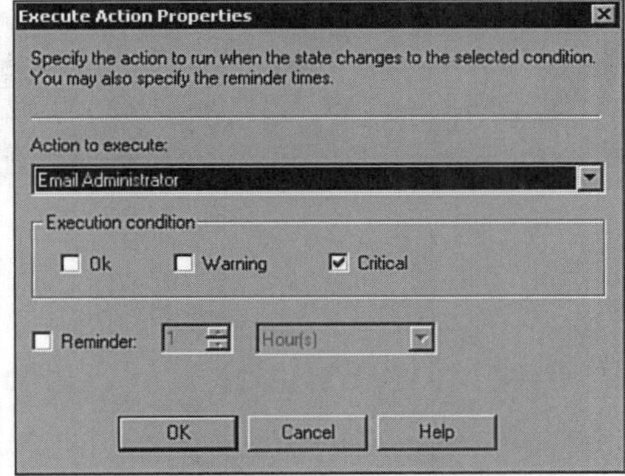

FIGURE 15.36
The Execute Action Properties dialog.

5. Select the action to execute from the Action to Execute combo box. Each action can be associated once per Data Collector node, Computer node, or Data Group node.
6. Select the Execute condition.
7. Select the reminder time if desired.
8. Click OK.

The Execute condition determines when the action will fire. If the Execute condition for an action is Critical, then any alerts set to a Critical state that are associated with this action fire. A reminder time is a period of time for Health Monitor to wait to fire the action again if it has not been cleared from the console. Figure 15.37 shows the Actions tab of a Data Collector with a number of associated actions.

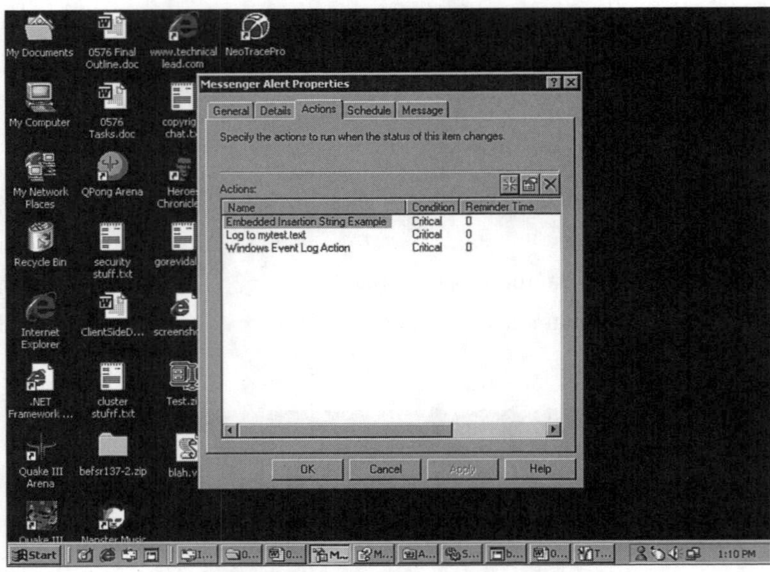

FIGURE 15.37
Actions associated with an alert.

Using Embedded Insertion Strings for Custom Action Messages

All actions support the creation of custom messages using insertions strings. The data from these insertion strings comes from the actions and the WMI event class associated with the action being fired. Insertions stings are used in message bodies for e-mail fields, event log entries, and command-line parameters.

Table 15.1 shows the list of supported insertion strings, their meanings, and whether they are supported on actions for nodes that are not Data Collectors. If an action is fired from a Data Collector, all the listed embedded codes are supported. Actions that fire from Health Monitor, Computer, and Data Group nodes support a subset of the embeddable codes. Note that the proper format for all these strings is %EmbeddedStatusEvent.<CODENAME>%, where CODENAME is the Name field in Table 15.1. For the EmbeddedCollectedInstance property, the correct form is %EmbeddedCollectedInstance.<PROPERTYNAME>%, where PROPERTYNAME is a property on the WMI instance that fired the action.

TABLE 15.1 Codes for Embedded Insertion Strings

Name	*Available On*	*Description*
`CollectionErrorCode`	Data Collectors	Error code from WMI. Not all instances will have data.
`CollectionErrorDescription`	Data Collectors	Error description from WMI. Not all instances will have data.
`CollectionInstanceCount`	Data Collectors	Number of instances collected. Not all WMI errors have more than one instance.
`GUID`	Data Collectors	A unique identifier for this event at this node.
`InstanceName`	Data Collectors	Equivalent to the `EmbeddedCollected Instance.Name` property. This comes from the WMI provider referenced in the alert.
`LocalTimeFormatted`	All	The time of the event in local time.
`Message`	All	This is the message specified from the Data Collector or the default message for other nodes.
`Name`	All	The name of the node that is generating the event.
`ParentGUID`	All	Unknown.
`State`	All	The state of the item from the WMI provider. Corresponds to the event ID in the event log.
`StatusGUID`	Data Collectors	Unknown.
`SystemName`	All	The server that generated the action.
`TimeGeneratedGMT`	All	Time in system time format, meaning it is not readable.
`EmbeddedCollectedInstance.<PROPERTYNAME>`	Data Collectors	When an action fires, it can look at the WMI instance that generated the event and use those properties in the message.

In this example, an action is created that logs an event to the NT event log. The same action can be associated with a Data Collector, Computer, or Data Group node. By associating an action with a Data Group and a Data Collector the behavior of the insertion strings becomes much more evident. For this example, perform the following tasks:

1. Right-click the Actions node in the Health Monitor console.
2. Select the New menu item.
3. Select the Windows Event Log Action menu item.
4. On the General tab, name this action Embedded Insertion Strings Example.
5. On the Details tab, change the error message to the text in Listing 15.2.
6. Click OK.
7. Right-click the Non-Synchronized Monitors data group.
8. Select the New menu item.
9. Select the Data Collectors menu item.
10. Select the Service Collector menu item.
11. On the General tab, name this alert `Messenger Alert`.
12. On the Details and Schedule tabs, leave everything set to defaults.
13. On the Actions tab, associate the Embedded Insertion Strings Example with this alert, leaving everything set to defaults.
14. Click OK.
15. Right-click the Non-Synchronized Monitors node.
16. Select Properties.
17. On the Actions tab, associate the Embedded Insertion Strings Example with this alert leaving everything set to defaults.
18. Click OK.
19. Stop the Messenger service on the server with the alert and action to cause the alert to trip and the action to fire.

LISTING 15.2 Text for the Error Message in the Embedded String Insertion Example

```
Embedded Insertion String Example:
Error Code From WMI= %EmbeddedStatusEvent.CollectionErrorCode%
Error Description from WMI= %EmbeddedStatusEvent.CollectionErrorDescription%
# of Instances Collected= %EmbeddedStatusEvent.CollectionInstanceCount%
GUID= %EmbeddedStatusEvent.GUID%
Instance Name= %EmbeddedStatusEvent.InstanceName%
Formatted Local Time= %EmbeddedStatusEvent.LocalTimeFormatted%
Message= %EmbeddedStatusEvent.Message%
```

LISTING 15.2 Continued

```
Name= %EmbeddedStatusEvent.Name%
Parent GUID= %EmbeddedStatusEvent.ParentGUID%
State= %EmbeddedStatusEvent.State%
Status GUID= %EmbeddedStatusEvent.StatusGUID%
System Name= %EmbeddedStatusEvent.SystemName%
GMT Time= %EmbeddedStatusEvent.TimeGeneratedGMT%

Embedded Collected Instance Data:
Service Name= %EmbeddedStatusEvent.EmbeddedCollectedInstance.Name%
Start Mode= %EmbeddedStatusEvent.EmbeddedCollectedInstance.StartMode%
Started= %EmbeddedStatusEvent.EmbeddedCollectedInstance.Started%
```

Associating the action with both a Data Collector and a Data Group node will show the differences in the messages reported in the event log. Listing 15.3 shows the message in the event log for when the action fired from the Service Monitor Data Collector.

LISTING 15.3 Event Log Message when the Data Collector Fires the Action

```
2/21/2001    11:10:23 AM     AC1      2

Windows
Source:  HealthMonitor


Embedded Insertion String Example:
Error Code From WMI= 0
Error Description from WMI=
# of Instances Collected= 1
GUID= {4E4BDA8E-BFFC-453A-949A-B7F94CC27E87}
Instance Name= Messenger
Formatted Local Time= 2/21/2001 11:10:23 AM
Message= Messenger service is Stopped: Critical condition.
(WMI Status: 0 )
Name= Messenger Alert
Parent GUID= {BBCC6E87-E1EA-47ee-AC4A-A5D635D0DB56}
State= 9
Status GUID= {8E4EB6F4-C929-4853-8E16-AD080CC3044D}
System Name= AC1
GMT Time= 20010221171023.000000+000

Embedded Collected Instance Data:
Service Name= Messenger
Start Mode= Auto
Started= FALSE
```

Listing 15.4 shows the error message generated when the action was fired from the data group.

LISTING 15.4 Event Log Message when the Data Group Fires the Action

```
2/21/2001   11:10:23 AM    AC1     2

Windows
Source:  HealthMonitor


Embedded Insertion String Example:
Error Code From WMI= <unknown>
Error Description from WMI= <unknown>
# of Instances Collected= <unknown>
GUID= {BBCC6E87-E1EA-47ee-AC4A-A5D635D0DB56}
Instance Name= <unknown>
Formatted Local Time= 2/21/2001 11:10:23 AM
Message= Non-Synchronized Monitors : Critical condition
Name= Non-Synchronized Monitors
Parent GUID= {@}
State= 9
Status GUID= <null>
System Name= AC1
GMT Time= 20010221171023.000000+000

Embedded Collected Instance Data:
Service Name= <unknown>
Start Mode= <unknown>
Started= <unknown>
```

Notice that none of the original message details are present in the data group–generated message. This is because the message generated here is actually a completely different event from the alert that triggered from the stopping of the Messenger service. Health Monitor cascades error messages in this fashion up the data group hierarchy to show a status change in the UI using a red X on the target data group or computer icon. This event represents the data group folder changing status as a result of the Messenger service being stopped. This same event would be generated for any status change of any collector in the Non-Synchronized Monitors data group folder.

Summary

Any Web farm can use Health Monitor 2.1's robust features to provide a complete monitoring suite. Health Monitor is a well-organized and thought-out administrator tool. It enables administrators to organize and manage the servers in a Web farm from a centralized console.

Administrators can create data groups to organize the different types of Data Collectors into focused and meaningful groups.

Data Collectors provide a suite of tools to perform the actual data retrieval of the monitored system. There are 11 Data Collector types, and each performs a service useful to the monitoring of a Web farm. From an HTTP monitor that can request and examine Web pages from a site to a generic WMI instance query, Health Monitor Data Collectors can look into any Web farm system and return its status. Once a Data Collector has gathered data, thresholds examine the returned data to see if criteria have been met that signify a status change. These criteria are miniprograms that run on an interval basis usually and provide automatic evaluations of specific Data Collector instances. Without thresholds, data is collected and ignored.

When a threshold does change the status of a collector, an action can fire in response. There are five types of actions, from sending an e-mail to running a custom VB script. An action is an administrator's virtual hand that can intercede and potentially correct known problems without directly involving an administrator. In the worst case, an action is a message that a problem exists to systems outside the Web farm.

There is a learning curve to use Health Monitor to its full potential. Understanding how to perform the variety of tasks for actions, Data Collectors, and thresholds helps in the planning and preparation of an overall monitoring strategy.

Performing Advanced Application Center 2000 Tasks

CHAPTER

16

IN THIS CHAPTER

This chapter covers how to use advanced features and functions of Application Center 2000. These tasks may or may not be useful for every Web farm, but the concepts in this chapter will help the administrator understand the complete picture of Application Center's feature list.

The goals of this chapter are to help you

- Learn to create custom event filtering to make inspection and management of the consolidated event views easier and more useful.
- Learn to define global folder and file exclusions for deployment. These exclusions allow administrators a finer-grain control over the deployment process.
- Learn to add performance counters to the global list of performance counters available in the cluster-wide performance monitor.
- Understand the ACLog database, including the tables, views, and jobs it runs on every member of an Application Center 2000 cluster.
- Learn to fire events when a server cluster status changes.
- Learn to use Health Monitor to run custom deployment scripts.
- Learn to use Application Center to deploy Site Server 3.0 membership sites.
- Learn how to configure security for the application in cross-domain deployment scenarios.

A number of these topics require tools that are available only on the Application Center 2000 Resource Kit. This toolkit has Application Center 2000 technologies that are not available anywhere else and is a mandatory read for any Web farm administrator that uses Application Center 2000.

Creating Custom Event Filtering

Application Center 2000 supports filtering events from its consolidated event views. This can be useful when certain applications constantly report useless information either because they are malfunctioning or because they make judicious, yet useless use of the event logs. To edit event filtering, perform the following steps:

1. Right-click the events node of the Application Center console and select Properties. Figure 16.1 shows this dialog box.

FIGURE 16.1
The event node's Events Properties dialog box.

2. Select the Exclusions button to launch the Event Exclusions dialog box, shown in Figure 16.2.

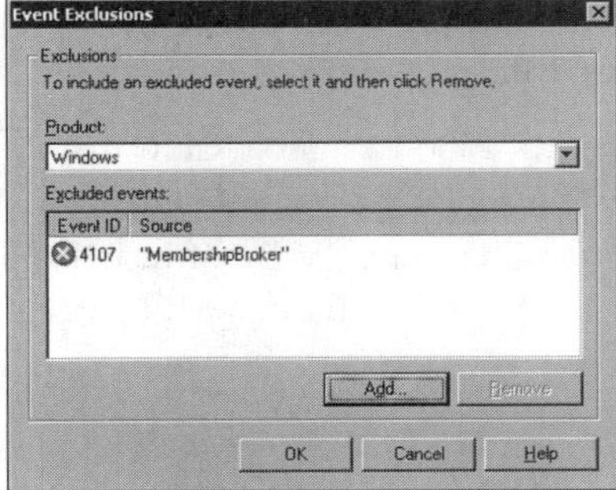

FIGURE 16.2
The Event Exclusions dialog box.

Use this dialog box to exclude a specific event message from being logged to the consolidated event views. This means that the event data does not make it to the Application Center 2000 data store, but it will continue to be logged into the event log as normal. To exclude a specific event, select the appropriate product: Application Center, Health Monitor, or, for all other events, Windows. Click the Add button and fill in the appropriate error information in the Add Event Exclusions dialog box, as shown in Figure 16.3. These exclusions apply only to future events. The existing events that meet the excluded criteria will continue to show up in event view until the consolidated archive period expires (15 days, by default).

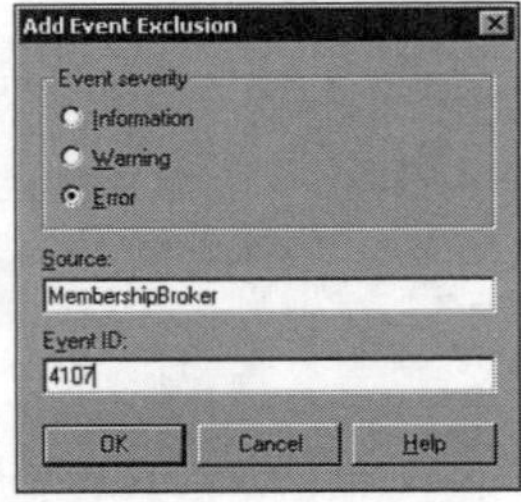

FIGURE 16.3
The Add Event Exclusions dialog box.

Application Center 2000 causes a couple of known problems with some of the more esoteric performance counter DLLs supplied with some of the more esoteric Microsoft products such as Site Server 3.0. Performance counters are implemented in a DLL supplied with the software being monitored. For example, Site Server 3.0 supplies a CDF generation tool that includes a performance counter DLL called CDPerf.DLL. Because this is a highly specialized feature, the majority of Web farms likely will not need to monitor the CDF generator. However, every Site Server 3.0 installation that installs Application Center 2000 will become painfully aware of this DLL. This DLL is incompatible with monitoring features of Application Center 2000, and it reports every 10 seconds that it failed to load correctly in the application log. This will fill up the log very quickly and make the consolidated event views quite useless.

Luckily, a program in the Windows 2000 Resource Kit, called the Extensible Counter List (EXCTRLST.EXE), can help. This tool is shown in Figure 16.4. To prevent CDFPerf.DLL from logging to the event log, scroll through the list of installed performance counters, select CDF Generator, and uncheck the Performance Counters Enabled option. This will stop the constant logging.

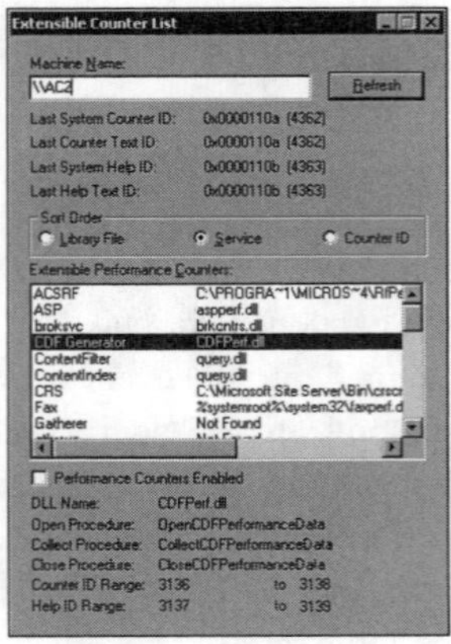

FIGURE 16.4
The Extensible Counter List management tool.

Defining File and Folder Exclusions for Synchronizations

Application Center 2000 supports the modification of deployment and synchronizations using file and folder exclusions. This feature provides a limited capability to prevent certain files and folders from being replicated by an application. File and folder exclusion is global to the cluster and cannot be applied at the single member level. Application Center 2000 supports the following three types of exclusions:

- Exclude a specific file, such as `d:\inetpub\wwwroot\postinfo.html`. This type of exclusion applies only to a full file path.
- Exclude a specific folder, such as `d:\inetpub\scripts`. This type of exclusion is useful to restrict well-known directories that contain known exploits.
- Exclude an entire class of files, such as `*.scc`. This will exclude all .scc files (a Source Safe configuration file that should never make it to production).

To use folder and file exclusions, complete the following steps:

1. Right-click the synchronizations node in the Application Center 2000 console.
2. Select Properties. Figure 16.5 shows the Synchronizations Property dialog box.

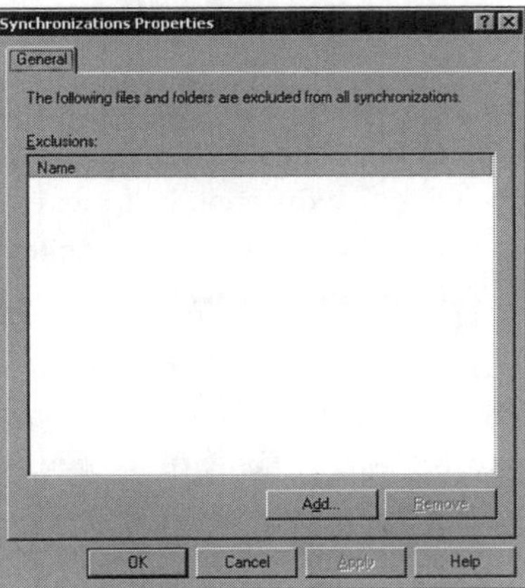

FIGURE 16.5
The Synchronizations Property dialog box.

3. Click the Add button, which displays the Add Exclusion dialog box shown in Figure 16.6.

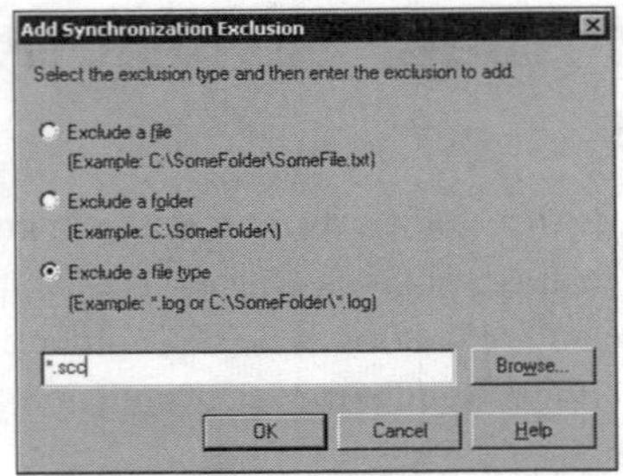

FIGURE 16.6
The Add Synchronization Exclusion dialog box.

4. Select the type of exclusion, enter the file path, folder path, or file type, and click OK.

> **NOTE**
>
> Folder and file exclusions do not support excluding a specific file globally. For example, it is not possible to exclude the postinfo.html file across all sites of a Web farm.

Adding Performance Counters to the Cluster-wide Monitor

Application Center 2000 has a robust consolidated cluster of performance views available from the console. These views provide five different historical trend views using the most important performance counters related to Web farm requirements. These views provide trending data for the last 15 minutes, 2 hours, 1 day, 1 week, and 3 month time periods.

Application Center 2000 supports the trending of 20 performance counters by default. These counters are some of the most important ones to trend for capacity planning and performance monitoring in a Web farm. Figure 16.7 shows some of the counters in the Add a Counter dialog box. Unfortunately, there is no simple way to add a new counter to trend. Administrators must perform a number of complicated steps, create a special document, and compile it to add a new counter to this list. These tasks are the focus of this section.

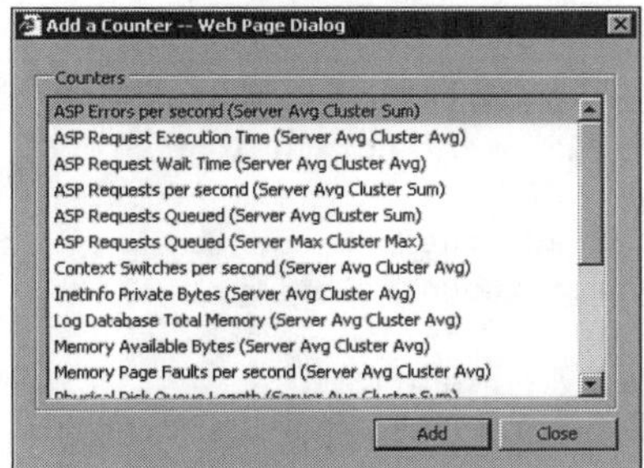

FIGURE 16.7
The list of available counters for performance views.

Listing 16.1 shows a simple VBScript block that can list all the counters currently installed. Application Center 2000 stores these counters in the `MicrosoftAC_CapacityCounterConfig` performance log class of the `MicrosoftApplicationCenter` WMI namespace. For Application Center 2000 to trend new counters, they must be added to this WMI section through a MOF file.

LISTING 16.1 Simple Script to List All the Installed Counters

```
Dim objLocator
Dim objService
Dim objCounters
Dim objCounter
Dim strCounterName

Set objLocator = CreateObject("WbemScripting.SWbemLocator")
Set objService = objLocator.ConnectServer(strComputerName,
➥"root\MicrosoftApplicationCenter")
objLocator.Security_.ImpersonationLevel=3

Set objCounters = objService.InstancesOf("MicrosoftAC_CapacityCounterConfig")
For Each objCounter in objCounters
strCounterName = objCounter.Name
wscript.echo(strCounterName)
Next
```

A MOF file is configuration file for WMI. MOF files are compiled with a program called MOFComp.exe, which compiles the MOF file and inserts the information into the specified WMI namespace. Listing 16.2 shows a simple MOF file to add the Web services bytes sent/sec to the trending charts. This would be useful to determine times when the most data is being sent to users of a Web farm.

LISTING 16.2 A Simple MOF File for Adding on Counter

```
// This specifies which namespace to add objects
#pragma namespace("\\root\\MicrosoftApplicationCenter")

//  This is the WMI class to add the new counter
instance of MicrosoftAC_CapacityCounterConfig
{
      Name = "Web Service Bytes Sent/Sec";
      CounterPath = "\\Web Service\\Bytes Sent/sec";
      CounterType = 1;
      Units = "bytes";
      AggregationMethod = 1;
      ClusterAggregation = 2;
    DefaultScale = 0;
};
```

Each MOF file entry for modifying these performance views must start with an instance of `MicrosoftAC_CapacityCounterConfig`. For each counter, each of the properties defined as explained in Table 16.1 must be present.

TABLE 16.1 Required Properties for `MicrosoftAC_CapacityCounterConfig` Data in a MOF File

Property	*Description*
`Name`	This is the human readable string of the counter name used to identify it in the performance view and database. It must be unique across all counters.
`CounterPath`	This is the path to the counter in PDH syntax with English names. The syntax is `\\PerfObject(ParentInstance/ObjectInstanc#InstanceIndex)\\Counter`.
`Units`	This is the human-readable string that describes the units for display purposes.
`CounterType`	This must be set to 1.
`AggregationMethod`	This is the method used in the rollup process to move data from one time period to another on a specific server. When data expires in the 15 minutes view, it is rolled up based on this value to the 1 hour view. Values can be 0–5:

TABLE 16.1 Continued

Property	*Description*
	0 = None 1 = Average 2 = Sum 3 = Last 4 = Min 5 = Max
`ClusterAggregation`	This is the method used in the rollup process to move data from one time period to another across the cluster. Values are the same as those for `AggregationMethod`.
`DefaultScale`	This is the scale to display the counter data in the UI as a power of 10.

From the previous MOF, an `AggregationMethod` of 2 averages the values when the counter is rolled up on the server from one time period to a longer period. A `ClusterAggregation` of 2 means to sum the values returned from each server and add them to the cluster-wide view value during the rollup process.

To add the new counter, add the previous text to a file called `ADDCOUNTER.MOF` and then compile it using `MOFCOMP.EXE`, as shown:

```
MOFCOMP.EXE ADDCOUNTER.MOF
```

This should produce the following output:

```
C:\>MOFCOMP.EXE ADDCOUNTER.MOF
Microsoft (R) 32-bit MOF Compiler Version 1.50.1085.0007
Copyright (c) Microsoft Corp. 1997-1999. All rights reserved.

Parsing MOF file: ADDCOUNTER.MOF
MOF file has been successfully parsed
Storing data in the repository...
Done!
```

After the counter is added to the WMI namespace, it must also be added to the ACLog database local to the cluster controller. Figure 16.8 shows the ACLog database in SQL 2000 Enterprise Manager expanded to the list of tables, selecting the Counters table and issuing the Return All Rows command.

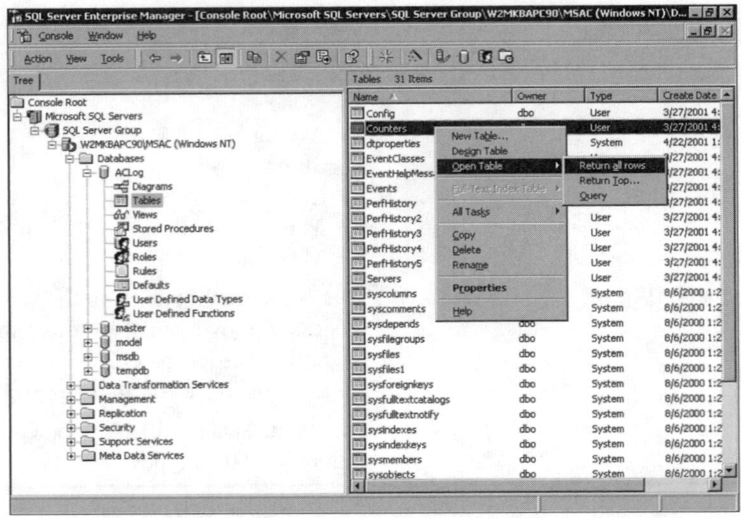

FIGURE 16.8

The Counters table in the ACLog database.

Return All Rows displays all the data in the Counter table. This data is a duplicate of the data in the WMI namespace that the UI uses to display. Add a new row and type in the same values in the columns as they are in the corresponding property of the MOF file. Figure 16.9 shows the new row being added to the Counters table.

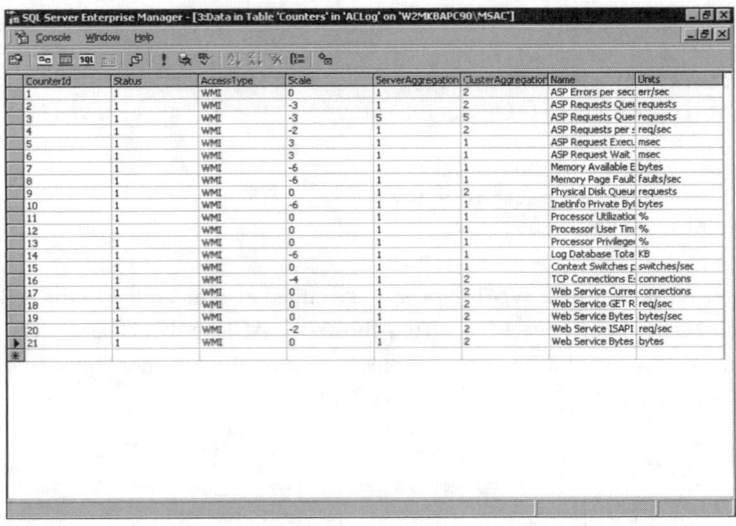

CounterId	Status	AccessType	Scale	ServerAggregation	ClusterAggregation	Name	Units
1	1	WMI	0	1	2	ASP Errors per sec	err/sec
2	1	WMI	-3	1	2	ASP Requests Que	requests
3	1	WMI	-3	5	5	ASP Requests Que	requests
4	1	WMI	-2	1	2	ASP Requests per	req/sec
5	1	WMI	3	1	1	ASP Request Exec	msec
6	1	WMI	3	1	1	ASP Request Wait	msec
7	1	WMI	-6	1	1	Memory Available E	bytes
8	1	WMI	-6	1	1	Memory Page Fault	faults/sec
9	1	WMI	0	1	2	Physical Disk Queue	requests
10	1	WMI	-6	1	1	Inetinfo Private By	bytes
11	1	WMI	0	1	1	Processor Utilizatio	%
12	1	WMI	0	1	1	Processor User Tim	%
13	1	WMI	0	1	1	Processor Privilege	%
14	1	WMI	-6	1	1	Log Database Tota	KB
15	1	WMI	0	1	1	Context Switches p	switches/sec
16	1	WMI	-4	1	2	TCP Connections E	connections
17	1	WMI	0	1	2	Web Service Curre	connections
18	1	WMI	0	1	2	Web Service GET R	req/sec
19	1	WMI	0	1	2	Web Service Bytes	bytes/sec
20	1	WMI	-2	1	2	Web Service ISAPI	req/sec
21	1	WMI	0	1	2	Web Service Bytes	bytes

FIGURE 16.9

Add a new counter to the ACLog database.

Now the new counter should be available in the Add a Counter dialog box for all the performance views, as shown in Figure 16.10. Select this new counter and click Add to add it to the current performance view. If the counter doesn't show up, restart the `WINMGMT` services using **`NET STOP WINMGMT`** from the command line, followed by **`NET START WINMGMT`**.

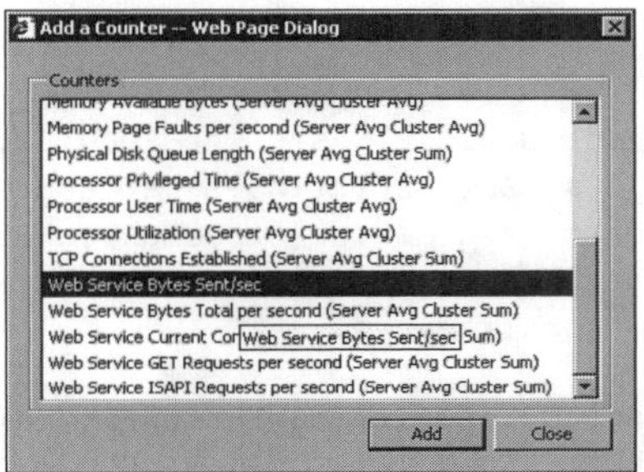

FIGURE 16.10
The new counter available in the Add a Counter dialog box.

Figure 16.11 shows the new counter data being displayed in the performance view. Notice that it just starts up, unlike the context switches per second counter data, which is available for the entire range of the graph. This is because the counter data didn't start collecting until it was added to both the database and the WMI namespace.

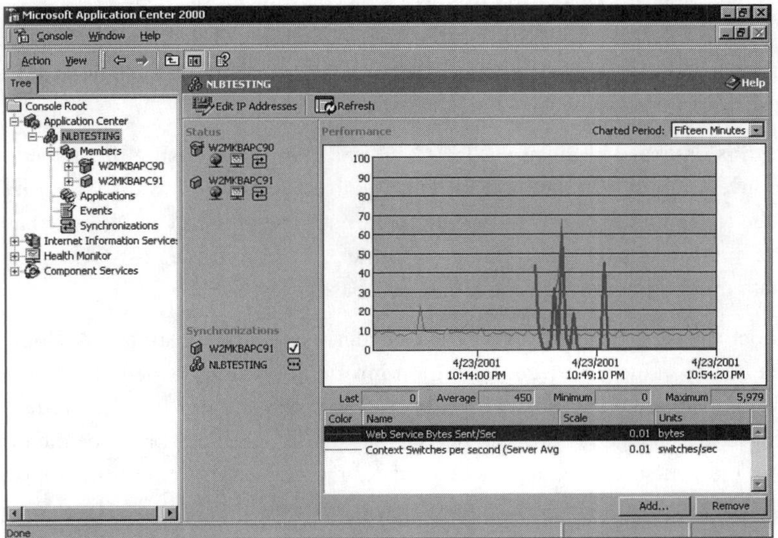

FIGURE 16.11
The new counter data in performance view.

Deleting a counter from performance view is simpler than adding one. First, it must be removed from the WMI namespace using the script in Listing 16.3.

Listing 16.3 Removing a Counter

```
Dim objLocator
Dim objService
Dim strCounterName
Dim strComputerName 'If this is blank, uses the local computer
Set objLocator = CreateObject("WbemScripting.SWbemLocator")
Set objService = objLocator.ConnectServer(strComputerName,
➥"root\MicrosoftApplicationCenter")
wbemLocator.Security_.ImpersonationLevel=3

objService.Delete("MicrosoftAC_CapacityCounterConfig.Name="""
➥+ strCounterName +"""")
wscript.echo "Deleted counter: " + strCounterName
```

This will not delete the counter data from the database; it will just stop the collection of data for this counter.

Understanding the ACLog Database

Application Center installs with performance and event logging for the Microsoft Data Engine (MSDE), a scaled-down version of SQL Server 2000. Application Center creates a named instance of SQL 2000 that is used for cluster information, event logging, and performance counter storage for all the console views. Whenever any node in the console is selected, the view pane executes queries against this database.

The name of this database instance is MSAC, so it is addressable using the named instance SQL 2000 convention: `SERVERNAME\MSAC`. This database uses Windows NT security so that any member of the local administrator group on the target server can access the database in this instance. The main database that Application Center creates and uses is ACLog. Figure 16.12 shows the data model diagram of the ACLog database.

The data model shows that the schema of the database is relatively simple. A Config table contains a single binary value where configuration information is embedded. A Servers table, at the center of all the rest of the tables, contains a single server entry for the server that the SQL Server 2000 MSAC instance is on. The PerfHistory tables store performance data that was logged during the course of the day for this cluster member in different time intervals. For example, PerfHistory stores the last 15 minutes of performance data. The Events tables contain the event history based on the event properties for a cluster.

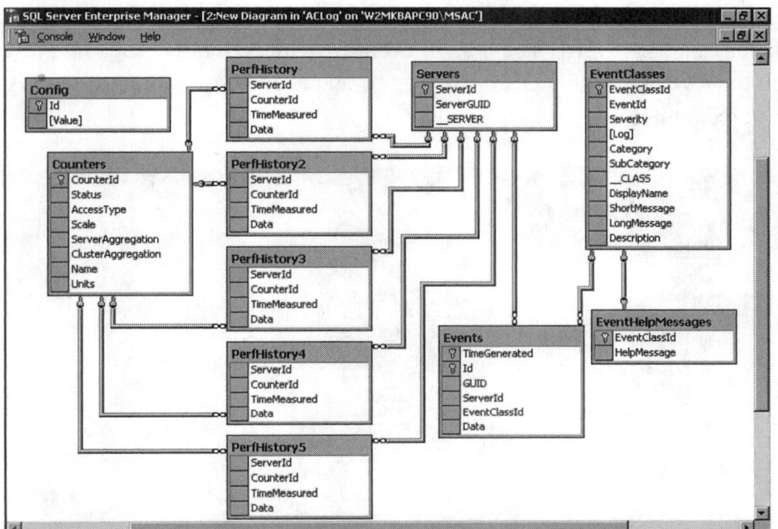

FIGURE 16.12

The data model of the ACLog database.

The Application Center 2000 console leverages a number of views, including EventView, EventDetailView, and the PerfHistoryViews. PerfHistoryView shows the last 15 minutes of activity and is used in performance view in the console to show the last 15 minutes of cluster activity. A number of scheduled jobs move the performance data from the other PerfHistory tables to maintain the data for the two-hour, one-day, one-week, and three-month views. Other jobs purge the Event database based on event node property settings from the console and rebuild the indexes.

Firing Actions When a Server's Cluster Status Changes

One of the most important events to occur in any Web farm is the addition or removal of members from the production mix. This is commonly referred to as bringing a server online or taking a server offline. Application Center 2000, with NLB and CLB clusters, fires WMI events that can be captured in Health Monitor for these status changes. From these events, any custom actions can be run. This provides an opportunity to e-mail administrators, run diagnostics programs, reset application state, or perform any other scriptable action.

Figure 16.13 shows the Synchronized Monitors (Application Center) section highlighted in Health Monitor. This is the section that has a preinstalled data collector for online and offline status changes of cluster members. The WMI event that fires is `MicrosoftAC_Cluster_Loadbalancing_Event`. The default event fires an action that logs to a text file called offline.log on the C: drive. Add a custom action to this event's Action tab to modify what happens when a server status changes.

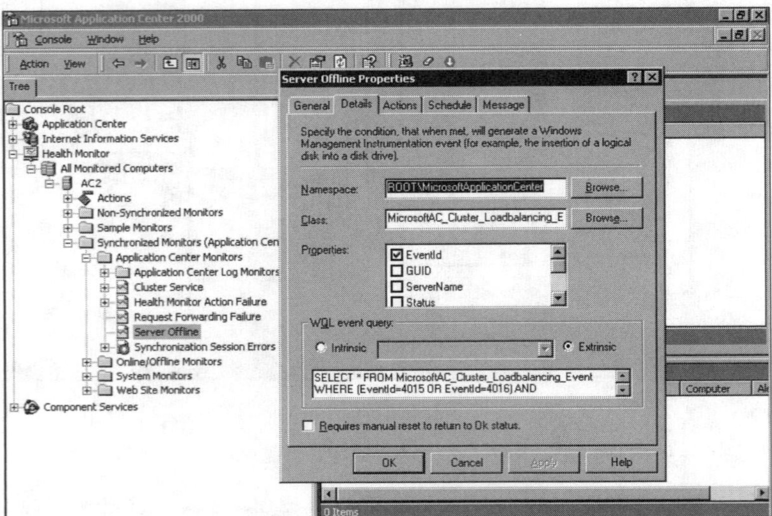

FIGURE 16.13
The Server Offline event in Health Monitor, with its Properties page.

With the default installation of Application Center, it is not possible to monitor load-balancing status changes of cluster members that use hardware load balancing. However, a good discussion of how to do this is available in the Application Center 2000 Resource Kit from Microsoft. The resource kit provides a command-line tool and some special MOF files that add the appropriate WMI events to manage the state of members that use hardware load balancers.

Using Health Monitor to Run Custom Deployment Scripts

Application Center 2000 lacks a key feature for customized deployment scenarios: launching scripts before, during, and after an application is deployed. There is no way in the GUI to associate a script action with an application. For that matter there is no way to associate a script action with an application. If an application's deployment requirements don't fit within the supported application resources (IIS metabase, Registry, DSN, file, and COM+

application), the only option is to use a named deployment. A named deployment is a deployment that has a well-known name. The deployment name is set when the deployment is created with the New Deployment Wizard or from the command line.

NOTE

Custom scripts can be run against specific servers because the name of the deployment is the server name. They can also be run during automatic cluster synchronization because that deployment is named after the cluster name.

Why the dependency on the deployment name? Application Center 2000 fires a series of WMI events during a replication session. These events are summarized in Table 16.2. The listed classes' full names come from the form `MicrosoftAC_Replication_Session_General_[EVENTTYPE]_Event`, where the event type is one of the WMI classes listed in the table. For example, `MicrosoftAC_Replication_Session_General_Success_Event` is from the class `Success`.

TABLE 16.2 WMI Events of Importance Fired During Replication

WMI Classes	*Description*
`Start`	This event fires at the start of every replication.
`Success`	This event fires at the successful end of every replication.
`Commit`	This event fires throughout the session at different replication stage changes.
`Failed`	This event fires when a replication job fails.

The only way to identify these events across synchronizations is by its name, which is a property on this WMI object called `ReplicationID`. Rather than simply associating a script with an application, the script must be associated with a deployment name and then the name must be reused any time the custom script needs to be run. Hopefully in future versions of Application Center 2000, a script item will be a standard resource for an Application Center application.

Listing 16.4 shows a script that will wait on a `Success` event to fire from the replication engine. Run this script on a cluster controller to catch the `Success` event.

LISTING 16.4 An Example of a Script That Handles a Replication Event

```
Dim strState, intCount, objEvents

Set objEvents = GetObject("winmgmts:root\MicrosoftApplicationCenter") _
    .ExecNotificationQuery ("select * from  " & _
    "MicrosoftAC_Replication_Session_General_Success_Event")

Set objReplicationEvent=objEvents.NextEvent
WScript.Echo  "EventID " & objReplicationEvent.EventID
WScript.Echo  "GUID " & objReplicationEvent.GUID
WScript.Echo  "ReplicationID " & objReplicationEvent.ReplicationID
WScript.Echo  "ReplicationJobID " & objReplicationEvent.ReplicationJobID
WScript.Echo  "Status " & objReplicationEvent.Status
WScript.Echo  "StatusMessage " & objReplicationEvent.StatusMessage
WScript.Echo  "TimeGenerated " & objReplicationEvent.TimeGenerated
WScript.Echo  "Type " & objReplicationEvent.Type
```

The `objEvents.NextEvent` command waits for the event to trigger before the script continues. To associate a script with an Application Center 2000 deployment using Health Monitor and Fire Script, perform the following steps:

1. Open the Health Monitor node in the Application Center 2000 console.
2. Right-click Actions and choose a new script action.
3. Click Browse and navigate to the target script action. Select the target script type.
4. Click OK to create the new action.
5. Right-click Synchronized Monitors (Application Center) and select New, Data Collector, WMI Event Query.
6. Set the namespace to `ROOT\MicrosoftApplicationCenter` and the class to `MicrosoftAC_Replication_Session_General_Success_Event`. Select the property ReplicationID because this is the name of the deployment.
7. Edit the WQL query so that it shows `Select * from MicrosoftAC_Replication_Session_General_Success_Event where Target='localhost'`.
8. Click the Actions property page and click the * button.
9. Choose the target actions and set the execute condition to Warning.
10. Press OK to close the WMI Event Query Properties page and create the new data collector.
11. In the Thresholds view for this new monitor, double-click # of Instances Collected and change the condition from # of Instances Collected to `ReplicationID`.

12. Change the Is Greater Than option to the Contains the Text option.
13. Change 0 to Fire Script.
14. Change the Following Will Occur field to The Status Changes to Warning.
15. Press OK.

Now whenever a deployment named Fire Script is created, the actions associated with this monitor will fire on the target member(s).

Deploying Site Server 3.0 Membership Sites with Application Center 2000

Existing Site Server 3.0 Web sites that use Personalization and Membership (P&M) can leverage Application Center 2000 to automate some of the P&M deployment tasks. This section assumes that the reader is familiar with the challenges of configuring P&M, but a brief overview helps explain how Application Center 2000 adds value to the process. P&M configuration is a two-step process on each member of the cluster and involves these steps:

1. Configuring a P&M server instance. This server is really just a collection of configuration information that includes a reference to a Windows NT SAM database or a Site Server 3.0 LDAP instance.
2. Mapping a P&M server instance to a specific Web site in IIS. This ties the P&M server configuration to a Web site and provides the Web site with a way to manage security and track users as they travel from page to page.

Configuration of the P&M server instance must be done manually on each server, either by hand or with the PMADMIN.VBS script. Although it might seem possible to leverage Application Center to transfer the registry settings and metabase entries that P&M uses, this does not work. A P&M server instance needs passwords for the membership management account and the membership proxy account. P&M stores this password information in the registry at `HKEY_LOCAL_MACHINE/SECURITY/Policy/Secrets`. The keys in this section are machine-specific; if they are replicated to other servers, they will not function.

Mapping of the P&M server instance is a step that can be automated and deployed by Application Center 2000. A mapping is simply a metabase entry, and Application Center 2000 supports the replication of any metabase path through the command-line tool AC.EXE.

NOTE

For more information on using the AC.EXE for Application Center 2000, see Appendix I, "Application Center Command-Line Reference."

The membership-mapping information is stored in the metabase at the /LM/Memebership/Mappings/W3SVC/<Web Site Virtual ID> key. The Web site virtual ID is the number that corresponds to the virtual ID of the Web site that is mapped to the P&M instance. Here is an example of using AC.EXE to add a metabase path to a membership mapping:

```
REM Add an IIS Resource
AC APPLICATION /ADDRESOURCE /NAME:MyApplication /RESOURCETYPE:IIS
/RESOURCEPATH:/LM/Membership/Mappings/W3SVC/3
```

This adds the mapping information for the Web site with the virtual ID of 3 to the application MyApplication. Figure 16.14 shows the MyApplication application resource list from the Application Center 2000 console. Notice that there is now a metabase entry icon with the label LM/Membership/Mappings/W3SVC/3.

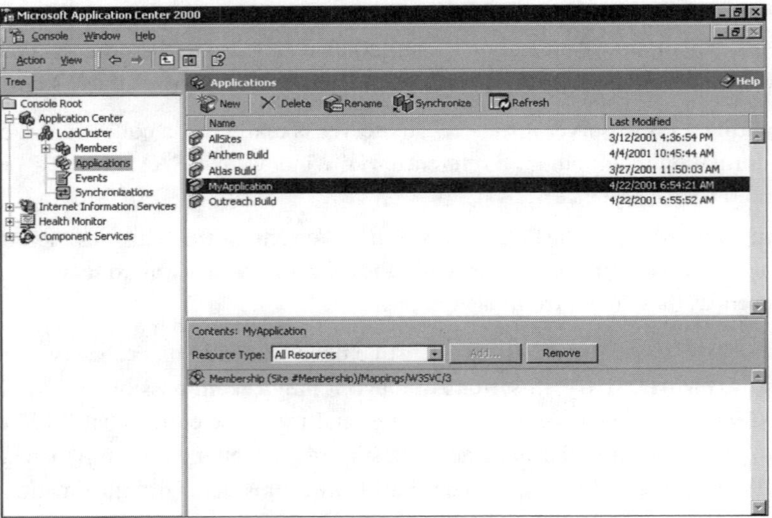

FIGURE 16.14

The membership mapping application resource entry.

To properly deploy a P&M site with Application Center 2000, take the following steps on the cluster controller:

1. Create the P&M server instance either manually or with the PMADMIN.VBS tool.
2. Map the P&M instance to the Web site either manually or with the PMADMIN.VBS tool.
3. Add the P&M mapping to the target application using the command-line tool AC.EXE.

On the members of the cluster, create the P&M server instance either manually or with the PMADMIN.VBS tool.

After the P&M server instance is created on the cluster members, deploy the application normally. The mapping will be installed automatically during Application Center 2000 metabase replication, eliminating a time-consuming step in the deployment of a Site Server 3.0 P&M site.

Configuring Security for Cross-domain Deployments

Application Center supports cross-domain deployments, but the main caveat is that security information that is tied to a domain does not get translated across domain boundaries. COM+ applications and IIS objects that have security configuration based on domain accounts will fail to deploy if the target is a cluster controller in a different security domain. For example, when Application Center 2000 verifies that a COM+ application has deployed correctly, it makes sure that the account information in the COM+ catalog is correct. When it tries to access an account from a different domain than the cluster controller is in, the deployment fails because the account information is unavailable.

Too often, administrators configure COM+ and IIS with domain accounts for convenience. Or, they feel that a local account does not have sufficient permissions to complete the tasks required of the application account. In most cases, this is not true. For a COM+ application, the security credentials that it uses, outside of role-based security, are primarily used for accessing local resources. Any account on a server has the proper access level to launch and access local resources by default. It is not even necessary for the user to be a member of any group on the local server for most COM+ application scenarios to have adequate permissions. This is actually a desired configuration because it makes application accounts relatively useless for anything other than the applications that they support. Beyond that, using local accounts makes deploying across domain boundaries easy with Application Center. The only requirement is that the server use mirrored accounts.

NEW TERM A *mirrored account* is two or more accounts that have the same username and password but that reside on separate servers. Mirrored accounts will have different security identifiers.

With a mirrored account, Application Center 2000 can successfully deploy a COM+ application or IIS object with security configuration across domain boundaries. Make sure that the account information does not specify a server name as in Figure 16.15. The AC1/ComPlusUser will not correctly deploy, even to other members in the cluster. Use ComPlusUser only, and the COM+ application will deploy anywhere a mirrored ComPlusUser account exists.

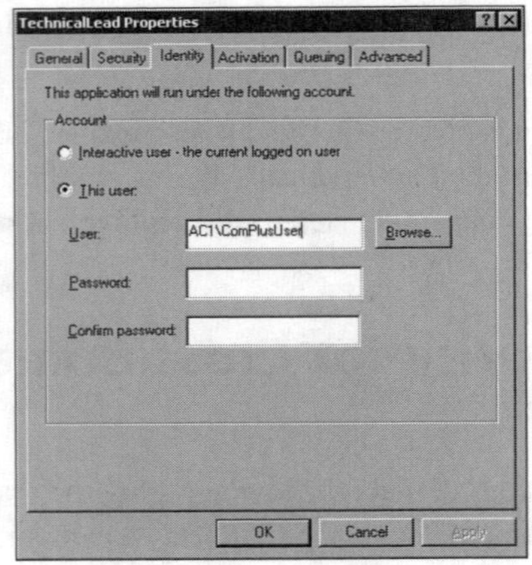

FIGURE 16.15
An improper configuration for mirrored accounts.

Use local mirrored accounts for security configuration. This means that every server in the deployment environment must have the same mirrored account information. This might seem like a considerable amount of work, but the reality is that with mirrored accounts, the security information for the application is done on a stager only once. Listing 16.5 shows a script to automate the creation of mirrored accounts on a server.

LISTING 16.5 Helpful Script to Create a Local User for Mirrored Accounts

```
' Create the COMPlusUser
CreateUser "COMPlusUser", "password", "COMPlusUser", "Application Account"
AddUserToGroup "COMPlusUser", "Guests"

'The following are the support functions for user creation
Function GetLocalServerName()
Dim WS
Set WS = CreateObject("WSCRIPT.NETWORK")
GetLocalServerName = WS.Computername
Set WS=nothing
End Function

Sub CreateUser(strUserName, strPassword, strFullName, strDescription)
Dim strServerName,
Dim myComputer
Dim newUser

'Get the local server name for the GetObject
```

LISTING 16.5 Continued

```
strServerName = GetLocalServerName

'Get the local computer object to create accounts
Set myComputer = GetObject("WinNT://" & strServerName)

On Error Resume Next
'Remove the old account if it exists
myComputer.Delete "user", strUsername
On Error Goto 0

' Create the new user account
Set newUser = myComputer.Create("user", strUsername)

' Set properties in the new user account
newUser.SetPassword strPassword
newUser.FullName = strFullName
newUser.Description = strDescription

'Commit the account information
newUser.SetInfo
End Sub

Sub AddUserToGroup(strUserName, strGroup)
Dim myGroup
Dim myUser
Dim strServerName

On Error Resume Next
'Get the local server name for the GetObject
strServerName = GetLocalServerName

'Get the group name from the local server
Set myGroup = GetObject("WinNT://" & strServerName & "/" & strGroup & ",group")

'Get the user from the local server
Set myUser = GetObject("WinNT://" & strServerName &
➥ "/" & strUserName & ",user")

'Add the user to the group
myGroup.Add(myUser.ADsPath)
End Sub
```

If using local accounts is not an option, cross-domain deployments from cluster controller to a controller with security dependencies will not work. Any IIS security configuration and all COM+ applications must be deployed by hand across security domain boundaries.

Summary

Application Center 2000 is an incredible tool for managing Web farms. The breadth of capabilities and customizability is huge and requires an understanding of diverse topics and esoteric technologies. Understanding the advanced features of Application Center 2000 better equips an administrator to deal with any challenges faced during the lifetime of a Web farm.

Introducing Windows Server Clusters

CHAPTER

17

IN THIS CHAPTER

Windows Server clusters provide the highest level of availability for applications that do not scale out. Without Windows Server clusters, these applications live on a single server, and their availability is tied to the failure rate of that server's hardware and software components. In a Windows Server cluster, these applications gain the capability to exist virtually across multiple servers, increasing their availability to that of two or more servers.

Windows Server clusters work by running specialized hardware and software components that are designed to make multiple independent computer systems behave as one unit. The hardware that Windows Server clusters use is called a *shared cluster storage device* because all members in the cluster attach to it directly and can gain control of the physical disks it manages. The Windows Cluster Server software knows how to manage access to this shared disk resource and through intracluster network communication makes decisions about application and cluster node availability in conjunction with data stored on the shared drives. Windows Server clusters are considered shared-nothing clusters that use shared disk storage to store the persistent state of a cluster. They don't use a distributed lock manager to control access to the physical disks and therefore are much simpler to configure and manage.

NEW TERM *Intracluster* network communication is the exchange of packets between two or more servers in a cluster for managing the state of the cluster as a single unit.

The Cluster service, a component of the Windows Server cluster's software, exchanges heartbeat and status information with other Cluster services on other nodes of the cluster. These status messages direct the activity of the cluster nodes and are used to determine when a node is offline, has a change to its cluster configuration, or has had a resource or hardware failure. This exchange of status messages between nodes in a Windows Server cluster is the fabric that makes these nodes unlike regular servers.

NEW TERM A *node* is a server that is a member of a Windows Server cluster. It can also be referred to as a *cluster node*.

The Cluster service also interacts with a Resource Monitor to access application resources that are a part of the cluster. These resources make up the application components that are virtualized by the Cluster service. A Resource Monitor provides a layer of abstraction and application protection because it exists outside the Cluster service process and because it intercepts all communication between real resources, such as physical disks, and the Cluster service. When a resource fails on a particular node, the Cluster service attempts to restart that service on the other nodes of the cluster. This is how Windows Server clusters increase the availability of the resources they manage.

The goals of this chapter are to help you

- Understand the software components involved in creating and managing Windows Server clusters.

- Understand the special hardware and software requirements of Windows Server clusters. Included is a discussion of the hardware compatibility list, OS support, shared disk technologies, and domain membership requirements.
- Understand the features of Windows Server clusters to help plan how to use them in a Web farm. Included is a discussion of availability, server cluster software components, clustering scenarios, virtual servers, server cluster resources, and the administrative console.

Windows Server Cluster Components

Windows Server clusters are made up of specialized software components and a shared external hard disk storage array. All Windows Server clusters share the following software components:

- A *Cluster service* that is a standard Windows NT service and is the brain of the cluster. This service is installed to all nodes of the cluster and controls the lifetime of applications and resources in the cluster. The Cluster service determines the status of cluster members and applications through intracluster communication and specific status events from cluster-aware applications. The Cluster service must run as a Windows NT domain account.
- *Resources and Resource Monitors* are the components that a Windows Server cluster manages. These components are virtualized representations of real resources that can be transferred from one node to the other. Examples of resources include file shares, network names, and SQL Server. The Resource Monitor sits between the Cluster service, in its own dedicated NT process, and a resource to protect the Cluster service from catastrophic resource failures during failover or from a poorly written resource's code.
- The *Cluster Administrator* is a console application that provides administrative support for managing the cluster. From this console all the resources, groups, and nodes of a cluster are configured, added, removed, and managed. The Cluster Administrator console also provides an accurate status of all the resources in the cluster in real-time.

Hardware and Software Requirements

Windows Server clusters have special hardware and software requirements for creating the cluster and for the applications that run on a cluster. These requirements include support for a subset of Microsoft's operating systems, two or more servers, shared disk technology, and NT domain membership.

Operating System Support

Installing and configuring Windows Server clusters requires Advanced Server 2000, Datacenter Server 2000 or Windows NT 4 Enterprise Edition. This book covers configuring for Windows

2000 Server platforms only. Windows Server clusters will not install onto Windows Professional 2000 or Windows Server 2000. When using Advanced Server, a two-node cluster is the only configuration supported and available. When using Datacenter Server 2000, up to four nodes can exist in a single cluster. Datacenter Server configurations are available only through OEM channels and are beyond the scope of this book. It is not possible to purchase Datacenter Server 2000 from Microsoft directly, so each vendor will have different setup and configuration options.

NOTE

For more information on Datacenter Server 2000 and for a list of certified OEM vendors, see `http://www.microsoft.com/windows2000/guide/datacenter/overview/default.asp`.

Server Architecture

Windows Server clusters on Advanced Server 2000 support two-node clustering only. It is recommended that the servers in a two-node cluster have identical hardware and software installed. This will minimize compatibility issues and simplify configuration. To receive technical support from Microsoft for Windows clusters, all hardware and software must comply with the hardware compatibility list.

NOTE

To check the hardware compatibility list, see `http://www.microsoft.com/hcl`. Search for "cluster" to see specific hardware requirements for Microsoft Cluster service.

Shared Disk Technologies

Windows Server clusters are shared-nothing clusters that rely on shared disk storage for persisting cluster state. This means that the servers in a cluster use a shared storage area to store configuration and status information about the resources installed on a cluster. Windows Server clusters call this shared status area the *quorum resource*. The quorum resource contains all the necessary information to restore a cluster node to service. This information is called the *cluster database*.

NEW TERM The *quorum resource* is a shared storage resource for Windows Server clusters. The quorum drive is where a cluster maintains a master copy of configuration data for all the nodes of the cluster.

Most shared disk clustering technologies have special configuration requirements due to the specialized nature of shared disk hardware. Most vendors have detailed instructions for properly configuring two or more servers to use the same set of shared drives. See Appendix H, "Configuring Shared Disk Technologies," for some general guidelines for configuring SCSI and fiber channel–based solutions. However, consult the shared disk manufacturer's installation guide for more detailed instructions.

Membership in a Domain

Windows Server clusters require that all members of a cluster be members of a valid Windows 2000 or NT4 domain. Windows Server clusters use domain accounts for the Cluster service and all clustered application resources. Windows Server clusters use domain accounts during failover scenarios. When one server's resources have moved to a different node in the cluster, these resources cannot acquire an ACL from a local server account on the failed node because the other node may not be available. This also means that domains with only one domain controller create a single point of failure for clustering. If the domain is unavailable, the Cluster service cannot properly manage the movement of resources from one node to another.

NEW TERM *Failover* is the process of transferring cluster resources, such as network names or SQL Server, from one node to another. Failover occurs when the cluster determines that a node in the cluster has become unavailable or that an application resource has failed.

Application Requirements

Windows Server clusters support only applications that use TCP/IP protocols for communication with clients. This includes clients that use DCOM, Named Pipes, and any other protocol that uses TCP/IP as its transport. Clustered applications must be able to specify the target for application-specific data. If the application cannot store its data on the shared drives of a cluster or in the Registry, it cannot participate in failover scenarios.

Clients of clustered applications must be able to reconnect if the network becomes unavailable. During failover and failback, the network presence of a cluster application will move from one node to the other. This move interrupts the connection of network clients and, if they don't attempt to reconnect after a network failure, even though the application resources are running on a new node in the cluster, clients will not automatically use them.

NEW TERM *Failback* is the reverse of failover. Failback occurs when a failed node reestablishes communication with the controlling node of a cluster (the node that has control of the quorum resource). Once the failback is initiated, all the original resources transfer back to the failed node, and the cluster is restored to its original state.

Clustering Feature Overview

The following sections outline some of the most important features of Windows Server clusters. These features are key to any successful Web farm. Understanding these features is the first step in realizing the power of Windows Server clusters. Features covered include

- Using Windows Server clusters to provide high availability for Windows applications such as SQL Server and custom applications.
- Using different clustering scenarios to take advantage of different configurations and fulfill application requirements.
- Using virtual servers to abstract the resolution of network resources from one server to a cluster.
- Describing the high-level resources available for clusters, including virtualized network names and physical disk subsystems that are shared across server clusters.
- Using the administrative console for an up-to-date graphical representation of the status of a cluster and simple management of clustered resources.
- Understanding the flexibility of configuring how clustered resources behave during failover scenarios.

High Availability

The goal of Windows Server clusters is to achieve high availability of mission-critical application components. High availability is achieved by using Windows Cluster service to remove single points of failure in application systems by making two machines appear as one. Any resource, such as file shares, NT services, SQL Server, or Exchange, can be clustered for high availability using Windows Server clusters.

NEW TERM A *resource* is a conceptual representation of an application component such as a physical disk drive or a network name. With Windows Server clusters, resources are said to be virtualized across the members of a cluster and can be owned by either node.

When a resource is in a clustered state, it can exist transparently on any node in a cluster. During failover, the Cluster service assures availability of these resources by starting them on the node that has control of the quorum resource. This means that even if the second node of the cluster is disconnected from the shared cluster storage, the resources it owns will come up on the first node. The Cluster service on the second node will shut down its resources until it can reestablish communication with the other node and the shared disk resources, eliminating potential conflicts for network-based access points.

Clustering Scenarios

Windows Server clusters provide considerable flexibility in arranging and using the resources available for applications. There are no set rules for how applications use the cluster nodes, and the capability to use cluster resources efficiently is purely a cost/benefit decision. A node that is serving resources is said to be "active." It is active because there are clients connected to the virtualized resources that are running on the node. A node that is not serving virtualized resources is said to be "passive." It is in a standby mode waiting for the first node to fail. This leads to two main clustering scenarios for application resources: Active/Active and Active/Passive. A third scenario involving only one machine provides no availability but does have some added capabilities for clustered resources.

Active/Active

In the Active/Active clustering scenario, both nodes of a cluster are actively serving client connections for different clustered resources. This is not a way to achieve scalability. A clustered resource is owned by one and only one node of a cluster at any one time. For example, an Active/Active cluster using SQL Server has two virtualized instances of SQL Server running across the nodes of a cluster.

During normal operation, each node of the cluster has a unique SQL Server instance that performs different database operations from the other. During a failover, the failed SQL Server instance is started on the other node, and two distinct instances of SQL Server run on the same physical node of the cluster sharing all node resources. In this situation, two SQL Server instances are highly available and each server fully utilizes its particular node during normal operations.

An Active/Active clustering scenario has the following advantages:

- Uses all hardware resources in a cluster.
- Common resource types can be organized across multiple machines for greater throughput during normal operation.

An Active/Active cluster scenario has the following disadvantages:

- During failover, resource performance could be affected if either node operates at over 50% capacity for scarce resources such as memory or CPU.
- Upgrades of clustered applications must be handled carefully and synchronized because most clustered applications don't support multiple versions of the same application on the same node.

Figure 17.1 shows an Active/Active clustering scenario with descriptions of application resources assigned to each node and what happens during failover.

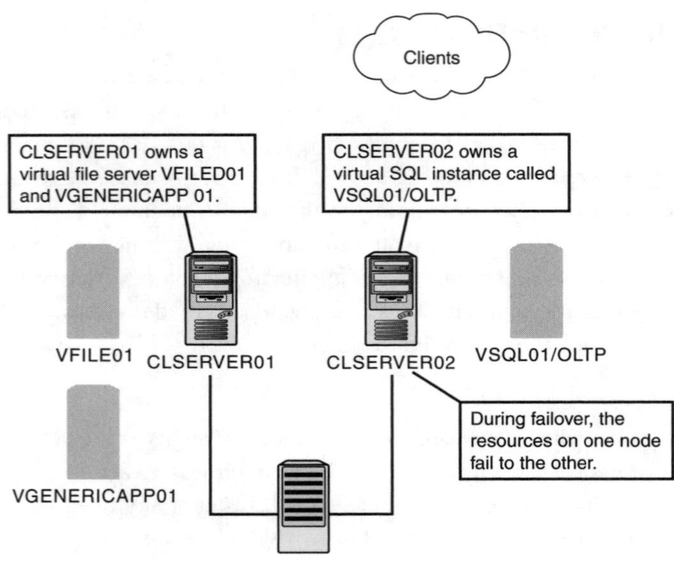

FIGURE 17.1
An Active/Active clustering scenario with sample resource assignments.

Active/Passive

In the Active/Passive cluster scenario, only one node at any given time is serving clustered resources for clients. This means that the passive node is a hot standby. For example, a cluster in Active/Passive mode could support a single instance of SQL Server. During normal operation that SQL Server instance runs on the first node of a cluster. During upgrades or failures, the second node of the cluster would perform the job of the first node.

An Active/Passive clustering scenario for application resources has the following advantages:

- If the hardware is identical for both nodes in a cluster, no performance degradation occurs during failover. This makes it easier to plan for upgrades.
- Mission-critical applications can be upgraded in a rolling fashion by failing resources to the active node and not failing back until the original node is upgraded.

An Active/Passive clustering scenario for application resources has the following disadvantages:

- Clustering hardware is wasted because one node in the cluster never hosts application resources.
- Clustering hardware that is not identical could affect performance of the clustered application during failover.

Figure 17.2 shows an Active/Passive cluster with sample resource assignments and what happens during failover.

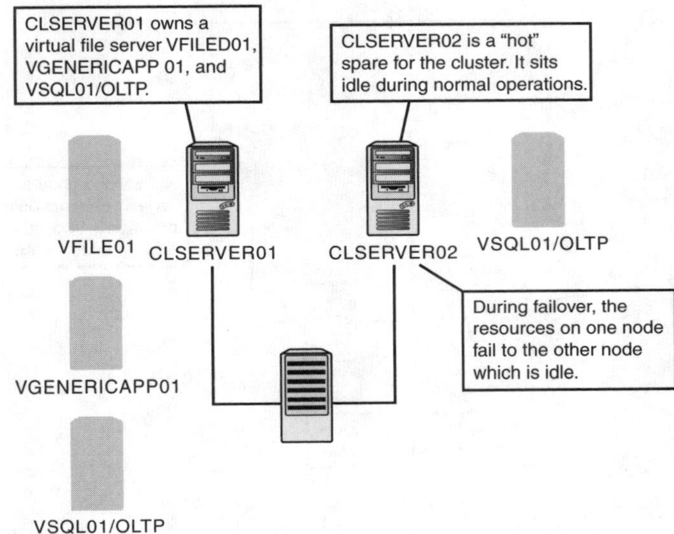

FIGURE 17.2
An Active/Passive clustering scenario with sample resource assignments.

Single Node

In a single-node cluster, none of the high-availability features of multiple machines acting as one are available. However, because Windows Server clusters enable the virtualization of application resources, it does provide an administrator with the capability to create a bank of virtual servers that is run on a single server. These virtual servers all act independently from a client perspective, but the administrator can manage them from one centralized console. A single-node cluster also provides the capability to add a second node in the future.

For example, a single-node cluster could host virtualized file servers for a corporation. Corporate users connect to the virtualized server for file sharing not aware that there is only one real server. From the administrator's perspective, all the servers and shares would be located on the same physical node, simplifying troubleshooting and management. Figure 17.3 shows a single-node cluster configured in this fashion.

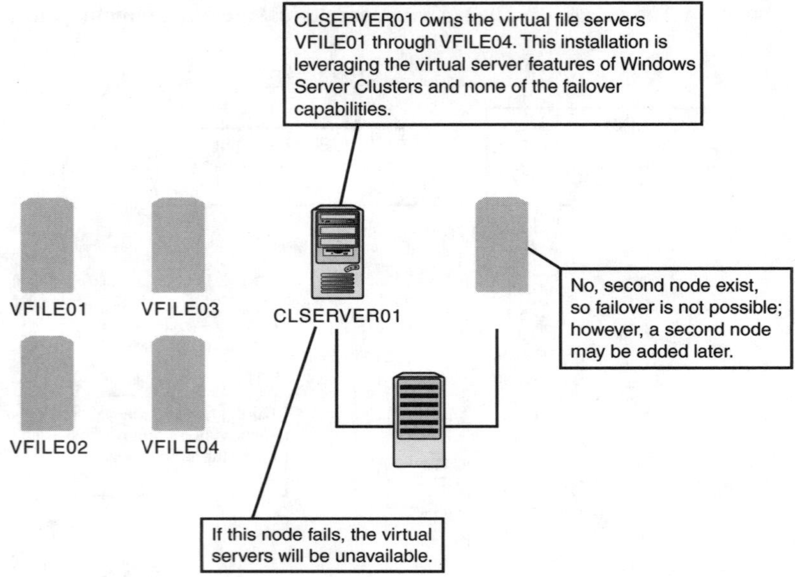
CLSERVER01 owns the virtual file servers VFILE01 through VFILE04. This installation is leveraging the virtual server features of Windows Server Clusters and none of the failover capabilities.
VFILE01
VFILE03
CLSERVER01
VFILE02
VFILE04
No, second node exist, so failover is not possible; however, a second node may be added later.
If this node fails, the virtual servers will be unavailable.

FIGURE 17.3
A single-node clustering scenario with sample resource assignments.

Console Management

Windows Server clusters have robust administrative console support for managing the resources, groups, and servers in a cluster. Administrators can treat the nodes in a cluster as one machine and manage which resources and groups belong to each node. The console is where all resources and groups are created and where information about the state of the cluster is displayed. Figure 17.4 shows the Cluster Administrator console.

The administrative console has a number of different organizational units or nodes for creating and managing different cluster objects. Each node type in the cluster console shows different information about the cluster. Some node types show different views of the same cluster information. Table 17.1 lists each node type, its parent node (if any), and a brief description of its function. Common administrative tasks for these nodes are covered in Chapter 19, "Clustering Application Resources."

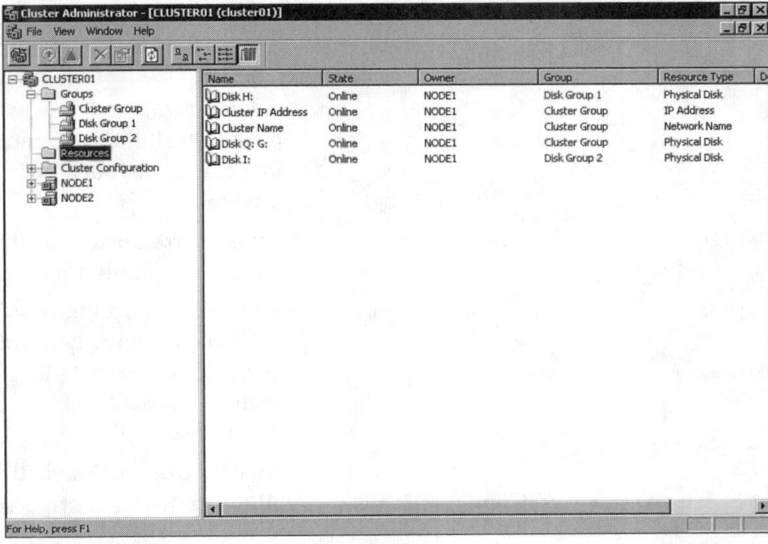

FIGURE 17.4
The Cluster Administrator console.

TABLE 17.1 Cluster Administrator Node Types

Node Type	*Parent Node*	*Description*
Cluster	None	The root node in the console. This node contains all other nodes and represents the top-level cluster object. Specify from this node the quorum resource and network for private intr-acluster communication.
Groups	Cluster	An organizational node that contains all the groups of a cluster. Create new groups and resources and configure new applications from this node.
Group	Groups	A group node that contains cluster resources and is where failover and failback policies are configured. All resources must belong to a group, and a group must be assigned to a cluster member by default.

TABLE 17.1 Continued

Node Type	*Parent Node*	*Description*
Resources	Cluster	An organizational node whose Details pane lists all the configured resources in a cluster and their current cluster status.
Cluster Configuration	Cluster	An organizational node that contains other configuration-only nodes.
Resource Types	Cluster	This node lists all the configuration-available resource types installed on a cluster. The list includes resources such as physical disk and SQL Server 7.0 (if installed).
Networks	Cluster Configuration	An organizational node that contains all the networks configured for a cluster.
Network	Networks	A configuration node for a specific network in a cluster. Networks are defined when creating a cluster and can be used for private (intracluster), public, or mixed use.
Network Interfaces	Networks	This node lists all the available network interfaces for all members of the cluster, their current states, and their configurations.
Cluster Member	Cluster	This node represents a physical server in the cluster. Overall membership and status of a node are controlled from this point. There is one Cluster Member node for each cluster member.
Active Groups	Node	This node lists the active or assigned groups for a particular member. This is usually a subset of the groups listed in the Groups node.
Active Resources	Node	This node lists the resources assigned to the groups for a particular Cluster node. This is usually a subset of the resources listed in the Resources node.

TABLE 17.1 Continued

Node Type	*Parent Node*	*Description*
Network Interfaces	Node	This node lists the network interfaces for a particular node in a cluster. This is a subset of the Network Interfaces node under the Cluster Configuration node.

Virtual Servers

One of the most useful features of Windows Server clusters is their capability to create virtual servers. Virtual servers appear as regular servers in an NT network. These servers have dedicated IP addresses and have the network footprint like a real server but without the dedicated hardware. Virtual servers enable administrators to create groups of servers from one server and direct users and applications to use those resources at the server-name level. This simplifies configuration and creates a layer of abstraction between the client and the server that gives Windows Server cluster its high-availability characteristics.

A virtual server is a combination of the IP address, a network name resource, and any clustered applications. These resources are then stored in the same group or folder from the cluster console and failover and failback are configured as a single unit. Creating resources and groups is covered in Chapter 19.

Cluster Resources

Windows Server clusters define special cluster components called *resources*. A resource can be a physical component such as a physical disk or a logical component such as a file share. All cluster resources can be brought online and taken offline through the Cluster Administrator. All cluster resources are managed in a cluster and can be owned only by a single node in the cluster at any given time.

A cluster resource is implemented with a special DLL called a *resource DLL*. A resource DLL is a cluster-aware program that provides well-known entry points that a Resource Monitor uses to communicate with the specified resource. A Resource Monitor provides a layer of abstraction and process isolation from the Cluster service to protect it from resource DLL failures.

Configuration features of cluster server resources include group assignment, preferred node ownership, and dependant resource designation. The following section describes some of the built-in cluster resources. Configuring these resources is covered in Chapter 19.

NEW TERM A *dependant resource* is a cluster resource that requires other cluster resources to function. Examples of dependant resources are SQL Server resources that require specific physical disks to operate or network names that depend on IP addresses to create a virtual server.

Physical Disk

A physical disk resource maps a cluster resource to a shared cluster storage disk drive. Physical disks can be owned by only one node at a time to prevent corruption. Physical disks have the same drive letter on all nodes of a cluster. As with all cluster resources, physical disks are members of groups, used by other resources as dependencies, and moved between nodes of the cluster.

Network Name

A network name cluster resource creates a new network identity for a cluster. This network name is like any other resource on the network; it will even register itself in dynamic DNS in a Windows 2000 domain. Use a network name and an IP resource in a group to create a virtual server that can failover from node to node.

Internet Protocol

The Internet Protocol resource type creates a virtualized IP address that exists on a network just like an IP address bound to a network adapter. Clients can connect to IP resources just as they would to real IP addresses bound to network adapters. To create a virtual server, use the IP resource with a network name in the same group.

Generic Application

The generic application resource enables the creation of cluster resources that failover for any standard Windows executable, including programs such as Notepad that are not cluster aware. A generic application resource has a few requirements: that the location of its configuration can be specified on shared cluster storage, that it be addressable by standard TCP/IP protocols, and that clients be able to reconnect when the virtual server housing the application is moved from one node to the other.

For a generic application resource to failover, it must be installed to both nodes of the cluster in the same place. If the application stores application or configuration data on a physical disk, this disk should be part of shared cluster storage. This enables the data for the application to failover with the application and ensures that the application starts up in the same state on the other node. An application with no special configuration or application data can be installed normally to the local hard drives of all cluster nodes. The only way to ensure that a generic application is functioning correctly and will failover successfully is to test it. See Chapter 19 for more information and an example of creating and testing a generic application resource.

Generic Service

The generic service resource is similar to a generic application resource except that it applies to Windows NT services. Cluster service does not understand how to determine if a service is functioning correctly, so it uses the state in a service manager to determine failover conditions. For example, if a service is stopped on its primary node, Cluster service becomes aware of the condition and starts the service on the other node.

For a generic service resource to failover, it must be installed to both nodes of the cluster in the same place. If the service stores service or configuration data on a physical disk, this disk should be part of shared cluster storage. This enables the data for the service to failover with the service and ensures that the service starts up in the same state on the other node. A service with no special configuration or application data can be installed normally to the local hard drives of all cluster nodes. The only way to ensure that a generic service is functioning correctly and will failover successfully is to test it. See Chapter 19 for more information and an example of creating and testing a generic service resource.

File Share

A file share cluster resource is a virtualized version of a standard Windows file share. Use file share resources to provide high-availability file share points. Use virtual servers and file share resources in conjunction to create many virtual file servers on a single cluster.

Print Spooler

The Print Spooler resource enables the clustering of printers. Clustering a printer requires a virtual server and a network-attached printer. Local printers attached to cluster members cannot failover to other nodes. Each virtual server can contain only one print spooler. Clients use the Print Spooler resource in the same way as they use a noncluster print spooler, by either network name or IP address. Drivers for the printer must be installed on both nodes of the cluster.

During failover, the current document being spooled is restarted on the failover node. When performing a manual move of the print spooler from one node to another, the Cluster service waits for pending jobs to finish before moving the resources.

Installing Windows Server Cluster Software

The software to configure and manage Windows Server clusters is installed from the Add/Remove Programs dialog in Control Panel. This will launch the Cluster Service Configuration Wizard. The Windows Server cluster software must be installed to each member of the cluster in succession. Details for completing this wizard for both cluster members is covered in Chapter 18, "Creating a Windows 2000 Server Cluster."

To install the administrative client only, run the `ADMINPAK.MSI` file from the `I386` directory of any Windows 2000 server product. Any NT or 2000 Professional or server product with the Cluster Administrator installed can connect to and administer any Windows Server cluster. To administer the cluster remotely, grant administrative privileges to a user to both members of a cluster. This can be accomplished by adding the target user to the Administrator group on both members of a cluster or by adding the user to a particular domain-level administrative group that has administrative privileges on both members of the cluster.

TIP

Administrative users must have Administrator privileges on both cluster members to administer the cluster.

Summary

Windows Server clusters have special software and hardware requirements that make them more difficult to configure and deploy initially. In the Windows 2000 server space, Windows Server clusters require at least Advanced Server 2000. They also require a shared disk subsystem, membership in a domain, and applications that use TCP/IP to communicate with clients. Windows Server clusters offer the only viable option for increasing the availability of applications that meet these requirements but have no built-in availability features.

Windows Server clusters have many special features. They have the capability to provide highly configurable clustering support, both for Active/Active clusters, in which both nodes in a cluster do the work, and for Active/Passive clusters in which one node is a "hot-swap" standby, giving the highest degree of availability. Cluster Server enables the creation of virtual servers. A virtual server is exactly like a real server from the perspective of its client but exists on a single node of a cluster.

Windows Server clusters provide the highest level of availability for the resources they manage. By enabling administrators to manage two servers as a single unit, clusters decrease the complexity of managing multiple servers and grant normally single-server applications in a Web farm such as Exchange and SQL Server the availability of two servers instead of one.

Creating a Windows 2000 Server Cluster

CHAPTER

18

One of the most challenging tasks for an administrator is the creation of a Windows Server cluster. This reputation of configuration complexity for server clusters is due to its special hardware requirements. Windows Server clustering requires a shared storage array and will not install to a server without such a device. Until recently, shared cluster hardware was both expensive and difficult to configure. This is slowly changing as vendors such as Compaq introduce Cluster in a Box, a specialized server line, that is perfect for small-to-medium size businesses that need the high availability of Windows Cluster Server. Compaq's Cluster in a Box is a self-contained unit with two servers and a shared storage array. Configuration is as simple as following the step-by-step instructions provided in the installation guide.

NOTE

The different requirements for configuring each vendor's shared storage solution and the installation of the drivers for accessing these storage devices are beyond the scope of this book. Consult the vendor documentation for specific details.

This chapter assumes that the nodes in the cluster have

- Windows 2000 Advanced Server installed.
- The shared storage driver successfully installed.
- The physical drives of the shared storage area visible from Disk Administrator.

CAUTION

Never turn on more than one node of the cluster at a time before installing Windows Cluster Server. Many shared storage devices can malfunction (some even catastrophically) without the special software that Windows Server cluster provides to share the disks across multiple servers.

The goals of this chapter are to help you

- Learn how to launch the Cluster Service Configuration Wizard on each node of a cluster. Each step in the wizard is covered in detail, including situations that arise only in certain conditions.
- Learn how to reboot a cluster, test the state of changing resources, and move groups to test that a cluster is functioning correctly.

Launching the Cluster Service Configuration Wizard

To install the software for a Windows Server cluster, launch the Control Panel Add/Remove Programs applet. Click the Components button on this dialog to display the Windows Components dialog box. From the list of Windows components, select the Cluster Service check box as shown in Figure 18.1.

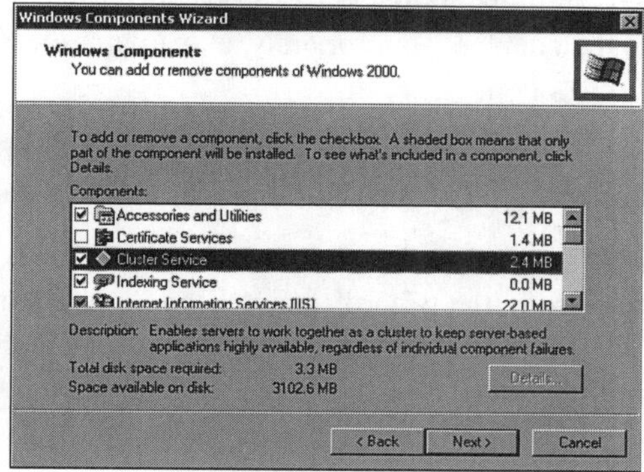

FIGURE 18.1
Selecting Cluster Service in the Windows Components dialog.

Clicking the Next button launches the Cluster Service Configuration Wizard. The following conditions will cause the Cluster Service Configuration Wizard to end prematurely:

- Attempting to install the Cluster service to a Windows 2000 Server or Windows 2000 Professional edition or nonenterprise version of the NT 4 Server operating system.
- Attempting to install the Cluster service to a server that does not have a shared cluster storage drive installed.
- Attempting to install the Cluster service to a server that is not a member of a valid NT or Windows 2000 domain.

Using the Cluster Service Configuration Wizard on the First Node

Before beginning the cluster wizard on the first node, complete the following steps:

1. Make sure the shared storage for the cluster is available and configured in Disk Administrator. This storage is just like any other storage and should have drive letters assigned; it must be formatted as NTFS.

2. Assign names to the drives that correspond to their intended drive letters. For example, name the I: drive `IDISK` or `IDRIVE`. This helps when configuring other members of the cluster.
3. Create a 100MB partition in the shared storage area and assign it the drive letter Q. This is for the quorum resource. Name this drive `QUORUM`.
4. Join the first cluster node to a Windows NT or 2000 domain.
5. Assign static IP addresses to all network adapters that are for cluster use. Make sure these network adapters are functioning correctly or the cluster wizard will not recognize them as valid. Name the adapters appropriately, using names such as `management`, `heartbeat`, `client`, and so on.
6. Create a unique domain user account with normal user privileges for use by the cluster.
7. Write down all this information for use on the second node of the cluster.

The Cluster Service Configuration Wizard (cluster wizard) must be successfully completed on each node in a cluster. The steps in the wizard change according to a number of conditions, including the number and type of network adapters and whether it is the first or second node. Figure 18.2 shows a high-level overview of the steps involved in completing the first node of a new server cluster.

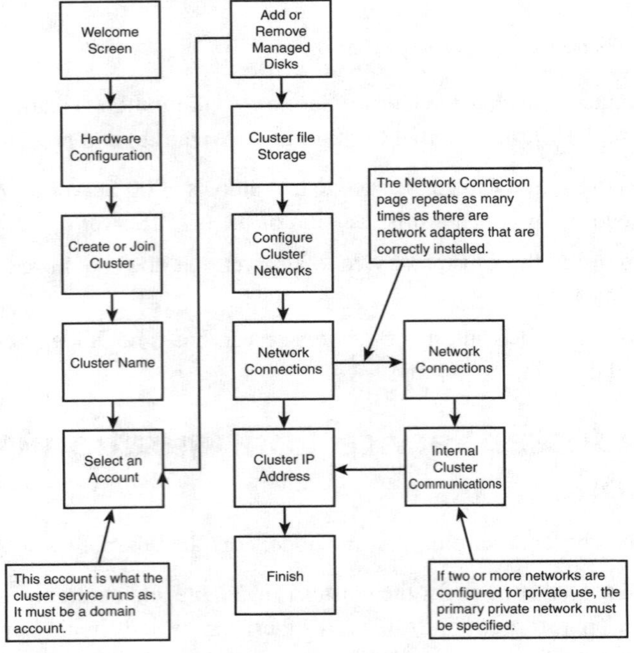

FIGURE 18.2

The path through the cluster wizard for the first node.

Accepting the Hardware Compatibility Requirements

After the welcome page, the wizard shows the Hardware Configuration page. In this page, Microsoft notifies the administrator that only certain approved cluster hardware is supported by Microsoft. This means that before choosing a Windows Server cluster solution, you should check the list at `http://www.microsoft.com/hwtest/hcl` and be sure that hardware used in the cluster is on this list. Figure 18.3 shows the Hardware Configuration page.

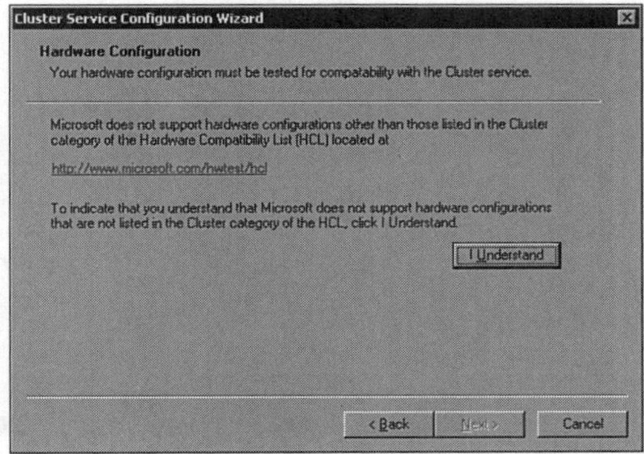

FIGURE 18.3
The Hardware Configuration page of the cluster wizard.

Click the I Understand button to enable the Next button to proceed to the Create or Join a Cluster page of the wizard.

Choosing to Configure the First Node

A cluster is a collection of computers or nodes. These nodes have special configuration and knowledge about the cluster they are part of. Creating a cluster requires a primary node. The primary node is no different from other nodes once the cluster is complete. It serves the role of cluster master while the other members join. Any member can be the primary node once cluster configuration is complete. Figure 18.4 shows the Create or Join a Cluster page of the wizard. On this page, choose to create the first node of the cluster by selecting the The First Node in the Cluster radio button and clicking the Next button.

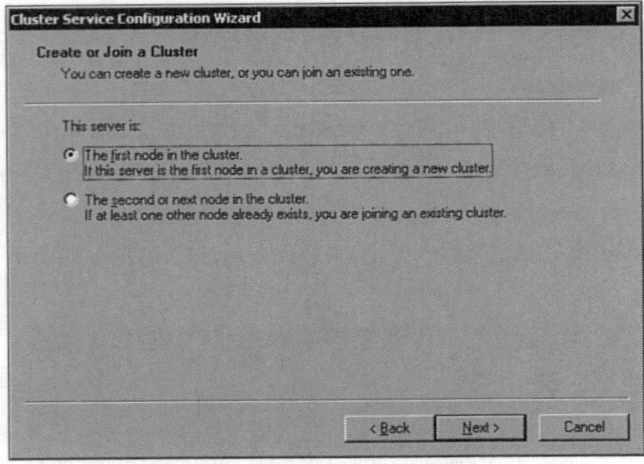

FIGURE 18.4
The Create or Join a Cluster page of the cluster wizard.

Choosing the Cluster Name

The cluster name is used to create the first virtual server in a Windows Server cluster. This name becomes a network-addressable entity that can be owned by any cluster member and represents the cluster. It is the network name that is used to address the configuration and management of a cluster locally or over the network. This name must be unique in the domain the cluster belongs to. For example, if a cluster is given the name `CLUSTER01` and the wizard finds a name conflict after checking the network, the wizard prompts for a different name. In a Windows 2000 domain with dynamic DNS enabled, this name will automatically register with DNS as the server's name does. This means the cluster name is addressable like a server on the network. A network name requires an IP address resource to be fully addressable over the network; this resource is configured later in the wizard.

Figure 18.5 shows the Cluster Name page of the cluster wizard. This is the network-addressable name that administrators use to administer a cluster remotely. It should be unique and descriptive of the cluster itself. Good examples of cluster names are `SQLCLUSTER01`, `FNPCLUSTER01`, and `EXCHGCLUSTER01`.

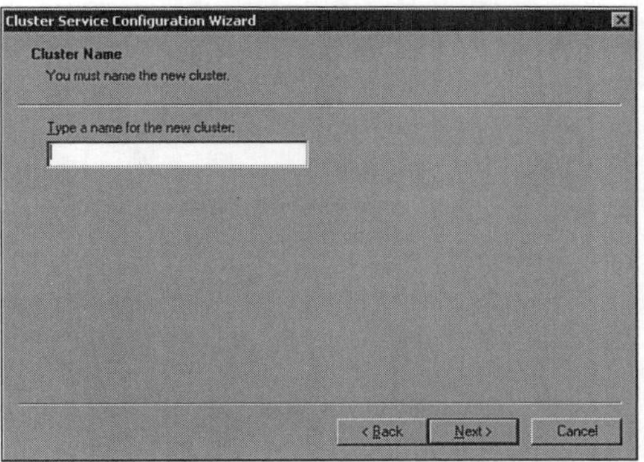

FIGURE 18.5
The Cluster Name page of the cluster wizard.

Selecting the Cluster Service Domain Account

Clusters require that a domain account be used on both nodes of the cluster to run the Cluster service. A domain account is required for all services or applications that require a user for access and authorization. During failover, local accounts on the failed node are unavailable. If a resource uses a local account from a specific node, it will fail to start because the security credentials of the user cannot be validated.

Figure 18.6 shows the Select an Account page of the cluster wizard. This domain account needs only normal domain user privileges because the wizard will grant Log On as a Service rights and add them to the local administrators group on each node.

TIP

Dedicate the cluster domain account to a cluster and do not use it for other services in the domain. In an environment with many clusters, each cluster should have its own domain account.

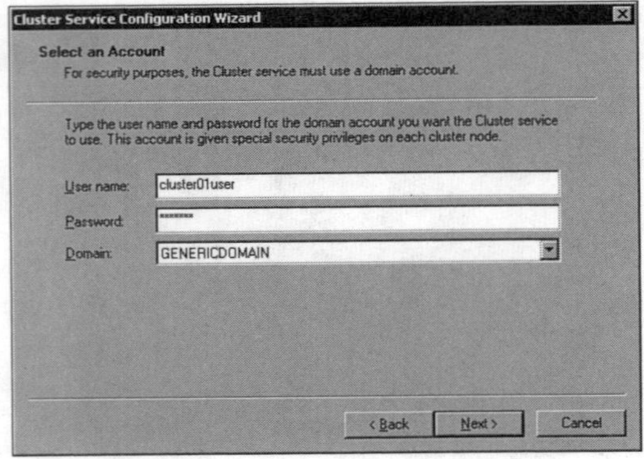

FIGURE 18.6
The Select an Account page of the cluster wizard.

Choosing Managed Disks from the Shared Drive Array

Clusters use shared managed disks for two reasons. Managed disks provide applications with a storage area that can move from node to node with the application. Cluster service uses a shared managed disk to store information about the state of the cluster. This shared drive dedicated to the Cluster service has a special name called the *quorum resource*.

Figure 18.7 shows the Add or Remove Managed Disks page of the cluster wizard. By default each configured managed disk is added to the cluster as a managed resource that can be shared across cluster nodes. Only in special circumstances should shared drives not be managed. To remove a drive from the managed section, click it and click Remove. To add a shared drive back to the managed pool, click the drive and click the Add button. There must be at least one shared drive for the quorum resource.

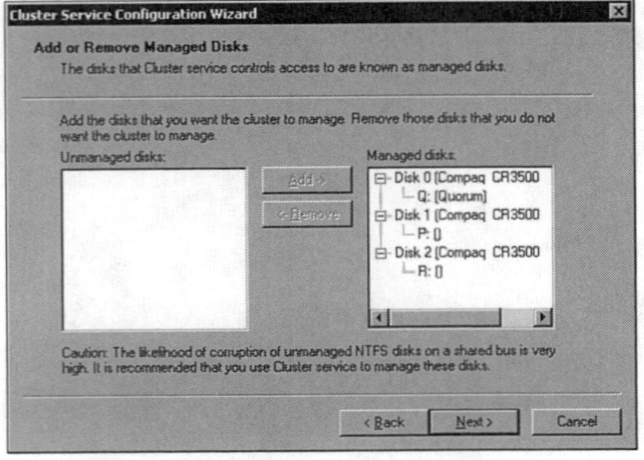

FIGURE 18.7
The Add or Remove Managed Disks page of the cluster wizard.

Selecting the Quorum Drive

The quorum resource is the brain of a Windows Server cluster. It is a node-independent shared storage area that contains all the data and configuration of the cluster in the cluster database. The cluster database contains a list of changes and events that have occurred on the cluster since it started.

To form a cluster, a node must be able to gain control of the quorum resource. This means that the physical drive resource that represents the quorum drive is owned by a particular node. Once this ownership is established, the cluster is formed. No other node will be able to access or take ownership of this resource as long as the original cluster node maintains ownership. For a second node to join a cluster, it must be able to communicate successfully through the cluster IP address with the node that owns the quorum resource, which ultimately is communicating with its Cluster service.

If at any time the second or a subsequent node loses contact with the node that owns the quorum resource, it will try to gain control of the quorum resource. This results in one of two possible scenarios:

- If the second node gains control of the quorum resource, all resources in the cluster are started on the second node because it is assumed the first node is out of service.
- If the second node fails to gain control of the cluster resource, then application resources on that isolated node are stopped. It is assumed that the node that still owns the quorum resource has started the resources that were on the isolated node.

If the quorum resource becomes unavailable to both nodes of the cluster, the cluster and its applications fail to start. This is unlikely because a cluster should have redundancy at the Hardware layer, including redundant drive controllers, a Raid 1, 5, 0+1, or 10 drive configuration, and redundant power.

Figure 18.8 shows the page in the cluster wizard where the cluster file storage drive or quorum resource is selected. The quorum drive must be at least 5MB in size, but Microsoft recommends 100MB.

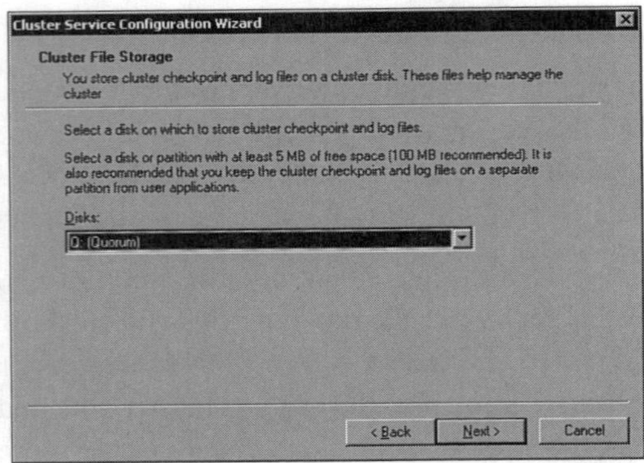

FIGURE 18.8
The Cluster File Storage page of the cluster wizard.

Configuring Cluster Networks

A Windows Server cluster requires network connectivity to function. Clusters must query the other nodes for current status information. Clients that use the cluster communicate with applications that run on the cluster. To meet these network requirements, a cluster has two network types: private and public.

A *private network* is used for intracluster communication. It is sometimes referred to as a heartbeat network because the type of traffic that is sent between nodes is periodic and pulse-like. These pulses are status messages that nodes send to one another. The private network is also used by the cluster to notify cluster nodes of resource allocation changes and failures. In a two-node cluster this network could simply be a cross-over cable between the two members.

A *public network* is used for managing the cluster remotely and accessing applications the cluster supports. This is the traditional network that is attached to a switch, router, or hub. It is sometimes referred to as the management network because all traffic from the Cluster Administrator travels through it to the cluster IP address.

All network adapters in a cluster should use static IP addresses because dependency on DHCP addresses can lead to cluster inconsistency. Consider a scenario in which a cluster node fails with a certain IP address, restarts, and receives a different IP address from the DHCP server. This could cause a delay as the name resolution is propagated throughout the network.

Make sure that the adapters have the correct binding order. Where there are two or more adapters and one is private, be sure it is bound after the public adapters. An improper binding order can cause delays in startup time and failure locating the domain controller for the domain account credential validation required by the Cluster service.

Network adapters serve three roles in a Windows Server cluster. A network adapter is either private, public, or mixed. Microsoft recommends that there be at least two network adapters that serve the private network role for intracluster communication. When there is a dedicated private network adapter and a single public network adapter, the public network adapter should be in the mixed role, as shown in Figure 18.9. This eliminates a single point of failure for cluster network operations by enabling Cluster service to use the public network adapter for heartbeat traffic if the dedicated private network adapter fails.

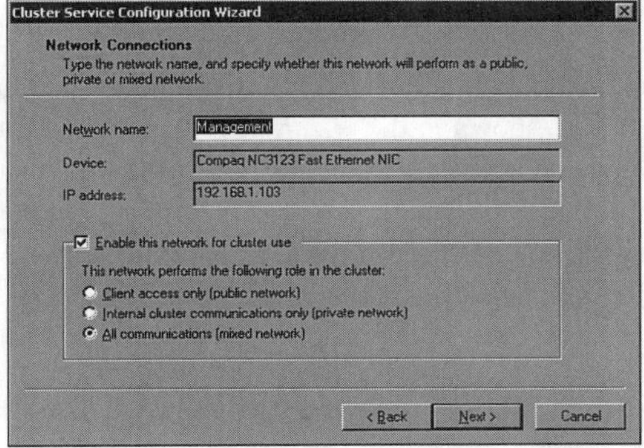

FIGURE 18.9
The Network Connections page of the cluster wizard.

Figure 18.9 is repeated for all valid network adapters in the first node. For a private network adapter, use the configuration settings shown in Figure 18.10. Notice that the network type is private. This network will be used by the cluster only for status and state communication between nodes. The subnet for the heartbeat network should be different from the public network.

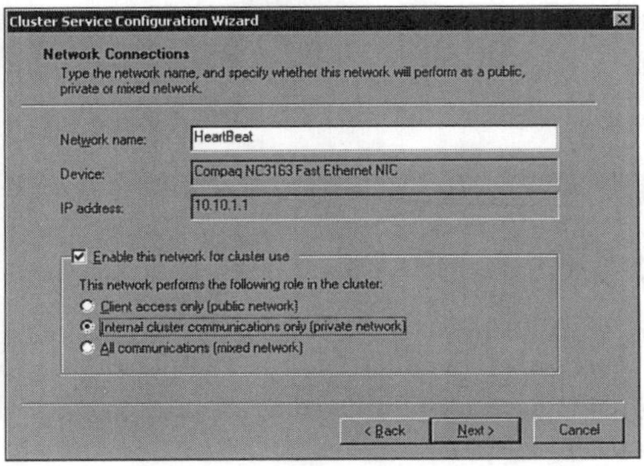

FIGURE 18.10
The Network Connections page of the cluster wizard for a heartbeat network.

CAUTION

When configuring networks for cluster use, make sure that every network adapter on the first node has a corresponding network adapter on all subsequent nodes and that they are all configured for the same physical network. Otherwise, other nodes will be unable to join the cluster.

Prioritizing Intracluster Communications

If a cluster has more than one network adapter configured for private cluster communications, then the page in Figure 18.11 is shown in the wizard. This page is used to configure the priority of different networks that can act as a private network. Networks that are dedicated as private show up at the top of this list by default, and it is recommended that these settings be accepted. To change the order of a network in the list, select the network and click the up and down buttons accordingly. As long as the first network in the list is available, it is used for all intracluster communication. The other network(s) in this list are used only during network failures.

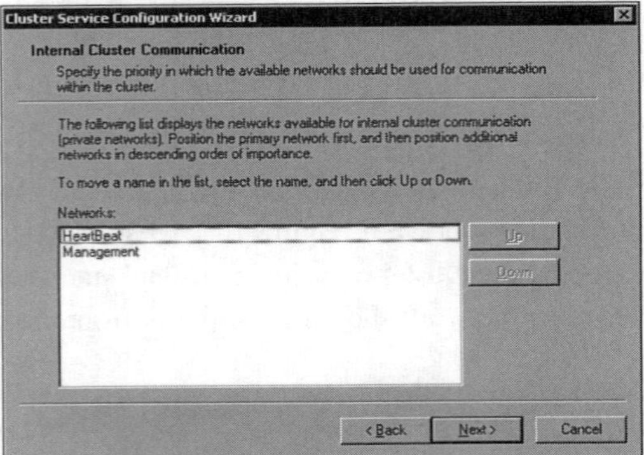

FIGURE 18.11
The Internal Cluster Communication page of the cluster wizard.

Configuring the Cluster IP Address

After specifying all cluster networks and their roles, the wizard creates the IP address for the cluster. The IP address resource is the second resource that is required for the virtual network-addressable cluster name that is used for remote administration and by other members of the cluster for joining the cluster initially.

Figure 18.12 shows the Cluster IP Address page of the cluster wizard. Specify an IP address, subnet mask, and the public network to use for this IP address. The IP address must match the IP address and subnet mask of the target cluster network.

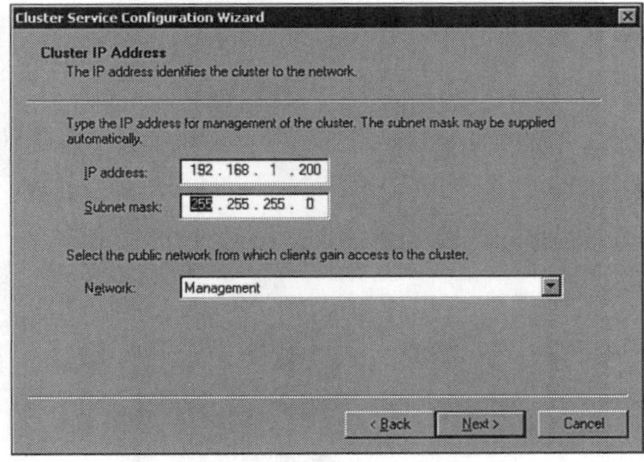

FIGURE 18.12
The Cluster IP Address page of the cluster wizard.

Completing the First Node Configuration

When the wizard is finished creating the new cluster, it creates certain entities in the cluster database.

It creates a group called the *Cluster Group* that contains the cluster name, the cluster IP address, and the quorum physical disk resource. This group symbolizes the virtual cluster name and is the heart of the Windows Cluster server. The node that owns this group is the master of the cluster.

Groups for each physical disk resource are created with the name Disk Group *n*. There are as many groups as there are unique physical disks. These groups are placeholders for the physical disk resources and can be deleted. The disk resources should be reassigned to the appropriate custom application groups.

Figure 18.13 shows the Cluster Administrator for a newly created cluster. Notice that Cluster Group is highlighted and contains the cluster IP address, the cluster name, and the quorum resource.

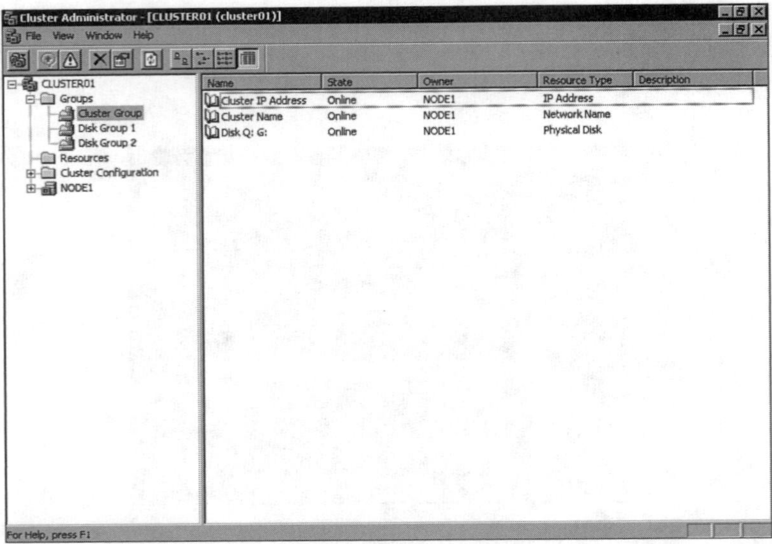

FIGURE 18.13
The Cluster Administrator for a new cluster.

Using the Cluster Service Configuration Wizard on the Second Node

Before beginning the cluster wizard on the second node, be sure to complete the following steps:

1. Make sure the shared storage for the cluster is available and configured in Disk Administrator. This storage is just like any other storage and should have drive letters assigned as they were on the first node. Do not reformat the drives.
2. Join the second cluster node to a Windows NT or 2000 domain.
3. Assign static IP addresses to all network adapters that are for cluster use. Make sure these network adapters are functioning correctly or the cluster wizard will not recognize them as valid network adapters. Give the adapters the same names as their corresponding adapters on the first node.
4. Make sure the first node is up and functioning. Try to ping the cluster name from the second node. The cluster wizard will use this name to contact the first node.

The Cluster Service Configuration Wizard must be successfully completed on the second node of a cluster for the node to join the cluster. Figure 18.14 shows a high-level overview of the steps involved in completing the second node of a server cluster. If there is an equal number of network adapters with appropriate configuration as in the first node, the wizard automatically assigns network adapters to cluster networks that are available. If they are not present, the user must specify which network adapter should be used for which cluster network. It is recommended that the cluster nodes be identical, so this configuration is not explored further.

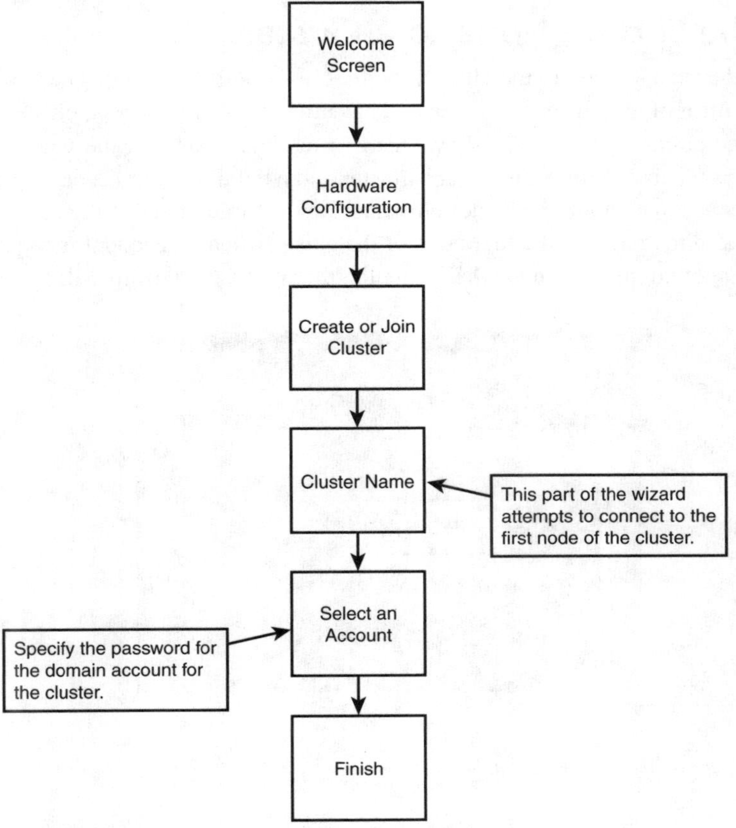

FIGURE 18.14
The path through the cluster wizard for the second node.

Choosing to Configure the Second Node

The second node is no different from other nodes once the cluster is complete. Figure 18.4 shows the Create or Join a Cluster page of the wizard. For the second node, on this page choose to add the second node by selecting the Second or Next Node in the Cluster radio button and clicking the Next button.

Joining the Second Node to a Cluster

When joining the second node to the cluster, the first node must be set up. The first node should be in control of all cluster resources and have the cluster IP address, cluster name, and quorum resource online. Figure 18.15 shows the Cluster Name page for the second node of the cluster. In this page, specify the name of the cluster and a valid domain account to connect to the cluster. This account should be an administrator on the target node. If the current interactive user is an administrator on the first node of the cluster, then no account is required. If the second node cannot connect to and authenticate the first node, the wizard will not continue.

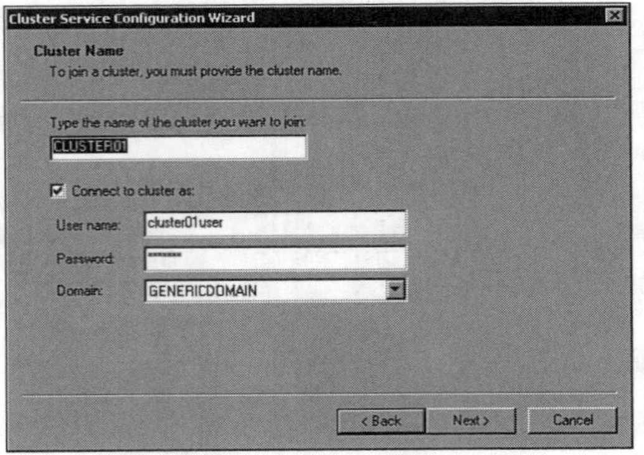

FIGURE 18.15
The Cluster Name page for the second node of the cluster wizard.

Selecting the Cluster Service Domain Account

Once the cluster wizard on the second node has connected to the Cluster service on the first node, it will gather information about the cluster and attempt to simplify the configuration of the second node. In Figure 18.16 the account name and domain of the cluster domain account are filled in. Type the password for the cluster account and click Next to complete this step of the wizard.

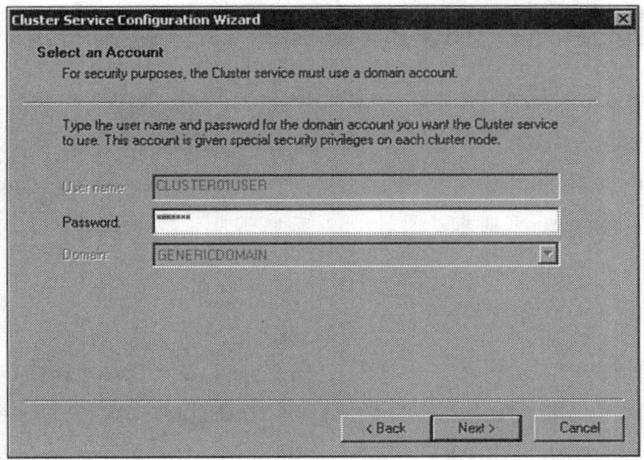

FIGURE 18.16
The Select an Account page for the second node of the cluster wizard.

Completing the Second Node Configuration

If the network adapters of the second node are equal in number to the first node and configured with the same settings (the subnet of the IP addresses and subnet masks must match), the configuration of the second node is complete. If there are not enough network adapters to equal the number of cluster networks defined on the first node, then the wizard cannot finish.

After Finish is clicked, the cluster wizard starts the Cluster service on the second node and adds the node to the cluster database. This process could take a few minutes, so be patient. Once the process is done, the Cluster Administrator shows a second node, as in Figure 18.17. The cluster is complete and should be tested.

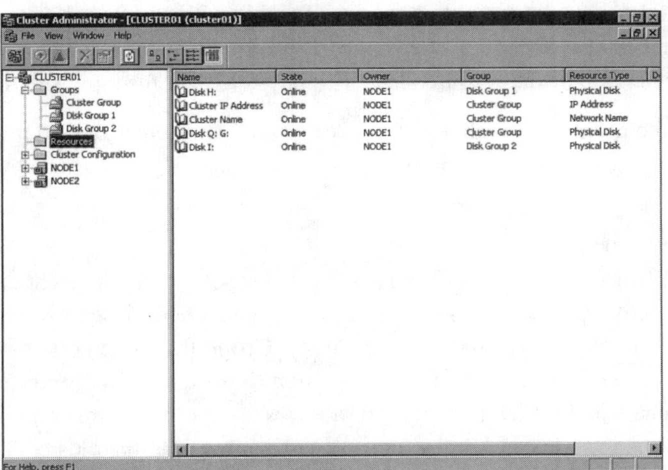

FIGURE 18.17
The Cluster Administrator for a two-node cluster.

Testing the Cluster

To test a newly created cluster, first reboot each node of the cluster one at a time and make sure the resources move from node to node. Once this is successful, take resources and groups offline through the Cluster Administrator. Finally, move groups from one node to the other through the Cluster Administrator.

Rebooting Cluster Nodes

Reboot each node of the cluster one at a time. Make sure the rebooted node comes up completely before rebooting the other node. This proves that the cluster nodes can successfully transfer ownership of the resources in a cluster, including the Cluster Group.

First reboot the second node and make sure that the Cluster Administrator shows it leaving the cluster and rejoining. Watch the computer node in the Cluster Administrator; when the Cluster service is unavailable, a red X is superimposed onto the node that has failed or is rebooting. This should happen in real-time. Other things to watch are the ownership of the groups in the cluster. When the node that owns the quorum resource is rebooted, the default Cluster Group should move from the rebooting node to the active node. Observe this change in real-time by watching the Details view of the Cluster Group. The Owner and State columns will change as the group is moved from one node to the other. The state should cycle through online, offline, online pending, and back to online. When the Cluster service is returning to service, the red X on the computer node is replaced by a red circle with a diagonal line.

Taking Resources Offline and Online

To take a resource offline, right-click the target resource and select Take Offline from the menu. This will take the resource out of service. Try this with a physical disk resource that is separate from the quorum resource. After taking it offline, try to access the resource from the node that had ownership of the resource last. The physical disk resource should be unavailable.

To bring a resource online, right-click the target resource and select Bring Online. If this is successful, the target resource is put into service.

Moving Groups

To move a group from one node to the other without rebooting a node, right-click the target group and select Move Group. This moves the group, as a reboot of the owning group does, to the other node of the cluster. Try moving the Cluster Group from one node to the other. This is the only time that a remote administrative connection to the cluster will freeze momentarily. This occurs because the network name and IP address are moving from one node to the other and during that time the Cluster Administrator loses contact with the cluster. The Cluster

Administrator will automatically reestablish connectivity to the cluster IP address and name when it returns to service on the node the group was moved to. Figure 18.18 shows the changes to resource state and ownership as a group moves from one node to the other.

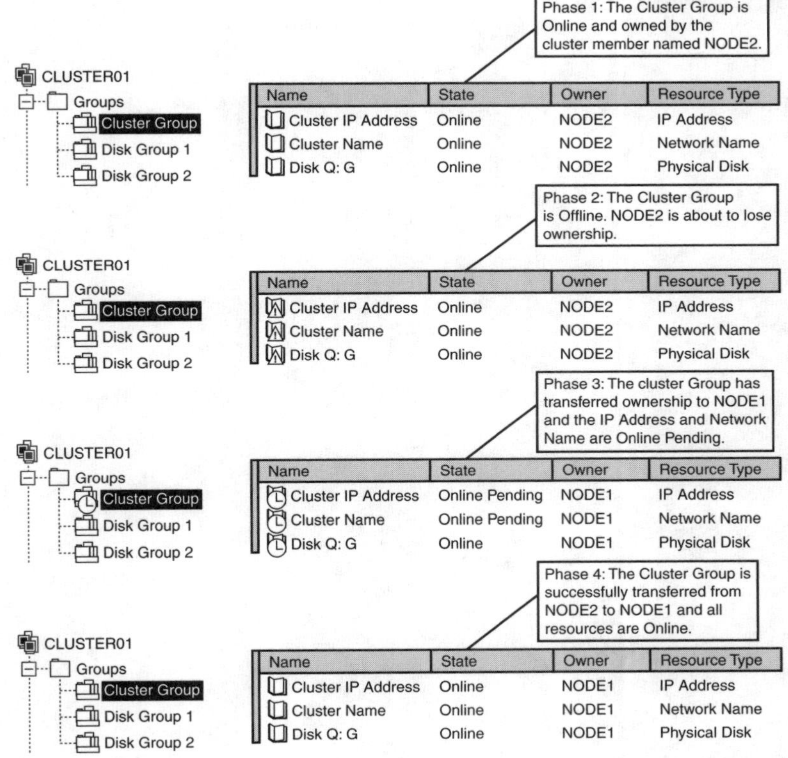

FIGURE 18.18
Moving a group.

Summary

Creating a Windows Server cluster is not as difficult as it seems. With careful planning, an understanding of server cluster requirements, and properly configured server hardware, the deployment is as simple as completing the cluster wizard.

The cluster wizard helps the administrator by providing a step-by-step process for creating each node in the cluster. The first node of the cluster is the most difficult because the cluster name and IP, its networks, and managed disks must all be configured. The second node is much easier, but it must have the same configuration as the first to join the cluster successfully.

Once the wizard is complete, testing the cluster is as simple as rebooting each node, changing resource state, and moving groups from node to node. Completing these tasks successfully means the server cluster is ready to provide a Web farm with the highest availability that Windows offers for application components such as file shares, generic services and applications, SQL Server, and Exchange.

Clustering Application Resources

CHAPTER

19

IN THIS CHAPTER

Windows Server clusters provide high-availability support for Windows applications. This support provides the administrator a way to organize the resources of a cluster into logical groupings. The configuration of cluster applications is done by creating cluster resources of different types and defining their behavior on the cluster.

Specific resources organized into groups define application units that can exist on any node in a cluster. These units are called *virtual servers*. Virtual servers provide a means for administrators to make a cluster appear as many different servers for simplified management of an application's and user's needs. Combined with the various cluster-aware resources, Windows Server clusters deliver the whole package for high-availability Windows 2000 servers.

The goals of this chapter are to help you

- Learn how to configure groups to manage the resources in a cluster. Topics include adding groups, assigning preferred group ownership, configuring failover, and failback parameters.
- Learn how to configure the resources of a cluster. Topics include adding and removing resources from the cluster and from groups, configuring dependent resources, configuring Registry replication, and configuring advanced resource parameters.
- Learn how to create and configure a Windows Cluster Server virtual server.
- Learn how to configure the different default resource types in a cluster, including Distributed Transaction Coordinator, generic Windows applications, generic Windows services, file shares, print spoolers, IIS virtual roots, COM+ applications, and Microsoft Message Queue services.

Configuring Groups

Groups are logical organizations of cluster resources that can be owned by any node in a cluster and define the objects that can failover and failback. Groups contain all dependent resources for a particular application type. For example, a group contains the network name and IP address resource for a virtual server along with the application-specific resource.

Windows Server cluster groups have the following characteristics:

- Groups store all cluster resources. No resource can be created without assigning it to a particular group.
- Groups provide the organizational element of failover and failback for a cluster. When a resource in a group fails, all the resources that are members of the same group move together from one node to the other.
- It is not possible to move resources from node to node outside the context of a group.

When a new group is created, there are no resources assigned to it. A new resource is added to the cluster, and part of that process is assigning it to one and only one group. The group's properties define how it behaves when resources it owns fail. All resources in a group inherit those properties and move with their group from node to node.

Adding and Removing a Group

To add a group to a cluster, perform the following steps:

1. Right-click any node in the Cluster Administrator.
2. Select the new menu item and then select Group.
3. In the New Group dialog, fill in the name of the new group and its description and click Next.
4. Select and order the nodes for preferred ownership and click Finish.

To remove a group from the cluster, perform the following steps:

1. Remove or delete all resources from the group. A group that contains resources cannot be deleted.
2. Right-click the target group and select Delete.

Moving a Group

To move a group from one node to the other, perform the following steps:

1. Right-click the target group.
2. Select Move Group.

Configuring Failover Parameters

Figure 19.1 shows the failover property page of a group. On this page, configure the failover thresholds and time period for a group. Failover thresholds are defined by how many times over a period of time a group automatically attempts to move from node to node during a failure. If this threshold is crossed during the time period, the Cluster service stops automatically attempting to restart the group and its failed resources on the other node. For example, a threshold of three times and a period of two hours means that if the group fails three times in a two-hour period, the Cluster service will no longer automatically move the group to the other node at the next failure. After the threshold is crossed, the group must be successfully restarted before the failover thresholds take effect again.

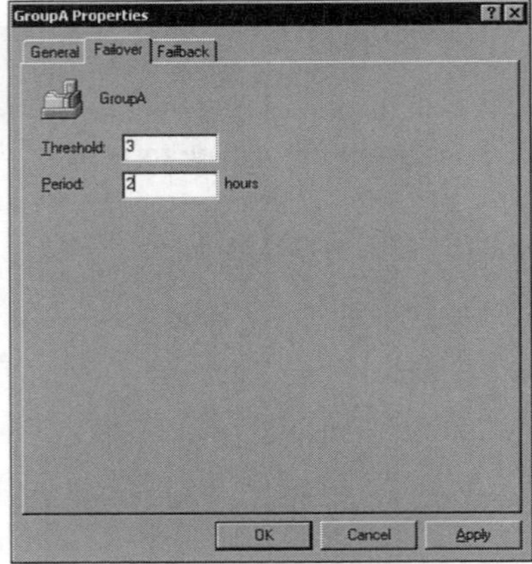

FIGURE 19.1
A group's Failover Properties page.

This feature is useful for preventing cluster thrashing. Cluster thrashing can occur when some resource dependency has been removed from the environment and, no matter how hard the cluster tries to bring the resource online, it will fail. If the failover process continually thrashes, then the cluster spends CPU, memory, and network resources trying to bring the resource back online. By establishing a failover threshold for a group, you can avoid thrashing.

Configuring Failback Parameters

Figure 19.2 shows the failback property page of a group, where you configure how a group behaves when the node it fails from is restored. If a group is prevented from failing back, it will move to another node unless an administrator explicitly moves it. If a group's preferred owner fails and the group allows failback, it will always return to its owner when it is restored to service. If a time period for failback is specified, then during that time the group will return to its preferred owner. If no preferred owner is specified, the group will not move.

Assigning Preferred Group Ownership

Preferred group ownership defines which node of a cluster is the primary owner of a specific group. This information is used when determining ownership during failback. For example, `GroupA`'s preferred owner is `Node1`, and `GroupA` is currently active on `Node1`. `Node1` is rebooted, which is equivalent to it failing. `GroupA` and its resources are stopped on `Node1` and moved to `Node2`. `Node1` returns to service, and the Cluster service on `Node1` reestablishes communication with the cluster. Cluster service looks at `GroupA`'s failback configuration and preferred ownership list, shown in Figure 19.3, to decide which node should own `GroupA`.

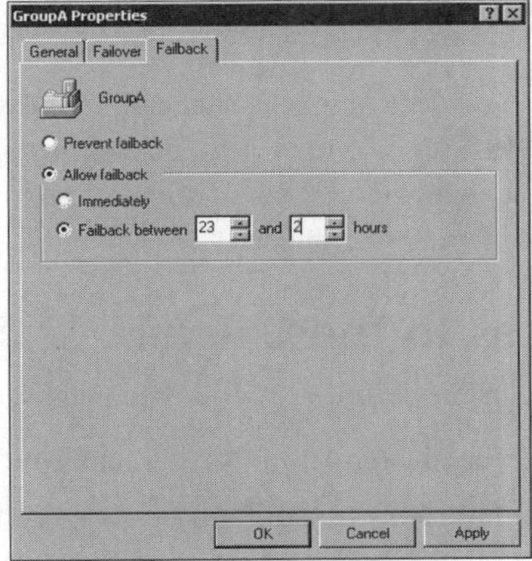

FIGURE 19.2
A group's Failback Properties page.

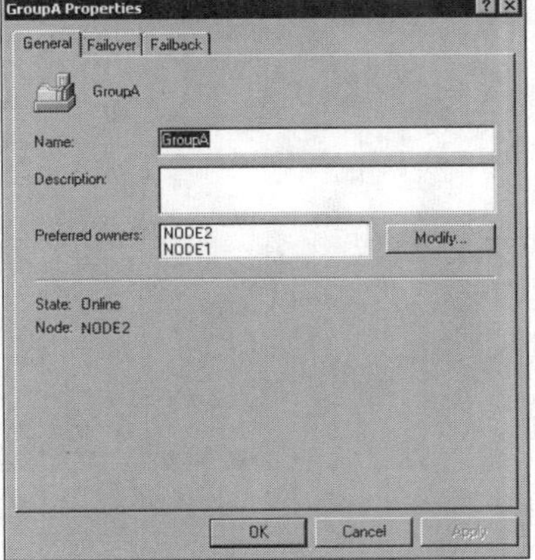

FIGURE 19.3
A group's General Properties page.

If `GroupA` is configured to allow failback immediately, then `GroupA` moves back to `Node1`, the topmost node in the preferred ownership list. If failback is prevented, then `GroupA` stays on `Node2` until an administrator initiates failback or `Node2` fails.

To modify preferred ownership click the modify button in Figure 19.3. From this dialog order the nodes in the cluster with the topmost being the preferred owner. Only one node needs to be added to establish a preferred owner.

Configuring Resources

Resources are the services, devices, applications, and application components of a cluster. Each resource type shares a default set of property pages and has pages that are specific to that resource type. This section covers the basics of adding and managing the properties and behaviors of resources in a Windows Server cluster.

Adding Resources to the Cluster

To add a resource to the cluster, perform the following steps:

1. Right-click any node in Cluster Administrator and select the New menu item.
2. Select Resource from the New menu item.
3. Complete the New Resource Wizard.

Figure 19.4 shows the first page of this wizard. This is where the name, description, resource type, and initial group membership are chosen.

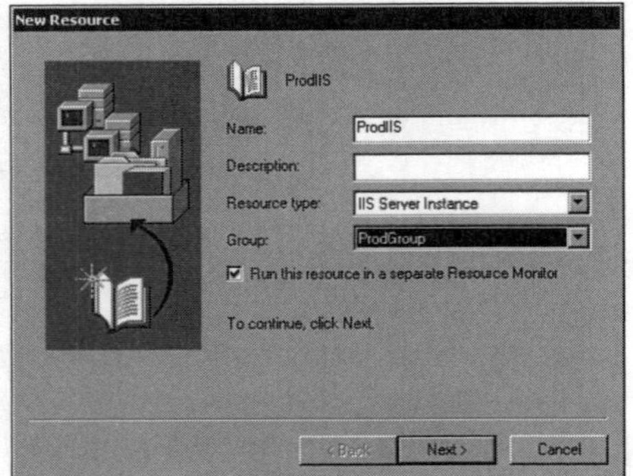

FIGURE 19.4
The first page of the New Resource Wizard.

Use the Run This Resource in a Separate Resource Monitor check box to isolate each resource in its own `RESRCMON.EXE` process. There is one `RESRCMON.EXE` process in which all resource DLLs are loaded. The `RESRCMON.EXE` process provides process isolation to the Cluster service from resource failures. Giving a resource its own `RESRCMON.EXE` process further isolates resources from one another. This is useful when a resource is causing cluster failures due to bugs in the resource DLL.

TIP

When adding new resources that aren't part of the built-in resources available with Windows Server clusters (such as SQL Server 2000) to an existing cluster, run these resources in their own RESRCMON.EXE process to ensure the highest availability of the cluster.

From the second page of the wizard, set the possible ownership of the resource. Ownership determines the nodes that can bring a resource online. In a two-node cluster, restricting ownership to a single node of the cluster effectively prevents the resource from failing over to the other node when the owning node fails. This type of resource has the availability of normal application on a single server.

Many resource types are dependent on other resources. Bringing a new resource online is dependent on specifying these dependencies. Set the dependencies of the resource from the third page of the wizard. Figure 19.5 shows the Dependencies page of the New Resource Wizard. To move resources from the Available Resources list box to the Resource Dependencies list box, double-click the resource for either list or select the resource and use the Add/Remove buttons.

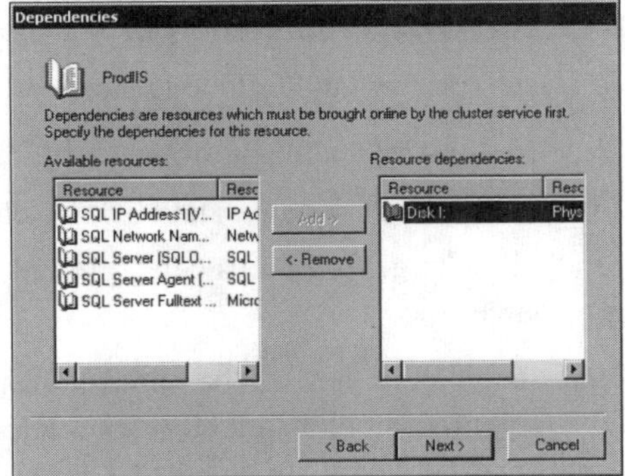

FIGURE 19.5
The Dependencies page of the New Resource Wizard.

Each resource type has a different set of dependency requirements. For example, a file share resource is dependent on a physical disk resource. In order to create a file share resource in a particular group, that group must contain a physical disk resource before starting the wizard. Because these dependencies are different for each resource, the requirements to complete the

New Resource Wizard change according to the type of resource selected. Creating each default resource type is covered in "Configuring Default Resources," later in this chapter.

Moving Resources to a New Group

To move a resource to a new group, right-click the target resource and select Move Group. If the resources have dependencies, those resources must move with the target resource to the new group. Figure 19.6 shows a physical disk resource moving from the `VSQL01` group to the `GroupA` group. Notice that the SQL IP address, network name, SQL Server, and SQL agent resources must be moved to `GroupA` as well.

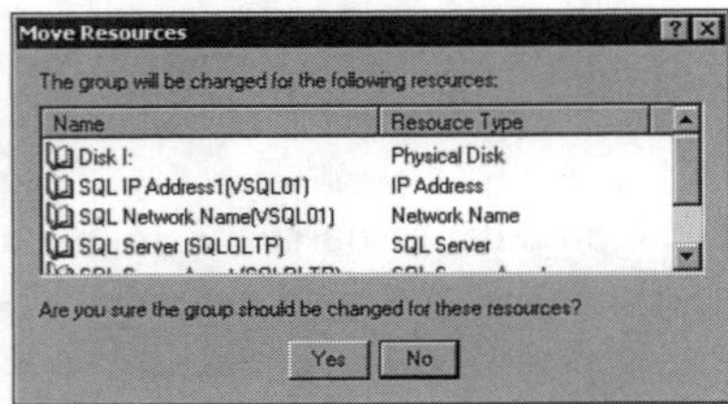

FIGURE 19.6
Moving resources to a new group that has dependencies.

Removing Resources from the Cluster

To remove a resource from a cluster, perform the following steps:

1. Right-click the target resource and select Take Offline.
2. Once the resource is offline, right-click it again and click Delete.
3. If other resources depend on the target resources being present in the group, click Yes to remove all these other resources too.

Resources must be in an offline state before they can be removed from a cluster. If other resources are dependent on the target resource, then it cannot be deleted until that dependency is removed or the other resource dependent on it are removed. Cluster Administrator will prompt to delete all dependent resources with a dialog similar to the Move Resource dialog. Be sure that it is okay to delete all the dependent resources before continuing.

Configuring Dependent Resources

Resources can be dependent on other resources by design or through configuration. This means that some resources require that another resource be present in the same group in order to be created. Configuration of dependencies is done in the same way except that the dependencies are specified by an administrator outside of resource-level requirements. It is useful to create these configuration dependencies to represent better the requirements of generic applications and services during failover and failback.

The dependencies property page for a resource is shown in Figure 19.7. The list of resources includes those resources that have already been specified as dependencies of this resource. To change the dependencies on this property page, click the Modify button. This launches a dialog similar to the dependencies page of the New Resource Wizard. Use the Add/Remove buttons to move resources around.

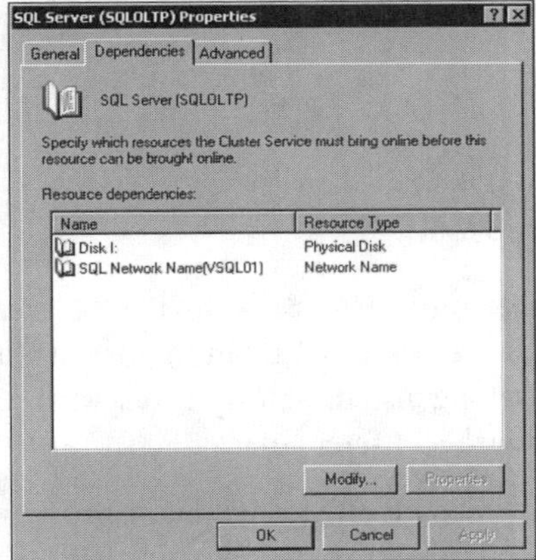

FIGURE 19.7
The Dependencies Property Page of a Resource.

> **NOTE**
>
> Resources cannot have cyclical dependencies. This means that no two resources can be dependent on one another. This is because Cluster services uses the dependency list of all resources in a group to determine the order in which resources must be brought online.

Controlling Group Failover when a Resource Fails

Cluster services uses the configuration settings on the Advanced property page of a resource to determine how to attempt to bring the resource back online after it has failed. Figure 19.8 shows this property page.

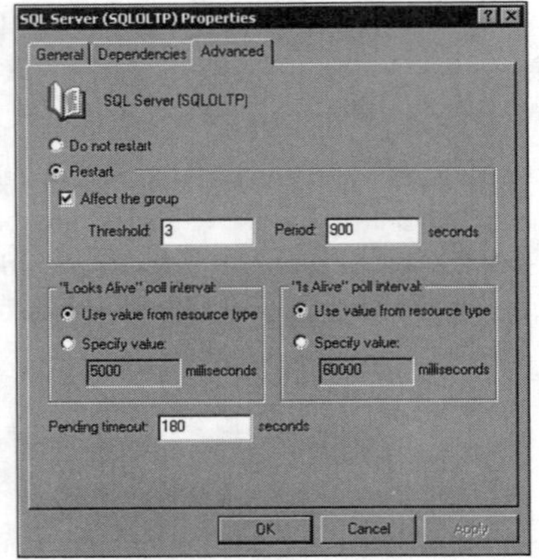

FIGURE 19.8
The Advanced property page of a resource.

The first setting to configure for a resource is whether Cluster service should attempt to restart the resource after it fails. Select Do Not Restart to prevent Cluster service from attempting to restart the resource. This setting also disables the Restart section; a resource with this setting cannot cause a group to fail to a different cluster node.

The failure of a resource by default affects the failover of a group. If Cluster service attempts and fails to restart a service three times in a row over a 900 second period, it will fail the entire group to another node, based on the preferred ownership list. Unselecting the Affect the Group check box effectively disables a resource's capability to cause the failover of the group to another cluster node. The Cluster service still attempts to restart the resource based on the threshold and period settings, but it will not move the group and the resource to another node. If the resources cannot be brought online, Cluster service leaves the resource in a failed state. Change the threshold and period settings on a case-by-case basis. The defaults should be appropriate for most resources.

Specifying "Looks Alive" and "Is Alive" Intervals

The other advanced settings to control for a resource are the Looks Alive and Is Alive polling intervals. Cluster service will poll resources periodically to check their status by asking the Resource Monitor(s) to invoke special methods on the resource DLLs. Each resource DLL is free to determine the appropriate checks for each poll interval type.

The Look Alive poll interval is intended to be a simpler check that does not do a full examination of a resource's status. The Is Alive poll is intended to be a much more thorough check of the resource's status for errors and other problems. Each of these checks places a burden on the resource and Cluster service, so use caution when changing from the defaults specified by each resource type. Usually these settings are changed only when a resource is having problems and must be checked more frequently for failures to keep the availability of the resource high.

When a Looks Alive or Is Alive poll determines that a resource has failed, the Cluster service will attempt to bring the resource up on the other node of the cluster, based on the restart parameters, preferred ownership settings, and group failover and failback settings—in that order. For more information on default intervals for each resource type, see "Configuring Default Resources," later in this chapter.

Creating a Virtual Server

Windows Server cluster can organize specific resources at the group level into a conceptual virtual server. A virtual server is composed of an IP address resource and a network name resource in the same group. These resources together with applications and other resources make up a virtual server.

Figure 19.9 shows a virtual server in the Cluster Administrator console. Notice that the group name is the same as the network name. This is for ease of management and is not required.

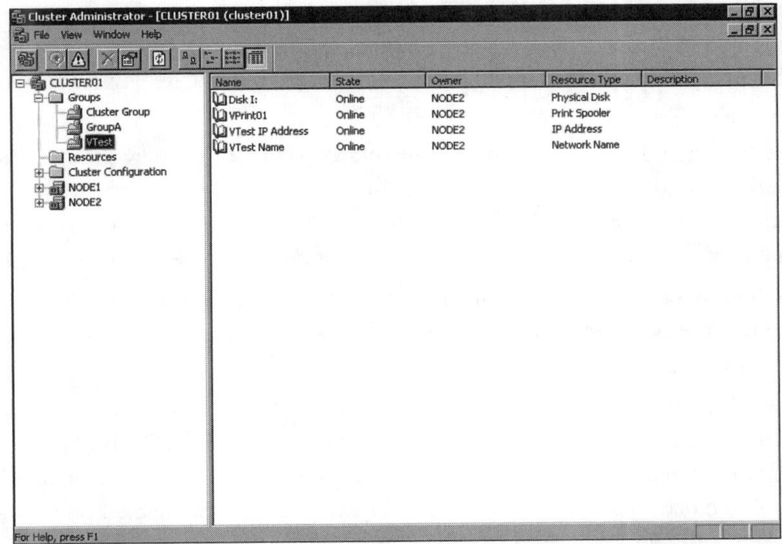

FIGURE 19.9
A virtual server in Cluster Administrator.

A virtual server is used to abstract the resources of a cluster into functional servers that have meaning to humans and applications but can hide the administrative names of servers. For example, clustering SQL 2000 requires a virtual server. The virtual IP and network name of the virtual server are used to reference the SQL server by clients. This makes it easier for users because virtual server names can be friendlier, such as `SQLORDERING`, whereas a cluster node's real name might be `NODE1` or `WIN2KCLUS01`.

A Windows Server cluster can have any number of virtual servers. A single cluster could have virtual server for SQL 2000, Exchange 2000, and file shares. There is a penalty at startup when the number of groups becomes large, because each resource and all groups must communicate their status to the Cluster service before coming online.

Because the concept of a virtual server is so valuable as a feature of Windows Server clusters, there is a special wizard provided in Cluster Administrator for its creation. Right-click on any node and select Configure Application to launch the Cluster Application Wizard. The Cluster Application Wizard encapsulates the following configuration steps:

1. Choose to create or use an existing virtual server. Creating a new virtual server results in additional steps in the wizard for configuring a network name, IP address resource, and a new or exiting group for these resources to be a member. Using an existing virtual server group (in this case, a virtual server is a group that contains at least one network name resource and its dependent IP address) eliminates the need to create a new group, a new network name, and an IP address. It skips the wizard to the Create New Resource Now or Later step.
2. Choose to create or use an existing resource group. Creating a new group adds a step to name and describe the group. Using an existing group will result in that group being tied to a new network name and IP address for the virtual server. The groups available to use for a new virtual server cannot contain any network name or IP address resources.
3. Name the group. This step happens only when a new group is created. This page is exactly like the New Group dialog that appears when adding a new group from Cluster Administrator.
4. Specify the network name and IP address. This step happens only when a new virtual server is being created. The name is the NetBIOS and DNS prefix for the new virtual server. For example, specifying `PRODSTUFF` here results in a NetBIOS name of `PRODSTUFF` and a DNS name (if Active Directory and Dynamic DNS are enabled on the domain for the cluster) of `PRODSTUFF.DOMAINNAME.COM`.
5. Specify Advanced Properties for the Group, Name and IP Address. This dialog enables the configuration of all the parameters of the group, network name, and IP address resources just as if they were created individually. Figure 19.10 shows this dialog. To configure a group's properties, select Resource Group Properties from the Categories list box and click Advanced Properties.

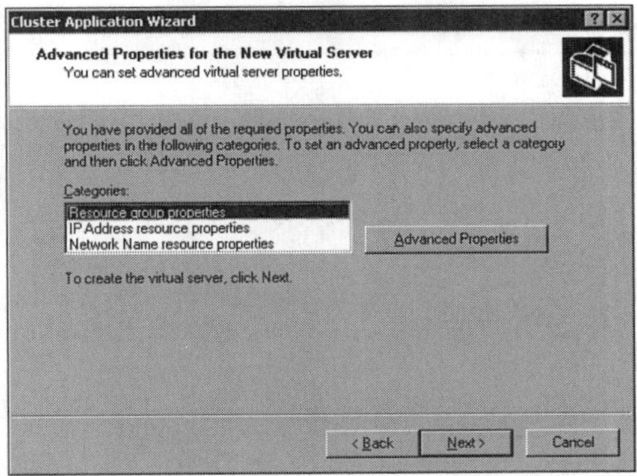

FIGURE 19.10
The Virtual Server Advanced Property page of the Cluster Application Wizard.

6. Create the Application Resource Now or Later. Here select Yes to configure the application resource for the new virtual server. Click No to finish the wizard and add resources to this virtual server later.
7. Pick Resource Type from the Available Resources drop-down combo box.
8. Name the application and configure its advanced properties. On this page, type the name and description for the new application resource. Click the Advanced button to configure the General, Dependencies, and Advanced property pages for a resource. These pages are the same as the ones that appear when examining properties for a configured application, except the page for the specific resource type is not present.
9. Configure Specific Resource Parameters. This page is the same as the property page for a specific resource and is different for each resource type.

Once this wizard is completed, depending on selections, the cluster could have a new group, IP address, network name, and specific resource assigned to it. Creating a virtual server for a Windows Server cluster is an easy way to add new applications to a cluster, simplifying many steps into one easy wizard.

Configuring Default Resources

Windows Server clustering supports a number of default resource types that are native to Windows 2000. Each of these types corresponds to common application elements that without Cluster service have no easy way to have high availability. Table 19.1 shows these default resources that are important for Web farm applications, their dependencies on other resources, and their default Is Alive and Looks Alive intervals.

TABLE 19.1 Some Properties for Default Cluster Resources

Name	*Required Dependencies*	*Suggested Dependencies*	*Looks Alive(ms)*	*Is Alive(ms)*
Physical Disk	None	None	5,000	60,000
MSDTC	Physical Storage, Network Name	None	60,000	120,000
IP Address	None	None	5,000	60,000
Network Name	IP Address	None	5,000	60,000
File Share	None	Physical Disk	5,000	60,000
Generic Application	None	Network Name	5,000	60,000
Generic Service	None	Network Name	5,000	60,000
IIS Service	IP Address	Network Name, Physical Disk	5,000	60,000
Message Queuing	Physical Disk	Network Name	60,000	120,000

Each resource may have a special property page that is added to the normal properties of a resource. The following section covers configuring each resource type, including any special requirements for bringing those resource online in a Windows Server cluster.

Configuring Distributed Transaction Coordinator

The Distributed Transaction Coordinator (DTC) is a single cluster instance resource. This means that only one DTC may be configured per cluster, and only one node at a time may have the DTC resource. The DTC has a special program that must be run on the node that owns the cluster group to add it to the cluster correctly. From the command line of this node, run `COMCLUST.EXE`. Once this finishes successfully, the MSTDC resource is added to the cluster group and brought online. This program must be run on all nodes so that during failover the MSDTC can start correctly.

Configuring File Shares

Figure 19.11 shows the property page for a file share resource. From this page, specify the share name, the share path, and a description of the share. To configure the number of users, click the Allow radio button and type a number. To set permissions on the share, click the Permissions button. This launches a standard file share permissions dialog.

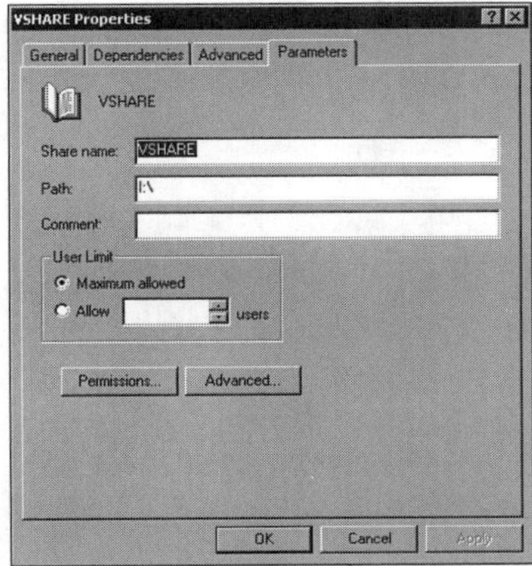

FIGURE 19.11
The File Share Resource Property page.

The Advanced button launches a dialog that allows the configuration of the different share types. There are three choices: Normal Share, Dfs Root, and Share Subdirectories. A normal share creates a single share that points to the path specified. Dfs Root creates a standalone Dfs root that has dependencies on a network name and IP address. Sharing subdirectories is an easy way to create a single file share resource, but share all the subdirectories under this resource as network shares. This means that the Cluster service has to poll only one cluster resource instead of potentially hundreds of resources.

Configuring a Generic Windows Application

Figure 19.12 shows the Parameters property page of a generic application. From this page, specify the program name of the application to run. If the application is not in the file search path then specify the full path. Specify the Start in directory and whether this application interacts with the desktop. In Figure 19.12, Notepad is used. If Interacts with Desktop is checked, then `NOTEPAD.EXE` will start on the owning node. If Notepad is closed from the console, another Notepad is instantly launched. If the application is failed to the other node, then Notepad is closed on the first node and launched on the second. If the application is accessible from the network, click the Use Network Name for Computer Name check box. This will provide the application with a network context of a virtual server. This box is available only if a network name is set as a dependency of this generic application resource.

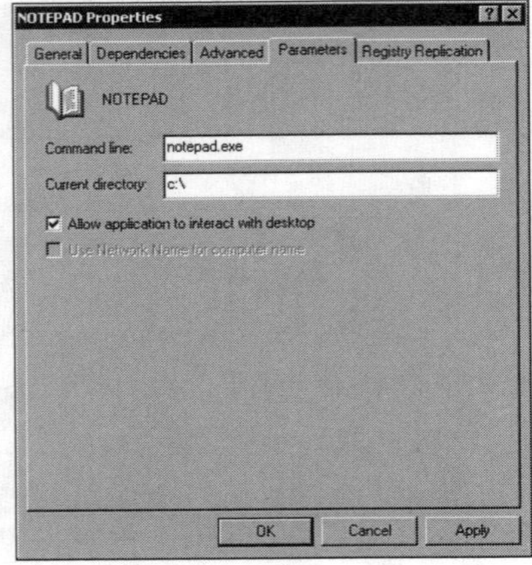

FIGURE 19.12

The generic application resource property page.

Figure 19.13 shows the second property page of a generic application: the Registry Replication page. If an application is dependent on Registry keys, specify them here. This ensures that these keys stay in sync during failover and failback. Registry keys must exist under `HKEY_LOCAL_MACHINE` they cannot be replicated. To add a key, click the Add button and type the path of the Registry key to replicate without typing `HKEY_LOCAL_MACHINE`. This automatically replicates all subkeys.

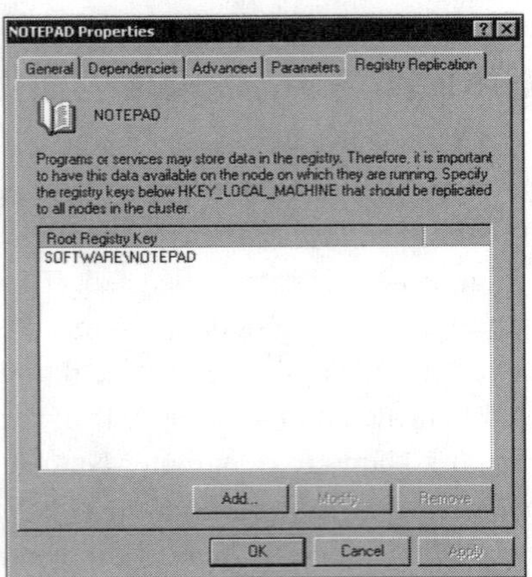

FIGURE 19.13

The Registry Replication property page of a generic application.

TIP

To help type long key names for Registry replication, use `REGEDIT.EXE` to browse to the desired key, right-click it, and select Copy Key Name. Then paste the key into the Add dialog and remove the text `HKEY_LOCAL_MACHINE\`.

Configuring a Generic Windows Service

Configuring a generic Windows service is similar to configuring a generic application. Figure 19.14 shows the generic service resource property page. From this page specify the service name (found by clicking properties of a specific service in the Service Control Panel applet), startup parameters, and whether to use a network name resource as its machine name context.

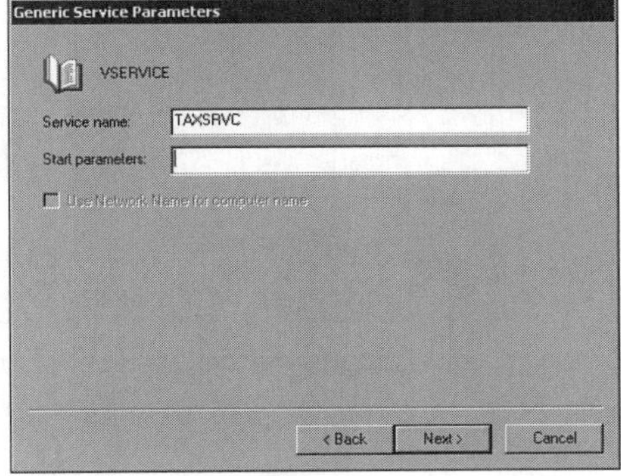

FIGURE 19.14
The generic service resource property page.

The state (started or stopped) of a generic service translates to the state of the resource (online or offline) in Cluster Administrator. Always manage generic services from the Cluster Administrator and not from the Services Control Panel applet. If a service is taken offline, it is stopped. During failover, the service is stopped on one node and started on the other. Cluster service does not stop a generic service from starting on both nodes; it only ensures that it has started on one.

Configuring IIS Virtual Roots

Windows Server clusters support high-availability IIS Web sites. This is different from load-balanced Web sites using Network Load Balancing or hardware load balancing. With Windows Server clusters, an IIS Web site that is clustered runs only on one node of the cluster at a time.

In this configuration there are no scalability gains. Even so, there are certain situations that might require that the Web site exist only on one server at a time. An example is when interfacing with a legacy application that doesn't support access from multiple Web servers.

Figure 19.15 shows the IIS Service Resource Property page. From this page, select FTP or WWW for a list of respective sites configured in IIS for this node. Select the IIS or FTP Web site to cluster using the IIS Server combo box. Use the Refresh button to reload the configured sites from the IIS metabase. Cluster Server mirrors the state of the IIS server (started/stopped) with the offline/online state of the IIS resource as it does with generic services.

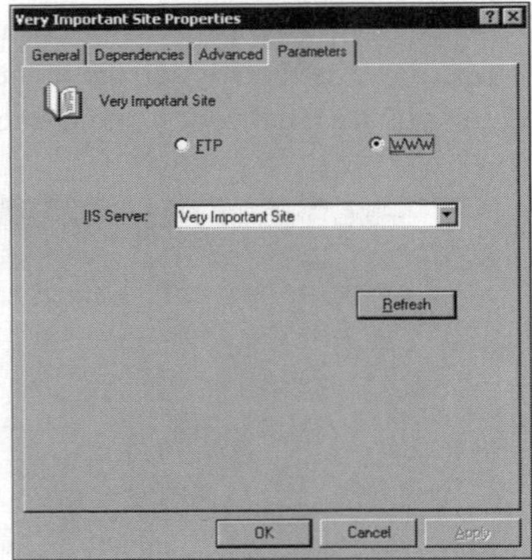

FIGURE 19.15
The IIS Service Resource Property page.

Clustering an IIS resource requires some extra configuration of IIS outside of Cluster Administrator:

- If the clustered Web site is not the default Web site (recommended), then the bindings in IIS must be configured so the Web site can start. This means that the default Web site either must be stopped or bound to a different IP address than the clustered site. It is recommended that the cluster site be bound to the IP address resource that it is dependent on. This IP address will not show up in the drop-down list in IIS but may be typed in manually.
- If the Web site configuration information is not identically configured on both nodes of the cluster, then the site will be unable to failover to the other node. Once again, the bindings should be set up as the first node.

CAUTION

If a cluster IIS resource is not bound to a specific IP address, then the site will respond to all IP address resources that are currently active on the same node that owns the IIS resource.

Configuring Microsoft Message Queue Service

Microsoft Message Queue is a distributed messaging broker that provides guaranteed delivery of messages even if target servers are unavailable at the time of message creation. Clustering message queue services creates a highly available centralized Message Queue repository.

A message queue resource has no special properties and is dependent on a physical disk and network name resource. Because message queue is integrated with Active Directory in Windows 2000, clustering message queue places some special requirements on the permissions of the Cluster service account. When the Cluster service first tries to bring the message queue service online, it attempts to create a new computer object in the `Computers` folder in the cluster's domain. It must have full control of the `Computer` folder for this creation to succeed. Once the message queue service is brought online, clients can use this virtual instance like a real instance of message queue on a real server. Windows Server clusters support as many virtual message queue servers as required.

Summary

Configuring and managing cluster resources is a straightforward task once the initial complexity of Cluster service is understood. Use groups to organize units of failover in the cluster. Configure failover and failback properties to best suit the needs of the resources in a group.

Resources represent the highly available application components supported on a cluster. Use resource ownership to help Cluster service decide the appropriate node of a cluster to bring the resource online. Specify dependencies to help Cluster service determine the order resources in the same group should be brought online to ensure that no resource failures occur because dependent resources were unavailable. Specify restart parameters so Cluster services know how many times to try to restart a resource before moving it to another node or marking it as failed. Use Looks Alive and Is Alive polling to check the status of a cluster resource periodically.

Cluster services supports many different default resource types. There are a number of key resources that help improve overall availability of a Web farm, including file shares, generic applications, generic services, IIS services, and message queues. Any Web farm that uses resources of these types can benefit from them being clustered using Windows Serverclusters.

Architecting Databases for Web Farms

CHAPTER

20

IN THIS CHAPTER

Data storage and retrieval drives a Web farm. Whether it is the presentation of products to order, the local weather, or the delivery of stock quotes, there is a database behind the Web servers that contains this knowledge. A database in a Web farm can track who you are, when you last visited, and when you leave. To customize content and create a rich user experience, customer data is stored in databases and accessed as the site is browsed. Every user requesting information from a Web farm accesses data from a database. As the user community of a Web site grows, the database must grow with it. This is no easy task because databases have special hardware and software requirements to achieve scale-up and scale-out.

A powerful, highly available, scaleable, and easily manageable database architecture is required for any Web farm to achieve success. The right technology choices have to be made up-front. These choices must strike a balance between cost and future growth potential. Unlike any other application area, the more money is spent on databases hardware, the better the long-term benefits are.

The goals of this chapter are to help you

- Learn about the options for distributing a database to support scalability
- Learn about the options for hardware technologies of robust and scalable database architectures
- Learn about the options for software technologies of robust and scalable database architectures

Understanding Database Distribution Options

Unlike the Web server, which commonly renders static images or forms populated with elements derived from a database, the contents of the database itself are undergoing constant change. In most cases, each Web server in a Web farm will store its own copy of the static code and content to be presented. The static nature of these objects, and the minimal space required to store them, contributes to the web server's candidacy for scaling out. In contrast, the database server houses a large volume of data that is not static. Each user expects that his view of the data presented is accurate and up-to-date, regardless of how many concurrent updates the database or databases are processing. The requirement to present this consistent drivesview of frequently changing data, and the sheer volume of the database, might limit the capability to scale out to multiple database servers. Scaling up, not out, remains the most common practice for managing database server capacity and performance requirements.

Adopting a scale-out strategy by replicating an entire database across multiple servers and distributing load across them could be an option, but four factors often prohibit this strategy:

- The cost of additional servers and storage
- The management of ongoing replication and synchronization routines
- Latency in the replication processes
- The lack of a true dynamic load-balancing utility across the multiple database servers

Two other popular alternatives exist for scaling database servers. The first is functional distribution, in which a database is segmented across functional boundaries, with separate database servers hosting various portions of the Web farms data (order processing, inventory, reporting, and so on). Availability is enhanced when data dependencies within the application layer are confined to the same functional boundaries that segment the database. Smaller servers are used for each distributed database. Drawbacks include these:

- Declarative referential integrity constraints can be enforced only by replicating necessary referential data to each server. Data integrity could be enforced programmatically rather than declaratively, but it might be less efficient and more difficult to maintain.
- Transactions that join databases from different servers are difficult to tune. Most query optimizers do not generate efficient execution plans for distributed queries.
- Cumulative network and server latency for remote database calls and distributed transactions can result in slow response times.

The second alternative to full replication is to partition the database. In this scenario, some logical segmentation of the business is chosen as the partition boundary. For example, this boundary could be set at a range of customer numbers or by warehouse locations, accounting periods, or geographic boundary. Each chosen segment would reside within its own database server, resulting in the distribution of overall load across multiple servers. The advantages and disadvantages of this model are very similar to those of the functional distribution model. Additionally, this model requires the development and implementation of a broker or director process to direct incoming database requests to the appropriate server.

Some database software vendors offer proprietary extensions to their core products, which allow multiple database servers to interact with a single physical database (such as Oracle Parallel Server). This strategy allows for one fault-tolerant database storage infrastructure to be built and accessed by multiple servers, eliminating the need for any data replication. Before choosing this option, be sure to analyze the software licensing and maintenance costs associated with this type of solution, compared to the hardware and administrative costs with a replication or distribution strategy. The reputation and support organization behind the particular vendor must also be considered. Many times such options also depend on specific operating systems or complex distributed lock-management systems.

Choosing Hardware Technologies for a Web Farm Database

Database technology is the oldest of any application layer of a Web farm. Databases were first drivesdeveloped on mainframes with the mind-set of a single box with a large computing engine. Even popular culture thinks of a database as a "thing" that exists on a giant mainframe. Microsoft SQL Server is the big player in the .NET world and was originally built for single-server situations. Microsoft SQL Server has its roots in Sybase SQL, a mainframe database.

Many of those original mainframe concepts and ideas still permeate modern database technology. For instance, queries against a single database are typically restricted to a single server; in other words, two separate server memory spaces cannot query the same database data. This is more a result of how databases are utilized than a lack of available technology to entice modification of this strategy.

Selecting Server Hardware

Numerous factors affect the server hardware decisions for Web farm database architectures. Unlike the more common scenario in the Web tier, the number of users and servers connecting to a database doesn't correlate to the hardware requirements. Deciding which hardware to use at the database tier is much more complex and is determined by the following criteria:

- The number of concurrent database sessions can impact Web farm database architectures because connecting and maintaining a connection to a database is one of the most expensive operations that an application can perform.
- Percentages of query types (inserts vs. updates vs. selects) can impact database architecture hardware requirements. Applications with large numbers of inserts and updates might need storage hardware with high write throughput, while applications that return large data sets would benefit from high read transfer rates.
- The number of database calls per Web interaction greatly impacts database and Web server performance. You must limit the number of round-trips from the database to the server; otherwise, the network connectivity to the database becomes the bottleneck.
- The size of typical result sets can impact database CPU performance, storage subsystem latency, and network latency.
- The total database size impacts the amount of disk storage required and the time that backup and restoration tasks take to complete. This is a key consideration for availability requirements because a backup that takes 24 hours to restore might justify a more expensive backup solution.

- Performance requirements greatly impact the architecture of a database. The more power lies under the hood, the better equipped a Web farm is to handle the explosive growth that is so common in Web farm environments.
- Availability requirements affect the hardware and software redundancy choices for the Web farm database architecture. High availability necessitates the move to clustered databases and redundant server hardware. Restore time from backup and time to propagate new and exiting application changes also impact availability decisions.
- Scalability requirements affect hardware and software scalability choices for the Web farm database architecture. Scaling a database means planning for scaleup by leaving room to upgrade memory, CPU, and so on. It also means leveraging special software technologies such as SQL Server Distributed Partitioned Views to achieve scale-out using partitioning technologies.

To meet these requirements, choices for database server hardware must be made carefully because this will be the most important equipment purchase for a Web farm. This hardware is the heart of a Web farm and the database, where all transactions are executed and all data is stored. Because databases don't rely on traditional scaling solutions, making the correct architectural decisions requires understanding unique hardware technology choices. The following list further highlights the importance of database hardware:

- *Web farm database hardware should have room for growth.* The database is the center of a Web farm. It is much easier to replace servers and perform upgrades in the other areas of a Web farm because availability is achieved through many servers doing the same tasks.
- *Web farm database hardware should be fault-tolerant.* Any failures of database hardware can bring down an entire suite of Web farm applications. Losing a single power supply could cause considerable downtime, and redundancy here is worth every extra penny.

Choosing Hardware That Has Room for Growth

With a Web farm database, a single server performs many tasks for many Web applications. Replacing this hardware completely is a migration task that can cause considerable headaches and downtime. Web farm database hardware should provide great performance but also maintain room for growth. Even in the best case of a Windows Server Cluster of databases, there comes a time when the cluster itself must be replaced, and migrating from one cluster to another is a more difficult migration effort.

A Web site that spends time waiting on the database to return data is an unused Web site. Four factors affect performance and growth:

- Disk I/O saturation
- Network latency
- Available CPU cycles
- Available RAM

Choose server hardware (CPUs, network interfaces, storage subsystems, and RAM) that exceed the requirements of the current applications supported. The goal of any Web application is to expand and grow. Sites add new features and gain users over the lifetime of a database. If Web servers become overstressed, it is easy to add more servers and scale out a Web tier, as shown throughout this book. Database hardware is different. Scale-out technologies for databases are just becoming a reality, and most of them are used to create impressive benchmarks. Real-world use is only for highly specific applications. General-purpose database servers rely on scale-up strategies for improving the performance of a database over its lifetime.

With this in mind, purchase hardware that meets the needs of the targeted applications considering 100% growth from the current requirements. Although this means more money up-front for hardware, planning for growth provides a cushion for expandability. When a Web site does reach critical mass, more likely the database tier will feel the pinch the most. To take this concept further, be sure that the database servers have room for growth in memory, disk I/O, expansion slots, and processors. Any good server hardware should be ready for the next wave of faster processors for the currently supported line. Being able to replace 500MHz processors with 750MHz processors is a great way to extend the lifetime of a database server.

Choosing Hardware That Is Fault-Tolerant

Build Web farm database servers for fault tolerance, with redundant hardware at critical single points of failure. The extra money spent on redundant power supplies, network cards, cooling, and disk subsystems can improve the availability of a server from 99% to 99.9%. Consider the following facts when making redundancy decisions:

- From experience, power supplies are the most common component to fail in a server. Use redundant power supplies to prevent unnecessary outages due to power surges and faulty equipment. The cost of adding a second power supply is a minimal cost when compared to the amount of downtime that a server without power causes. Optimally, each power supply should be connected to a separate protected electrical circuit.
- From experience, disk drives are the second most common component to fail in a server. Disk drive subsystems use a Redundant Array of Independent Disks (RAID) to add fault tolerance and increased I/O throughput to what is normally a fault-prone technology.
- Redundant network connections provide a greater level of availability, eliminating single points of failure by providing two network adapter levels and two cables to the network backbone. A cable failure is also a common occurrence and can be minimized with redundancy.

- Cooling systems, such as fans, can fail, leaving a system in a dangerous condition. A computer that runs hot can cause random errors in programs and eventually lead to hardware failure of the CPU and motherboard. Two or more fans give a cushion to replace a fan that has broken.
- The environment hosting the servers must be safe and reliable. Constant availability is required for all electrical, lighting, and air-conditioning systems.

If a system fails and requires a server to be powered down to replace the faulty component, the outage experienced is almost as bad as not having redundant hardware at all. Hot-swappable technologies eliminate the need to power down a server in the event of a component failure. Cooling systems, power supplies, and even disk subsystems are hot-swappable on most server hardware. Hot-swappable memory and CPU chips are less common but are becoming an important feature in some modern server hardware.

Using a Redundant Array of Independent Disks (RAID)

RAID stands for Redundant Array of Independent Disks. RAID is a technique that combines commodity hard drives into a collection, or array, of disks. Different combinations of disks in an array can improve performance or reliability, or both. These combinations are called RAID levels. RAID is used throughout a Web farm for many different applications. This section covers general RAID types and their uses. Although only some RAID levels are suited for Web farm databases, it is important to understand RAID fully to make the right decisions for all parts of the Web farm.

NEW TERM A *RAID level* is a particular combination of disks in an array. Common RAID level designations are RAID-1, RAID-5, and RAID 0+1.

In what is known as the "RAID" paper, Patterson, Gibson, and Katz (at the University of California Berkeley) originally introduced RAID in 1987. Here they described the RAID architecture broken into levels 1 through 5. Each RAID level uses a slightly different combination or technique to improve redundancy and throughput. Later third parties have developed RAID levels 0+1, 6, 7, 10, and 53 (50). Each level has inherent strengths and weaknesses, and the newer levels have been developed for more modern application needs. However, it is wrong to assume that RAID 10 is better than RAID 1. Choosing a RAID level for a particular application depends on criteria and need.

RAID uses combinations of multiple techniques to achieve redundancy and improve I/O throughput. The first of these techniques is called striping. Striping is the process of breaking data that would normally exist sequentially on a single disk across multiple disks. This allows simultaneous access to normally sequential data with increased performance, but it decreases reliability because, if one disk fails, all the data is lost. Figure 20.1 shows a striped set of disks and the access to data across all drives at once.

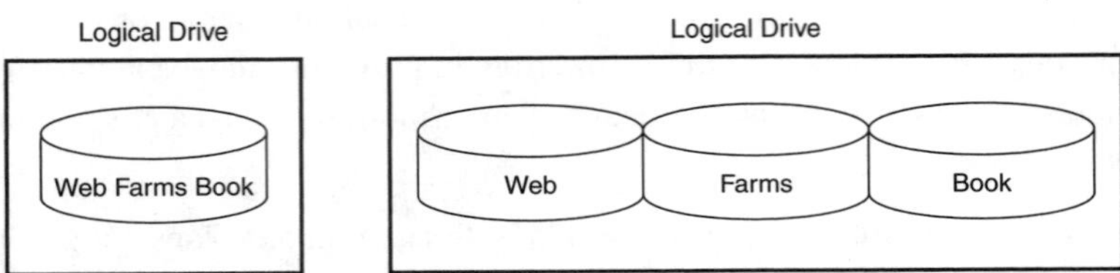

FIGURE 20.1
A striped set of disks vs. a normal disk.

NEW TERM *Striping* is the technique of breaking a sequential stream of data or blocks of varying sizes into multiple sets across multiple drives, allowing for simultaneous access and increased bandwidth to data.

The second technique that RAID uses is called mirroring. Mirroring is the duplication of the same data across multiple disks—hence, a mirror image of the data is created. Complete mirroring provides total redundancy of data at the cost of double the disk space. Many of the RAID levels attempt to address this by using parity error-checking techniques to provide less than 100% duplication but still 100% recoverability in case of failures. Figure 20.2 shows a full mirrored set of disks and the corresponding data distribution.

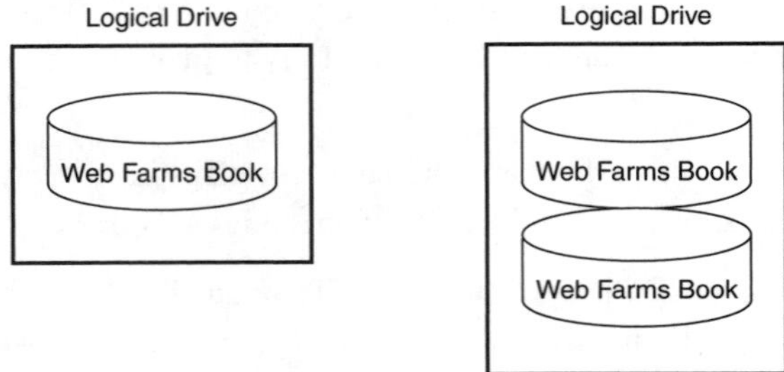

FIGURE 20.2
A mirrored set of disks vs. a normal disk

NEW TERM *Mirroring,* or *duplexing,* is the technique of duplicating a block of data across multiple drives, allowing redundancy and recoverability of data during failures.

Combining mirroring and striping techniques produces the different RAID levels. For example, RAID 1 is complete mirroring of data for total redundancy, while RAID 5 stripes data across multiple drives and uses parity data for redundancy.

RAID Levels

The following sections describe the different RAID levels available on the market today. Each level's pros, cons, and appropriate application use are covered. RAID level availability is a function of the hardware or software providing the RAID capability. Be sure to investigate what RAID levels a storage device supports before purchasing it. It is important to understand a few terms when considering RAID technologies:

- *Transfer rate* is the rate at which a single write or read operation is completed. This transfer rate applies only to contiguous operations.
- *Transaction rate* is the rate at which multiple unique requests are made to a RAID configuration. A transaction starts a transfer.
- *ECC* stands for error correction code and is used to restore lost data in some RAID configurations.

RAID-0

RAID-0 is striping of disks without redundancy and fault tolerance. This provides high performance throughput and no wasted space. The failure of a single disk in a RAID-0 array means that the entire set is unusable and that data can be recovered only through restoring from backup. RAID-0 was not one of the original RAID configurations, but it is important to understand for RAID 0+1 and RAID 1+0 configurations. Table 20.1 summarizes the characteristics of RAID-0 configurations.

TABLE 20.1 Characteristics of RAID-0 Configurations

Topic	*Summary*
Pros	Striping is a high-performance technique because I/O access (both read and write) is spread across many drives and channels.
	It saves on costs because all disk storage is 100% utilized in the array.
	Parity calculation is eliminated.
	RAID-0 is simple and easy to implement in software or hardware.
Cons	No fault tolerance exists, so the R in RAID is not really used here.
	One drive failure means loss of all data in array.
	The RAID-0 block size is often not supported by standard drives or OS; special controllers or OS might be necessary.
Storage Utilization	This equals n disks × disk capacity.
Web Farm Uses	OS and Data disk on highly redundant server farms like Web and streaming media clusters that can afford loss of single server while disk is recovered.

Figure 20.1 shows a typical RAID-0 configuration because it is only a striped set.

RAID-1

RAID-1 is pure mirroring of disks. This provides a high read rate because data can be read from both disks but at the cost of storage. It takes twice the amount of storage as RAID-0 to equal the same amount of storage on RAID-1. In the original RAID paper, RAID-1 was the reference point that the other RAID levels were derived from. With disks costs lowering in recent years, the cost of RAID-1 is still high but not prohibitive. Table 20.2 summarizes the characteristics of RAID-1 configurations.

TABLE 20.2 Characteristics of RAID-1 Configurations

Topic	*Summary*
Pros	As long as both disks in a mirrored pair don't fail, all data integrity is maintained.
	RAID-1 allows for simultaneous reads per mirrored pair for increased performance.
	Read transaction rate is *n* times the number of disks in the mirror set. Write transaction rate is the same as that for a single disk and higher than RAID-3 or RAID-5.
	Disk replacement is simple; replace the bad disk, and copy the contents of its mirror partner to it.
	Design is simple to understand and implement. It is supported by both hardware and software.
Cons	Twice as much storage, space, and power is needed to equal the capacity of a RAID-0 array.
	Usable storage capacity is 50% true capacity.
	Software solutions might burden the CPU and OS.
	Transfer rates are the same as those for single disks.
Storage Utilization	This equals n disks $\times$ disk capacity $\div$ 2
Web Farm Uses	OS and Data disk on Application server, domain controller, or other server that may not have high redundancy at the server layer.

Figure 20.2 shows a typical RAID-1 configuration because it is only a mirrored set.

RAID-2

RAID-2 configurations use striping in combination with Hamming Code ECC. As data is written to the striped sets of disks, a corresponding ECC word is recorded on the ECC disks. When data is read from the array, the Hamming Code is used to verify the correctness of the data. Figure 20.3 shows a RAID-2 configuration.

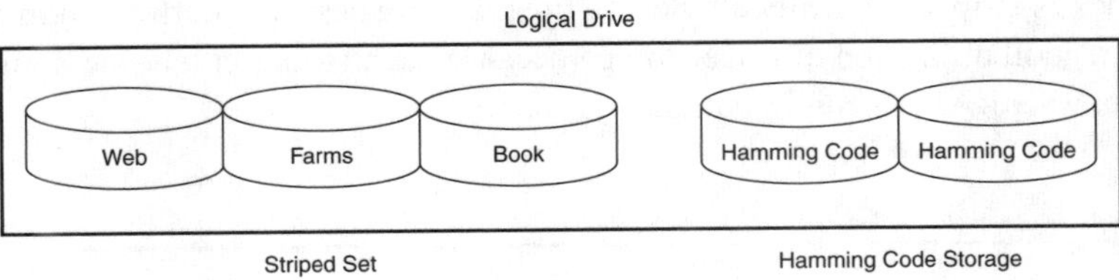

FIGURE 20.3
A RAID-2 configuration.

RAID-2 is not used much today because there are many limitations to this configuration. The number of Hamming Code ECC disks required is high, and the transfer rates needed makes this an unattractive error-correction methodology. The Hamming Code error detection adds unneeded controller complexity for detection of data corruptions. It is intended for use with disk drives that lack the built-in error detection offered by manufacturers today. RAID-2 is no longer considered commercially viable. Table 20.3 summarizes the characteristics of a RAID-2 configuration.

TABLE 20.3 Characteristics of RAID-2 Configurations

Topic	*Summary*
Pros	Data correction is accomplished in real time when a Hamming Code comparison fails the data is corrected at that point.
	RAID-2 can provide very fast transfer for writes and reads rates.
Cons	RAID-2 can require a large amount of Hamming Code disks, sometimes approaching RAID-1 requirements.
	Only obscure commercially implementation is possible because other forms of RAID are as fast and easier to implement.
	Controller technology is more complex and requires the capability to calculate Hamming Codes in real time.
Storage Utilization	This equals $n \times$ number of disks – the space required for Hamming Code ECC storage. It is dependant on implementation and transfer rates.
Web Farm Uses	No uses exist, when compared to other RAID levels.

RAID-3

RAID-3 is the first RAID level that uses parity calculations and striping for increased redundancy and throughput. RAID-3 provides for high transfer rates for reads and writes because every data block is striped, typically a byte at a time, and requests are performed in parallel. It also provides a good utilization of drive storage because each stripe set has one parity disk. Figure 20.4 shows a RAID-3 configuration.

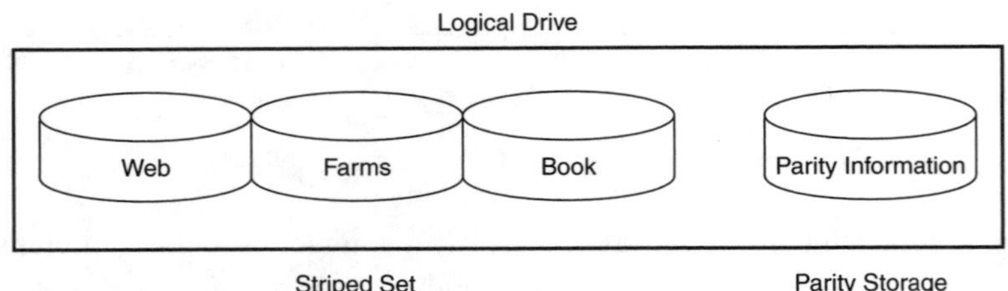

FIGURE 20.4
A RAID-3 configuration.

RAID-3 uses sector-sized stripes and drive arm synchronization between the disks of the array. Parity information is used to recover data on a single failed disk with an EOR (exclusive OR) operation to the data on the other disks. Parity calculation requires a read to every disk to calculate parity, so write transaction rate is only slightly better than that of a single disk.

TABLE 20.4 Characteristics of RAID-3 Configurations

Topic	*Summary*
Pros	High read and write transfer rates are involved.
	Only one drive is used per striped set for parity information.
	Single disk failures don't affect performance or operation in the array.
Cons	RAID-3 does not support loss of more than one drive in the array.
	The writes transaction rate is not much better than single disk.
	Complex hardware controllers are required to implement successfully.
	Recovery of failed disk can be time-consuming because regeneration of the failed disks requires reading all data on all disks.
	RAID-3 is difficult to implement due to block size and spindle synchronization requirements for all disks.

TABLE 20.4 Continued

Topic	*Summary*
Storage Utilization	This equals (n disks – 1) × the capacity of each disk.
Web Farm Uses	No uses exist in a Web farm. Other RAID levels are better.

RAID-4

RAID-4 is similar to RAID-3 in that it uses larger blocks of data. This eliminates some of the problems of read transaction throughput of RAID-3 because transactions on blocks of data can be performed simultaneously across multiple drives in the stripe set. However, write transactions are worse because blocks of data are written sequentially and depend on the parity drive. RAID 5 has replaced RAID-4 because it uses a single parity drive as RAID-3 does. Figure 20.5 shows a RAID-4 configuration.

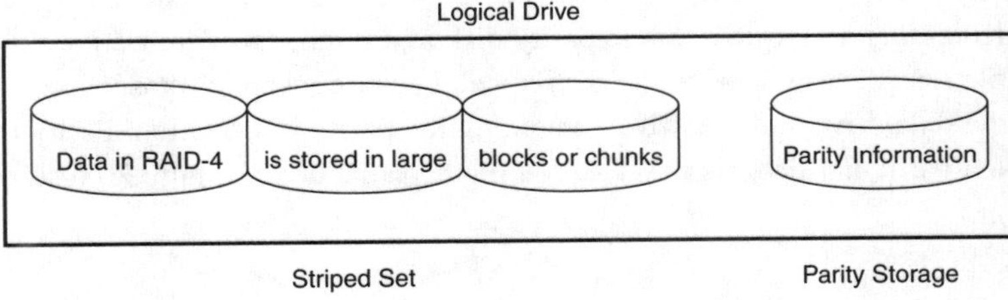

FIGURE 20.5
A RAID-4 configuration.

Table 20.5 summarizes the characteristics of a RAID-4 configuration.

TABLE 20.5 Characteristics of RAID-4 Configurations

Topic	*Summary*
Pros	The read transaction rate is high.
	The read and write transfer rate is high.
	Only one drive is used per striped set for parity information.
	Single disk failures don't affect performance or operation in the array.
Cons	The block read transfer rate is equal to that of a single disk if controllers don't read from striped set simultaneously.
	The write transaction rate is poor.

TABLE 20.5 Continued

Topic	*Summary*
	Hardware implementations are required and are very complex and expensive.
	Recovery of failed disks can be time consuming because regeneration of the failed disks requires reading all data on all disks.
Storage Utilization	This equals (*n* disks – 1) × the capacity of each disk.
Web Farm Uses	No uses exist; use RAID-5 instead.

RAID-5

RAID-5 is historically the most popular RAID configuration. It has better write performance than RAID-2, -3, or -4 because it is an independent collection of disks (the striped set) with distributed parity information across all the disks. This distribution of parity data reduces the contention surrounding access to a single parity disk and improves write transaction performance. Multiple reads and writes can be overlapped because a single transaction uses two drives, at most: the data drive and the drive containing the parity information. Parity information for the data on a particular drive is never stored on the same drive. Figure 20.6 shows a RAID-5 configuration.

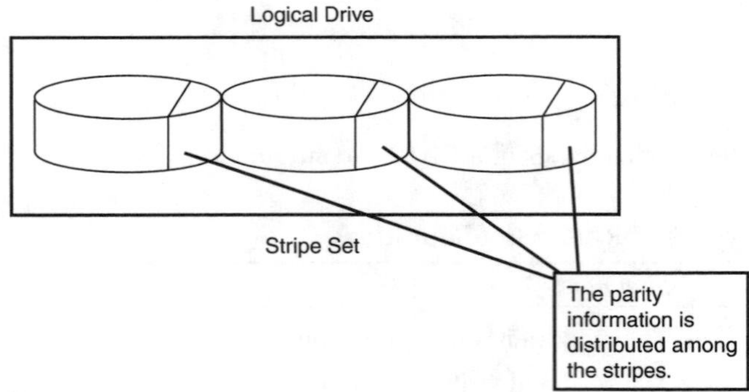

FIGURE 20.6
A RAID-5 configuration.

In RAID-5, the disks' arms and data access are not synchronized. This allows the disks to serve different data requests independently. The number of disks in an array corresponds directly to the number of independent requests a RAID-5 configuration can handle. Table 20.6 summarizes the characteristics of a RAID-5 configuration.

TABLE 20.6 Characteristics of RAID-5 Configurations

Topic	*Summary*
Pros	The read transfer and transaction rates are high. The write transaction rate is much better than in RAID-3 or RAID-4. Parity data takes equivalent space as on RAID-3 and RAID-4 configurations. Great fault tolerance exists.
Cons	Single disk failures affect performance or operation in the array minimally. Complex design requires hardware implementation. Only single disk failure can be sustained before loss of data occurs. Recovery of failed disk can be time-consuming.
Storage Utilization	Equals (*n* disks – 1) × the capacity of each disk.
Web Farm Uses	RAID-5 is useful for all Web farm equipment. It is considered now to be the "poor man's choice" for RAID solutions in a Web farm because it gives the best price/performance/redundancy ratio. The only solutions that are better are potentially RAID 0+1 and RAID-10.

RAID 0+1

RAID 0+1 is a configuration of disks that results in entire stripes of RAID-0 configurations being mirrored together as a RAID-1 configuration. When data is read from a mirrored striped set, it can come from either disk in the mirror and can be transferred from many separate disks in the stripe set. Data is written to all disks in the striped set and is mirrored. Figure 20.7 shows a RAID 0+1 configuration.

This technique provides the best of both worlds from the perspective of a RAID-0 and RAID-1 transfer and transaction. Redundancy is equivalent to RAID-5. The main drawbacks to RAID 0+1 are that it is as expensive as RAID-1 and can sustain only one drive failure. Drive failure also reduces the array to a RAID-0 state.

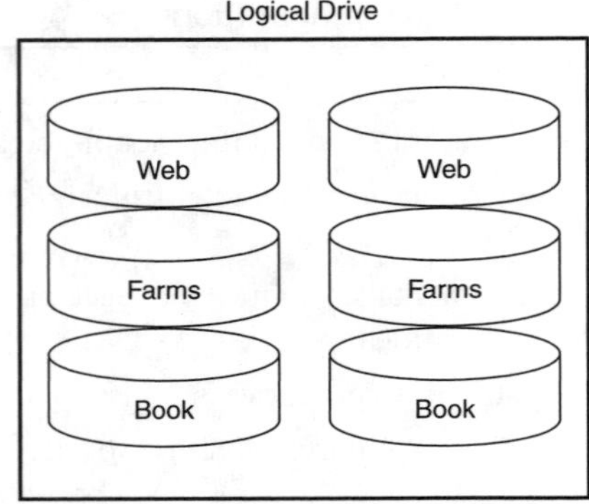

FIGURE 20.7
A RAID 0+1 configuration.

TABLE 20.7 Characteristics of RAID 0+1 Configurations

Topic	*Summary*
Pros	Fault tolerance is the same as that of RAID-5.
	Transfer and transaction rates are high because of striping.
	The same disk space is used as with RAID-1, but four disks are required to start rather than two.
Cons	Loss of a single drive reduces the configuration to a RAID-0 state with no fault tolerance and affects performance of the array.
	All drives must move together, reducing overall sustained throughput.
	It is very expensive to implement and requires double the disk space.
Storage Utilization	This equals n disks ÷ 2 × the capacity of each disk.
Web Farm Uses	Web farm databases lack support for RAID-10 configurations.

RAID-10 or 1+0

A RAID-10 or 1+0 (RAID-10) configuration provides the best combination of mirroring and striping in use today. A RAID-10 configuration is said to be mirrored disks striped together. This provides the throughput of a RAID 0+1 solution with the reliability of RAID-1. Figure 20.8 shows a RAID-10 configuration.

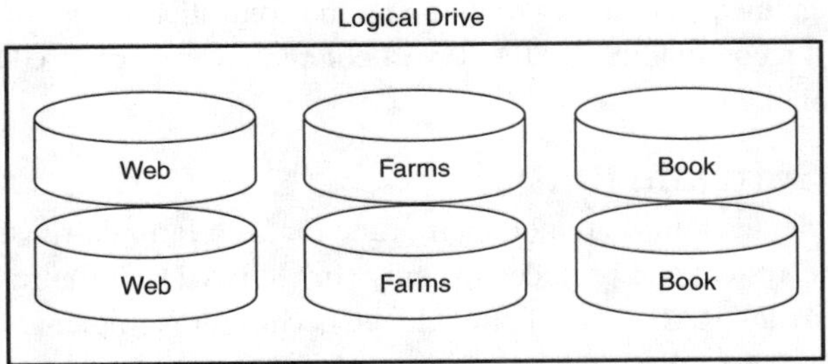

FIGURE 20.8
A RAID-10 configuration.

Because multiple mirrored sets are striped together, a single drive from each mirrored set can fail without affecting the data availability of the entire array. Second, performance is only minimally impacted because the loss of a single drive in a mirror does not affect all the other mirrored pairs. RAID-10 arrays have the same overhead as RAID-1 solutions. Table 20.8 summarizes the characteristics of a RAID-10 configuration.

TABLE 20.8 Characteristics of RAID-10 Configurations

Topic	*Summary*
Pros	RAID-10 uses the same fault tolerance as RAID-1.
	Transfer and transactions rates are the highest because of the combination of RAID-0 and RAID-1.
	Multiple drives can fail as long as at least one member of each mirror set remains available.
Cons	All drives must move together, reducing overall sustained throughput.
	Very complicated controller technology is involved.
	RAID-10 is very expensive to implement and requires double the disk space.
Storage Utilization	This equals n disks ÷ 2 × the capacity of each disk.
Web Farm Uses	Highly available, high-volume Web farm databases can be used.

For Web farm database architectures, RAID-10 is the best choice for a RAID configuration. RAID-10 provides the highest availability of any RAID solution, with incredible transfer and transaction rates due to the multiple parallel access points to data. It is an expensive solution requiring specialized equipment and almost twice the storage capacity of a RAID-5 solution.

As the cost of storage media continues to drop and the controller technology supporting RAID-10 becomes more of a commodity, RAID-10 will completely replace RAID-5 in the Web farm in critical application areas.

Hardware vs. Software RAID

Software RAID implementations are not appropriate for Web farm databases. Software RAID adds overhead to the system and provides for only simple RAID configurations such as RAID-0 and RAID-1. Hardware RAID is the better choice because it is implemented in hardware and is much faster than software RAID. Most hardware RAID implementations have a variety of RAID levels available, and some support hot-swapping of failed disk and automated disk rebuilding capabilities. Hardware RAID has become much more of a commodity in the last few years and is worth the extra dollars.

Using Advanced Storage Solutions

Choosing a RAID solution is only part of the hardware decision for Web farm database architectures. The second choice is whether to use storage inside the database server or to use an advanced form of external storage. The following section discusses the three main choices for external storage: shared storage arrays, storage area networks, and network-attached storage.

Shared Storage Arrays

A shared storage array (SSA) is the simplest of all external storage solutions. An SSA is typically a vendor-specific rack-mountable collection of drive bays that have the following characteristics:

- An SSA has a simple interface for connecting drives with controllers, usually SCSI, but some support Fibre Channel configurations.
- An SSA has a limited number of ports for connecting servers to the external storage. These ports typically don't support connections to other expansion devices such as Fibre Channel switches.
- An SSA is used to create a basic Windows Server Cluster, providing the shared quorum resource and the shared physical disk resources for a database.
- An SSA has limited management and flexibility, but most support hot-swappable drive replacement and various RAID configurations.
- An SSA typically has a vendor-specific and proprietary specification for accessing the drives in the array.

An SSA is an inexpensive starting point for Web farm database architectures' external storage needs. It is the minimum requirement for the storage solution of a Windows Server Cluster. An SSA will provide limited capability to expand a database's storage capability and provide enough flexibility to allow a Web farm database to grow. If other, more robust external storage solutions are not in place (such as a SAN), an SSA is a safe and acceptable choice for a new Web farm.

Storage Area Networks

A storage area network (SAN) is a specialized network that connects data storage devices to servers and has the following characteristics:

- A SAN is a high-speed network, typically in the 1Gbps range. This network is like a computer bus for storage that is shared by many servers.
- A SAN uses specialized network hardware for backbone communication, such as industry-standard Fibre Channel switches.
- A SAN provides a layer of abstraction between the storage device and the servers, allowing the physical disk configuration to grow, shrink, or change based on need.
- A SAN supports standard data-management tasks, including archiving of data, sharing of data across servers, disk mirroring, and backup and restore.
- A SAN can interoperate with existing shared storage arrays and network attached storage devices.

Web farm database architectures use a SAN to provide a flexible, expandable, and manageable data network. The storage needs of a successful Web farm will grow over time. As transaction volumes increase, the amount of storage and time required to perform backups increases. The speed at which data is retrieved and the overall performance of queries can decrease due to I/O problems with standard disks in high-volume environments. A SAN provides flexibility and ease of management to grow the storage available to handle the increased transactions and backups. High performance is maintained by adding or replacing components that become overburdened (switches, controllers, disks, and server adapters). Figure 20.9 shows a simple SAN with storage and servers connected through a Fibre Channel switch.

The number of servers needing access to data also grows over time, and a SAN accommodates this growth by providing switch-based port access to data and the capability to add storage and controllers as new devices on the SAN. A Web farm with a SAN provides a simple mechanism for growth. A SAN defines a plan for growing storage needs and makes decisions about adding storage and controllers simple.

NOTE

For more information on storage area networks, see the Storage Networking Industry Association's Web site, `http://www.snia.org/`.

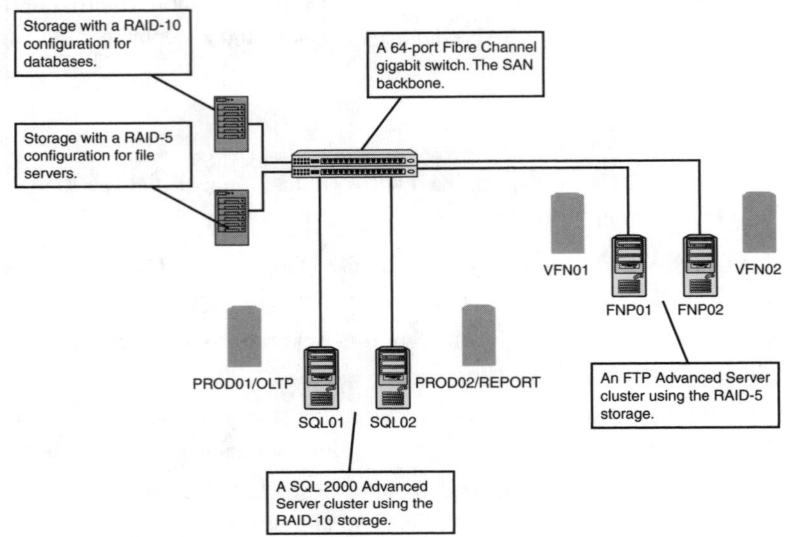

FIGURE 20.9
A SAN for a Web farm.

Network-Attached Storage

Network-attached storage (NAS) is a device that acts like a file server without the overhead of operating system software and server hardware. NAS has the following characteristics:

- NAS is a network-addressable set of physical disks with the capability to connect to an Ethernet network and have at least one IP address.
- NAS is typically implemented using the most popular network file access protocols, including Microsoft's Internetwork Packet Exchange (IPE) and NetBEUI, Sun's Network File System, and Novell's IPE.
- NAS devices appear as servers on the network and either have standard file share points or mapped drives or can be accessed with fully qualified paths.
- NAS devices have management software that allows the creation of file share points and configuration of security access permissions for the different network and security systems supported.
- NAS uses RAID to provide redundancy and performance improvements when accessing data.
- NAS can use a SAN to provide the physical disk storage or, in some cases, could be a component of a SAN.

A NAS is a fully redundant, highly available network file share point that provides a simple plug-and-play methodology for network file access. A Web farm database would not use a NAS for its database storage. However, Web farms have other uses for NAS, including the storage of database backups, a file share for common data for Web sites or other applications that support a Web farm. Figure 20.10 shows a NAS in use as an intermediary backup device for a database, before writing the backup to tape. These "hot" backups provide for a faster restore from the last known good backup of a database than a slower tape device can offer. In this example, the tape backup may be used as an off-site backup for recovery from disaster or catastrophic failure.

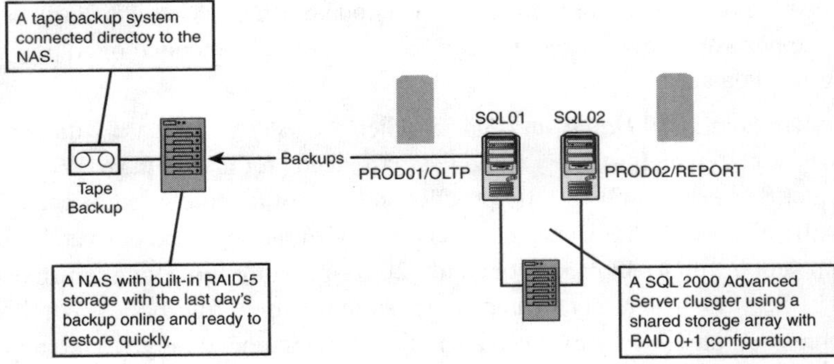

FIGURE 20.10
A NAS device as a backup point for a Web farm database.

Choosing Software Technologies for a Web Farm Database

The software that a Web farm database uses is just as important as the hardware. Without robust and flexible software, the best hardware configuration has no chance to handle a growing Web farm. Assuming that the database is SQL Server 2000, two choices must be made in relation to software:

- Pick the correct version of Windows based on the number of CPUs required, maximum memory utilization, and whether the Web farm database is in a Windows Server Cluster.
- Pick the clustering configuration for the Windows Server Cluster that will support a Web farm database.

Choosing a Windows 2000 Operating System Version

Three Windows 2000 operating systems can support Web farm database architectures:

- *Choose Windows 2000 Server* when a single server configuration is desired. Windows 2000 Server supports up to four CPUs and 4GB of memory. Windows 2000 Server cannot be used in a Windows Server Cluster. It is recommended that all mission-critical databases supporting Web farm applications use a Windows Server Cluster for high availability of the server hardware and SQL Server application.
- *Choose Windows 2000 Advanced Server* when a clustered configuration is desired. Windows 2000 Advanced Server supports up to eight CPUs and 8GB of memory. With Advanced Server, it is possible to create two node clusters. Windows 2000 Advanced Server supports Windows Server Clusters and is the recommended operating system for all Web farm databases.
- *Choose Windows 2000 Datacenter Server* when a clustered database with two eight-CPU machines is not enough to support the database needs for a Web farm. Windows 2000 Datacenter Server is an OEM-only product and cannot be purchased directly from Microsoft. Windows 2000 Datacenter Server configuration varies per vendor but, in general, can support up to 32 processors and 32GB of memory in a single instance. In a Windows Server Cluster, Datacenter Server supports up to four nodes. Windows 2000 Datacenter Server is a very expensive solution recommended only for the highest-volume sites.

Choosing a Windows Cluster Service Configuration

Assuming that an Advanced Server is the choice for operating system and the database is in a Windows Server Cluster, there are two types of configurations:

- *Choose Active/Passive* when high availability is the goal even during the highest transaction volume. In the active passive configuration, instances of SQL Server only are active on one node in a two-node cluster at a time. This means that as long as utilization on the single node of the cluster is less than 100%, the second node (with identical hardware) will be capable of handling the volume during failover. The choice for Active/Passive is less of an issue because it is so easy to install and configure instances of SQL Server 2000. See Chapter 21, “Clustering SQL Server 2000,” for more details on how to install and configure SQL 2000 on a cluster.
- *Choose Active/Active* when high availability and maximum hardware utilization are important. An Active/Active configuration is the best utilization of clustered hardware because both nodes in the cluster are handling database requests. Each instance of SQL 2000 handles different databases, so this doesn’t allow a single database to scale to mul-

tiple servers. However, it does provide an application that needs multiple database the capability to split these databases to multiple servers for the highest throughput. Active/Active configurations tend to run the risk of overutilization of a single node, so be careful that utilization on either node never exceeds 50% for long periods of time. If this does happen, the database might become unavailable during failover because of the overutilization of a single node in the cluster.

Neither of these choices makes any recommendations for the number of instances of SQL Server to run on a single cluster. Nothing precludes an Active/Passive configuration from running two instances of SQL server on the same node in the cluster. Most normal Active/Passive configurations will run one instance on a single node. Figure 20.11 shows this configuration.

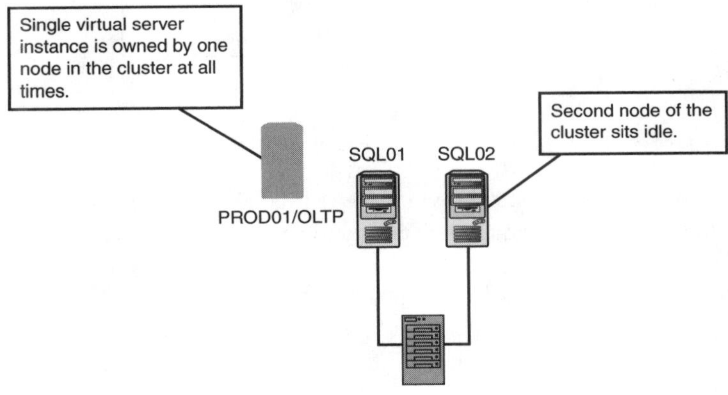

FIGURE 20.11
An Active/Passive Web farm database with one SQL Server 2000 instance.

A second form of Active/Passive configuration makes much better use of cluster hardware by running a second instance of SQL 2000 on the "passive" node of the cluster, housing a staging version of the production database. This means that both nodes of the cluster are used, but the passive node only supports a staging environment. During failover, utilization of the staging environment must be controlled and minimized so that the production database is not impacted. This also provides an identically configured box for the staging environment for stress testing. This configuration does cause some difficulties when upgrading versions of the operating system or SQL 2000, but as long as a testing area is available to stage these upgrades, the gain in availability might be worth the risk, while not wasting server hardware. Figure 20.12 shows an Active/Passive configuration with two separate deployment stages.

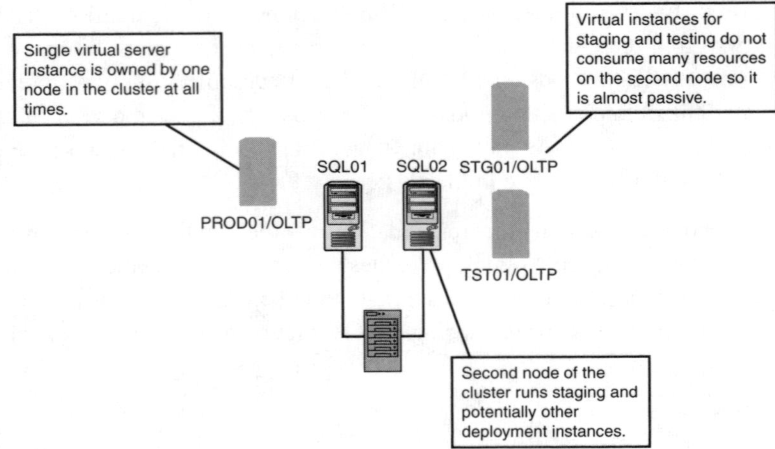

FIGURE 20.12

An Active/Passive Web farm database with multiple deployment instances.

Finally, Active/Active configuration runs two or more production instances of SQL 2000 on a cluster. Each node is assigned a primary owner of an instance. Because each instance runs on its own node of the cluster, SQL Server 2000 can fully utilize it. Numerous risks are associated with this configuration, including loss of availability of the cluster during failovers if one node does not have the capability to handle the work of two. Figure 20.13 shows an Active/Active configuration.

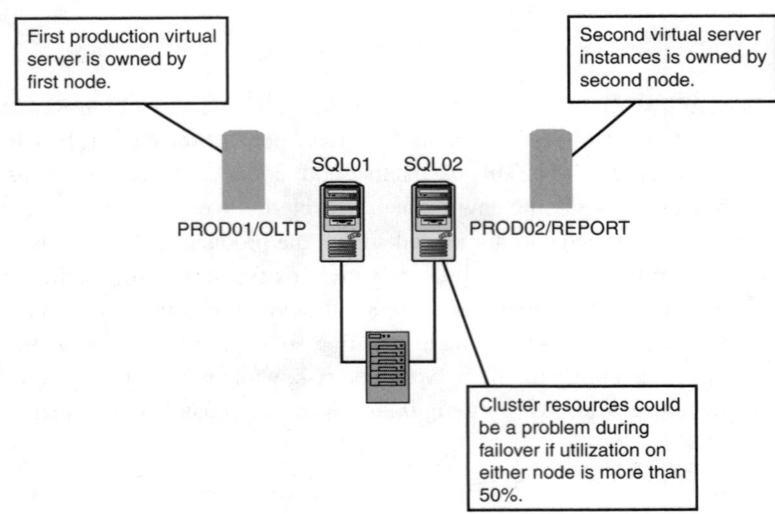

FIGURE 20.13

An Active/Active Web farm database with multiple production instances.

Summary

Web farm database architectures are the key component to successful Web farm applications. The hardware of database architectures provides the Web farm foundation. Functional database distribution or data portioning facilitates database scaling by proving a means for administrators to manage load against a database server farm. The RAID configuration used for database storage must provide high availability and great performance for the Web farm applications. Advanced storage solutions can offer flexibility and growth potential for the storage needs of a Web farm. Together with redundant server hardware, the picture of a highly available and manageable Web farm database architecture is clear.

The software of a Web farm database uses the hardware to provide the real application-level functionality. The choice of operating system for the server hardware determines the maximum number of processors and amount of memory available for database server software such as SQL 2000. The operating system also determines whether a database server can run in a clustered configuration for the highest level of availability. Windows Server Clusters provide the capability to run a database in Active/Passive mode for high availability and guaranteed failover capacity of mission-critical applications and in Active/Active mode for complete utilization of expensive database hardware.

Taken together, the software and hardware of Web farm database architectures form the heart of a Web farm application. If this heart is healthy and robust, with the capability to grow, the impact of a successful Web site on a database architecture can be minimized. Because replacing the heart of a Web farm is a major logistical and availability challenge, picking the best hardware and software is a critical decision that should be made only after careful consideration.

Clustering SQL Server 2000

CHAPTER

21

IN THIS CHAPTER

Clustering a SQL Server 2000 installation is the final step in building an architecture for a Web farm that can sustain system outages and failures in hardware and software at the database tier. Clustering increases the availability rating of a Web farm because the database is no longer a single point of failure, and a Web farm is protected from a hardware failure on the database server. A Web farm needs a highly available database tier to complement Web and application servers that achieve high availability with Application Center 2000 or hardware base load balancing technologies.

SQL Server 2000 provides rich built-in support for Window Server clusters. SQL Server 2000 in conjunction with a Windows Server cluster delivers the highest availability for mission-critical database applications on the Windows 2000 platform. Through the setup program for SQL Server 2000, administrators configure and install SQL Server to one node of a cluster, and the setup program takes care of the rest. There is never a situation in which a mission-critical database should not be clustered and run from a Windows Server cluster.

The goals of this chapter are to help you

- Understand how SQL Server 2000 failover clustering works with a Windows Server cluster. Topics include preparing a cluster for SQL Server 2000 and how to use multiple instances of SQL Server 2000 on a server cluster.
- Learn how to manage instances of SQL Server 2000 on a Windows Server cluster. Included are step-by-step instructions for installing, uninstalling, and configuring a SQL Server 2000 instance on a cluster using the SQL Server 2000 setup program. This section describes the complete setup process for the clustering aspect of SQL Server 2000.

Understanding SQL Server 2000 Failover Clustering

Creating a high availability SQL Server has come a long way from the days of clustering SQL Server 7.0. Gone is the special cluster wizard that created the virtual server instances. Gone are the difficulties and risks in applying service pack upgrades and hot fixes. Gone is the SQL Server 7.0 cluster limitation of two virtual SQL instances. SQL Server 7.0 was very hard to cluster and very hard to maintain once clustered. That is not the case with SQL 2000.

NEW TERM A *failover cluster* is a SQL Server 2000 instance installed to nodes on a Windows Server cluster. These special instances of SQL Server can move from node to node in a Windows Server cluster for high availability.

Creating a SQL Server failover cluster is an integrated setup option for SQL Server 2000 Enterprise Edition. Enterprise Edition is required for all scenarios involving Windows Server clusters and will be referred to as SQL Server 2000 for the remainder of this chapter. During setup, SQL Server 2000 examines the target server and determines if it is running a Windows Server cluster. If it detects a valid installation, the Setup Wizard installs SQL Server 2000 and creates the correct cluster resources for a failover cluster.

NOTE

Using failover clustering requires SQL Server 2000 Enterprise Edition.

Using Multiple Instances on a Cluster

One of the most useful features of SQL Server 2000 is the capability to install multiple, separate instances to the same physical server. Each instance of a SQL server contains a separate directory for its binaries and program files. A server with multiple instances will have a separate copy of the SQL Server binaries for each instance.

NOTE

SQL Server 2000 supports two types of instance installations for failover clustering: default and named.

A default instance uses the network name of the virtual server group that the instance is associated with. For example, a default instance installed into a cluster group that contains a network name resource `VSQL` is addressed from clients using the `VSQL` name. This is the equivalent configuration to a Windows Server cluster with SQL Server 7.0 installed. In fact, SQL Server 7.0 only supports instances that have names that are equivalent to the network name resource.

There can be only one default instance per server cluster whether that instance is SQL Server 2000 or SQL Server 7.0. The default instance in SQL Server 2000 is equivalent, from the application perspective, to a clustered installation of SQL Server 7.0. It is not possible to install a default instance of SQL Server 2000 side by side with a SQL Server 7.0 installation. To do this requires a named instance of SQL Server 2000.

A named instance combines the network name of the target virtual server group and the SQL Server 2000 instance name to create a uniquely addressable name. That name is assigned during the setup process for a failover cluster and is used in the creation of the copies of the binaries, service names, and Registry entries for a named instance of SQL Server. For example, if the network name resource of the target cluster group is `VSQL`, and the SQL Server 2000 instance name is `PROD`, then the unique instance name is `VSQL\PROD`. Use this full name in connection strings and when connecting to the instance from the SQL Server tools.

NOTE

SQL Server 2000 supports 16 unique installation instances (including the default instance) in each Windows Server cluster.

The install path for an instance on a server cluster must be available for both nodes of the cluster during setup. This means that the install path must exist on a local drive and be creatable on both nodes of the cluster. Failover clustering setup will fail if the other nodes in the cluster cannot support the installation because of disk space limitations and duplicate instance names (that are not clustered, for example).

Preparing a Cluster for SQL Server 2000

A SQL Server 2000 failover cluster requires a few preinstall configuration steps on the target cluster:

1. Define a group that will hold the resources required for a clustered SQL Server 2000 instance.
2. Create the physical disk resources for the databases on the shared drive array, making sure they have the same drive letters on both nodes of the cluster, and add them to the group.
3. Configure the private networks as described in Chapter 18, "Creating a Windows 2000 Server Cluster."
4. Create a domain user account and assign it to the Administrator group of each node in the cluster.

From here, complete the Setup Wizard to install an instance of SQL Server on a Windows Server cluster.

Managing Instances of SQL Server 2000 on a Windows Server Cluster

Use the SQL Server 2000 setup program to install, upgrade, or remove SQL Server 2000 instances. The setup program is a simple wizard that treats managing instances across multiple nodes in a cluster like a single server. This means that the setup program for a single cluster instance needs to be run only once to install or remove it from all nodes in a cluster.

CAUTION

Install a clustered instance of SQL Server 2000 to only one node of the cluster. This node should own the shared drives that store the system databases. Running the setup program on a second node and creating the same named instance will cause the failover capabilities of SQL Server 2000 to malfunction.

Installing SQL Server 2000 to a Windows Server Cluster

To install a clustered instance of SQL Server 2000, run the setup program from the SQL Server 2000 CD. If it does not launch automatically, select `AUTORUN.EXE` from the `root` directory. From the main setup screen, select SQL Server 2000 Components. From the next screen, select Install Database Server. This launches the SQL Server 2000 Setup Wizard.

The first step in the Setup Wizard is to choose the type of server installation. Figure 21.1 shows the Computer Name page of the Setup Wizard. From this page, select the virtual server instance to have the Setup Wizard create or use an existing virtual server active on this node of the cluster. If the virtual server exists, the setup program checks to be sure that the cluster group does not already contain an instance of SQL Server associated with that virtual server. If the cluster does not have that virtual server instance, the setup program will create the network name and IP address resource later during the setup process.

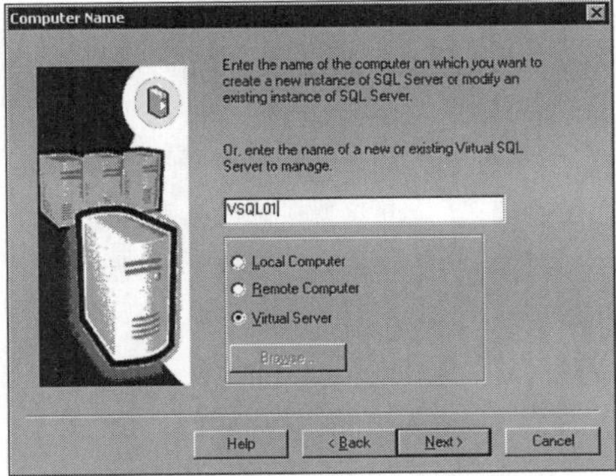

FIGURE 21.1
The Computer Name page of the SQL Server 2000 Setup Wizard.

Click through the User Information and Software Licensing page of the Setup Wizard to the Failover Clustering page. Configure the mixed and public cluster networks used to communicate with this SQL Server instance. Figure 21.2 shows this page. Select the cluster network to use for this IP address from the Network to Use combo box. Type the IP address for the subnet associated with each cluster network in the IP Address box. The subnet mask is programmatically assigned from the configuration information stored in the cluster. Click the Add button for each network that will be associated with this instance. A SQL Server instance can have any number of cluster networks associated with it for greater redundancy.

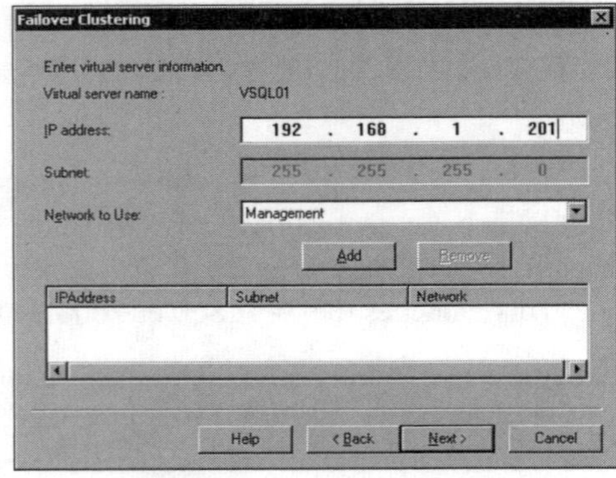

FIGURE 21.2
The Failover Clustering page of the SQL Server 2000 Setup Wizard.

The next page of the Setup Wizard is the Cluster Disk Selection page. This page displays all the cluster groups that contain physical disk resources but not existing instances of SQL Server. Select the cluster group that contains the shared drives that are used by SQL Server to store the databases for this instance. Figure 21.3 shows the Cluster Disk Selection page.

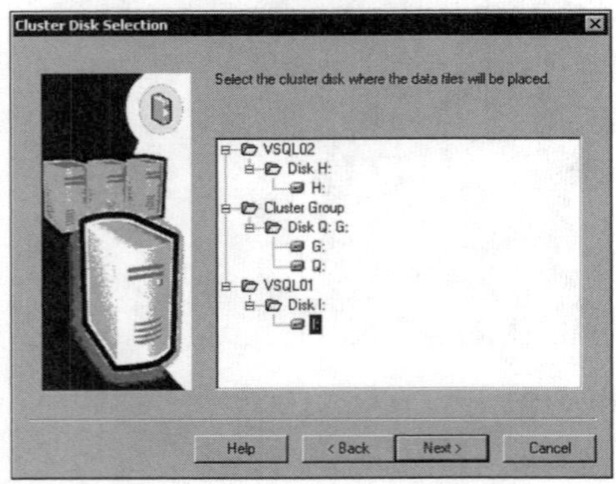

FIGURE 21.3
The Cluster Disk Selection page of the SQL Server 2000 Setup Wizard.

CAUTION

Do not use the cluster group that contains the quorum resource for a SQL Server 2000 instance. The quorum physical disk resource should be used to store the cluster database and track cluster state.

The next page of the Setup Wizard is the Cluster Management page. The setup program installs, either locally or remotely, this new instance of SQL Server to the nodes chosen on this page. By default, the setup program installs new instances to all nodes in the cluster. Nodes that are not available show up in the Unavailable Node list box for the following reasons:

- They are unable to join the cluster correctly due to failed network connectivity, hardware failure, or failure of the Cluster service to start.
- The node already contains an instance of SQL Server with the named or default instance being created.

To add a node from the Available Nodes list box, select the node and click the Add button. To remove a node from the Configured Nodes list box, select the node and click the Remove button. For failover to work correctly, a SQL Server 2000 instance must be installed on at least two nodes.

The next page of the Setup Wizard prompts the administrator for valid credentials on the remote node that has administrative privileges for installing the instance. This account should be a member of the local Administrator group on all nodes of a cluster. The domain account that the SQL Server 2000 instance runs as should have sufficient privileges to complete the installation on the remote node(s).

The rest of the wizard proceeds the same as the installation of a non-clustered SQL Server 2000 instance. The Services Account page, shown in Figure 21.4, has an effect on the setup in regard to a clustered instance. The clustered services must run as a domain account that is a member of the local administrators account on both nodes of the cluster. It is possible and recommended to use a different account from the domain account that is used for the Cluster service itself.

It is important to consider in advance the SQL Server options to be installed on a clustered instance. It is not possible to change these options once the clustered instance is installed. Because the setup program installs the instance on remote nodes, it does not support changing the installed options at a later date. To change options for a clustered instance, it must be removed completely from the cluster and reinstalled.

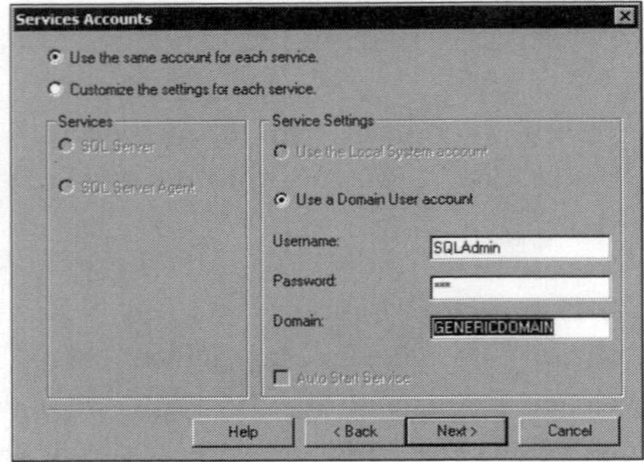

FIGURE 21.4

The Services Account page of the SQL Server 2000 Setup Wizard.

After the SQL Server 2000 instance has been installed successfully to the nodes in the cluster, Cluster Administrator shows the new resources that have been added to the cluster group that contained the physical disk resources for the databases of the new instance. Figure 21.5 shows this cluster group with its network name, IP address, SQL Server, SQL Server Agent, and SQL Server FullText cluster resources configured and online.

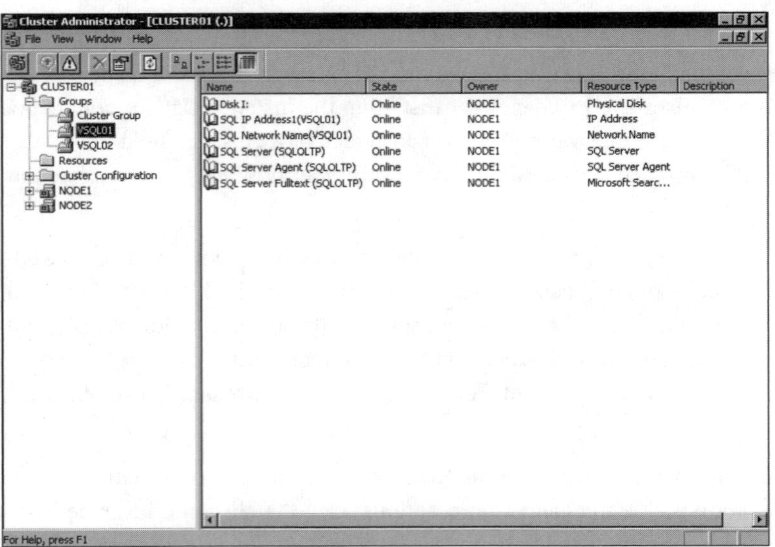

FIGURE 21.5

A SQL Server 2000 instance in Cluster Administrator.

Maintaining SQL Server 2000 on a Windows Server Cluster

Once a SQL Server 2000 instance is clustered properly, use the setup program to change cluster settings. Settings that can be modified include the cluster networks supported by this instance of SQL Server and the nodes of the cluster with the instance installed.

To maintain a SQL Server 2000 instance, perform the following steps:

1. On the Computer Name page, select Virtual Server and type the name of the instance in the Instance Name text box and click Next.
2. On the Installation Selection page, select Advanced options and click Next.
3. On the Advanced Options page, select Maintain a Virtual Server for Failover Clustering and click Next.
4. If changing network information, reconfigure the IP addresses for each public or mixed cluster network in the Failover Clustering page. At this point, new networks for the cluster can be configured and old networks changed or removed. When satisfied with the cluster network configuration click Next.
5. To change the node the instance is installed on, move the nodes around on the Cluster Management page. Any nodes that are moved from Configured Nodes to Available Nodes will have the instance uninstalled. Once the instance is removed from a node, it can no longer failover to that node.

NOTE

It is not possible to change which cluster disk the system database is installed on using this portion of the Setup Wizard. To change the system disk location, the instance must be completely removed from the cluster.

Removing SQL Server 2000 from a Windows Server Cluster

Removing a SQL Server instance from a cluster can be done only through the setup program. There are no entries in the Add/Remove Programs section of Control Panel for virtual server instances of SQL Server 2000. To remove a installation, perform the following steps:

1. On the Computer Name page, select Virtual Server and type the name of the instance in the Instance Name text box and click Next.
2. On the Installation Selection page, select Upgrade, Remove, or Add Components to an Existing Instance of SQL Server 2000 and click Next.

3. On the Instance Name page, select the instance of SQL Server to remove. In the case of a virtual server, there is only one possible instance, so select it and click Next.
4. On the Existing Installation page, select the only available option, Uninstall Your Existing Installation and click Next.
5. On the Remote Install page, type in an account that has administrative privileges on the remote nodes in the cluster and click Next to finish the wizard.
6. The virtual server network name, IP address, and SQL Server components are all removed after the wizard finishes.

NOTE

Virtual Server instances cannot have individual components added or removed after the initial setup. To do this, remove the virtual server instance completely and reinstall.

Summary

SQL Server 2000 makes clustering databases for high availability a simple task. Integrated completely with the setup program, clustering a database application has never been easier. It is as simple as installing a single instance of SQL Server 2000 to a standalone server. On a cluster, the setup program handles installing the instance to all specified nodes in the cluster and creating the virtual server resources on the cluster. After the setup program is complete on one node of the cluster, there are no special or extra steps needed to enable a SQL Server 2000 instance to work across all nodes of the cluster.

Failover clustering is a SQL Server term that means *high availability*. With a failover cluster, a SQL database never needs to be unavailable again. Failover clustering eliminates the single point of failure that is the traditional server database model. Simple to understand and built on top of the multiple instances feature of SQL Server 2000, failover clustering is the right choice for any mission-critical database application.

Maintaining a Cluster

CHAPTER

22

IN THIS CHAPTER

Even high-availability clusters in a Web farm require regularly scheduled maintenance. A neglected cluster node is much more likely to fail than one that has proper care and maintenance. The servers in the cluster should be maintained in the same fashion as any other Windows 2000 server, with a few exceptions. Cluster nodes require special care when dealing with the clustered applications and the cluster software.

Once a cluster is in production, there will be times that cluster nodes must be rebooted, new service packs applied, and hardware replaced or upgraded. It is during those times that proper understanding of cluster technology and best practices will shorten or eliminate the downtime and return a cluster to service. In some cases, with best practices, a cluster can be maintained without any effect on its applications other than the move from one node to another. In such cases, the power and value of Windows Server clusters is best demonstrated.

The goals of this chapter are to help you

- Learn how to perform a graceful failover and reboot of a cluster.
- Learn how to change the configuration parameters of the quorum drive and recover a corrupt quorum log.
- Learn how to perform many of the common administrative tasks that are required to maintain a cluster over its lifetime. This includes adding storage to the shared drive array, evicting nodes from the cluster, and applying services packs.

Clustering Best Practices

The following section describes a myriad of clustering best practices. Use of best practices come up in the course of operating a cluster. Following these guidelines reduces downtime and the risk of serious cluster failures. Windows Server clusters are complicated beasts; don't become complacent when working with them outside of regular operations. Always follow best practices when performing any of the following tasks.

Performing Graceful Failovers and Reboots

When a cluster node loses power unexpectedly, the Cluster service on the remaining nodes notices that the node is no longer responding when there is no reply to the UDP heartbeat message sent every 1.2 seconds. Groups currently assigned to that node are immediately transferred to the next node in their preferred ownership list and brought online. This loss of power is considered a catastrophic event that could result in catastrophic failure of data and hardware on the cluster. Clearly sudden power removal (pulling the plug) is not a best practice.

A less catastrophic event is the graceful shutdown of a cluster node through the Start menu at the console. This enables Windows to shut down device drivers, services, and applications running on the node systematically. This is an acceptable way to reboot a cluster node, but it is not a best practice. When the cluster service on a node is stopped, it initiates failover for all the groups it owns and terminates itself. It does not wait for the groups it owns to return to service on other node members successfully. If the failover fails for any reason and the original owner is in the process of rebooting, the groups could change to a completely failed state. In that case, the cluster applications are no longer available and the Windows Server cluster has failed to provide high availability to its applications.

The best practice for graceful failover and node reboot is to fail the groups manually and ensure that the resources in those groups are working on the other node before rebooting the original node. This ensures that the applications in the groups assigned to the rebooted node continue to function while their primary owning node is rebooted. If the failover fails, then the owning node is still available for the resource to return to service. Check the event log on the node that could not bring the resources online for clues as to why the failover failed.

Windows Server clusters support command-line configuration of a cluster. A command-line script can be created that fails the groups manually, and another script can be used to check the status of those groups. Scripting is a great way to establish and ensure that the best practice is followed. Listing 22.1 shows a command-line script for failing over two groups in a cluster. This cluster is a two-node cluster with nodes named `NODE1` and `NODE2`. It has three groups, `Cluster Group`, `VSQL01`, and `VSQL02`.

LISTING 22.1 Using the Command Line to Failover Groups

```
REM ***Moves the Cluster Group to the second node
Cluster cluster01 group "Cluster Group" /moveto:NODE2
REM ***Moves the VSQL01 group to the second node
Cluster cluster01 group "VSQL01" /moveto:NODE2
REM ***show the status of the groups and quit
Cluster cluster01 group "Cluster Group" /status
Cluster cluster01 group "VSQL01" /status
```

The result of this script is that all the groups in the cluster are now active on `NODE2`, and `NODE1` is ready to reboot. To verify that there are no active groups on the cluster, use the Cluster Administrator to expand `NODE1` in the tree and select the `Active Groups` folder. This folder should be empty.

When `NODE1` returns to service, repeat the procedure and move all the active groups from `NODE2` to `NODE1`, make sure the resources come up properly, and then reboot `NODE2`. Following this procedure keeps the cluster resources available and prevents a cluster from returning to service in a corrupted state.

Accessing the Cluster Administrator when Cluster Resources Fail

The cluster group contains the cluster resources that represent the cluster on the network. These resources typically include the network name and IP address of the cluster instance and usually the quorum drive resource. These resources grouped together represent the cluster administrative interface. Normally the cluster name is used to connect to the cluster. However, if the cluster network name and IP address cannot be brought online, then the network name is not accessible. If the IP address fails also, then the cluster administrative controls cannot be accessed from a remote location.

To access the cluster from a node in the cluster without using the network names, perform the following steps:

1. In Cluster Administrator, select the File menu and select Open Connection. This launches the Open Connection to Cluster dialog, shown in Figure 22.1.
2. Instead of typing the name of the cluster or browsing for the cluster name, type a single period. This tells the Cluster Administrator to try to connect to the local instance of Cluster Server.

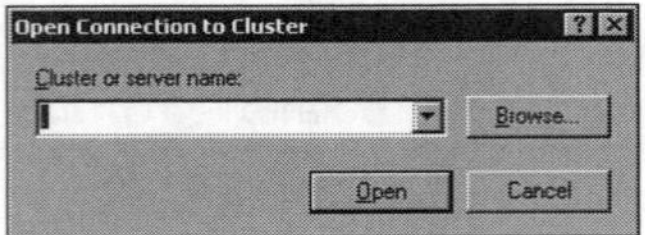

FIGURE 22.1
Connecting to a local cluster with Cluster Administrator.

Changing the Quorum Drive Configuration

During the course of a cluster's lifetime it should be necessary to change the location of the quorum drive only for hardware failures or data corruption. The location of the quorum drive is controlled through the properties of the root node in Cluster Administrator (the cluster name). To change quorum properties, right-click the cluster node and select the Properties menu item. Figure 22.2 shows the quorum disk property page for a cluster. Select the new physical disk resource for the quorum drive from the Quorum Resource combo box. If the physical disk resource has more than one logical partition, then select the appropriate partition from the Partition combo box. The defaults for Root Path and Reset Quorum Log are appropriate and should not be changed unless necessary (either physical disk corruption or extended diagnostics).

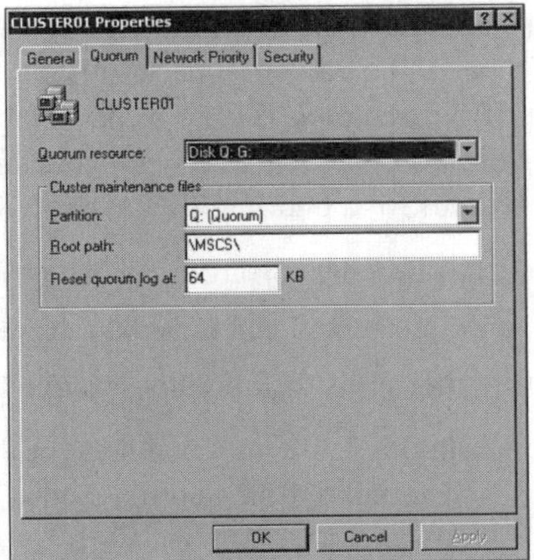

FIGURE 22.2
The quorum property page of a cluster.

After the new location of the quorum is selected, the changes happen immediately. The target disk now contains all the necessary data for a quorum resource and is the new brain of the cluster.

Recovering from a Corrupted Quorum Disk

If the Cluster service fails to start, there could be a problem accessing the quorum resource. The first step is to make sure that the cluster is actually in a failed state. Sometimes cluster nodes have problems when they are improperly shut down while obtaining the cluster resource. If this occurs, it can appear that the cluster is malfunctioning. If all the resources and nodes in a cluster are not functioning properly, perform the following tasks:

1. Shut down all nodes in the cluster as gracefully as possible and turn them off.
2. Turn off the shared drive array if it has its own power source.
3. Turn on the shared drive array and one node of the cluster and allow it to come up completely.
4. Bring up Computer Management and look in the Services section to see if the Cluster service failed to start.
5. If it did start, then launch the Cluster Administrator and connect to the local instance (as described in the section "Accessing the Cluster Administrator when Cluster Resources Fail" earlier in this chapter). If the local instance comes up, make sure that all resources are online and try to bring online those that have failed. If everything comes online, the quorum resource should be fine. Bring up the second node and return to it the resources it normally supports.

If the Cluster service failed to start, check the event log for any messages from `ClusSvc`. If none of these messages point to anything obvious, check in Explorer that the drive that has the quorum resource is accessible. If the event log is clear or does not state that the quorum resource is corrupt and the drive is accessible, it is still possible the quorum resource is corrupt. There are three possible reasons for a quorum resource failure:

- The quorum resource data has become corrupted but the physical disk is not failing.
- The file system information is corrupted and must be repaired.
- The physical disk hardware that holds the quorum resource has failed or is failing.

To determine the start of the quorum drive, use only one node of the cluster. Power down the second node for all these tests. To determine if the quorum data is corrupted, perform the following tasks:

1. Find the Cluster service in the Computer Management, Services and Applications, Service section.
2. Right-click the Cluster service and select Properties.
3. In the startup section of the main property page, type **`fixquorum`**.
4. Start the service.
5. Once it starts, stop the service, remove the startup parameter, and restart the service. The Cluster Administrator should now be able to connect to the local instances of Cluster service and bring the resources of the cluster online.

If it fails to start, then the file system may be corrupt or the physical disk may have failed. Run `CHKDSK` on the quorum drive to determine if the file system is corrupt. `CHKDSK` cannot run on a drive that is currently locked by the Cluster service, so if the service is locked starting, add the `startup` parameter, `-noquorumlogging`. This will enable the `CHKDSK` program to check the quorum drive even with the Cluster service started. If `CHKDSK` succeeds without errors, test the physical hardware as recommended by the manufacturer. If none of these tests show problems with the quorum resource, it is likely the quorum resource is fine. Make sure to remove any `startup` parameters from the service properties before continuing.

Evicting a Node from the Cluster

It is sometimes desirable to completely remove a node from a Windows Server cluster. This process is called *evicting a node from the cluster*. An evicted node is no longer a participant in any cluster activities and cannot own cluster resources. To evict a node from the cluster, right-click the node in Cluster Administrator and select Evict Node.

Once the node is evicted, uninstall the Cluster service, detach the node from the shared drives (as long as it is properly terminated), and perform whatever maintenance is required. When the maintenance is complete, reattach the shared drive and reinstall Cluster service to join the node back to the cluster.

Adding Storage to a SCSI Shared Drive Array

At some point in the life of a cluster it may become necessary to increase the capacity of the shared storage array. Drive arrays support many different methods for replacing failed hardware and increasing capacity without affecting availability. This section assumes that this functionality is not available, so check with the array vendor for techniques relating to more advanced hardware. The steps described here should work with all storage arrays, and when performed by prepared administrators should minimally impact the cluster availability.

Changing storage configuration in a shared drive array is accomplished in two distinct ways:

- Increasing the capacity of existing drives by replacing them with larger drives.
- Adding new drives to the shared storage array.

When increasing the capacity of existing drives, cluster groups and resources that have dependencies on the drives being replaced must be removed from the cluster. To accomplish this task, perform the following steps:

1. Delete or move all the applications and their data to other storage in the array.
2. Remove the physical disk resource from the cluster.
3. Following the best practices described in the earlier section "Performing Graceful Failover and Reboots," power down the nodes instead of restarting them.
4. Power down the last node of the cluster.
5. Remove the old drives and add the new ones.
6. Power up one node of the cluster and make sure the cluster service starts and all the existing resources come on line.
7. Use Disk Administrator to configure the drive(s) in the shared array.
8. Add the new physical disk resource to the cluster and reconfigure the removed applications.
9. Power up the second node and test the cluster by moving the new resources from node to node.

To add new capacity to a shared drive, perform the following steps:

1. Following the best practices described in "Performing Graceful Failover and Reboots," power down the nodes instead of restarting them.
2. Power down the last node of the cluster.

3. Add the new drives to the shared array.
6. Power up one node of the cluster and make sure the cluster service starts and all the existing resources come on line.
7. Use Disk Administrator to configure the drive(s) in the shared array.
8. Add the new physical disk resource to the cluster and add the new drive(s) to the appropriate groups, or create new ones for new applications.
9. Power up the second node and test the cluster by moving the new resources from node to node.

NOTE

If the drive being replaced or upgraded is the quorum drive then follow the steps in the earlier section "Changing the Quorum Drive Configuration" before following the steps in this section.

Controlling Cluster Diagnostic Logging

Windows Server cluster logs diagnostic data to a log file. This is called the *cluster log*. It is a record of all the actions that have transpired on every level of a cluster. Each resource logs actions and activities to this log. This log is separate from the quorum log, which is stored on the quorum drive and used by the cluster as a database to track configuration changes to the cluster and its applications.

Cluster service creates a system-level environment variable called `ClusterLog`. The value of this variable is a path to the log file. This path is `c:\winnt\cluster\cluster.log` by default. Change this path to have the cluster log diagnostic information to another location. Remove the environment variable to completely disable cluster diagnostic logging.

Applying a Windows Service Pack to a Cluster

Applying a Windows service pack to a cluster is an important task for maintenance of any cluster. First failover all the resources from the node to be upgraded to other nodes in the cluster. Make sure these resources successfully failover by checking their status in the Cluster Administrator. Run the service pack setup and let it apply itself to the idle cluster member. When the service pack finishes, the cluster node will reboot. When the cluster node returns to service and successfully returns to the cluster, failover all the groups to this node to ensure that everything is still functioning correctly. If any resources fail to come up on the upgraded node, do not apply the service pack to the other nodes until those resource issues have been resolved. Once all resources are functioning, apply the service packs to the remaining nodes.

NOTE

For the highest availability, apply a service pack to one node of the cluster at a time. Make sure that all resources are moved from the upgraded nodes before applying a service pack.

Summary

Best practices ensure the high availability of Windows Server cluster applications. It is a complicated software technology that can be maintained properly and in a safe manner. The most important best practice to follow is to make changes to a cluster one node at a time. Upgrades are easy to deal with and enable applications to remain available on other nodes when only one cluster node is active. When troubleshooting, many problems can be resolved by shutting down the other nodes in a cluster and making a single one work correctly. Never deal with multiple nodes in a cluster when there is an option to deal with one. Making changes to all cluster nodes at once is not the best practice and could result in complete failure of the cluster.

Most maintenance tasks can be completed in such a way that ensures the cluster's continued availability for the applications in a Web farm. This above everything else is the primary goal of any Windows Server cluster installation. If basic Windows Server cluster maintenance tasks required significant downtime, the value a Windows Server cluster adds to a Web farm would be minimal.

Securing a Web Farm

CHAPTER
23

Securing the Web farm is a critical success factor for any online business. Security provides auditing of who and what was done to the internals of Web farm. Security protects company property and customer information. Security guarantees that a malicious hacker will have much difficulty in disrupting the day-to-day operations of a Web farm.

Without proper security precautions, the availability of a Web farm application is put at dire risk. Not only is security a vehicle for improving the availability of a site, but it also is key in driving process and procedures for running the Web farm operations. Security policy and procedures are critical part of any Web farm design.

For some, security policy and procedure is a roadblock to achieving a goal. To others, it is a means to an end. Somewhere in the maelstrom that surrounds security-related problems is a philosophy that provides the best level of comfort for the end users and administrator's alike. Achieving the balance is the constant goal of the information security architect.

The goals of security for a Web farm are defined and upheld by the information security architect and encompass the following three concepts:

- *Confidentiality* says that communications between to entities are secret and assured to be between the actual identities of the entities.
- *Integrity* says that the message sent is the message received.
- *Availability* says that the entities in the Web farm to communicate with are present when communication is desired.

As a whole, securing a Web farm is as important as securing a real business. No sane proprietor would leave the keys in the front door, customer data open to access, or the combination to a safe unprotected. It is no different for a Web farm and all its ancillary data and functionality. Take a look at some of the goals to accomplish while exploring Web farm security.

The goals of this chapter are to help you

- Understand the "defense in depth" security philosophy to provide layers of independent security defenses in a Web farm.
- Establish security policies, including passwords, for administrators and applications and understand application accounts as well.
- Harden a Windows 2000 server so that common security vulnerabilities are eliminated and a server is ready to serve content to the Internet.
- Use a firewall in a Web farm. This includes understanding firewall fundamentals, benefits of firewalls, and how to harden a firewall with solid security policies and reasonable access restrictions to best address administrator security concerns and application developer requirements.

Understanding Defense in Depth

All successful security architectures are built from a philosophy. Even in the physical world, a security philosophy permeates how people obtain access to resources. Each resource commands a different level of protection, depending on its perceived value and worth. Clearly a difference in security access is required when checking out a book in the library as compared to reading documents marked "Top Secret" in the CIA. These security philosophies for access to physical systems translate into similar security philosophies for Web farms.

For example, multiple levels of security protect funds in a bank. First, all banks keep money locked in safes. Then, to access the money stored in the safe, customers must supply credentials that validate who they are and what accounts belong to them. Finally, banks maintain logs of all transactions and video surveillance of all activities.

Another important point about physical security systems is that each one operates independently of the other. In the bank example, money is secured in a safe independent of the security procedure for accessing the money. Likewise, the logging and surveillance happens extraneous to the other security operations. A criminal wanting access to money must bypass more than one security system to compromise the funds in a bank.

What defense in depth means for a Web farm is exactly what it means for physical systems. Defense in depth protects a Web farm by providing multiple levels of independent security.

NEW TERM *Defense in depth* is a security philosophy that is used in secure systems. It operates on the principle that multiple independent levels of security protect important resources.

Another way to think about defense in depth is to use concentric circle to represent different layers of security, as in Figure 23.1. Here, to obtain access to the data in the middle of the circles, a hacker would have to breach each layer independently.

Defense in depth is a good philosophy for Web farm security for a number of important reasons. If all that stands between a hacker and a Web farm's credit card data is a single layer of security, then the job of hacking a site is relatively simple. No security layer is completely foolproof, either, so multiple layers increase the time for a hacker to break into a Web farm. If every layer is hardened independently, then each layer is as big a challenge as the next. Increasing the time to hack a site with multiple security layers makes intrusion detection during break-ins more likely before a site's defenses are compromised.

Organizations that rely on a defense in depth security policy are never lulled into believing that they have a secure site. The time and money required creating and implementing a security policy of this magnitude forces an organization to remain current with security issues on all fronts. The security administrator must understand vulnerabilities at the network layer, at the firewall, in the operating system, and in the applications on the servers in the Web farm.

Constant attention and investigation into new vulnerabilities easily requires a full-time resource. To be familiar with the latest hacks means monitoring security newsgroups, mailing lists, and Web sites. When a security hack has been identified, quick and decisive action must be taken because the hackers are just as diligent about new attacks as the security administrator. In general, defense in depth forces an organization to have a deeper understanding of security issues on all levels. This attention to security matters reveals vulnerabilities in places likely missed by Web farms with no security philosophy.

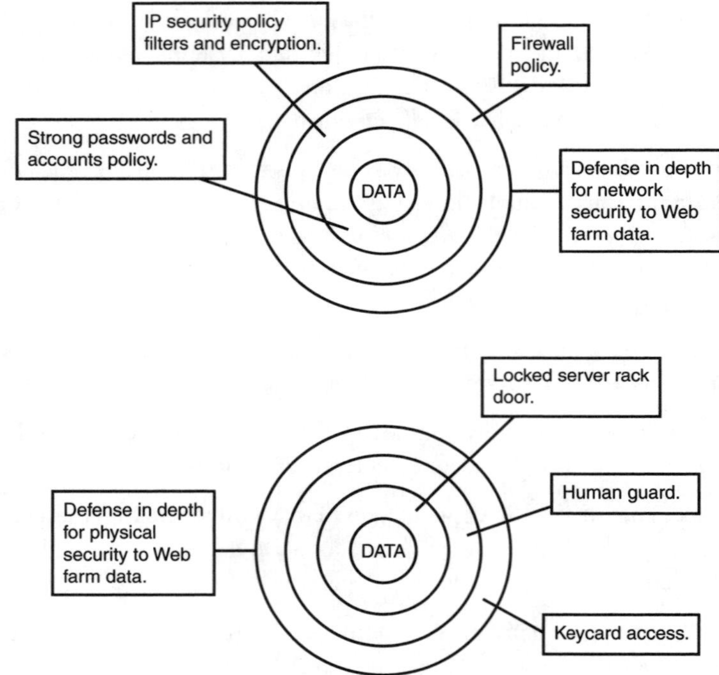

FIGURE 23.1
Defense in depth using multiple layers of security.

Establishing Security Policies

Security policies define how people are permitted to interact with the servers and network hardware of a Web farm. All policies define identification procedures and access or use privileges. Identification procedures test whether an individual is known by the secure systems of a Web farm. These systems could be a firewall, a router, a Web server, or a database server. Use privileges define what types of actions a user who is properly identified can perform.

User authentication procedures start by requesting a user for identification. This identification can come in many forms: a user ID a driver's license, a fingerprint, a retina scan, an employee application, and so on. A password is used to validate a users identification. The concepts of identification and validation combine to create the authentication process. It is through authentication that initial access is granted or denied by the security process. Prompting for identification creates a boundary between regions. In the NT world, this request for authentication is referred to as a challenge.

There are three factors used in all forms of authentication:

- Something known like a password, combination or PIN.
- Something possessed like a SecurID toke, crypto key, ATM card.
- Something personal such as a retinal scan, fingerprint, or DNA.

These factors are listed in order of effectiveness from worst to best. Having only one factor is bad, especially when it is a password. It is best to have multiple factors, sometimes referred to as two-factor authentication.

For example, some corporations have two-factor authentication to obtain access to corporate resources. The first authentication happens on the employee's first day through filling out paperwork and presenting government identification information such as a driver's license. From this authentication, the employee is issued an employee ID badge: a security token that is something possessed, a factor in authentication. The process of receiving the badge is the authentication; from that day forward until the employee leaves, this badge is a physical security token that represents this one-time authentication. An ID badge defines use criteria for whatever physical domain the badge protects. This ID card grants access to protected areas, but the user is never challenged again to prove who he is. This ID badge security token never expires.

The second authentication factor that a user must answer is a network logon. In this authentication, a user must enter a username and password to access the resources on a network. This authentication also creates a security token for resources on the network and is the second factor in the two-factor authentication process for a new employee. This security token is used to map back to a resource access list to grant or deny use privileges. In either case, the user presents identification information and, in return, receives a security token that defines who he is.

NEW TERM A *security token* is the result of a successful user authentication process. A security token is used to obtain access to a resource; it can be as simple as an ID badge for a building or as complex as a username and password for a network or server.

A user could be granted access to a network but denied use of some resources on that network, just like having an ID badge in a more sophisticated company that can be programmed to grant access to some rooms and not others. In understanding the difference between authentication and authorization, remember that authentication points are defined by granting a token. An access or use right is established when a token is examined to determine privileges. If an employee walks around a building and must use an ID badge to enter a room, this is a use right because there was no challenge. Card readers that share the same access control lists are said to exist in the same security domain. The same is true for networks. Network resources that share the same authorization lists exist in the same security domain.

NEW TERM A *security domain* is a group of resources that share and understand how to use the same security token to grant or deny authorization to users.

Within a security domain, administrators define access control lists (ACL). An ACL is a list of users or groups allowed to access a resource. In the case of an ID badge, each location, guarded by badge readers, has a list of users to grant a particular token entry to. In the case of a Windows 2000 security domain, ACLs apply to such tasks as logging onto servers, using printers, reading file shares, launching programs, using COM+ applications, debugging programs, and so on. An access control list is a list of the users and groups that can use each resource.

NEW TERM *Access control lists* are lists of users and groups that define who can use a particular resource in a Windows 2000 security domain.

Defining Physical Security Policies

A physical security policy is as important as a network security policy when protecting resources in a Web farm. All the hardened firewalls and servers in the world with awesome network security policies cannot protect a Web farm from an intruder walking up to the server console and gaining access.

Protect servers by requiring a secured use point with an ID badge. If an ID badge system is not practical, then have the operations staff police enter the operations center and require individuals who enter to identify themselves and sign in. Do not allow unknown or visiting people to travel unaccompanied into the server room. Use common sense when protecting the physical location of the Web farm.

Defining Network Security Policies

The most likely place for an intruder to gain unauthorized access to a Web farm is through a network connection. Most Web farms attach to at least two networks: a secure network that is used by administrators to manage and update the farm, and the Internet. Both of these networks can represent many security domains.

Organizing Security Domains

Access to a Web farm from a secure network is usually predicated on the fact the secure network and the Web farm network are aware of one another. In some cases, the security token from one network is useable on the other. This relationship is called a trust. A security domain can trust that the users that are on one domain are valid on another.

NEW TERM A *trust* is a relationship definition between two security domains that grants users in one domain access to resources in another.

Managing this relationship is important for defining the security policies that administrators must use and implement to do their job. This policy also protects the Web farm from users or intruders on the secure network. Security domain architectures for Web farms are either shared or dedicated.

Shared Web Farm Security Domain

A number of ways exist to organize security domains around a Web farm network. In shared security domain architectures with secure and insecure network access points, there are two security domains. Figure 23.2 shows a two-domain model for a Web farm. The Internet is a separate security domain. The application layer of the Web farm issues challenges to users from the Internet. These challenges include anonymous access, authentication with a username and password, or a cryptographic certificate-based mechanism. With all authentication schemes on a Web farm, the challenge points are exposed to the Internet and are insecure. In the second domain, which covers the Web farm and the administrative support infrastructure, a standard Windows 2000 forest provides a network challenge, and administrators' and users' access rights are broken out with standard Windows 2000 account privileges and rights. This model requires a tight hand over user privileges because limiting access to servers requires careful management of user rights.

Dedicated Web Farm Security Domain

Another likely scenario for constructing security domains for a Web farm is with a dedicated Web farm security domain. In this case, the Internet is still involved, as shown in Figure 23.3, with the same types of challenges for authentication. A security domain is dedicated to the Web farm and an administrative domain. The Web farm domain separates the administrative support roles from the service account roles into a separately managed domain. The Web farm domain is explicitly told which accounts to grant access to from the administrative domain through a one-way trust. Accounts in the Web farm domain cannot access resources in the administrative domain. Accounts in the Web farm domain are limited to service accounts, the accounts that the Web farm applications use to obtain security tokens in the Web farm domain. Management of access to resources is easier because administrator roles in the administrative domain are not necessarily administrators in the Web farm domain. This model supports multiple administrative security domains.

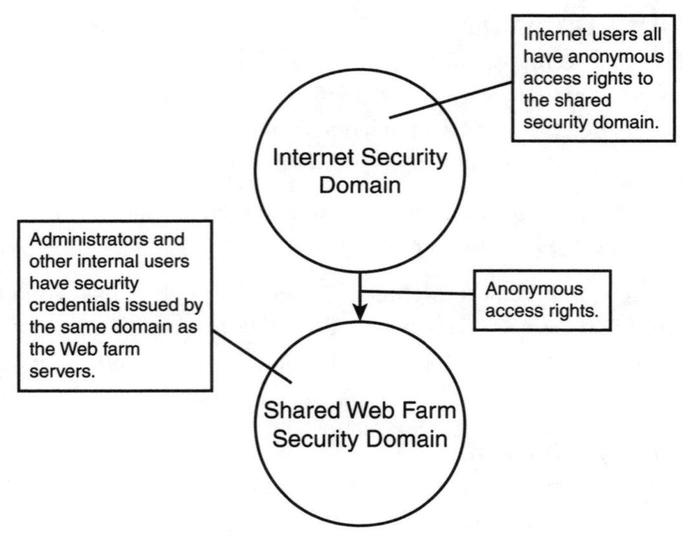

FIGURE 23.2
A shared security domain in a Web farm.

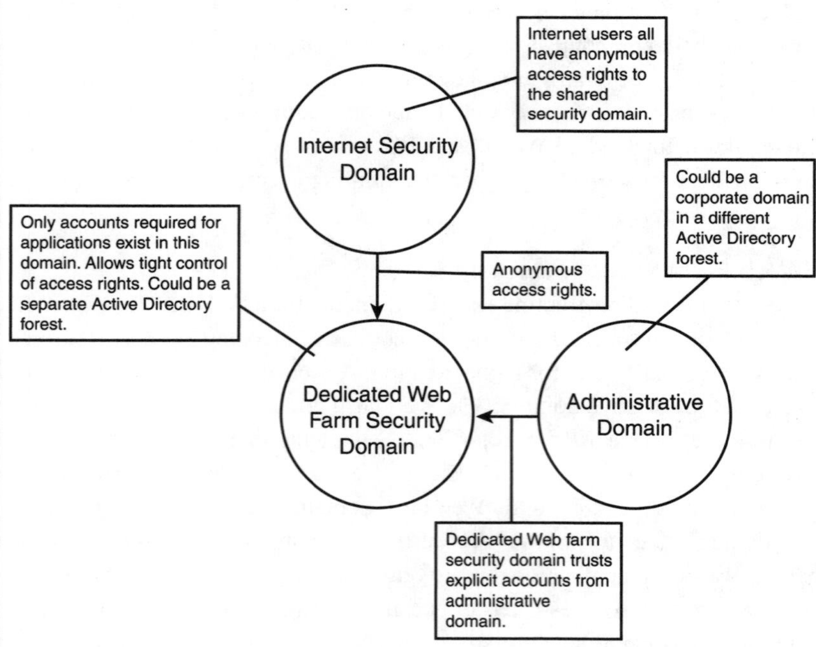

FIGURE 23.3
A dedicated Web farm security domain.

Defining Administrative Accounts

Administrators need the authority to investigate, configure, and troubleshoot a Web farm to do their job. The easiest way to assign administrative rights in a Windows 2000–based security domain is to make all the administrators members of the Domain Admins group. This group is all-powerful and has the rights to all servers in the network. This right is granted at the time a system joins the domain because the joining process adds the Domain Admins group to the local Administrators group of a server.

A more secure way to organize administrators is by application. Each application should have its own administrative group in the security domain. Instead of adding administrators to the Domain Admin group, add the administrators, whether they are members of the deployment team, operations, or support, to this group. Then explicitly add this group to the administrator's group of the servers that make up the application. Create this group as a domain local scope group in a Windows 2000 security domain. A domain local group can consist of domain accounts and other domain local groups from a single domain in a Windows 2000 forest. Domain local groups cannot contain members or groups from other domains.

A domain local group per application is the most appropriate group structure for administering a Web farm because it forces a grant-right policy rather than a deny-right policy. With a grant-right policy, each server that is added to the farm must have the appropriate domain local groups added to the local administrator group of each machine. In a deny-right policy, such as what happens when a server joins a domain, restriction of rights requires steps that, in most cases, are easier to forget than when an administrator must explicitly grant rights.

For example, if a Web farm supports three applications, the security domain of the Web farm has three domain local groups. Add each of the groups to the local administrator group of all the servers that each application uses. If two applications share a server, then add both groups to that server's administrator group.

Never use these accounts for application purposes. When administrators leave, these accounts must be disabled, without fear of breaking an application in production. Make sure that administrators follow good password practices and change passwords frequently. Password policy can be set using the Domain Security Policy console found on a Windows 2000 domain controller.

Defining Service Accounts

A service account is a broad term meaning any account that is used by an application to access resources in a secure fashion or as a particular user type. Service accounts are used throughout Windows 2000 in IIS, COM+, Application Center 2000, SQL Server 2000, and so on. An administrator typically defines a new account for each system and, upon service installation, provides the account name and password to the service so that it can store it on the system and use it as needed. In other cases, as with IIS, the installation program creates local accounts and assigns random passwords to these accounts; then it uses this account to access secure resources. For anonymous users to gain access to files on the Web site, they use this account.

In an anonymous access Web site, the security principle that is used to access resources is typically the anonymous user account. IIS 5.0, when it manages this account, acts as the local system and can gain access to any resource locally and any COM+ resource remotely that does not have security authorization turned on (the default setting). This is the preferred method for configuring anonymous access sites because creating Windows 2000 accounts for these users and granting them access is difficult to manage and usually is overkill.

However, to access resources locally, COM+ applications and other applications must act as some security principle called a service account. For custom services accounts, there are two methodologies for defining these accounts:

- Create a domain-level user and set all the applications and services security to assume the role of this user. The user can be simply a member of the Domain Users group and can be granted administrative access to the local machines that require it. Never over grant access levels and assign service accounts administrative privileges unless mandated by the application. Most service accounts need user access levels only. Applications that require administrative access will state this explicitly.
- Create local accounts and, when required, match the passwords and account names across multiple servers. This is actually the preferred method for Application Center 2000 deployments that must travel across security domains. Application Center 2000 will not deploy COM+ applications that use domain accounts as service accounts across domain boundaries, even when two-way trusts are established.

Either model is a viable alternative, depending on the security requirements and domain model in use. Never use these accounts to log on or access servers interactively—and if when using the local account model, these accounts can be denied the right to access this computer from the network, effectively eliminating the danger of someone leaving the company using these accounts to cause harm.

Creating a Corporate Security Team

Every organization, especially one that supports Web farms, should have a team of individuals dedicated to developing, responding, and fixing security-related issues. This team should have an information security architect who is familiar with the issues surrounding network and Web security to help guide the corporation toward a successful and secure Web farm.

Hardening a Windows 2000 Server

Windows 2000 is one of the easiest servers in the world to set up and configure. The simplest path through the Windows 2000 install program has one security question: the password for the administrator account. Other than joining a domain from the setup, there is no further opportunity to manage the security configuration during the default install.

With this ease of configuration and setup comes a price in security. The default configuration for Windows 2000 is not suitable for any secured environment. It is geared toward showing off the features of Windows 2000 with the greatest of ease. Microsoft's philosophy, good or bad, is open the server wide and expect the administrator to lock it down. Of course, this goes against the security philosophy of denying all features not explicitly allowed.

The process of denying all features not explicitly allowed is called hardening a server. Hardening removes unneeded features, services, accounts, and configuration. Hardening adds secure configuration and defines the applications, users, and servers that have access to secured resources. Different types of servers have different hardening needs. All servers should have some base form of server hardening, the degree of which is determined by the type of Web farm and the applications it supports.

NEW TERM *Hardening a server* is the process of removing unneeded features, services, configuration, and security information from a server and explicitly allowing applications, users, and servers access to the secured resources.

General Best Practices for Server Hardening

Server hardening is a two-phase process. In the first phase, after the server is built, there are a standard series of configuration changes, tuned to a particular environment that each server should go through. The second phase is the ongoing maintenance due to new security fixes and configurations to protect against new attacks. These changes fall into the following categories:

- *Remove unneeded accounts and groups.* These are likely default account information that, if unused, is like a cluster of apples waiting to be picked from the tree by a hacker. Don't delete accounts or groups required by an application or operating system service, like the IUSR_<machinename> account used by IIS for anonymous access.
- *Rename administrative and guest accounts.* Everyone knows that the administrator account for Windows by default is Administrator. Rename this account using a security policy. The guest account is disabled by default, but, if it is needed, be sure to change its name.
- *Remove unneeded network drivers.* By default, Windows 2000 installs and enables Microsoft Network and File and Print for all network adapters. Be sure that these are needed before leaving them on. These are powerful tools for users and hackers alike.

- *Remove or disable unneeded services.* Windows 2000 installs numerous services that are not needed in a majority of Web farm scenarios. Services that are candidates for removal or disabling include Alerter, Messenger, Distributed File System, and any other unused services. On an Internet server, disable FTP and SMTP if they are not used. Don't leave powerful application services around—the only people who will use them if your users don't need them are hackers.
- *Use security policies.* Security policies simplify and organize the hardening process. Almost all security configurations can be managed by security policies. Security policies are discussed in the upcoming section "Applying Security Policies to Windows 2000."
- *Use TCP/IP filters or IP Security policies.* These can further control access to a server. The filters prevent the flow of traffic to and from the server based on protocol type (TCP, UDP, and so on), port, and IP address. These filters are explained in "Applying Security Policies to Windows 2000," later in this chapter.
- *Keep up with security fixes and new attacks.* Join important industry mailing lists, including Microsoft Security Notification Service and NTBugTraq.

NOTE

Visit `http://www.microsoft.com/technet/security/notify.asp` to join the Microsoft Security Notification Service. To join the NTBugTraq mailing list, visit `http://www.ntbugtraq.com`.

Applying Security Policies to Windows 2000

Windows 2000 supports security templates and their application for quickly securing a server. A number of tools use security templates, including the Local Security Policy Editor, the Group Policy Editor, and the Security Configuration and Analysis snap-in. These tools edit and apply security templates to servers or groups of servers. The Security Configuration and Analysis snap-in is particularly useful because it compares the current security policy with the settings in predefined template before it is applied.

TIP

To use the Security Configuration and Analysis snap-in, open a new MMC (use mmc.exe) and add it to the console.

Using the Security Configuration and Analysis Tool

Figure 23.4 shows the Security Configuration and Analysis (SCA) snap-in with the HISECWEB.INF security template loaded. A security template is just a simple text file that contains information about security and configuration policies. This text file can then be applied to a server and the security policy can be adjusted without a reboot.

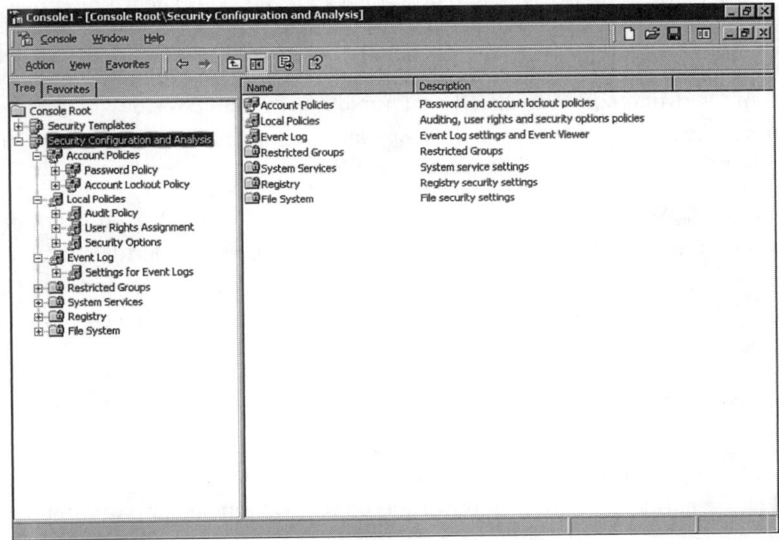

FIGURE 23.4
The Security Configuration and Analysis snap-in.

The SCA must have a local database file to store the template comparison. To create a new database, perform the following tasks:

1. Right-click the SCA root node.
2. Select Open Database and type a name for the new database file. This creates a new database and prompts for a security template to import.
3. Select a template and click OK.

To analyze the impact of a security template on the current system, right-click the SCA root node and select Analyze Computer Now. This will compare the imported template(s). Policies that are different show up with a red X on the side of the policy name. Policies that are the same have a green check next to the policy name.

To apply a security template, right-click the SCA root node and select Configure Computer Now. This applies the template loaded to the local computer. To apply security policy to a group of servers, use the Group Policy Editor and put all the servers in a separate organization unit in the Active Directory. Apply the group policy to the unit using the Active Directory Users and Computers console.

Understanding the HISECWEB Template

Security templates are not panaceas, but they do simplify the management of a Web farm. One template of particular usefulness is the HISECWEB.INF file. This security template is recommended by Microsoft to secure a Web server, or any other server exposed to the Internet. If you are looking for a security template to help out your Web Farm management, check this template out on the Microsoft Web site. This template is available for download from Microsoft at `http://download.microsoft.com/download/win2000srv/SCM/1.0/NT5/EN-US/hisecweb.exe`.

Be sure to check all Web applications after applying a security template. It is possible for some of the settings to have disabled features that an application needs. Don't hesitate to change settings that are not appropriate for a particular environment. A number of particularly interesting settings in the HISECWEB.INF template are not necessary for all Web environments:

- The password policy settings can cause problems and might be excessive. If Web applications use local accounts that have limited rights, it is a bad idea to have expiring passwords.
- The requirement for signed drivers could make updating the Web server problematic. Be sure that the hardware manufacturer of the server equipment supports signed drivers because HISECWEB.INF makes this a requirement.
- Terminal services are disabled, eliminating all remote administration. To allow administration in a multi-homed environment like those discussed in Chapter 4, "Planning a Web Farm Network," configure the IP Security filtering policy on the network adapter that is accessed from the Internet, and deny terminal services access by blocking the Remote Desktop Protocol (RDP) port (port 3389). More information on IP Security policies is presented in the section "Configuring IP Security Filtering," later in this chapter.
- The HISECWEB.INF template disables the following services: Alerter, Clipbook, Computer Browser, DHCP Client, Fax Service, Internet Connection Sharing, Irmon, Messenger, Netmeeting Remote Desktop, Remote Access Auto Connection Manager, Remote Access Connection Manager, Remote Registry Service, Task Scheduler, and Terminal Services. Telnet was overlooked in this version but should be disabled as well.

HISECWEB.INF does not rename the administrator account or guest account. This can be done from a security policy also, either by using a custom one or by modifying HISECWEB.INF. Figure 23.5 shows the SCA and where this configuration exists. To rename these accounts, double-click the policy Rename Administrator Account, click the Enable Policy button, and type the new account name in the text box provided. After this policy is applied to the target machine, these accounts will be renamed automatically. When modifying the HISECWEB.INF template to meet a Web farm's needs, save it as a new security template and apply it locally or as a group policy to multiple servers at once.

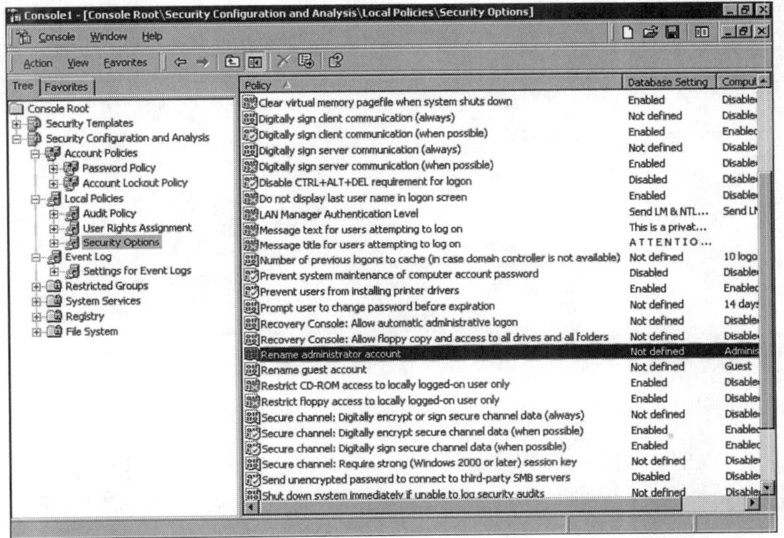

FIGURE 23.5

Renaming the Administrator and Guest accounts.

Configuring TCP/IP Filtering

Windows 2000 supports rudimentary, global TCP/IP filtering. This filtering allows for the configuration of rules that restrict access to a server on all adapters that have TCP/IP installed, based on TCP and UDP ports and specific IP protocols. For instance, a valid TCP/IP filter would allow traffic only to port 80. This would mean that the server, on all adapters, rejects any other traffic, including administrative, network logons. This is a useful tool for simple networks and single-adapter boxes. In a multiple-adapter configuration in which one network adapter is used by anonymous or Internet traffic and the other is used for administrative traffic, the more flexible IP Security policy is more appropriate.

The TCP/IP filtering configuration is found in the advanced properties of a network adapter configuration. To locate the TCP/IP Filtering dialog box in Figure 23.6, perform the following tasks:

1. Right-click My Network Places and select Properties to bring up Network and Dial-up connections.

2. Right-click any available adapter and select Properties.
3. Select the TCP/IP protocol and click the Properties button.
4. Click the Advanced button and select the Options tab.
5. On the Options tab, select TCP/IP Filtering and click the Properties button.

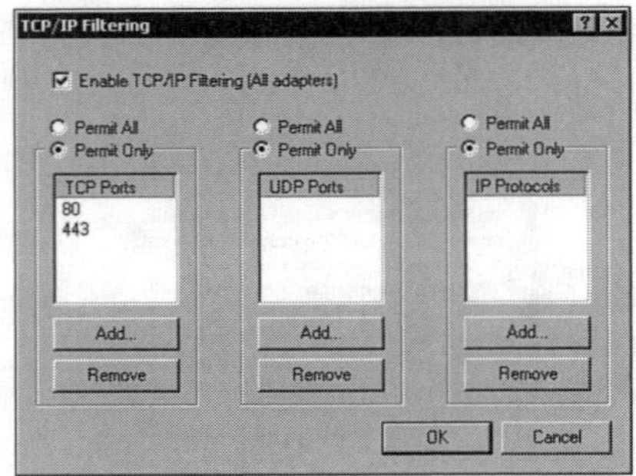

FIGURE 23.6
The TCP/IP Filtering dialog box.

Configuring the TCP/IP Filtering dialog box is simple. By default, all ports and protocols are available. To restrict the server to ports 80 and 443, perform the following steps:

1. Click the Permit Only radio button above the TCP Ports list box.
2. Click the Add button under the TCP Ports list box.
3. Type **80** and click OK.
4. Now type **443** and click OK.
5. Click OK to close and accept the configuration.

Remember that this filter is global and applies to all network adapters. Applying a rule to a remote machine could make it inaccessible.

CAUTION

Applying a TCP/IP filter rule to a machine remotely, such as while using terminal server, could make it inaccessible.

Configuring IP Security Filtering

IP Security is a new feature of Windows 2000 that greatly expands networking the security features. IP Security extends the features of TCP/IP filtering and adds secure and encrypted communications. For Web farms, the most important part of IP Security policies is its advanced packet filtering and blocking capabilities, called IP Security filters.

NEW TERM An *IP Security policy* is an association of filters and filter actions that define how IP Security interacts with incoming and outgoing network packets on a server. Only one policy can be active at a time, but any number of configured polices can be created.

Creating an IP Security Policy Using the Local Security Policy UI

Creating a new IP Security policy using the UI is a three-step process. First, create the filters that pertain to the types of network traffic that a Web farm server wants to watch. Then create the actions that IP Security should take when a filter criteria is met by an incoming or outgoing network packet. Finally, create the policy object and associate the filters and actions together. In this section, the goal is to create a blocking filter for all traffic and a pass-through filter for HTTP.

To create IP Security policy, filter a list, and filter actions, use the Local Security Policy snap-in under Administrative Tools in the Start menu. Figure 23.7 shows this snap-in. Highlighted in this figure is the IP Security Policies on Local Machine node. Visible in the right-click menu is the selection Manage IP Filter Lists and Filter Actions. Select this option to launch the Manage IP Filter Lists and Filter Actions dialog box.

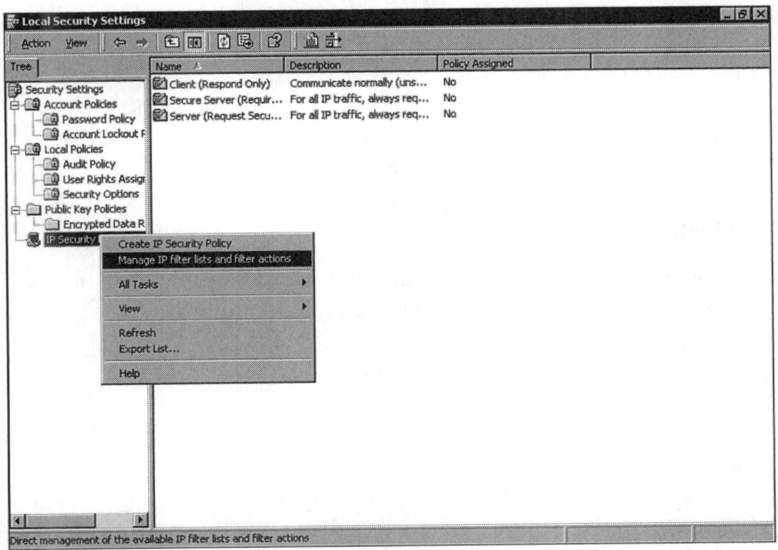

FIGURE 23.7
The Local Security Settings snap-in.

Figure 23.8 shows the Manage IP Filter Lists and Filter Actions dialog box. Filter lists are simply a grouping of 1 to *n* independent network packet filters. A filter is a rule that defines the types of network traffic, source addresses, and destination addresses inspected by IP Security. Filters specify nothing about what IP Security should do if it sees traffic that matches the criteria specified in a filter. This list of filters is global and can be used by any number of different IP Security policies. For example, a valid filter would be to watch traffic from any IP address to a specific IP address on port 80 using TCP protocol.

NEW TERM An *IP Security filter* is a network traffic criterion that has protocol, destination, and source address information. IP Security filters watch the network traffic specified by a filter and fire filter actions when a criterion is met.

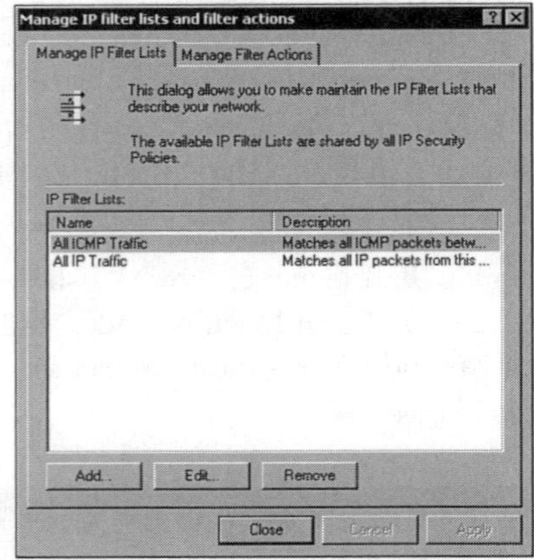

FIGURE 23.8
The Manage IP Filter Lists and Filter Actions dialog box.

To add a new filter list, click the Add button under the IP Filter Lists list box. This launches the IP Filter List dialog box, shown in Figure 23.9

This dialog box maintains a list of filters through standard Add/Remove buttons. Type **Filter All** into the name text box to identify this filter list. Add a description to better clarify the intent of this filter.

TIP

Uncheck the Use Add Wizard box to disable the IP Security filter and filter action wizards. These wizards are nice, but it is more valuable to use the straight UI for this example.

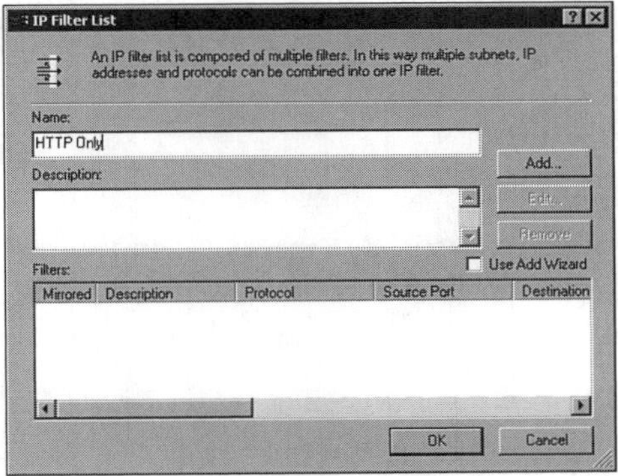

FIGURE 23.9
The IP Filter List dialog box.

Creating the First Filter

The first filter should watch all traffic to and from the box on all protocols. This is the filter that will use the Block filter action created in the next section to stop all traffic to the server. To create the first filter for this example, uncheck the Use Add Wizard check box and click the Add button. This launches the Filter Properties dialog box, shown in Figure 23.10.

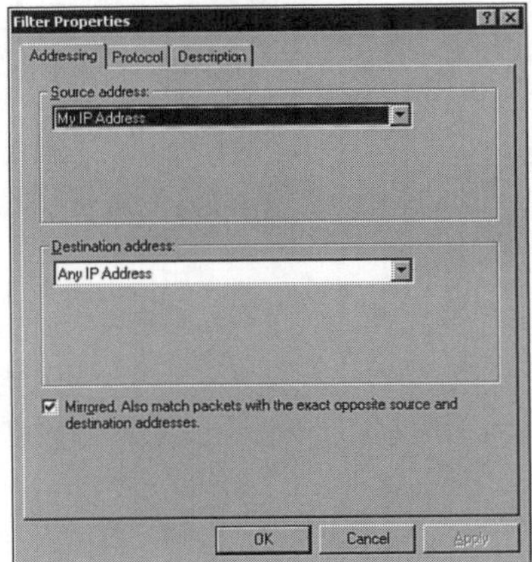

FIGURE 23.10
The Filter Properties dialog box.

To create the first filter, perform the following tasks:

1. Click the Add button on the IP Filter List dialog box.
2. Leave the Addressing and Protocol tabs at their defaults.

3. On the Description tab, type **Filter All Traffic** in the Description text box.
4. Click OK to create the filter.
5. Click OK to create the filter list.

Creating the Second Filter

The second filter is to watch traffic destined to the server for local IP addresses and port 80, the HTTP port. This filter, in conjunction with the first filter, will block all traffic except HTTP traffic to the server. To create the second filter, perform the following tasks:

1. Click the Add button to create a new IP filter list; call it HTTP In Only.
2. Click the Add button on the IP Filter List dialog box.
3. On the Addressing tab, leave the defaults.
4. On the Protocol tab, shown in Figure 23.11 change the protocol to TCP, and select the From the Port radio button. Type **80**.
5. On the Description tab, type **Filter Incoming HTTP** in the Description text box.
6. Click OK to create the filter.

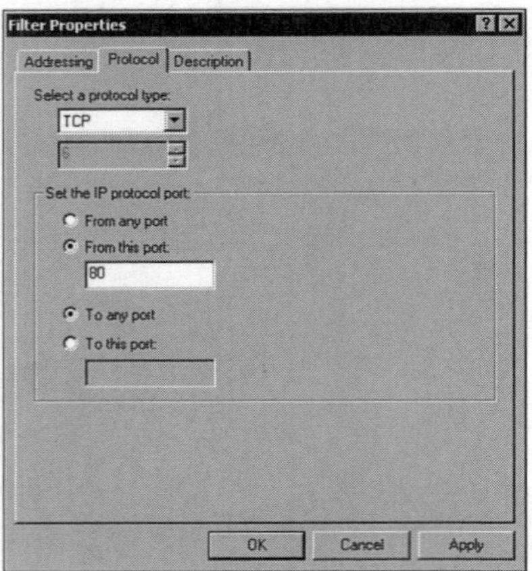

FIGURE 23.11
The Protocol tab of the Filter Properties dialog box.

At this point there should be two new filter lists in the Manage IP Filter list and filter actions dialog as shown in Figure 23.12.

Now create a new action called Block by performing the following tasks:

1. Select the Manage Filter Actions tab of the Manage IP Filter Lists and Filter Actions dialog box.

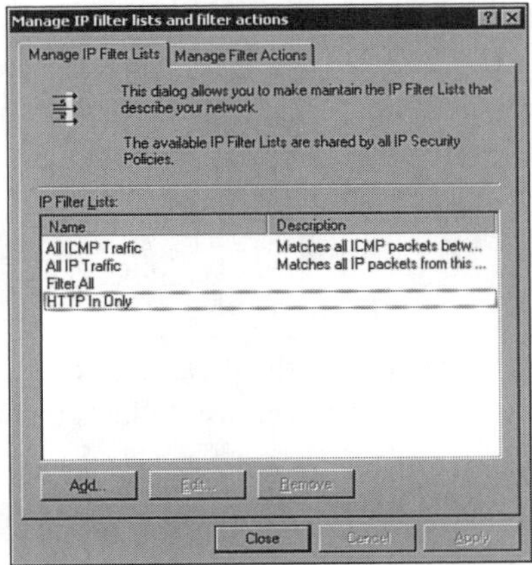

FIGURE 23.12
The Manage IP Filter Lists and Filter Actions dialog box with new lists.

2. Click the Add button below the Filter Actions list box. This launches the New Filter Action Properties dialog box, as shown in Figure 23.13.
3. Select the Block Radio button.
4. Switch to the General tab and name the filter action Block.
5. Click OK to create the action.
6. Close the dialog box and prepare to create the IP Security policy.

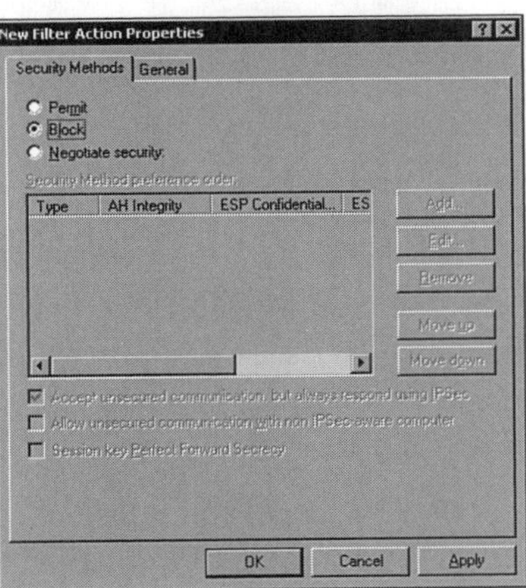

FIGURE 23.13
The New Filter Action Properties dialog box.

Creating the New IP Security Policy

Now that the filters and filter actions are in place, it is time to create the new IP Security policy. The IP Security policy associates the filters with actions to complete the server hardening. To create a IP Security policy from the UI, perform the following tasks:

1. Right-click the IP Security Policies on Local Machine node in the Local Security Settings snap-in, and select Create IP Security Policy. This launches the IP Security Policy Wizard.
2. Click through the wizard, accepting all the defaults and responding Yes to any dialog boxes. These are not important for IP Security Policies that implement IP filtering.
3. On the last page of the wizard, leave the Edit Properties check box checked. This launches the IP Security Policy Properties dialog box shown in Figure 23.14.

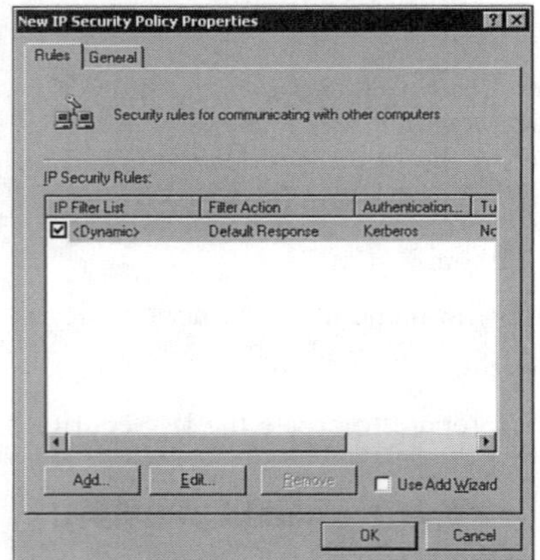

FIGURE 23.14
The IP Security Policy Properties dialog box.

This is the dialog box that associates filters and actions with a specific policy. These associations of filters and actions are called IP Security rules. The first rule that this policy needs is one that blocks all traffic. This follows the security philosophy of denying any unnecessary services that aren't explicitly allowed. To add the first new rule to an IP Security policy, perform the following tasks on the server console:

1. Click the Add button under the IP Security Rules list box. This launches the New Rule Properties dialog box.
2. From the IP Filter List tab, select the filter list named Filter All.
3. Switch to the Filter Action tab and select the action named Block.
4. Click OK to accept the rule.

Now the first rule is in place. If no other rule is added, the target server will be completely unavailable from normal network traffic. Add the second rule to allow incoming HTTP traffic by performing the following steps:

1. Click the Add button under the IP Security Rules list box. This launches the New Rule Properties Dialog again.
2. Select from the IP Filter List tab the filter list named HTTP In Only.
3. Switch to the Filter Action tab and select the action named Permit.
4. Click OK to accept the rule.

Now the policy is complete. Click OK to accept the policy. The new policy now shows in the details view of the IP Security Polices on Local Machine node in the Local Security Settings snap-in. Right-click the policy name and select Assign to enable this policy. IP Security policies take effect immediately. To test this policy, try to launch a browser from the target server. No HTTP traffic is allowed out. Next, launch a browser from a different server and browse to the target server. The Web service should respond, but the server will not respond to traffic on any other port but 80.

This example creates a very simple rule that, in most cases, will not be useful in the real world. More complicated and useful rules are created using the command-line tool IPSECPOL.EXE.

Creating an IP Security Policy Using IPSECPOL.EXE

The command line-configuration tool for IP Security policies is located in the Windows 2000 Resource Kit. It is called IPSECPOL.EXE, and it is very useful for quickly creating complicated policy, including all the necessary filters and actions.

In this example, a multiple-adapter server is configured with a very useful IP Security policy. The goals are simple:

- Block all ports but 80 and 443 from the adapter that connects to the Internet (protected by NAT and a firewall, of course). This will lock down the front-rail adapter except for Web traffic.
- Allow all traffic to the adapter that connects to the secure network for administrative purposes.

IPSECPOL.EXE works at the filter and rule levels, automatically creating the policy container. Each command adds a filter and a filter action with the same name. This creates extra actions and filters than when using the UI, but the ease of use makes it worth the extra clutter. Listing 23.1 shows the entire script for creating this IP Security policy. Use `IPSECPOL.EXE -?` for more general information on this tool.

LISTING 23.1 Creating an IP Security Policy with IPSECPOL.EXE

```
REM DELETE ALL EXISTING POLICY
IPSECPOL.EXE \\machinename -w REG -p "DMZWeb" -o


REM BLOCK FRONT RAIL COMPLETELY
IPSECPOL.EXE \\machinename -x -w REG -p " DMZWeb " -r "LockDownFR" -n BLOCK -f
172.19.21.*/255.255.254.0+*


REM ALLOW HTTP INTO FRONT RAIL
IPSECPOL.EXE \\machinename -x -w REG -p " DMZWeb " -r "HTTPFRIN" -n PASS -f
172.19.21.*/255.255.254.0:80+*::TCP 172.19.21.*/255.255.254.0:443+*::TCP


REM ALLOW HTTP OUT FRONT RAIL
IPSECPOL.EXE \\machinename -x -w REG -p " DMZWeb " -r "HTTPFROUT" -n PASS -f
*:80+172.19.21.*/255.255.254.0::TCP *:443+172.19.21.*/255.255.254.0::TCP
```

This example assumes that the front-rail subnet is 172.19.21.* and that the back-rail subnet is 172.19.20.*. Four lines of script produce the complete IP Security policy for locking down the front-rail network adapter of a DMZ Web server. This policy would take a long time to create with the UI. The next sections describe each command in detail.

Deleting the Policy

```
IPSECPOL.EXE \\machinename -w REG -p "DMZWeb" -o
```

This command deletes a policy named DMZWeb from the target machine. This is done only for convenience because it will delete all the associated filter lists and actions for that policy. Use this when interactively trying to get a command-line policy correct. The `REG` keyword means to use the registry of the local machine. Table 23.1 summarizes this command line.

TABLE 23.1 Summary of the Delete Policy Command

Command	*Description*
`\\MachineName`	Used to target a specific machine. Can be blank for the local machine. Must have administrative privileges on target machine.
`-w REG`	Deletes the information about this policy from the registry of the target machine rather than from the directory service in an Active Directory domain.
`-p "DMZWeb"`	Identifies the policy that is the target of the command.
`-o`	Deletes the policy.

Blocking the Front Rail Completely

```
IPSECPOL.EXE \\machinename -x -w REG -p " DMZWeb " -r "LOCKDOWNFR" -n BLOCK -f
172.19.21.*/255.255.254.0+*
```

This command shuts down all traffic to and from the 172.19.21.* subnet. In the case of this multiple-adapter Web server, the front-rail adapter uses that subnet. This command effectively shuts off this adapter. Table 23.2 summarizes any new commands issued for this action. This switch is of particular interest because it defines a new filter:

```
-f 172.19.21.*/255.255.254.0+*
```

The syntax for the filter command is as follows:

```
Source IP/Source Mask (+|=) Destination IP/Destination Mask(::Protocol)
```

Here, + means to create a two-way rule and = means to create a one-way rule (traffic flows from source to destination). The `(::Protocol)` optional qualifier means to restrict the filter by protocol and can be TCP, UDP, ICMP, or RAW. The source and destination IP can use `*` to mean "any" and `0` to mean "any local IP addresses." Table 23.2 summarizes this command line.

TABLE 23.2 Summary of the LOCKDOWNFR Command

Command	*Description*
`-x`	Sets the policy to active. Use -y to not set it to active.
`-r "LOCKDOWNFR"`	Specifies the name of the filter action and filter list that this command creates.
`-n BLOCK`	Is equivalent to picking the Block radio button on the New Filter Action Properties dialog box. This blocks all traffic that meets the criteria specified by the `-f` command.
`-f 172.19.21.*/255.255.254.0+*`	Filters for traffic to and from any IP address and the front-rail subnet.

Allowing HTTP Traffic In

```
IPSECPOL.EXE \\machinename -x -w REG -p " DMZWeb " -r "HTTPFRIN" -n PASS -f
172.19.21.*/255.255.254.0:80+*::TCP 172.19.21.*/255.255.254.0:443+*::TCP
```

This command explicitly allows traffic for ports 80 and 443 into the server. Table 23.3 summarizes the `HTTPFRIN` command.

TABLE 23.3 Summary of the `HTTPFRIN` Command

Command	*Description*
`-r "HTTPFRIN"`	The name of the filter action and filter list that this command creates.
`-n PASS`	Is equivalent to picking the Permit radio button on the New Filter Action Properties dialog box. This passes through all traffic that meets the criteria specified by the `-f` command.
`-f 172.19.21.*/255.255.254.0:80+*::TCP`	Allows in all TCP traffic destined for port 80.
`172.19.21.*/255.255.254.0:443+*::TCP`	Allows in all TCP traffic destined for port 443.

Allowing HTTP Traffic Out

```
IPSECPOL.EXE \\machinename -x -w REG -p " DMZWeb " -r "HTTPFROUT" -n PASS -f
*:80+172.19.21.*/255.255.254.0::TCP *:443+172.19.21.*/255.255.254.0::TCP
```

This command explicitly allows traffic for ports 80 and 443 out of the server. This would be an optional rule because it is not necessary to allow browsing activities from a server. The rule is necessary in scenarios in which the Web server connects to other Web servers for things such as .NET Web services. Table 23.4 summarizes the `HTTPFROUT` command.

TABLE 23.4 Summary of the `HTTPFROUT` Command

Command	*Description*
`-r "HTTPFROUT"`	Gives the name of the filter action and filter list that this command creates.
`-n PASS`	Is equivalent to picking the Permit radio button on the New Filter Action Properties dialog box. This passes through all traffic that meets the criteria specified by the `-f` command.
`-f *:80+172.19.21.*/255.255.254.0::TCP`	Allows out all TCP traffic destined for port 80 on a remote Web server.
`*:443+172.19.21.*/255.255.254.0::TCP`	Allows in all TCP traffic destined for port 443 on a remote Web server.

Securing IIS on a Web Server

Microsoft has created a document available on the Web that contains procedures for securing IIS on a Web server. This document is called the Secure Internet Information Services 5 Checklist; it is located at `http://www.microsoft.com/technet/security/iis5chk.asp`. This document describes basic best practices for securing a IIS server such as removing unneeded ISAPI mappings, the admin Web site, example application and so on. Leverage this document and the information in this chapter to create a highly secure Web server.

Using a Firewall

Firewalls protect Web farms from unauthorized network access. They are the keepers of the doorway into a Web farm allowing only authorized traffic in and letting only authorized traffic out. This gateway is a critical component to any successful and secure Web farm. Without it, all the Web farm resources would have to perform the duties of the firewall and would have to be very hardened against attacks.

This section breaks the discussion of firewalls into four parts:

- Firewall concepts are presented, expanding and clarifying the role of a firewall in the Web farm.
- Benefits of the firewall to the servers and applications in a Web farm are covered.
- Best practices are presented, without discussing any particular firewall type, for creating firewall policies.
- Hardening the firewall server above and beyond the hardening of a standard server is discussed, to protect the firewall from known attacks and exploits.

Understanding Firewalls

A firewall is a system designed to control the user and system access to and from a network. Firewalls are located at the gateways between networks and are a collection of related programs that perform different network packet-management tasks. Firewalls typically perform four separate packet-management tasks:

- *Blocking and filtering network packets* by doing simple address and port inspection of every packet sent between the networks it bridges. These packets must meet criteria specified by security policies that are rules on the firewall. Management tools or command-line utilities are used to specify rules depending on the firewall vendor. By default, firewalls disallow all traffic, so they must have rules applied to be of any use.
- *Managing well-known application protocols* such as HTTP, FTP, or Telnet through application gateways. Rules apply to specific ports, and some firewalls can inspect and remove protocol-specific information such as HTTP cookies.

- *Managing network traffic flow at the network protocol (TCP* or UDP) *level*. If firewall rules allow two hosts to connect, then packets flow between hosts is unimpeded as long as the connection remains opened.
- *Hiding the true internal network addresses* as a proxy server. Firewalls using this capability intercept all messages entering and leaving the network and translate them to the appropriate target or destination address.

Firewalls help protect server and applications from malicious or unauthorized use by controlling the flow of information between networks. Without firewalls, networks servers are susceptible to probing by any user without regard to intent or purpose. Figure 23.15 shows a firewall with a Web farm.

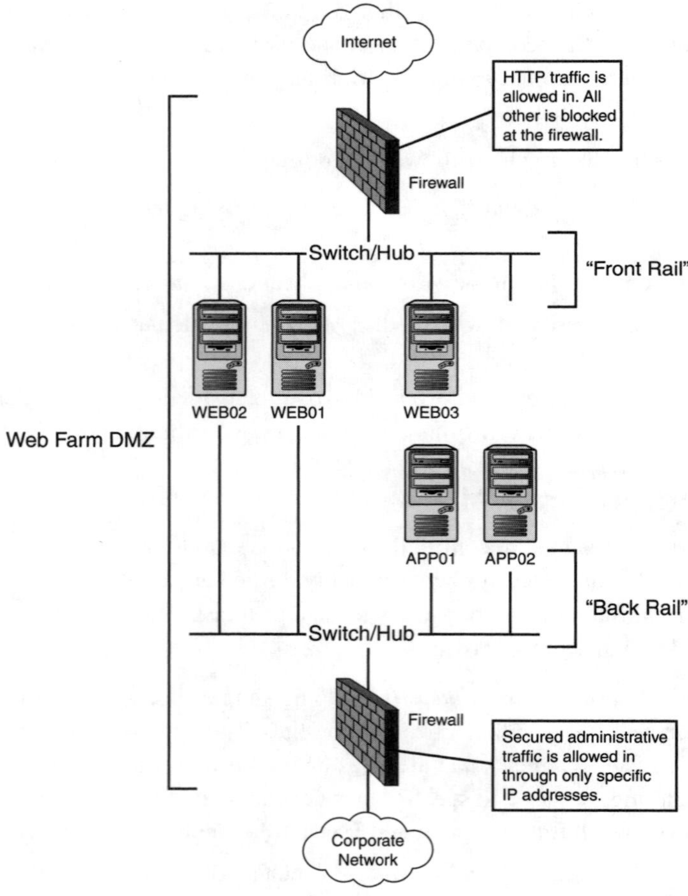

FIGURE 23.15
A firewall in a Web farm.

Understanding Firewall Benefits

Implementing a firewall in a Web farm is not an easy task. It requires a dedicated set of servers (for redundancy), special software or hardware for load balancing, and an administrator with skill in firewall configuration. These extra costs are outweighed by the following benefits:

- *Conserves server resources* by reducing the overall traffic that a server must examine. Because of application gateway management, entire application-type packets such as `PING` and `TRACEROUTE` never reach target servers.
- *Hides servers from other networks,* including the Internet. By using Network Address Translation (NAT), a server behind a firewall never binds its network adapters to an Internet-addressable IP.
- *Protects servers from well-known attacks* by shielding them from access to specific ports such as NetBIOS, SNMP, and other oft-exploited ports.
- *Hides server information* from other networks. This prevents unwanted users from port-scanning well-known Internet IP addresses and finding lists of available servers to attempt to hack. Firewalls will just drop and not respond to packets that contain information that is not allowed through a firewall because of its rule set.
- *Warns of possible attacks* like an early warning system. Firewalls can log all traffic, and programs or users inspect these logs looking for traffic that is suspect, such as repeated failed attempts to access unusual ports or services.

Setting Policies on a Firewall

All messages entering or leaving a Web farm network must pass through a firewall. The firewall examines and blocks those that do not meet specified security criteria. Each firewall product has different rule types and administrative tools for controlling these policies. Most have rules that allow blocking of specific application ports, port ranges, IP addresses, IP address ranges, TCP traffic, and UDP traffic.

With those general rules follow these best practices:

- Manage traffic flow granularly by creating more rules rather than less. If you need to have some Web servers respond to `PING` and not others, create two groups with separate rules, one that allows only HTTP traffic and one that allows HTTP traffic and `PING`.
- Deny all services not explicitly allowed. Don't open up a server for HTTP traffic (port 80) when it is a dedicated FTP (port 21) server. Open ports are doors into servers waiting to be opened, so define a rule that denies access to all ports except 21 for a dedicated FTP server.
- Allow traffic to flow only in the direction needed. A Web server does not need to browse the Web (typically this is true, but there are exceptions), so allow HTTP traffic to the box and don't allow the box to send HTTP traffic.

- Define IP address ranges that have known security policies where possible so that new servers "inherit" the rule sets of similar servers. This allows the addition of new Web servers that have IP addresses in the range supported, and no firewall changes are required.
- Maintain logs of traffic that is not allowed or expected for troubleshooting and intrusion detection purposes.
- Apply security policies to groups for easy maintenance. Leverage the group-creation features of a firewall. It is much easier to create a group that has specific policies than to create a specific policy for each server behind a firewall. Changing the rule used for a specific server requires moving the server from one group and placing it in another.

Hardening a Firewall

Following best practices and hardening a standard server are important. Following best practices for a firewall is critical. The firewall is a Web farm sentry on the Internet. If it is not secure, then the Web farm it protects is not secure. A firewall should be hardened just like any other Windows server. However, administrators should harden a firewall beyond a standard server and apply the following best practices:

- Make a firewall completely standalone. It should not be a member of a domain or have any other distinguishing characteristics.
- Do not install anything else on the firewall server but firewall software.
- Remove all unneeded services from the firewall.
- "Stealth" the firewall so that it does not accept connections from anywhere. This is done by adding rules to the firewall's rule base. The firewall is a hop along a path to somewhere else; it should never be the destination. This includes ICMP (PING) traffic. Anyone scanning a firewall should receive no response from the firewall and have no indication that the firewall exists.
- Do not register the IP address of an Internet firewall with a DNS hosting service. Knowing this IP address is not necessary to access a Web farm.
- Do not allow remote access from the Internet for firewall administrators. Any door to administrators is a door for anyone on the Internet if they determine the password.

Summary

A secure Web farm is a successful Web farm. A secure Web farm means that corporate resources are safe and that susceptibility to hackers and attacks from the Internet is less likely. A secure Web farm is aware that security policy is important and tries to maintain a heightened awareness to current security issues and is always ready to change when a new attack becomes a reality. Security is the most overlooked but critical aspect of managing a Web farm.

Using defense in depth as a security philosophy is the first step toward a secure Web farm. Defense in depth means that when one layer of security, such as a firewall, is compromised, there is another layer, such as IP Security policy, waiting for the hacker. This philosophy doesn't prevent break-ins, but it does slow hacking down so that detecting it becomes possible.

Establishing security policies means thinking about different types of secure access and creating the appropriate policy to facilitate it. Whether it is administration of a Web farm domain or a corporate security team, policy defines appropriate behavior in a secure Web farm.

The process of hardening a server follows the security idiom, "Deny all access except that which is explicitly required." This process closes the door to hackers because unused system services are no longer available for exploitation or control. Many powerful tools can harden a Windows 2000 server, including security templates such as HISECWEB, TCP/IP filtering, and IP Security. A hardened server is an important chink in the armor of a secure Web farm.

Finally, firewalls provide a reliable sentry that guards the Web farm from the Internet. Through packet filtering and blocking, application masking, address translation, and proxy services the firewall is a key component in the defense in depth philosophy. Without a firewall, every server in the Web farm is potentially exposed to the Internet. Firewalls make administrating security simple because they abstract the Web farm from the Internet and inspect and block any network packet that does not fit the application needs of the Web farm. Firewalls are the single most important element in a highly secured Web farm.

Appendices

IN THIS PART

Preparing for ASP.NET

APPENDIX

A

IN THIS APPENDIX

The Microsoft .NET application framework is a set of development tools for building .NET applications and services. ASP.NET is a collection of .NET framework classes designed to help build Web applications that bring the benefits of the .NET framework to the Web farm application development space. These benefits include the following:

- *All code is compiled* to MSIL and then JIT compiled to machine code at runtime. This is a change from ASP 3.0, where code in ASP pages is executed as interpreted script. ASP.NET applications are much more efficient than their ASP 3.0 counterparts. This affects simple troubleshooting because code does not have to exist on the server. Only DLL files that contain the Web application need to be deployed with the HTML code.
- *The full functionality of the operating system is available* to Web applications. In ASP 3.0, calling a Windows API had to be done from a COM component because script languages did not support accessing Windows API directly. The .NET framework contains hundreds of classes that wrap the Windows API, and all the classes are available to Web programmers. This means that ASP.NET applications can be much more powerful but also potentially more dangerous. It is more likely that a poorly written ASP.NET application could do something to affect the box, such as overload the CPU or use all available memory.
- *XML and SOAP are the basis for interoperability and communication* between distributed systems. Datasets, SOAP services, .NET Remoting, configuration services, and other .NET framework services are all XML based. These XML forms make working with and configuring ASP.NET applications as simple as using Notepad to edit a text file. With XML at the center of everything, interoperability with legacy systems is easy. SOAP is a disconnected protocol for remote procedure calls (RPC) that can use HTTP as a transport. SOAP is therefore much more firewall friendly than classic RPC. Most implementation is configured to use port 80 by default, but SOAP is not limited to port 80 or even HTTP, as it is possible to send SOAP messages through any transport mechanism.
- *It is caching centric*. ASP.NET has a built-in object and page cache. This greatly reduces the load of dynamic pages because portions that don't change frequently or have only a few forms are cacheable. Administrators or developers can specify through XML configuration how often and how long an ASPX page is cached and what criteria are used to shuffle objects in and out of cache. Caching eliminates network roundtrips to database and application services and greatly improves the throughput of any Web-based application.

Deployment Impact of ASP.NET on a Web Farm

ASP.NET supports XCOPY deployment. *XCOPY deployment* is the idea that all it takes to move a Web site from a development environment to production is to XCOPY the Web directory from one server to another. ASP.NET stores all its configuration information in a file called `WEB.CONFIG`. This file is a simple XML document that contains all the information needed to configure and run an ASP.NET site. In an ASP 3.0 application, this information would be in the metabase, Registry, and COM+ catalog, but it is not possible to XCOPY the metabase, Registry, or COM+ catalog. Hence, with that information in an XML file, it can be duplicated with XCOPY.

A number of new file extensions have been added to ASP.NET. Developers and administrators should understand the purposes of each of these new file types. Table A.1 describes the different file types in ASP.NET.

TABLE A.1 New File Extensions in ASP.NET

Extensions	*Description*
ASAX	The `GLOBAL.ASA` version in ASP.NET. There is one `GLOBAL.ASAX` file per Web application in ASP.NET.
ASCX	An ASP.NET server control. The `ASCX` file is an encapsulation of HTML and code that behaves as a unit and is reusable across multiple `ASPX` sites. A good example is a footer or header control for a page.
ASHX	Unknown at this time.
ASMX	A Web service. This is the extension and application type that uses `SOAP` to communicate with distributed clients.
ASPX	The new ASP page. It does all the work and is compiled.
AXD	Unknown at this time.
DISCO	A Web service discovery file used to catalog all the Web services at a particular URL level in a Web site.
VSDISCO	Unknown at this time.
REM	A .NET remoting file. Used to point .NET class creation to remote servers.
SOAP	A .NET remoting file for remote creations that use `SOAP`.
CONFIG	An XML document that contains configuration data. The `.INI` of .NET.
CS, VB	`VB` and `C Sharp` source files.
WEBINFO	Unknown at this time.

How ASP.NET Integrates with IIS 5.0

ASP.NET sits on top of IIS 5.0 by using the ISAPI filter and extension architecture. There is one main DLL file, `ASPNET_ISAPI.DLL`, that implements the required filter and extension DLL entry points.

When installed, ASP.NET adds a new global filter named ASPX. This filter is used by ASP.NET to hook the ISAPI filter process so that ASP.NET code can participate in the preprocessing steps of normal ISAPI filters but with managed code. These preprocessors are called *HTTP Handlers* in .NET and are added into the filter chain in the `WEB.CONFIG` file.

ASP.NET also adds the file extensions from Table A.1 to the Application Configuration, App Mappings tab. These are the ISAPI extension mappings that are used after ISAPI filtering is complete to execute the ASP.NET Web site code. The `WEB.CONFIG` file is used to determine where this extension code runs, either in the IIS process itself or completely out of process in a new hosting runtime for ASP.NET called `ASPNET_WP.EXE`.

Addressing Custom Code Problems in ASP 3.0

APPENDIX

B

IN THIS APPENDIX

Bad coding practices in ASP 3.0 include long ASP scripts, the use of interactive code including visual ActiveX controls in ASP, the use of dynamic SQL commands directly in ASP, and storing ActiveX objects in session or application state.

Long ASP Scripts Cause Web Server Slowdowns

Long ASP scripts can tax the CPU on a Web server. If too much ASP is attempted in one request, the Web browser could timeout before completing the script. Make sure that any ASP script requests can finish in a reasonable amount of time under heavy load.

Listing B.1 shows an example of a long ASP script that can cause server slowdowns. Notice the large number of loops and calculations. These calculations should be done inside a component to complete the request in a minimal amount of time. Long ASP scripts like this are difficult to debug and troubleshoot.

LISTING B.1 A Long ASP Script

```
'***Process Order
Dim I,J,K
Dim orderObject
'***get the order object from a database for this user. Not shown here
'Pull out all the items from the submitted form
For I = 1 to Request.Form(Request.Form.Count)
        If Request.Form(I) <> 0 then
OrderObject.Add Request.Form(I)
Next
'…
'Loop through all the items and total them up NOT SHOWN
'Loop through all the items and calculate tax NOT SHOWN
'Loop through all the items and check inventory NOT SHOWN
'At this point, with database hits and other calculations, the
'script is in danger of timing out, especially if there is a
large number of items.
```

Interactive Code Can Lock Threads in IIS

Using interactive code inside ASP is another common cause of Web server failures. Developers sometimes use message boxes within code to alert themselves to errors in execution or when a particular event happens. These message boxes make it easy to debug code before it moves into production. However, if they are not removed before the code goes to the production environment and they are executed within the scope of an ASP request, the message boxes will not be visible on the server. Instead, one of the 25 or so threads that IIS uses to execute ASP code is effectively locked because the thread that was executing the script is waiting for a user to close the message box. If other COM objects were created with this locked thread in other pending requests, those requests will timeout because certain Apartment-Threaded COM objects are tied to the thread that created them. Listing B.2 shows an example of a COM object that has interactive code being used in IIS.

LISTING B.2 Interactive Code That Locks IIS

```
'objBad displays a message box for an error condition
Dim objBad
Set objBad = CreateObject("Ordering.Validation")

'If OrderID is zero then the Validate function displays a message box
Obj.Validate Request.Form("OrderID")

'if validate displays the message box, this code stops executing in this
'thread and it is locked.
```

Dynamic SQL Commands Are Bad Practice

Using dynamic SQL commands puts an extra load on the SQL server when compared to stored procedures because the SQL server must parse the command and then dynamically generate the result set. In addition, dynamic SQL statements hide from database administrators the types of queries that are being executed against a database. Listing B.3 shows a dynamic SQL statement being executed in ASP.

LISTING B.3 Embedded SQL Code and Fix

```
'ADO Objects Created Elsewhere
'This command objects executes a dynamic SQL statement
ADOCommand.Execute "SELECT * FROM AUTHORS WHERE fn_name =
➥'" & Request.Form("name") & "'"
```

These SQL commands are a serious point of vulnerability. A malicious user could submit bogus data through a form post that could accidentally be included in the dynamic SQL statement that is being created in the ASP page. If possible, isolate all access to a SQL server database with stored procedures such as in Listing B.4.

LISTING B.4 Use Stored Procedures from ASP

```
'ADO Objects Created Elsewhere
'This command objects executes a stored procedure statement
ADOCommand.Execute Array((Request.Form("au_name")), "spAuthorByName"
```

Storing Apartment-Threaded COM Objects in Session State Causes Thread Contention

Storing Apartment-Threaded COM objects in session state seems like a good idea, but this is a bad practice. The code in this type of COM object (VB COM objects are Apartment-Threaded) must be executed on the same thread that created it. Listing B.5 illustrates storing a COM object in session. This block of code executes on a thread A.

LISTING B.5 Storing an Object in Session State

```
Dim objBad
Set objBad = CreateObject("VBCOM.Object")
'This stores the object off in session
Session("objVB") = objBad
```

Now that `objBad` is in a session state variable called `objVB`, it is available for this user on his next request. However, different threads handle repeated requests by the same user. If thread B runs code that uses an object stored in session by thread A, the COM libraries must thread switch into A. Thread B waits for thread A to become available and then passes processing onto thread A so the COM object can be accessed. If thread B is waiting on thread A at the same time thread A is waiting on thread B, a deadlock occurs and both threads timeout their requests. This is a perfect example of code that works great with one user but fails under load and can cause the entire server to become unresponsive.

There are special types of COM objects that can be stored in session or application state. However, they require special synchronization for an environment that is multithreaded like IIS and are not recommended. Create the component when it is needed and destroy it when it is no longer used, as in Listing B.6.

LISTING B.6 Proper Use of Apartment-Threaded COM Objects in ASP

```
Dim objGood
Set objGood = CreateObject("VBCOM.Object")
'Do some work
objGood.Work
'Destroy the component
Set objGood = nothing
```

Hardware Load Balancing Vendors

APPENDIX

C

The following is a list of the major hardware load balancing vendors in alphabetical order.

Alteon (Nortel Networks)

50 Great Oaks Boulevard

San Jose, CA 95119

WWW: www.alteonwebsystems.com

E-mail: info@alteon.com

Phone: (888) 258-3662

Fax: (408) 360-5501

Cisco Systems, Inc.

170 W. Tasman Drive

San Jose, CA 95134-1706

WWW: www.cisco.com

E-mail: info@cisco.com

Phone: (800) 553-6387

Fax: (408) 526-4100

Coyote Point Systems

3350 Scott Boulevard

Building #20

Santa Clara, California 95054

WWW: www.coyotepoint.com

E-mail: info@coyotepoint.com

Phone: (650) 969-6000

Fax: (408) 654-2927

F5 Networks, Inc.

401 Elliott Avenue West

Seattle, WA 98119

WWW: `www.f5.com`

E-mail: `info@f5.com`

Phone: (888) 882-4447 (88BIGIP)

Fax: (206) 272-5556

Foundry Networks, Inc.

2100 Gold Street

P.O. Box 649100

San Jose, CA 95164-9100

WWW: `www.foundrynetworks.com`

E-mail: `info@foundrynet.com`

Phone: (888) 887-2652 (TURBOLAN)

Fax: (408) 586-1900

Radware, Inc.

575 Corporate Drive, Suite 205

Mahwah, NJ 07430

WWW: `www.radware.com`

E-mail: `info@radware.com`

Phone: (888) 234-5763

Fax: (201) 512-9774

Scaling Out SQL Server 2000

APPENDIX

D

SQL Server 2000 supports a technique for scaling out a single database to multiple database servers, called *distributed partitioned views*. This new feature in SQL Server 2000 enables a database to be split across multiple servers, and standard load balancing technologies can be used to scale out the database. The form of a shared-nothing cluster is called a *federation of database systems*. Each node is an independent entity with dedicated disk capacity.

Scaling out SQL Server 2000 is accomplished with distributed partitioned views and application-specific changes. It is not possible simply to mark a database as distributed, copy it to multiple database servers, and run queries against a virtual network name. Instead, a single view must be broken into easily identifiable groups and then distributed across all the databases. For example, a view with a single table has a primary key that is used to partition the data. The range of values that each server handles is identified when the view is created. The process for creating a distributed partitioned view is described in detail in the SQL Server 2000 Books Online.

From an application standpoint, every server has access to all the data, but under the covers, SQL Server 2000 directs queries and requests to the appropriate server based on this primary key value. With this new technology, it is possible to scale out SQL Server when transaction demands of individual tables outgrow a single server.

Using the WLBS.EXE Command-Line Interface

APPENDIX

E

IN THIS APPENDIX

WLBS

WLBS.EXE is the command-line tool to manage Network Load Balancing clusters. Every aspect of Network Load Balancing can be managed from the command line. Use the following syntax for issuing commands with WLBS.EXE:

```
WLBS <command> [<cluster>[:<host>] [/PASSW [<password>]] [/PORT <port>]]
```

Type **WLBS** with no parameters for command line help. The [<cluster>[:<host>] [/PASSW [<password>]] [/PORT <port>]] portion of the usage syntax is for accessing a cluster remotely. Remote administration is disabled by default, and Microsoft recommends against enabling it. See Chapter 5, "Using Microsoft Network Load Balancing in a Web Farm," to learn how to enable remote administration. All commands in this reference assume that the command is issued locally. To make a command target a remote cluster, add

```
vclustername /PASSW password /PORT 2504
```

To target a particular member, add

```
vclustername:hostname /PASSW password /PORT 2504
```

where hostname is either the dedicated IP address or host priority number. PORT 2504 is the default port and can be changed in the Registry at HKEY_LOCAL_MACHINE\SYSTEM\CurrentControlSet\Services\WLBS\Parameters. Change the RemoteControlUDPPort DWORD value to the desired port number.

help

Launches the Windows help for Network Load Balancing.

```
Wlbs help
```

ip2mac <cluster>

Returns information about an existing cluster on the network.

```
Wlbs ip2max vclustername
```

The command returns the following information about a cluster:

```
WLBS Cluster Control Utility V2.3. (c) 1997-99 Microsoft Corporation
Cluster:     vclustername
Multicast MAC: 03-bf-ac-10-fa-0c
Unicast MAC:   02-bf-ac-10-fa-0c
```

This information is useful for network configurations that require port locking and manually entered ARP entries.

reload

Forces the local Network Load Balancing configuration to reload from the Registry. This command can only be issued locally.

```
Wlbs reload
```

query

Queries the target cluster member for its status.

```
Wlbs query
```

This command returns

```
Host 32 converged with the following host(s) as part of the cluster: 31, 32
```

when the member 32 is successfully converged with the cluster. It will also return information if the cluster member is stopped. Table E.1 shows the different states that SUSPEND, RESUME, START, STOP, and DRAINSTOP put the cluster in and how to reverse the command. If cluster operations are stopped, then the cluster member does not handle traffic. Cluster control determines if the cluster can accept administrative commands.

TABLE E.1 The Different States of a Cluster

Command	*Cluster Operation*	*Cluster Control*	*Reverse*
STOP	Stops cluster operations	No effect	START
START	Starts cluster operations	No effect	STOP
SUSPEND	Stops cluster operations	Stops cluster control	RESUME and START
RESUME	No Effect	Starts cluster control	SUSPEND
DRAINSTOP	After connections, end STOP cluster operations	No effect	START

display

Displays all the configuration information about the current cluster. May be issued only locally. This command will display the Registry information for WLBS, the last five event log entries, IP configuration information (same as issuing IPCONFIG /ALL), and the information from the QUERY command.

```
Wlbs display
```

suspend

Suspends all cluster operations and remote control capabilities. The only way to restart cluster control operations is by issuing a RESUME command. A START command is required to start cluster operations.

```
Wlbs suspend
```

resume

Resumes all cluster control operations after a SUSPEND command. It does not start the cluster operations (receiving traffic). This must be done with a START command.

```
Wlbs resume
```

start

Starts cluster operations on a member so the member may receive traffic again.

```
Wlbs start
```

stop

Stops cluster operations on a member so the member no longer receives traffic.

```
Wlbs stop
```

drainstop

Stops cluster operations by not accepting any new connections and waits for the current connections to terminate. This command can be interrupted with a STOP or START command.

enable <port> | ALL

Enables a particular port if specified. Specify ALL to enable all ports. Use this to start cluster operations on a specific port, such as port 80.

```
Wlbs enable 80
```

disable <port> | ALL

Disables a particular port if specified. Specify ALL ports to disable all ports. Use this to stop cluster operations on a specific port, such as port 80.

```
Wlbs disable 80
```

drain <port> | ALL

Same as DRAINSTOP except it can be done per port.

```
Wlbs drain 80
```

Well Known Certificate Authorities

APPENDIX

F

These authorities are installed by default to Internet Explorer 5.0 and above. Purchasing a certificate from one of these authorities ensures seamless integration for secure transactions using SSL. Users will not need to install a new root certificate to establish a secure connection to a Web server with a certificate purchased from one of these vendors.

Entrust Technologies, Inc.

4975 Preston Park Boulevard

Suite 400

Plano, Texas 75093

WWW: `www.entrust.com`

E-mail: `entrust@entrust.com`

Phone: (888) 690-2424

Fax: (972) 943-7305

Equifax, Inc. (EquifaxSecure)

WWW: `www.equifaxsecure.com`

E-mail: `secure.server@equifax.com`

Phone: (877) 857-7640

GlobalSign

Haachtsesteenweg 1426, Chaussée de Haecht

B-1130 Brussels, Belgium

WWW: `www.globalsign.com`

E-mail: `info@globalsign.com`

Phone: +32 2 724 36 36

Fax: +32 2 724 36 37

Thawte

P.O. Box 17648

Raleigh, NC 27619-7648

WWW:	`www.thawte.com`
E-mail:	`info@thawte.com`
Phone:	(919) 831-8400
Fax:	(919) 743-3340

VeriSign

1350 Charleston Road

Mountain View, CA 94043

WWW:	`www.verisign.com`
E-mail:	`internetsales@verisign.com`
Phone:	(650) 429-5512
Fax:	(650) 961-7300

Supported IIS 5.0 HTTP Error Responses

APPENDIX

G

This appendix lists all the error responses that an IIS server can give.

TABLE G.1 IIS 5.0–Supported HTTP Error Responses

Error	*Explanation*
400	Bad Request. A generic error, IIS will return a more specific error in most cases.
401;1	Unauthorized: Login Failed. Occurs when basic authentication fails because of incorrect usernames or passwords.
401;2	Unauthorized: Login Failed Due to Server Configuration. Occurs when a user does not send credentials to the server when requested.
401;3	Access Denied by ACL on Resource. Occurs when a client is successfully authenticated but tries to access a secured resource he doesn't have permissions.
401;4	Unauthorized: Authorization Denied by Filter. Occurs when an ISAPI filter extending an authentication request denies access to a file on the server.
401;5	Unauthorized: Authorization by ISAPI or CGI Application Failed. Occurs when an ISAPI or CGI program extending an authentication request denies access to a file on the server.
403	Unauthorized: User Does Not Have Authorization to View the Directory or Page Requested.
403;1	Forbidden: Execute Access Forbidden. The file requested has been marked to not allow execute access permissions.
403;2	Forbidden: Read Access Forbidden. The file requested has been marked to not allow read access permissions.
403;3	Forbidden: Write Access Forbidden. The file cannot be written to the directory specified due to access permissions.
403;4	Forbidden: SSL Required. The page requested requires the use of HTTPS.
403;5	Forbidden: SSL 128 Required. The page requested requires high security to access.
403;6	Forbidden: IP Address Rejected. The IP address of the incoming request was rejected.
403;7	Forbidden: Client Certificate Required. The page requested requires a client certificate to access.
403;8	Forbidden: Site Access Denied. The DNS address of the incoming request has been blocked from accessing this site.
403;9	Forbidden: Too Many Users Are Connected. The Web server is overloaded.
403;10	Forbidden: Invalid Configuration. The CGI, ISAPI, or other executable program requested cannot be run from this directory.
403;11	Forbidden: Password Change. The password currently in use was changed during the last request and must be reentered.

TABLE G.1 Continued

Error	*Explanation*
403;12	Forbidden: Mapper Denied Access. A directory mapped to in this site denied access to the credentials supplied.
403;13	Forbidden: Client Certificate Revoked. The client certificate in use by this browser has been revoked.
403;14	DEFAULT, Forbidden: Directory Listing Denied. The request to browse the directory was denied.
403;15	Forbidden: Client Access Licenses Exceeded. The number of client access licenses for this server has been exceeded.
403;16	Forbidden: Client Certificate Untrusted or Invalid. The client certificate in use is invalid or untrusted.
403;17	Forbidden: Client Certificate Has Expired or Is Not Yet Valid. The time stamp on the client certificate is invalid.
404	File Not Found. The file request is unavailable or incorrect.
405	Resource Not Allowed. The page requested cannot be displayed because the page address is incorrect.
406	Not Acceptable. The resource you are looking for cannot be opened by your browser.
407	Proxy Authentication Required. Authentication with a proxy server is required before this request can be serviced.
412	Precondition Failed. The request was not completed due to preconditions that were set on the page requested.
414	Request—URI Too Long. There is a problem with the page requested, and it cannot be displayed.
500	Internal Server Error. There is a problem with the page requested, and it cannot be displayed.
500;12	Application Restarting. The page requested cannot be retrieved because the application is restarting.
500;13	Server Too Busy. The number of requests in the queue to the server has made it too busy.
500;15	Requests for `global.asa` Not Allowed. The `global.asa` file may not be retrieved.
500;100	Internal Server Error—ASP Error. An error occurred in the ASP processing engine.
501	Not Implemented.
502	Bad Gateway.

Configuring Shared Disk Technologies

APPENDIX

H

IN THIS APPENDIX

Using Shared SCSI

It is possible to use basic SCSI technology to create a shared storage system. In a two-node cluster, a shared SCSI system consists of an external SCSI drive enclosure connected to two servers by either a normal SCSI cable, a y-cable, or a Trilink connector.

A SCSI bus is simply a chain of devices, each with a unique ID, that share a path to and from the CPU and memory on a server. When two or more servers share a SCSI bus, special termination semantics enable successful resource sharing. Correctly configuring a shared SCSI bus has the following challenges:

- Each device, including the two controllers and all hard drives, must have a unique SCSI ID. If any two devices share the same ID, they will compete for control of the bus and cause failures during install of the second node of the cluster.
- The SCSI bus must be properly terminated. This means that each segment (the portion that connects an adapter to the storage) must have exactly two points of termination. In a two-node cluster, this means that there are exactly four points of termination. Terminating a SCSI bus is accomplished using either internal termination in SCSI adapters, with Y cables, or with Trilink connectors.

Terminating a SCSI Bus Using SCSI Adapters

This is not the preferred method of termination. The points of termination are the shared drive array and the internal cluster member SCSI adapters. Because a SCSI segment must always have two points of termination, detaching the server from the shared storage array can break the cluster.

Terminating a SCSI Bus Using Y-Cables or Trilink Connectors

A y-cable or Trilink connector provides the best solution for terminating a shared SCSI bus. Figure H.1 shows a two-node cluster with a y-cable configuration. In this configuration, even with the node detached from the y-cable, there are always two points of termination. This gives the most flexibility and prevents the SCSI bus from failing during catastrophic node failures that require a node to come offline.

Using Fiber Channel

Fiber channel connections to cluster storage work in the same way as SCSI connections except that fiber channel solutions are much simpler. In fiber channel there are no termination problems, and each fiber channel controller comes with a unique ID so there is no need to configure it. Fiber channel uses switch technology to connect all the devices, so configuration is as easy as setting up a standard network switch.

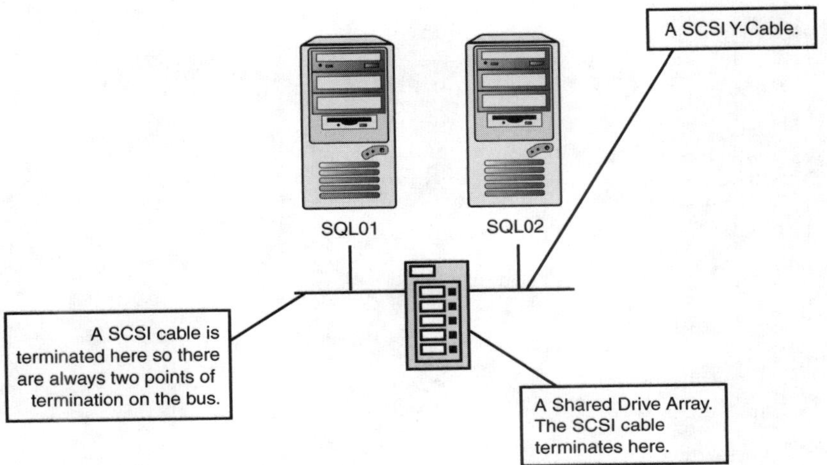

FIGURE H.1
A shared SCSI Windows cluster using y-cables.

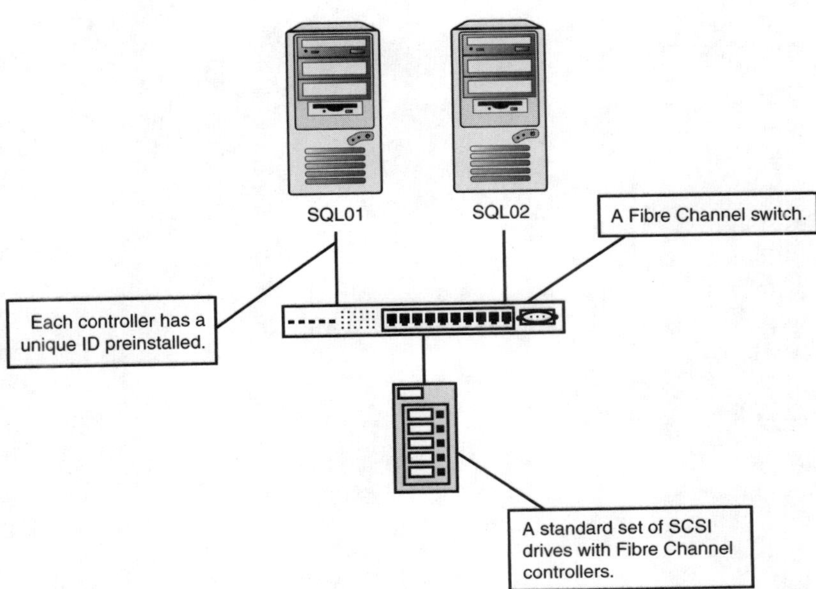

FIGURE H.2
A fiber channel Windows server cluster.

Application Center Command-Line Reference

APPENDIX

I

IN THIS APPENDIX

AC

AC.EXE is the command-line interface for Application Center 2000. From this tool, administrators can script most of the actions that can be accomplished using the GUI interface. Type the following at the command prompt to see a the list of commands supported:

```
AC
```

AC supports the following five different command groups:

- **Application**—Used to manage, create, and delete applications for deployment
- **Cluster**—Used to manage the creation of clusters and their membership
- **Deploy**—Used to launch deployments of applications to cluster members
- **CLB**—Used to manage component load balancing features in a COM+ cluster
- **LoadBalance**—Used to manage the status of members in a cluster

When the parameters to a specific command are listed in the following sections, these conventions apply:

A parameter not enclosed in any type of bracket is required.

```
/NAME:application_name
```

A parameter enclosed in brackets (`[` and `]`) is considered optional.

```
[/MEMBER:membername]
```

Multiple parameters enclosed in curly braces (`{` and `}`) means that at least one of the commands is required.

```
{/NAME:application_name | /GUID:application_GUID}
```

Multiple parameters enclosed in brackets (`[` and `]`) means that to use either command, both must be used.

```
[/USER:username /PASSWORD:password]
```

To prevent the command that issue prompts from prompting interactively, use `/Y`.

AC APPLICATION

The `AC APPLICATION` command can be used to create, delete, and list applications in a cluster, as well as add and remove resources to an application. The `AC APPLICATION` command is the only way to add resources unavailable from the GUI, such as metabase entries to an application.

/CREATE

Use AC APPLICATION /CREATE to create a new application for an Application Center 2000 cluster. Here is an example of using the AC APPLICATION /CREATE command:

```
AC APPLICATION /CREATE /NAME:MyApplication /USER:Admin /PASSWORD:guessme
```

This command creates a new application called MyApplication using the user Admin and password guessme. The AC APPLICATION /CREATE command has the switches shown in Table I.1.

TABLE I.1 Parameters for the AC APPLICATION /CREATE Command

Parameter	*Description*
[/MEMBER:membername]	Targets the application creation on a specific member cluster.
/NAME:application_name	Specifies the name of the new application. Be descriptive.
[/MEMBERONLY]	Targets the application only on a specific member.
[/USER:username /PASSWORD: password]	Shows a user that has administrative privileges on the target member. Must come as a /PASSWORD:password pair.

/DELETE

Use AC APPLICATION /DELETE to delete an application from an Application Center 2000 cluster. The following line shows an example of using the AC APPLICATION /DELETE command:

```
AC APPLICATION /DELETE /NAME:MyApplication /USER:Admin /PASSWORD:guessme
```

This command deletes the application called MyApplication using the user Admin and password guessme. The AC APPLICATION /DELETE command has the switches shown in Table I.2.

TABLE I.2 Parameters for the AC APPLICATION /DELETE Command

Parameter	*Description*
[/MEMBER:membername]	Targets the application deletion on a specific member cluster.
{/NAME:application_name | /GUID:application_GUID}	Specifies the name or GUID of the application to be deleted. Application GUIDs can be found with the /LIST command.
[/MEMBERONLY]	Targets the application command only on a specific member.

Table I.2 Continued

Parameter	*Description*
`[/USER:username /PASSWORD:password]`	Shows a user that has administrative privileges on the target member. Must come as a `/PASSWORD:password` pair.

/LIST

Use `AC APPLICATION /LIST` to display the list of applications on Application Center 2000 cluster or a specific member. Here is an example of using the `AC APPLICATION /LIST` command:

```
AC APPLICATION /LIST /USER:Admin /PASSWORD:guessme
```

This command lists all the applications for a cluster or a single member, as shown here:

```
Name                                    Identifier
-----------------------------------------------------------------------------
AllSites                                {2E3D9AEB-26BD-4F33-8EC4-D6907F0F152D}
TechnicalLead.com                       {735FB3EE-4A9A-4823-BCBC-8AE511E235DC}
Simple Application                      {C5164108-D627-4590-978E-917DCBC8F781}
MyApplication                           {011986F2-0081-4BA8-869C-0666B5020865}
```

The `AC APPLICATION /LIST` command has the switches shown in Table I.3.

Table I.3 Parameters for the `AC APPLICATION /LIST` Command

Parameter	*Description*
`[/MEMBER:membername]`	Targets the application creation on a specific member cluster.
`[/MEMBERONLY]`	Targets the application only on a specific member.
`[/USER:username /PASSWORD:password]`	Shows a user that has administrative privileges on the target member. Must come as a `/PASSWORD:password` pair.

/ADDRESOURCE

Use `AC APPLICATION /ADDRESOURCE` to add a resource to a specific application in a cluster. It supports adding the five resource types from the command line, including IIS, file paths, registry entries, DSNs, and COM+ applications. Listing I.1 shows an example of each type of resources added to MyApplication using the `AC APPLICATION /ADDRESOURCE` command.

LISTING I.1 Examples of Using the AC APPLICATION /ADDRESOURCE Command

```
REM Add an IIS Resource
AC APPLICATION /ADDRESOURCE /NAME:MyApplication /USER:Admin /PASSWORD:guessme
➥ /RESOURCETYPE:IIS /RESOURCEPATH:/LM/Membership/Mappings/W3SVC/3

REM Add a COM+ Application Resource
AC APPLICATION /ADDRESOURCE /NAME:MyApplication /USER:Admin /PASSWORD:guessme
➥ /RESOURCETYPE:COMPlusApp /RESOURCEPATH:

REM Add a DSN Resource
AC APPLICATION /ADDRESOURCE /NAME:MyApplication /USER:Admin /PASSWORD:guessme
➥/RESOURCETYPE:DSN /RESOURCEPATH:TLDBConnect

REM Add a File Path Resource
AC APPLICATION /ADDRESOURCE /NAME:MyApplication /USER:Admin /PASSWORD:guessme
➥/RESOURCETYPE:FileSystem /RESOURCEPATH:C:\AppData

REM Add a Registry Resource
AC APPLICATION /ADDRESOURCE /NAME:MyApplication /USER:Admin /PASSWORD:guessme
➥/RESOURCETYPE:Registry /RESOURCEPATH:
➥"HKEY_LOCAL_MACHINE\SOFTWARE\TechnicalLead"
```

These commands add the specified resource types to the MyApplication application using the user Admin and password guessme. The AC APPLICATION /ADDRESOURCE command has the switches shown in Table I.4.

TABLE I.4 Parameters for the AC APPLICATION /ADDRESOURCE Command

Parameter	*Description*
/RESOURCETYPE:Type	Can be one of the following: • IIS, for metabase entries • FileSystem, for file paths • Registry, for registry paths • DSN, for DSNs • COMPlusApp, for COM+ applications
/RESOURCEPATH:Path	Specifies the path to the specified application types. Format is based on type. See Listing I.1 for more details.
[/MEMBER:membername]	Targets the application creation on a specific member cluster.
{/NAME:application_name | /	Gives the name or GUID of the application to

TABLE I.4 Continued

Parameter	*Description*
`GUID:application_GUID}`	add the resource to.
`[/MEMBERONLY]`	Targets the application only on a specific member.
`[/USER:username /PASSWORD:password]`	Shows a user that has administrative privileges on the target member. Must come as a `/PASSWORD:password` pair.

/REMOVERESOURCE

Use `AC APPLICATION /REMOVERESOURCE` to remove a resource from a specific application in a cluster. It supports removing the five resource types from the command line, including IIS, file paths, registry entries, DSNs, and COM+ applications. Listing I.2 shows an example of each type of resources being removed from MyApplication using the `AC APPLICATION /REMOVERESOURCE` command.

LISTING I.2 Examples of Removing a Resource with the `AC APPLICATION /REMOVERESOURCE` Command

```
REM Remove an IIS Resource
AC APPLICATION /REMOVERESOURCE /NAME:MyApplication /USER:Admin
➥/PASSWORD:guessme /RESOURCETYPE:IIS /RESOURCEPATH:
➥/LM/Membership/Mappings/W3SVC/3

REM Remove a COM+ Application Resource
AC APPLICATION /REMOVERESOURCE /NAME:MyApplication /USER:Admin /PASSWORD:
➥guessme /RESOURCETYPE:COMPlusApp /RESOURCEPATH:MyCOMApp

REM Remove a DSN Resource
AC APPLICATION /REMOVERESOURCE /NAME:MyApplication /USER:Admin /PASSWORD:
➥guessme /RESOURCETYPE:DSN /RESOURCEPATH:TLDBConnect

REM Remove a File Path Resource
AC APPLICATION /REMOVERESOURCE /NAME:MyApplication /USER:Admin /PASSWORD:
➥guessme /RESOURCETYPE:FileSystem /RESOURCEPATH:C:\AppData

REM Remove a Registry Resource
AC APPLICATION /REMOVERESOURCE /NAME:MyApplication /USER:Admin /PASSWORD:
➥guessme /RESOURCETYPE:Registry /RESOURCEPATH:
➥"HKEY_LOCAL_MACHINE\SOFTWARE\TechnicalLead"
```

These commands remove the specified resource types from the MyApplication application using the user Admin and password guessme. The AC APPLICATION /REMOVERESOURCE command has the switches shown in Table I.5.

TABLE I.5 Parameters for the AC APPLICATION /REMOVERESOUCE Command

Parameter	*Description*
/RESOURCETYPE:Type	Can be one of the following: • IIS, for metabase entries • FileSystem, for file paths • Registry, for registry paths • DSN, for DSNs • COMPlusApp, for COM+ applications
/RESOURCEPATH:Path	Gives the path to the specified application types. Format based on type. See Listing I.2 above for more details.
{*/NAME:application_name* | */GUID:application_GUID*}	Specifies the name or GUID of the application to remove the resource from.
[/MEMBERONLY]	Targets the application only on a specific member.
[/USER:username /PASSWORD:password]	Shows a user that has administrative privileges on the target member. Must come as a /PASSWORD:password pair.

/LISTRESOURCES

Use AC APPLICATION /LISTRESOURCES to list the resources in a particular application. Here is an example of using the AC APPLICATION /LISTRESOURCES command:

```
AC APPLICATION /LISTRESOURCES /NAME:MyApplication /USER:Admin /PASSWORD:guessme
```

This command lists the resources of the application called MyApplication using the user Admin and password guessme. This produces output in the following form:

```
Type            Path
-------------------------------------------------------------------------
COMPLUSAPP      /Applications/{9DB611BD-2F03-40B2-91D1-E0D68F77269E}
DSN             TLDBConnect
IIS             /LM/Membership/Mappings/W3SVC/3
REGISTRY        HKEY_LOCAL_MACHINE\SOFTWARE\TechnicalLead
```

The AC APPLICATION /LISTRESOURCES command has the switches shown in Table I.6.

TABLE I.6 Parameters for the AC APPLICATION /LISTRESOURCES Command

Parameter	*Description*
[/MEMBER:membername]	Targets the application creation on a specific member cluster.
{/NAME:application_name | /GUID:application_GUID}	Specifies the name of the application to list the resources of.
[/MEMBERONLY]	Targets the application only on a specific member.
[/USER:username /PASSWORD:password]	Shows a user that has administrative privileges on the target member. Must come as a /PASSWORD:password pair.

AC DEPLOY

Use AC DEPLOY to create, delete, and list the current deployments active in a cluster, as well as add and remove members from the synchronization loop in a cluster. The AC DEPLOY command is the only way to stop a synchronization that is currently in progress.

/START

Use AC DEPLOY /START to start a new deployment. Here is an example of using the AC DEPLOY /START command:

```
AC DEPLOY /START /DEPNAME:DEPLOY /SOURCE:AC1 /SOURCEUSER:Admin
➥/SOURCEPASSWORD:guessme /TARGETS:AC2 /TARGETUSER:Admin
➥/TARGETPASSWORD:guessme
```

This command creates a new deployment called DEPLOY. Its goes from AC1 to AC2 and synchronizes all applications in the cluster. Here is another example of using the AC DEPLOY /START command:

```
AC DEPLOY /START /DEPNAME:DEPLOYCOM /SOURCE:AC1 /SOURCEUSER:Admin
➥/SOURCEPASSWORD:guessme /TARGETS:AC2 /TARGETUSER:Admin
➥/TARGETPASSWORD:guessme /APPNAME:MyApplication /COMPLUS /WAIT
```

This command creates a new deployment called DEPLOYCOM. It deploys the application MyApplication, along with an COM+ application in MyApplication in a synchronous fashion. The AC DEPLOY /START command has the switches shown in Table I.7.

TABLE I.7 Parameters for the AC DEPLOY /START Command

Parameter	*Description*
[/DEPNAME:depname]	Gives the name of the deployment.
[/SOURCE:sourcename]	Specifies the source server for the deployment.
/SOURCEUSER:username /SOURCEPASSWORD:*|pwd]	Shows a user that has administrative privileges on the source server. Must come as a /SOURCEPASSWORD:password pair.
[/TARGETS:targetname1, targetname2,...]	Specifies the target servers for the deployment.
/TARGETUSER:username /TARGETPASSWORD:*|pwd]	Shows a user that has administrative privileges on the target server(s). Must come as a /TARGETPASSWORD:password pair.
[/APPNAME:appname1,appname2,... | /APPGUID:appguid1,appguid2,...]	Shows the applications to deploy, either by application name or by application GUID. If this is not specified, it will synchronize all applications on the cluster.
[/NOACL]	Does not deploy ACLs. Be careful because this will change the properties of Web files to have the permission that will prevent access from anonymous users.
[/COMPLUS]	Deploys COM+ applications.
[/WAIT]	Forces the deployment to happen synchronously.

/LISTDEPLOYMENTS

Use AC DEPLOY / LISTDEPLOYMENTS to list the most recent deployments on a cluster, whether active or not. Here is an example of using the AC DEPLOY /START command:

```
AC DEPLOY /LISTDEPLOYMENTS
```

This command returns a listing of the most recent deployments on the server where the command was executed. Listing I.3 shows the results of this command.

LISTING I.3 The Results of the AC DEPLOY /LISTDEPLOYMENTS Command

```
Replication Job:
Name:            DEPLOY
Source:          AC1
Status:          Succeeded
Targets:         AC1
Applications:    AllSites, MyApplication
```

LISTING I.3 Continued

```
Replication Job:
Name:             12:38:45 04/21/01
Source:           AC1
Status:           Succeeded
Targets:          AC2
Applications:     MyApplication

Replication Job:
Name:             AllSites
Source:           AC1
Status:           Succeeded
Targets:          AC2
Applications:     AllSites
```

The `AC DEPLOY /LISTDEPLOYMENTS` command has the switches shown in Table I.8.

TABLE I.8 Parameters for the `AC DEPLOY /LISTDEPLOYMENTS` Command

Parameter	*Description*
`[/SOURCE:sourcename]`	The source server to retrieve the deployment list from.
`/SOURCEUSER:username /SOURCEPASSWORD:*|pwd]`	A user that has administrative privileges on the source server. Must come as a `/SOURCEPASSWORD:password` pair.

/TERMINATE

Use `AC DEPLOY /TERMINATE` to stop a deployment job in progress. Here is an example of using the `AC DEPLOY /TERMINATE` command:

```
AC DEPLOY /TERMINATE /DEPNAME:DEPLOY
```

This command terminates a deployment called DEPLOY that is running on the local server. This command changes the status of the deployment to stopped as reported by `/LISTDEPLOYMENTS` or from the GUI. The `AC DEPLOY /TERMINATE` command has the switches shown in Table I.9.

TABLE I.9 Parameters for the `AC DEPLOY /TERMINATE` Command

Parameter	*Description*
`{/JOBID:jobid | /DEPNAME:depname}`	The JobID or deployment name to cancel.
`[/SOURCE:sourcename]`	The source server to terminate the deployment on.

TABLE I.9 Continued

Parameter	Description
[/SOURCEUSER:username /SOURCEPASSWORD:*|pwd]	A user that has administrative privileges on the source server. Must come as a /SOURCEPASSWORD:password pair.

/ENABLESYNC

Use AC DEPLOY /ENABLESYNC to stop a deployment job in progress. Here is an example of using the AC DEPLOY /ENABLESYNC command:

```
AC DEPLOY /ENABLESYNC /SOURCE:AC1
```

This command enables synchronizations on the source server. This command is equivalent to checking the check box Include This Member in Synchronizations on a specific member's property dialog box. The AC DEPLOY /ENABLESYNC command has the switches shown in Table I.10.

TABLE I.10 Parameters for the AC DEPLOY /ENABLESYNC Command

Parameter	Description
[/SOURCE:sourcename]	The source server to enable synchronizations.
[/SOURCEUSER:username /SOURCEPASSWORD:*|pwd]	A user that has administrative privileges on the source server. Must come as a /SOURCEPASSWORD:password pair.

/DISABLESYNC

Use AC DEPLOY /DISABLESYNC to stop a deployment job in progress. Here is an example of using the AC DEPLOY /DISABLESYNC command:

```
AC DEPLOY /DISABLESYNC /SOURCE:AC1
```

This command disables synchronizations on the source server. This command is equivalent to not checking the check box Include This Member in Synchronizations on a specific member's property dialog. The AC DEPLOY /DISABLESYNC command has the switches shown in Table I.11.

TABLE I.11 Parameters for the AC DEPLOY /DISABLESYNC Command

Parameter	Description
[/SOURCE:sourcename]	The source server to disable synchronizations on.
[/SOURCEUSER:username /SOURCEPASSWORD:*|pwd]	A user that has administrative privileges on the source server. Must come as a /SOURCEPASSWORD:password pair.

/STATUS [:ALL]

Use AC DEPLOY /STATUS [:ALL] to return a list of the synchronization settings for a specific member of the cluster or with all members using the /STATUS:ALL form. Here is an example of using the AC DEPLOY /STATUS:ALL command:

```
AC DEPLOY /STATUS:ALL
```

This command returns the text in Listing I.4.

LISTING I.4 The Results of the AC DEPLOY /STATUS:ALL Command

```
Synchronization status
Member                                 Synchronization
-------------------------------------------------------------
AC1                                    Enabled
AC2                                    Enabled
```

The AC DEPLOY /STATUS [:ALL] command has the switches shown in Table I.12.

TABLE I.12 Parameters for the AC DEPLOY /STATUS [:ALL] Command

Parameter	*Description*
[/SOURCE:sourcename]	The source server to list the synchronization status.
[/SOURCEUSER:username /SOURCEPASSWORD:*|pwd]	A user that has administrative privileges on the source server. Must come as a /SOURCEPASSWORD:password pair.

AC LOADBALANCE

Use AC LOADBALANCE to manage load balancing for members whose clusters use network load balancing or component load balancing. Members can be taken offline brought online, the NLB weight changed and that status of the member queried with the AC LOADBALANCE command.

/ONLINE

Use AC LOADBALANCE /ONLINE for load balancing the target member of the cluster. Here is an example of using the AC LOADBALANCE /ONLINE command:

```
AC LOADBALANCE /ONLINE
```

This command puts the target member's load-balancing status to an online state from either a suspended or an offline state. Here is another example of using the AC LOADBALANCE /OFFLINE command:

```
AC LOADBALANCE /ONLINE /MEMBER:AC1 /MEMBERONLY
```

This command puts AC1's load-balancing status to online only if it is in a suspended state. /MEMBERONLY will not allow a cluster member to come back online from an offline state. The AC LOADBALANCE /ONLINE command has the switches shown in Table I.13.

TABLE I.13 Parameters for the AC LOADBALANCE /ONLINE Command

Parameter	*Description*
[/MEMBER:member_name]	Specifies The member to turn load balancing on.
[/USER:username /PASSWORD:*|pwd]	Shows a user that has administrative privileges on the target server. Must come as a /PASSWORD:password pair.
/MEMBERONLY	Changes the status from suspended to online. Does not work if load balancing is completely offline.

/OFFLINE

Use AC LOADBALANCE /OFFLINE to suspend load balancing on the target member of the cluster. Here is an example of using the AC LOADBALANCE /OFFLINE command:

```
AC LOADBALANCE /OFFLINE
```

This command puts the target member's load-balancing status to an offline state from either a suspended or an online state. Here is another example of using the AC LOADBALANCE /OFFLINE command:

```
AC LOADBALANCE /OFFLINE /MEMBER:AC1 /MEMBERONLY /DRAIN:10 /Y
```

This command puts AC1's load-balancing status to suspended only if it is not in a offline state. /DRAIN:10 means that it will take 10 minutes before the state of the cluster members goes to suspended. During that time, no new connections are made to the cluster, and existing ones terminate normally. /MEMBERONLY will not allow a cluster member to go to a suspended state from an offline state. The AC LOADBALANCE /OFFLINE command has the switches shown in Table I.14.

TABLE I.14 Parameters for the AC LOADBALANCE /OFFLINE Command

Parameter	*Description*
[/MEMBER:member_name]	Specifies the member to turn load balancing off.
[/USER:username /PASSWORD:*|pwd]	Shows a user that has administrative privileges on the target server. Must come as a /PASSWORD:password pair.
/MEMBERONLY	Changes the status from online to suspended. Does not work if load balancing is completely offline.

TABLE I.14 Continued

Parameter	*Description*
`[/DRAIN:time]`	Specifies the time, in minutes, to wait for the connections on a cluster close. No new connections are allowed to the cluster after the command is executed.

/SETNLBWEIGHT:weight

Use `AC LOADBALANCE /SETNLBWEIGHT:weight` to set the weight of the target server to a relative value between 1 and 100. Here is an example of using the `AC LOADBALANCE /SETNLBWEIGHT:weight` command:

```
AC LOADBALANCE /SETNLBWEIGHT:80
```

This command puts the target member's load-balancing weight to 80. This does not mean that the member handles 80% of the traffic. It is a relative number based on the percentage of all the other weights combined. The `AC LOADBALANCE /SETNLBWEIGHT:weight` command has the switches shown in Table I.15.

TABLE I.15 Parameters for the `AC LOADBALANCE /SETNLBWEIGHT:weight` Command

Parameter	*Description*
`[/MEMBER:member_name]`	The target member to change the NLB weight on.
`[/USER:username /PASSWORD:*|pwd]`	A user that has administrative privileges on the target server. Must come as a `/PASSWORD:password` pair.

/STATUS [:All]

Use `AC LOADBALANCE /STATUS [:All]` to return the load-balancing status of a target member. Or, with `/STATUS:ALL`, every member's status is returned. Here is an example of using the `AC LOADBALANCE /STATUS [:All]` command:

```
AC LOADBALANCE /STATUS:ALL
```

This command lists the status of all members of the cluster. Listing I.5 shows the results of this command.

LISTING I.5 The Results of the `AC LOADBALANCE /STATUS:ALL` Command

```
Load balancing Settings for AC1:
    Load balancing: enabled
    Status: online
```

LISTING I.5 Continued

```
    Weight: equal
Load balancing Settings for AC2:
    Load balancing: enabled
    Status: online
    Weight: equal
```

The `AC LOADBALANCE /STATUS [:ALL]` command has the switches shown in Table I.16.

TABLE I.16 Parameters for the `AC LOADBALANCE /STATUS [:ALL]` Command

Parameter	*Description*
`[/MEMBER:member_name]`	The target member to check the load balancing status on.
`[/USER:username /PASSWORD:*|pwd]`	A user that has administrative privileges on the target server. Must come as a `/PASSWORD:password` pair.

AC CLUSTER

`AC CLUSTER` allows the administrator to manage an Application Center 2000 cluster from the command line. A cluster can be created or deleted, new members can be added, the cluster controller can be moved to another member, the NICs of a server can be listed, and the cluster database for a member can be purged.

/CREATE

Use `AC CLUSTER /CREATE` to create a new Application Center 2000 cluster on the target server. Here is an example of using the `AC CLUSTER /CREATE` command:

```
AC CLUSTER /CREATE /NAME:TESTCOMAPP /CONTROLLER:AC1 /TYPE:COMPLUSAPP
➥/LOADBALANCING:CLB /MANAGEMENTNIC:0
```

This command creates a new COM+ cluster named TESTCOMAPP on AC1 that uses CLB. Notice that it requires a NIC ID that can be found from using the `AC CLUSTER /LISTNICS` command. Here is another example of the `AC CLUSTER /CREATE` command:

```
AC CLUSTER /CREATE /NAME:TESTWEB /CONTROLLER:AC1 /TYPE:WEB /LOADBALANCING:NLB
➥/MANAGEMENTNIC:0 /LBNIC:1 /CLUSTERIPADDRESS:192.168.1.200 /
➥CLUSTERIPSUBNETMASK:255.255.255.0 /AFFINITY:NONE
```

This command creates a new NLB Web cluster named TESTWEB. The management and load-balancing NIC must be specified along with a cluster IP address. The `AC CLUSTER /CREATE` command has the parameters shown in Table I.17.

TABLE I.17 Parameters for the `AC CLUSTER /CREATE` Command

Parameter	*Description*
`[/CONTROLLER:controller_name]`	Specifies the server to use as the cluster controller for the new cluster. If nothing is specified, a new cluster is created on the server issuing the command.
`/NAME:cluster_name`	Specifies the name of the new cluster. This will be the virtual name in an NLB cluster.
`[/DESCRIPTION:cluster_description]`	Gives a description of the cluster and its purpose.
`[/USER:username /PASSWORD:password]`	Shows a user that has administrative privileges on the target cluster controller. Must come as a `/PASSWORD:password` pair.
`/TYPE:Web | ComPlusApp | ComPlusRouting`	Specifies the type of cluster to create—either a Web, COM+, or COM+ routing cluster.
`/LOADBALANCING:NLB | CLB | Other | None`	Specifies the type of load-balancing support for a cluster.
`/MANAGEMENTNIC:nic_id`	Gives the ID of the management NIC.

If the `/LOADBALANCING` parameter is set to NLB, the parameters in Table I.18 are used to further specify how NLB should be set up.

TABLE I.18 Additional Parameters for `AC CLUSTER /CREATE` When `/LOADBALANCING:NLB` Is Specified

Parameter	*Description*
`/CLUSTERIP:ip` `/CLUSTERIPSUBNETMASK:subnet_mask`	Gives the cluster IP address and subnet mask. These parameters are required and must be specified together.
`[/DEDICATEDIP:ip` `/DEDICATEDIPSUBNETMASK:subnet_mask]`	Gives the dedicated IP address and the subnet mast. Optional; must be specified together.
`[/AFFINITY:Single | ClassC | None]`	Specifies the type of NLB affinity.
`/LBNIC:nic_id`	Specifies the cluster NIC used for load balancing by NLB.

TABLE I.18 Continued

Parameter	*Description*
`[/KEEPNLBSETTINGS]`	Retains and upgrades the existing settings in an NLB cluster that hasn't used Application Center 2000 in the past.

/DELETE

Use `AC CLUSTER /DELETE` to delete an existing Application Center 2000 cluster on the target server. Here is an example of using the `AC CLUSTER /DELETE` command:

```
AC CLUSTER /DELETE /CONTROLLER:AC1
```

This command deletes the cluster on AC2. The `AC CLUSTER /DELETE` command has the parameters shown in Table I.19.

TABLE I.19 Parameters for `AC CLUSTER /DELETE` Command

Parameter	*Description*
`[/CONTROLLER:controller_name]`	Specifies the cluster controller whose cluster should be deleted.
`[/USER:username /PASSWORD:password]`	Shows a user that has administrative privileges on the target cluster controller. Must come as a `/PASSWORD:password` pair.

/ADD

Use `AC CLUSTER /ADD` to add a new server to an existing Application Center 2000 cluster on the target server. Here is an example of using the `AC CLUSTER /ADD` command:

```
AC CLUSTER /ADD /CONTROLLER:AC1 /MEMBER:AC2 /MANAGEMENTNIC:0 /NOSYNCADD
➥/DISABLELOADBALANCING
```

This command adds the server AC2 to a COM+ cluster using CLB whose controller is AC1. Notice that it requires a NIC ID that can be found from using the `AC CLUSTER /LISTNICS` command. Here is another example of the `AC CLUSTER /ADD` command:

```
AC CLUSTER /ADD /CONTROLLER:AC1 /MEMBER:AC2 /MANAGEMENTNIC:0 /LBNIC:1
```

This command adds AC2 to an NLB Web cluster controlled by AC1. The management and load-balancing NIC must be specified. The `AC CLUSTER /ADD` command has the parameters shown in Table I.20.

TABLE I.20 Parameters for the `AC APPLICATION /ADD` Command

Parameter	*Description*
`[/CONTROLLER:controller_name]`	Specifies the cluster controller of the target cluster to add the member to.
`[/MEMBER:member_name]`	Gives the server name of the new member to add to the cluster.
`[/USER:username /PASSWORD:password]`	Shows a user that has administrative privileges on the target cluster controller. Must come as a `/PASSWORD:password` pair.
`[/NOSYNCONADD]`	Doesn't synchronize the new member with the cluster controller automatically.
`[/DISABLELOADBALANCING]`	Does not perform load balancing on the new cluster member. Its status will be offline.
`/MANAGEMENTNIC:nic_id`	Gives the ID of the management NIC.

If the target cluster uses NLB, then the parameters in Table I.21 are used to further specify how NLB should be set up on the new members.

TABLE I.21 Additional Parameters for `AC CLUSTER /ADD` with an NLB Cluster

Parameter	*Description*
`[/DEDICATEDIP:ip /DEDICATEDIPSUBNETMASK:subnet_mask]`	The dedicated IP address and the subnet mast. Optional; must be specified together.
`/LBNIC:nic_id`	The cluster NIC used for load balancing by NLB.

/REMOVE

Use `AC CLUSTER /REMOVE` to remove a server from an existing Application Center 2000 cluster. Here is an example of using the `AC CLUSTER /REMOVE` command:

```
AC CLUSTER /REMOVE /MEMBER:AC2
```

This command removes the server AC2 from whatever cluster it is a member of. The `AC CLUSTER /REMOVE` command has the parameters shown in Table I.22.

TABLE I.22 Parameters for the AC CLUSTER /REMOVE Command

Parameter	*Description*
[/MEMBER:member_name]	Specifies the server name member to remove from the cluster. If this is not specified, the local server is removed from a cluster.
[/USER:username/PASSWORD:password]	Shows a user that has administrative privileges on the target cluster controller. Must come as /PASSWORD:password pair.
[/FORCE]	Removes the server even if it cannot be reached. Should run AC CLUSTER /CLEAN on the target server.

/SETCONTROLLER

Use AC CLUSTER /SETCONTROLLER to designate a server that is a member of a cluster but not the controller as the new controller. Here is an example of using the AC CLUSTER /SETCONTROLLER command:

```
AC CLUSTER /SETCONTROLLER /MEMBER:AC2
```

This command sets the server AC2 as the new cluster controller. The AC CLUSTER /SETCONTROLLER command has the parameters shown in Table I.23.

TABLE I.23 Parameters for the AC CLUSTER /SETCONTROLLER Command

Parameter	*Description*
[/MEMBER:member_name]	Specifies the server name member to remove from the cluster. If this is not specified, the local server is removed from a cluster.
[/USER:username /PASSWORD:password]	Shows a user that has administrative privileges on the target cluster controller. Must come as a /PASSWORD:password pair.
[/FORCE]	Forces the new server to become the cluster controller even if the original controller cannot be contacted. Run AC CLUSTER/CLEAN on the old controller in this case, and rejoin it to the cluster.

/CLEAN

Use AC CLUSTER /CLEAN to reset a cluster member or controller back to its original state. The local SQL Server 2000 instance is also purged and reset to the install condition. This command can be run only on the target server; it may not be run remotely. Here is an example of using the AC CLUSTER /CLEAN command:

```
AC CLUSTER /CLEAN
```

The AC CLUSTER /CLEAN command has the parameters shown in Table I.24. This parameter is valid only for clusters that use NLB in managed mode.

TABLE I.24 Parameters for the AC CLUSTER /CLEAN Command

Parameter	*Description*
[/KEEPIPS]	Retains the IPs that are on the cluster adapter

/LISTMEMBERS

Use AC CLUSTER /LISTMEMBERS to list the members of a cluster. Here is an example of using the AC CLUSTER /LISTMEMBERS command:

```
AC CLUSTER /LISTMEMBERS
```

This command lists all the members of a cluster, their current status, and which is the controller. Here are the results of this command:

```
Members for cluster TESTWEB:
--------------------------------------------------------------
AC1             Online          Alive           Controller
AC2             Online          Alive
```

The AC CLUSTER /LISTMEMBERS command has the parameters shown in Table I.25.

TABLE I.25 Parameters for the AC CLUSTER /LISTMEMBERS Command

Parameter	*Description*
[/MEMBER:member_name]	The server name of the member to get the list of cluster members from. If this member is not the controller, it will contact the controller and return the same list.
[/USER:username /PASSWORD:password]	A user that has administrative privileges on the target cluster controller. Must come as a /PASSWORD:password pair.

/LISTNICS

Use AC CLUSTER /LISTNICS to list the NICs on a target server. Here is an example of using the AC CLUSTER /LISTNICS command:

```
AC CLUSTER /LISTNICS /COMPUTER:AC1
```

This command lists the NICs on AC1. This list can be used to provide the /LBNIC and /MANAGEMENTNIC parameter values for other AC CLUSTER commands. Here are the results of this command:

```
Network adapters on   AC1
0 : [00000000] Compaq NC3163 Fast Ethernet NIC
1 : [00000001] Compaq NC3163 Fast Ethernet NIC
```

The first number is the number to use in the /LBNIC and /MANAGEMENTNIC commands. The AC CLUSTER /LISTNICS command has the parameters shown in Table I.26.

TABLE I.26 Parameters for the AC CLUSTER /LISTNICS Command

Parameter	*Description*
[/COMPUTER:computer_name]	Specifies the target computer to query the NIC information.
[/USER:username/PASSWORD:password]	Shows a user that has administrative privileges on the target cluster controller. Must come as a /PASSWORD:password pair.

AC CLB

Use AC CLB to manage the CLB routing list on the cluster controller of a Web/COM+ routing cluster. This command can set all members of the list, load the members from a COM+ cluster, add members one by one, remove a single member, or list the members in the routing list.

/SETCLBMEMBERS

Use AC CLB /SETCLBMEMBERS to set the routing list members of a cluster. Here is an example of using the AC CLB /SETCLBMEMBERS command:

```
AC CLB /SETCLBMEMBERS /COMPLUSMEMBERS:AC3,AC4
```

This command adds the servers AC3 and AC4 to the routing list on the target cluster. The AC CLB /SETCLBMEMBERS command has the parameters shown in Table I.27.

TABLE I.27 Parameters for the AC CLB /SETCLBMEMBERS Command

Parameter	*Description*
[/ROUTINGMEMBER:routingmember]	A COM+ routing cluster member.
[/ROUTINGUSER:username /ROUTINGPASSWORD:*|pwd]	A user that has administrative privileges on the target routing member. Must come as a /ROUTINGPASSWORD:password pair.
/COMPLUSMEMBERS:member1, member2, member3,..	A list of COM+ application servers that are a part of a the routing list.

/LOADCLBMEMBERS

Use AC CLB /LOADCLBMEMBERS to set the routing list with all the members of a COM+ cluster. Here is an example of using the AC CLB /LOADCLBMEMBERS command:

```
AC CLB /LOADCLBMEMBERS /COMPLUSMEMBERS:AC3
```

This command adds the servers AC3 and AC4 to the routing list on the target cluster because they are both members of the COM+ cluster that AC3 is a member of. The AC CLB /LOADCLBMEMBERS command has the parameters shown in Table I.28.

TABLE I.28 Parameters for the AC CLB /LOADCLBMEMBERS Command

Parameter	*Description*
[/ROUTINGMEMBER:routingmember]	A COM+ routing cluster member.
[/ROUTINGUSER:username /ROUTINGPASSWORD:*|pwd]	A user that has administrative privileges on the target routing member. Must come as a /ROUTINGPASSWORD:password pair.
/COMPLUSMEMBER:member1	A COM+ application server that is a member of a COM+ cluster.
[/COMPLUSUSER:username /COMPLUSPASSWORD:*|pwd	A user that has administrative privileges on the target routing member. Must come as a /COMPLUSPASSWORD:password pair.

/ADDCLBMEMBER

Use AC CLB /ADDCLBMEMBER to add a single server to the routing list of a cluster. Here is an example of using the AC CLB /ADDCLBMEMBER command:

```
AC CLB /ADDCLBMEMBER /COMPLUSMEMBER:AC3
```

This command adds the server AC3 to the routing list on the target cluster. The AC CLB /ADDCLBMEMBER command has the parameters shown in Table I.29.

TABLE I.29 Parameters for the AC CLB /ADDCLBMEMBER Command

Parameter	*Description*
`[/ROUTINGMEMBER:routingmember]`	A COM+ routing cluster member.
`[/ROUTINGUSER:username /ROUTINGPASSWORD:*|pwd]`	A user that has administrative privileges on the target routing member. Must come as a `/ROUTINGPASSWORD:password` pair.
`/COMPLUSMEMBER:complusmember`	A single COM+ application server to add to the routing list.

/REMOVECLBMEMBER

Use `AC CLB /REMOVECLBMEMBER` to remove a single server from the routing list of a cluster. Here is an example of using the `AC CLB /REMOVECLBMEMBER` command:

```
AC CLB /REMOVECLBMEMBER /COMPLUSMEMBER:AC3
```

This command removes the server AC3 from the routing list on the target cluster. The `AC CLB /REMOVECLBMEMBER` command has the parameters shown in Table I.30.

TABLE I.30 Parameters for the AC CLB /REMOVECLBMEMBER Command

Parameter	*Description*
`[/ROUTINGMEMBER:routingmember]`	A COM+ routing cluster member.
`[/ROUTINGUSER:username /ROUTINGPASSWORD:*|pwd]`	A user that has administrative privileges on the target routing member. Must come as a `/ROUTINGPASSWORD:password` pair.
`/COMPLUSMEMBER:complusmember`	A single COM+ application server to remove from the routing list.

/LISTCLBMEMBERS

Use `AC CLB /LISTCLBMEMBERS` to list the servers in the routing list of a cluster. Here is an example of using the `AC CLB /LISTCLBMEMBERS` command:

```
AC CLB /LISTCLBMEMBERS
```

This command displays the routing list on the target cluster. Listing I.6 shows the results of this command.

LISTING I.6 The Results of the `AC CLB /LISTCLBMEMBERS` Command

```
CLB routing list for cluster AC
AC3
AC4
```

The `AC CLB /LISTCLBMEMBERS` command has the parameters shown in Table I.31.

TABLE I.31 Parameters for the `AC CLB /LISTCLBMEMBERS` Command

Parameter	*Description*
`[/ROUTINGMEMBER:routingmember]`	A COM+ routing cluster member.
`[/ROUTINGUSER:username /ROUTINGPASSWORD:*|pwd]`	A user that has administrative privileges on the target routing member. Must come as a `/ROUTINGPASSWORD:password` pair.

INDEX

SYMBOLS

A

E

K-L

M

N

O

P

Q-R

S

T

U

V

W

X-Y-Z